Shakespeare in Print

Shakespeare in Print is the first ever comprehensive account of Shakespeare publishing and an indispensable research resource. Andrew Murphy sets out the history of the Shakespeare text from the Renaissance through to the twenty-first century, from the twin perspectives of editing and publishing history. Murphy tackles issues of editorial and textual theory in an accessible and engaging manner. He draws on a wide range of archival materials and attends to topics little explored by previous scholars, such as the importance of Scottish and Irish editions in the eighteenth century, the rise of the educational edition and the history and significance of mass-market editions. The extensive appendix is an invaluable reference tool which provides full publishing details of all single-text Shakespeare editions up to 1709 and all collected editions up to 1821. The listing also provides full details of a selected range of major editions beyond these dates to the present day.

ANDREW MURPHY is Reader in English Literature at the University of St Andrews. He is author of *Seamus Heaney* (second edition, 2000) and *But the Irish Sea Betwixt Us: Ireland, Colonialism, and Renaissance Literature* (1999), and editor of *The Renaissance Text: Theory, Editing, Textuality* (2000).

Shakespeare in Print

A History and Chronology
of Shakespeare Publishing

ANDREW MURPHY

University of St Andrews

CAMBRIDGE
UNIVERSITY PRESS

PUBLISHED BY THE PRESS SYNDICATE OF THE UNIVERSITY OF CAMBRIDGE
The Pitt Building, Trumpington Street, Cambridge, United Kingdom

CAMBRIDGE UNIVERSITY PRESS
The Edinburgh Building, Cambridge, CB2 2RU, UK
40 West 20th Street, New York, NY 10011–4211, USA
477 Williamstown Road, Port Melbourne, VIC 3207, Australia
Ruiz de Alarcón 13, 28014 Madrid, Spain
Dock House, The Waterfront, Cape Town 8001, South Africa

http://www.cambridge.org

First published 2003

Printed in the United Kingdom at the University Press, Cambridge

Typeface Ehrhardt 11/13 pt.   *System* LATEX 2$_\varepsilon$ [TB]

A catalogue record for this book is available from the British Library

Library of Congress Cataloguing in Publication data
Murphy, Andrew.
Shakespeare in print: a history and chronology of Shakespeare publishing / Andrew Murphy.
    p.   cm.
Includes bibliographical references and index.
ISBN 0 521 77104 8 (hardback)
1. Shakespeare, William, 1564-1616 – Criticism, Textual.   2. Early printed books –
Great Britain – Bibliography.   3. Shakespeare, William, 1564-1616 – Bibliography.
4. Shakespeare, William, 1564-1616 – Chronology.   5. Great Britain – Imprints.
6. English imprints.   I. Title.
PR3071.M87 2003
822.3'3–dc21   2003046033

ISBN 0 521 77104 8 hardback

For Gerard

Contents

viii   *Contents*

Acknowledgements

All books incur debts, but a book such as *Shakespeare in Print* acquires creditors at a rate of profligacy that would shame a drunken gambler. These pages serve to acknowledge only my major debts – I hope the many other people who have helped with the book in one way or another, and whose names do not appear here, will forgive the oversight and accept a less personal expression of genuine gratitude.

My first word of thanks goes to my St Andrews colleagues, who have greatly facilitated work on this project over the course of several years. Robert Crawford and Nick Roe helped to nurture the book and Neil Rhodes was an exemplary reader of the entire manuscript – his comments and his consistent support and encouragement have been a wonderful gift. Rachel Heard served as research assistant on the project, funded by a grant from the British Academy. Her work was, in every respect, first rate.

My thanks also to those who encouraged the project in its earliest stages, especially Tom Berger, Graham Holderness, Randy MacLeod, Laurie Maguire and Leah Marcus. Reverend Dr Jim Rigney provided moral support and generously supplied materials. Parts of the book were read by Lukas Erne, Trevor Howard-Hill, John Jowett, Richard Knowles and Paul Werstine and I am very grateful to all of them for their feedback. Stanley Wells served as both an informal and a formal reader of the book and his feedback and advice were invaluable and greatly contributed to strengthening the text. I would also like to thank those scholars who were kind enough to share with me pre-publication copies of their work, especially Lukas Erne, Trevor Howard-Hill and Richard Knowles (again) and David Scott Kastan, Edward Ragg and Jean Addison Roberts.

Many of those involved in the *New Variorum* project were extraordinarily generous in providing me with assistance. Paul Werstine patiently answered complicated questions about obscure editions. In an extended series of emails, Richard Knowles shared both his general textual wisdom and his revisions to the *Variorum Handbook*. The *Variorum Hamlet* editors – Bernice Kliman and Eric Rasmussen – provided me with a copy of one of their primary research files and Judy and Dick Kennedy also very generously allowed me access to some of their *Midsummer Night's Dream* materials. I am also very grateful to a large number of other *New Variorum*, *Arden* 3 and *New Cambridge Shakespeare* editors who took the trouble to respond to requests for information – my apologies that I cannot list all of them individually here.

Work on this book could not have been carried forward without the generous support of several funding agencies. I wish to thank the Bibliographical Society, the British Academy, the Carnegie Trust for the Universities of Scotland and the Shakespeare Birthplace Trust for providing research grants. My particular thanks to the Leverhulme Trust, for awarding me a fellowship which enabled me to take a year out from teaching to work on the book and also for funding an extended trip to a range of UK libraries.

I have run up debts to many libraries: my home library at St Andrews (my particular thanks to Christine Gascoigne and the staff at Special Collections), the Edinburgh University Library, National Library of Scotland, British Library, University of London Library, University of Hertfordshire Library, Cambridge University Library, Trinity College Cambridge Wren Library, Bodleian Library, Birmingham Central Library, Trinity College Dublin Library, National Library of Ireland, Library of Congress and the University of Michigan Library. My thanks to the staff of all of these institutions. A particular word of thanks must go to Susan Brock at the Shakespeare Centre Library at Stratford-upon-Avon for her kind assistance and to Stanley Wells for helping with my visit there. I am also grateful to Martin Maw, who facilitated my work at the Oxford University Press archives and to Edwin Moore, who helped me access the Peter Alexander files at HarperCollins in Glasgow.

One expression of institutional gratitude remains outstanding and that is my enormous debt to the Folger Shakespeare Library. Kathleen Lynch, Carol Brobeck, Barbara Mowat and the staff of the library and of the Folger Institute made me feel welcome and at home from the very first moment I arrived at East Capitol Street, SE. I was delighted to receive a fellowship from the Folger in support of my project and was humbled when I discovered that the award would be issued in the names of Myra and Charlton Hinman. Betsy Walsh was extremely accommodating in searching out materials while I was at the Folger and in chasing up last minute queries when I was on the other side of the Atlantic. The desk staff at the library were models of indulgent patience when I submitted ticket after ticket demanding to see complete runs of obscure multi-volume editions. Fellow readers made working at the library an intellectual and companionable pleasure and my particular thanks go to regular Supreme Court diners (and occasional Hawk and Dove drinkers) Fernando Cioni, Lukas Erne, Steve May and Kirk Melnikoff. My thanks also to Dympna Callaghan, Jay Halio, Margaret Rose Jaster, David Scott Kastan, Laurie Maguire, Stephen Orgel, Jean Roberts, Bruce Smith, Peter Stallybrass, Alden and Ginger Vaughan and all the other scholars who made me feel welcome in Washington, and to Leah Marcus and Linda Gregerson for inviting me to speak at Vanderbilt and Ann Arbor while I was in the US. I would also like to thank Jacqueline Belanger, Peter Holland, Andrew Nash and Ramona Wray for invitations to give talks on material drawn from this book at the Centre for Editorial and Intertextual Research (University of Cardiff), the Shakespeare Institute, the Institute for English Studies (University of London), and Queen's University Belfast.

I am greatly indebted to my Cambridge editor, Sarah Stanton, who fruitfully shaped this book by encouraging me to rethink the original proposal and who efficiently guided the book through to publication. The comments provided by the press readers at various stages during the book's genesis were enormously helpful. Jan Sewell cast an eagle eye over the chronological appendix and offered many invaluable corrections and Maureen Leach was a speedy and very helpful copyeditor. Thanks are also due to Sarah (and to Elisabeth Leedham-Greene) for facilitating my work on the Cambridge University Press archives at the press itself and at the Cambridge University Library.

It is traditional in acknowledging those who have helped with a work of scholarship to include a rider exempting them from all responsibility for errors which remain in the text. In a book such as this, which includes so much factual information, it would be a great convenience to be able to blame others for any errors in the pages that follow. Sadly, however, for all the mistakes that may – and I dare say *will* – be found in this book, I can only hold my wrists out and say: 'it's a fair cop, gov; I'll come quietly'.

Finally: a word of thanks to everyone outside the Shakespearean or academic orbit who made life pleasurable while the book was underway. My particular thanks to Vincent Durac, Susan Manly, Gill Plain, Rhiannon Purdie and Andrew Roberts and Sally Kilmister. Frank and Elaine Hayes supplied a copy of F1 2001, which (together with a copy of GT2 provided by the book's dedicatee) was a vital tool as the book was being written. Tina Kelleher took me to see Cal Ripken play for the Orioles. Chen and Lili Liebstein (and Luz, Don, Jorge, Chino, Claudia, Mika and Divi) made Washington truly feel like a home away from home. Charonne Ruth has, as ever, been a staff and a star. *Shakespeare in Print* is dedicated to Gerard Murphy: my oldest friend and encourager.

Andrew Murphy
East Neuk of Fife

Abbreviations

AEB	*Analytical and Enumerative Bibliography*
Ath.	*The Athenæum*
Bks.	*The Bookseller*
CUP	Cambridge University Press
DNB	*Dictionary of National Biography*
ER	*Edinburgh Review*
ESTC	RLG, English Short Title Catalogue database, copyright British Library and ESTC/NA (see http://www.rig.org/cit-est.html).
JEGP	*Journal of English and Germanic Philology*
Lib.	*The Library*
MARDIE	*Medieval and Renaissance Drama in England*
MLA	Modern Language Association
MLR	*Modern Language Review*
MP	*Modern Philology*
MR	*Monthly Review*
N&Q	*Notes & Queries*
NLS	National Library of Scotland
OUP	Oxford University Press
PBA	*Proceedings of the British Academy*
PBSA	*Papers of the Bibliographical Society of America*
PH	*Publishing History*
PMLA	*Publications of the Modern Language Association*
RES	*Review of English Studies*
SB	*Studies in Bibliography*
SQ	*Shakespeare Quarterly*
SS	*Shakespeare Survey*
TCD	Trinity College Dublin
TLS	*The Times Literary Supplement*

WorldCat	WorldCat bibliographic database. Published by Online Computer Library Center (OCLC) (see http://www.oclc.org/firstsearch/instruction/citing/mla.shtm).
F	Folio
F1	First Folio
F2	Second Folio
F3	Third Folio
F4	Fourth Folio
Q	Quarto
Q0	Remnant of a lost quarto
Q1	First Quarto
Q2	Second Quarto
Q3	Third Quarto
Q4	Fourth Quarto

PART I | Text

Introduction

The year 1864 marked the three-hundredth anniversary of Shakespeare's birth. Various schemes were proposed for celebrating the occasion. A committee was formed with the intention of commissioning a public statue of the playwright. The publishing trade journal, *The Bookseller*, poured scorn on the idea, accusing the committee members of empty pomposity: 'self-seeking', the journal complained, 'was their only motive; [the aim of] the proposal to raise a statue was, that the pedestal might be sufficiently large to convey their names to posterity'.[1] *The Bookseller* suggested an alternative form of tribute to the committee's vainglorious plan. 'It would not form a bad Shakespearian monument', the journal suggested, 'if a copy of all the editions of his works and comments upon them were collected and piled together.' 'A tribute of this kind', the journal noted, 'would be more rational than a senseless pillar or column of stone.'[2]

It is interesting to contemplate the manner in which *The Bookseller*'s imagined monument would have evolved century by century. In 1664, a column of Shakespeare editions would have been somewhat more than 150 volumes high. By 1764, something in the region of 500 books could have been heaped on top of each other. At the time of the three-hundredth anniversary, the number of volumes forming the column would already have been approaching the point where counting the individual texts would have been difficult, as editions proliferated at an unprecedented rate, in America as well as Britain, and, indeed, elsewhere throughout the world. By 1964, the exponentially multiplying building materials would have produced a monument rivalling that biblical 'tower, whose top may reach unto heaven'. And still there was no end in sight, despite the optimism of one textual scholar who, at the mid-point of the twentieth century, looked forward to the day when 'the accumulation [of bibliographical facts] will reach the limits of human endeavour and the fact-finding be exhausted'. When that day arrived, he predicted, 'the final capstone [could] be placed on Shakespearian scholarship and a text achieved that in the most minute details is as close as mortal man can come to the original truth'.[3] Such twentieth-century dreams of an edition of Shakespeare so compellingly definitive that it would bring the editorial process to an end proved no more, indeed, than fantasy, and so still, uncapped, the tower of editions continues inexorably to rise. Like Bruegel's famous vision of Babel, Shakespeare's monument is destined to remain forever in an unfinishable state. When 2064 arrives, whole new strata of materials will have joined the accumulated tons of rag fibre, woodpulp and ink: plastic, silicon, magnetic media . . . who can say what else.

If the accumulated mass of Shakespeare editions is indeed a kind of Tower of Babel, then the aim of *Shakespeare in Print* is to chart a journey from the lowest floors to the unfinished heights. But the journey time available is relatively short, the building massive, and the rooms myriad. For these reasons, John Velz has described the business of writing a book such as this as an 'awesome task'.[4] Other scholars have, very sensibly, confined themselves to an individual room or two or to parts of particular floors. Thus, for instance, Margreta de Grazia, Peter Martin and Peter Seary have devoted entire books to the work of a single Shakespeare editor, and Simon Jarvis and Marcus Walsh have written about Shakespeare editing in extended periods of a single century.[5] Arthur Sherbo has produced a covey of books which, taken together, constitute a history of Shakespeare editing over a stretch of several decades.[6] At the risk of overloading a fanciful extended metaphor, it might be said that still other scholars have offered a non-stop elevator ride from the bottom of the tower to the top, providing snatched glimpses of each floor along the way. So, for example, a slightly breathless Paul Werstine presents a complete history of Shakespeare editing in a bravura thirty-page essay entitled 'William Shakespeare' in the MLA's *Scholarly Editing: A Guide to Research*, and Barbara Mowat attempts to cover the same general territory in about half that number of pages in a chapter contributed to Margreta de Grazia and Stanley Wells' *Cambridge Companion to Shakespeare*. With a deal more space to spare in his masterful short monograph, *Shakespeare and the Book*, David Scott Kastan lingers lovingly on certain floors, but then shoots silently past others, attending most closely to material that holds for him a broader theoretical significance.

By contrast with the work of these scholars – which I find entirely admirable and to which (as will repeatedly be seen in the chapters that follow) I am enormously indebted – my own aim in this book is to offer, for the first time, an extended single volume study that covers the entire history of Shakespeare publishing century by century, and which treats every period in some detail. It is inevitable that this book – lengthy though it is – will itself miss much along the way. Doubtless there will be readers who will consider it an unforgivable omission that I have neglected to discuss some particular edition, or that I have treated of another in a condensed and hurried manner. However, I hope that such readers may also feel that if – to lean again on my Bruegellian metaphor – I rush too quickly past particular rooms, or fail even to push open the door to many another, then, in compensation, I also attempt a considered exploration of certain areas where the settled dust of decades' neglect has seldom enough been disturbed by the tread of scholarly enquiry. So, for example: it is striking that so much recent scholarship on the history of Shakespeare publishing has concentrated exclusively on the eighteenth century (the work of de Grazia, Martin, Seary, Jarvis, Walsh and Sherbo referred to above is all concerned with this period). By contrast, very little sustained attention has been paid to Shakespeare publishing in the nineteenth century.[7] There is a certain irony in the fact that scholarly work has been oriented in this way, given that it was precisely in the nineteenth century that the Shakespeare text became – from a publishing point of view – a genuinely popular commodity, to be mass-produced, mass-marketed and mass-distributed. *Shakespeare in Print* attempts to redress such imbalances as this by devoting a roughly equal measure of attention to every phase of the extended history of Shakespeare publishing.

Setting out the scope of my project and its general parameters is relatively easy, defining its precise focus is a touch more difficult. An alert reader may already have noticed that, in this introduction, I have tended to slide back and forth between speaking of editing and of publishing, writing interchangeably of editions and of texts. As this duality indicates, the history of the reproduction of Shakespeare's texts could potentially be approached from two distinctive perspectives. What John Velz characterised as 'awesome' was, in fact, the 'task of writing a comprehensive history of the Shakespearean *editorial tradition*' (emphasis added) and one could indeed write a study of the history of the Shakespeare text which focused exclusively on the history of editing, on what the most important of Shakespeare's editors have done to the text century by century and how the general theory of editing has evolved over the course of this time period. But books, of course, are not just edited, they are also – as Jerome J. McGann, D. F. McKenzie and others have forcefully reminded us – *produced*.[8] They appear in different formats, in different quantities, in different places, aimed at different markets, under a variety of different circumstances. So: one could also write a study of the Shakespeare text that focused exclusively on the history of Shakespeare publishing, on how publishers have handled the text in different ways over time. I have, however, felt very strongly in writing this book that an exclusive focus either on editing or on publishing would not produce an adequate general history of the reproduction of Shakespeare's texts.

Editorial history has tended – certainly at least until very recently – to have a certain teleological cast to it.[9] Thus, the best Shakespeare editors are seen as being those who have helped to advance the theory of Shakespearean editing in some way, who have, we might say, stepped along the road that leads towards ever more advanced conceptions of the editorial project. This view of editing thus resonates with what S. M. Parrish has characterised as 'the Whig interpretation of literature'.[10] The eighteenth century provides a convenient example. From the point of view of editorial history, Shakespeare publishing in the eighteenth century is dominated by a succession of editors, running from Nicholas Rowe to Edmond Malone, and the achievements of each editor in turn can be weighed, to see how much of a contribution he has made to the development of the editorial tradition. The logic of this framework necessarily suggests that some editors merit far more attention than others and that some deserve hardly any attention at all. For instance, in 1743–4, Sir Thomas Hanmer, one time Speaker of the House of Commons, published an edition of Shakespeare's works with the university press at Oxford. Hanmer was not well versed in contemporary editing theory and, textually, his edition is decidedly undistinguished. Writing of his text in 1933, R. B. McKerrow observed that

> Hanmer seems to have known little and cared less about such matters as early editions or the language of Shakespeare's time, and attempted to reform the text by the light of nature alone, with the result that though his conjectural emendations are sometimes ingenious and seem at first sight attractive, the work as a whole can hardly be regarded as a serious contribution to Shakespearian scholarship.[11]

McKerrow's judgement is perfectly reasonable in the context of the terms of reference that he is applying here – the terms of reference, that is, of editorial history. But there is more – much more – to Hanmer's edition than McKerrow's dismissive assessment suggests. Hanmer's was the first English Shakespeare edition to be published outside the city of London and the first to be produced by a university press. It was also an enormous commercial success, quickly selling out its print run, and subsequently changing hands at an ever-increasing price as the years went by.[12] Furthermore, it enjoyed an extended afterlife, immediately spawning a range of other editions. The Tonson cartel, indignant at what they saw as an encroachment on their private property, reacted to the Oxford edition by appropriating the Hanmer text and reissuing it in a cheap octavo London edition in 1745. Hanmer's edition thus became part of the important larger-scale battle over copyright which raged during the course of the eighteenth century. Another publisher – John Osborn – produced a duodecimo edition of the Hanmer text in 1747. The Tonson cartel bought up this edition too, and reissued it with a substitute title page. The pocket-sized volumes proved popular and so the cartel decided to reprint them in 1748, 1751 and 1760. In 1770–1, Oxford University Press itself issued a second edition of Hanmer's text and this too proved a commercial success. By 1892, one bookseller in London was offering the second Oxford Hanmer edition for 30s. at a time when he was selling a copy of Nicholas Rowe's 1709 text – described as a 'Very rare Edition' – for exactly one third of this price.[13]

A history of Shakespeare editing would very largely overlook Hanmer's edition. It would also pass over texts considered, in editorial terms, to be 'derivative', which is to say, editions that simply reproduce an existing text without further conscious editorial intervention. But, again, these texts have their own particular significance. To take a nineteenth-century instance: the London publisher John Dicks was prompted by the tercentenary of Shakespeare's birth to add his own few modest blocks to *The Bookseller*'s Shakespeare monument.[14] He issued individual plays at the price of two for a penny. It is not entirely clear what edition his texts were based on, but certainly they were derivative. Dicks shifted 150,000 play texts in this way. He then drew his individual texts together into a 2s.-collected volume and sold 50,000 copies of this edition. He next moved this collected text into paperback format and sold a staggering 700,000 further copies – in the space of about two years. These sales figures might be compared with the equivalent figures for high-profile editorially significant editions. The towering academic edition of the nineteenth century was the Clark and Wright text, produced as a joint venture by Macmillan's and Cambridge University Press, and issued at around the same time as Dicks' texts. Alexander Macmillan had initially thought to print just 750 copies of this edition. In the event, he increased the print run to 1,500 copies, but he did not think it a worthwhile investment to produce stereotype plates so that further issues could easily be released. Looking at these figures, we can see that in just two years Dicks' 2s. and 1s. editions sold, between them, 1,000 times the original projected print run of the most editorially significant edition of the nineteenth century. In 1864, *The Bookseller* predicted that texts of Shakespeare would 'be poured upon the country until every person has possessed himself of a copy'.[15] If *The Bookseller*'s prediction proved to be accurate, then the imprint carried by the flood of Shakespeares washing through the country was 500 times more likely to be that of the obscure John Dicks, rather than of the prestigious house of Macmillan or the Cambridge University Press.[16] Dicks' derivative text thus made an enormous contribution to the wide dissemination and popularisation of Shakespeare's works, and yet his name finds no place in standard histories of the reproduction of the text.[17]

I am suggesting, then, that a thorough and useful account of the history of Shakespeare's texts cannot be written from the perspective of editorial history alone. But it is also true, of course, that an exclusive focus on publishing history would be equally unbalanced. For example: from a publishing point of view, Alexander Pope's 1723–5 edition was a dismal flop. It failed to attract a convincing number of subscribers – even Swift and Arbuthnot did not sign up for the set – and a significant portion of the edition remained unsold some four decades after publication, when outstanding stock was sold off at auction at around one tenth of the original price.[18] Quite a contrast, we might say, with Thomas Hanmer's edition. Yet no one who truly understands the history of Shakespeare publishing would suggest that Pope's edition lacks significance simply because it was a commercial failure. Pope systematised and regularised the text – especially the metre – in ways that persisted in the canon for decades, if not centuries. His edition provoked Lewis Theobald to write the first ever book devoted exclusively to Shakespearean editorial concerns: *Shakespeare Restor'd*. Additionally, he prompted Theobald to produce his own edition of the plays – an edition which, some would argue, helped significantly to lay the groundwork for much later textual work. Pope's edition is thus absolutely central to the early history of Shakespeare editing – and therefore to the general history of the Shakespeare text – even if his edition had little immediate commercial impact.

One might also make the point here that attempting to write an account of the Shakespeare text exclusively from the perspective of publishing history would be a very difficult task indeed, given the sheer volume of Shakespeare editions that have been issued over the course of the past four centuries. Anyone seeking to write a history of these texts needs some kind of stable navigation points – otherwise Shakespearean history would run the risk of becoming a record of just one damn text after another. This book takes as its fixed navigation points those editions which are consensually regarded as being textually significant – the editions, in other words, that any serious editor of Shakespeare would be expected to consult. But the book does not confine itself simply to travelling the shortest line between these beacon texts; it also attends to a broad range of other editions not normally covered in survey histories of the editorial tradition.

Shakespeare in Print, then, attempts to meld editing and publishing history, in order to produce as multifaceted an account of the history of the reproduction of the Shakespeare text as possible. As already indicated, the book discusses all of the editions that are commonly regarded as being textually important and it gives some account of why these editions are considered to be significant. So, a reader working through this volume will discover that the 'editor' of the Second Folio retrieved Greek and Roman names and many foreign language phrases and bits of dialogue that had been lost in the First Folio; that Edward Capell was the first editor to build his own text from the ground up, instead of marking up a copy of his predecessor's edition; that Charles Knight valorised the First Folio texts over their Quarto counterparts; that the editors of the 1986 Oxford text privileged what they considered to be the most 'theatrical' versions of the plays. Such a reader will also be able to reconstruct, from this book, a general history of the evolution of Shakespearean editorial theory, from the work of the earliest anonymous quarto and folio 'editors', to Pope's aesthetically oriented reframing of the text, through Malone's insistence on the documentary and the authentic, on to the formulation of a would-be scientific approach (initially in the New Shakspere Society and then, more coherently, in the work of the New Bibliographers), thence to the impact on the editorial project of the evolution of social and poststructural conceptions of textuality and, finally, to the reshaping of editorial concerns in the light of the emergence of electronic modes of publishing.

In tandem with this focus on editors and editing *Shakespeare in Print* also attends closely to the wider context of Shakespeare publishing, examining peripheral, derivative and popular editions. So this book finds room to trace the history of eighteenth-century Scottish and Irish editions of Shakespeare and indicates why these editions are important; it maps out a history of cheap Shakespeare publishing in the nineteenth century; it logs the emergence of schools and expurgated editions. Just as a history of editors and editing is combined here with a history of the theory of editing, so I also attempt to combine the history of popular and peripheral editions with a certain element of general historical contextualisation of the business of producing texts. In covering the eighteenth century, for example, I try to place the emergence of opposing strands of Shakespeare publishing – metropolitan/Celtic, prestige/popular – in the context of battles over the exact legal status of Shakespeare's text and the dispute over the precise meaning of copyright. Likewise, publishing trends in the nineteenth century are discussed in the context of the broadening of the educational franchise and technological advances which very significantly reduced the cost of producing editions. In charting the rise of Shakespeare publishing and editing in America, I have tried to sketch some of the history of book collecting in the United States, since no serious editing work could be undertaken in America until the necessary materials had been accumulated in easily accessible libraries. Part of the aim of this book, then, is to set the extended narrative of Shakespeare publishing within something of its greater historical and cultural contexts.

The book also attempts – where it can – to give some attention to the quotidian logistics of editing and publishing. *Shakespeare in Print* draws – in many instances for the first time – on a range of archival materials connected with the publication of particular editions. I have made use of the Macmillan archives at the British Library, the archives of Oxford and Cambridge university presses, the Routledge archives at the University of London Library, Edward Dowden's papers at Trinity College Dublin, the John Dover Wilson and David Nichol Smith papers at the National Library of Scotland, and many other manuscript sources. These materials provide an insight both into the intellectual formation of the edited text and into the logistics of bringing an edition to press and to the marketplace. For example, a series of letters exchanged between David Nichol Smith and W. W. Greg, coupled with the Oxford University Press Shakespeare files, serves neatly to indicate the shift in editorial conceptions which occurred in the opening decades of the twentieth century. Smith, increasingly influenced by the emergent New Bibliography, grew frustrated with the traditionalist Walter Raleigh, with whom he was trying to create a new edition for the Oxford press. Raleigh thought that the best new edition would simply present a corrected transcription of the First Folio, but Smith strongly disagreed. The intellectual tensions between the two scholars ultimately proved to be irresolvable and had the effect of sinking the project (at least as it was originally conceived). From a somewhat different perspective, Edward Dowden's papers help to remind us that even those editions that are driven by the best intellectual motives still have their commercial context, as Dowden – dismayed by the sales figures for his inaugural *Hamlet* volume – quickly withdrew from the general editorship of the *Arden Shakespeare*, on the grounds that the series was unlikely to enjoy much enduring success. In slightly more mundane terms, I have also drawn on archival materials to provide details of print runs and sales figures for some editions – for example, tracking the *Globe Shakespeare* through the Cambridge University Press prizing books (effectively the company's publication ledgers) to discover exactly how many copies of it were printed over a period of about half a century.

I have said that *Shakespeare in Print* attends to this kind of backstage logistical history *where it can* and the qualification is important to note here. The editors and publishers of editions of Shakespeare are legion. But few enough of them have left much of a trace behind. The extensive collection of Macmillan materials held at the British Library is very much the exception rather than the rule. Even this well-preserved archive is incomplete, as the process used by the company in the nineteenth century for mechanically making copies of its outgoing correspondence was imperfect, with the result that some volumes of Macmillan letters held by the British Library now consist entirely of blank pages. The experience of having fastidious librarians deliver neatly bound blank books to one's desk in the rarefied atmosphere of the British Library manuscript reading room is not without its own peculiar surreal charm, but one cannot help registering a sense of genuine loss also. Other major archives are subject not to the whim of imperfect reproduction technologies, but to the pressing need that working publishing companies necessarily feel to save on storage space. In the case of one archive that I visited, many file covers indicated that the enclosed contents had been 'weeded', which is to say that documents had been removed and destroyed, in order to slim the files down. For some commercial publishers – notably corporate multimedia giants who inherit once venerable imprints like the small change of great legacies – the conservation of archives may seem a useless frivolity: why spend money to preserve the past if the past cannot be made to generate a speedy profit? Some other archives have survived in fragmentary form by chance, such as a Thomas Nelson ledger preserved in the Edinburgh University Library and an account book for the 1853–65 James Orchard Halliwell edition in the same collection (the latter acquired when the university bought a set of Halliwell materials that had originally been held by the Public Library of Penzance). Other archives have, like the Library of Alexandria, suffered at the hands of history itself: a call to one London publisher to enquire about materials relating to their nineteenth century editions of Shakespeare was met with the response that all of their early records had been destroyed in the Blitz. The archival material presented here should, then, be treated with a certain degree of caution. This is the material – or some of it, at least – which happens to have survived. It may be difficult to say to what extent, exactly, it is representative of the culture of Shakespeare publishing more generally.

In addition to the archival limitations discussed in the previous paragraph, a further problem might also be noted here. John Sutherland has identified a tendency in certain forms of publishing history to concentrate on, as he has put it, 'picking the lowest apples' on the tree.[19] Sutherland's vivid metaphor indicates, as I take it, an overreadiness among some scholars to scavenge in archives for easily useful material and to leave behind the mass of other, less immediately accessible data. I must plead guilty here to being myself something of an archival scrumper. I have tended in many instances to look to archives for material which easily fits with the narrative line of this book, declining, in many cases, to ascend through dense branches of accounting figures and convoluted reprint histories. The Routledge archives held at the University of London Library provide a nice indication of what some of these largely unclimbed documentary limbs might look like.[20] The library holds six of the company's late-nineteenth-century Publication Books. They cover the period 1850–1902, but they do not run in strict sequence – many volumes overlap in their periods of cover. A very wide range of Shakespeare entries is included: Hazlitt's, Knight's Pictorial, the *Shakspere Companion Histories*, Campbell's, the *Illustrated*, Staunton's, the Guinea, the Edition de Luxe, the Blackfriars, the Shilling, Routledge's, the Sir John Gilbert, the Mignon, the *Ariel*. Some of these texts were published in multiple editions; some were published in multiple issues; some were issued in multiple sizes and/or configurations; some were issued in parts. Complex lines of accounting and production figures run through the ledgers like a bubbling stream of black ink, and mapping a complete publication history of any one of these editions would be a major undertaking. Untangling such histories lies outside the scope of this present volume, so the more closely detailed data included in such archives remain – for now, at least – an underexplored resource (at least from a Shakespearean point of view).

I have set out the scope and objectives of *Shakespeare in Print* and I have also touched on some of the book's limitations. There are a further set of specific omissions that I would also like to register here. An early attempt to include a broad-brush history of translations of Shakespeare's texts into other languages proved to be unsatisfactory, as the topic is far too great and too complex to be treated in a useful way in a study of this kind. For instance, the earliest translation of Shakespeare into Italian would appear to be a set of three texts (*Othello, Macbeth* and *Coriolanus*), produced by Giustina Renier-Michiel, commencing in 1798. But Renier-Michiel's command of English was not particularly good, so her edition was effectively an Italian reworking of Pierre Le Tourneur's 1776 French edition of the plays. Various other editions followed Renier-Michiel's, but it was not until the middle of the nineteenth century that a satisfactory Italian translation of the plays was produced.[21] Given the complexity of such histories, I have limited myself here to discussing English-language texts. I should note, however, that I have also concentrated on charting the history of editions of Shakespeare published in Britain and Ireland and in the United States. But, of course, the production of English-language editions has not been confined to these locations, and the history of the publication of Shakespeare editions in, for example, Canada, Australia and the Indian sub-continent still remains to be unravelled.[22] I should also make clear that the focus of this book is on the printed text of Shakespeare's own plays. For this reason, theatrical adaptations are very largely ignored and theatrical issues more generally are not much attended to either. I also have very little to say about illustrations, beyond commenting briefly on some of the very earliest illustrated texts and noting the fact that pictorial editions became much more economical to produce – and therefore became much more popular – in the nineteenth century. Illustration, like translation, is a very large-scale topic in its own right, a topic which would merit a complete study in itself.[23]

These are the aims and the general parameters of the main text of *Shakespeare in Print*. The text is supplemented by a chronological appendix which provides a listing of major editions from the Renaissance through to the beginning of the twenty-first century. A separate introduction is provided for this appendix, indicating the scope and rationale of the entries included in the listing. Each text included in the chronological appendix is assigned its own number and references to editions in the main body of the book are keyed to this numbering system. Such reference numbers are signalled by the symbol '§' in the main text of the book.

The names of Shakespeare's editors are legion; who now remembers H. Bellyse Baildon, Henry Ten Eyck Perry, N. Burton Paradise, Thomas M. Parrott or Virginia Gildersleeve? Or who remembers that George Santayana, Algernon Swinburne and George Saintsbury produced editions of Shakespeare texts, or that Sir Walter Scott and Lewis Carroll commenced work on Shakespeare editions which they never finished?[24] Editions of the playwright's work have been produced in every conceivable form and format, ranging from the 'Elephant folios' of Halliwell's 1853–65 edition to the miniature volumes of a William Pickering text, printed in 'Diamond Type', of which the *Dublin University Magazine* observed that it 'seems exclusively intended for sale in the kingdom of Lilliput, or for the benefit of opticians in general'.[25] The text has been edited and amended in a wide variety of different ways, from modern-spelling editions to old-spelling editions, to an edition of *Shaekspeer'z Hamlet*, being 'A Vurshon in Nue Speling, Edited Bie P. A. D. MacCarthy' and 'Publisht on Behaaf ov Dhe Simplified Speling Sosiëty bie Sur Iezak Pitman & Sunz, Ltd' in 1946.[26] Editions have ranged from the humble to the exalted, from Thomas Johnson's cheap pocket-book texts, clandestinely exported from the Netherlands into England at the beginning of the eighteenth century, to 'the finest edition of *Hamlet*, I dare to say, in the world', specially edited by John Dover Wilson for the German millionaire Count Harry Kessler, with illustrations by Edward Gordon Craig, seven copies being printed on vellum, 'fifteen on imperial Japanese paper, and three hundred on hand-made paper'.[27] Editions have been issued by university presses and by fly-by-night publishers; Mills and Boon – best known in the UK for sentimental romances – once issued an illustrated text of *Henry V*, edited by C. R. Gilbert, Rector of Seagrave.[28] The texts have been turned into comic books and the BBC once considered providing the petrol company Exxon with cut-price copies of the plays to give away to its customers.[29] So many widely distributed editions were available at the close of the twentieth century that, in 1992, the Open University in the UK issued a volume entitled *Which Shakespeare? A User's Guide to Editions*.[30] It would be impossible to cover all of this rich history in detail in a single-volume study such as this. I do hope, however, that enough of the story is told here to make the journey to the top of the Shakespearean Tower of Babel seem worth the effort of the climb.

I   The early quartos

In 1585, at the age of twenty-one, Shakespeare grew tired of the limited prospects available to him in Stratford and he set off on foot for London, taking about four days to complete the hundred-mile journey. Once arrived in the city, he called in at the lodgings of Richard Field, a fellow Stratfordian, some three years older than himself, who had made the same journey to London in 1579.[1] Field had apprenticed himself to the printer, George Bishop, but had quickly transferred to the service of the Huguenot Thomas Vautrollier, who maintained printing establishments in both London and Edinburgh. Through Field, Shakespeare was able to find employment in the print trade, most likely at the press of Henry Denham, who, at the time, was just embarking on the considerable task of printing Holinshed's *Chronicles*. Shakespeare worked as a proof-reader at Denham's, in the process making the acquaintance of Denham's apprentice, William Jaggard, whose own firm would, much later, be responsible for printing the first collected edition of Shakespeare's plays. During this time, Thomas Vautrollier died and Field, recently emerged from his apprenticeship, married Vautrollier's widow Jacqueline and took over the business. Shakespeare, in his spare time, frequently returned to his friend's shop and helped out with the printing.

The connections which Shakespeare established during his years in the printing trade were central to his career as a writer. From proof-reading Holinshed's *Chronicles*, he gained a thorough knowledge of British history. At Field's he would certainly have discovered North's translation of Plutarch's *Lives*, which had been published by Vautrollier and subsequently by Field himself and which would serve as the source-book for Shakespeare's Roman plays. At his friend's shop he may also have come across James VI of Scotland's *Essayes of a Prentice in the Diuine Art of Poesie*, which Vautrollier had published in Edinburgh in 1584. In this way, Shakespeare may have become familiar with the aesthetic theories of the future royal patron of the Globe company. When Shakespeare came to publish his own work, it was his old friend Field who served as publisher.

All of this, of course, makes for a good story. But, like many narratives which seek to fill in the blank space of Shakespeare's 'lost years', it amounts to little more than wishful speculation advanced by a commentator with a vested interest in the tale being told. This story of Shakespeare's career in the print trade was set out in 1933 in a lecture entitled 'Shakespeare: Once a Printer and Bookman', delivered at Stationers' Hall by the appropriately named Captain William Jaggard, who bolstered his argument with some 'five hundred supporting quotations'.[2] The truth of Shakespeare's relations with the world of publishing is, however, altogether more fragmentary and uncertain. With the likely exception of his early narrative poems (and possibly his sonnets) – and in marked contrast with contemporaries such as Ben Jonson – Shakespeare seems to have concerned himself little with the publication of his own writings.[3] Indeed, as Douglas A. Brooks has observed (echoing many other commentators) 'Shakespeare seems to have been singularly indifferent about whether and how the plays he wrote made it into print' – an indifference which Richard Dutton suggests may have derived from a sense of loyalty to the company for which he served as principal playwright: 'The short answer . . . to why Shakespeare never published his own plays is quite likely to be that he was a company man, too identified with an ethos in which any removal of company property warranted expulsion from its ranks, too bound to a small group by ties that went beyond a mere contractual framework.'[4]

It is true, however, that the Stratfordian Richard Field (who was indeed Thomas Vautrollier's apprentice and marital successor) was the first person ever to publish a text by Shakespeare. He registered the narrative poem *Venus and Adonis* with the Stationers' Company on 18 April 1593, publishing it some time later in the same year. The balance of probability suggests that it was Shakespeare himself who brought the poem to Field. *Venus and Adonis* was likely written at a time when the London theatres were experiencing one of their routine bouts of closure, owing to a particularly virulent outbreak of the plague, so that Shakespeare was obliged, in J. M. Robertson's evocative phrase, 'to boil his pot by his pen'.[5] *Venus and Adonis* sold for 1*s.*, which was about three times the average price for a book of its size (the 1609 *Sonnets* volume, by contrast, appears to have sold for 5*d.*). Francis R. Johnson speculates that 'the high price was due to the book's being classified under *erotica* rather than to Shakespeare's as yet unmade reputation'.[6] The inflated sale price notwithstanding, it is unlikely that Field would have paid the poet much for the text, but this would not have been Shakespeare's primary aim in having the work published. The poem is dedicated 'To the right honourable Henrie Wriothesley, Earle of Southampton, and Baron of Titchfield'

(§3, dedication). Wriothesley was just nineteen years old at the time, a ward of the powerful William Cecil, Elizabeth's Lord High Treasurer, with whom he had a turbulent relationship. The motivation for dedicating the poem to Southampton would in large measure have been mercenary. Shakespeare – the largest segment of his income cut off as a result of the shut-down of the theatres – would have hoped for a financial return on his dedication. Much later, an anecdotal tradition would take hold suggesting that Southampton had given Shakespeare the fabulous sum of £1,000 (the equivalent of about 150 years' salary for a teacher at the time).[7] The truth of this story is highly questionable, but, nevertheless, it does seem likely that he received some form of return for the *Venus and Adonis* dedication, since, in the very next year, he dedicated a second narrative poem – *The Rape of Lucrece* – to the same patron. The somewhat more intimate tone of the *Lucrece* dedication – 'The love I dedicate to your Lordship is without end; whereof this pamphlet without beginning is but a superfluous moiety' (§5, dedication) – may indicate that the effect of the *Venus* dedication had been to bring Shakespeare favourably to Southampton's notice.

By the time *Venus and Adonis* appeared under his imprint, Richard Field was well established in the London trade. His name initially appears on the title page of the books he produced in the capacity of publisher. In 1588, *The Copie of a Letter Sent out of England to Don Bernadin Mendoza* appears as printed 'by I. Vautrollier for Richard Field', 'I. Vautrollier' being Thomas's widow, Jacqueline. This formulation serves usefully to remind us of the permeability of the distinction between publishing and printing that existed in the Renaissance period. Both trades were regulated by the same body, the Stationers' Company, but while some members of the company specialised exclusively in printing and some exclusively in publishing, many others combined the two activities to varying degrees. Field's career fits into this last category: of the approximately 295 books that he printed, he served as publisher for about 112, with the remaining 183 being published by other members of the Stationers' Company.[8] By 1589, Field was producing books under his own imprint and in this year he served as printer and publisher of George Puttenham's *Arte of English Poesie*. In the same year he printed two books for John Harrison the elder, who would later figure in Field's publishing and printing of Shakespeare's poems.

While by no means primarily a printer or publisher of literary texts, Field nevertheless had a hand in the production of many important contemporary literary works. He was frequently employed by the publisher William Ponsonby, printing the first complete edition of *The Faerie Queene* for him in 1596. In the same year, Field printed Spenser's *Fowre Hymnes* and *Daphnaida* and two years later he printed a folio collection of Sir Philip Sidney's works for Ponsonby. In advance of working with Shakespeare, Field had direct experience of closely collaborating with another poet during the course of the printing process. In 1591 he printed Sir John Harington's translation of Ariosto's *Orlando Furioso*.[9] A substantial portion of the manuscript which Harington provided for Field has survived and it offers a fascinating insight into author-printer relationships in the period. Harington includes several instructions in the text directed at the printer, at one point requesting that 'a spare leafe' be inserted between the twenty-third and twenty-fourth books of the translation. At another point, he addresses the following complex request directly to Field himself:

> Mr ffeld I dowt this will not come in in the last page, and thearfore I wowld have [yow?] immedyatly in the next page after the fynyshinge of this last booke, with some prety knotte. to set down the tytle, and a peece of the Allegory as followeth in this next page. / I would have the allegory (as allso the appollygy and all the prose that ys to come except the table [)] in the same printe that Putnams book ys./

W. W. Greg observes that, 'Whether Field interpreted his wishes correctly I do not know: what he did was to place a "prety knotte", in the shape of a printer's ornament, below the notes to canto XLVI, and continue immediately with the heading and text of the Allegory.'[10]

Whether Shakespeare was so particular in his instructions to Field, we do not know, but *Venus and Adonis* duly appeared in 1593, with the title page indicating that it was 'Imprinted by Richard Field' and that copies were 'to be sold at the signe of the white Greyhound in Paules Church-yard'. Paul's Churchyard was the centre of the London bookselling trade and the shop located at the sign of the white greyhound belonged to John Harrison the elder, to whom Field would transfer the publishing rights to the poem on 25 June of the following year. Only one copy of Field's first edition of *Venus and Adonis* is known to have survived. It was purchased by Edmond Malone in 1805, and he wrote on the flyleaf: 'Bought ... at the enormous price of Twenty five Pounds.'[11] The scarcity of the volume may point to its popularity, since it is an irony of publishing history that genuinely popular printed materials tend to be much handled and circulated, to the point where they disintegrate and drop from sight. As Sidney Lee observed in the introduction to his 1905 facsimile reprint of the poem, 'wholesale mortality is doubtless the penalty the work paid for its popularity and accessibility. The copies were eagerly read and re-read, were quickly worn out and were carelessly flung away' (§972, p. 54).

Certainly, the number of editions which followed on from the 1593 original is an index of the book's popular success. Field produced a second edition of the poem for Harrison in 1594, acting now as printer to Harrison as publisher. A third edition followed, probably in 1595 (the only extant copy lacks a title page) and by the year following Shakespeare's death (1617), a total of ten editions had been published. By 1636, the fifteenth edition appeared in diminutive sextodecimo format. Harrison was also the publisher (and Field the printer) of Shakespeare's *Rape of Lucrece*, which, while not as popular as *Venus and Adonis*, nevertheless had run through six editions by the year of Shakespeare's death. In 1627, *Venus and Adonis* became the first Shakespeare text to be published outside London, when John Wreittoun produced an octavo edition of the poem in Edinburgh.[12] In the second half of the century, only one edition each of the two poems appeared – *Lucrece* in 1655 and *Venus and Adonis* in 1675. The poems resurfaced in 1707, somewhat incongruously included in the fourth volume of *Poems on Affairs of State*, sandwiched between 'The Miseries of England, from the Growing Power of her Domestick Enemies' and 'The First Anniversary of the Government under his Highness the Lord Protector'.

Further evidence of the poems' popularity in Shakespeare's lifetime is provided by the fact that selections from the texts became something of a staple of Renaissance anthologies. In 1600, Robert Allott published his *England's Parnassus* anthology and he included among his selections thirty-nine passages from *Lucrece* and twenty-six from *Venus and Adonis*. In the same year, John Bodenham's *Belvedere* included ninety-one passages from *Lucrece* and thirty-four from *Venus*. In 1601 another of Shakespeare's poems, 'The Phoenix and the Turtle', was included in the collection *Loves Martyr or, Rosalins Complaint*. Poems by Shakespeare were also included in a compilation volume entitled *The Passionate Pilgrime*. The exact publishing history of this volume is somewhat obscure. An edition of the text was published in 1599, but it appears to have been based on an earlier edition, only one copy of which now survives, preserved at the Folger Shakespeare Library. The surviving copy of the first edition is incomplete and lacks a title page, so it cannot be accurately dated, but it is likely that both editions were issued in the same year.[13] The second edition was printed by William Jaggard (whose firm would later be closely associated with the production of the 1623 First Folio) and Jaggard printed a further edition in 1612. The title page of the second edition of this collection attributes authorship to 'W. Shakespeare', though only a small number of the poems in the collection are known to have been written by Shakespeare. The attribution is repeated in the third edition, where the title is expanded to *The Passionate Pilgrime.*

Or Certaine Amorous Sonnets, betweene Venus and Adonis, newly corrected and augmented. By W. Shakespeare. the third Edition. Whereunto is newly added two Loue-Epistles, the first from Paris to Hellen, and Hellens answere backe again to Paris. This new edition added some further poems, taken (without attribution) from Thomas Heywood's *Troia Britanica, or Great Britaines Troy*, which Jaggard had printed in 1609. In his *Apologie for Actors*, published in 1612, Heywood castigated Jaggard for the misattribution of his work to Shakespeare, indicating that Shakespeare too was displeased with the claims made on the volume's title page:

> Here likewise, I must necessarily insert a manifest iniury done me in that worke [*Troia Britanica*], by taking the two Epistles of *Paris* to *Helen*, and *Helen* to *Paris*, and printing them in a lesse volume, vnder the name of another . . . [But] as I must acknowledge my lines not worthy of his patronage, vnder whom he hath publisht them, so the Author I know much offended by M. *Iaggard* (that altogether vnknowne to him) presumed to make so bold with his name.[14]

It seems possible that Jaggard may have responded to protests either from Heywood or from Shakespeare, since, of the two surviving copies of the 1612 *Passionate Pilgrime*, one (held at the Bodleian) includes a second title page, which omits Shakespeare's name.

Heywood's complaint against Jaggard may possibly offer some tentative evidence of Shakespeare's own direct involvement in the publication of what has become his best-known volume of poems – the *Sonnets* collection – in 1609.[15] Of the poems by Shakespeare in the *Passionate Pilgrime* collection – which included some of the sonnets[16] – Heywood says that Shakespeare 'since, to do himself right, hath published them in his own name'.[17] The publisher of the 1609 volume, Thomas Thorpe, registered the text as 'a booke called Shakespeares sonnettes' and the same formula is repeated on the volume's title page: *Shakespeares Sonnets. Neuer before Imprinted* (if it is more than just a piece of puffery, '*Neuer before Imprinted*' here must presumably indicate the collection as a whole).[18] It may well be that this foregrounding of possessive authorship is what Heywood is pointing to when he refers to Shakespeare's having 'published' the poems 'in his own name'.[19] For all Francis Meres' early praise of Shakespeare's 'sugred sonnets' (then in circulation only among his 'private friends') in *Palladis Tamia* (1598), the 1609 volume seems not to have been a great commercial success. Thirteen copies of the volume have survived intact – by contrast, as we have seen, with the single fragment of the first edition of the very popular *Venus and Adonis*.

It took more than thirty years for the poems to appear in another edition, with John Benson finally republishing them in *Poems Written by Wil. Shakespeare. Gent* (1640). Benson derived his text partly from Thorpe's 1609 volume, though he omitted some of the poems included there. He also added some non-Shakespearean poems, taken from Jaggard's *Passionate Pilgrime*. In a prefatory epistle to the reader, Benson stressed – somewhat perplexingly, the modern reader may feel – the sedate clarity of the poems: '*in your perusall you shall finde them* Seren, *cleere and eligantly plaine, such gentle straines as shall recreate and not perplexe your braine, no intricate or cloudy stuffe to puzzell intellect, but perfect eloquence*' (§130, *2ᵛ).[20] The logic of Benson's claim (assuming that we take it to be anything more than just a conventional blurb) becomes clearer when we realise that he altered the text of the poems and the overall shape of the collection to achieve a general regularisation of effect. Many individual sonnets were combined into twenty-eight-line units, with somewhat anodyne titles being added: 'True admiration' (A4r), 'Youthfull glory' (A6r), 'A bashfull lover' (B5r), 'Two faithfull friends' (C5ᵛ). In some instances, poems are re-gendered to avoid sexual complexities, though Margreta de Grazia has argued that the extent and significance of this regendering has been exaggerated by many editors and critics.[21] Benson's vision of the poems proved to be an enduring one. The sonnets were not republished during the course of the seventeenth century, but when companion volumes of the poems were produced to accompany eighteenth-century editions of the plays it was, in almost every case, Benson's collection which served as the base text.[22] The first occasion on which 'the 1609 text was properly instated as the sole authoritative text of Shakespeare's sonnets' (§1676, p. 44) was when Edmond Malone edited the poems for his supplement to the 1778 Johnson–Steevens edition.

Looking back on the early history of the publication of his poetry from a twenty-first-century perspective, we may be inclined to feel that, with the possible exception of his fellow Stratfordian, Richard Field, Shakespeare was singularly poorly served by his publishers and printers. We should remember, however, that no concept of 'copyright', in its modern sense, existed in Shakespeare's time. 'Ownership' of texts was confined to publishers, who established their right to produce a work by licensing it with their professional body, the Stationers' Company; a publisher might additionally guarantee ownership of the text by paying a further fee to have the title entered in the Stationers' Register.[23] An author who brought a new work to a publisher would be paid for the text – sometimes, in part at least, by being given copies of the printed book – but this payment secured outright ownership of the text. The publisher might well transfer the rights to the text to a fellow publisher (as Field transferred his rights to *Venus and Adonis* to John Harrison the elder), but having once received the initial payment the author then ceased to have any further interest (in the legal sense) in the text. As Douglas A. Brooks has nicely observed: 'In early modern London, the death of the author was in some sense merely a workaday hazard of publication.'[24]

In the case of theatrical scripts, a further transactional layer intervened between the writer and the publisher. Plays for commercial production were, for the most part, commissioned by theatre companies from a pool of jobbing playwrights, many of them working collaboratively to produce scripts.[25] The going rate for a new play in Shakespeare's time appears to have been somewhere between £5 and £8.[26] Once purchased, the play became the property of the theatre company who might, if they chose, sell the play in due course to a publisher. Of course, from 1594 onwards, Shakespeare was in a rather different position from his fellow writers, in that he was a shareholder in the theatre company for which he wrote, and so he did, effectively, indirectly maintain partial ownership of his plays as performance texts. Earlier in his career, however, the situation was quite different.

The first play of Shakespeare's to be published was *Titus Andronicus*, which was printed by John Danter and was 'to be sold by Edward White & Thomas Millington'. As with most play texts produced during the Renaissance, it was published in quarto format and it probably sold for about 6*d*.[27] Like the majority of play texts published before 1600, the volume contained no indication of authorship – about ten editions of plays by Shakespeare published before 1600 would likewise appear without the playwright's name, a fact which serves to re-emphasise for us the differences between Renaissance and modern conceptions of authorship and textuality.[28] Danter, who ran a small-scale business out of Duck Lane in Smithfield, had registered the play some months before he printed it. Of the eighty titles he entered in the Stationers' Register, over half would appear to have been ballads, none of which seems to have survived.[29] Danter did, however, apparently have a strong connection with Thomas Nashe, for whom he printed several issues of *Strange News*, together with *The Terrors of the Night* (1594) and *Have With You to Saffron Walden* (1596). Nashe seems to have lived with Danter for a spell and in *Have With You to Saffron Walden* he defends Danter's wife against Gabriel Harvey's characterisation of her as a shrew.

An unflattering portrait of Danter himself is provided in the anonymous play *The Returne from Pernassus*, part two, which would seem to have been composed in 1601, some two years after Danter's death. Shakespeare himself had been much invoked in the first part of the play, as one of the characters, Gullio, is given to quoting from the poet and from his contemporaries, with or without acknowledgement. Ingenioso (probably himself a figure for Thomas Nashe) says of him at one point, 'Marke, Romeo and Iuliet: o monstrous theft, I thinke he will runn throughe a whole booke of Samuell Daniells.'[30] Danter appears as a character in part two of the *Returne* and he haggles with Ingenioso about the sale of a manuscript. Ingenioso offers Danter a book which he tells him 'has much salt and pepper in the nose: it will sell sheerely vnderhand, whenas these bookes of exhortations and Cathechismes lie moulding on thy shopboard'. Danter grudgingly offers Ingenioso 40*s.* for the book, together with an 'odde pottle of wine'. However, when Ingenioso makes clear to Danter that the book on offer constitutes 'A Chronicle of *Cambrige* Cuckolds', Danter perks up and exclaims: 'Oh, this will sell gallantly. Ile haue it whatsoeuer it cost.'[31] It is hard to say, of course, whether this portrait of Danter is accurate or malicious – after all, he was dead when it appeared and could not defend himself against such playful malevolence. However, if there is some element of truth in this image of the publisher, we might say that it is no surprise that he would be attracted to a sensationalist tale of horror such as *Titus Andronicus.* We do not know whether *Titus*, like the fictional *Cambridge Cuckolds*, 'sold gallantly', but a second edition was called for in 1600 and a third appeared in 1611. However, no further separate edition was published during the course of the seventeenth century. Of Danter's original first edition, only one copy now survives, which was discovered in Sweden in 1904 and purchased by Henry Clay Folger in the following year. The second and third editions were both published by Edward White, who, we will recall, Danter's title page identified, together with Thomas Millington, as a vendor of the text. White would seem to have claimed ownership of the play following Danter's death, but Millington also appears to have laid claim to it.[32] Whoever had the superior case, it was Millington who transferred the title to Thomas Pavier (of whom we will hear much more in chapter 2) on 19 April 1602. Pavier does not seem ever to have published an edition of the play.

  Titus Andronicus was one of two Shakespearean plays produced by John Danter. The second text was *Romeo and Juliet*, which was published in 1597, with a title page reading: *An Excellent conceited Tragedie Of Romeo and Iuliet. As it hath been often (with great applause) plaid publiquely, by the right Honourable the L. of Hunsdon his Seruants* (Q1, §15, title page).[33] Again, as in the case of *Titus Andronicus*, there was no attribution of authorship, and the stressing of the performance lineage of the text, its popular reception, and the aristocratic sponsorship enjoyed by the theatre company, are typical of play-script title pages from this period.[34] A second edition of *Romeo and Juliet* (Q2) appeared two years later, in 1599, this time published by Cuthbert Burbie and printed by Thomas Creed. Like Richard Field, Creed had been employed by William Ponsonby, for whom he produced editions of such works as the second part of Robert Greene's *Mamillia* (1593), Machiavelli's *Florentine History* (1595) and Edmund Spenser's *Colin Clouts Come Home Again* (1595). The title provided in the Burbie/Creed edition of *Romeo and Juliet* broadly follows the conventions registered in Danter's first edition (by this time, Lord Hunsdon had become the Lord Chamberlain, and so the company's name is duly upgraded): *The Most Excellent and lamentable Tragedie, of Romeo and Iuliet. Newly corrected, augmented, and amended: As it hath bene sundry times publiquely acted, by the right Honourable the Lord Chamberlaine his Seruants.* However, the inclusion of the phrase 'newly corrected, augmented, and amended' is significant, in that the purpose of this formula may have been to draw attention to important differences between the 1597 and 1599 texts. By comparison with the Second Quarto, the First Quarto is a significantly shorter text, as it lacks about 800 lines that are found in the Second Quarto, thus making it about one third shorter in total. Scene six of act II is also significantly recast between the two versions and there are notable alterations or reframings of the dialogue in III.1.145-61, IV.5.42-95, V.3.224-69 and elsewhere.[35]

Romeo and Juliet is not the only Shakespearean text to appear in two significantly variant versions. In 1603, Valentine Simmes published an edition of *Hamlet* for Nicholas Ling and John Trundell, which differed considerably from a further edition printed for Ling by James Roberts in the following year. The 1604 edition (some copies of which are dated 1605), is announced on the title page as 'Newly imprinted and enlarged to almost as much againe as it was, according to the true and perfect Coppie' (§50, 51, title page). Likewise, Thomas Creed printed an attenuated version of *The Merry Wives of Windsor* for Arthur Johnson in 1602; this text was reprinted in 1619, but an alternative and more expansive version of the text was produced for Richard Meighen by Thomas Harper in 1630. In Meighen's edition the text is described on the title page as 'Newly corrected'. This latter edition was effectively a reprint of the text which had been presented in the First Folio collected edition of Shakespeare's plays published seven years earlier in 1623. The First Folio also offered alternatives to some other texts which had previously appeared in significantly different quarto versions. *Henry V*, for example, had been published three times in attenuated quarto editions – in 1600, 1602, and 1619 (falsely dated 1608) – before a more expansive text was included in the First Folio. Likewise, the First Folio offered greatly expanded versions of *2* and *3 Henry VI*, which had appeared in earlier versions as, respectively, *The First part of the Contention betwixt the two famous*

Houses of Yorke and Lancaster and *The true Tragedie of Richard Duke of Yorke*. Thomas Millington had published the former of these texts in 1594 and 1600 and the latter in 1595 (unusually, in octavo format) and 1600 and Thomas Pavier had combined the two texts as *The whole contention betweene the two famous houses, Lancaster and Yorke* in an edition of 1619. Two other First Folio texts also offered significant – though considerably less extensive – variants on their quarto predecessors: *King Lear* (which had been published by Nathaniel Butter in 1608 and by Pavier in 1619) and the highly popular *Richard III*, which had run through six editions in advance of the First Folio (three published by Andrew Wise, in 1597, 1598 and 1602, and three by Matthew Lawe, in 1605, 1612 and 1622).[36]

The group of variant texts is rounded out by two further plays. The First Folio's *Taming of the Shrew* mirrors in certain respects a play entitled *The Taming of a Shrew*, which was published in 1594 by Peter Short for Cuthbert Burbie. The differences between the texts in this instance, however, are so pronounced that the plays have generally been regarded as separate entities, even as scholars have failed to agree on what exact relationship exists between them. Finally, we have the case of *Pericles*. It was omitted from the First Folio and did not appear in a collected edition of the plays until the second issue of the Third Folio in 1664. It had by then, however, been published six times in quarto. This play shares many of the features which are thought to be characteristic of the attenuated texts, with its brevity and perceived unevenness being taken as an indication that this, too, may be a compacted version, but one for which a more expansive alternative has not survived.

The short texts were formally classified as a group and labelled – some would say unjustly – as 'bad quartos' by A. W. Pollard in 1909.[37] The question of how these plays came to appear in two variant versions and of how exactly these versions found their way into print has puzzled Shakespearean scholars for centuries. Eighteenth-century editors tended generally to favour the view that the shorter plays were produced in advance of their longer counterparts and that they constituted 'first drafts' which Shakespeare subsequently worked over to produce the later, more polished and expansive versions. Alexander Pope was the first editor to adopt this view, specifically in relation to *Romeo and Juliet*, though, as Harry Hoppe has noted, Pope's position was complicated by his 'theory that many of the quartos contain added matter inserted by the actors after they had performed the dramas and had the prompt-books in their possession for a long period'.[38] Thus, while believing the Second Quarto to be Shakespeare's later version of the First Quarto, Pope nevertheless frequently substituted the First Quarto material for the Second Quarto in order to eliminate passages which he felt were '*unworthy of* Shakespear', laying the blame for these base passages at the feet of the players who, he observed acidly, were (in the manner of Procrustes) capable of 'either lopping, or stretching an Author, to make him just fit for their Stage' (§194, VI, p. 333, I, p. xvii). As Hoppe notes – again most specifically in relation to *Romeo and Juliet* – the first-draft theory was sustained by succeeding eighteenth-century editors such as Hanmer, Capell and Malone and on through the work of nineteenth-century scholars such as Singer, Knight, Verplanck, Ulrici, Hudson, Staunton, and Spedding.[39]

While Pope's theory generally found support among succeeding editors, his immediate successor, Lewis Theobald, tentatively offered an alternative explanation. Theobald suggested that, rather than the longer texts being expansions of their shorter counterparts, the shorter texts might, in fact, be abridged texts, with the abridgement resulting from inadequate rendering of the longer originals by copyists who had acquired the texts by using short-hand transcription: 'many Pieces were taken down in Short-hand, and im-perfectly copied by Ear, from a *Representation*' (§206, I, pp. xxxvii–xxxviii).[40] Theobald's notion was taken up by John Payne Collier in his 1842–4 edition of Shakespeare. Collier, who worked for much of his life as a journalist, had himself been a parliamentary reporter, and was proficient in shorthand.[41] The strength of interest in stenography in the latter half of the nineteenth century is indicated by the following passage from a letter which the *Variorum* editor H. H. Furness wrote to his sons in 1885:

> I received a telegram this eveg [sic] from 'L.F. Austin, Chicago' [the actor Henry Irving's agent, who was on tour with Irving in the US at the time] asking me to reply by telegraph whether or not I believed the first Quarto (the telegram spelled it 'quarter') of Hamlet was obtained by shorthand during representation. What a queer idea! to telegraph a question of that sort, on Sunday too! I suppose there had been some dispute & I am the referee. Has a note on Shakespeare ever been telegraphed before, I wonder? I have replied 'Aye' but it took thirty five words to say it.[42]

Furness' 'aye' must, however, be treated with considerable caution. Certainly a number of shorthand systems were available in the Renaissance period. Timothy Bright, in *Characterie, An Art of Short, Swift, and Secret Writing* (1588) offered one such system and Peter Bales, in *The Writing Schoolmaster* (1590), which set out a system known as 'brachygraphy', of-fered another. A more satisfactory system was advanced by John Willis, in his *Stenography* of 1602 (too late, of course, for the possibility of its having been used in producing many of the short quartos). Stenography was indeed used in the copying of sermons in the Renaissance period, but whether it was ever used for transcribing plays is much more difficult to establish.[43] One clear piece of evidence in favour of its use in the theatre appears to have been provided by Thomas Heywood, who included a prologue to a '*Play of Queene* Elizabeth' – probably his *1 If You Know Not Me You Know Nobody* – in his *Pleasant Dialogues and Dramas* (1637). In this prologue, Heywood commented on the mutilated quality of an earlier printed text of the play (Nathaniel Butter had first published it in 1605): 'some by Stenography drew / The plot: put it in print: (scarce one word trew:)'.[44] Heywood's testimony notwithstanding, a number of scholars writing in the first half of the twentieth century seriously called into question the possibility that shorthand could serve to explain the existence of attenuated play texts. William Matthews challenged the theory in a series of considered articles published in the 1930s. Matthews makes clear that the variants found in the short quartos are simply not of the kind that use of Bright or Bales' shorthand systems would have produced. Furthermore, he also argues that no one using either of these systems could have coped with a rate of speech of 150 to 200 words per minute, which he estimates to have been the average on the Renaissance stage.[45]

Matthews' conclusions were supported by G. N. Giordano-Orsini, who carried out an analysis of Heywood's *If You Know Not Me* and concluded that 'it seems fair to claim that either Heywood's assertion that it was by stenography that this play was put in print must be regarded as mistaken, or if stenography was used it was supplemented from the memories (and perhaps the "parts") of two or more actors'.[46] The general thrust of Giordano-Orsini's analysis is to suggest that the quality of the text is determined by exactly which actors are present on stage at any given time. When certain actors are present, the quality of the text is good; when they are absent, the quality of the text diminishes greatly. In advancing this analysis, Giordano-Orsini is clearly indebted to the work of W. W. Greg, who, in a 1910 study of the 1602 short-quarto version of *Merry Wives of Windsor*, noted 'the very unusual accuracy with which the part of mine Host is reported' and suggested that the 1602 text represented a version of the play which had been reconstructed from memory by the actor who had played the part of the Host, who then illicitly sold the text to the publisher (§1042, p. xxxvii).[47] Greg's original speculative formulation was complexly constructed – Laurie E. Maguire identifies thirteen separate interlocking elements in his analysis – and was advanced with a certain degree of tentativeness.[48] The idea of 'memorial reconstruction' was, however, subsequently taken up by a wide range of other commentators, with the result that it quickly became established as a critical commonplace. Paul Werstine notes that 'by the 1950s the idea that all imperfect texts were transmitted into print by reporters who memorially reconstructed plays had such a grip on textual criticism that it could survive any self-contradiction and explain almost any phenomenon'.[49]

The memorial theory leaned rather heavily on some broad generalisations concerning Renaissance theatrical and publishing practices. In the first instance, it exhibited something of an antitheatrical bias, as the lower ranks of Renaissance actors were imagined as being shiftless and dishonest. John Dover Wilson's identification of the bit-part actor who played Voltemar/Voltemand as the 'culprit' responsible for cobbling together the First Quarto *Hamlet* is typical in this regard:

> one phrase which he places in Hamlet's mouth . . . may . . . be
> unhesitatingly quoted as an authentic specimen of Voltemarian style. The
> phrase is 'drinking drunke.' Does it tell us the secret of the pirate's
> impecuniosity and his shifty devices to turn a dishonest penny? The First
> Grave-digger dismisses him with 'Go get thee to Yaughan's.' Possibly he
> knew the toper's haunts. . . . Let us leave the rascal drinking, if not drunk,
> at Yaughan's and pass on to the original copy which he mangled.[50]

Perhaps Wilson was correct: maybe bit-part actors in Shakespeare's time were indeed impecunious, bibulous and untrustworthy. At a deeper level, however, Wilson's jesting comment points to a general tendency within analyses based on the memorial reconstruction hypothesis. Such analyses often tend to rely on a high degree of speculative guesswork, in the absence of clear hard evidence. We may again take Wilson's work on *Hamlet* as an example here. He attributes to his reporter the mangling of 'to be or not to be', but then faces the question 'how comes Voltemar to be on the stage at this juncture?' Here is his response to his own enquiry:

> The answer is, I think, that Ophelia is saying her prayers during the
> soliloquy, that for this properties in the shape of a *prie-dieu*, and perhaps a
> simple altar, were necessary, and that Voltemar, possibly in his 'churlish
> priest' costume, had to make the required arrangements at the beginning
> of the scene.[51]

Reading this, it is hard not to feel the force of Fredson Bowers' rather uncharitable observation that Wilson's 'highly speculative mind produced more random insights than it did comprehensive working hypotheses that have stood the test of informed scrutiny'.[52] But one might also say that many of the explicatory structures built on the foundation of memorial reconstruction by scholars less flamboyant than Wilson are just as highly speculative.

The memorial theory is also problematic from the perspective of publishing history. Memorial reconstruction is predicated on the notion that there was a ready market for printed plays and that publishers were eager to get hold of the texts of popular works, so that they could tap into this market and turn a quick profit – so eager, in fact, that they were willing to resort to any means, fair or foul, to lay their hands on play scripts. Peter Blayney has, however, radically interrogated this set of assumptions. Blayney's analysis of Renaissance publishing practices reveals that only a very small number of new plays were published each year (an average of just 4.8 per annum in the final two decades of Elizabeth's reign) and that play publishing represented only a tiny percentage of overall publishing activity.[53] He also notes that, of the plays that were published, few were sufficiently commercially successful to justify being quickly reprinted. The reprint interval is indicative of the rate at which a text would have sold out its printrun, making back a publisher's upfront investment and, eventually, generating a profit. On the basis of his analysis of reprint evidence, Blayney argues that 'no more than one play in five would have returned the publisher's initial investment inside five years. Not one in twenty would have paid for itself during its first year – so publishing plays would not usually have been seen as a shortcut to wealth.'[54]

Blayney's findings make clear that, from the point of view of the economics of publishing, the notion of publishers paying bit-part actors to cobble together clandestine versions of stage plays in order to turn a speedy profit seems rather unlikely. Blayney's conclusions are supported by Laurie E. Maguire's rigorous analysis of the forty-one Renaissance plays which have at one time or another been identified as being memorially reconstructed. Maguire notes that evidence internal to the texts themselves suggests that only one of these plays (Marlowe's *Massacre at Paris*) can be said with any high degree of certainty to have been a memorial reconstruction and she argues that this text was probably assembled by a branch of the Strange's/Admiral's Men while performing away from London – not by a rogue actor (or actors) seeking to defraud theatrical colleagues.[55] Part of the problem with memorial reconstruction is, in a sense, its own ingenuity: it attempts to explain a wide variety of textual phenomena according to a single, elegant narrative. As Stephen Urkowitz, among others, has noted, Renaissance textuality is rarely open to such simple analysis:

> we may consider that the printed scripts of plays usually represent a confluence of pressures and contributions generated by an extended literary, theatrical, and publishing community: authors, shareholders, journeyman actors, apprentice boys, playhouse scribes and bookkeepers,

> different versions of chronicle histories, rival playwrights, theatrical
> censors, publishers, compositors setting from the initial manuscript copy,
> proof-readers, compositors setting from printed and possibly annotated
> copy in later quartos, and compositors setting Folio copy.[56]

Perhaps the best – albeit unsatisfactory – explanation that can be provided for
the divergent texts is that they offer variant conceptions of the plays, marked
by complex theatrical and extra-theatrical histories and arriving into print
by routes which are not amenable to a single explicatory narrative.[57] In this
sense, they testify to the diversity of textual culture at a time when the
commercial theatre was still in its infancy and when the contours of print
culture were just beginning to become established.[58]

Having mapped out some of the history of how Shakespeare's texts first
made it into print, we will move on to consider exactly who the readers
of these books might have been.[59] We have already noted that the typical
price of a quarto play text would be likely to have been 6*d.*; by the standard
of Renaissance wage rates this was quite expensive. Skilled craftsmen in
London in the period would typically have been paid about 16*d.* a day. Thus,
as Richard Altick has noted:

> a man who had seen *Hamlet* at the Globe and wanted to read it at his
> leisure would have had to spend between a quarter and a half of his day's
> earnings. With that same sixpence he could have bought two dinners or
> gone back to the Globe (if he were content to stand in the pit) for six
> more performances.[60]

Peter Blayney has provided some rather neat evidence indicating that publishers had the more prosperous, and more literate, end of the economic
spectrum in view when they brought out editions of plays. Blayney notes
that, by the end of the sixteenth century, roman type had largely displaced
blackletter, but that blackletter continued in use for certain types of publication. One area in which blackletter persisted was in the horn-book from
which children first learned their alphabet. This contrasted with the use
of roman type in Latin primers, such as Lily's *Grammar*. Blayney argues
that this fact 'apparently led the book trade to associate roman type with
a higher level of literacy and education than blackletter' and he notes that
works aimed at those who were less educated – 'jestbooks, works for the instruction and improvement of the young, certain kinds of sensational news
pamphlets, and above all, ballads' – were printed in blackletter. Blayney
presents some striking figures indicating the rapid decline in the use of
blackletter in play-text printing, noting that, between 1583 and 1592, 'nine
out of twenty plays (45 percent) were printed in blackletter, but in 1593–1602

the proportion dropped to ten out of seventy-six (13 percent)', and there-after the overwhelming majority of plays were printed in roman.[61] We can assume from this evidence that publishers quickly came to distinguish play texts from other sorts of popular entertainment publications, such as ballads and jestbooks.

Thomas Bodley, of course, famously excluded plays from the library which he helped to establish at Oxford University, classing them among the 'many idle bookes & riffe raffes . . . which shall neuer com into the Librarie', and fearing 'the harme that the scandal will bring vnto the Librarie, when it shalbe giuen out, that we stuffe it full of baggage bookes'.[62] It is clear from some of the recorded reactions to Shakespeare's work, however, that his books at-tracted a highly literate readership. Gabriel Harvey, the inveterate annotator, wrote in the margins of an edition of Chaucer that he acquired sometime after 1598: 'The younger sort takes much delight in Shakespeares Venus, & Adonis: but his Lucrece, & his tragedie of Hamlet, Prince of Denmarke, haue it in them, to please the wiser sort.'[63] Likewise, in his *Palladis Tamia* (1598), Francis Meres, in addition to claiming, on the basis of his poetry, that 'the sweete wittie soule of *Ovid* liues in mellifluous & hony-tongued *Shakespeare*' also elevated the playwright's dramatic work to an equivalent status with the classics by noting that 'As *Plautus* and *Seneca* are accounted the best for Comedy and Tragedy among the Latines: so *Shakespeare* among the English is the most excellent in both kinds for the stage.'[64] But Shakespeare's reader-ship extended beyond what might be considered a metropolitan or academic coterie. Sir Thomas Barrington of Essex left a record of the books he pur-chased between 1635 and 1639, ranging from the 'theological, tractarian and philosophical' through to Latham's *Falconry*, Gervase Markham's *Faithful Farrier* and to such titles as *The Swedish Intelligencer*. His purchases also ran to several literary works, including George Herbert's *The Temple* and (in December 1637) the two parts of Shakespeare's *Henry IV* and a copy of the second folio.[65]

Evidence that the reading of dramatic texts was not the exclusive province of men and that women may well have made up a very significant proportion of the readers of play texts is provided in Humphrey Moseley's preface to his Beaumont and Fletcher folio of 1647. Moseley justified his restriction of the volume to plays which had not previously appeared in print by commenting that, to have done otherwise 'would have rendred the Booke so Voluminous, that *Ladies* and *Gentlewomen* would have found it scarce manageable, who in works of this nature must first be remembred'. As Peter Blayney has observed, an 'unqualified "must be remembred" might have been simple gallantry, but "must *first* be remembred" suggests that Moseley envisaged a readership in which women outnumbered men'.[66] Further evidence of female readership is provided in an early seventeenth-century letter from one Ann Merricke to her friend, Mistress Lydall, in which she laments not being able to attend the London theatre:

> I cu'd wish my selfe with you, to ease you of this trouble, and with-all to see the Alchymist, which I heare this terme is revis'd, and the newe playe a freind of mine sent to Mr. John Sucklyn, and Tom: Carew (the best witts of the time) to correct, but for want of these gentile recreationes, I must content my selfe here, with the studie of Shackspeare, and the historie of woemen, All my countrie librarie.[67]

Later in the century, in 1664, Margaret Cavendish wrote the first ever critical essay to be published on Shakespeare – Letter CXXIII of her *Sociable Letters*.[68]

Use of the printed texts of the plays was not exclusively confined to the realm of the study. A 1611 Star Chamber trial for sedition throws up interesting evidence for the use of the texts in provincial performance. Sir Richard Chomeley's players – a provincial acting company made up of recusants – were accused of having presented a seditiously pro-catholic play, *Saint Christopher*, at Gowthwaite Hall in Nidderdale in Yorkshire during the Christmas season of 1609. Of interest in the current context is the testimony of one of the players, William Harrison, that, in addition to *Saint Christopher*, 'one of the playes acted and played was Perocles prince of Tire, And the other was Kinge Lere'. Harrison goes on to insist that 'these plaies which they so plaied were vsuall playes And such as were acted in Common and publicke places and Staiges . . . and such as were played publicly and prynted in the bookes'. Speaking specifically of *Saint Christopher* and attempting to establish its credentials as a play which had been endorsed for publication by the appropriate authorities, Richard Simpson (one of the family whose members made up the core of the company) insisted that their performance of it was 'played according to the printed booke or Bookes' and that 'the booke by which [they] did act . . . was a printed book, And they onelie acted the same according to the contents therein printed, and not otherwise'.[69] No copy of *Saint Christopher* has survived, but the first quartos of *Lear* and *Pericles* were, at the time, both recent London publications: Nathaniel Butter had published *Lear* in 1608 and Henry Gosson had brought out *Pericles* in the following year.[70]

It seems clear then, that, at least in a limited way, printed play texts were being used as the basis for creating performance scripts outside of London. Some additional evidence in support of this conclusion is provided by Thomas Middleton's *Mayor of Quinborough*, where reference is made to thieves who 'only take the name of Country-Comedians / To abuse simple people with a printed play or two, / Which they bought at *Canterbury* for six pence'.[71] There have been some suggestions that printed texts may have been used as promptbooks in the London theatres also, but W. W. Greg has been sceptical of this view, indicating that 'It is by no means certain that the prompter would have found a quarto convenient' and noting that a printed text 'would offer less room for annotation, and the prompter, used to a "book" with from fifty to eighty lines to a page, might feel less at home with a quarto half the size, which would entail more turning of the leaves and restrict his freedom to look ahead'. On the other hand, Greg observes, 'if their prompt-book were accidentally destroyed or lost, or if it merely became worn with use, [the players] would be likely enough to substitute a printed edition if one was available'.[72]

By the 1640s, of course, the printed text was the *only* form that plays could take. In September of 1642, an order from parliament temporarily forbade the performance of plays on the grounds that 'publicke Sports doe not well agree with publike Calamities'.[73] In 1644, the Globe was pulled down and the ban on performances was officially made permanent in 1647. In that same year, Moseley's Beaumont and Fletcher edition obliquely made reference to the civil war and the ban on performance, offering the printed volume as a substitute for live theatre: 'For, since ye saw no *Playes* this Cloudy weather, / Here we have brought Ye our whole Stock together.'[74] In the case of Shakespeare, however, the theatrical interregnum largely coincided with a significant decline in publishing activity. None of Shakespeare's plays was published during the course of the 1640s and only three plays appeared in print in the following decade: *Merchant of Venice* in 1652 and *King Lear* and *Othello*, both in 1655 (the *Lear* text was the first to bear a woman's name in its imprint, that of Jane Bell). With the restoration of the monarchy in 1660, a revived theatrical culture quickly begin to emerge. The first plays to be performed at the earliest of the Restoration London theatres – an open air venue called the 'Red Bull' – included *The Merry Wives of Windsor*, *Othello* and *Henry IV*. The repertoire of a smaller company at the Phoenix in Drury Lane included *Pericles*.[75] Michael Dobson has argued, however, that, early in the Restoration period, 'Shakespeare's plays, among the oldest in the repertory, seemed anomalous' and he cites the well-known example of John Evelyn's 1661 diary comment: 'I saw *Hamlet* Pr: of Denmark played but now the old playe began to disgust this refined age: since his Majestie being so long abroad.'[76] The *Hamlet* that Evelyn saw and disliked was almost certainly a version of the play that had been produced by William Davenant, who served as an important link between the Restoration and the ante-bellum theatre. Davenant had been Charles I's poet laureate and, from 1660, he led the Duke's Men, one of the two principal Restoration companies. Davenant's version of *Hamlet* was published in 1676, with the title page indicating that the text was given 'As it is now Acted at his Highness the Duke of York's Theatre' (§140, title page).[77] By contrast with many later Restoration adaptations, the 1676 *Hamlet* is reasonably faithful to Shakespeare's original, though some of the language has been moderated to make it more suited to the tastes of a contemporary audience. Hazleton Spencer has noted 'a number of cases of the literalization of figures of speech and the toning down of especially vigorous language'.[78] In performance, the play was very extensively cut and the printed text carries the following note:

> To the Reader.
> This Play being too long to be conveniently Acted, such Places as might be least prejudicial to the Plot or Sense, are left out upon the Stage: but that we may in no way wrong the incomparable Author, are here inserted according to the Original copy with this Mark ".
>
> (§140, unpaged)

Spencer notes that 'In general the cutting is done with a view to retaining what is dramatic, and lopping off the lyric and sententious passages which have now become elocutionary arias for Hamlet.'[79] Other acting-version texts followed this players' quarto *Hamlet*: *Othello* (1681) and *Julius Caesar* (1684), both as 'now Acted at the Theater Royal' (§143, 146, title page), and *1 Henry IV* (1700), 'As it is Acted at the Theatre in Little-Lincolns-Inn-Fields by his Majesty's Servants' (§158, title page).[80]

The 1676 *Hamlet* was reprinted in 1683, 1695 and 1703, and in 1718 a second series of performance *Hamlet*s was initiated, based on a text established by Robert Wilks, who offered a set of cuts which differed from Davenant's. Henry N. Paul notes that 'The history of this text and its printings is a long one. It was constantly reprinted in duodecimo for theatrical uses, each successive reprint being made from the preceding printing with the usual accumulation of printer's errors which this process entails.'[81] Paul traces the history of this text forward to 1761. The evident success of these acting texts points to a persistent niche market within Shakespeare publishing, as performance editions of the plays have reappeared over the centuries. The best-known theatrical editions include Bell's 1773 (and later) texts 'of Shakespeare's Plays, as they are now performed at the Theatres Royal in London. Regulated from the Prompt Books of each House', which Charles H. Shattuck observes were 'widely used for promptbook-making for two or three decades'. Shattuck notes the persistence of the genre well into the nineteenth century:

> Kemble's acting editions of the separate plays in his own repertoire were printed and reprinted in the 1790's and down to about 1815, and they generally displaced Bell for professional uses. After the turn of the century 'standard' acting editions proliferated: Mrs. Inchbald's about 1808, Oxberry's by 1820, Cumberland's about 1830 and after, Hinds English Stage in the later 1830's, Thomas Hailes Lacy's from the 1840's to about 1864 . . . In the 1850's Charles Kean revived the Kemble practice of publishing his own versions of the plays as he staged them, and after him Charles Calvert, Henry Irving, and others followed suit.[82]

From the early twentieth century onwards, a new version of the theatrical edition emerged with the appearance of film tie-in editions, such as the 'motion picture edition, illustrated with photographs' of *Romeo and Juliet*, published in 1936 and based on George Cukor's film of the same year, or the 1996 Kenneth Branagh *Hamlet* edition, which includes a screenplay and film diary. A curious variation on this publishing phenomenon appeared in 1998, when the film *Shakespeare in Love* prompted the release of an editorially stripped-down version of the *New Penguin Shakespeare* edition of *Shakespeare's Sonnets*, to capitalise on a rekindled interest in Shakespeare's 'love poetry'.[83]

Penguin's love poems volume marks the long and complex road of Shakespeare publishing stretching between the early poetry editions of the 1590s and our own era of multiplicitous editions targeted at diverse market segments. The primary aim of this chapter has been to explore the history of the single text editions of Shakespeare's works in their first century of publication. Many of the earliest editions of the texts of Shakespeare and his fellow playwrights were seen largely as publishing ephemera – 'baggage bookes', as Thomas Bodley put it. In 1616, however, Ben Jonson lent a certain respectability to dramatic works, by including the text of his plays in the folio volume of his collected works. While Jonson's gesture was received with a certain degree of scepticism by some of his contemporaries – one wit remarked 'Pray tell me *Ben*, where doth the mystery lurke, / What others call a play you call a worke' – it nevertheless paved the way for other large-scale collected editions of Renaissance play texts.[84] Within three years of the appearance of Jonson's volume, plans would be in hand to issue a collection of Shakespeare's plays.

At the very beginning of the twentieth century, A. W. Pollard 'had the pleasure of making the acquaintance of a German gentleman who had found,
among the treasures of a library formed by a book-loving ancestor . . . a
volume containing nine quarto plays with all of which Shakespeare's name
has been connected'. The gentleman made his way to London and, soon,
Pollard tells us,

> the fat little volume was in my hands, and as I took it out of its wrapping
> I felt as if my new acquaintance had brought an old friend with him, for
> on the plain brown calf cover I saw stamped in gold EDWARD GWYNNE,
> the name of a well-known seventeenth-century collector, who frequently
> marked his books in this way.[1]

The first two plays in the volume – the variant versions of *2* and *3 Henry VI* –
were grouped together under the single title *The Whole Contention between
the two famous houses of York and Lancaster* and the other plays were also
provided with individual title pages, which indicated a variety of imprints
and dates. Like *The Whole Contention*, the *Henry V* and *Merry Wives* texts
included in the volume were also based on variant quartos. The other plays in
the collection were *The Merchant of Venice*, *King Lear*, *A Midsummer Night's
Dream*, *Pericles*, and the apocryphal plays *A Yorkshire Tragedy* and *Sir John
Oldcastle*. A few years later Pollard came across another Shakespeare volume,
containing the same selection of texts, but bound in a different order. Struck
by the coincidence, Pollard sought evidence for the existence of other such
volumes. He found that the Capell collection at Trinity College Library,
Cambridge had the exact same set of plays bound into two volumes and
that the Garrick collection at the British Museum also had a set of the ten
plays, bound individually. Enquiries farther afield led to the discovery that
the University of Virginia had at one time owned a single volume set of
the plays, which had been presented to the university by Thomas Mann
Randolph, the son-in-law of Thomas Jefferson. The volume had, however,
been lost in a fire in 1895.[2]

Endeavouring to explain the existence of these discrete sets of variously dated texts, Pollard tentatively suggested that the plays dated earlier than 1619 'belonged to unsold stock, and that the news of the forthcoming folio of 1623 caused them to be thrown on the market as what we now call a "remainder" '.[3] The notion of 'remainders' is, however, somewhat anachronous in an early seventeenth-century context, since it was not until late in the next century that the practice of remaindering began significantly to develop, with Thomas Tegg playing a leading role ('I was the broom that swept the booksellers' warehouses', he tells us).[4] Within two years of Pollard's suggestion, however, W. W. Greg advanced an entirely different explanation for the existence of the quarto collections. Greg discovered certain peculiarities in the various plays that made up the sets. The most notable feature he observed was that the plays were all printed on a mixed stock of paper and that a similar mixture of sheets was evident in texts supposedly printed at different times and by different printers. Greg concluded from this evidence that the plays must all have been produced at the same time by the same printer and that the earlier dates and some of the imprints were therefore falsified, with the intent to deceive.[5] In 1910, William J. Neidig provided further proof that the quartos had all been produced in the same print shop and that they had been printed more or less consecutively. Neidig observed that he 'proposed to apply to the study of the printed page a system of exact measurements not unlike the modern Bertillon system of measuring criminals'.[6] We will come on to the question of just who the 'criminals' were in this case in a moment, but let us first observe Neidig's detective work in action. Neidig analysed a set of precisely calibrated photographs of the title pages of the quarto texts and he noticed that certain parts of many of these pages could be mapped onto each other, producing an exact match. Thus, for example, a composite photograph of the supposed 1600 *Merchant of Venice* and the 1619 *Pericles* reveals that the attribution line 'Written by W. SHAKESPEARE', the 'HEB DIEU HEB DDIM' printer's device, and the initial 'Printed' of the imprint matched each other exactly. Neidig therefore concluded that

> The compositor of these two quartos . . . used a single setting of type for the printing of his title-pages except in the upper portions. After the first title-page was printed, this economical compositor simply 'fatted' the entire lower half of the page and made it do duty for the second – made a 'pick-up' of it, or 'lifted' it, in order to avoid the labor of resetting the type and quads of which it was constructed.[7]

Neidig traced his 'economical' compositor's tracks through a total of seven of the nine quartos and by observing changes to the type he was able to establish the order in which the plays were printed. A further piece of confirmatory evidence in support of Greg's and Neidig's analyses was offered some decades later by Allan H. Stevenson who, as he tells us, 'On a perfect morning in July, when I might have been bowling on the greens of Arroyo Seco', instead examined the Huntington Library copies of the 1619 quartos and discovered what he took to be traces of figures in some of the watermarks, indicating the year in which the paper was manufactured. Thus, for example, *Henry V*, supposedly 'Printed for T. P. 1608' appeared to have a watermark dated 1617 or 1619.[8]

Who, then, was responsible for printing and for publishing these plays, and what reason did they have for resorting to the ruse of false imprints? The publisher can be identified readily enough. The rights to at least half of the plays included in the collection were owned by Thomas Pavier and it is, indeed, his initials that appear most frequently on the title pages. Evidence from the ornaments and typestock used indicates that the printer of the texts was William Jaggard. Pavier and Jaggard had collaborated in the past, when, in 1601, they had jointly published *A View of all the Right Honourable the Lord Mayors of this Honorable Citty of London*, which Jaggard (who was the author of the short volume) had dedicated to the then sitting lord mayor, Sir William Ryder.[9] They also collaborated on publishing a number of play texts in 1605, including *The Fair Maid of Bristow*, *The First Part of Hieronimo* and *Captain Thomas Stukeley*.[10] The two publishers evidently remained lifelong friends, as Jaggard later named Pavier as overseer in his will.[11] The Pavier joint venture was not Jaggard's first hazard in Shakespearean publishing – as we have already seen, he was the publisher of the *Passionate Pilgrime* poetry collection which had attracted Thomas Heywood's (and possibly Shakespeare's own) bitter complaint.[12]

If it is easy enough to identify the principal agents behind the 1619 collection, it is much more difficult to say exactly why they proceeded as they did. Pavier was perfectly entitled to publish many of the plays included in the collection. He owned the rights to the two plays that made up the *Whole Contention*, together with the rights to the apocryphal *Yorkshire Tragedy* and *Sir John Oldcastle* and the variant quarto of *Henry V*.[13] *Pericles* is a rather complicated case, in that it was entered in the Stationers' Register to Edward Blount in 1608. Blount never published the play, but Henry Gosson did issue two editions in 1609, and in 1611 another edition appeared, with an imprint indicating that it was printed 'by S. S.' – probably the former draper Simon Stafford. Greg suggested that since 'The first edition contravened the entrance . . . clearly no copyright was recognized [and the] copy was derelict.'[14] The situation does not, however, seem to have been quite as clear-cut as this and it is possible that Pavier had some sort of claim to the text, perhaps, as Gerald D. Johnson speculates, arising from his association with Henry Gosson, with whom he had entered into a ballad-publishing partnership.[15] At any rate, his ownership of the text seems later to have been accepted as legitimate.[16] The rights to *Merry Wives* were held by Arthur Johnson, whose name is included on Pavier's title page, together with the correct date, so in this instance it would appear that Pavier had secured Johnson's consent to the reprint. Nathaniel Butter held the rights to *King Lear* and Pavier and Butter had collaborated in publishing editions of *If You Know Not Me* in 1608 and 1610 and would continue to collaborate after 1619. As in the case of Johnson, then, it would appear that Pavier came to some arrangement with Butter regarding *Lear* and Butter's name appeared on the title page, though, in this case, the imprint was dated 1608, the year in which Butter produced his own first edition of the play. The final two texts included in the collection were *Midsummer Night's Dream* and *The Merchant of Venice*, the rights to which had been owned by Thomas Fisher and Thomas Hayes (or 'Heyes'), respectively. Neither of these plays had been reprinted since their original editions of 1600 and both Fisher and Hayes were dead by 1619. *Merchant* had originally been entered to James Roberts, who assigned the copy to Hayes on 28 October 1600, and who had printed the 1600 edition for him. William Jaggard had taken over James Roberts' business in around 1608 and so may have felt that he had some sort of slender claim on the rights to *Merchant*.[17] In any event, the play was included in the Pavier collection with a James Roberts imprint, dated 1600. The same procedure was followed with *Midsummer Night's Dream*, though here the Roberts connection was even more slender – he had simply been the printer of the 1600 edition. A summary of all of this information is provided in table 2.1.

Pavier has sometimes been characterised as a rogue printer on the basis of the 1619 collection (in 1902 Sidney Lee went so far as to describe him as 'a publisher of evil repute' – see §914, 'Introduction', p. xv). In fact, however, with the exception of some difficulties with the authorities early in his career, Pavier was a well-respected member of the publishing trade and served as Assistant Warden and Under Warden for the Stationers' Company – indeed in the very year in which the quartos appeared Pavier was elected to the Court of Assistants of the Company.[18] Play-text publication represented only a tiny proportion of his output and his more usual stock-in-trade was, as Gerald D. Johnson has noted, 'reprints of popular sermons such as *A Jewell for the Eare* and *Gods Arrowe Against Atheists*, and of devotional tracts such as *The Doctrine of the Bible* and *A Garden of Spirituall Flowers*'.[19] Of course public piety is no guarantee against private iniquity, but, as Johnson

Table 2.1 *Ownership and publication details for the Pavier quartos collection*

Title	Ownership	Imprint	Date	Sigs.
The Whole Contention	Pavier	Printed at London, for T. P.	n.d.	A–Q4
Pericles	Unclear – Pavier or derelict	Printed for T. P.	1619	Tit., R–Aa4, Bb1
A Yorkshire Tragedy	Pavier	Printed for T. P.	1619	Tit., A–C4, D1-3
The Merchant of Venice	Thomas Hayes (dec.), acquired from James Roberts (1600); claimed by Lawrence Hayes (1619)	Printed by J. Roberts	1600	A–K4
The Merry Wives of Windsor	Arthur Johnson	Printed for Arthur Johnson	1619	A–G4
King Lear	Nathaniel Butter	Printed for Nathaniel Butter	1608	A–H4
Henry V	Pavier	Printed for T. P.	1608	A–G4
Sir John Oldcastle	Pavier	London printed for T. P.	1600	A–K4
A Midsummer Night's Dream	Thomas Fisher (dec.); probably derelict	Printed by Iames Roberts	1600	A–H4

has further noted, if the falsified dates and casuistically contrived imprints in the 1619 quartos were intended to deceive Pavier's publishing brethren, then the deception was perpetrated with singular ineptitude, since, unlike other examples of counterfeit printing from the period, the Pavier quartos make little enough effort to imitate the title pages of the texts being copied.[20] If Pavier was attempting to work around the blind side of anyone it was probably the King's Men theatre company that he had a wary eye on, rather than the Stationers' Company. In the year in which the Pavier quartos appeared, the King's Men had sought the help of the Lord Chamberlain in securing their interest in their textual property. On 3 May 1619, the Court of the Stationers' Company recorded consideration of a letter from the Lord Chamberlain which led them to proclaim that 'It is thought fitt & so ordered That no playes that his Ma^tyes players do play shalbe printed w^thout consent of some of them.'[21] It is impossible to say whether the King's Men were responding directly to Pavier in making this move and, if so, how it was that they got wind of his undertaking.[22] In any event, the falsified title pages would appear to have shielded Pavier well enough from the wrath of the King's Men and Johnson has suggested that they may have provided Pavier with enough of a fig leaf for the officers of the Stationers' Company to have overlooked the affair: 'Since there is no record that anyone protested, it must be assumed that the ruse succeeded, or that, as is more likely, the officers of the Company simply winked at the affair.'[23]

Pavier may have been motivated to embark on his collection in the first instance because he had spotted a potential gap in the publishing market. Shakespeare had died in 1616 and none of his plays had appeared in print since 1615. The English history plays were clearly very popular, with the variant text of *Richard III*, together with *1 Henry IV* and *Richard II* all clocking up five editions each by that year. Pavier may have thought that he could build on that popularity by reissuing his own Shakespearean histories – the variant *2* and *3 Henry VI* – and perhaps felt that it would be a timely move to combine these plays with a selection of other Shakespearean titles which would provide a substantial volume of selected plays. That Pavier clearly had a collection in mind is indicated by the signature numbers of the first three plays included in the set (see table 2.1). Pavier, as we have seen, provided a single title page for the Henry plays, but he also signed the two plays in sequence (A-Q4). Likewise, *Pericles*, the next play to have been printed, continues the signature sequence established by the Henry plays, indicating that it is being thought of as part of the same volume as the first two plays. After *Pericles*, the sequence is abandoned and the remaining plays are signed individually – perhaps this provides a clue as to when exactly it was that Pavier realised his project might be likely to fall foul of the King's Men's proprietorial tendencies. After *Pericles* the plays are no longer being thought of as belonging to a single sequential volume.

It is conceivable that the action taken by the King's Men may have been prompted by their having themselves spotted the very same market gap that Pavier had identified. They too, it seems, were weighing the sales potential of a volume that would draw together the plays of their recently deceased leading playwright.[24] Or, to put it in less crudely commercial terms, they may have been contemplating the possibility of erecting a kind of textual monument to the memory of their departed colleague and friend. The project was driven forward by John Heminge and Henry Condell – fellow actors and sharers in the King's Men. Shakespeare, in his will, had left 'to my ffellowes John Hemynge Richard Burbage & Henry Cundell xxvj[s] viii[d] A peece to buy them Ringes'.[25] On the death of Burbage in 1619 Heminge and Condell assumed the leadership of the King's company.[26] Heminge in particular seems to have been commercially enterprising as, in addition to acting with and helping to run the King's Men, he was also the proprietor of a tap-house which adjoined the Globe.[27] The tap-house, like the Globe itself, was a victim of the fire of 1613. A contemporary ballad describes how 'with swolne eyes, like druncken Flemminges, / Distressed stood old stuttering Heminges' and regrets that no shower of rain assisted in putting out the fire 'Nor thou, O ale-howse, neither', before going on to note 'Had itt begunne belowe, sans doubte', the wives of Burbage, 'Henry Condye' and Heminge 'for fear had pissed itt out'.[28]

Heminge and Condell drew together the texts of thirty-six of Shakespeare's plays, for inclusion in a single volume of folio size, published in 1623; eighteen of the plays had not appeared in print before this collection.[29] The plays were organised into three categories: Comedies, Histories, and Tragedies, creating some anomalies, such as the inclusion of *Cymbeline* among the tragedies; the redesignation as histories of some plays described as tragedies in quarto (such as *Richard II*, *Richard III*, *3 Henry VI*); and the reconceiving of some plays on historical subjects as tragedies (e.g., *Macbeth* and the Roman plays). Commenting on the rationale for organising the texts in this way, Stephen Orgel has observed:

> Some of the Shakespearean chronology would doubtless have been forgotten by 1623 . . . and associating all the plays according to their subject matter, which was the system employed for those concerned with English history, might well have proved excessively arbitrary. But just as grouping his epigrams together under the rubric of the classical genre seemed to Jonson to confer a special dignity on his favourite poems, so the genres themselves, at any rate those of comedy and tragedy, must also have had the attraction of classical forms for Shakespeare's first editors, conferring the dignity of ancient drama on the work of their fellow actor.[30]

In addition to being afforded a classical framework, *Mr. William Shakespeares Comedies, Histories, & Tragedies* was also the first folio-size volume ever to be dedicated entirely to play texts (Jonson's 1616 folio was not exclusively dramatic). Traditionally, the folio format had been reserved for works of a serious nature and in the 1630s William Prynne commented sniffily in *Histrio-Mastix* that

> *Some Play-books since I first undertooke this subject, are growne from* Quarto *into Folio; which yet beare so good a price and sale, that I cannot but with griefe relate it, they are now (e) new-printed in farre better paper than most Octavo or* Quarto *Bibles, which hardly finde such vent as they.*

In the marginal annotation to his text Prynne further complains '(e) Shackspeers Plaies are printed in the best Crowne paper, far better than most Bibles'.[31] Prynne's sense of indignation notwithstanding, the folio format may not necessarily in itself have been intended as a gesture of aggrandisement, since the sheer quantity of text involved would almost certainly have ruled out any other format for a single volume edition.[32] As Charlton Hinman has pointed out:

> Unless these thirty-six plays were to be set forth in a type so small as hardly to be readable, the single volume that was contemplated would have to be a very large one at best. Only the capacious pages of a folio would be at all suitable; and a book of something like 1,800 pages would be required anyway, unless double columns as well as pages of maximum size were used [which, of course, they were].[33]

The publishers of the volume are identified in the colophon as 'W. Jaggard, Ed. Blount, I. Smithweeke, and W. Aspley'. Jaggard's involvement has seemed to many to be surprising, given his less than illustrious Shakespearean track record, but he had theatrical connections of long-standing, having acquired the monopoly of playbill printing when he took over the business of James Roberts.[34] Furthermore, Peter Blayney has noted that Jaggard would have been well-placed to negotiate with some of those who held the rights to a number of the plays.[35] With Pavier, obviously, he was well connected and, as we have seen, Pavier held the rights to *2* and *3 Henry VI* and *Henry V* (the fact that these were all variant texts had no bearing on the rights issue) and he may also have had a claim to *Titus Andronicus*. Nathaniel Butter and Arthur Johnson seem to have been persuaded to allow the inclusion of their texts of *Merry Wives of Windsor* and *King Lear* in the 1619 collection, so, again, Jaggard might well have been helpful in persuading them to agree to the inclusion of texts of these plays in the First Folio.[36] Two of the publishers listed in the First Folio colophon would appear to have been drawn into the syndicate precisely because of their Shakespeare holdings. John Smethwick owned *Hamlet, Romeo and Juliet, Love's Labour's Lost* and *The Taming of the Shrew* (indirectly, by virtue of owning the rights to *A Shrew*) and William Aspley owned *Much Ado About Nothing* and *2 Henry IV*. A summary of the ownership rights and prior publication history of the plays is provided in table 2.2.

Smethwick and Aspley seem not to have played a very active part in the venture and the title page of the Folio indicates that it was 'Printed by Isaac Iaggard, and Ed. Blount'. This imprint is misleading in that Blount was a publisher, not a printer. The printing was carried out entirely by the

Table 2.2 *Ownership and publication details for the texts included in the First Folio. Plays are listed in the order in which they appear in the Folio*

Title	Ownership in 1623	Publication History
The Tempest	Blount & Jaggard	First published in Folio
The Two Gentlemen of Verona	Blount & Jaggard	First published in Folio
The Merry Wives of Windsor	Arthur Johnson	Q1 1602; Q2 1619 (both variants)
Measure for Measure	Blount & Jaggard	First published in Folio
The Comedy of Errors	Blount & Jaggard	First published in Folio
Much Ado About Nothing	William Aspley	Q 1600
Love's Labour's Lost	John Smethwick	Q1 1598; possible other edition predating Q1, now lost
A Midsummer Night's Dream	Thomas Pavier or derelict	Q1 1600; Q2 1619
The Merchant of Venice	Lawrence Hayes	Q1 1600; Q2 1619
As You Like It	Blount & Jaggard	First published in Folio
The Taming of the Shrew	John Smethwick (by virtue of owning *Taming of a Shrew*)	*The Shrew* first published in Folio. *A Shrew* published: Q1 1594; Q2 1596; Q3 1607.
All's Well that End's Well	Blount & Jaggard	First published in Folio
Twelfth Night	Blount & Jaggard	First published in Folio
The Winter's Tale	Blount & Jaggard	First published in Folio
King John	John Dewe might have had a claim to the text, on the basis of his having been the most recent publisher of a separate play, *The Troublesome Reign of King John*	First published in Folio *Troublesome Reign* published: Q1 1591; Q2 1611; Q3 1622.
Richard II	Matthew Law	Q1 1597; Q2, Q3 1598; Q4, Q4a 1608; Q5 1615
1 Henry IV	Matthew Law	(Possible early edition, of which only an undated fragment survives); Q1 1598; Q2 1599; Q3 1604; Q4 1608; Q5 1613; Q6 1622
2 Henry IV	William Aspley	Q1, Q1a 1600
Henry V	Thomas Pavier	Q1 1600; Q2 1602; Q3 1619 (all variant)
1 Henry VI	Blount & Jaggard	First published in Folio

Table 2.2 (*cont.*)

Title	Ownership in 1623	Publication History
2 Henry VI	Thomas Pavier	Q1 1594; Q2 1600; Q3 1619 – jointly with *3HVI* as *Whole Contention* (all variant)
3 Henry VI	Thomas Pavier	Octavo 1 1595; Q ed. 2 1600; Q ed 3 1619 – jointly with *2HVI* as *Whole Contention* (all variant)
Richard III	Matthew Law	Q1 1597; Q2 1598; Q3 1602; Q4 1605; Q5 1612; Q6 1622 (all variant)
Henry VIII	Blount & Jaggard	First published in Folio
[*Troilus and Cressida*]	Henry Walley (but Jaggard had a very tenuous claim, via James Roberts)	Q 1609
Coriolanus	Blount & Jaggard	First published in Folio
Titus Andronicus	Derelict (though Thomas Pavier may have had a slender claim)	Q1 1594; Q2 1600; Q3 1611
Romeo and Juliet	John Smethwick	Q1 1597 (variant); Q2 1599; Q3 1609; undated Q4, possibly 1622
Timon of Athens	Blount & Jaggard	First published in Folio
Julius Caesar	Blount & Jaggard	First published in Folio
Macbeth	Blount & Jaggard	First published in Folio
Hamlet	John Smethwick's title appears to have been recognised	Q1 1603 (variant); Q2 1604/5; Q3 1611
King Lear	Nathaniel Butter	Q1 1608; Q2 1619
Othello	Thomas Walkley	Q1 1622
Antony and Cleopatra	Blount & Jaggard	First published in Folio
Cymbeline	Blount & Jaggard	First published in Folio

Jaggards, with Isaac, William's son, playing a central role; William himself had gone blind, probably as early as 1612.[37] Blayney notes that, at the time the Folio project was conceived, Isaac Jaggard was in his late twenties and had published just three books, and he suggests that it is 'fairly safe to guess that Isaac Jaggard was the one who first suggested the venture but that Blount was the principal investor'.[38] Blount was in his fifties at this time and had served his apprenticeship with William Ponsonby – the publisher

of Spenser and Sidney, among others. Blount took over the business when
Ponsonby died in 1603. He was, as W. W. Greg puts it, 'a man of some
literary aspiration and had written several . . . trifles under his own name:
he had been a friend of Marlowe and regarded himself as in some sense his
literary executor'.[39] David Scott Kastan has nicely observed of him that 'as
the English publisher of Marlowe, Montaigne, Cervantes, and Shakespeare,
Blount might be said to have invented, if not precisely the Renaissance for
England, at least its first Great Books course'.[40]

Blount and Isaac Jaggard entered sixteen of the thirty-six Folio plays in
the Stationers' Register on 8 November 1623, shortly before the book was
offered for sale to the public. The plays in question were: *The Tempest, Two
Gentlemen of Verona, Measure for Measure, The Comedy of Errors, As You Like
It, All's Well that Ends Well, Twelfth Night, The Winter's Tale, 1 Henry VI,*[41]
*Henry VIII, Coriolanus, Timon of Athens, Julius Caesar, Macbeth, Antony
and Cleopatra* and *Cymbeline*. Peter Blayney has noted, perhaps a bit harshly,
that it 'is a striking testimony to the nature of Edward Blount's interest
in Shakespeare's plays that although he had himself registered *Antony and
Cleopatra* in 1608, by 1623 he had apparently forgotten that he owned it'.[42]
Blount had also registered *Pericles* in 1608, but it was omitted from the
First Folio, perhaps because no alternative to the apparently defective text
provided in the 1609 and 1611 editions was available, or perhaps because
it was not considered to be substantially a product of Shakespeare's pen.[43]
Two Noble Kinsmen, which Shakespeare wrote in collaboration with John
Fletcher, was also omitted from the volume (though another Fletcher collaboration, *Henry VIII*, was included).[44] Two other plays which may have
been excluded are *Love's Labours Won* (attributed to Shakespeare in 1598
and listed in a bookseller's daybook five years later, though no copy of it
has ever been discovered) and *Cardenio*.[45] This latter play was performed at
court on 20 May and 9 July 1613 and was entered in the Stationers' Register
by Humphrey Moseley in September 1653, attributing the play to Fletcher
and Shakespeare. Moseley never published the play, but Lewis Theobald
claimed to have had access to manuscript copies of it in creating his *Double
Falsehood* in 1727.[46]

While the book actually appeared late in 1623, it seems clear that the
process of planning and producing it began much earlier. In the previous
year, John Bill's London edition of the *Mess-Katalog* of the Frankfurt book
fair, issued under the title *A Catalogve of svch bookes as have beene published,
and (by authoritie) printed in English, since the last Vernall Mart, which was in
Aprill 1622. till this present October 1622*, included the following entry: 'Playes,
written by M. *William Shakespeare*, all in one volume, printed by *Isaack*

Iaggard, in fol.'[47] The book was still 'in press' when this notice appeared, with work on the volume probably having commenced in either February or March of 1622. Progress on the Shakespeare volume was retarded by the fact that it was not the only large project occupying the Jaggard shop during 1622 and 1623. The Jaggards' men seem to have been working on at least three other significant volumes at the same time as they were producing the First Folio: Augustine Vincent's *A Discovery of Errors*, André Favyn's *Theatre of Honour* and William Burton's *Description of Leicestershire*. In addition to these volumes, the Jaggards' men would also have been occupied with occasional pieces of minor printing, such as the jobbing work which would have come the firm's way by virtue of William's being the official printer to the City of London (a privilege which Isaac succeeded to on his father's death). There is some evidence to suggest that work on the Folio was entirely suspended from mid-July to the end of September 1622, owing to the pressure of other work.[48]

The question of how many different compositors worked on setting up the text of the First Folio was first raised by Thomas Satchell in 1920, in a letter sent to *The Times Literary Supplement* from Kobe, Japan. Satchell noted consistencies in variant spelling patterns in the Folio text of *Macbeth* and suggested that one possible explanation for this might be that the 'manuscript was set by two compositors, who each took half, and carried out their own ideas in the spelling'.[49] These compositors were, for convenience, labelled 'A' and 'B'. Satchell's limited analysis was built upon by numerous later scholars, and by 1963 Charlton Hinman, using spelling tests similar to Satchell's own, had identified a total of five different compositors. He even went so far as to hazard a guess at what the name of one of the compositors might have been. Noting that compositor 'E' seemed routinely to be confined to setting up text from printed copy; that he made a greater than usual number of mistakes; and that his work seemed to be subjected to a higher level of proof-reading, Hinman suggested that this compositor might well have been an apprentice, and he identified John Leason, bound to William Jaggard on 4 November 1622 (and his first apprentice for over eight years) as the likeliest candidate.[50] Subsequent analyses of the text have raised the total number of compositors thought to have worked on the text to nine.[51]

Hinman carried out his analysis at the Folger Shakespeare Library, making use of the Library's extensive collection of First Folios, which runs to in excess of eighty copies. In examining the volumes, he used a piece of optical collating equipment which he had himself designed, drawing on his experience of working in military intelligence in the Second World War. Military analysts had thought of using a process of alternating projections of successive photographs of enemy fortifications to determine whether bombs had hit their targets. Areas of damage – effectively areas of difference between the two otherwise identical images – would create a kind of kinetic effect in the visual field of the observer. The technology available at the time was inadequate to this military application, but Hinman made use of the general principle in constructing his own collating machine.[52] Hinman's first collator was assembled 'from bits taken from Giles Dawson's son's Erector set, two slide projectors, and sundry electric motors, mirrors, etc.'.[53] It had initially been estimated that collating the Folger copies would be a forty-year project, but Hinman's machine enabled the task to be completed in just nineteen months, with Hinman himself, together with Giles Dawson, devoting four hours a day to the collation.[54] Hinman's study was the most detailed examination of the volume (perhaps indeed of *any* book) that had ever been carried out.[55] By meticulously tracking the distribution patterns of repeatedly used damaged type pieces throughout the First Folio he was able to reconstruct in great detail the manner in which the book was printed and the way in which it proceeded through the Jaggards' shop.[56] Whereas previously scholars had thought that the volume had been set page by page in the sequence in which the pages would appear in the finished book, Hinman demonstrated that it was, in fact, set by formes.[57] The book is a folio in sixes and Hinman discovered that, as a general rule, the compositors proceeded from the inner forme of sheet three 'backwards' to the outer forme of sheet one. This working method cut down on the amount of type needed and helped to strike a balance between composition and presswork; it also meant that type could be distributed more quickly.[58] Proceeding in this way did, however, mean that the copy needed to be cast off accurately and any errors in casting off were likely to cause problems for page make-up.[59] Hinman identified several pages where text is condensed or spacing expanded to compensate for casting-off errors. He also noted that, in some instances, single pentameter lines were broken into two short lines in order to fill up excessive space. In other instances, half lines were tagged onto the preceding full line to save space. In the case of p. 365 of *Antony and Cleopatra* (sig. ZZI^r), two speeches by Proculeius follow on immediately one from the other and Hinman speculated that a stage direction, separating the two speeches and indicating the capture of Cleopatra, has been deleted by the compositor in order to save space on a crowded page.[60]

The question of exactly what texts the Jaggards' compositors worked from in setting up the volume is a rather vexed one. Heminge and Condell claimed in their address to the readers of the folio that 'as where (before) you were abus'd with diuerse stolne, and surreptitious copies, maimed, and deformed by the frauds and stealthes of iniurious impostors, that expos'd them: euen those, are now offer'd to your view cur'd, and perfect of their limbes' (A3r). In one reading this claim suggests that the First Folio texts are independent of the quartos (or, at least, of the most poorly reproduced quartos). However, it is clear that in some instances the Folio compositors made direct use of printed quartos and that some of these quartos would appear to have been annotated by reference to manuscript copies of the plays held by the King's Men. Gary Taylor notes that *Much Ado, Love's Labour's Lost, Midsummer Night's Dream* and *Merchant of Venice* 'were reprinted with little change except to stage directions and speech-prefixes', but that in the case of *Richard II*, 'the manuscript was more thoroughly compared with a printed text, so that dialogue readings were sporadically altered, in addition to the systematic alteration of stage directions and speech-prefixes'.[61] In other instances, the compositors worked directly from manuscript copy alone. The manuscript was of various kinds – in some cases perhaps author's papers, in others a transcript of some sort. Throughout much of the twentieth century, it was considered a relatively easy matter to distinguish between different kinds of manuscript sources, and in particular to distinguish between authorial 'foul papers' and theatrical 'prompt books'.[62] However, the stability of these categories has increasingly come to be interrogated and it is difficult to draw firm conclusions regarding the exact nature of manuscript copy.[63] It seems safest at this point simply to say that Jaggards' compositors worked from a mixed collection of textual sources.

Hinman's analysis enabled him to determine the particular order in which the plays were set. In very broad general terms, the plays were printed in the order in which they appear in the finished volume, but there were, however, significant anomalies in the order of proceeding, some of which take us back to the issue of who owned the rights to the individual plays. The first major jump in the setting sequence occurred close to the end of the Comedies section when the compositors moved forward to *King John* (the first play of the Histories section), skipping over both *Twelfth Night* and *The Winter's Tale*. They then returned to *Twelfth Night*, but then again jumped forward to set part of *Richard II* (the second of the Histories) before moving back to set *The Winter's Tale*, thereby completing the Comedies. In this instance, no rights issues were involved (neither play had been registered or printed before) and Hinman speculates that 'some short-lived trouble over the copy itself' lay at the root of the problem.[64] Having set both *King John* and about half of *Richard II* in advance of completing work on the Comedies, we would expect Jaggard's men to have moved directly from *The Winter's Tale* to the conclusion of *Richard II* and on to the first and second parts of *Henry IV*.

In fact, however, they began instead to set *Henry V*, moving on through the first two Henry VI plays and the early segment of *3 Henry VI*, before finally 'doubling back' to complete *Richard II* and to set *1* and *2 Henry IV*. The rights to two of the 'stalled' plays – *Richard II* and *1 Henry IV* – were held by Matthew Law (who also owned the rights to *Richard III*) and Hinman speculates that the Folio syndicate had some difficulty in agreeing terms with him.[65] The matter does, however, seem to have been resolved quickly enough and printing proceeded through to the end of *Richard III*. A further delay occurred before the last of the Histories, *Henry VIII*, was printed, but again this would appear to have been caused by the unavailability of copy, since no rights issues were involved.[66]

The printing of the Tragedies proceeded smoothly until the compositors came to the end of *Romeo and Juliet* – the third play in the section. *Troilus and Cressida* was intended to be the next play in the sequence, but it seems clear that the publishers were unable to agree terms with Henry Walley, who held the rights to the play. The verso of the final page of *Romeo and Juliet* originally contained the opening page of *Troilus*, but this was cancelled and a new set of pages substituted, with *Timon of Athens* taking the place of *Troilus*. The dispute over *Troilus* was not resolved until very late in the printing process. Jaggard and Blount may well have stumbled upon the key to the issue when they entered their Folio texts in the Stationers' Register in November of 1623. In addition to making the entry, the clerk also searched through the register for details of other entries relating to Shakespeare. In the process, he would have discovered that, though Walley and Richard Bonian entered *Troilus* in 1609 (in advance of their edition of that year) James Roberts had provisionally registered it much earlier, in February of 1603. We have already seen, of course, that Roberts' business had been taken over by Jaggard in 1608 and so he could have argued that he had some legal interest in the play. While the discovery might not have been enough for Jaggard to be able to feel that, as Greg puts it, he was 'in a position to snap his fingers at Walley', it nevertheless considerably strengthened his negotiating hand and the play was hastily included in the volume – so hastily that its title never appeared in the contents page.[67] The text could not be inserted at the end of the Tragedies, because the final play, *Cymbeline*, had already been printed and it included the volume's colophon on its last page, which therefore logically had to be the final page of the book. The play was therefore placed at the head of the Tragedies section. In printing *Troilus*, some of the sheets in which the play was backed against *Romeo and Juliet* were used, with the final *Romeo* page being crossed out. After a time, a prologue for the play (which had not been included in the 1609 quarto) was discovered and this prologue was substituted for the superfluous *Romeo* page, with the first page of *Troilus* being reset as the verso page of this cancel leaf. The net effect of the disturbance caused by *Troilus* was that the Folio appeared in three distinct states: (i) lacking *Troilus* entirely; (ii) including *Troilus*, with the redundant *Romeo* page crossed through and the prologue omitted; (iii) including *Troilus*, with a single cancel leaf eliminating the *Romeo* page and the prologue included.[68]

The completed book was, then, ready for sale by the very end of 1623. A copy of the volume bound in plain calf probably cost about £1 – a substantial sum, given that the annual income of an ordinary clergyman at the time might have been somewhere between £10 and £20.[69] To offer a somewhat different point of comparison, the cost of the folio was roughly equivalent to the cost of forty-four loaves of bread.[70] There has been much debate concerning exactly how many copies of the volume would have been printed. A 1587 ordinance of the Stationers' Company limited the print run (from a single setting of type) of the vast majority of books to no more than 1,500 copies and Hinman thought – on the basis of the necessity of balancing composition and presswork – that a likely figure for the Folio would be about 1,200 copies.[71] Blayney has, however, argued that Hinman's logic in arriving at this figure is flawed and has suggested that

> Given the price and the unprecedented nature of the Folio, it would have been foolhardy to risk printing as many as 1200 copies – and Blount's career shows few signs of foolhardiness. If substantially fewer than 500 copies had been printed the unit cost would have been impractically high – but since the book sold out in nine years, the actual figure was probably closer to 500 than to 1200. A guess of 750 copies seems realistic.[72]

As Blayney notes here, however many copies of the First Folio were printed, it would appear to have sold sufficiently well to have warranted a second edition within nine years. By the time this second edition came to be published both William and Isaac Jaggard were dead. Isaac died early in 1627 and in June of that year his widow, Dorothy, assigned her inherited publishing rights to Thomas and Richard Cotes. Thomas was the second apprentice that William Jaggard had taken on and, with the help of his brother, he took over the Jaggard printing house and made a great success of the business. E. E. Willoughby notes that 'in the heyday of their career they probably surpassed in production all the other printers of London except the King's Printer'.[73] By 1630, the Cotes brothers held not only Jaggard's share of the sixteen Jaggard–Blount Shakespeare rights, but they had acquired Pavier's copies as well – by transfer from Robert Bird, who had secured Pavier's rights from his widow in 1626. Blount had transferred his rights to Robert Allot in 1630, so the Second Folio proceeded in much the same way as the First: Thomas Cotes was identified as the printer, as Isaac Jaggard had been, and Robert Allot served in place of Blount as the principal publisher. Again, as in the case of the 1623 edition, the volume included a colophon which listed the names of the entire syndicate. In this case 'John Smethwick, William Aspley, Richard Hawkins, Richard Meighen, and Robert Allot'. Smethwick and Aspley were, of course, survivors from the first edition and Hawkins and Meighen entered the frame by virtue of having acquired, respectively, Thomas Walkley's rights to *Othello* and Arthur Johnson's rights to *Merry Wives*. In a departure from the practice established in the First Folio, the Second Folio was issued with five separate title pages. In each case, the imprint begins 'Printed by *Tho. Cotes*, for' and this is followed by the name and address of one of the five publishers identified in the colophon. Giles E. Dawson has estimated that 'among existing copies those bearing the Allot imprint outnumber, by something like two to one, all the others together' – as one might expect, given Allot's dominant role in the project.[74] In publishing the volume, the Cotes brothers added a new poem to the preliminaries, written by the son of one of their neighbours – John Milton. It was the first English poem of Milton's to appear in print.

In the preface to his own edition of 1790 Edmond Malone suggested that the compiler of the Second Folio 'was entirely ignorant of our poet's phraseology and metre, and that various alterations were made by him, in consequence of that ignorance, which render his edition of no value whatsoever' (§357, I, Preface, p. xx). Later commentators have, however, been more generous in their assessment of the volume. In 1924 Allardyce Nicoll noted that it is with the Second Folio that we 'first come upon an attempt to "edit" Shakespeare'. This is not wholly true, in that many individual texts were in some sense 'edited' when they were reissued in new quarto editions, but Nicoll is certainly correct in suggesting that the Second Folio represents the first attempt to revisit the text of most of the Shakespearean canon in a relatively systematic manner.[75] Nicoll argues that whoever was responsible for preparing the text of the Second Folio had certain clear strengths as an editor – not the least of which was a command of languages and a good knowledge of classical mythology. Nicoll notes that in *Love's Labour's Lost* 'a whole sentence in Latin, nonsensical and meaningless in the First Folio, has been perfectly corrected, while corrupted Roman and Greek names throughout have been amended'. Likewise, the sense of the French language scenes in *Henry V* is much improved and, in the Tragedies, 'all through, Roman and Greek names are conjured out of the often meaningless collections of consonants and vowels as the First Folio presented them. "Pantheon" is thus captured from "Pathan", "Acheron" from "Acaron", "Phoebe" from "Thebe", and, as a final triumph, "heart of Actium", from "head of Action".'[76] An extensive comparative analysis of the seventeenth-century folios was published by M. W. Black and Matthias Shaaber in 1937, under the auspices of the MLA. Black and Shaaber confirmed the general view of the Second Folio advanced by Nicoll. While noting that the volume was 'so badly printed and seems to have received so little proof reading after it was set up that in it we are not surprised to find every conceivable kind of typographical error in plentiful numbers', nevertheless, they observe, the person responsible for assembling the volume 'was the first of Shakespeare's editors, and not the least brilliant', demonstrating 'considerable alertness, ingenuity, and tact'.[77] In addition to confirming this editor's particular strengths in language and mythology (they note that he restored 'Hiperion' from 'Epton' in act V, scene ii of *Titus*), they also demonstrated his abilities in restoring defective metre and in adding entrances and exits.[78] Paul Werstine has summarised the enduring achievements of the volume by noting that 'About six hundred editorial changes originating in the Second Folio continued to claim a place in early twentieth-century editions'.[79]

While the Second Folio was published just nine years after its predecessor, it would take more than three decades for the collection to be issued for a third time. The Third Folio appeared in 1663, with an imprint indicating that it was 'printed for Philip Chetwinde' and the printers have been identified as Roger Daniel, Alice Warren and either John Hayes or Thomas Ratcliffe.[80] Chetwind was a clothworker by training and he had married Robert Allot's widow, Mary, in 1637. He initially encountered some difficulty when he tried to move into the field of publishing, making use of the Allot rights, but by 1653 he was publishing under his own name. His books included several Welsh language texts (for example, Thomas Powel's *Cerbyd Iechydwriaeth*) which were produced for him by printers such as Sarah Griffin, John Streater and Ellen Cotes.[81] Ellen Cotes was the widow of Richard Cotes, whose brother Thomas was also by this time deceased. She was thus the inheritor of both the Jaggard half of the Jaggard–Blount Shakespeare rights (Chetwind, of course, holding the other half) and of Pavier's Shakespearean copies. It seems odd, then, that she was neither involved in printing the Third Folio, nor was she (or any other publisher holding rights in Shakespeare's plays) mentioned anywhere in the volume. Perhaps Chetwind and Cotes had arrived at some sort of informal arrangement – as Henry Farr has noted, 'it hardly seems possible that Chetwind could have brought out the volume without her acquiescence'.[82]

A second issue of the Third Folio appeared in the following year, augmented with, as the title page tells us, 'seven Playes, never before Printed in Folio' (§136, title page). The plays in question were *Pericles*, *The London Prodigal*, *Thomas Lord Cromwell*, *Sir John Oldcastle*, *The Puritan Widow*, *A Yorkshire Tragedy* and *Locrine*. While *Pericles* has generally been accepted as being at least partly the work of Shakespeare, the other addenda to the Third Folio have not and Thomas Lounsbury commented with dryly xenophobic wit in 1906 that 'No one indeed in these modern times is likely to stand up unqualifiedly for the genuineness of any of the numerous plays once attributed to the dramatist, but now utterly discarded, unless it may be an occasional German.'[83] Comparing the Third Folio with the Second, Black and Shaaber observed that it

> does more credit to the printing house which turned it out and is largely free from gross typographical errors. But from the fact that it unintentionally omitted a great many words, we infer that the proof reading given it was not sufficiently careful to catch unobtrusive compositor's errors. The editor, furthermore, was not nearly so aggressive as the editor of F2 and did not feel free to go further than to correct blunders that make nonsense of meaning, grammatical improprieties, and archaic diction.[84]

Black and Shaaber registered a total of 943 editorial changes made in the Third Folio, a little more than 300 of which had, they reckoned, been accepted by editors up to the early twentieth century.[85]

The Third Folio is a relatively scarce book and it has been suggested that a significant proportion of the copies printed may have been destroyed in the Great Fire of London in 1666. Several stationers' shops and printworks were lost in the fire, including those of Alice Warren and John Hayes.[86] Many booksellers placed their stocks in the crypt of St Faith's, beneath the choir of St Paul's Cathedral, but the flaming roof of the cathedral broke through the sealed vault and, as John Evelyn tells us, the books 'were all consumed, burning for a weeke following'. The loss to stationers was estimated at some £200,000.[87] It may perhaps have been the loss of a large number of copies of the Third Folio which prompted the issuing of a further edition of the collection in 1685.

By 1685, the ownership of the plays had again changed hands. Eleanor Cotes' rights passed to John Martin and Henry Herringman in August of 1674. Martin died in 1681 and his widow, Sarah, assigned his rights to Robert Scott (about whom little is known) in 1683. While Eleanor Cotes is known to have owned half the rights to the texts originally registered by

Jaggard and Blount, it seems that Martin and Herringman believed that they had acquired these plays outright – Dawson suggests that this belief may have been prompted by a set of transactions not included in the Stationers' Register.[88] In any event, by 1685, Henry Herringman was clearly the dominant rights-holder and his name appears as publisher on all of the title pages to the Fourth Folio. As in the case of the Second Folio, a variety of title pages was produced, with different imprints. One imprint reads simply 'for *H. Herringman*' and the other two read: (i) 'for *H. Herringman, E. Brewster, and R. Bentley*' and (ii) 'for *H. Herringman, E. Brewster, R. Chiswell, and R. Bentley*'. Dawson speculates that Herringman must have been 'the principal if not the sole capitalist in the publication' and suggests that the 'other booksellers' names were probably small investors, each receiving a stipulated number of copies'.[89]

The Fourth Folio differs from the Second and Third in that it is not a page-for-page reprint of the 1623 original. The volume falls into three divisions, each with separate signatures and pagination: the Comedies; the Histories plus the Tragedies up to and including *Romeo and Juliet*; and the remainder of the Tragedies, together with the apocryphal plays added in 1664. The three sections are clearly the work of three distinct printshops and a certain degree of inconsistency in the editorial work carried out in the three sections would seem to indicate that the text was handled somewhat differently by the staff at each of the three printworks. Black and Shaaber concluded that the data derived from their analysis of the volume indicated that

> the editor of the second division was the most alert and the most successful of the three, but they show very little difference among the three revisers in the aims they pursued. Their minds were fixed on the job of printing under their superintendence, not on Shakespeare's plays; their object was to produce a creditable specimen of the printer's art and a book that buyers could read with ease.[90]

Some editions of the Fourth Folio show an odd anomaly: sixteen-and-a-half sheets in the middle section of the book appear in some copies without the side and foot rules that normally serve to frame the text. Giles Dawson has designated the copies containing this anomaly as the 'Fifth Folio' and he speculates that the new version of the text came into being sometime around 1700, when it was discovered that the original printer responsible for the middle segment of the book had underprinted some of the sheets which made up his section. In order for complete copies of the volume to be assembled, this shortfall had to be made up and the missing pages were newly set up and printed.[91] Eric Rasmussen has noted that the reprinted pages 'correct dozens of errors in F4, modernise hundreds of spellings and punctuations, and systematically introduce the use of apostrophes in possessives'.[92]

Dawson's suggestion of a final folio text completed somewhere around 1700 offers us a neat cut-off point for our narrative in this chapter. The 'Fifth Folio' would be the last single volume edition of the plays for the best part of a hundred years. It would also be the last text to be assembled 'anonymously', as it were – its editorial work carried out by unknown printshop functionaries, concerned, as Marvin Spevack has put it, 'not so much to restore the "true text" or to elucidate it as to make it immediately accessible, correct, and natural' (§1603, I, 'Introduction', unpaged). The eighteenth century would be dominated by multi-volume editions of Shakespeare and those editions would be the work of named editors who, for the most part, would be asked to take on the role of the editor because of their existing public profile as cultural figures. They would also help to reconfigure the general conception of the editorial project.

3   The Tonson era 1: Rowe to Warburton

The publisher Jacob Tonson the elder cut a rather unprepossessing figure. As Kathleen Lynch has observed, 'he was unattractive in appearance, unrefined in manners. He was heavy-jowled, corpulent, slovenly, "left-legged" and awkward in gait, loud-voiced and blustering. He would flatter no one.' And yet, as Lynch further observes, Tonson

> was accepted on his own hearty terms by the members of the exclusive Kit-Cat Club, the most famous of all literary clubs, which he founded and presided over. The noblemen and gentlemen of the club, many of whom regarded literary pursuits as a diverting pastime, found Tonson a comical dog, delightful in his cups and capable of matching wits with the wittiest.[1]

Tonson was also the founder of one of the eighteenth century's most formidable publishing houses. The Tonsons were the primary publishers of all of the major editions of Shakespeare produced in the first seven decades of the century.

Jacob Tonson the elder was born in 1655, the grandson of a bookseller who specialised primarily in legal texts. At the age of fourteen he was apprenticed to the London publisher Thomas Basset and he was admitted to the freedom of the Stationers' Company in 1678. Shortly after gaining his freedom he set up shop at the Judge's Head in Chancery Lane and in the following year he co-published, with Abel Swalle, an edition of John Dryden's adaptation of *Troilus and Cressida*. Securing Dryden as a client was Tonson's first major coup as a publisher and Dryden remained a Tonson author for the rest of the century. Tonson's second major success as a literary publisher came in 1683, when he purchased a half share in *Paradise Lost* from Brabazon Aylmer. By 1690, Tonson owned the poem outright and it consistently turned a healthy profit for him. Late in his career, when asked which poet brought him the greatest revenue, he instantly replied 'Milton'.[2] The fourth edition of *Paradise Lost* appeared in 1688, co-published by Tonson and Richard Bentley. Bentley had been a member of the partnership responsible for issuing the Fourth Folio three years previously and he was also involved in publishing some single-play Shakespeare editions. In 1695 he brought out his own edition of the players' quarto of *Hamlet* and this text was also issued with an alternative title page, in which the names 'H. Herringman, J. Tonson, T. Bennet, and F. Sanders' were added to the imprint. This would seem to have been Tonson's first minor venture into the field of Shakespeare publishing.

It is impossible to say whether Tonson's role in the Bentley *Hamlet* represents the first indication of a desire to set Shakespeare beside Milton on the Tonson roster of canonical authors. If it does, then we can say that it took Tonson the best part of a further decade and a half before the title deeds to Shakespeare (or the greatest part of him) could be lodged beside those to Milton. He acquired his majority stake in Shakespeare through a kind of commercial pincer movement. As we have seen in the previous chapter, the largest segment of Shakespeare rights (the core of which was the texts originally owned by Blount and Jaggard) had, by 1674, passed into the hands of Henry Herringman and John Martin.[3] Tonson paid £140 for over 100 Herringman copies on 20 May 1707, thus acquiring the first half of the Martin–Herringman tranche of Shakespeare rights. Martin's copies had passed in the first instance to Robert Scott, who entered into a partnership with his brother-in-law William Wells. Scott's copies would appear ultimately to have passed to Wells' son and daughter, George and Mary, and, on 20 October 1709, Tonson purchased some 380 Wells copies for £100, in the process reuniting the Martin–Herringman rights.[4] The Tonson firm was never the exclusive owner of all of Shakespeare's plays, but it was very much the dominant partner within the cartel which published Shakespeare for the better part of the eighteenth century.

By the time Jacob the elder acquired his majority stake in Shakespeare, the Tonson firm was well established as a premier literary publisher. In 1703, Tonson's nephew, another Jacob (for convenience, Jacob II), inherited a half share in his father, Richard's, publishing business and he may at that time have entered into partnership with Jacob the elder (as the lineages of the Tonson family are somewhat complex, a basic family tree is included here as figure 3.1). Six years later, in 1709, Tonson published some of Alexander Pope's poems in an anthology entitled *Poetical Miscellanies*. Hearing of this, the dramatist William Wycherley commented to Pope: 'I approve of your making Tonson your Muse's Introductor into the world . . . who has been so long a Pimp, or Gentleman-Usher to the Muses.'[5] If Tonson was pimping for Pope in 1709, he was also in the process of acting as Gentleman-Usher for Shakespeare, seeking to make his recently acquired property available to the public in a new edition, to supersede the now near quarter-century-old

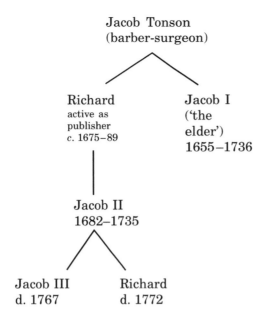

Jacob Tonson
(barber-surgeon)

Richard
active as
publisher
c. 1675–89

Jacob I
('the
elder')
1655–1736

Jacob II
1682–1735

Jacob III
d. 1767

Richard
d. 1772

Note: The bulk of the firm's copyrights were sold after Jacob III's death; Jacob III's brother Richard played very little part in the business.

Figure 3.1 Basic Tonson family tree.

Fourth Folio. At around this time, Tonson relocated his business to the Strand, and began using 'Shakespeare's Head' as his shop sign and trademark.

In commissioning and publishing his first Shakespeare edition in 1709 Tonson broke with the pattern established by the four seventeenth-century folios in several important respects. In the first instance, the format of the edition was different: the bulky single-volume folio was displaced by a set of six octavos, with a few sets being printed up on larger paper.[6] The loss of what had been a prestige format (at least for the seventeenth century) may have been compensated for by the fact that the text was now accompanied by forty-five engraved illustrations, most of which were indebted to contemporary fashion and stage practice, with, for instance Troilus and Cressida being represented 'frankly taking a curtain call'.[7] Elsewhere, as Peter Holland has noted, 'Othello has carefully placed his decorated three-cornered hat on a convenient table before murdering Desdemona and Hamlet has made a token gesture of dressing mad by allowing his stocking to be "down-gyved" but without adjusting his wig.'[8] The 1709 text also offered, for the first time, a biography of Shakespeare, largely drawn from anecdotes gathered by Thomas Betterton, whose 'Veneration for the Memory of *Shakespear* [had] engag'd him to make a Journey into *Warwickshire*, on purpose to gather up what Remains he could of a name for which he had so great a value' (§168, I, p. XXXIV).

Though the materials for the biography had been largely compiled by Betterton, the text itself was written by Nicholas Rowe and here we encounter the most significant departure from previous practice effected by Tonson. As we have already noted, the seventeenth-century folios were seen through the press by anonymous printing-house functionaries, whose primary aim was, as Black and Shaaber have put it, 'to produce a creditable specimen of the printer's art and a book that buyers could read with ease'.[9] Tonson, by contrast, shifted the work of preparing the text into a wholly separate sphere, engaging Rowe for the task because of his established literary reputation (and foregrounding his role on the title page: '*The Works of Mr. William Shakespeare; in six volumes. Adorn'd with cuts. Revis'd and corrected, with an account of the life and writings of the author. By N. Rowe, Esq*'). He also sought outside assistance for Rowe while the work was underway, placing an advert in the *London Gazette* and the *Daily Courant* for March of 1709, announcing that if

> any Gentlemen who have Materials by 'em, that may be serviceable to this Design, will be pleased to transmit 'em to Jacob Tonson, at Gray's-Inn-Gate, it will be a particular Advantage to the Work, and acknowledg'd as a Favour by the Gentleman who has the Care of this Edition.[10]

Rowe, for his part, became the first person since Heminge and Condell to set out a textual programme in the preliminaries to his edition. Dedicating the edition to the Duke of Somerset, he noted the pleasure that the Duke had often taken in Shakespeare, but observed that what he would find in this edition would be a 'new and improved' version of the playwright's works:

> I have taken some Care to redeem him from the Injuries of former Impressions. I must not pretend to have restor'd this Work to the Exactness of the Author's Original Manuscripts: These are lost, or, at least, are gone beyond any Inquiry I could make; so that there was nothing left, but to compare the several Editions, and give the true Reading as well as I could from thence. This I have endeavour'd to do pretty carefully, and render'd very many Places Intelligible, that were not so before.
>
> (§168, I, A2r–A2v)

This brief statement of Rowe's maps out in small compass some of the central issues that editors of Shakespeare would wrestle with during the course of the eighteenth century (and, indeed, beyond). Rowe registers the fact that Shakespeare's original manuscripts have perished and that the printed texts that survive from the dramatist's own era very frequently constitute variant witnesses to the plays which they preserve. Furthermore, he notes, the texts are in many places obscure or unintelligible and thus in need of correction. A succession of editors from Rowe forwards would struggle with the issue of how exactly the early printed witnesses should be sorted relative to each other and also with the question of what, precisely, constitutes 'correction', and whether it is possible (or even desirable) to attempt to produce an edition which would in any meaningful sense represent an accurate approximation of Shakespeare's lost original manuscripts.

While his preliminary statement certainly raised issues that were absolutely central to the editorial project, Rowe himself seems, in practice, not to have been greatly troubled by these questions. He based his edition on the text of the Fourth Folio, occasionally making reference to other texts – as D. Nichol Smith observes, he 'made such emendations here and there as readily occurred to him on a leisurely perusal' of his available materials.[11] Noticing that Fourth Folio *Hamlet* lacked a scene that was present in the quarto line of texts (IV.ii, where Fortinbras appears with his army), he restored the bulk of the scene in his own edition, drawing on one of the late players' quartos.[12] Likewise, he restored the prologue to *Romeo and Juliet*, copying it from the 1637 quarto, but printing it at the end of the play rather than at the beginning. Beyond this, he also seems to have made some use of a quarto edition of *King Lear* and to have derived occasional readings from either the First or Second Folio.[13]

Rowe also regularised the Shakespearean text in a variety of different ways, many of which persisted in the text well into the twentieth century. For this reason, Peter Holland has argued that, up until the closing decades of the twentieth century, 'Rowe's edition was the single greatest determinant on the way Shakespeare's plays appeared in collected editions, in some respects even more important than the early quartos or the First Folio' (§1710, I, p. vii). Rowe increased the number of indicators of location included in the text, in some cases taking his cue from Restoration adaptations of the plays.[14] He also introduced act and scene divisions for all plays, thus foregrounding their literary quality as printed texts, at the expense of their theatrical lineage – something the dramatist William Congreve was also at this time doing in preparing his own three-volume *Works* for publication by Tonson in 1710.[15] He included a 'dramatis personae' list for all of the plays, using ordering principles based on social rank and gender. Thus, as Barbara Mowat has observed:

> We have no way of knowing how Shakespeare would have listed the characters for any of his plays – though one doubts that he would have listed . . . 'Escalus, Prince of Verona' and 'Paris, kinsman of Escalus' before any of the other characters in *Romeo and Juliet*, or that he would have placed 'Claudius, King of Denmark' above Hamlet – and far, far above Gertrude.[16]

As Mowat points out, Rowe's principles of ordering – odd though they may seem when delineated in this way – nevertheless persisted for a very long time within the editorial tradition.[17]

The price of Rowe's edition was 30*s.*, just 50 per cent more than the likely typical price of the First Folio almost a hundred years previously. Relatively speaking, however, this would still have been an expensive purchase. Robert D. Hume has pointed out that the cost was equivalent to 'the total weekly salary of Thomas Newman, prompter to the Drury Lane company' and that 'all house servants earned less, most of them a lot less'.[18] Rowe included the apocryphal plays in his collection but, in keeping with the tradition of the folios, he excluded the poems. The sales opportunity provided by this omission was seized upon by Edmund Curll, a rogue publisher who seems blithely to have survived every recrimination which his activities brought upon his head. He was famously tossed in a blanket by the boys of Westminster school for printing a Latin oration by one of their number without permission; Pope administered an emetic to him as repayment for another infraction; he was imprisoned, set in the pillory, and repeatedly lampooned in print.[19] And yet, as Ralph Straus puts it, 'Pachydermatously Curll continued to exist.'[20]

In preparing to publish the poems, Curll mimicked Tonson's *Daily Courant* advert with one of his own which promised 'a Gratification from J. Baker at the Black Boy in Pater-Noster-Row' to anyone contributing to the improvement of the notes.[21] Curll's shadowing of Tonson continued in the text itself, which was issued in a size and format making it appear to be an additional seventh volume to Rowe's edition. The volume was advertised as being 'printed exactly as the Plays, and some on large paper to compleat sets'.[22] The text was compiled by Charles Gildon, a hack writer who had fallen into Curll's service and whose 'nightly drudgery by candlelight' eventually led to complete blindness.[23] Gildon added to the poems 'An Essay on the Art, Rise and Progress of the Stage in Greece, Rome and England', sets of remarks on the poems and the plays, and a glossary. The poems themselves were pulled together from a variety of sources. In the case of the sonnets, for example, Gildon reproduced Benson's 1640 text, rather than that of Thorpe's 1609 edition. Giles Dawson notes that Gildon's text of the poems was subsequently reproduced some fourteen times (the last being a supplement to the 1808 Boston edition) and its impact was long-lasting:

> Until 1780 no edition of the collected poems printed in England . . .
> contained the genuine *Sonnets* in their original form. During most of the
> 18th century, therefore, the only form in which a person could buy the
> *Sonnets* was in the deformed Benson version, which would have died
> quietly in 1640 if Curll had not dug it up and given it a new life.[24]

Rowe's 1709 edition was sufficiently successful to warrant a second issue in the same year, in which the 'size, type, alphabets, total number of pages, and frontispieces to all intents correspond with the first edition'.[25] Just five years later, Tonson published another version of Rowe's text, with new illustrations and an index consisting of 'a Table of the most Sublime Passages in this Author' (§181, I, title page).[26] The most significant change was, however, in the format of the edition: having shrunk Shakespeare from folio to octavo, Tonson now further reduced him to duodecimo. In switching format, Tonson may have been responding to a series of individual play editions which had been issued in the Hague by Thomas Johnson (of whom we will hear more in chapter 5), under the series title 'A Collection of the Best English Plays'. Johnson's texts were in octavo format and were advertised as providing 'small Volumes fit for the pocket'.[27] Tonson may well have registered Johnson's move as indicating a potential broadening of the market and may have reconfigured his wares accordingly. H. L. Ford has suggested that the two versions of the Rowe edition served quite distinct functions:

> In the large mansions in town and country the 1709 edition reposed in
> state in the library, but often the owners of these were again the
> customers for the smaller and cheaper edition, either for their own use or
> for the amusement of the then large household staff attached to their
> residences: some copies do turn up marked specifically for 'The
> Housekeeper's Room'.[28]

Curll again provided a matching poems' volume for the 1714 edition, but this time Tonson drew him directly into the project, issuing some copies of the edition with a cancel title page indicating that it was in nine volumes (rather than eight) and including Curll's name in the imprint.[29]

Four years after Rowe's third edition appeared, Jacob the elder left London for Paris, where he was to remain for the better part of two years. Before leaving, he assigned his copyrights to Jacob II, for the sum of £2,597 16*s*. 8*d*.

Kathleen Lynch suggests that this move served as an indication that Tonson's 'life as a publisher was over'.[30] In broad general terms this is true, but Jacob I retained his interest in Shakespeare, and in the early 1720s he was back in England, participating in the preparation of another new edition. The new text was again placed in the hands of a well-established and highly regarded literary figure: the man for whom Tonson had served as literary 'pimp' just over a decade previously, Alexander Pope. Harry M. Geduld has suggested that Pope found Jacob the elder's 'experience invaluable on important textual matters' and that Tonson 'acted in an advisory capacity' throughout.[31]

The first public indication that Pope's edition was underway came in a note in the *Weekly Journal* for 18 November 1721, observing that the 'celebrated Mr. Pope is preparing a correct Edition of Shakespear's Works; that of the late Mr. Rowe being very faulty'.[32] This announcement was followed up some months later by another call to the general public for assistance, published in the *Evening Post* for 3–5 May 1722. The notice indicates that 'if any Person has any Editions of the Tempest, Mackbeth, Julius Caesar, Timon of Athens, King John, and Henry the 8th; printed before the Year 1620', they should be brought to 'J. Tonson, in the Strand', and the owners will there 'receive any Satisfaction required'.[33] Tonson and Pope might have waited until doomsday for the requested texts to be delivered to them, since all of these plays had, as we have already seen, appeared in print for the first time in the 1623 folio. It is, of course, a touch unfair to mock Tonson and Pope for the lack of knowledge indicated by the *Evening Post* advert. After all, it would be the best part of another two decades before anyone would attempt a systematic bibliography of known Shakespeare editions (and even this would, somewhat incongruously, form part of a volume entitled *New Memoirs of the Life and Poetical Works of Mr. John Milton*).[34] But the slip is revealing nonetheless, in that it indicates that the centre of gravity of Pope's edition was not historically located. As we shall see, the sensibility which Pope brought to the task of editing Shakespeare was aesthetic rather than textual or bibliographical – hardly a surprising tendency, we might feel, in the foremost poet of his generation.

Where Rowe offered passing comments on his editorial programme in his Dedication to the Duke of Somerset, Pope provided his readers with an extended Preface in which he discussed the nature of the task facing him as editor. During the course of the Preface, he laments what he takes to be the deeply unsatisfactory state of the text and he places the blame for this squarely on the shoulders of Heminge and Condell and their theatrical colleagues. Referring to the First Folio, he observes:

This edition is said to be printed from the *Original Copies*; I believe they meant those which had lain ever since the Author's days in the playhouse, and had from time to time been cut, or added to, arbitrarily. It appears that this edition, as well as the Quarto's, was printed (at least partly) from no better copies than the *Prompter*'s *Book*, or *Piece-meal Parts* written out for the use of the actors.

(§194, I, p. xvii)

Pondering the implications of this, Pope asks: 'how many faults may have been unjustly laid to [Shakespeare's] account from arbitrary Additions, Expunctions, Transpositions of scenes and lines, confusion of Characters and Persons, wrong application of Speeches, corruptions of innumerable Passages by the Ignorance, and wrong Correction of 'em again by the Impertinence, of his first Editors?' (§194, I, p. xxi).

By his own reckoning, then, Pope faced a monumental task in redeeming the text from the corrupt state into which it had fallen. Writing to Judith Cowper in November 1722, when the text was about one quarter completed, he represented his editorial policy as being cautious and conservative: 'I have never indulged my own Conjectures, but kept meerly to such amendments as are authorized by the old Editions in the authors life time.'[35] However, because Pope essentially regarded all early editions of Shakespeare as sharing wholly equal status (and equal liability to corruption), the editorial principle mapped out here in effect provided him with licence unsystematically to pick and choose among variant texts as some particular readings appealed to him more than others. These readings were spliced into his base text – a copy of Rowe's edition (probably the 1714), which he marked up for the printers.[36] But Pope went further than selecting from among variant readings. Convinced that the plays were rife with actorly interpolations, he cut sections of text from all but ten of the plays, convinced that the lines and passages concerned had never been written by Shakespeare. In most cases, the excised text was 'degraded' to the bottom of the page, but in some instances lines were simply cut out without attention being drawn to the fact. *Love's Labour's Lost* was a particularly vexing text for the poet – as Peter Seary has observed, the play's 'unrelenting word-play . . . did not appeal to eighteenth-century sensibilities'. Pope degraded some 222 lines of the text 'and signified his general disapprobation of four complete scenes by marking them with triple daggers'.[37] In all, over the course of the entire edition, Pope degraded a total of some 1,560 lines.

Like Rowe before him, Pope also regularised the text in various ways. He retained Rowe's dramatis personae lists with very little amendment and he further advanced Rowe's policy of systematically dividing the plays into acts and scenes, following the Italian and French practice of 'marking a new scene whenever a character of importance enters or leaves the stage'.[38] Again in common with Rowe (and with the 'editors' of the later folios), he continued the process of modernising spelling and punctuation. His most noteworthy set of regularising changes came, however, in the area of versification. Pope consistently sought to smooth out irregularities in the metre, in an attempt, as T. R. Lounsbury rather uncharitably puts it, 'to reduce everything to the measured monotony of eighteenth-century versification'. To this end, 'words were inserted in the verse, words were thrown out, or the order of the words was changed', emendations which Lounsbury estimated 'mounted into the thousands'.[39] Pope was also occasionally greatly exercised by the problem of Shakespeare's persistent anachronisms. In this matter, he tended to draw the line in the oddest of places. Happy enough to accept a Caesar who plucked open his doublet, Pope was nevertheless unwilling to countenance any references to hats in the ancient world, as R. B. McKerrow notes:

> finding 'hat' four times in the plays on classical subjects, twice in
> *Coriolanus*, once in *Timon of Athens*, and once in *Julius Caesar*, Pope in the
> first three cases altered 'hat' to 'cap'. In the fourth there was a difficulty;
> the phrase was 'Their hats are pluck'd about their ears', and I suppose
> that he did not quite see how one could do this with a cap. Still 'hat' could
> not be allowed to stand, so he cut the word out and substituted a dash.[40]

The overall effect of Pope's editorial work is to provide us with, as D. Nichol Smith has observed, 'such an edition as he presumes Shakespeare would have given us had he brought it out with Jacob Tonson', or, as Lounsbury put it, with characteristic acerbic wit: 'Shakespeare berouged, periwigged, and attired generally according to the fashionable literary mode of the eighteenth century'.[41] But, again, this is an excessively harsh judgement and – more than this – it fails adequately to engage with Pope's project in its own terms. In the Preface to his edition, Pope identified 'the better half of Criticism' as being 'the pointing out of an Author's excellencies' and he carried out this function in relation to Shakespeare by identifying 'the most shining passages' with quotation marks placed along the margin or, 'where the beauty lay not in particulars but in the whole scene', by a star placed at the beginning of the scene (§194, I, p. xxiii).[42] The primacy of the aesthetic informed Pope's attitude to textual as well as critical matters, and it was the aesthetic codes of his own contemporary culture that most concerned him, rather than those of the Renaissance period. While admiring Shakespeare immensely, Pope also likened his work to a building filled with 'dark, odd, and uncouth passages', with many elements of the structure being 'childish, ill-plac'd, and unequal to its grandeur' (p. xxiv). The task Pope set himself was, in a sense, to modernise and upgrade this property, to make it comfortably fit for eighteenth-century habitation. Marcus Walsh has thus justly observed that

> Pope's choice of an aesthetic orientation was wholly reasonable within his historical context. He conceived his business as the mediation of Shakespeare, the author of a past and less cultivated age, to readers in his own . . . There seems little point in asking whether his judgments are consistent with aesthetic criteria that Shakespeare might have used. They are not, because Pope's orientation is not authorial.[43]

Pope's edition was published in six volumes in 1725. Tonson again seems to have had his eye on a double market for the text, as he initially issued it in large quarto format, then reduced it to duodecimo for the second edition, which appeared three years later. The downshift in format may also reflect a general failure of the expensive quarto text to achieve satisfactory sales. Pope's was the only quarto edition of Shakespeare undertaken by the Tonson cartel and solicitations for subscriptions 'called out a miserably disappointing response'.[44] Even Swift and Arbuthnot failed to subscribe. Some 140 sets remained unsold as late as 1767, when they were disposed of for just 16s. per set – not much more than a tenth of the original price.[45]

As in the case of Rowe's 1709 text, the edition itself excluded the poems, but, once again, a seventh volume issued by another set of publishers and printed in the same format and style, soon filled the gap. This volume was prepared by 'the physician turned literary hack, George Sewell' and consisted very largely of a recycling of Gildon's original Curll volume.[46] A year after Pope's edition was published a further volume appeared which also contrived to look like an extension to the edition. Far from complementing Pope's text, however, this 1726 quarto bore the following combative title:

> *Shakespeare Restor'd: or, A Specimen of the Many Errors as well*
> *Committed, or Unamended, by Mr Pope in his Late Edition of this Poet.*
> *Designed not only to correct the said Edition, but to restore the True Reading*
> *of Shakespeare in all the Editions ever yet publish'd.*

The author of this 194-page attack on Pope was Lewis Theobald, a lawyer by training who had enjoyed some limited success in the commercial theatre. He was responsible for an adaptation of *Richard II*, performed at Lincoln's Inn Fields in 1719 and published in 1720. The Prologue to Theobald's play might well have seemed to indicate a certain potential textual kinship between himself and Pope:

> *Immortal* Shakespear *on this Tale began,*
> *And wrote it in a rude, Historick Plan,*
> *On his rich Fund our Author builds his Play,*
> *Keeps all his Gold, and throws his Dross away*;
> *Safe in this Aid, he can no* Thunder dread,
> Fenc'd with the *God's* own *Laurel* round his Head.[47]

For Theobald the dramatist, as for Pope the editor, Shakespeare's text consists of a combination of precious materials and trash. Each sets out to eliminate the latter and to fashion a more seemly edifice from the former. But when Theobald turned textual critic he shifted his ground, in the process effecting an important reconceptualisation of the Shakespearean editorial process.

Shakespeare Restor'd was, as Marcus Walsh has put it, 'an extraordinary piece of detailed and strenuous critical analysis'.[48] The bulk of the book (some 132 pages) was given over to a critique of Pope's text of *Hamlet*, but in the remainder of his volume Theobald commented on almost all of the other plays as well. Theobald singles out for criticism those places where Pope has

> *substituted* a *fresh Reading*, and there was no Occasion to depart from the
> Poet's Text; where he has *maim'd* the Author by an unadvis'd
> *Degradation*; where he has made a *bad* Choice in a *Various Reading*, and
> degraded the better Word; and where he, by *mistaking* the *Gloss* of any
> Word, has given a wrong Turn to the Poet's Sense and Meaning.[49]

Pope was stung by the attack and he responded by lampooning Theobald in verse. In the first instance, in a satiric fragment published in his *Miscellanies* volume in March 1728, he linked Theobald with Sewell and all other jobbing editors, mocking their work as mere empty pedantry:

> Pains, Reading, Study, are their just Pretence,
> And all they want is Spirit, Taste, and Sense.
> *Commas* and *Points* they set exactly right;
> And 'twere a Sin to rob them of their *Mite*.
> In future Ages how their Fame will spread,
> For routing *Triplets*, and restoring *ed*.
> Yet ne'er one Sprig of Laurel grac'd those Ribbalds,
> From sanguine *Sew*[*ell*] down to pidling *Tibbalds*:
> Who thinks he *reads* when he but *scans* and *spells*,
> A Word-catcher, that lives on Syllables.[50]

Pope returned to the attack later in the same year, in the first edition of the *Dunciad*, published anonymously to begin with, but later owned by the poet.

Here Theobald appears as the chosen favourite of the goddess Dulness and he lists the tedious work through which he honours her:

> Here studious I unlucky Moderns save,
> Nor sleeps one error in its father's grave,
> Old puns restore, lost blunders nicely seek,
> And crucify poor *Shakespear* once a week.
> For thee I dim these eyes, and stuff this head,
> With all such reading as was never read;
> For thee supplying, in the worst of days,
> Notes to dull books, and Prologues to dull plays;
> For thee explain a thing 'till all men doubt it,
> And write about it, Goddess, and about it.[51]

Despite his withering parodies, Pope was forced, albeit grudgingly, to concede that a great number of Theobald's criticisms were indeed just and he incorporated some 106 of his corrections into the second edition of his own text, also published in 1728.[52]

Coming back to *Shakespeare Restor'd* itself, we can say that a clear indication of the fact that Theobald was bringing a different sensibility to the business of Shakespearean textual scholarship is provided by his favourable invocation of the work of Richard Bentley.[53] Bentley was one of the foremost classical scholars of his day and he had produced important editions of Horace (1711), Terence (1726) and Manilius (1739).[54] Classical and biblical commentators had a long tradition of grappling with complex textual issues, including problems of the relative authority of multiple witnesses, the precise nature of textual corruption and the limits of editorial correction. The dispute between Pope and Theobald betokens, to some extent, the migration of advanced textual disputation from the classical and biblical realm into the arena of national literature, as eighteenth-century culture began to shift towards the secular and the vernacular.[55] Tracing the lineage of the textual models inherited by eighteenth-century editors of secular texts, Marcus Walsh indicates a very interesting doctrinal division in post-Reformation biblical studies between, on the one hand, a Catholic approach which vested authority in oral tradition and foregrounded the church itself as the arbiter of scriptural meaning and, on the other, a Protestant (and, specifically, an Anglican) approach which 'defended the determinate meaning, the comprehensibility, and the reliability of transmission of Scripture'.[56] What Walsh identifies here is, we might say, a difference in textual attitude between a paradigm which privileges social meaning constructed over time through the force of tradition, and a contrasting paradigm which privileges historically rooted meaning, intelligible through a process of textual recovery. Though one would want to resist a fatuous analogy which maps these divisions neatly onto the Catholic (and fortuitously named) Pope and his Protestant adversary, it can, nevertheless, be argued that, while Pope sought a text which resonated with the consensual aesthetic values of his own society, Theobald was much more interested in endeavouring to relocate the text within its own historical moment, pledging fidelity to the integrity of the text and seeking to explain difficulties by appealing, wherever possible, to a greater textual and cultural historical context.[57] Some of the general outlines of Theobald's approach can be glimpsed through Pope's parodic distortions of his position. 'Pains, Reading, Study' are indeed what textual criticism involves for Theobald, rather than acuity of poetic vision, since it is only by engaging in 'all such reading as was never read' that an editor can hope to achieve any kind of accurate sense of an author's own textual and linguistic environment. By achieving such an understanding, an editor might hope to be able to illuminate a text by *explaining* its obscurities (thereby 'Old puns [and other meanings] restor[ing]') rather than emending them out of existence. For Theobald, to 'Explain a thing . . . and write about it' – even at great length, if necessary – is indeed of primary importance, since it is through explanation that readers are brought to accommodate their understanding to the text, rather than the text being compelled to accommodate itself to the reader's capacity to understand.

Theobald intended to follow up *Shakespeare Restor'd* with another volume of textual readings and commentaries on Shakespeare, but 'Earnest Sollicitations' were, he tells us, made to him that he should give the subscribers to the proposed volume 'the Poet's Text corrected' (§206, I, p. lxiii). In the 1728 second edition of his controversial *Double Falsehood* (a 'lost' Shakespeare play for which he claimed to hold manuscript copy), Theobald made his change of intentions public:[58]

> I am honor'd with so many powerful Sollicitations, pressing Me to the Prosecution of an Attempt, which I have begun with some little Success, of *restoring* SHAKESPEARE from the numerous Corruptions of his Text: that I can neither in Gratitude, nor good Manners, longer resist them. I therefore think it not amiss here to promise, that, tho' *private Property* should so far stand in my Way, as to prevent me from putting out an *Edition* of *Shakespeare*, yet, some Way or other, if I live, the Publick shall receive from my Hand his *whole* WORKS corrected, with my best Care and Ability.[59]

Theobald's comment on the possibility that 'private Property' might stand in the way of his edition is interesting, as it indicates that, at the time of

writing, he did not know who would publish the edition or whether the
Tonson cartel would allow it to proceed. In the first half of 1730, his friend
Charlotte West, Lady de la Warr, acted as intermediary between Theobald
and the Tonson group, though they failed to agree terms – in part because
the second edition of Pope's text had been published hardly two years previously, but also, perhaps, because Pope himself had been writing to the
publishers, attempting to dissuade them from employing Theobald.[60] As
the Tonson negotiations stalled, Theobald was approached by a rival cartel
who indicated their willingness to publish his edition. Hearing of this, the
Tonson group decided to close with Theobald, sensing that an enforced defence of their rights to the text would prove to be a messy business (an issue
we will take up in greater detail in chapters 5 and 6). As his payment,
Theobald was to receive 400 sets of the edition on demy and a further 100
sets on royal paper, at a cost to the publishers of about £600, but offering
Theobald a potential income from sales of 1,100 guineas.[61] This was one of
the highest payments made to an editor during the course of the eighteenth
century – Pope, by contrast, had been paid just £100.[62] Theobald clearly
had reason to be thankful for the negotiating skills of Lady de la Warr, but,
equally, his publishers must have been keenly aware of the commercial value
of the controversy which Theobald and Pope's very public arguments had
provoked.

Pope's edition, as noted, was not entirely a solo effort. Jacob the elder
would appear to have placed his accumulated literary expertise at the poet's
disposal and Pope himself writes that he had 'got a Man or two . . . at Oxford
to ease me of part of the drudgery of Shakespear' and also that, in London,
he planned to 'get together Parties of my acquaintance ev'ry night, to collate
the several Editions of Shakespear's single Plays'.[63] Theobald, too, had his
collaborators. He entered into a correspondence so intense with Reverend
William Warburton (later Bishop of Gloucester) that he almost began to
fancy him as a lover. The flood of letters between them, Theobald tells
him, 'bring[s] back to my mind the time of a love-correspondence; and the
expectation of every fresh Letter from you is the joy of a mistress to me'
(of Warburton we will hear much more in due course).[64] In his Preface, he
also acknowledged the assistance of Hawley Bishop and of Styan Thirlby of
Jesus College, Cambridge, who granted Theobald 'the Liberty of collating
his Copy of *Shakespeare*, mark'd thro' in the Margin with his own Manuscript
References and accurate Observations' (§206, I, p. lxv). Thirlby had published an edition of Justin Martyr in 1721 and probably himself intended to
produce an edition of Shakespeare, but a quirkily irascible temperament and
an excessive fondness for alcohol seem to have prevented him. Some years
later, in 1745, he was pictured by a contemporary in the following terms:

'an old man at six in the evening in a striped satin nightgown and cap I took to be Dr. Thirlby or such a sort of body that does not inhabit our poor earth nor subjects itself to our whims'.[65] Thirlby was not always entirely pleased with the acknowledgements he received throughout the text of Theobald's edition, especially when his name was attached to notes, based on his ideas, but written by Theobald himself. Against one such note in his copy of Theobald's edition, Thirlby wrote, with characteristic bad-temperedness:

> I wish, Sr, you wd not give reasons for me. This is so far from a reason of mine, that I do not understand it. Cd you not have made this emendation your own as well as so many others of mine? You had displeased me far less than by printing my name into this stupid note.[66]

Of the material contributed to the edition by Warburton, Thirlby was even more dismissive. Against one of Warburton's notes, he wrote: 'Stupid wretch . . . You needed not to have put his name to this note. Every sentence of it shews who wrote it. Other men may have wrote as great nonsense but no other man ever wrote such.' Against Warburton's glossing of 'Hold good my complexion' in *As You Like It* as 'let me not blush', Thirlby wrote: 'i.e. let me not let a fart'.[67]

Like Pope before him, Theobald set out his editorial programme in his Preface. He answered Pope's jibes at 'all such reading as was never read' by foregrounding the extent of his acquaintance with Shakespeare's contemporary textual world:

> to clear up several Errors in the Historical Plays, I purposely read over *Hall* and *Holingshead*'s Chronicles in the Reigns concern'd; all the Novels in *Italian*, from which our Author had borrow'd any of his Plots; such Parts of *Plutarch*, from which he had deriv'd any Parts of his *Greek* or *Roman* Story: *Chaucer* and *Spenser*'s Works; all the Plays of *B. Jonson*, *Beaumont* and *Fletcher*, and above 800 old *English* Plays, to ascertain the obsolete and uncommon Phrases in him: Not to mention some Labour and Pains unpleasantly spent in the dry Task of consulting Etymological *Glossaries*.
>
> (§206, I, pp. lxvii–lxviii)

Theobald's comment about the dry business of consulting glossaries points to his keen awareness of the fact that language shifts and evolves over time. In this he can be contrasted with Pope, who slated the First Folio for its lack of eighteenth-century spelling: 'every page is . . . scandalously false spelled, and almost all the learned or unusual words [are] intolerably mangled' (§194, I, p. xv). Simon Jarvis aligns Theobald's work in this regard with that of

Joseph Scaliger on the classical languages, and registers Theobald's recognition that 'the criteria of correctness by which English syntax and lexicon are to be judged may be historically variable'.[68] Another important editorial principle mapped out in Theobald's Preface concerned the use of analogous passages as a means of explication: 'I have constantly endeavoured to support my Corrections and Conjectures by parallel Passages and Authorities from himself, the surest Means of expounding any Author whatsoever' (§206, I, p. xliii). Elucidation by parallel passages, as R. B. McKerrow noted, has 'been followed by every commentator upon Shakespeare since his day'.[69]

In common with Pope, Theobald used as his base text a copy of his predecessor's edition. Theobald received from Tonsons a copy of the second Pope edition, with blank pages interleaved and he used these pages for the text of his notes (some of these volumes have survived in the collections of the British Library and Winchester College).[70] Because he used Pope as his base text, many of Pope's changes persisted into Theobald's edition and this is particularly true in the area of versification, where Theobald silently accepted most of the alterations which Pope made to harmonise the metre with eighteenth-century poetic practice. Lounsbury suggests that Theobald's acquiescence in this matter arose from his sincerely sharing 'in the belief of his age in [Pope's] unassailable supremacy as a master of verse, and in the propriety of applying his superior skill to the rectification of Shakespeare's text'.[71]

A number of scholars have raised the question of why it was that Theobald should have chosen Pope's edition as his base text – especially given the level of hostility that existed between them. After all, in the Preface to his edition, Theobald said of Pope that he would 'willingly devote a part of [his] Life to the honest Endeavour of quitting Scores' with the poet (§206, I, p. xxxvii). Peter Seary has suggested that the Tonson cartel obliged Theobald to use Pope's edition, because they were endeavouring to shore up their claim to the rights in the Shakespeare text. Seary maps out a repeated gap of about fourteen years between new editions across the first extended series of Tonson texts and he relates this to the 1709 *Act for the Encouragement of Learning*, which limited the basic term of copyright to a period of fourteen years. He thus suggests that the logic of the cartel's position was that the editorial work in each new edition was effectively reconstituting an existing property and thereby extending its legal lifespan. 'Theobald's choice of copy', he concludes, 'must be attributed to circumstances of publishing history and not to ignorance.'[72] While there is a certain elegance to Seary's suggestion, Simon Jarvis has questioned the validity of his claim. The connection back to Pope is, not surprisingly, nowhere advertised in Theobald's edition and so it is hard to see exactly how the Tonson cartel would have imagined that the link could have been legally established if necessity so demanded. As Jarvis notes, in the case of a dispute, 'it is hard to imagine a magistrate sufficiently bored, insane, or malicious to have the texts collated with each other, or to hear such evidence were it presented'.[73] In any case, as will be seen in chapter 5, since the major London publishers were, at this time, heavily engaged in arguing for the continued existence of *perpetual* copyright, it is unlikely that they would have been willing to concede that the effect of the 1709 act had been to limit the period of ownership of literary property to a set of fixed terms. It is much more likely, then, as Jarvis argues, that Theobald's choice of text indicates a certain essential lack of clarity in his attitude towards textual matters. While generally opposing Pope's aestheticism and condemning his lack of systematic study of the earliest printed Shakespeare texts, Theobald himself never developed either a wholly programmatic view of the relationships among the earliest texts or a sense of the exact implications of those relationships. He seems to have retained a general feeling of respect for inherited notions of the centrality of the 'received' text (i.e., the text moulded by and inherited from the editorial tradition) and his attitude towards the business of correcting that text appears at times to have been self-contradictory: Jarvis has thus concluded that

> Theobald's editorial theories and practices are in many respects still eclectic ones: as much material as possible from early Quartos and the First Folio is to be gathered and used to correct a text whose basis is Pope's second edition of 1728; decisions as to whether the Quarto or Folio readings should have priority in disputed cases are often made on the basis of a variety of aesthetic or linguistic, rather than bibliographical, criteria.[74]

If Theobald's position was somewhat muddled, the general principles of his textual programme were nevertheless foundational for much of what followed in Shakespeare editing for the next several centuries. The effect of Pope's witty attacks on him was to damage Theobald's reputation among his immediate editorial successors, even as they quite happily drew upon his work. The general public perception of the relative merits of the first three eighteenth-century editors is reflected in a question and answer which appeared in *The Weekly Oracle: or, Universal Library*, a sort of 'ask the experts' magazine of the 1730s. The questioner asked: '*Which Edition would you advise me to, as most likely to come at the Author's genuine Work*, Rowe's, Pope's, or Theobald's?', to which the *Oracle* replied:

> Mr. *Rowe* does not seem to have been a Critic of any Distinction:
> Mr. *Pope*'s Taste, we are inclined to think preferrable to both the other;
> but Mr. *Theobald* has spared no Labour, whatever he may want in Taste:
> However, he has embarrassed his Volumes with many useless,
> impertinent, and bad Notes.[75]

The *Oracle*'s comment on Theobald's notes is significant. Rowe had presented his readers with a clean page, containing his version of Shakespeare's plays, formatted according to the conventions of the early eighteenth-century and – in common with the seventeenth-century folios – lacking in annotation.[76] Pope's text was elegantly printed on the wider expanse of a quarto page, with generous margins. Some text, as we have seen, was demoted by Pope to the bottom of the page and there were some annotations, but they were relatively sparse. The primary goal, for Pope, was still to present the Shakespearean text in as clear a fashion as possible. Theobald made a break with this general convention. In his edition, annotation became both more frequent and more intrusive on the page. To take the instance of *Love's Labour's Lost* – the second text in volume II: the play runs to ninety-six pages in total; fifty-five of those pages include annotations; in eight instances, the annotations occupy more than 50 per cent of the page, crowding upwards against the text itself. Where Theobald led, others would follow and progressively more and more of the page space would be annexed for annotation. As we will see in the next chapter, Samuel Johnson, in his 1765 edition, initiated a new tradition of 'variorum' editions, which self-consciously incorporated the observations of crowded lines of previous commentators on the edition page. It is in these editions that the origins of scholarly *mise-en-page* can be found (at least for English secular texts). But this emerging dispensation was not without its critics. One late eighteenth-century reviewer observes, for instance, that 'all these inestimable notes are printed at the bottom of the page, so that a reader, at all inquisitive, can scarcely keep his eyes from them, and is frequently drawn into the whirlpool, in spite of all his efforts'.[77] As the century drew to a close, a gathering chorus of such criticism was heard and we shall see in chapter 9 that, by the beginnings of the nineteenth century, publishers had begun to heed these critical voices.[78]

Returning to Theobald, one can say that, by the end of the nineteenth century, his central importance to the editorial tradition was beginning to receive greater recognition. John Churton Collins lamented the attitude of those editors who made mention of Theobald 'as a gentleman might refer among his friends to a shoe-black who had just amused him with some witticism while polishing his boots' and he celebrated Theobald's foundational achievements as an editor.[79] In his British Academy Shakespeare lecture of 1933, R. B. McKerrow dubbed Theobald 'the true founder of modern Shakespearian scholarship'.[80] In addition to helping to shape editorial theory, Theobald has also left his mark on Shakespeare's text in more immediate ways. Comparing Theobald's text with the Globe edition (which served as standard for almost a century after its first appearance in 1864), R. F. Jones estimated that some 150 of Theobald's substantial emendations had been accepted into the later edition. Among these emendations is his celebrated changing of Mistress Quickly's 'a Table of greene fields' to 'a babbled of green fields', in *Henry V*.[81] The success of Theobald's edition in his own century is also evidenced by the fact that it was the most frequently reprinted of all of the Tonson editions. By 1773, his text had been issued some eight times by London publishers.

Theobald's was the last new Shakespeare edition undertaken by Jacob the elder and his nephew. Jacob II died in 1735 at the age of fifty-two, at which point the publishing firm passed into the hands of his son, Jacob III, whose brother Richard played only a minor role in the affairs of the business. Jacob the elder died in the following year and a contributor to the *Gentleman's Magazine* at the time memorialised him with an extended bibliographic conceit:

> . . . he who many a scribbling elf
> *Abridg'd*, is now abridg'd himself.
>   When heav'n review'd th'*original text*,
> 'Twas with erratas few perplex'd:
> Pleas'd with the copy 'twas *collated*,
> And to a better life *translated*.[82]

When Jacob III decided to produce his own first Shakespeare edition he turned to Reverend William Warburton to act as editor.[83] Warburton, as we have already seen, had carried on extensive correspondence with Theobald when Theobald was working on his edition. In 1738 Warburton was providing entries for an encyclopaedic dictionary being co-edited by his fellow cleric Thomas Birch and on 30 September of that year he wrote to Birch desiring that he 'would mention [his] intent of giving an edition of Shakespeare's Plays' and providing sample materials in connection with the edition.[84] Birch duly announced the text in the 'Shakespeare' entry of the *General Dictionary, Historical and Critical* (1739) and he included Warburton's sample in the text.[85] By January of 1743, Warburton was telling Birch that 'for my amusement, from time to time [I] go on in preparing Shakespeare for the press', but it would be another four years before the edition finally appeared.[86]

In spite of the close friendship enjoyed by Warburton and Theobald, the two had quarrelled following the appearance of Theobald's edition, as Warburton felt that his contribution to the text had not been adequately acknowledged. In writing the Preface to his own edition, Warburton launched a mean-spirited attack on his former friend, who had died in 1744. 'As to Mr. *Theobald*', he wrote, 'who wanted Money, I allowed him to print what I gave him for his own Advantage: and he allowed himself in the Liberty of taking one Part for his own, and sequestering another for the Benefit, as I supposed, of some future Edition' (§231, I, p. x).[87] He then proceeded to rehash Pope's parodic characterisation of Theobald, claiming that he

> was naturally turned to Industry and Labour. What he read he could transcribe: but, as what he thought, if ever he did think, he could but ill express, so he read on; and, by that means got a Character of Learning, without risquing, to every Observer, the Imputation of wanting a better Talent.
>
> (§231, I, p. xi)

Warburton's alignment with Pope was also advertised on the title page of his edition, where the text is attributed jointly to both of them, and in his Preface the reverend editor claimed that Pope (who, like Theobald, had died in 1744) 'was desirous I should give a new Edition of this Poet, as he thought it might contribute to put a stop to a prevailing folly of altering the Text of celebrated Authors without Talents or Judgment' (§231, I, p. xix). This claim of Warburton's was referenced with a footnote reading 'See his Letters to me', which Styan Thirlby mocked in his own copy of Warburton's edition, in a marginal comment reading 'You might as well have said see my arse in a band box.'[88]

Warburton did indeed follow in Pope's footsteps in the sense that his orientation as an editor was almost entirely aesthetic. His changes to the text were legion and he frequently emended passages which were, in the original, perfectly intelligible. Thus, in *Hamlet*, Ophelia's 'virgin crants' became 'virgin chants', Hamlet imagines taking arms against 'assail of troubles' rather than 'a sea of troubles', and his line 'That roars so loud and thunders in the index' becomes 'that roars so loud it thunders to the Indies'; in *As You Like It*, Rosalind recalls Orlando's kissing 'as full of sanctity as the touch of holy *beard*', rather than 'the touch of holy *bread*'; and, in *Romeo and Juliet*, in an emendation equally characteristic of a bishop, perhaps, Capulet's praise of the Friar, 'All our whole city is much bound to him' becomes 'All our whole city is bound to hymn.'[89] A classic Warburton emendation is his changing, in *Macbeth*, of 'And prophecy' to 'Aunts prophesying'. As Allardyce Nicoll sardonically notes, the 'context [shows] the force of this brilliant emendation':

> The night has been unruly: where we lay,
> Our chimneys were blown down, and, as they say,
> Lamentings heard i' the air, strange screams of death,
> *Aunts* prophesying with accents terrible
> Of dire combustion and confused events.[90]

Warburton also frequently twisted words into new and unheard of configurations, which he then glossed in his notes. Such coinages include 'fraine', 'pouled', 'geap', and 'to gaude'.[91] A contemporary critic, addressing Warburton, observed: 'instead of Critical Remarks, thou hast given thy Readers scarce any thing but bold Conjectures, and trifling Emendations of the Text, supported with *Corinthian Brass* and *Effrontery*'.[92]

From beyond the grave, Theobald might well have enjoyed a hearty last laugh at Warburton's expense. Just as he himself had presented *Shakespeare Restor'd* as a supplement to Pope's edition, so, in 1748, did Thomas Edwards publish a volume which purported to be *A Supplement to Mr Warburton's Edition of Shakespear. Being the Canons of Criticism, and Glossary, Collected from the notes in that celebrated work, and proper to be bound up with it*. In place of Theobald's scholarly earnestness, however, Edwards deployed a parodic wit worthy of Pope himself, as he slyly complimented his reverend adversary by noting that he must do him 'the justice to say, that, however he may be slandered by the ignorant or malicious Tartufes, it is very apparent that he has not interrupted his more serious studies by giving much of his time and attention to a playbook'.[93] The greater portion of Edwards' text was taken up with his 'canons of criticism' – a set of textual principles which he claimed to have abstracted from Warburton's editorial practice. The first half dozen canons provide a good flavour of the whole collection:

> CANON I.
> *A Professed Critic has a right to declare, that his Author wrote whatever he thinks he should have written, with as much positiveness as if he had been at his elbow.*
>
> (p. 12)
>
> CANON II.
> *He has a right to alter any passage which he does not understand.*
>
> (p. 13)
>
> CANON III.
> *These alterations he may make, in spite of the exactness of measure.*
>
> (p. 20)

CANON IV.
Where he does not like an expression, and yet cannot mend it, he may abuse his author for it.

(p. 21)

CANON V.
Or he may condemn it as a foolish interpolation.

(p. 22)

CANON VI.
As every author is to be corrected into all possible perfection, and of that perfection the profess'd critic is the sole judge; he may alter any word or phrase, which does not want amendment, or which will do, *provided he can think of any thing, which he imagines will do better.*

(pp. 22–3)

As books on textual criticism go, Edwards' *Canons of Criticism* (as it became known by its third edition) was something of a runaway best-seller, notching up seven editions by 1765 and becoming 'the most frequently published piece of Shakespearean criticism in the eighteenth century'.[94] The popularity of Edwards' volume provides a neat indication of the extent to which secular and vernacular editorial culture had changed over the course of less than half a century. Textual attitudes that seemed broadly acceptable in a Rowe or a Pope were, by mid-century, regarded as ridiculous when practised by a Warburton. As a result of this, the editors of the second half of the century would much more commonly align themselves with the textual principles formulated by Theobald, even if they paid him little more than grudging homage in the process.

4   The Tonson era 2: Johnson to Malone

Warburton's edition would appear not to have been a great commercial success for the Tonson cartel. They never reprinted the text and, for the best part of two decades, they relied instead on new releases of older editions to serve the Shakespeare market.[1] This may be the reason why, when Jacob III eventually did publish his second wholly new edition, he returned to his great-uncle's formula and appointed the leading literary figure of the day, Samuel Johnson, as editor. Johnson's interest in the text of Shakespeare was of long standing. In 1745, he published a pamphlet entitled *Miscellaneous Observations on the Tragedy of Macbeth*, which included 'Proposals for printing a new edition of the plays of William Shakespear', in ten 'small Volumes', the subscription price to be 'one Pound five Shillings in Sheets'.[2] The publisher of this projected edition was to be Edward Cave, the son of a Rugby shoemaker who had scraped together enough money to set up a small printing office at St John's Gate in London, where he established one of the most successful periodicals of the eighteenth century, the *Gentleman's Magazine*. Johnson contributed extensively to Cave's journal and he 'had a room set apart for him at St. John's Gate, where he wrote as fast as he could drive his pen, throwing the sheets off, when completed, to the "copy" boy'.[3] When Jacob III got wind of the plans of Cave and his then little-known editor, he wrote the publisher a letter in which politesse and threat were mixed in equal measure. Asserting the cartel's exclusive rights to the text of Shakespeare, Tonson suggests that 'if you call on me any afternoon about four or five o'clock, I doubt not I can shew you such a title as will satisfy you, not only as to the original copy, but likewise to all the emendations to this time'. Observing that he regards Cave as 'a man of character', he continues 'I had rather satisfy you of our right by argument than by the expence of a Chancery suit, which will be the method we shall take with any one who shall attack our property in this or any other copy that we have fairly bought and paid for.'[4] Whether Cave accepted the invitation to drop by the shop at 'Shakespeare's Head' in the Strand and view the evidence proffered is not recorded – either way, he abandoned plans for his own edition.

By the middle of the next decade Johnson had established his literary reputation and credentials. His *Dictionary* was published in 1755 and, within a year, a new prospectus for a Johnson edition of Shakespeare was issued, to be published by the Tonson cartel. It would be the best part of another decade before the edition itself was published, prompting the satirist Charles Churchill to chide Johnson on behalf of his subscribers, in a poem entitled 'The Ghost':

> He for subscribers baits his hook
> And takes your cash; but where's the book?
> No matter where; wise fear, you know,
> Forbids the robbing of a foe;
> But what, to serve our private ends,
> Forbids the cheating of our friends?[5]

While Churchill's accusations of cheating are entirely unfair, Johnson does seem to have been less than completely efficient when it came to the business of handling subscriptions. Asked by Tonson whether he could provide an account of the total number of his personal subscribers, Johnson is reported to have replied that he could not, for two very good reasons: 'I have lost all the names and spent all the money. It came in small portions, and departed in the same manner.'[6]

In his Tonson prospectus, Johnson, like Pope before him, offered a highly pessimistic assessment of the state of the text inherited from Shakespeare's contemporaries:

> It is not easy for invention to bring together so many causes concurring to vitiate a text . . . no books could be left in hands so likely to injure them, as plays frequently acted, yet continued in manuscript: no other transcribers were likely to be so little qualified for their task as those who copied for the stage, at a time when the lower ranks of the people were universally illiterate: no other editions were made from fragments so minutely broken, and so fortuitously reunited; and in no other age was the art of printing in such unskilful hands.[7]

For Pope, such pessimism had served as justification for extensive intervention in emending the text, but Johnson, when he came to the business of editing, was wary of Pope's methods, observing of his illustrious predecessor that 'he rejected whatever he disliked, and thought more of amputation than of cure' (§283, I, C8r). Ruefully noting that the 'allurements of emendation are scarcely resistable', Johnson nevertheless determined as far as possible to avoid that editorial 'unhappy state, in which danger is hid under pleasure'

(§283, I, E3r). 'As I practised conjecture more', he tells us, 'I learned to trust it less; and after I had printed a few plays, resolved to insert none of my own readings in the text. Upon this caution I now congratulate myself, for every day encreases my doubt of my emendations' (§283, I, E1v).

Like many of his contemporaries, Johnson wrote of Theobald with condescending derision, characterising him as 'a man of narrow comprehension and small acquisitions, with no native and intrinsick splendour of genius' and styling him as 'weak and ignorant . . . mean and faithless . . . petulant and ostentatious' (§283, I, D1r–v). As Johnson's comments on emendation make clear, however, he had a great deal more in common with Theobald himself than with his adversaries. Like Theobald, Johnson favoured the prescription that obscure readings should, as far as possible, be retained and explained, rather than emended, as he observed:

> It has been my settled principle, that the reading of the ancient books is probably true, and therefore is not to be disturbed for the sake of elegance, perspicuity, or mere improvement of the sense. For though much credit is not due to the fidelity, nor any to the judgement of the first publishers, yet they who had the copy before their eyes were more likely to read it right, than we who read it only by imagination.
>
> (§283, I, E1r)

Johnson did, however, disagree with Theobald on one issue of fundamental importance. While Theobald, as we have seen, paid close attention to the earliest copies of Shakespeare's plays, he did not have a strong sense of how exactly these texts might be sorted relative to each other. Johnson thus notes that Theobald, in listing the editions he consulted, suggests that one might regard 'the two first folios as of high, and the third folio as of middle authority'. Johnson characterised this position as fundamentally flawed, observing that 'the first is equivalent to all others, and . . . the rest only deviate from it by the printer's negligence. Whoever has any of the folios has all, excepting those diversities which mere reiteration of editions will produce' (§283, I, D1v). In making this observation, Johnson set out a principle that would become absolutely fundamental to editorial theory for the next two-and-a-half centuries: that printed texts can be arranged into a logical sequence and that the text presumed to be closest to the author's own original has an authority which outweighs that of all other editions. It is because of his articulation of this basic proposition that R. B. McKerrow hailed Johnson as the scholar 'alone of all the early editors . . . to have seen clearly the principles on which textual criticism of printed books must be based'.[8] However, while Johnson articulated this principle, he did not necessarily follow through on it in practice. Though he registered the primacy of the First Folio, he nevertheless did not use it as the foundation for his own edition. Instead, he based his text on an eclectic combination of Warburton's edition and the 1757 fourth edition of Theobald. Arthur M. Eastman has observed that Johnson's 'use of two different sources within the same play, within the same act, even within the same scene, and his willingness to omit important notes because he lacked the sixth volume of Theobald's Shakespeare point to no policy but that of expediency'.[9] While in theory, then, Johnson pledged fidelity to what he identified as the earliest authoritative text, in practice he remained faithful to the traditional custom of privileging the received text (or, somewhat confusingly in this case, two very different received texts).

Marcus Walsh has quite rightly observed that by at least registering that editions could be arranged into a hierarchy of authority, Johnson 'served to move Shakespearean editing further, and more decisively, towards an authorial orientation' and hence away from the alignment favoured by Pope, where the aesthetic codes of contemporary society function as a determining factor in the editorial process.[10] However, like his predecessors, Johnson also invested heavily in regularising the plays for his contemporary audience, providing, for instance, numerous additional stage directions to clarify the action. Eastman has estimated that Johnson may have made something in the region of between 14,000 and 15,000 changes to the text. Most of these changes were relatively minor in nature and involved a systematising of certain features of the text. Thus, Eastman notes that 'he got rid of a great deal of punctuation, particularly the hundreds of pairs of parentheses that his precursors had used either in lieu of dashes or commas or, as if to emphasize thought divisions, along with them'.[11] He also helped to clarify the text by cutting up a large number of extended sentences which had traditionally been strung together using semicolons, and, where his 'precursors had printed quotations without any mark to differentiate them from surrounding words[,] Johnson quite regularly italicized quotations'. The overall effect, Eastman argues, was to 'clarify and illuminate the drama's highest pleasure to the untrained reader, to keep his fancy easily and uninterruptedly aloft. It was, as was no Shakespeare before it, a Shakespeare for the laity.'[12]

Eastman is certainly correct to suggest that Johnson must have kept the general reader in mind as he prepared his text, but he did not, at the same time, lose sight of the more specialist reader. Johnson's edition appeared in the wake of a half century of detailed Shakespearean textual commentary. While he acknowledged that much of this commentary (and the disputes which it fuelled) was overheated, occasioning 'the most arrogant ostentation, and . . . the keenest acrimony' (§283, I, D7r), nevertheless, he recognised the value of a great deal of the work produced by his predecessors. For this reason, his edition seeks to provide a 'summation' of the best of that material; he includes in his text the prefaces of Pope, Theobald, Hanmer and Warburton, together with Rowe's 'Life' and as many of his predecessors' notes as he felt were useful to his reader, making, as Colin Franklin has observed 'almost a full page on the many occasions when Johnson opposed Warburton who opposed Theobald'.[13] Johnson was also the first editor to include the text of Shakespeare's will in his edition – the existence of which was noted in 1737.[14] The 1765 edition has thus been characterised as the first 'variorum' edition and it gave rise to a long series of texts stretching onward to 1813, and with many additional versions spun off along the way.

The immediate inheritor of Johnson's *Shakespeare* was George Steevens, who was primarily responsible for the second edition of the text, published in 1773. By this time, the Tonson firm had been wound-up. Jacob III died in 1767 and the bulk of the Tonson copyrights were sold off following his death, the Shakespeare rights fetching £1,200 (by contrast with an 85 per cent share in Dryden, which sold for £100 and half the rights to Ben Jonson, which brought in just £60).[15] Jacob's brother Richard survived him by five years, but, despite his initials being included in the imprint, he had never been much involved in the publishing business, dedicating most of his energies instead to his political career (he served as a member of parliament, initially for Wallingford and subsequently for New Windsor).[16] By 1767, then, the Tonson era had effectively come to an end and Steevens' revision of Johnson would be undertaken under different auspices.

Before Steevens produced his second edition of Johnson's text, however, one final Shakespeare edition did appear with the Tonson name included in the imprint. Published in 1767–8, just as the old firm was being shut down, the editor of this text was Edward Capell. The contrast between Capell and Johnson is striking. Where Johnson was the bon vivant centre of literary London, Capell was a rather isolated, eccentric figure. Though reportedly as a young man he was 'a professed beau' and 'knew where the *bona-robas* were' (knew so well that his constitution 'suffered ultimately from these *inamoratas*') he later lived an isolated existence.[17] A contemporary, Samuel Pegge, described him as '*all over Shakespeare*' and observed that, being 'too *opiniatre* and dictatorial' in his conversation, he alienated such few friends as he made and became, later in life, 'almost an anchorite'. His social habits at home seem fussily suited to the fastidious business of what

Pope characterised as the 'dull duty of an editor'. Pegge tells us that when a friend came to call on him

> he was desired to leave his cane in the vestibule, lest he should either dirt the floors with it, or soil the carpet. No one but himself was permitted to stir his fire, or snuff his candles; and to remove and misplace the most trifling thing in his room was a heinous offence.[18]

Like Theobald, Capell was a lawyer by training, but in 1737 he was appointed to the office of Deputy Inspector of Plays, thereby gaining practical experience with theatrical scripts. He would appear to have begun work on his edition of Shakespeare some considerable time before it appeared in print. In the manuscript copy of his edition, preserved (together with his excellent collection of folios and quartos) in the Wren Library at Trinity College, Cambridge, the plays are individually dated, the earliest (*Merry Wives of Windsor*) being inscribed 25 November 1749.[19] From the first, the Tonson cartel seem to have been less than enthusiastic in their attitude to Capell's undertaking. He was paid a fee of £300 for his work, by contrast with the subscription arrangements enjoyed by Theobald and Johnson, both of whom possibly netted in excess of £1,000 for their efforts.[20] While Capell's edition was ambitious, it was also problematically fragmented. Colin Franklin observes of the edition itself (published in octavo) that the 'wide margins of these charming books gave them the appearance of large-paper copies'.[21] Capell returned to an older tradition of *mise-en-page* by keeping his text free from annotation, thus presenting a clear page. His edition was, in fact, annotated, but the notes were included in a wholly separate set of volumes, published later than the edition itself. The first volume of notes appeared in 1774, but the sales were so poor that Capell withdrew the book from circulation, compensating the publishers (E. and C. Dilly) for their loss.[22] He then produced a two-volume set of notes, published by subscription in 1779, but again sales were less than he had hoped for. It was not until 1783 that the full three volumes of his commentary were in print, under the stewardship of John Collins, Capell himself having died in 1781. The long delay in bringing the notes and commentary to print meant that the rationale of Capell's edition was not immediately understood. Furthermore, as Gary Taylor has observed, 'Even modern scholars sympathetic to Capell's ambitions find his consortium of publications damnably frustrating to use.'[23] The problem is compounded by the fact that Capell employed a unique set of markers and symbols in his edition, such as setting 'what is added without the authority of some ancient edition' in black letter (§304, I, p. 48). To add further to the odds stacked against Capell, his writing – especially when contrasted with the fluid elegance of his immediate predecessor, Johnson – was generally rather pedestrian and colourless, though he hardly deserves Johnson's snide put-down that, like Caliban, 'he doth gabble monstrously', or James Boswell the younger's later observation that 'Never was there a writer who appeared to have taken more pains to show that language . . . was not intended to communicate our ideas.'[24] As in the case of Theobald, recognition of Capell's strengths would come much later. In 1861, J. O. Halliwell would issue a pamphlet offering *A Few Words in Defence of the Memory of Edward Capell*, in which he characterised the editor as 'one of the most acute, sensible, and learned of all Shakesperian critics . . . the first who had a true knowledge of the correct philological criticism of the text of our great dramatist'.[25]

For all of its problems, Capell's edition did indeed present some unique and important features. Crucially, he was the first Shakespearean scholar radically to interrogate the notion that editors should use the received text as the basis for their own edition. Thus, he observes of Rowe that he 'went no further than to the edition nearest him in time, which was the folio of 1685, the last and worst of those impressions' (§304, I, pp. 13–14). He goes on to argue that 'the superstructure cannot be a sound one, which is built upon so bad a foundation as that work of Mr ROWE´s; which all [subsequent editors] in succession, have yet made their corner-stone'. 'The truth is', he asserts, 'it was impossible that such a beginning should end better than it has done: the fault was in the setting-out' (§304, I, p. 19). Capell himself became the first Shakespearean editor to produce a text from the ground up, relying on the earliest printed editions.[26] According to a contemporary reviewer, he was said to have 'actually copied every play of his author at least ten times with his own hand'.[27] If this is true, then nine of these copies have since perished, but, as we have already noted, Capell's own hand-written manuscript of his edition has indeed survived as part of his bequest to Trinity College Cambridge.

While breaking with the received text, Capell also went some distance towards recognising the fact that the earliest editions might be arranged into a sequence of diminishing authority. In this, his work complements Johnson's, though he did not see Johnson's edition until his own work was very far advanced. Arranging the early texts he consulted into a table of editions, he makes the following comments on the relationships among the early quartos and among the folios:

> The quarto's [sic] went through many impressions, as may be seen in the
> Table: and, in each play, the last is generally taken from the impression
> next before it, and so onward to the first; the few that come not within

this rule, are taken notice of in the Table: And this further is to be observ'd of them: that, generally speaking, the more distant they are from the original, the more they abound in faults; 'till, in the end, the corruptions of the last copies become so excessive, as to make them of hardly any worth. The folio too has it's [sic] re-impressions . . . and they tread the same round as did the quarto's.

(§304, I, pp. 13–14)

As in the case of Johnson, however, his registering of this principle is not necessarily a sign that he followed it in practice, and McKerrow, for one, sees little difference in Capell's editorial approach and that of his predecessors, arguing that he still juggles readings in search of the one that he finds most appealing, cleaving to 'the idea that if an editor likes a reading, that reading is (a) good, and (b) attributable to Shakespeare'.[28]

Though ultimately falling back, in many instances, on aesthetic criteria of judgement, Capell's work nevertheless registers a continuing trend in eighteenth-century editing towards the purely textual and bibliographic. This trend is further marked in the work of Charles Jennens, a wealthy eccentric who took to editing Shakespeare at the age of seventy and published editions of five individual plays between 1770 and 1774. His original intention was to edit all of the plays, but his advanced years bested him; he died in 1773 and his final text, *Julius Caesar*, was published posthumously.[29] Initially, Jennens presented his work anonymously, though, in a moment either of tongue-in-cheek whimsy, or gross self-indulgence (or both), he included the following dedication in the first of his editions, *King Lear*:

> To Charles Jennens, Esq., at Gopsal, Leicestershire, under whose patronage, by access to whose library, and from whose hints and remarks, The Editor hath been enabled to attempt an Edition of Shakespeare, the same is inscribed, with the greatest gratitude, by his most oblig'd, and obedient humble servant the Editor.
>
> (§315, unpaged)

In the Preface to his *Lear* edition, Jennens noted that 'it will appear to anyone who will give himself the trouble of examination that no fair and exact collation of *Shakespeare* hath yet been presented to the public' (§315, a4r) and the primary focus of all of his Shakespearean endeavours lay precisely in the area of collation. Jennens' was, as Steven Urkowitz has noted, 'the first attempt to provide readers with a complete collation, on the page, of all the variants between the early editions, and with a full record of the editorial decisions of his eighteenth-century predecessors' and he grappled with 'the problems of presenting the complex and detailed evidence of the early texts' in the pages of his editions.[30] His work has received high praise from a number of modern commentators, with John Velz styling him 'the most careful and intelligent collator in the century'.[31] Velz has also observed that Jennens' commentary is 'pithy, reasonable, and sometimes brilliant'.[32] Again, like so many other eighteenth-century editors, while he carried out an enormous amount of very valuable textual spade-work, he was less successful in following through on the logic of his own position, and the emendations which appeared in his own text were very often, once again, not motivated by fully bibliographic criteria. Thus Gordon Crosse has noted that, for example, his alteration of *Lear*'s 'Or image of that horror . . . Fall and cease' to 'O image of true honour . . . Fair and chaste' indicates that 'he did not understand the difference between necessary emendation and random guessing'.[33]

Jennens' edition of *Lear* was dissected with savagely acute wit in the December 1770 issue of the *Critical Review*. The reviewer, calling to mind the underground motions of the Ghost in *Hamlet*, characterised Jennens as a 'worthy pioneer', but asked 'who ever heard of a victory obtained by the efforts of pioneers only? or of any particular thanks returned to those useful but inglorious burrowers before an army?' The greater part of the impression would, he suggests, likely 'continue to encumber the warehouse of the printer, till it has been thoroughly perused by those silent and industrious critics the Worm and the Mouse, to whose contemplation we suppose the world will be content to resign it'. As for the editor himself, the reviewer suggested that he would be happy to recommend Jennens 'to Messrs. Evans, Courtier, or some other peruke makers of eminence, in whose service he would meet with no small encouragement for selecting with accuracy the black hairs from the white ones'.[34] Jennens responded to his critics in what Gordon Crosse describes as 'a foolish and angry pamphlet', published in 1772.[35] A contemporary account suggested that Jennens had his pamphlet read aloud to him every day for a month and 'kept a constant eye on the newspapers, that he might receive the earliest intelligence of the moment at which [his critics] should have hanged and drowned themselves in consequence of his attack on their abilities'.[36]

The author of the *Critical Review*'s attack on Jennens certainly did not either hang or drown himself. The reviewer in question was George Steevens, who would serve, as we have already seen, as principal editor of the second edition of Johnson's *Shakespeare*, published in 1773, and such delectable malice was his stock-in-trade throughout his career – in one of his editions, he 'glossed indecent expressions in the text with obscene notes to which he affixed the names of two eminently respectable clergymen, Richard Amner and John Collins, with both of whom he had quarrelled'.[37] Born of wealthy parents in 1736, Steevens attended Eton and King's College, Cambridge and, having inherited the family fortune in 1768, he set about a career as an independent scholar, specialising mainly in Shakespeare.[38] John Nichols' memoir of him indicates a man whose fastidiousness in life's small details made him fit, like Capell, for the minutiae of complex editorial work. Every day, Nichols tells us, he would walk from his home on Hampstead Heath into the centre of London, where he met with various friends; he 'then hastened to the shop of Mudge and Dutton, the celebrated watch-makers, to regulate his watch'.[39]

Steevens' first published work on Shakespeare would appear to have been the forty-nine notes he contributed to the appendix of Johnson's 1765 edition.[40] In the following year, he published, with the Tonsons, a collection of *Twenty of the plays of Shakespeare, being the whole number printed in quarto during his life-time, or before the restoration*. Most of the texts for this four-volume collection were provided by David Garrick. Steevens' interest in reproducing these early texts highlights the fact that, while he baited Jennens for his burrowing antiquarianism, he nevertheless recognised the value of the earliest editions and the need for these texts to be more widely known. In addition to the plays included in his collection, Steevens also provided a text of the 1609 edition of the sonnets which, as we have seen in chapter 3, had dropped out of circulation as a result of Gildon's selecting Benson's 1640 edition of the poems as the base text for his supplement to Rowe's edition.[41] Steevens held no very high opinion of the sonnets, however, and he would later drop them from his own 1793 edition, famously observing that 'the strongest act of Parliament that could be framed, would fail to compel readers into their service'.[42]

In the same year that his quartos collection appeared, Steevens issued proposals for a new edition of Shakespeare. The prospectus was dated 'February 1 1766'. Johnson's edition had been published just a few months previously, in October 1765, and Capell's edition was currently in press, so it seems that, having largely withdrawn from new Shakespeare initiatives for the best part of two decades following the Warburton edition, the Shakespeare cartel found itself engaged in one last great efflorescence in the dying years of the Tonson era.[43] Steevens tactfully avoids criticising Johnson in his prospectus, instead attributing any shortcomings in the 1765 edition to the failure of others to come forward and offer their help to the editor. Had Johnson, he writes, 'met with the assistance he had reason to expect from the Public, in aid of his own great abilities, all further attempts at the illustration of [Shakespeare], had been as unnecessary as vain'.[44] 'A perfect edition of the Plays of Shakespeare', Steevens asserts, 'requires at once the assistance of the Antiquary, the Historian, the Grammarian, and the Poet' and he desires that all those wishing to offer contributions to the new edition should direct their letters 'to be left at Mr. Tonson's in the Strand'. Steevens' call for assistance certainly drew a number of collaborators into the project and, partly as a result of the contributions made by other Shakespeareans, the new edition of Johnson's text ran to ten octavo volumes, where the original had been eight.

In his prospectus, Steevens asserted that he would 'not lay himself under any obligations to prepare his work in a limited time' and it was six years before the edition appeared in print. By then, of course, the Tonson firm had been wound up, and, in his 'Advertisement to the Reader', Steevens paid tribute to the memory of Jacob III, 'a man', he writes, 'whose zeal for the improvement of English literature, and whose liberality to men of learning, gave him a just title to all the honours which men of learning can bestow' (§332, I, E7r). '[L]et it not be thought', he concludes, 'that we disgrace Shakespeare, by joining to his works the name of TONSON' (§332, I, E7v). A huge array of names were joined to the works of Shakespeare on the title page to Steevens' own edition – in all, thirty-six publishers are identified in the imprint and Colin Franklin has suggested that this indicates the trade's 'closing ranks after the death of Jacob Tonson'.[45] It may also, however, be a sign of the banding together of London publishers in the face of increasing challenges to monopolist understandings of the nature of copyright. As we shall see in the next two chapters, the London trade's claim that copyright was perpetual was finally overturned in the year immediately following the Johnson–Steevens edition. The banding together of large numbers of London publishers to produce the principal new editions of Shakespeare appearing in the final quarter of the eighteenth century begins, in this context, to look a bit like the turning of the Londoners' publishing wagons into a final circle.[46]

Capell's edition had appeared while Steevens was working on his own text and Steevens offers a slighting comment on his immediate predecessor's work in the 'Advertisement' which served as preface to his edition. Noting that Capell's commentary volumes were as yet unpublished, he observes that, while he has glanced at Capell's text of *2 Henry VI*, he decided on the basis of this cursory sampling that it was 'of little consequence to examine any further'. 'This circumstance is mentioned', he asserts, 'lest such accidental coincidences of opinion, as may be discovered hereafter, should be interpreted into plagiarism' (§332, I, E6v, E7r). Capell himself did not see matters in quite these terms and when John Collins published the full edition of Capell's commentaries, Collins rebuked Steevens for having 'dress'd up his volumes throughout, by appropriating to himself, without reserve, whatever suited his purpose from [Capell's] edition'. Collins goes on to note that a comparison of Johnson's original texts with Steevens' subsequent editions reveals, precisely, 'a regular system of plagiarism, upon a settl'd plan, pervading those later editions throughout'.[47] Collins was probably overstating the case here, but it certainly is true that, as G. Blakemore Evans puts it, Steevens engaged in 'heavy filching from Capell'.[48] In the 1773 edition, Steevens reiterates, without acknowledgement, Capell's principle that an accretive received text inevitably leads to an accumulation of errors, criticising Rowe just as Capell had done:

> The want of adherence to the old copies, which has been complained of, in the text of every modern republication of Shakespeare, is fairly deducible from Mr Rowe's inattention to one of the first duties of an editor. Mr Rowe did not print from the earliest and most correct, but from the most remote and inaccurate of the four folios.
>
> (§332, I, E3r)

While (re)articulating this principle, Steevens did not, unlike Capell, follow through on its logic: he used Johnson's edition as his base text 'constantly compared with the most authentic copies' (§332, I, E3r).

The faint odour of plagiarism seems to have clung to Steevens even in the public imagination. An anonymous play entitled *The Etymologist* was published shortly after Samuel Johnson's death, and the text was dedicated to various people, including 'all the commentators that ever wrote, are writing, or will write, on Shakespear: and particularly to that commentator of commentators, the conjectural, inventive, and collatitious, G. S. Esq.' In the play, an Irish servant of Johnson's observes to a fellow countryman that 'Master Stavans has used my master main ill in his Shaksper business; he heard all he had to say on the subject, and clapt his own name to half of it.' His compatriot's wry response is: 'your master [is] not so ill used neither; a man is well off now-a-days if he gets half what belongs to him'.[49]

Whatever the truth of the allegations made against him, Steevens continued to revise his text, publishing a new edition in 1778. In producing this edition he enlisted the help of Isaac Reed. In some respects, Reed made an unlikely bedfellow for Steevens as he was, without a doubt, the most retiring and modestly self-effacing of eighteenth-century Shakespearean editors (though it may be for this very reason that Reed seems to have been the only contemporary with whom Steevens never quarrelled). In the year in

which the first Johnson–Steevens–Reed edition appeared, Reed wrote to
John Nichols and confessed:

> I declare I have such a horror of seeing my name as Author or Editor, that
> if I had the option of standing in the pillory, or in standing formally
> before the publick in either of those lights, I should find it difficult to
> determine which to choose . . . I heartily detest all the squabbles and
> paltry tricks which are used by authors against one another, and which no
> one who gives his name to the publick has a right to suppose himself
> insignificant enough to be exempt from.[50]

Reed maintained his cherished anonymity in the various Steevens' editions
in which he had a hand. In the 1778 text, no reference is made to him at
all on the title page, and in subsequent editions he is identified only as 'the
Editor of Dodsley's Collection of Old Plays' – a project with which he and
Steevens had been jointly involved.[51]

In 1783, Steevens wrote to Reed, asking him to assume control of the
next planned revision of the text, observing 'I send you the fixtures of the
old Shop, together with as much of the good will of it as lies in my power
to bestow.'[52] Steevens provided Reed with 'some 445 additions, revisions
and omissions in his own 1778 notes'.[53] Enhanced annotation was, for Reed,
the cornerstone of the new edition, as he makes clear in his (anonymous)
'Advertisement':

> Since the last Edition of this Work in 1778, the zeal for elucidating
> Shakspeare, which appeared in most of the gentlemen whose names are
> affixed to the notes, has suffered little abatement. The same persevering
> spirit of enquiry has continued to exert itself, and the same laborious
> search into the literature, the manners, and the customs of the times,
> which was formerly so successfully employed, has remained
> undiminished. By these aids some new information has been obtained,
> and some new materials collected. From the assistance of such writers,
> even Shakspeare will receive no discredit.
>
> (§343, I, pp. 1–2)

The printers' text for the edition has survived and William C. Woodson has
mapped out the manner in which new annotations were added to the 1778
base text. Notes were sent 'by Malone, Whalley, Henley, Henderson, Mason,
and Reynolds, who included their commentary in letters or in small sheets
ready for pasting. The letters were cut apart and tipped in, with the verso
notes transcribed onto the margins of the appropriate pages'.[54] Reed himself
contributed eight notes to the prolegomena and somewhat more than 200 to
the plays themselves, all signed 'Editor'.[55]

In the *Monthly Review*, the publishers of the 1785 edition (much the same coalition as had produced the previous Steevens text) were taken to task for the edition's shoddy workmanship. The printing is, the reviewer observes, 'very negligently, we were going to say, shamefully, executed. The paper is bad, and the type worse. The letters are scarcely legible in some places, because there is not ink sufficient to stain the paper; and in others, because it is so redundant as to run into blots.' Much of the work, the reviewer suggests, 'would disgrace a common school-book'. Nevertheless, the review ends positively by noting that 'the present edition . . . with "all its imperfections on its head," is far superior to any that have preceded it'.[56]

Johnson himself died in 1784, but his name continued to appear on the title pages of the Steevens–Reed sequence. Though he had handed control of the text over to Reed for the 1785 edition, Steevens himself resumed central place behind the counter of 'the old Shop' for the new edition of 1793. He did this, in part, because he had, in the interim, fallen out with fellow Shakespearean Edmond Malone and he wished to use the new edition as a public platform for carrying forward their quarrel. Steevens attacked Malone partly by proxy, making use of Joseph Ritson. Ritson was a disgruntled scholar who had himself wished to produce an edition of Shakespeare, issuing proposals in 1783 for an edition that would 'with regard to the correctness of the text, be infinitely superior to any that has yet appeared'.[57] The 'eight duodecimo volumes' that Ritson projected never appeared and he was forced to content himself by lobbing verbal missiles at those editors who did manage to get their work into print. He savaged the 1778 Johnson–Steevens–Reed in *Remarks, Critical and Illustrative on the Text and Notes of the Last Edition of Shakspeare* (1783), observing that Johnson and Steevens should together be sent to 'the regions of oblivion and disgrace'.[58] In 1788, he attacked Reed's 1785 revision in *A Quip Modest* and, in 1792, he launched a direct assault on Malone, claiming that he wished 'to rescue the language and sense' of Shakespeare 'from the barbarism and corruption they have acquired in passing through the hands of this incompetent and unworthy editor', and caricaturing Malone as a '*Paddy from Cork*' Irishman.[59] Malone was furious at the attack and his own copy of Ritson's pamphlet 'abounds with evidence of personal animus, with insults underlined or marked and defiant marginal comments ornamenting almost every page'.[60] He responded with his own pamphlet, in the form of *A Letter to the Rev. Richard Farmer, D.D.*, Master of Emmanuel College, Cambridge, one of the most respected scholars of the day, and author of the highly influential *Essay on the Learning of Shakespeare*. By this time, Steevens and Ritson had been reconciled and, in preparing his own new edition, Steevens drew heavily upon Ritson's work, including his criticisms of Malone. In all, Steevens added about 450 notes by Ritson to the edition, some 150 of them drawn from his attack on Malone. As a consequence, Ritson wrote to Steevens on 2 April 1793, modestly offering 'his best thanks for Mr. Steevens's obliging and valuable present of his elegant edition of Shakespeare; as well as for the honour he has done Mr. Ritson, in allotting to his crude and trivial observations a station of which they are evidently unworthy'.[61]

In addition to recycling Ritson's criticisms of Malone, Steevens also directly attacked Malone's editorial principles in his 'Advertisement' to the edition. Like Capell, Johnson, and, indeed, Steevens himself in his earlier incarnations, Malone insisted on the priority of the First Folio and he strongly rejected the notion that the Second Folio had any authority. Steevens now reversed his own earlier position, arguing against the elevation of the First Folio and making a case for recognising the merits of the Second. In the first instance, defending emendations based on the eighteenth-century editorial tradition, he observes:

> we have sometimes followed the suggestions of a Warburton, a Johnson, a Farmer, or a Tyrwhitt, in preference to the decisions of a Hemings or a Condell, notwithstanding their choice of readings might have been influenced by associates whose high-sounding names cannot fail to enforce respect, viz. William Ostler, John Shanke, William Sly and Thomas Poope.
>
> (§375, I, pp. xii–xiii)[62]

More seriously, he argues that 'it is on all hands allowed that what we style a younger MS. will occasionally correct the mistakes and supply the deficiencies of one of better note, and higher antiquity' and he asks why it should not be the case that 'a book printed in 1632 be allowed the merit of equal services to a predecessor in 1623' (§375, I, p. xxvi). He concludes his discussion of the issue by noting, with sweetly malicious satisfaction, that 'no stronger plea' in favour of the Second Folio 'can be advanced, than the frequent use made of it by Mr. Malone', who, he asserts, has drawn heavily on it in his text, despite his dismissal of it as worthless (§375, I, p. xviii).

Steevens' clash with Malone represents, in a sense, the final collision of two different visions of textual scholarship, as the century drew to a close. Ironically, Malone's conception of the Shakespearean editorial process was moulded, in the first instance, in work that he undertook under Steevens' auspices. Born in Ireland and educated at Trinity College Dublin, Malone, like Theobald and Capell before him, originally trained as a lawyer, though he took little pleasure in making the rounds of the Munster Circuit as a barrister. Much like Steevens, Malone was the beneficiary of a family inheritance which granted him, from 1776, an annual income of about £1,000.[63] Within a year he had completed his first editorial project (an edition of Goldsmith) and had relocated to London to embark upon the life of an independent scholar. Once in London, he made the acquaintance of Steevens and a contemporary of the pair characterised them as 'two laborious commentators on the meaning of words and phrases: one dull, the other clever, but the dullness was accompanied by candour and a love of truth, the cleverness by a total absence of both' (it should doubtless be clear enough by now which was which).[64] Malone contributed an essay offering 'An Attempt to Ascertain the Order in Which the Plays of Shakespeare Were Written' to the 1778 Johnson–Steevens–Reed edition and he followed this up, two years later, with a two-volume supplement to the edition, providing an account of the Elizabethan theatre; a reprint of Arthur Brooke's *Tragicall Historye of Romeus and Juliet* (1562) (a copy of which he had borrowed from Edward Capell); the 1609 text of the sonnets; and the seven apocryphal plays included in the second issue of the Third Folio.[65] In February 1782, Malone published *Cursory Observations on the Poems Attributed to Thomas Rowley*, in which he helped to expose the supposed medieval works of 'Rowley' as a contemporary forgery, perpetrated by Thomas Chatterton. His methods of meticulously historicised enquiry in this study were typical of his approach and would be brought into play again in 1796 when he exposed William Henry Ireland's Shakespeare forgeries.[66] These methods would also be deployed in his textual and editorial work, where he very largely eschewed received tradition in favour of documentary research and rigorous archival enquiry.

In August 1783 Malone wrote to John Nichols, requesting that he make a minor correction to a piece of Malone's that had been published in the *Gentleman's Magazine*, and asking him that at the same time he might add 'that you are happy to hear that this *ingenious gentleman*, or whatever else you please to call him, had undertaken, and is now preparing a new Edition of Shakspeare, with select notes from all the Commentators'. Such a notice would serve, Malone feels, 'better than a direct advertisement'.[67] Just about seven years later, in September 1790, Isaac Reed noted in his diary a meeting with James Boswell, who tells him that 'Malone would finish his Edition of Shakespeare in a fortnight' and the edition did, indeed, appear shortly before the end of the year.[68] The text was accompanied by an innovative compendium of scholarly resources, including many new materials which Malone had unearthed during the course of his extensive archival researches. Peter Martin observes that, with 'his *Account of the English Stage*, the extracts taken from Aubery's manuscripts, Henslowe's diary, Herbert's Office-book, and the revised essay on the order of the plays, the work possessed an unprecedented originality and authority'.[69] Likewise, Margreta de Grazia has registered the catalogue of 'firsts' achieved by Malone's edition:

> It was the first to emphasize the principle of authenticity in treating Shakespeare's works and the materials relating to them; the first to contain a dissertation on the linguistic and poetic particulars of Shakespeare's period; the first to depend on facts in constructing Shakespeare's biography; the first to include a full chronology for the plays; and the first to publish, annotate, and canonize the 1609 Sonnets. While it is always possible to locate adumbrations of these interests in earlier treatments, it is in this edition that they are first clearly articulated – and articulated together as an integral textual schema.[70]

In terms of the actual text presented, Thomas Tyrwhitt, the classicist and Chaucer editor, had suggested to Malone that he should make the First Folio his standard and that a copy of the First Folio should be 'actually sent to the press, with such corrections as the editor might think proper' (§357, I, p. xliv). Malone rejected this suggestion, in part because he regarded some of the quartos which preceded the First Folio as being of higher authority than the 1623 text. He strongly reaffirmed the principle that the earliest texts possessed an authority quite distinct from that of their successors, arguing that (with the exception of those cases where 'the author corrects and revises his own works') 'as editions of books are multiplied, their errours [sic] are multiplied also; and . . . consequently every such edition is more or less correct, as it approaches nearer to or is more distant from the first' (§357, I, p. xiii). By contrast with Capell, however, Malone did not build his edition from the ground up, preferring, ironically it might be felt, to use a copy of the 1785 Johnson–Steevens–Reed as his base text.[71] He did, however, meticulously collate his base text against the relevant early editions:

> I determined, after I had adjusted the text in the best manner in my power, to have every proofsheet of my work read aloud to me, while I perused the first folio, for those plays which first appeared in that edition; and for all those which had been previously printed, the first quarto copy, excepting only in the instances of *The Merry Wives of Windsor* and *King Henry V*, which, being either sketches or imperfect copies, could not be wholly relied on; and *King Richard III.* of the earliest edition of which tragedy I was not possessed. I had at the same time before me a table

which I had formed of the variations between the quarto and the folio. By this laborious process not a single innovation, made either by the editor of the second folio, or any of the modern editors, could escape me.

(§357, I, pp. xliv–xlv)

Despite his heavy emphasis on what he styled the 'authentick' text, Malone was still willing, like his predecessors, to make a number of silent changes aimed at regularising the text. Thus, Simon Jarvis notes that there 'are some features of the Quarto and Folio texts which Malone himself finds unacceptable on grammatical grounds, notably disagreement in the number of subject and verb'. Elsewhere, Jarvis observes, he 'silently supplies missing accusatives to pronouns and silently brings the tenses of verbs into conformity'.[72] For this reason, Jarvis argues that, despite his innovative methodologies, residual traces of traditional editorial practices persist in Malone. In making this argument, Jarvis breaks with the Foucauldian view of Malone presented by de Grazia, who proposes, in *Shakespeare Verbatim*, that Malone's work needs to be seen not as an evolution of eighteenth-century practice but as a radical break with a prior tradition, initiating a wholly new textual dispensation. Malone's innovations, de Grazia argues, 'do not extend earlier interests, as the use of a graduated chronological scale implies; they render them obsolete'.[73]

While de Grazia's argument is certainly compelling and is elegantly conceived, in the broader context of eighteenth-century editorial practice, Malone's work does, in fact, seem an evolution of the positions mapped out earlier by Theobald and Capell and, as Jarvis has noted, it also seems clear that Malone never fully escapes from a lingering eighteenth-century sense of the importance of the received text and an aesthetic project which seeks, as Jarvis puts it, 'to participate in the polishing of the English tongue and that tongue's most impressive monuments'.[74] The difficulties of de Grazia's position are exposed when she attempts to dismiss Capell's innovations as lacking meaning outside of the later context of Malone's methodologies, as she argues that 'the importance of Capell's break with the received text was not discernible until it could be placed within a schema as comprehensive and consistent as Malone's'.[75] It is hard not to feel that a certain element of special pleading is being indulged in here, in order to uncouple Capell and Malone and to set them into wholly distinct editorial categories. Malone's more general unacknowledged debts to Capell also go largely unregistered by de Grazia, even though they were recognised by contemporaries. A writer in the *Monthly Review* observed of Capell that

> while he was diving into the classics of Caxton, and working his way
> under ground, like the river mole, in order to emerge with all his glories;
> while he was looking forward to his triumphs; certain other active spirits
> went to work upon his plan, and digging out the promised treasures, laid
> them prematurely before the Public, defeating the effect of our critic's
> discoveries by anticipation. Steevens, Malone, Farmer, Percy, and a
> whole host of literary-ferrets, burrowed into every hole and corner of the
> warren of modern antiquity, and overrun all the country, whose map had
> been delineated by Edward Capell.[76]

In 1792, Malone issued proposals for 'a new and splendid edition' of Shakespeare, 'in fifteen volumes, royal octavo'. Interestingly, in this edition, the plays were to be 'arranged in the order in which they are supposed by Mr. Malone to have been written'.[77] Subscriptions were to be taken by G. G. J. and J. Robinson and James Heath. The Robinsons were leading members of the cartel who, in the following year, published Steevens' revision of the Johnson–Steevens–Reed text and, discouraged by the sales figures for that edition, George Robinson cancelled Malone's contract.[78] A second Malone edition was, indeed, published, but not until 1821, nine years after his death. His work on the edition was completed by the younger James Boswell, whose father had received much assistance from Malone during their long years of friendship. Boswell had begun helping Malone when the veteran editor's sight started to fail.[79] As Arthur Sherbo has noted, he brought much to the edition himself, 'not solely in the ordering and presentation of unfinished and scattered materials left by Malone but also in additions to the prolegomenous matter and to the commentary'.[80] On occasion, his interventions had unfortunate consequences, in that his changes resulted in 'several instances where the text is at variance with Malone's note to it'.[81] Boswell followed Malone's plan of presenting the plays in presumed order of composition, but could not bring himself to extend this scheme to the English history plays which, anomalously, are presented in order by reign.

In 1844, George Henry Lewes, writing in the *Westminster Review*, dismissed the Malone–Boswell edition in the following terms:

> We can nowhere point to such an accumulated mass of industry, which is
> at the same time such a mass of rubbish. It is impossible to conceive a
> greater amount of stupidity, drivelling, pedantry, senseless learning,
> collected into one work. Note upon note, blunder upon blunder,
> conjecture upon conjecture, drivel upon drivel: without order, without
> method, wearisome, tantalizing, and profitless.[82]

Lewes' views were not, however, typical of the response which the text received. The twenty-one volume edition achieved a remarkable position of dominance during the course of the nineteenth century, and even as late as 1928 D. Nichol Smith would write of it that 'it is still the standard complete edition'. (In making this observation, Smith was curiously ignoring the Cambridge edition of 1863–6 and its 1864 Globe spin-off.)[83] Together with the final revision of the Johnson–Steevens–Reed text, which also ran to twenty-one volumes and which was completed by William Harris, Librarian of the Royal Institution, the Malone–Boswell text became a staple of the nineteenth-century reprint trade.

Four folio texts supplied the demand for collected editions of Shakespeare in the seventeenth century. Over the course of the eighteenth century, by contrast, some fifty collected editions were published with London imprints. And where the seventeenth-century texts were prepared for the press by anonymous functionaries, the eighteenth century witnessed the birth of the editor, and the emergence of intense theoretical disputation in the realm of secular editing – the birth, we might say, of bibliography (in the narrowly specialist sense of the word). The result of the endless wrangling among editors and of the freighting of the text with accumulated layers of commentary was to prompt a reaction against the editorial enterprise among a number of commentators. As early as 1749, John Holt complained that 'No Author has suffered more' at the hands of his commentators 'than our deservedly admired SHAKESPEAR: Who, though a Modern, has been explained into Obscurity, and though he wrote in a living Tongue, has been rendered unintelligible by his commentating Editors.'[84] Likewise, in 1765, Benjamin Heath criticised 'a race of criticks' who treated Shakespeare injuriously:

> Under the specious pretence of re-establishing his genuine text, they have given it us mangled and corrupted, just as their own particular turn of imagination prompted, or the size and pitch of their own genius suggested to them; and by discarding the traditionary reading, and interpolating their own fanciful conjectures in its place, they have, to the utmost of their power, endeavoured to continue the corruption down to distant posterity.[85]

Some twenty years later, the publisher John Bell echoed Holt's complaint that 'SHAKESPEARE has been *illucidated* into *obscurity*' and, by the century's end, T. J. Mathias was imagining Shakespeare as Actæon, pursued 'By fell 𝔅𝔩𝔞𝔠𝔨 𝔏𝔢𝔱𝔱𝔢𝔯 𝔇𝔬𝔤𝔰' of critics, including *Pamphagus*-Warburton, 'a dog of most voracious appetite, who snaps at and devours everything digestible or indigestible'.[86] At the end, Mathias, 'out of breath', abandons the chase, because he 'wish'd not *to be in* at SHAKSPEARE´S death'.[87] Noting that the latest edition of Shakespeare has grown to fifteen volumes, Mathias sardonically observes that it 'will not be too much to hope for an edition in *Fifty* volumes quarto, printed on a *wire-wove paper, glazed, and hot pressed*'.[88] Mathias points here to new developments in printing technology which would, indeed, play an important role in Shakespeare publishing across the nineteenth century. Before we come on to discuss these issues, however, we must first double-back, to consider what else was happening in eighteenth-century Shakespeare publishing, outside the realm of the mainstream editions parodied by Mathias in his poem.

5   Copyright disputes: English publishers

We have already noted that, on the death of Jacob III in 1767, the Tonson majority share in the rights to Shakespeare was sold at auction for £1,200. The Shakespeare rights were just one of 600 lots and the grand total realised by the sale was £9,550 19s. 6d.[1] Auctioning of publishing rights was a common practice at the time and a contemporary estimate suggests that, between 1755 and 1774, London publishers traded rights to the total value of some £50,000.[2] Cyprian Blagden has observed of these auctions that 'the behaviour of booksellers, as buyers, gives no indication of any fear that they were not putting their money into gilt-edged and eternal securities'.[3] Before the end of 1774, however, the majority of these supposed gilt-edged bonds (including those guaranteeing ownership of the texts of Shakespeare) would be worth little more than the paper they were printed on, as a result of a case brought before the House of Lords which produced a definitive clarification of the exact parameters of British copyright.[4] At a stroke, the publishing landscape changed dramatically. As Mark Rose has put it, the 'works of Shakespeare, Bacon, Milton, Bunyan, and others, all the perennials of the book trade that the booksellers had been accustomed to treat as if they were private landed estates, were suddenly declared open commons'.[5] This revolutionary redistribution of publishing property was not achieved in a single, easy victory, however. The 1774 ruling was less a definitive guillotine-blade chop than the final culmination of a long guerrilla campaign, during the course of which the most princely London publishers had been assailed, in the first instance, by a motley collection of small-time English renegades and, secondly (and more successfully), by a more organised conglomerate of Scottish insurgents, determinedly seeking to carve out a niche for the products of their own burgeoning publishing industry. In this chapter, we will attend mostly to the activities of the English challengers, while in chapter 6 we will turn our attention to the Scots (and also to their colleagues across the Irish Sea).

To understand the grounds on which the disputes regarding ownership of publishing rights proceeded, it is necessary first to map out briefly some of the history of the mechanisms of control which prevailed within the realm of publishing. As was noted in chapter 1, the publishing trade in England was regulated by the Stationers' Company, which was granted a monopoly on printing by Mary I in 1557. The intention of this grant was to allow the Company to regulate the activities of its guild members, and also – and more importantly from the crown's point of view – to ensure that the Company acted as the government's agent in controlling access to the medium of print, thereby making possible 'the better tracking down and punishment of producers and purveyors of heretical writings'.[6] Established mechanisms of publishing control were – in common with many other legal and political processes – disrupted by the Civil War and subsequent Interregnum. Following the restoration of the monarchy, new legislation was introduced in 1662, with the intention of, as the title of the act expresses it, '*Preventing Abuses in Printing Seditious, Treasonable and Unlicensed Books and Pamphlets, and for Regulating of Printing and Printing-Presses*'. The legislation instituted a new position of Surveyor of the Press, who was granted extensive powers of censorship.[7] It also reaffirmed traditional strict limitations on the expansion of the publishing trade, confining the number of master printers (excluding the king's and university printers) to twenty and also setting limits for the numbers of presses, journeymen, and apprentices.[8]

   The 1662 act was time-limited and thus needed to be renewed by parliament on a routine basis. By the 1690s, however, opposition to the terms of the legislation was growing. On the one hand, the partisan political control of the press which the position of Surveyor made possible came to be resented. On the other, the limitations on printing imposed by the act were seen as a restraint on trade, creating, in effect, a constraining monopoly. John Locke was particularly active in campaigning against the act, objecting to the control exercised over the press by 'ignorant and lazy stationers', as he styled the London publishers.[9] The net result of such opposition was that the act was allowed to lapse by parliament and it expired on 3 May 1695. Alvin Kernan notes that, following the expiration of the act, 'the number of printers grew steadily, and by 1724 there were 75 printers in London, plus at least 28 more in the provinces'.[10] Fearing the consequences of expansion and deregulation, the established London publishers lobbied hard for the speedy reintroduction of governmental controls. Their earliest efforts met with little success, with four bills failing to clear parliament between 1695 and 1698 and a further two bills foundering in 1699 and 1701.[11] In January of 1710, the MP Edward Wortley made a further attempt to introduce legislation and his bill finally succeeded, becoming the *Act for the Encouragement of Learning, by Vesting the Copies of Printed Books in the Authors or Purchasers of such Copies, during the Times therein mentioned.* John Feather has observed that to 'those members of the trade who had agitated for new legislation ever since the old Printing Act had finally lapsed in 1695 it represented a substantial victory, granting them the rights they sought while not reimposing the irksome requirements of pre-publication censorship'.[12] The extent of the London publishers' satisfaction with the new dispensation is registered in the fact that on 1 May 1710 the Stationers' Company voted to bear the expenses incurred during the bill's passage through parliament.[13]

There was, however, one element of the new legislation which, had they thought about it more closely, might have caused the Londoners to keep their corporate wallet firmly in pocket. Among the additions made to Wortley's bill during the course of its passage through parliament was a clause setting limits on the duration of copyright. Under the old regime, of course, copyright was perpetual, but the 1710 act imposed a limit of twenty-one years for works already in print and of fourteen years for new books, renewable for a further fourteen if the author were still alive. These limitations probably indicate a persisting sense among parliamentarians that the monopolist position of the London publishers should in some measure be challenged. In framing the 1710 act, parliament would appear to have taken as its model the 1623/4 Statute of Monopolies, which 'forbade monopolies except in the special case of grants of privilege to the inventors of new manufactures: existing grants of this sort were allowed to continue for twenty-one years, and new grants could be made for a period of fourteen years'.[14] In the event, the Londoners seem to have concluded that the time limits were a bridge that they would somehow contrive to cross when they came to it and, as Alvin Kernan has observed, after the passage of the act, 'all went on, as they had before, selling and purchasing what the booksellers and authors still assumed to be perpetual rights in books old and new'.[15]

The Tonson cartel's rights to Shakespeare were, under the terms of the act, due to expire in 1731 and challenges to the cartel's monopoly began to occur from the mid-1730s onward. Earlier in the century, however, the Tonsons had something of a foretaste of what was to come, when their exclusive rights to Shakespeare were threatened by a certain Thomas Johnson. Johnson is something of a shadowy figure. He was probably born around 1677 and seems to had some sort of Scottish connection, either through his own family or through his wife, Jane Weems.[16] He lived in the Hague from 1701 until 1728, when he relocated to Rotterdam where he had 'a very large shop & warehouse full of very good books to a considerable value'.[17] He served, as Warren McDougall has noted, as 'an important link between [Edinburgh University] professors and European scholarship' and his letters to Professor

Charles Mackie have survived in the Edinburgh University archives.[18] The letters throw an interesting light on Johnson's publishing activities, particularly in the context of the 1710 act. The act, as John Feather has indicated, 'implied, but did not state, that it was illegal to import any English-language books into England and Wales if they had been previously printed there', but it was 'specific in permitting the import of books in classical or modern foreign languages'.[19] Johnson seems to have been generally familiar with the provisions of the act and he brought a certain level of creativity to the business of giving the impression that he and the ships he hired sailed on the right side of legality. He regularly reprinted English works and exported them to Edinburgh, but he took the precaution of disguising them, against the possibility that any legal question might arise. On 13 October 1719, he writes to Mackie: 'your Bale . . . will be pretty Cargo: the English books are put between the leaves of the Latin & French ones in such a way as they'l not be easily seen at ye Custom house, but you must get your Cousin to separate them, to whom I send books also in your parcel'.[20] In the same letter, he requests of Mackie:

> Give my service to Mr. G. Stewart ye Bookseller, tell him he may have of Prior's & Swift's works or 4th vol. of Homer if he'd direct me by whom to send them, but I cannot venture 'em at my risque not knowing what master to trust or to what port to send 'em safe.

Johnson sent Mackie a wide range of books, including, according to an invoice enclosed with a letter of 21 January 1721, copies of Swift's *Works* and Pope's *Homer*. There is no record in the correspondence of his sending on editions of Shakespeare, but he was in fact a Shakespeare publisher.

Sometime around 1710, Johnson had the idea of issuing *A Collection of the Best English Plays*. Initially, he seems to have hedged his bets about the legality of what he was doing and the first tranche of Shakespeare texts included in the *Collection* (some of them Restoration adaptations) carried an imprint which simply read 'LONDON, Printed in the Year 1710', though many of them did include Johnson's own characteristic printer's device. By 1711, Johnson was venturing a touch more boldly to include on his title pages the imprint: 'Printed for T. JOHNSON, Bookseller at the Hague'. Johnson's *Collection* was originally envisaged as a ten-volume set running to a total of forty plays, but it was supplemented between about 1714 and 1718 by a further two volumes, increasing the total number of plays to forty-eight. The plays sold individually for either 6*d*. or 8*d*.[21] A second issue appeared between 1720 and 1722, consisting of sixteen volumes and including a further sixteen plays. Johnson's business ultimately passed into the hands of H. Sheurleer, who reissued the collection in 1750.[22] We have already noted in passing that Johnson produced his texts in octavo format, 'Neatly & correctly printed, in small volumes fit for the pocket', and that this may well have prompted the Tonson cartel to begin producing smaller-scale reprints of their own editions.[23] A further innovation was his publishing the plays in his collection individually over time, with volume titles subsequently released, for binding the texts into a complete set. As we will see, this procedure would be followed by another Shakespearean upstart, in the mid-1730s.

The Tonson cartel seem not to have taken any action against Johnson – presumably it would have been difficult for them to do so, given that he was permanently based in the Netherlands. While their scaled-down version of Rowe's edition, published in 1714, was probably a response to Johnson, by 1723, they had returned to lavish Shakespeare publishing, with Pope's grand, expensive quarto edition. The high cost of Pope's edition did not go unremarked. An unsigned article in *Mist's Journal* for 20 March 1725 noted an advertisement by the publishers indicating that non-subscribers to the edition would be charged an extra guinea to purchase Pope's text. The *Mist's Journal* writer noted, tongue-in-cheek, the further additional costs which a purchaser might expect to incur:

> The Binding, fit for a Lady's Toilet, or a Beau's Library, will not come to above two Guineas more; so that any *Beau* or *Belle* may have a compleat Set of *Shakespear*, finely gilt, and letter'd at the Back, and which will look very pretty thro' a Glass Scrutore, for about seven Pounds seven Shillings Sterling.[24]

The finely judged sarcasm continues, as the writer observes that

> Indeed, some Persons may object, that if another Bookseller had been the Publisher of this *Shakespeare*, he might have sold it, ready bound, that is, with a plain binding, for about forty Shillings, have been able to pay Copy-Money out of that, and yet have gain'd a good Bookseller's Profit by it. – But let your slovenly Scholars and poor Rogues, who buy Books only to read, complain and make this Remark. The People of the *Beau Monde* look upon Books no otherwise than as the neat Furniture of a Closet, and are of Opinion they are not to be esteem'd according to their intrinsick Worth, but, like Toys, bear a Value and a Price according to the Shop they come from.

The serious point behind the satire is made explicit when the article's author registers the pernicious effect of monopoly publishing: 'where a Bookseller has the Property of a Copy vested in him, such a Book cannot be had from any person but himself or from those that sell it under him; and therefore the Publick is obliged to come up to his Price'. He goes on to call for an edition of Shakespeare to be provided 'at a reasonable Price', noting that he would 'take fifty Shillings to be too much', and commenting sharply in the next number of the journal that Tonson 'owes the Publick a good Edition of that Work, since the last publish'd by him, and which he sold dear enough, was, by much, the most incorrect and faulty that ever yet came out'.[25]

The *Mist's Journal*'s call for an affordable edition of Shakespeare did not draw forth an immediate response, but the consequences of pricing books out of the reach of the average person certainly struck Cornelius Cotes, who in 1734 established an odd periodical entitled *Cotes Weekly Journal; or, the English Stage-Player*. In the introduction to his inaugural number, Cotes comments on the 'Usefulness of Plays in general' and laments that 'it requires more Expence to be furnished with a complete Collection of them, than is agreeable to the Circumstances of the Bulk of Mankind, especially to bear it all at once'.[26] In establishing his journal, Cotes had hit upon a novel scheme for addressing this problem. His periodical, priced at 2*d*., provided 'the most authentic Intelligence both Foreign and Domestic' and combined it with, as a supplement, a folio sheet containing part of the text of a play. Regular purchasers of the journal would be able to collect complete plays on a week-by-week basis. The domestic news printed included a very handy list of 'Casualties of this Week', which provided details of their cause of death. Thus, issue no. 7 includes the following helpful figures:

> Burnt at St. John's in Southwark 1. Drowned in the River Thames 6. Excessive Drinking 2. Found dead in the Street (a Male Infant) 1. Fractured his Scull by a Fall from the Yard of a Ship 1. Hang'd himself (being Lunatick) 1. Kill'd by a Fall from a Ladder 1. Overlaid 1. Threw herself out of a Window (being Lunatick) 1.[27]

The first play to be published by Cotes was *Julius Caesar*. Sadly, however, he appears to have managed a total of just two plays in all (the second was Fielding's *The Miser*) and the journal seems to have folded after only nine issues. The rather condescending tone which Cotes adopted towards his intended readership (not to mention his conservatively minded political programme) may have had something to do with the venture's rather short life:

> This Design has a natural Tendency to spread Politeness over the most vulgar and obscure Parts of Town and Country; and an illiterate Artificer or Peasant, of good natural Parts, may learn to be as much delighted with the Works of Shakespeare, Dryden, &c. as with dabbling in Politics, perusing idle Tales and romantick Histories, or any other Diversions.

Thus, by this Means, the Manners of Persons in low Life will be insensibly polished and improved, and an Air of Gentility and Complaisance render their Conversation with one another more agreeable than ever, and at the same time recommend them to the Notice and Esteem of their Superiors; and how vastly more innocent and entertaining will their friendly Debates be, about the Sentiments of this or that particular Dramatic Author, than political Controversies.[28]

Cotes was not the only one concerned about the fact that the London publishers were maintaining the cost of books at an excessively high level. In the year following his venture, an organisation was launched which drew its title from the 1710 copyright act: the 'Society for the Encouragement of Learning'. One of the members of the group, the Earl of Egmont, discusses the plans of the society in his diary and indicates a sense of bitterness at what he perceives to be the sharp practice of some of the dominant publishers of the time:

I was made acquainted this day [17 March 1735] with a subscription of ten guineas a man by divers noblemen and gentlemen in favour of ingenious authors to rescue them from the tyranny of printers and booksellers, who buy their works at a small rate, and while they almost starve then make fortunes by printing their labours. Thus Jacob Tonson the bookseller got very many thousand pounds by publishing Dryden's works, who hired himself to write for a starving pay.[29]

Part of the society's programme involved subsidising the publication of certain worthy texts, and it anticipated the procedures of later organisations such as the Malone Society by seeking to establish a guaranteed circle of subscribers. The society met with no great success, however, and it was disbanded in 1749 having achieved very little. Nevertheless, its very existence serves to indicate a general level of frustration with the manner in which readers and authors alike were perceived as being exploited by the large publishing houses.[30]

At about the same time as Cotes was attempting to provide cheap plays for 'the Bulk of Mankind' and the Earl of Egmont and his noble and gentle friends were banding together to support struggling authors, another English publisher was making determined efforts to supply affordable texts of Shakespeare to a popular audience. This publisher was Robert Walker, who, throughout his career (which stretched from about 1729 to 1752) consistently (and gleefully) served as a thorn in the side of his London brethren. He was, as Giles E. Dawson has observed, 'one of the first publishers to specialize in the production of good books in the cheapest possible form,

his almost unvaried method being to issue them in weekly penny parts'.[31]
He also published newspapers and was a dealer in patent medicines – his
west-country agent, Joseph Collett, advertised that, in addition to 'any Books
printed by R. Walker', he also sold 'Bostock's Cordial, Daffey's Elixir, Ward's
Pectoral Tincture, the Hippo Drops [and] Ointment for Piles'.[32] Walker began publishing editions of individual Shakespeare plays in 1734. At the
time, the standard price for a printed play was about 1*s*., but Walker published his plays in parts, at a penny a sheet. Since the average play ran
to four or four and a half sheets, this meant that a complete play could
be had for fourpence or fourpence ha'penny – less than half the standard
price.[33]

While the Tonson cartel appear largely to have ignored Johnson's continental ventures and Cotes' failed experiment, they were incensed by Walker's
actions. The Tonsons' lawyer, Briggs, was instructed to write to Walker, informing him that 'Mr. Tonson would spend 1000*l*. before he should go on,
and likewise have him lock'd up in a Gaol, and that it would be the ruin of
him and his Family.' After receiving the letter, Walker went to see Tonson.
The publisher being 'at that time ill of the Stone', Walker gave his servant
a message to pass on to him, calmly informing him that 'he would try the
Issue by Consent with Mr. Tonson, either at Law or Equity'. Apparently
possessing a clear understanding of the 1710 act (clearer, as it would turn
out, than many eighteenth-century judges), he insisted that 'no Person had
any Right or Property in' Shakespeare's plays. Walker's position can only
have added to Tonson's physical discomfort.[34] Given his defiant attitude,
Tonson could hardly risk initiating legal proceedings against him, since, if
Walker's reading of the 1710 act was confirmed by the courts, then all of the
rights which the Tonsons held in long-established texts would be rendered
wholly worthless. In other circumstances, Tonson might have considered
a Chancery suit, since, in Chancery, establishing that 'a presumptive right
existed and that it was being injured, or was likely to be injured' was sufficient to secure an interim injunction, which could then be used to tie up
the defendant in legal red tape, often for several years.[35] However, in the
case of Walker, Tonson seems to have felt that even this course of action was
too risky, and soon enough Walker was defiantly proclaiming, in an advertisement included in one of his editions: 'They have . . . had the Assurance
to say, that they would sue me for that which they have no Right to, why
don't they do it? Here is Term come, and no Bill in Chancery, nor Action
at Common Law.' Walker assured Tonson and his colleagues that he 'was
not one of those poor Noodles who would be frightned by their insolent
Threats'.[36]

Fearful of the consequences of going to law against such a defiantly auda-
cious opponent, Tonson settled on a double strategy for tackling Walker. In
the first instance, he told Walker that he 'would undersell him till he had put
him down'.[37] Anticipating twentieth-century business practices in both the
publishing and airline industries, Tonson produced a 'spoiler' series, selling
his texts initially at 3*d*. a play. When this did not deter Walker, he dropped
his price still further, to just a penny a play. The plays were printed in bulk
in an attempt to flood the market and thus crowd out Walker's wares. At the
same time, Tonson secured a statement from Chetwood, the prompter for
the Theatre Royal in Drury Lane, condemning Walker's series as 'useless,
pirated and maimed'. This statement was published in the preliminary pages
of the Tonson cheap editions. Tonson also made use of such pages in some
of his texts to launch further attacks on his opponent, as when he announces
that

> *Whereas one* R. Walker *has proposed to Pirate all* Shakespear'*s Plays; but*
> *through Ignorance of what Plays are* Shakespear'*s, did, in several*
> *Advertisements propose to print* OEDIPUS KING of THEBES, *as one of*
> Shakespear'*s Plays; and has since printed* TATE´S KING LEAR *instead of*
> Shakespear'*s, and in that and* HAMLET *has omitted almost one half of the*
> *Genuine Editions printed by* Tonson *and Proprietors. The World will*
> *therefore judge how likely they are to have a compleat Collection of*
> Shakespear'*s Plays from the said* R. Walker.[38]

Walker gave back as good as he got, using the preliminary pages to his
editions to launch his own attacks against Tonson and his allies, describ-
ing Chetwood's statement as 'FOOLISH, FALSE, SCANDALOUS, and
A GROSS IMPOSITION ON THE PUBLICK' and brazenly printing
'*A Specimen of some of* Tonson'*s Omissions and Blunders in the Tragedy of King
Lear, which render the same useless and unintelligable*' [sic].[39] Despite Tonson's
best efforts, Walker persisted in his project, and succeeded in issuing the entire canon. He also followed Thomas Johnson's practice of releasing volume
title pages so that the plays could be gathered into a seven volume set. Tonson,
as Giles E. Dawson has noted, kept pace with Walker, 'issuing his own ru-
inously competitive editions as fast as Walker's appeared – faster, indeed,
for while at the beginning he followed, producing play for play, before long
he dropped this course and proceeded at his own speed to finish well ahead
of his antagonist'.[40] The net result of this battle was that, for the first time
ever, the market was flooded with cheap editions of Shakespeare. Dawson
has tentatively suggested that this situation may well have contributed to
a rise in Shakespeare's popularity from the end of the 1730s onward. It is

certainly the case that, within just a year or two of the Walker–Tonson battle, the influential 'Shakespeare Ladies Club' was formed and they soon 'persuaded the managements of Drury Lane and Covent Garden to engage in a significant series of Shakespearian revivals'.[41] Likewise, Dawson notes that 'Garrick began acting in 1741 and soon showed an awareness of a demand for more and better Shakespeare.'[42] Noting the prominence of Shakespearean adaptations in the early decades of the eighteenth century, Robert D. Hume has observed of the Tonson–Walker dispute that very abruptly

> not only were *all* the plays within the reach of virtually any would-be
> buyer, but something like original texts were readily available to anyone:
> Shakespeare no longer had to be seen through the filters of Davenant and
> Dryden and Tate. No single factor can be said to account for the
> Shakespeare boom of the eighteenth century, but the availability of cheap
> and semi-authentic texts of the whole (expanded) canon must have been a
> crucial factor in making Shakespeare much more widely and more truly
> known.[43]

Jacobs I and II both died as the contest with Walker was drawing to a close. It was a few years before Jacob III was faced with a new Shakespeare edition which challenged the Tonson cartel's monopoly. This edition was very different in kind from Walker's undertaking. Where Walker was a small-time operator producing cheap and cheerful duodecimos for the popular market, the next challenge to the cartel's supremacy was initiated by no less a figure than Sir Thomas Hanmer, Speaker of the House of Commons. Hanmer conceived his edition as '*another small monument designed and dedicated to* [Shakespeare's] *honour*' (§224, I, p. v). Monumental it certainly was: complete in six lavish, well-produced quarto volumes, with thirty-six illustrations, and published by the Clarendon Press at Oxford University.

Hanmer thought of himself as a serious editor. In a memoir of the Speaker's life, Sir Henry Bunbury suggested that he 'probably turned his thoughts [to editing Shakespeare] soon after the publication of Theobald's edition of 1733', noting that he himself possessed 'a copy of this work, with corrections and notes on the text of every play in the baronet's handwriting'.[44] Hanmer's annotated Theobald edition has been preserved in the Folger Library, but Giles E. Dawson has argued that the marked-up text which Hanmer sent to the printers was more likely to have been a copy of the 1725 Pope edition.[45] Hanmer certainly followed Pope in degrading unsatisfactory passages, noting that he '*hath ventured to discard but few more upon his own judgment*', including '*that wretched piece of ribaldry in King* Henry V. *put into the mouths of the* French *Princess and old Gentlewoman, improper enough as it is all in* French *and not intelligible to an* English *audience, and yet that perhaps is the best thing that can be said of it'* (§224, I, p. III).[46] Pope himself paid a visit to Oxford in 1743 and he saw the text being produced at the Clarendon Press. He wrote to Warburton, telling him that he was only able to have a close look at one sheet, 'in the Margins of which were no various readings or marks for references of any sort, but a fine well-printed Text that coverd a multitude of Faults'.[47] Pope's comments are, in fact, characteristic of the general view which critics have taken of Hanmer. Malone dismissed him with a single sentence: 'Of Sir Thomas Hanmer it is only necessary to say, that he adopted almost all the innovations of Pope, adding to them whatever caprice dictated' (§357, I, p. lxvi). The editors of the 1863–6 *Cambridge Shakespeare* styled him a 'country gentleman of great ingenuity and lively fancy, but with no knowledge of older literature, no taste for research, and no ear for the rhythm of earlier English verse [who] amused his leisure hours by scribbling down his own and his friends' guesses in Pope's Shakespeare' (§587, I, p. xxxii). Even the historian of the Oxford University Press, Harry Carter, characterised Hanmer's as 'an edition fit neither for scholars nor for schoolboys. It was a luxurious edition fit only for bibliophiles'.[48]

As is perhaps appropriate for a bibliophile's edition, Hanmer's *Shakespear* has, in general, been better regarded for its illustrations than for its text. Thirty-one of the images were designed by Francis Hayman and subsequently engraved by Hubert Gravelot, who added a further five illustrations of his own design.[49] Hanmer's agreement with Hayman has survived and it indicates that the editor was a rather rigorous task-master who drove a hard bargain. The second clause of the agreement specifies that if all of the commissioned illustrations are not completed within the narrow timeframe specified in the document, 'the said Francis Hayman shall not be entitled to receive any payment or consideration whatsoever for any part of the said work'.[50]

If Hanmer drove a hard bargain with his illustrator, he was rather more generous in his dealings with his publisher. Writing to Dr Smith, the Provost of Queen's College, Oxford, Hanmer noted that he was willing to absorb the cost of the illustrations himself and that he was undertaking the edition for no personal 'honour, reward, or thanks', but 'for the honour of Shakespear' and he hoped that the edition might be in some 'degree profitable to the University, to which I shall always retain a gratitude, a regard, and a reverence'.[51] The edition was an unusual undertaking for the university press – as Harry Carter points out, no book had ever been published before 'at the University's expense and sold by subscription'.[52] Carter provides a breakdown of the press' costs in producing the edition and they afford an

Table 5.1 *Oxford University Vice-Chancellor's expenditure and receipts for Sir Thomas Hanmer's edition of Shakespeare. (Carter History, I, p. 303.)*

	£	s.	d.
Paper, 560 reams of Royal	800	0	0
The printers' bill	305	0	0
Copperplate printing	24	7	6
Engraving, to Gravelot	14	14	0
A corrector's journey to London	2	2	0
For the pressmen to drink Sir Tho. Hanmer's health	2	2	0
Correctors	84	0	0
Caslon, letter-founder	39	2	0
Wood, pressman, for delivering copies	6	6	0
Binding and delivering Sir Tho. Hanmer's copy	6	1	0
	1,283	14	6
Receipts from sales			
1744–5, 575 sets	1,811	5	0
1745–6, 6 sets	18	18	0
1746–7, 3 sets, being the last	9	9	0
	1,839	12	0

interesting insight into the expenses involved in such a publishing venture (not least the two guineas spent on drinking the editor's health, which may, perhaps, not have been a standard feature of more commercially oriented publishing in the period). Carter's breakdown is reproduced in table 5.1. As the accounts indicate, the edition sold out smartly and quickly recovered its basic costs. Its success might well have afforded Hanmer a wry smile of satisfaction, if he was aware of Pope's dismissive assessment of his venture. As we have already noted, some 140 copies of Pope's first edition remained unsold in 1767, when they were disposed of for the knockdown price of 16*s.* each (cheap enough to have pleased even *Mist's Journal*, we might surmise). By that time, as Oxford University Press archivist Martin Maw has noted, 'a second-hand copy of Hanmer's could fetch ten pounds – a fabulous sum'.[53]

The commercial success of his edition may have provided a small crumb of comfort to Hanmer in his dismal final years. A widower, he married, late in life, the daughter and heir of Thomas Folkes of St Edmondbury in Suffolk.[54] His new wife was much younger than he and was not well treated by Hanmer. Eventually she left him for a younger man, Thomas Hervey. A property dispute between the young couple and the older man led to an exchange of pamphlets, during the course of which great laundry-loads of dirty linen were washed in the public arena of print. In an open letter to

Hanmer, Hervey made accusations which, while delicately (if not slightly ludicrously) phrased, are nevertheless still somewhat shocking in their kiss-and-tell explicitness. Hervey says that he posed certain questions to Lady Hanmer,

> in as decent Terms as I could find to express myself; which, tho' they made her blush (poor Wretch!) I remember made her laugh. What, said I, did he never attempt to consummate? Did he never try to *pin* the matrimonial *Basket?* Upon which, she averr'd to me, she could not certify you was a Man, if she was called upon for such an Attestation; that you once made some little Feint towards joining of your Persons, on the Wedding-night, and the next Morning begg'd Pardon for her Disappointment; but, from that Time took no more Notice of her than if you had forgotten her Sex.[55]

Hervey's pamphlet is curiously haunted by Hanmer's position as an editor, as on a number of occasions he draws upon Shakespearean examples to elucidate his arguments. Referring to a sickness he has suffered, Hervey observes 'was I visionary or superstitious, I should be apt to think it had been judicially inflicted on me (as the Ghost tells *Hamlet*) *to whet my almost blunted Porpose*'.[56] Hervey's pamphlet drew out a pro-Hanmer reply, which in its turn prompted a further pamphlet styled 'a proper reply to a late scurrilous pamphlet, entitled, a proper reply to a letter from the honourable Thomas Hervey'. This latter pamphlet was entitled *Measure for Measure*.

While Hanmer was, as Hervey might have put it, *assailed by a sea of* matrimonial *troubles*, the *slings and arrows* that he might have expected – on the basis of Robert Walker's experience – to have been fired at him from the house of Tonson never seem to have materialised. There is no record of Jacob III and the rest of the proprietors making any immediate move directly against Hanmer or his publisher. As Giles E. Dawson has pointed out, the printing of Hanmer's text took more than a year, 'during which time Tonson could hardly have remained in ignorance that such a project was afoot' – especially, we might add, since one of his own Shakespeare editors had seen the text being printed.[57] Dawson concludes that, since the university 'would scarcely infringe a sound copyright', the press must have come to the same conclusion as Walker – that the text was freely available for reprinting – and the Tonson cartel must have been chary of taking on so grand an opponent (and an adversary that had traditionally enjoyed certain special privileges when it came to printing).

The Tonson cartel did not entirely bend in the face of the venerable Clarendon Press, however. The year after the final volume of Hanmer's edition appeared (1745) the cartel produced their own octavo version of his text, including an 'Advertisement from the Booksellers' in the preliminary pages, which runs in part:

> This edition is exactly copied from that lately printed in *Quarto* at *Oxford*; but the Editor of that not having thought proper to point out the Alterations he has made from the former Copies, we were advised to mark those Passages in the Text thus, ' ' and place the discarded Readings at the bottom of the Page, as also to point out the Emendations made by Mr. *Theobald*, Mr. *Warburton*, and Dr. *Thirlby*, in Mr. *Theobald*'s Edition, which are used by this Editor. The changes in the disposition of the Lines for the Regulation of the Metre are too numerous to be taken particular notice of.
>
> (§225, I, A2r)

The note continues with an attack on Hanmer written by Warburton, who some have thought, for this reason, to be the editor of the edition, though Arthur Sherbo has argued against this conclusion.[58]

The Hanmer edition clearly rankled with Jacob III. We have seen that, in 1745, he warned Edward Cave off an edition which he proposed to undertake with Samuel Johnson.[59] Tonson was keen to impress on Cave that his manner of dealing with the university was exceptional and that he would take a wholly different line with anyone else who sought to move in on his Shakespearean territory.[60] Inviting Cave to call on him, he informs him that he will explain the 'reasons why we rather chuse to proceed with the University by way of reprisal for their scandalous invasion of our right, than by law, which reasons will not hold good as to any other persons who shall take the same liberty'. Tonson sternly informs Cave that, under all other circumstances, a Chancery suit 'will be the method we shall take with any one who shall attack our property in this or any other copy that we have fairly bought and paid for'.[61]

Cave, as we have already seen, was unwilling to stand up to Tonson – perhaps he had other fish to fry, as publisher of the highly successful *Gentleman's Magazine*. Two years later, however, in 1747, another publisher came along who was made of sterner stuff, possessed, it seems, of more of the spirit of a Walker than a Cave. This publisher was John Osborn, who reissued Hanmer's text in nine duodecimo volumes. Tonson again threatened, but it seems that Osborn was not for turning. If the account of the affair included in pamphlets published by Alexander Donaldson in 1764 and 1767 is to be believed, the cartel were obliged by Osborn to 'strike their flag'.[62] Osborn reportedly answered the cartel's threats by asserting that 'if they talked any more to him in that Style, he would print a Dozen of Books to which they had such pretended Rights'.[63] The cartel were obliged to make a deal with Osborn. They agreed to purchase a large portion of his edition from him, which they then reissued with cancel title pages, with their own names in the imprint. In addition, they reportedly arranged to pay Osborn an annual pension, 'to buy him off from reprinting upon them'.[64] All in all, a good day's work from Osborn's perspective.[65] But the cartel had reason to be pleased as well, since the handily sized volumes proved to be popular and Tonson and his associates reissued them in 1748, 1751, and 1760, making Hanmer's text one of the most reprinted of the eighteenth century.

The university press itself issued a revised edition of Hanmer in 1770–1, again in quarto format. The rationale for the edition was explained in an advertisement included in the preliminaries:

> The great demand . . . of the publick for so elegant an edition induced the delegates of the university press to set about this republication: in which the inaccuracies of the first impression in punctuation and spelling are carefully adjusted; and, in order to obviate such other objections as have been made to it, at the end of each volume are annexed the various readings of the two most authentick publishers of our author's plays, Mr *Theobald*, and Mr *Capell*.
>
> (§321, I, a2r)

The edition was produced under the stewardship of Thomas Hawkins, Chaplain of Magdalen College, who added a table of emendations and a glossary.[66] Colin Franklin notes that the 'whole production showed Oxford at its laziest and finest; choosing the version everyone (Capell above all) condemned, adding scholarly equipment neatly but in such a way that it was the greatest nuisance to use; achieving artistically the most delightful edition of Shakespeare'.[67] The dominant characteristic of the early ventures of the university press into the field of Shakespeare publishing seem to have been a preponderance of style over substance. In the nineteenth and twentieth centuries, however, both Oxford and Cambridge university presses would invest heavily in producing editions of real scholarly merit.

With the exception of the Clarendon second edition, the Shakespeare cartel seems not to have been quite so much troubled by English rivals after an accommodation had been reached with Osborn. In the interval between Jacob III's death in 1767 and the landmark House of Lords judgement of 1774, a small number of non-cartel English editions, or part editions, did, however, appear. Perhaps this was an indication that, without a Jacob Tonson at the helm, the cartel was unwilling to press its exclusivist claims quite so vigorously. Or perhaps it was a sign that everyone concerned was beginning to feel the advance breeze of the winds of change that were about to blow through the realm of publishing, bringing the imperial powers of the monopolists to an end. Charles Jennens issued his texts between 1770 and 1774. While his intention was to produce editions for the whole canon, it may have been felt that his eccentric texts were likely to secure only a minority readership. In 1768 another edition of the complete plays was produced outside of London, in Shakespeare's native Warwickshire. The edition's imprint indicated that it was published in Birmingham by Robert Martin and it included the names of a number of sales agents throughout the country. This text is sometimes styled the 'Stratford Shakespeare', as it is thought to have been produced on the initiative of Garrick and to have been offered for sale in Stratford during the course of Garrick's Shakespeare Jubilee in 1769. The text, Franklin observes, 'was really another issue of Warburton's Pope'.[68] Robert Martin's brother, William, would later provide printing materials for John Boydell's grand Shakespeare project.[69] Martin's text was one of two editions produced in Birmingham at this time. The second is undated, but is thought to have been issued sometime in the period 1768–70. The publisher is identified in the imprint as N. Boden and, again, a list of sales agents is provided. Little else is known about this rare edition. Nine volumes were planned, but only five would seem ever to have appeared. In 1772, a new edition of Theobald's text was issued in London, published by Crowder, Ware and Payne. This, however, would seem simply to be a spin-off from the cartel's own publishing activities, since Payne's name appears in the imprint of a large number of cartel editions.

The last non-cartel edition to begin appearing in advance of the House of Lords ruling was that produced by John Bell, commencing in 1773. During the course of a fifty-year career, Bell 'plied each of the associated book and newspaper trades – as printer, publisher, bookseller, typefounder, bookbinder, and journalist – usually practicing several of them simultaneously'.[70] His Shakespeare edition was dedicated to Garrick, 'as a grateful, tho' small, return, for the infinite pleasure, and extensive information, derived from your exquisite performance, and judicious remarks' (§331, I, p. iv). The text was intended to have a strong theatrical flavour and advertised itself as providing the plays 'As they are now performed at the Theatres Royal in London; Regulated from the Prompt Books of each House, by Permission' (title page). Catherine Alexander has noted that the nature of the project shifted as it proceeded and that from volume six Bell 'began to reprint the plays which were rarely or never part of the theatrical repertoire'. Alexander observes that each of the plays 'continued to be prefaced with an engraving of a dramatic moment and an introduction but, lacking cast lists for Drury Lane and Covent Garden, the most tangible link with performance disappeared'.[71]

Bell's editor, Francis Gentleman – 'the raffish actor, playwright, poet, and teacher of oratory' – sought in various ways to render the text more morally acceptable to readers, anticipating the later efforts of Henrietta and Thomas Bowdler.[72] The rationale for Gentleman's changes is set out in the 'advertisement' which prefaces the first volume of the edition:

> Shakespeare's admirers, even the enthusiastic ones, who worship him as *the god of their idolatry*, have never scrupled to admit that his most regular pieces produce some scenes and passages, highly derogatory to his incomparable general merit; he frequently trifles, is now and then obscure, and, sometimes, to gratify a vitiated age, indelicate: but can any degree of critical taste wish the preservation of dark spots, because they have grown upon dramatic sunshine? is not the corrective hand frequently proved to be the kindest? critics, like parents, should neither spare the rod, nor use it wantonly.
>
> (§331, I, p. 5)

Unlike the Bowdlers, however, Gentleman was not systematic in the way in which he approached the business of expurgation. Sometimes offending words or passages are deleted, sometimes placed in parentheses, or italics, or quotation marks; at other times they are completely ignored, so that, for instance, Prince Hal quite happily calls Falstaff a 'whoreson, obscene, greasy, tallow catch' and Falstaff, in turn, calls him a 'bull's pizzle'. As Noel Perrin has observed, if 'a foolish consistency is the hobgoblin of little minds, Gentleman had one of the largest minds of his century'.[73]

Although Gentleman's efforts may have caused Bell's edition to be 'classed with Hanmer's as the worst of the century', it proved to be a remarkable commercial success and the run sold quickly.[74] Bell had hit on a good publishing formula: well-produced books, with attractive illustrations, sold at a moderate price. Once the end of perpetual copyright was confirmed by the 1774 Lords' decision, Bell quickly set about applying his formula to the wide range of texts which were now confirmed as being in the 'public domain'. In 1776 he launched his 'Poets of Great Britain Complete from Chaucer to Churchill' series, running to a total of 109 volumes, priced at 1s. 6d. each, together with his 'Bell's British Theatre' in twenty-one volumes, published in

6*d*. weekly parts.[75] He also produced several more Shakespeare texts. In his 1786–8 edition he became the first Shakespeare publisher to abandon the use of the long 's', adopting the modern form instead.[76] He also used the term 'Prolegomena' for the preliminary materials which served as the first two volumes of the edition, establishing a practice that would be much repeated. The text and other materials were issued in parts and a contemporary review indicated that the edition could be assembled in whatever manner suited the buyer:

> The purchaser . . . may arrange the plays into volumes in what order he pleases: – this was judiciously contrived. The works of the great Poet may be bound up separately, and the Notes and Commentary on each play may be collected in another set of volumes, and so placed as to correspond with the series of the plays. He may then read the text, and let himself be carried away by the current of the poet's imagination, without that frequent interruption of notes, which is apt to distract the mind, and weaken the impression made by the Author.

The reviewer pointed out the utility of an edition whose volumes were 'not only fit for the library, but for a pocket-companion'.[77] The idea of a multi-purpose Shakespeare had already been taken up by John Stockdale in 1784. Stockdale published the first single-volume Shakespeare to have appeared since the Fourth Folio and his eye was fixed upon much the same market as Cornelius Cotes had settled on many years previously. Noting that 'there is still a numerous class of men to whom [Shakespeare] is very imperfectly known' and that many 'of the middling and lower ranks of the inhabitants of this country are either not acquainted with him at all, excepting by name, or have only seen a few of his plays, which have accidentally fallen their way', Stockdale's editor, Samuel Ayscough, expresses the hope that his own edition might help to bring such people into the Shakespearean fold (§346, A2r). By the same token, however, he notes that it is not only the uninitiated who might find his volume useful:

> It will be found serviceable even to those whose situation in life hath enabled them to purchase all the expensive editions of our great dramatist. The book now offered to the public may commodiously be taken into a coach or a post-chaise, for amusement in a journey. Or if a company of gentlemen should happen, in conversation, to mention Shakspeare, or to dispute concerning any particular passage, a volume containing the whole of his plays may, with great convenience, be fetched by a servant out of a library or a closet.
>
> (§346, A2v)

Returning to Bell's own text, we can say that he certainly had high aspirations for his 1785–88 edition. In his 'Reasons *for Printing this* WORK, *and* Observations *on it's* [sic] *Propriety*', printed in the individual parts, he observed that he was 'ambitious of producing a Work which may attract the admiration of all Europe, in hopes of deriving a proportionate share of reputation and advantage to himself' (§349, unpaged). Likewise, in an address 'To the PUBLIC', he asserts that 'THIS Work is intended to supersede the necessity for any other Edition whatever, as it will be calculated to gratify every class of Readers.' This was, of course, a vain ambition: Bell's enterprise served as a model for many others, and cheap reprints of Shakespeare and other canonical texts soon became a staple of the publishing trade. As Charles Knight later observed, Bell 'raised up a series of rivals and imitators, who went upon the same principle of giving the common reader nicely-printed small volumes, with embellishments by first-rate artists'.[78] John Cooke followed Bell in producing sixpenny volumes of the work of the British poets and Richard Altick has registered the impact which these volumes had:

> William Hone, John Clare, Henry Kirke White, Thomas Carter, Leigh Hunt, and William Hazlitt all left records of their purchases. 'How I loved those little sixpenny numbers containing whole poets!' Hunt exclaimed late in life. 'I doated on their size; I doated on their type, on their ornaments, on their wrappers containing lists of other poets, and on the engravings from Kirk. I bought them over and over again, and used to get up select sets, which disappeared like buttered crumpets; for I could resist neither giving them away, nor possessing them.'[79]

In terms of Shakespeare, the effect of the text's being confirmed as public property was to prompt a multiplication of editions, so that the early stately parade of Tonson texts, progressing through a monarchical succession of editors, gradually gave way to a crowded rush of competing editions. By 1804, the publishers Sharpe and Symonds found it necessary to apologise for producing yet another edition of Shakespeare, by claiming that there was no need for them to apologise for producing yet another edition of Shakespeare (a formula which would be much repeated in the period):

> Though the editions lately published, of the Plays of our immortal Dramatist, have been numerous beyond all precedent, the Proprietors of [this] edition consider any apology for adding to the number as perfectly unnecessary. Its intention is obviously to facilitate and extend the knowledge of an Authour, of whom England has just reason to be proud.
> (§407, unpaged)

To note this proliferation of editions is, in a sense, however, to get ahead of ourselves, since we have not yet charted the process leading up to the House of Lords ruling which resulted in the texts of Shakespeare and others being released into the public domain. To trace these developments we must move northward from England, across the border into Scotland (and also westward, across the Irish Sea).

6   Copyright disputes: Scottish and Irish publishers

We have seen in the previous chapter that, while the Westminster parliament attempted, in 1710, to codify and regulate the issue of copyright, a certain vagueness in the wording of the legislation (coupled with the established London trade's desire to maintain its traditional privileges) led to a protracted series of disputes concerning the exact meaning and force of the 1710 act. Difficulties over the meaning of the act itself were compounded by the complexities of enforcing it within the hybrid polity of the eighteenth-century British Isles. Scotland had dissolved its own national parliament and entered into union with England and Wales in 1707. The 1710 act did therefore apply to Scottish publishers. However, Article XIX of the Treaty of Union guaranteed the continuance of the Scottish legal system, which was significantly different from its English counterpart – not least because the Scots had Roman law as part of their common law, which the English did not.[1] As late as 1806, Lord Chancellor Erskine would observe that 'I know something of the law but of Scotch law I am as ignorant as a native of Mexico.'[2] In these circumstances, it was perfectly possible that the English and Scottish courts might well arrive at very different conclusions regarding the meaning and implications of the copyright legislation.

Ireland offers something of a mirror image of Scotland in this period. Though the Irish too had been possessed of their own distinct legal system – the *brehon* law codes – this system had been entirely suppressed as English control over the island was tightened during the course of the seventeenth century. Thus, by the eighteenth century, English law wholly prevailed in Ireland. However, by contrast with Scotland, Ireland *did* retain its own parliament – albeit a parliament constrained in its powers and largely subordinate to its Westminster counterpart. As in the case of Scotland, Ireland represented a disjunct element within the greater entity of the British state (if 'state' is indeed the right word for this uneasy conglomeration of national units). The 1710 act was neither passed through the Irish parliament, nor extended to Ireland by Westminster. Ireland was, therefore, unlike Scotland, not subject to its terms.

Ireland's legal location outside the structures of copyright created a situation which, as La Tourette Stockwell has observed, was 'particularly advantageous to the Dublin printers', in that 'a book, which it was illegal to print in England without a copyright, might without a copyright be readily printed in Ireland'.[3] In this climate, Irish publishing flourished. The prosperity of the trade is neatly indicated by the report of a 'riding of the franchises' at Drogheda in 1728. In the procession of the guilds, the reporter observes:

> Stationers, Cutlers and Painters Stainers did by far excel, for a Printer, as Master, who had made on purpose an exceeding neat little Dutch Press, and the Frames and Cases fixed on a very handsome Carriage neatly painted, and drawn by six fine Horses and Trappings, the Compositor and two Press-Men at Work, and Printed two fine Poems in Praise of Printing, which were distributed as they went along.[4]

The text of one of the poems printed on the carriage ran in part:

> Let Glad Hibernia Hail the Noble Art
> That mends the Mind, and cultivates the Heart!
> New tune the Harp, with Permanence secure,
> And charm inspiring Muses to thy Lure;
> The Rare Machine let all her sons revere,
> Nor doubt an Elzever and Stephen here;
> While latest Times, Newton, Entire shall boast,
> Nor Mourn an Addison, like Livy, lost![5]

Later in the century Sir William Hamilton would observe that 'He never found a book or a whore in anyone's house since he came to Dublin.'[6] One would have to say in response to this that Sir William cannot have looked very hard, at least as far as books are concerned, since Ireland itself certainly provided a lucrative market for native publishers.[7] It was, however, quite a small market compared with the much larger one which lay on Ireland's eastern doorstep. Thus, as Richard Cargill Cole has observed, while 'the Irish booksellers aimed their reprints at their own people', 'it was not long before they saw they could increase their sales by exporting some of their production to Britain'.[8]

The question of whether it was legal for Irish publishers to export into Britain is a rather vexed one. John Feather notes that the 1710 act 'implied, but did not state, that it was illegal to import any English-language books into England and Wales if they had been previously printed there'.[9] In exporting reprints of works still within their copyright period the Irish were certainly sailing close to the legal wind, though it is by no means clear whether they were, in fact, breaking the law. By March 1734, complaints by London publishers against their Irish counterparts were being brought to the attention of the Westminster parliament. The Irish were underselling the Londoners by, in some cases, as much as 40 per cent, and were making significant inroads in the provincial markets.[10] Though himself a victim of the reprint trade, Jonathan Swift defended the Irish publishers against English criticism, observing 'If I were a Bookseller in this Town, I would use all Safe Means to reprint London Books and run them into any Town in England that I could.'[11] Within a few years of Swift's making these remarks, however, Westminster took action, passing a further piece of copyright legislation in 1739. This act specifically forbade the importing of any book published in Britain in the previous twenty years, under penalty of 'the forfeiture of the sheets for damasking, a fine of £5, and a fine of double the value of every book, one half of which was to go to the Crown, the other half to whoever sued for it'.[12] While the act certainly hampered Irish exports, a clandestine trade nevertheless still continued.[13]

English publishers were most concerned about Irish reprints of new works, including fiction. By the mid-century the novelist Samuel Richardson, himself a printer, raised the oddly Borgesian possibility of the consequences of a Dublin reprint appearing in advance of the London publisher's original from which it was copied: 'And who can say, that, if they can get it out before him, they will not advertise, that *his* is a Piracy upon *theirs*?'[14] In addition to reprints of contemporary fiction, the Irish publishers were also turning out standard canonical texts, including editions of Shakespeare. George Grierson would appear to have been the first Irishman to have ventured into the field of Shakespeare publishing.[15] Grierson was, as Henry R. Plomer has observed, 'the first and most distinguished of several generations of a family of printers' based in Dublin.[16] He served as king's printer in Ireland from 1733 and, as E. R. McClintock Dix has noted, the 'output of his press was considerable and varied' and included 'much of great importance'.[17] He was married to Constantia Phillips, a polymath who died at the age of just twenty-six, and who was 'an excellent scholar, not only in Greek and Roman literature, but in Hebrew, divinity, history, philosophy and mathematics'.[18] She was a member of Swift's Dublin circle and is thought to have been the author of the 1728 poem on printing quoted above.[19]

Grierson began publishing editions of Shakespeare in 1721, when texts of *Julius Caesar*, *Othello* and *Hamlet* appeared under his imprint. In 1723 he issued *1 Henry IV* and in that same year his fellow Dubliner, George Ewing, published an edition of *Macbeth*.[20] Ewing included in this latter text a list of 'Plays sold by George Ewing at the Angel and Bible in Dames-Street, opposite the Castle-Market'. Three Shakespeare titles appeared on the list: *Julius Caesar*, *Othello* and *Hamlet*, and this would suggest that Ewing had accepted some of Grierson's stock for sale. This arrangement may possibly have represented the first steps towards a joint Shakespearean venture between the two publishers. In 1725 Grierson published a second edition of *Othello* and printed an edition of *The Tempest* for Ewing. In this latter text, the publishers jointly presented a prospectus for a new edition of Shakespeare which was 'In the Press, and will be speedily publish'd.' The eight-volume edition was offered for sale 'in half Binding for a *British* half Crown payed at the Subscription for each Volume' (§193, unpaged prospectus). The total cost of the edition would therefore have been just £1 sterling. The text was issued in 1725–6 and, as the prospectus and the edition's title page made clear, it was a straight reprint of Pope's edition. The Pope set, as we have seen, might have cost (depending on the binding and on whether one had been a subscriber) as much as seven guineas to purchase. The price comparison, in one sense, is hardly a fair one, since the London text was a lavish quarto and Tonson had, of course, to pay Pope for his editorial labours, while the Dubliners produced a no-frills octavo, without having to pay Pope a penny. Still, the difference in price offers a clear indication of the potential threat which Irish publishers presented to their London counterparts.

The Grierson–Ewing edition attracted a total of some 150 subscribers, three of whom purchased multiple copies (Richard Bettesworth six, and Robert Allen and Ish. Baggs two each).[21] The list includes twenty clergymen (one of them the Bishop of Ossory) and fourteen women. Six subscribers indicated connections of one sort or another with Trinity College Dublin and there was a scattering of military personnel, such as Colonel James Hamilton, Quartermaster Blashford Wynne and Lieutenant Zobel. Advertisements included in the edition indicated just how extensive were Grierson and Ewing's publishing interests. The lists of 'books printed for and sold by' the two publishers included Hodgson's *Navigation*; Milton's *Paradise Lost* and *Regained*, 'with Cuts, in Octavo or Twelves'; Cheynes' *Essay on Health*; and an anonymous play entitled *What d'ye callit, a Tragi-comi-pastoral Farce*, together with a wide range of other play-texts.[22] In 1726 Grierson and Ewing published the Sewell poems volume as a supplement to their Shakespeare edition.

Where Grierson and Ewing led the way, a great many others followed. Between 1725 and the end of the century, some forty-seven Irish publishers were involved in producing editions of Shakespeare. Between them, they published almost eighty different texts, most of them single-play editions, but also including seven sets of complete works (or complete plays).[23] The most popular individual plays were those which had been the first published by Grierson: *Othello* (ten editions); *Hamlet* (nine editions); and *Julius Caesar* (eight editions). *Macbeth* clocked up six editions and *Romeo and Juliet* and *1 Henry IV* ran to five each. Shakespeare publishing was mostly confined to Dublin, but not exclusively so.[24] Eugene Swiney published an edition of *Macbeth* in Cork in 1761 and, two years later, Phineas and George Bagnell issued *Othello* in the same city. Swiney, interestingly, was a Catholic printer, at least one of whose publications – Charles O'Conor's *Case of the Roman-Catholics* – was suppressed by the city authorities.[25] James Magee also published a pair of Shakespearean texts in Belfast later in the century (a *Hamlet* edition and an edition of Garrick's adaptation of *Romeo and Juliet*). Swiney offered his customers in Cork an extensive range of Shakespearean wares, including Warburton's edition (probably the Dublin reprint which followed hard on the heels of the London edition of 1747) and texts of *As You Like It*, *Coriolanus*, *Hamlet*, *Julius Caesar*, *King Lear*, *Richard III*, *Henry IV* (part not specified), *Much Ado*, *Merry Wives*, and *Timon of Athens*.[26] The likely price of these editions is indicated by a notice included on the final page of Thomas Moore's 1731 text of *1 Henry IV*, which advertises a range of 'Plays sold singly at a British sixpence' (§204). The list includes Moore's own editions of *Hamlet* and *Othello*, published in the same year. The same price of 'a British six-pence' is provided in an advertisement included in Abraham Bradley's edition of *Merry Wives*, in 1739 and in Philip Crampton's 1746 edition of *1 Henry IV*. As we have already seen, the typical price for a single play in London at the time was 1*s*., so the Irish publishers were undercutting their English counterparts by 50 per cent.

The second collected edition of the plays to be published in Dublin was produced by John Smith and Abraham Bradley in 1739. Smith was an Ulster Presbyterian who had studied at the University of Glasgow, where he became acquainted with the philosopher Francis Hutcheson, who, as we will see, would later influence the Scottish publishers Robert and Andrew Foulis.[27] The Smith–Bradley edition ran to seven duodecimo volumes and a number of texts from the edition were spun off as individual play texts, as is indicated by the pagination of the single-play editions and by the appearance of catchwords on the final pages of some individual texts (for instance, the final page of the 1739 *Timon of Athens* has the catchword 'TITUS').[28] The National Library of Ireland copy of the Smith and Bradley set offers an interesting early example of 'bowdlerisation', with offending words and passages crossed through and blotted out.[29]

Smith and Bradley's text was followed by the Dublin reprint of Warburton's edition, proposals for which were issued by Edward and John

Exshaw on 23 May 1747.[30] In their prospectus, the Exshaws noted that they
had originally intended to publish a reprint of Hanmer's text, but, hearing of
Warburton's edition, and recognising him to be 'one of the justest Criticks
this Age or any other ever produced', they concluded that they 'should hold
themselves inexcusable, were they to publish any other'.[31] The Exshaws seem
to have been more gifted as publishers than they were as judges of critical
merit – they proposed a speedy turn-around for their venture, promising
to provide the first volume by June, with the remaining seven volumes to
be delivered within four months of the date of the prospectus (that is, by
23 September). Subscribers were to pay 4*s*. 4*d*. Irish up front and 1*s*. $7\frac{1}{2}d$.
'on the Delivery of each Volume in Half binding'. This brought the total
cost of the edition to 17*s*. 4*d*. Irish, or just 16*s*. sterling. The title page
of the edition indicates that the Exshaws were joined in their venture by
a range of other Dubliners, including George and Alexander Ewing, the
Smiths, and a number of smaller players, most of whom had published the
occasional individual Shakespeare play under their own imprint. The cartel
clearly anticipated that their edition would be marketable outside of the capital, and the Exshaw proposals identified subscription agents in seven towns
and cities throughout the island: 'Mr. *Sullivan* and Mrs. *Pilkington* in *Cork*;
Mr. *John Hay* and Messrs. *Joy* in *Belfast*; Mr. *Stevenson* in *Newry*; Mr. *Dickie*
in *Armagh*; Mr. *Ferrar* and Mr. *Walsh* in *Limerick*; Mr. *Louis* in *Derry*; and
Mr. *Ramsay* in *Waterford*, Booksellers' (§232).

While the third Dublin collected edition appeared just eight years after
the second, it would be the best part of two decades before the fourth Irish
edition appeared, in 1766. This edition was, again, produced by a cartel
of Dubliners, with John Exshaw and J. Leathley surviving from the original partnership. Where the 1747 edition had been a reprint of Warburton,
the new edition reproduced Johnson's 1765 text. The Dubliners somewhat
cheekily included an advertisement indicating that their edition was, in fact,
rather to be preferred to its London equivalent:

> THE Publishers have not omitted any opportunity of making this
> Edition as compleat as possible: They have carefully corrected a large
> *Errata* in that printed in London; and also, with great pains and trouble
> have distributed into their proper places, a number of curious Notes, sent
> to Mr. JOHNSON by some of his learned Friends, and by him inserted in
> an Appendix: They have also made some valuable Additions from the
> Twenty Plays of SHAKESPEARE, lately published by that ingenious
> Critic GEORGE STEVENS, Esq; by which means they hope to give this
> *Edition* a preference to any now extant.
>
> (§286, I, unpaged)

The time-lag between the third and fourth Dublin editions may in part be accounted for by the fact that it matched a similar gap in new Shakespeare publishing in London. As we have already noted, following the appearance of Warburton's edition, the Tonson cartel confined themselves to reprinting old texts until they embarked on Johnson's *Shakespeare*. So, between 1747 and 1765 there simply were not any wholly new London editions for the Irish trade to reprint. There may, however, have been one other factor in this equation. With the notable exception of Thomas Johnson in the Netherlands and the irrepressible Robert Walker in London, Irish publishers essentially had a free run of the Shakespearean reprint trade during the early part of the eighteenth century. Scottish publishers, doubtless conscious of the fact that – unlike the Irish – they were subject to the provisions of the 1710 act, were very slow to become involved in Shakespeare publishing. They could, in fact, quite legitimately have begun producing editions from 1731, when the Tonson cartel's rights expired. However, as we have seen, the exact meaning of the terms of the 1710 act were a matter of some considerable dispute, and the Scots stayed their hand a further twenty-one years before venturing to produce editions of Shakespeare.[32] Once they did begin publishing such editions they were, of course, offering competition to both the Londoners and the Irish. The first Scottish editions started to appear in 1752 and it may well be that the market for Irish reprints contracted somewhat as a result, prompting a certain slow-down in the rate of Irish production.[33]

The first Scottish publisher to produce editions of Shakespeare in the eighteenth century was Robert Foulis of Glasgow.[34] Born on 20 April 1707 (quite literally in the dying days of Scottish independence), Foulis was apprenticed as a barber in 1720.[35] His master was – rather humorously from a Shakespearean point of view – a certain Alexander Leggat, for whom he made 'a natural wig and a tie-wig as his "essay"'.[36] Where George Grierson enjoyed high cultural connections 'by proxy', as it were, through his accomplished wife Constantia, Robert Foulis was culturally well-connected in his own right. While working at his trade in Glasgow he attended, in his spare time, the lectures of Francis Hutcheson, Professor of Moral Philosophy at Glasgow University. Hutcheson has been dubbed the 'father' of the Scottish Enlightenment and he is said to have 'inflamed [Foulis'] desire for knowledge' and to have 'suggested to him the idea of becoming a bookseller and printer'.[37] Foulis' younger brother, Andrew, who would later join him in the publishing trade, officially enrolled as a student at the university and subsequently taught Greek, Latin and French in Glasgow. Robert Foulis established himself as a bookseller at the university in 1741, turning publisher in the same year and producing an edition of Cicero's *De Natura*

Deorum. David Murray somewhat romantically pictured the Foulis book-shop as 'a pleasant lounge, in which professors and students were accustomed to meet, dally with the books, talk over the topics of the day, and discuss questions of philosophy with the printer'.[38] In the following year, the philosophically minded printer set up his own press, and in 1743 he became the official printer to the university. He quickly set about establishing Glasgow as a centre for high quality publishing and printing, acquiring type from Alexander Wilson and John Bain, who had set up a letter foundry at St Andrews in 1742, moving their operation to Camlachie, close to Glasgow, in 1744. Wilson and Bain's types were said to excel the work even of Caslon.[39]

In 1744, Foulis produced a celebrated edition of Horace, the pages of which were reportedly 'hung up on the college walls with a reward appended for every mistake discovered'.[40] The Foulis press became renowned for its editions of the classics and Henry Curwen observed in the nineteenth century that in 'the course of thirty years they produced as many well printed classics as Bodoni of Parma, or Barbon of Paris, and their books, in exactness and beauty of type, almost rival the Aldine series'.[41] The Foulis brothers began issuing individual Shakespeare plays from 1752. As Foulis himself noted, the project was conceived as a collected-plays edition, but the texts were released individually, in order of critical importance: 'the plays are all printed so as to sell separately [and] we are going on with the rest [volume one having already been completed] not in order, but first with those which are most esteemed'.[42] As in the case of their Irish counterparts, the text provided by the Foulis brothers was entirely derivative, being a straight reprint of Pope's second edition (which was duly acknowledged on the title pages). The complete text was issued in 1766, in octavo and duodecimo configurations.[43] The cost of the Shakespeare editions was £1 12*s.* for the larger set and just 16*s.* for the smaller.[44]

At the same time as he was publishing his first edition of Shakespeare, Robert Foulis was also carrying forward an ambitious scheme to set up an academy of the arts in Glasgow, with the intention of publishing examples of the work produced there. The Earl of Northumberland's secretary, Harvock, attempted, early in the process, to dissuade him from the venture, writing to him in December 1753:

> I cannot help thinking that my Lord is of my opinion, that a correct and well-printed Book would be more agreeable to us from your Press than any thing else. These will ornament, and with great lustre too, as well as real profit, the Libraries of Popes and Princes, while your Prints lye

> mouldering in a Dusty Corner . . . I really believe from what I have seen
> and heard, that . . . all men of Sense, wish you more success in Printing
> than in Painting and Sculpture.[45]

Harvock was prophetic, but Foulis was stubborn in his commitment to the
scheme. Ultimately it led to his financial ruin – a precedent which John
Boydell might later have done well to have contemplated.

While the Foulis edition was in progress in Glasgow, another edition
of Shakespeare was making its way through the press in Edinburgh. This
edition appeared in 1753 and, like the second Foulis edition, it ran to eight
volumes. Unlike the Foulis text, or the Dublin texts that had appeared up
to this point, however, it was not simply a straight reprint of a London
edition. The cartel who published the text – 'W. Sands, Hamilton & Balfour,
Kincaid & Donaldson, L. Hunter, J. Yair, W. Gordon, and J. Brown' –
employed an editor to prepare the text for them, with Warburton's edition
serving as copytext. This editor set about his task with a relatively light
hand, following his source very closely, but nevertheless showing a certain
independence of mind. John Velz has concluded of his work on *Julius Caesar*
that there are '10 original substantive readings' in the text, together with
'careful collation (of Hanmer against Warburton, chiefly), and a striking
anticipation of Johnson's punctuation'.[46] Pope and Warburton's practice of
degrading 'suspected' passages and marking notable speeches with inverted
commas was followed in this edition. The text was provided with a 'Scots
Editors Preface', in which culture and commerce are mingled in explaining
the rationale for the venture: 'THE distinguished character of SHAKESPEAR
as a dramatic writer, the great demand for his works among the learned
and polite, and a laudable zeal for promoting home manufactures, were the
principal motives for undertaking an edition of his works in *Scotland*' (§252,
I, p. i). The gentle hint of national pride here resurfaces later in the preface,
when the writer observes of the text that

> though it is not intended to affirm, that this edition is free from faults, yet
> such care has been taken, that 'tis thought it may well vie with any of
> those hitherto published in *England*; at least, we flatter ourselves, it will
> not be found inferior either in beauty or correctness.
>
> (§252, I, p. vi)

Exactly who was the Scots Editor who took pride in his ability to produce
a text that could comfortably stand side-by-side with the best of English editions? Traditionally, he has been identified as Hugh Blair, the Scottish divine
who served as Professor of Rhetoric and Belles Lettres at the University of

Edinburgh, where he played a key role in what Robert Crawford has styled the 'Scottish invention of English literature'.[47] This identification has been made on the basis of a note included in a 1795 reprint of the Edinburgh text, which reads: '*This Edition of* SHAKESPEARE *is correctly printed from the famous Edition* 1753, *by Dr.* Hugh Blair' (§380, 381, I, unpaged). Warren McDougall has, however, drawn attention to some evidence which calls into question Blair's supposed role in producing the text.[48] In 1765, the Edinburgh publisher Alexander Donaldson (of whom we will hear much more shortly) acrimoniously dissolved a partnership that he had entered into with the printer John Reid. During the course of a complex legal dispute occasioned by the split, Donaldson sought to recover part of the proceeds from the sale of some books which had been disposed of by Reid's creditors. Among the contested volumes was an incomplete set of Warburton's edition. Donaldson claimed that he distinctly remembered how this set had come into his possession, and how he had passed it on to Reid, so that he 'might make out an estimate of the expence of printing them, as [Donaldson] had some intention of publishing an edition' of Shakespeare.[49] Somewhere between the two offices, one volume of the set had been mislaid; Donaldson did not proceed with the edition, and the remaining volumes were not returned to him by Reid. Reid's version of events was completely different and he set out his side of the story in his deposition to the court:

> An edition of Shakespear's works was printed by Mess. Murray and Cochran in 1753, from Pope and Warburton's edition. The Respondent had the sole management of that edition, selected the notes, enlarged and altered the index, prefixed a catalogue of the beauties observed by Mr Dodd, gave an index of them, and a list of the various readings, and wrote the Scots editors preface; and he preserved the copy from which it was printed, and caused it to be rebound after the work was entirely finished. This copy the Respondent afterwards lent out in volumes to different persons of his acquaintance; which gave occasion to one of the volumes being lost. And were it necessary, the Respondent could prove, and he is ready to do so if necessary, his having lent it out at different times, long prior to the year 1760.[50]

It is difficult to know which of these two accounts to take at face value. On the one hand, Donaldson was a tough-minded and uncompromising businessman, probably quite capable of being creatively economical with the truth when it suited him, but, on the other hand, Reid was being hard-pressed by his creditors at the time and the 'shop value' of £2 8s. which had been placed on the incomplete Warburton set might well have weighed heavily on his mind.[51] If Reid was indeed telling the truth it is hard to avoid feeling that he missed his vocation in becoming a printer – perhaps a career as an editor might have suited him better and might have helped to keep him out of the courts.

By contrast with Reid, Donaldson had a very clear head for business. He was the son of a Drumsheugh weaver, who reportedly bequeathed him some £10,000, which he used to set himself up as a bookseller and publisher. This was not a wholly new departure for the family, as Donaldson's grandfather had also been involved in the print trade, notably as publisher of the *Edinburgh Gazette* between 1699 and 1705.[52] He began work as a publisher in 1750, becoming, in this same year, a burgess of Edinburgh. He was probably the 'Donaldson' whose name appeared in the imprint of the 1753 Shakespeare edition. He certainly sold the edition at his Edinburgh shop, offering it at a price of £1 2s., or £1 8s. 'neatly bound in red turkey'.[53] The edition was thus more expensive than the 1747 Dublin text, but it was still significantly cheaper than contemporary London editions. Donaldson was clearly motivated by a mixture of a desire for profit and a desire to see intellectual property made more widely accessible. In his testimony against Reid, he observed that their partnership had come about in the first instance because he had 'formed a resolution of establishing a printing-house of his own; whence he expected not only considerable advantage to himself, but a benefit to the public, by lowering the prices of so useful an article of commerce'.[54]

Donaldson would be the one who would take the fight over the exact meaning of copyright directly into the backyard of the London publishers. In 1759, the Londoners, increasingly frustrated by the swelling tide of Scottish and Irish reprints, initiated a plan to drive the wares of the Scots and Irish from provincial English bookshops. On 23 April 1759, the London bookseller John Whiston wrote to John Merrill, who sold books in Cambridge, informing him that 'We have *a scheme now entered into* for totally preventing the sale of Scotch and Irish books, which were first printed in England.'[55] The general details of the scheme were outlined for Merrill in this and subsequent letters and the plan was made public in a letter circulated to all English provincial booksellers in November 1759, signed by John Wilkie, the London booksellers' agent for their trade sales. Wilkie begins by noting that the Londoners had 'for some years past been greatly injured in their property, by sundry persons fraudulently and clandestinely in England, and openly in Scotland and Ireland, reprinting and vending' books to which the Londoners claimed exclusive rights. Wilkie warned that this situation would no longer be tolerated and that legal action would be taken against anyone selling such reprints. The threat was coupled with an offer to come to terms with booksellers who might already be holding reprint stock: the Londoners were willing to buy in such books 'at the real price they cost you, and give you in return to the same value in the genuine editions of the said books, at the lowest market-price'. There was, however, a condition attached: anyone taking up the offer must 'engage not to purchase or vend any such pirated editions for the future'.[56] To back up their threats, the London publishers created a 'war chest' which was to be used for funding law suits against offending booksellers. The fund ran to some £3,150. The largest contributor was Jacob Tonson III, who subscribed £500. He was followed by Andrew Millar – a key figure, as we shall see, in the battle over copyright – who gave £300.[57]

That the Londoners' scheme clearly had some effect is indicated by the fact that it ultimately prompted Alexander Donaldson to make a bold countermove. In 1763, he expanded his operations by opening a shop in London itself. He explained his reasons for this move in a notice included in a pamphlet which he published a year later, entitled *Some thoughts on the state of literary property*:

> This is to give notice, that ALEX DONALDSON, from *Edinburgh*, has now opened a shop for cheap books two doors east from *Norfolk-street*, in the *Strand*, where they are sold from thirty to fifty *per cent*. under the usual *London* prices. – The *London* booksellers . . . having prevented their brethren from dealing with him, have forced him, in self-defence, to establish this shop. – Good allowance is made to merchants who buy for exportation, and to country booksellers.[58]

The author of the pamphlet was not identified and it may well have been written by Donaldson himself. The writer vigorously assailed the London monopolists and, like Walker some years before, insisted that their reading of the implications of the 1710 act was wrong-headed and perverse. Referring specifically to the Londoners' recent initiative and to the Whiston and Wilkie letters, the author writes: 'Amongst the books mentioned . . . are Shakespear, Milton, and Hudibras. – We shall be glad to know what exclusive right the *London* booksellers have to these articles, some of them printed above one hundred years ago', and he strongly denies that exclusive rights attach to any of these works, insisting, on the basis of the provisions of the 1710 act, that they 'may safely be published and sold all over Great Britain, without infringing the laws'.[59]

In arguing against the Londoners' claims to exclusive rights in standard canonical texts, the author of the pamphlet cites the example of one of their

own brethren, John Osborn, who, he reports, 'some years ago . . . they had
threatened, prosecuted, and tried every other artifice, to intimidate . . . from
printing Shakespear, and other works; but all to no purpose; he was not
to be wrought upon so easily, and they were obliged at last to strike their
flag'.[60] Osborn was, as we have already seen, the London publisher, who,
in 1747, produced a nine-volume octodecimo edition of Hanmer's Oxford
text of Shakespeare, and who stood his ground when threatened by the
Tonson cartel.[61] The episode is given even greater prominence in a second
anonymous pamphlet, entitled *Considerations on the nature and origin of literary property*, published under Donaldson's imprint in 1767, where a more
extended account of the matter is provided:

> Mr. Osborne Bookseller in Pater Noster Row, London . . . printed an
> Edition of Shakespear, in Opposition to one undertaken by some of the
> most noted Booksellers in London, and most active Champions of the
> Common Law. Him they prosecuted, and threatened, in the most terrific
> Manner; but Mr. Osborne having calmly answered, That, if they talked
> any more to him in that Style, he would print a Dozen of Books to which
> they had such pretended Rights. They immediately, and justly, took
> alarm, and were glad to take the half of the Impression off his Hands, at
> the Price he was pleased to put upon it, besides allowing him, as it is said,
> an annual Pension, which he enjoys to this Day, to buy him off from
> reprinting upon them.[62]

Perhaps emboldened by his recollection of Osborn's experience,
Donaldson became himself more actively involved in Shakespeare publishing following the appearance of his second pamphlet on copyright. In 1768,
his name appears on the title page of Robert Martin's Birmingham edition,
as London agent for the text (Martin was himself Scottish). In the following
year, he reprinted the 1753 Scottish edition, in collaboration with fellow
Edinburgh publisher Walter Ruddiman. One year after this, he issued a series of single play editions. The texts included in this series were *Hamlet*,
The Tempest, *The Winter's Tale*, *Richard II*, *Richard III* and, a touch unex-
pectedly, *1 Henry VI*.[63] In the next year, 1771, in a characteristically bold
move, he again reissued the 1753 edition, this time adding a dedication to
David Garrick, in which he observes: 'THIS edition claims your patronage
in a particular manner, because it is exactly printed from the one published
at Edinburgh in 1753, which I have heard you honour with your approbation' (§323, Dedication). In a complex cultural move, Donaldson makes
use here of the foremost English Shakespearean of the day to gain an en-
dorsement for his Scottish text of Shakespeare, and his British publishing

ambitions are signalled by an imprint which indicates that the text is 'Printed by A. DONALDSON, and sold at his Shop, corner of Arundel-Street, Strand, London; and at Edinburgh.'

Donaldson's flurry of Shakespearean publishing occurred after the death of Jacob Tonson III. It may be for this reason that he would not appear ever to have been called to legal account for his activities by the Shakespeare cartel. In common with his fellow countrymen he was, however, the subject of much litigation throughout his career, complaining at one point that he had 'had to struggle with the united force of almost all the eminent booksellers of London and Westminster' and that 'above one hundred of the most opulent booksellers [had], in their turn, been plaintiffs against' him.[64] Court cases against Scottish publishers had been initiated as early as 1738, when Andrew Millar instituted proceedings in the Court of Session in Edinburgh against twenty Edinburgh and nine Glasgow publishers, charging them with infringing his copyright in Thomson's *Seasons*. Millar eventually dropped the action, but the case provided an interesting foretaste of developments to come.[65] Millar was ironically himself a Scot and he would later acquire the Tonsons' shop in London (a resonantly symbolic move on his part).[66] Both Millar himself and the presumed rights to Thomson's *Seasons* would remain at the centre of the copyright debate for the next several decades.

In 1743, Millar was back in the Court of Session, joined by sixteen other London publishers. Again, 'a small army of Scots' (as Warren McDougall puts it) was to be taken legally to task for reprinting a number of works to which the Londoners laid claim.[67] Listed among the ranks of this Scottish army was Robert Foulis. Millar's lawyers set out what would be a central plank of the Londoners' argument during the course of the next several decades: that they possessed common law property rights in the texts which they had purchased; that these rights were therefore perpetual; and that the 1710 act merely provided additional protections. The Scots were defended by Henry Home, later Lord Kames, himself, as it happens, a Shakespeare enthusiast, who would quote the dramatist liberally in his literary textbook *Elements of Criticism* (1762).[68] Home characterised the Londoners as 'perhaps a Dozen or half a Dozen People of over-grown fortunes' and he accused them of attempting, not just to stifle competition, but of endeavouring to crush the growing Scottish printing trade in the bud:

> There is somewhat else at Bottom with the Pursuers, than merely
> Reparation for pretended Incroachments upon their Privileges. The Art
> of Printing is daily improving in *Scotland*, at least in *Edinburgh* and
> *Glasgow*; and the Defenders, picked out amongst a great many

Booksellers, are they who are pushing on this Branch of Commerce with all Vigour. *Hinc illae lacrymae.* The Art of Printing has been so long confined to *London*, that the Booksellers there begin to consider it as an exclusive Monopoly, which they alone are intitled to deal in.[69]

The Lords of Session eventually ruled against the Londoners, and Millar and his co-plaintiffs, rather in the manner of 'Proud Edward's army', were sent 'homeward / Tae think again'. Further skirmishes in the Edinburgh courts also went against the Londoners and it became clear that their case would never be favoured by Scottish law, not least because the Scottish judges were unwilling, on the basis of their own legal codes, to entertain the notion of immaterial property, which served as the foundation for the Londoners' argument (which is to say, the Londoners argued that, in purchasing rights they were acquiring a property which had an existence quite distinctive from the physical text itself). The Scottish judicial system reaffirmed its position several times and, as late as 1773, in *Hinton* v. *Donaldson*, the Scottish Lord Kennet prefaced yet another judgement against a London publisher by observing 'I will not meddle with the law of England, in the first place, because I do not profess to understand that law; and secondly, because I think it ought to have no influence in determining upon the law of Scotland.'[70]

Failing to have their reading of the 1710 act affirmed by the Scottish courts, the Londoners largely abandoned the fight in Scotland itself and retrenched south of the border, where they hoped for better results in the English courts. As McDougall has observed, the 'Scots were left free, in the main, to reprint and distribute within Scotland books on which the copyright had expired or to which, in their opinion, it did not apply.'[71] Ultimately, Millar and his fellows did find favour in the English courts, at least for a time. In 1766, Millar initiated a lawsuit against Robert Taylor, who had published an edition of the *Seasons*. Millar had purchased the rights to Thomson's work in 1729 and so a strict reading of the 1710 act would have suggested that these rights had expired in 1757, at the end of an initial copyright term of fourteen years, renewed for a further and final fourteen years. However, in its judgement of April 1769, the Court of King's Bench found in favour of Millar by a majority of three to one, confirming that 'rights in copies were merely a form of property, and like all property existed for ever'.[72] The idea of perpetual copyright thus achieved a clear legal status in England and, as Gwynn Walters has observed, 'After *Millar* v. *Taylor* perpetual copyright was the law of the land.'[73] The dissenting opinion came from Justice Sir Joseph Yates, whose reading of the situation had much in common with that of his legal colleagues across the border in Scotland, in that he argued that 'it was the essence of property that it was defensible against trespass, and therefore ideas were not a piece of property' and that there was 'no common law protection for rights in copies, but only the limited protection granted by Parliament in 1710'.[74] The Londoners might have done well to ponder these points, as these precise issues would return to vex them again.

Millar himself died while the Taylor case was in progress and his executors sold his Thomson copyrights at auction to Thomas Beckett and fourteen partners for £505 in June of 1769 (Millar himself had paid £242 for them).[75] Donaldson was excluded from the Millar sale, but, persisting in his own reading of the 1710 act, he had issued his own edition of the *Seasons* in the previous year and, as John Feather observes, he 'ostentatiously put it on sale in London', in effect goading the trade into taking action against him.[76] Having acquired the Thomson rights, Beckett and his partners duly obliged, filing a bill in Chancery against Donaldson and drawing on the *Millar* v. *Taylor* judgement in making their case. In November 1772, Chancery found in favour of Beckett and granted an injunction against Donaldson. The Scottish publisher immediately appealed to the House of Lords. The case prompted much popular interest and it was recognised that the outcome would have considerable consequences. Burke, Goldsmith and Garrick, among other literary and cultural figures, were said to have attended the deliberations.[77] Lord Camden, addressing the House, asserted that, if the Londoners had their way: 'All our Learning will be locked up in the Hands of the *Tonsons* and the *Lintots* of the Age, who will set what Price upon it their Avarice chuses to demand, 'till the Public become as much their Slaves, as their own Hackney Compilers are.'[78] Of course, there were no publishing Tonsons left at this point, but Camden's comment registers the extent to which the firm had dominated the English literary world for most of the eighteenth century and had become virtually a byword for monopolist commercial domination. On 22 February 1774, the Lords found in Donaldson's favour. As it happens, they agreed with the Londoners' argument that a common law right of property in a text did indeed exist, but they concluded that that right was negated by the 1710 statute. They further concluded that, as a consequence, copyright extended only for the limited periods specified by the act.[79] As Richard Altick has observed, the ruling 'killed the legal fiction of perpetual copyright' once and for all.[80] If a traditional tale passed down in the Donaldson Edinburgh printworks is to be believed, the publisher's triumph 'was celebrated by a procession in Edinburgh; all concerned paraded the streets with music, flags, etc.'.[81] Efforts to have the effects of the decision negated through the introduction of new legislation reinstating the status quo ante were rigorously opposed and ultimately failed. Lord Camden, again, commented that the London trade had maintained their position 'by most iniquitous oppressions' and that they had

> exercised it to the disgrace of printing; that they were monopolists, and if the line of justice and equity were drawn, it would be, that those who had deprived others of their right for a series of years, should make compensation to all those they had injured by such conduct.[82]

W. Forbes Gray has characterised the 1774 Lords ruling as 'the Magna Charta of literary property, for it decreed that any person was at liberty to print and sell works of which the statutory term of copyright had expired, on the simple ground that all such works were public property'. It is for this reason that Gray concludes that the 'cheap book – the book which is popular and sells by the thousand just because it is cheap and attractive – was virtually the creation of Donaldson'.[83] As we have seen at the conclusion of the previous chapter, the effect of the Lords ruling was to prompt an acceleration of Shakespeare publishing, so that, by 1788, a writer in the *Monthly Review* was observing that 'By men of cold and phlegmatic constitutions, it may be thought that the rage for Shakespeare has been carried to excess; and that editions have multiplied so fast, that the Public may now be said to be, not only encumbered, but distracted, with variety.'[84] A simple statistical analysis indicates that, while in the half century between 1725 and 1774, some thirty-one collected plays or complete editions of Shakespeare were published in England, in the half century following (1775–1824), the equivalent figure is about sixty-two editions. In the immediate wake of the Lords ruling, then, collected-edition Shakespeare publishing doubled. A more rapid acceleration would occur in the final three quarters of the nineteenth century, as technological advances made printing much cheaper and as the reading public grew significantly in size.

The Donaldson ruling had somewhat paradoxical implications for the Scots and the Irish, in that, while it confirmed their right to reprint public-domain texts and to sell their editions into the English market, it also confirmed that English publishers could engage in this trade as well. While the Scots held their own reasonably well in the open market, the Irish faltered somewhat. Irish editions of Shakespeare tail off dramatically in the final decades of the eighteenth century. From a high of fourteen items published in the 1750s, Irish Shakespeare texts drop away considerably later in the century. One of just two items published in the 1780s was an edition of *Much Ado About Nothing*, produced by John Parker, with a title page reading 'Bell's Edition' – we have already seen that John Bell was one of the first English publishers to begin taking advantage of the new regime initiated by the 1774 ruling. If Parker's text is an indication that the Irish were seeking to join what they could not beat, then confirmation may come from the fact that, in the same decade, John Magee, publisher of the *Dublin Evening Post*, agreed to act as Bell's agent in Ireland. In 1785, he was offering a twelve-volume set of Bell's edition on cheap paper for just 12*s*.[85]

As the century drew to a conclusion, the Irish trade was delivered two fatal blows. In 1795, the Irish parliament imposed a large increase in the duty on imported paper. It was a well-intentioned, but utterly wrong-headed move. The objective was to foster a native Irish papermaking industry (and, more pragmatically, to raise additional tax revenue). Irish papermakers were, however, unable to provide enough materials to sustain the book trade and the increased cost of imported paper cut away the Irish publishers' ability to produce competitively priced books. The final death-blow for the Irish publishing industry came five years later, when, in the wake of the 1798 uprising, the Irish parliament was dissolved and Ireland was formally incorporated into the United Kingdom. As a result of the Act of Union, the provisions of the 1710 copyright act were extended to Ireland. As Richard Cargill Cole has observed, the Act of Union

> gave the *coup de grâce* to the dying Irish reprint industry and with it the Irish book trade in general. . . . The new London reprints had already taken from booksellers in Ireland much of the reprint business for works whose copyright had expired . . . For the new works of the Romantic Age by Sir Walter Scott, Robert Burns, William Wordsworth, and Lord Byron, the Union meant that the Irish booksellers could not issue cheap reprints but would be obliged to pay the London publishers for publication rights.[86]

As Cole further notes, the dissolution of the Irish parliament also helped to deprive Irish publishers of a large segment of their native market.[87] If Sir William Hamilton, in the mid-eighteenth century, failed to find either a book or a whore in any Dublin house he entered, by the early decades of the nineteenth century the reduction of Dublin's status from a capital with its own parliament to, effectively, a provincial backwater, meant that there were fewer houses in which expensive commodities such as books might be likely to find a home (though one imagines that prostitution probably operated according to a somewhat different set of commercial imperatives). By the mid-nineteenth century, the historian Sir John Gilbert reported that the number of books published in Ireland since the union had declined by about 80 per cent.[88]

Irish publishers did manage two final collected editions of Shakespeare in the last decade before union. In 1794, John Exshaw issued a reprint of Edmond Malone's 1790 edition in sixteen volumes. Malone's response to the appearance of this edition in his native country has not been recorded. Certainly, in 1793, he had strongly denounced a London reprint edition, the title page of which gave the impression that he had been the one responsible for its abridged notes.[89] Three years before the Irish Malone edition appeared, William Jones published a reprint of the second edition of Samuel Ayscough's Shakespeare, which had been published by Stockdale in London in the previous year (1790). Jones styled his text the 'ROYAL IRISH EDITION of SHAKSPEARE' and, as in the case of the 1766 Dublin reprint of Johnson's edition, he took the trouble cheekily to point out 'the principal objects which render his publication more valuable than that of Mr Stockdale'. Jones' improvements were rendered

    I. By prefixing the very elaborate preface of Dr Johnson, which contains not only a critical dissertation on the genius and writings of Shakspeare, but a summary of the merits and opinions of all preceding Editors.
    II. By adding to the life given by Mr Rowe, the Postscript of Dr Johnson, the additional Anecdotes furnished by Steevens and Malone, and Extracts from Dr Farmer's Essay on the Learning of Shakspeare.
    III. To heighten the whole by the embellishment of sculpture, a highly finished Head of Shakspeare is added, from an original picture in the Chandos collection, the genuine production of an Irish artist.

The edition also included the dedication and preface from the First Folio and Jonson's commendatory verses. Even with all these extras, and 'notwithstanding the obvious superiority at which he . . . aimed', Jones managed to offer the text for sale at one third less than Stockdale (§362, I, pp. i–ii). The Jones edition included some nine and a half pages of subscribers' names, a good many of them booksellers. The likely extent of distribution of the text is usefully indicated by the fact that Jones included the number of copies subscribed by each bookseller. The figures for booksellers whose location is identified are provided in table 6.1. Other booksellers – presumably mostly Dublin-based – accounted for a further 265 copies of the edition.

The Jones edition did not just circulate in Ireland – in common with many eighteenth-century Irish reprints, it also made its way across the Atlantic to America. Five sets of the edition went to the Philadelphia bookseller William Prichard and seven sets were sent to Connecticut. Samuel Campbell offered the edition for sale in New York and a second Philadelphia bookseller, Patrick

Table 6.1 *List of bookseller subscribers to William Jones'*
1791 edition whose location is specified in the subscribers list

Bookseller	Location	Number of copies subscribed
James Cuming	Newry	12
George Douglas	Derry	20
Anthony Edwards	Cork	35
Mrs Finn	Kilkenny	50
Joseph Gordon	Newry	7
William Magee	Belfast	36
A. Watson and Co.	Limerick	7
Thomas Ward	Lisburn	16
Thomas Walsh	Armagh	2
Total		185

Byrne, also advertised it for sale.[90] As we shall see in the next chapter, the
Jones edition also served as the base text for the first complete edition of
Shakespeare published in America itself: the Bioren and Madden Philadelphia edition of 1795. This transatlantic relocating of the Jones text was
entirely fitting, since the collapse of the Irish publishing trade led to the
mass migration of Irish print workers to America. Early Irish migrants included Hugh Gaine, a former apprentice of the printer James Magee who,
as already noted, published some Shakespearean texts in Belfast. As early as
1761, Gaine was 'advertising for sale a number of pamphlet plays, suitable
for taking to the theatre' – these included editions of *King Lear* and *The
Tempest* and Garrick's *Catharine and Petruchio*.[91] At about this time he also
became the exclusive broker for New York theatre tickets.[92] Gaine's fellow
Irishman, John Dunlap was another early emigrant to America, where he
ultimately served as the official printer of both the Declaration of Independence and the Constitution. Thomas Kirk, who served his apprenticeship in
Cork, arrived in New York in 1790 and by 1803 he had established printing
and bookselling businesses in both Brooklyn and New York, where he would
ultimately establish the city's largest bookshop. As Cole notes,

> In his earlier years in Brooklyn and New York he reprinted Richardson's
> *Pamela* for three different publishers, Hugh Blair's *Rhetoric* twice, an
> important text book used at both Harvard and Yale for many years,
> Samuel Johnson's *Rambler*, Isaac Watt's *Hymns*, and William Hazlitt's
> *Eloquence of the British Senate* twice. Among the twenty-eight works he

published in 1813 were reprints of such important English writers as Edmund Burke, Shakespeare, Robert Southey, and four works by the popular English moralist Hannah More.[93]

By the time of the Act of Union, some thirty-nine Irish print workers had already settled in America and they were quickly joined by another sixty-two print migrants.[94] As the Irish sought pastures new across the Atlantic, they contributed in various ways to the dissemination of Shakespeare in the newly independent United States – a territory hitherto to a great extent largely indifferent to the attractions of Shakespeare. The nineteenth century, as we shall see, would witness the gradual rise of the United States as an important power in Shakespearean publishing (as in so much else).

7   American editions

Writing of the history of 'Shakespeare in America', George B. Churchill observed in 1906 that a 'people that is winning soil out of the wilderness and defending itself against savages has no thought of literature, much less of stage-plays'. While one might baulk at Churchill's imperial characterisation of colonial America as a wasteland inhabited by savages, nevertheless, his broad general point is valid: the harsh reality of life in the American colonies dictated that these territories were not a fertile ground for literature or theatre. Churchill goes on to note that the pragmatic considerations which served to block the emergence of a vigorous literary culture in the colonies were compounded, in many cases, by an ideologically determined resistance to literature in general and to theatre in particular:

> Massachusetts was a Puritan state, founded by the kin of those men who in England attacked so bitterly the stage of Shakespeare. Pennsylvania was a Quaker colony, and the serious views of the Quaker gave no more countenance to the drama than did the austere and ascetic Calvinism of the Puritan.[1]

It comes as no great surprise, then, to discover that no performance of a Shakespeare play would appear to have been staged in the colonies before the middle of the eighteenth century. The Murray-Kean company performed Colley Cibber's adaptation of *Richard III* in New York in March 1750 and, in December of the following year, Robert Upton's company staged a performance of Shakespeare's *Othello* in the same city.[2] If performances of Shakespeare were thin on the ground, so too were editions of the plays and one commentator has observed that there is 'no evidence that there was a copy of Shakespeare's plays in Massachusetts during the seventeenth century'.[3] This contention might well be true of the other American colonies as well, with one notable exception. An inventory of a certain Captain Arthur Spicer, a Virginian lawyer and justice of the peace, drawn up in 1699, includes a copy of *Macbeth* – probably either the 1673 quarto or Davenant's 1674 adaptation.[4]

Records of the existence of editions of Shakespeare in New England gradually emerge over the course of the eighteenth century. In the 2 July 1722 edition of the *New England Courant*, the paper's editor, James Franklin, proudly announces that the journal's staff 'are furnish'd with a large and valuable collection of Books'. He goes on to list 'a small part of our Catalogue', which includes 'Shakespear's Works', together with an eclectic selection of texts, including 'Aristotle's Politicks', 'The Turkish Spy', 'Art of Thinking', 'St Augustine's Works' and 'Burnet's Theory of the Earth'.[5] In the following year, Harvard University library produced its first catalogue, listing a recently purchased copy of the 1709 Rowe edition.[6] By the 1740s Yale too had acquired an edition of Shakespeare, courtesy of the Irish philosopher George Berkeley, who provided the college with a gift of a diverse collection of over one thousand books, including several volumes of plays and other literary texts.[7] In the Yale library catalogue produced in 1743, the Shakespeare edition is included under the heading 'books of diversion'.[8] Three years later, Benjamin Franklin purchased a copy of the Hanmer edition for the Library Company of Philadelphia.[9]

The private ownership of Shakespeare editions also spread over the course of the century. William Byrd II – like Arthur Spicer, a Virginian – built up a considerable library at his home on the James River. The collection ran to in excess of 3,000 volumes and included folio editions of Jonson, Spenser, Beaumont and Fletcher and Shakespeare. Byrd had lived in England between 1684 and 1692 and E. E. Willoughby has suggested that his Shakespeare edition may have been a copy of the 1685 Fourth Folio.[10] Byrd employed a librarian to oversee the collection, who he 'was wont to address as "Most Hypocondriack Sir"'. Carl L. Cannon speculates that the librarian's 'melancholy may have been due to Byrd's frugality with candles, which left the poor librarian in almost Cimmerian darkness'.[11] Twenty years after Byrd's death, in 1764, editions of Shakespeare were common enough in the colonies to be caught up in a moment of cultural circulation which might at one time have made a New Historicist literary critic weak at the knees. Captain Thomas Morris of His Majesty's 17th Regiment of Infantry was sent to Pontiac's village near Naumee Rapids, where he encountered a native American who made him 'a present of a volume of Shakespeare's plays'. Morris noted, in Churchillian mode, that this was 'a singular gift from a savage'. Progressing onward on his journey, Morris later had a lucky escape, thanks to his absorption in his Shakespeare volume:

> on the seventh of September in the morning we got into easy water and
> arrived at the meadow near the Miamis fort, pretty early in the day. We

were met at the bottom of the meadow by almost the whole village, who brought spears and tommahawks in order to despatch me; even the little children had bows and arrows to shoot at the Englishman who had come among them; but I had the good fortune to stay in the canoe, reading the tragedy of Anthony and Cleopatra, in the volume of Shakespear, which the little chief had given me, when the rest went on shore, though perfectly ignorant of their intention, I pushed the canoe over to the other side of the river.[12]

It was rather unfortunate for Captain Morris' compatriots, we might feel, that they did not share his enthusiasm for Shakespeare. Just five years after Morris' lucky escape, a contributor to the *New American Magazine or General Repository* set out the essentials for tranquil colonial country living. His list included 'a well stocked farm, six slaves, a gracious wife, opportunity to revere God and country' and a library of his favourite authors, identified as 'Swift, Shakespeare, Pope, Young, Addison and Gay'.[13]

The editions of Shakespeare passing through the hands of these colonial country squires, native chiefs, English soldiers, and ivy league students were, of course, like Byrd's folio, imported texts, either London editions or, as we have already seen, reprints commonly offered for sale by immigrant Irish bookmen. It would be much later in the century before a native tradition of Shakespeare publishing established itself in America. Printing itself first came to the English colonies in 1638, when Joseph Glover imported a press to Cambridge, Massachusetts.[14] The press was set up by Stephen Daye and his sons, under the auspices of the president of Harvard. The first book produced in the colonies was issued two years later. This was the 'Bay Psalm Book', 'an entirely new translation from the Hebrew of a great body of religious verse'. In 1662 the press issued an original piece of poetry, Michael Wrigglesworth's 'Day of Doom', but this too was a religious text, characterised as 'a terrible theology expressed in an equally terrible versified production'.[15] One of the greatest achievements of the Cambridge press was a translation of the Bible into one of the native American languages, carried forward by John Eliot, and known as the 'Eliot Indian Bible'.[16] The New Testament appeared in 1661 and, two years later, the complete text was published. As printing extended throughout the colonies, the ideological project of spreading the Christian gospel ran in parallel with the more mundane business of the kind of jobbing work that was the meat and drink of the majority of printers: 'Warrants of all sorts, indentures, bill heads, bills of lading, insurance and other ships' papers', together with almanacs, and 'ready reckoners' which served to make sense of the complex range of currencies being used throughout colonial America (including English pounds, the paper currencies of individual colonies, Spanish money, and tobacco). In due course, local newspapers also provided regular work for colonial printers. But, as Lawrence C. Wroth has observed, the 'book or pamphlet of purely literary intention was relatively rare in the early days of American printing'.[17]

As the eighteenth century progressed, the American printing industry became increasingly self-sufficient, spurred in part, later in the century, by the non-importation resolutions prompted by the colonists' break with Britain.[18] The first American-made press was produced for William Goddard of Philadelphia in 1769 and, by 1775, Story and Humphreys of the same city were advertising a book entitled the *Impenetrable Secret* which they patriotically claimed had been produced using materials wholly manufactured in Pennsylvania. By the end of the century this latter territory in particular was well served by papermakers and typefounders. It comes as little surprise, then, to find that the very first American complete works of Shakespeare should have been produced in Philadelphia, by the publishers Bioren and Madan, in 1795. An edition of the playwright's works had, in fact, been advertised five years earlier, in the *Gazette of the United States* for 19 May 1790, the advert running:

SHAKESPEARE

To the very many editions of our immortal bard, one is in agitation by the Blue-Stocking Club, which consists of many of the first rate male and female geniusses, to be entitled, 'The Ladies Shakespeare.' The plan of this edition is to be a familiar criticism on the sensibilities, rather than the language or learning of the author – somewhat in the stile of Addison's critique of Milton – to be useful to all who have any relish for the poet, or moral writer.[19]

Nothing would seem to have come of this project, though a couple of individual play editions did appear in Boston in advance of the 1795 Philadelphia text. *Hamlet* and *Twelfth Night* were produced in the Massachusetts capital for David and John West in 1794. Both were abridged theatrical texts, substantially based on Bell's 1773–4 edition. The *Hamlet* provides the abridged text of the play only, while the *Twelfth Night* edition included some sixty-six notes, culled from Bell's edition.[20]

The 1795 Philadelphia complete works was the first edition of Shakespeare to be produced outside of Britain and Ireland and the preface sets out the text's objectives: 'In preparing this work for publication, the editors have exerted themselves as much as possible, by an elegant type and good paper, to do credit to the American press. Conscious of their solicitude to deserve approbation, they hope that their efforts have not been entirely unsuccessful' (§382, I, p. xii). For all its American ambitions, however, the text was heavily marked by a certain Celtic lineage. The base text for the edition was, as we have already noted, the William Jones Dublin reprint of Samuel Ayscough's second edition.[21] The glossary for the Philadelphia text was probably drawn from a 1792 edition produced by a Scottish conglomerate headed by W. Gordon of Edinburgh. The preface to the edition includes a page long quote (§382, I, pp. xi–xii) from the Scottish divine and academic, Hugh Blair, whose highly popular *Lectures in Rhetoric and Belles Lettres*, which drew on Shakespearean examples, has been credited with serving to establish a presence for Shakespeare in the American college curriculum, in advance of the emergence of departments of English literature at American universities.[22] The edition was very lightly annotated and eschewed any significant discussion of textual issues. This reluctance to enter into the textual undergrowth was glossed in the preface as characteristically American: 'An American reader is seldom disposed to wander through the wilderness of verbal criticism. An immense tract of excellent land, uncultivated, and even unexplored, presents an object more interesting to every mind than those ingenious literary trifles, that in Europe are able to command so much attention' (§382, I, p. x).

Alfred Van Rensselaer Westfall has tentatively identified the editor of the 1795 text as Joseph Hopkinson, a prominent Philadelphia lawyer, observing that his work on the edition 'leaves little to [his] credit', as he hardly did more than 'hand the printer a glossary from one edition, the text from a second, and a few notes from a third'.[23] Either Hopkinson or Bioren and Madan's compositors did, however, modernise the spelling of the text, perhaps inspired by the reforms which had been advocated by the lexicographer Noah Webster. A persisting American resistance to theatre and the perceived frivolity of literature is perhaps registered in the fact that the bulk of the preface to the edition is taken up with a defence of Shakespeare's works against the charge of immorality. The editor is particularly keen to distinguish Shakespeare's work from that of the Restoration dramatists who succeeded him:

> The more carefully that we compare Shakespeare with his successors, the more shall we be convinced, that as a moral writer he was infinitely superior to any one of them, and that the reproaches which have been thundered from the pulpit against the stage, cannot reasonably be applied to the stage of Shakespeare.
>
> (§382, I, p. vii)

Westfall's criticisms of Hopkinson's lack of initiative as an editor are perhaps a touch unfair, given that the materials required for conducting original work in Shakespearean editing and annotating simply did not exist in America during the eighteenth century and, indeed, would not exist until well into the next century. There was little else that the Philadelphia editor could do, other than to reconfigure the materials that came to hand in the form of editions imported from Britain and Ireland. In this respect, the Philadelphia edition established a procedure that would be followed in the next several collected editions published in the US. The 1802 Boston edition, for example, was again a reprint of a reprint, this time taking the 1792 Gordon edition as its base text, but adding notes from the 1773 Johnson–Steevens edition, and with the text of the poems taken from Bell's 1774 volume.[24] The principal terms of publication were set out as follows:

1. This Work shall be comprised in sixteen numbers, or eight duodecimo volumes.
2. The numbers will be published monthly, or oftener, if possible, and sent to the dwellings of subscribers in town, neatly stitched in covers.
3. Each number will contain about 200 pages, and consist of two and three plays, with Dr. Johnson's notes.
4. The price to subscribers will be *thirty-eight cents*, – payment on delivery. To non-subscribers *fifty cents*.

(§402, front wrapper of no. 1)

As in the case of a number of similar ventures in Britain, the plays were individually paginated to facilitate the sale of single texts, to complement sales by part, volume, and set. Thus *Merchant of Venice*, for example, was offered for sale for 25 cents, 'stitched in blue'.[25] The subscribers' list for the complete edition runs to about 350 names, a bit more than 10 per cent of whom were associated with Harvard.[26] The vast majority of subscribers are Boston-based, with a small handful of others sprinkled throughout New England – for example Nathaniel Appleton of Salem, Cazneau Bayley of Portsmouth, Thomas Procter of New York, and a number of subscribers associated with Rhode Island College. The tight concentration of the bulk of the edition's sales in a single region – indeed, a single city – is indicative of the lack of readily available distribution networks in the US in this period. It would be some time before publishers could envisage producing editions aimed at a broader regional market, let alone a national American market.

If the first two American collected editions were almost entirely derivative in nature, a third edition, published in 1805–9 was somewhat more ambitious in its aims. Much of the editorial work on the edition was carried forward by

Joseph Dennie and an announcement in the 11 February 1804 issue of the American literary journal *Port Folio*, signalled the publisher's intention to 'surpass the London edition in neatness of mechanical execution, and rival it in fidelity and correctness'. The edition was priced at $1.50 per volume to subscribers (in boards) or $1.75 to non-subscribers and the advertisement noted that this price compared favourably with currently available imports: 'The inferior copy of the last London edition, in 21 vols. boards, sells for FIFTY-ONE DOLLARS; more than double the price of the proposed edition.'[27]

Dennie's ambitions for the edition were further signalled in an advertisement indicating that he was

> particularly desirous of inspecting the *first* folio edition. This is probably very scarce, and may be found only in the cabinet of some *distant* virtuoso. But the owner of this rare book will be very gratefully thanked, if the Editor can have permission to consult it, for a short season.[28]

Dennie also advertised for copies of various key critical works, together with a Shakespeare concordance.[29] Whether he ever secured access to these books is hard to say – indeed, it is difficult to know whether there would have been a copy of the First Folio available anywhere in the US at the time when he was working on his edition. At any rate, Dennie's experience with the edition seems not to have been an entirely happy one – he had a falling out with one of the publishers, as he was disappointed with the quality of the volumes which were being produced, and he appears to have dropped out of the enterprise for several volumes. Of Dennie's own achievement, Westfall has concluded that, while 'he may have desired to do scholarly study, his notes, in the end, as they had to be, were chiefly conjectural. They contain some interesting and illuminating suggestions, but no new information. Some of them are commonplace and valueless.'[30] Sales of the edition were poor and the sheets were repackaged in a number of different ways in subsequent years, in an attempt to dispose of the stock.

The Boston edition of 1802 met with a greater level of commercial success, in that a second edition of the text was issued after just five years. This new edition was a paginal reprint of the original and, again, it drew a high number of its subscribers from academic circles. More than half of the then currently enrolled students at Harvard – a total of ninety-nine – subscribed, making up just over 50 per cent of all subscribers. Twenty-eight students from Brown also subscribed, as did seventeen from Union and seven from Dartmouth.[31] A further Boston edition appeared in 1810–12, based on the 1803 Johnson–Steevens–Reed. The chief distinguishing feature of the edition is that each play is illustrated by a wood-cut engraving by Alexander Anderson, making it the first American illustrated edition of Shakespeare.[32] Another American first was achieved in 1813, when John T. Buckingham printed the first single-volume Shakespeare edition to appear in the US. Buckingham produced the edition for Charles Williams of Boston and Joseph Delaplaine of Philadelphia and some copies of the edition were provided with an imprint naming the publisher as 'Eastburn, Kirk & Co. New York', an indication, as Westfall has noted, that, at least at a regional level, 'trade connections were developing and marketing facilities extending'.[33] Buckingham himself, in a note included in the volume, indicates that the edition was also produced in six miniature volumes – an early instance of the nineteenth-century vogue for diminutive editions which would flourish on both sides of the Atlantic.

The recycling of the same text into a variety of different editions accelerated dramatically – in both the UK and the US – with the rise of stereotype printing. In stereotyping, a mould is taken from the composed forme and this mould is then used to produce a metal plate, which can be employed to run off second and subsequent editions without the necessity for any further setting of type. The method was known in the Netherlands as early as the sixteenth century and limited use was made of the technique in Paris in the eighteenth century.[34] In Britain, the Edinburgh goldsmith William Ged experimented with stereotyping in the 1720s and 1730s, but several of his publishing partners conspired against him, fearing the consequences of the invention for the printing trade. As George A. Kubler has noted, he 'encountered every possible form of opposition from the compositors who, when they corrected one fault, purposely made half a dozen others, and the pressmen, when the masters were absent, battered letters in aid of the compositors'.[35] Ged's career ended in failure, but interest in the method was revived in Scotland by Andrew Foulis – a partner, as mentioned in chapter 6, in the Glasgow firm which began issuing editions of Shakespeare in the 1750s. Foulis and Andrew Tilloch – a doctor of jurisprudence who served as editor of the *Philosophical Magazine* – perfected a method of stereotyping which they then sold on to the innovative London printer, Charles Mahon, Lord Stanhope. Stanhope set up a commercial stereotyping enterprise at the beginning of the nineteenth century, under the direction of Andrew Wilson, conducting his early experiments at the Shakespeare Press in London.[36] In 1809, Wilson printed the first stereotyped edition of Shakespeare, for the publishers Vernor, Hood and Sharpe.[37]

By the early decades of the nineteenth century, stereotyping had crossed the Atlantic and the effect of the method is neatly illustrated by the history of the first American stereotyped edition of Shakespeare, which was published initially in New York in 1817–18, by Henry Durell, who issued a second edition in 1818. In 1821, the same plates were used to produce a further edition, but this time with the imprint 'Collins and Hannay'. This firm reissued the text several times, running off editions from the plates in 1823, 1824, 1825 and 1826. Some time after this, the plates changed hands again and, in 1835, Dearborn of New York issued the text, configuring it in six volumes instead of ten. The plates would then appear to have passed into the hands of Harper's, who ran off an edition from them in 1839 and then subsequently used them as the basis for further editions produced in 1843, 1850, 1854, 1859, 1860, 1867, and 1868.[38] The history of the Durell plates serves to illustrate both the extent to which the American Shakespeare market was growing over the course of the nineteenth century and also the increasing ease with which standard texts could be used to satisfy this market.

While reprints of British texts flourished in the US in the nineteenth century, a desire to produce a text which would offer a distinctively American contribution to Shakespeare studies also persisted. In 1836, Hilliard, Gray and Co. of Boston published an edition for which O. W. B. Peabody served (anonymously) as editor. Peabody was a Harvard graduate who failed as a lawyer, becoming instead first a journalist and then a Unitarian preacher. He made Samuel Weller Singer's 1826 London edition the base text for his own edition, Singer's text having, by the 1830s, displaced Johnson–Steevens–Reed as the preferred edition for reprinting. While his edition was heavily indebted to Singer, Peabody did attempt some original, independent textual work. In the 'Advertisement' to the text, the publishers claimed that the editor has 'preferred, in general, to follow the readings of the folio edition of 1623, with which the text of [Singer's] edition has been carefully compared' (§481, I, 'Advertisement', paged 6*). It is not clear exactly where Peabody could have located a copy of the First Folio – most documented American copies of the volume date from later in the century (Thomas Barton's copy was, for instance, purchased in 1845), but it has been suggested that Peabody may have used one of the facsimiles of the First Folio published in London early in the nineteenth century.[39] Even with some version of the First Folio in hand, however, there was a limit to what Peabody could achieve without having access to a much greater range of early texts and a supporting library of secondary materials. Westfall characterises Peabody's achievement as modest: 'His edition is not epoch-making because he did little more than reprint Singer's text. He was not a Shakespearean scholar. He was a student and editor, who was asked to prepare an edition of Shakespeare.'[40] Jane Sherzer is, however, more generous in her assessment, observing that, while 'the text, on the whole, remains Singer's and ... the original work is meager', this 'in no wise impairs the fact that here, for the first time in America, is sounded the true note for a correct editing of the Shakespearian text'. Thus, for Sherzer, Peabody 'must be regarded as the father of textual criticism in America'.[41]

Whatever the scholarly merits of Peabody's text, it was certainly a commercial success, with its stereotype plates being used to issue reprints for several decades. Peabody's immediate successor as an ambitious editor of Shakespeare was Gulian C. Verplanck, whose work was, by contrast, a commercial failure, largely because it was dogged by bad luck, including, as Richard Knowles has noted, 'a change of publishers and two printing-house fires', the second of which destroyed the plates.[42] Verplanck was a New York lawyer and congressman and his edition was issued serially in 138 parts between 1844 and 1847. The original publisher was the engraver H. W. Hewet, but the project was taken over by Harper's after just over ten plays had been completed. Verplanck himself, in his 'Preface', poses the question 'What can be the use of any more editorial labour upon Shakespeare, and especially by an American editor?' (§488, I, p. v). His response is that, given the extent of the advances made by contemporary British critics – especially in the work of John Payne Collier – an edition which synthesises this material specifically for an American audience seems necessary:

> It, therefore, appeared highly desirable, and at the same time not at all difficult, to combine many of the merits of the several best and latest English editions in an American edition, – compressing all the results of modern Shakespearian criticism into such a compass as would render them accessible and convenient to numerous readers, whose want of leisure, or inclination, or of means, might prevent them from consulting the voluminous labours of the European commentators.
>
> (§488, I, p. vi)

Verplanck abandoned the popular Singer text, in favour of Collier's edition of 1842–4. He did not, however, follow Collier slavishly. As he observes in his 'Preface', he was 'gradually led to adopt a revised text, not exactly corresponding with that of any preceding edition' (§488, I, pp. vi–vii). Like Peabody, Verplanck generally privileged the First Folio, restoring some folio readings which had been emended by Collier. He was well acquainted with what he characterised as the 'higher Shakespearian criticism, in which this century has been so prolific' and was influenced by such critics as 'Coleridge, Ulrici, Schlegel, Mrs Jameson [and] Hallam' (§488, I, p. ix). Sherzer concludes that, 'As an editor Verplanck far surpasses Peabody' and that his edition 'is based upon sound principles'. With a patriotic sense of the value of hard-headed American intellectual pragmatism, she observes that he displayed 'some independence, if not originality, and a clear and virile mind that breathes at times thro' the dreary wastes of European criticism like a fresh western wind'.[43]

Such intellectual virility as Sherzer identifies in Verplanck may also have been part of the mental apparatus of Henry N. Hudson, who came to Shakespearean criticism and editing after an early life spent as a farmer and coach-maker. Certainly, in 'English in Schools', Hudson observed of gaining an honest living that it 'is the *best* thing that any man does, as, on the other hand, shining intellectually is the poorest thing that any man does, or can possibly learn to do'.[44] Hudson's varied career continued with stints of school teaching in Kentucky and Alabama, followed by ordination as an Episcopal minister and service as chaplain to the New York Volunteer Engineers during the Civil War, before he was appointed to a professorship at Boston University, where he lectured on Shakespeare. A contemporary account indicates that Hudson was a memorable speaker and teacher:

> with a facial expression peculiar and striking[,] not at all an elocutionist, he stood before his audiences and classes as if charged with a kind of electric light, burdened with a kind of volcanic energy, struggling to find exit in flashes or volumes of expression; in his own untaught and untrammeled way, by tones, emphasis and accent, gestures, contortions and gyrations, getting for himself the utterance he sought and inspiring his hearers and pupils with his own enthusiasm.[45]

Hudson published an eleven-volume edition of Shakespeare in Boston between 1851 and 1856. Unlike predecessors such as Dennie and Peabody, Hudson did not particularly aspire to breaking new ground as far as the text itself was concerned. Indeed, even from a literary critical perspective, his aims were disarmingly modest, as he observed in his *Lectures on Shakespeare*: 'if I know my own mind, I have rather studied to avoid originality than to be original'.[46] For all his declared lack of originality, however, Hudson contrived to produce an edition which was serviceable and popular, with each play provided with an introduction which synthesised much of the current criticism of the text. The edition was well received, with Edward S. Gould, in the *North American Review* observing that 'as to the size of volume, typographical arrangement, completeness of explanatory notes, and full analysis of the characters of the plays, with their histories, Mr. Hudson's work may safely challenge competition with the long array of his predecessors'.[47] Gould registers Hudson's lack of originality, but manages to offer the editor a generous compliment in the process: 'Chronologically speaking, [his] method of analyzing the poet's characters is *after* that of Coleridge and of Mrs. Jameson;

but Mr. Hudson has so improved on his models, that he is but little more indebted to them, than Shakespeare was to his predecessors for the plots of his plays.'[48] A revised version of Hudson's edition was published in 1871, and in 1881 he produced a new edition, published by Ginn, Heath & Co. of Boston under the title the 'Harvard Shakespeare', in which the text was to be 'set forth on conservative principles but without dotage or bigotry'.[49] The complete Harvard edition was offered to teachers for an introductory price of $25.[50]

The popular success of Hudson's editions, coupled with the widening proliferation of cheap commercial reprints, indicates the extent to which Shakespeare's works had finally gained a solid foothold in American culture by the middle decades of the nineteenth century. In 1843, for example, the curtain of the St Charles Theatre in New Orleans included the pointedly symbolic image of Shakespeare being borne aloft on the wings of an American eagle.[51] Four years later, in a more literal gesture of cultural appropriation, P. T. Barnum attempted to buy Shakespeare's family home in Stratford, intending to transport it back to America.[52]

By 1849, the battle lines between a British imperial Shakespeare and a Shakespeare absorbed into the cultural system of the American republic were being very clearly drawn in the streets of New York city. The British actor William Charles Macready and the American Edwin Forrest staged competing productions of *Macbeth* – Macready at the Astor Place Opera, Forrest at the Broadway Theatre. Rivalry between the two productions prompted an American sense of national pride and fostered deep anti-British feeling. Thus, Forrest's declaiming the lines 'What rhubarb, senna or what purgative drug will scour these English hence?' was received with sustained cheering from the Broadway audience. Macready's performance, by contrast, was greeted with 'an avalanche of eggs, apples, potatoes, lemons, and, ultimately, chairs hurled from the gallery'.[53] An attempt to mount a second performance of Macready's production led to a riot outside the theatre, prompting the militia to open fire on the crowd. Twenty-three people were killed, including the printers George A. Cutis and Timothy Burns.[54]

American theatrical appropriations of Shakespeare at the mid-century were gradually matched by quite literal American appropriations of early modern Shakespeare texts, as a culture of antiquarian book collecting began to take hold in the US. James Lenox (1800–80) acquired two copies each of the First Folio, the Third Folio and the Fourth Folio and seven copies of the Second Folio, in addition to several early quartos. Another particularly strong collection was that established by Thomas Pennant Barton (1803–69), who possessed fourteen pre-1623 quartos, together with all four folios, his copy of the First Folio being 'one of the finest known'.[55] In 1842, the London book dealer Thomas Rodd wrote to the American, noting that Barton had (at that point) accumulated thirteen early quartos and commenting that this was 'a very respectable number for a private collection and certainly unmatched on your side of the Atlantic'.[56]

It was the existence of these collections that made possible the first genuinely innovative American edition of Shakespeare – Richard Grant White's twelve-volume text, published in Boston between 1857 and 1866. In his Preface, White acknowledges the access he has been granted to original source texts by Barton and Lenox:

> The copy of the folio of 1623 which I have constantly used is that in the Astor Library, which is the well-known copy formerly in the collection of the Duke of Buckingham at Stowe. But I have also, whenever it seemed desirable, had the privilege of examining the admirable copy of the first folio, now in the noble Shakespearian library of Mr Thomas P. Barton of New York, which entire collection, indeed, has at all times been open to me for consultation when the limits of my own humbler shelves were reached . . . To Mr. James Lenox my readers as well as myself also owe much for the very generous and unreserved manner in which he placed his collection of the early quartos – the value of which is hardly known except to the best informed bibliographers – entirely at my service.
>
> (§502, I, pp. xxi–xxii)

White set out his editorial methodology in his Preface, indicating that, like many other Americans before him, his instinctive inclination was to privilege the the First Folio text, but without uncritically elevating it above all others:

> the text of the present edition is founded exclusively upon that of the first folio, and has been prepared, in the first instance, as if no other edition of authority had appeared since that was published, although afterward the readings of every edition, ancient and modern, and the suggestions of every commentator, have been carefully examined, adopted when they appeared admissible, and recorded when they were deemed worthy of preservation.
>
> (§502, I, pp. ix–x)

His work on the edition was interrupted by the Civil War and the final volume to appear (volume one of the complete set) was published after the conflict had drawn to a conclusion. In another gesture of amalgamating Shakespeare to American concerns, White figures his edition as a post-war 'peace-offering', noting that his project has been finished 'under the glad auguries of a peace and a prosperity which we may reasonably hope will never again be . . . interrupted' (§502, I, p. xxxiv).

White's edition was well received by American critics, with James Russell Lowell declaring in the *Atlantic Monthly* (in 1859, when the edition was part published) that 'in acute discrimination of æsthetic shades of expression, and often of textual niceties, Mr. White is superior to any previous editor' and concluding 'Mr. White has thus far given us the best extant text, while the fullness of his notes gives his edition almost the value of a *variorum*.'[57] The merit of White's work was acknowledged by Shakespeareans on the other side of the Atlantic as well. Writing to Macmillan's in July of 1875, Edward Dowden advises on the publication of a volume of Shakespeare illustrations, suggesting that they be accompanied by 'a careful selection of appropriate extracts . . . from the best English, American, French & German critics'. Under the heading '<u>American</u>', the only critics listed are Hudson and White.[58] In his 1939 survey of *American Shakespearean Criticism*, Westfall observed that, encountering White's work, 'the reader feels that here at last is an American scholar working with the library resources which are available to him [in the US], and producing results which, for independence, originality, and scholarship, may be compared with those of English and German critics'.[59] In this sense, American Shakespeare criticism can be said to have come of age with White's work.

George B. Churchill observed of White in 1906 that he 'was indeed the real pioneer in American Shakespearean scholarship, he blazed a path in which all who followed him have walked in safety'.[60] It seems a bit excessive to claim for White that he made the world safe for Shakespeare studies, but Churchill's essential argument that White opened a space for others to occupy is entirely valid. The editor who most clearly moved into this space was Horace Howard Furness. Furness was born in 1833 and trained as a lawyer, practising in Philadelphia. He first developed an interest in Shakespeare when he was in his mid-teens, as he indicated in responding to the question 'How did you become a Shakespeare Student?' later in life:

> I cannot but think that I have been peculiarly favored in my introduction to Shakespeare. When I was about fourteen or fifteen years old, during two winters between 1847 and 1849, Mrs Kemble gave, here in Philadelphia, two series of Readings, and to both of them, with infinite kindness she sent me a card of admission. Thus to this gracious lady and venerated friend I owe the memory, vivid to this hour in many a scene and line, of her inimitable revelations of more than half of all of Shakespeare's plays.[61]

In 1860, Furness joined the Shakspere Society of Philadelphia, the Society having been founded by a group of city lawyers some eight years previously. The society was in some respects a touch dilettante in its approach to its activities, holding an annual feast in honour of Shakespeare's birth, but celebrating it in the last week of December because 'terrapin, canvas-back ducks, and venison then abound, where as there is no good thing edible to be found in April'. It was, by all accounts, Furness who persuaded the society to move the date of the dinner back to the actual month of Shakespeare's birth.[62]

Their close concerns with the gastronomic aspect of Shakespeare studies notwithstanding, the society did, in fact, bring a considerable degree of seriousness to their activities. They gathered together a substantial library of books, with each member possessing his own copy of the 1821 Malone–Boswell edition, which they used as their base text. They also drew on material from other editions and critical works in the course of their discussions, with individual members taking responsibility for specific texts. Thus, when they studied *Julius Caesar* in 1862, for example, Furness was called upon to make a particular study of Warburton's edition, Johnson's 1765 text, and the German edition of Nicolaus Delius.[63] It was this method of working that turned Furness' mind towards the possibility of creating a new variorum edition which would supersede the Malone–Boswell text. Preparing for the Society's projected study of *Hamlet*, Furness, as he later wrote,

> made a mighty Variorum . . . cutting out the notes of five or six editions, besides the Variorum of 1821, and pasting them on a page with a little rivulet of text. 'Twas a ponderous book, of Quarto size and eight or nine inches thick – I took great delight in burning it some years ago. But the work revealed to me that it was high time to begin a new Variorum, that we might start afresh.[64]

Taking this cut-and-paste *Hamlet* as a model, Furness set to work on producing an edition of *Romeo and Juliet*. The Philadelphia publisher J. B. Lippincott agreed to produce the volume, his interest prompted in part by a desire to enter a text in the 1873 International Industrial Exhibition in Vienna. As Furness prepared his text for the press, Lippincott provided him with experimental proofs, offering different layouts, styles, and combinations of type size. 'Eight times did I remodel the first twenty pages of that volume', Furness later wrote, 'as it now stands, it seems a task of no special difficulty, but no one who has not tried it, can imagine what entanglements impeded me at every step, and how appalling the mass of my materials loomed up before me'.[65] In addition to his problems with the layout of the text, Furness also ran into difficulties with the text itself. Needing some base text to serve as the core of the edition, he hit upon the plan of reproducing that of the magisterial Cambridge edition, published in nine volumes between 1863 and 1866.[66] Furness announced the details of his venture in a letter published in *Notes and Queries* on 22 January 1870, noting that for several years 'all of us Shakespeare students have felt the need of an edition which should set forth the labours, both in text and commentary, of our learned modern editors with the same satisfactory clearness and precision that the textual varieties of the Qq. and Ff. are given in that invaluable edition of the Cambridge editors, Messrs. Clarke [sic] and Wright'.[67] Wright took offence at what he interpreted as an act of editorial piracy in Furness' use of the Cambridge text (an offence compounded by what he considered a misleading implication in Furness' announcement that the Cambridge text did not provide a collation of editions subsequent to the 1821 variorum) and he registered a public protest in the pages of the *Athenaeum*. There followed a number of brisk public exchanges between the two editors, but, in the end, they arrived at a private reconciliation. In the interim, Furness had decided to drop his plan of reproducing the Cambridge text, preferring instead to construct his own text. As the series progressed, he eventually came to reject this method of proceeding also and with his *King Lear* volume he moved closer to providing an unmodernised and minimally edited reproduction of the First Folio text, a procedure which he consistently followed from *Othello* onward.

The inaugural *Romeo and Juliet* volume appeared in 1871 and it provided a massive collection of materials. As James M. Gibson indicates, it ran to

> over three hundred pages of text, textual notes, and commentary plus appendices on the source of the plot, the date of the play, the text, the costuming, and excerpts from foreign criticism by the likes of Philarete Chasles, Albert Cohn, Lessing, Goethe, and Ulrici, criticism too general to be placed elsewhere in the volume. Forty-four editions of the play – four folios, five quartos, and thirty-five editions from Rowe (1709) to Keightly and the Cambridge Edition (1865) – were collated and all textual variants were noted. Following each textual variant appeared a list of which editors had adopted or rejected the various readings and who was the first to adopt each reading. One hundred and fourteen critical and exegetical works – seventy-five English, thirteen French, and twenty-six German – in addition to the above editions were scoured for commentary and explanatory notes. All this, plus a full reprint of the Danter Quarto, or bad quarto of 1597 that varied too greatly from the other early editions to be placed in the collation, took exactly 480 pages, in the publisher's words 'a library of the costliest Shakespearian literature'.[68]

Furness was roundly praised for his achievement by critics and scholars and Lippincott won an honourable mention in Vienna, in the Division of Publishers of Educational Books. The volume was not, however, a commercial success, in part because of the high retail price of $7.50. Concerned about the price, Furness – who had by this time come into a family inheritance – agreed to subsidise the project, paying for the stereotype plates of the plays himself. In this way, he was able to convince Lippincott to drop the price of the volumes to just $3 each (later the price would rise again to $4 per volume). While his partnership with Lippincott persisted over the decades Furness nevertheless was embittered by the publisher's consistent placing of profit above all other concerns and in writing to fellow American Shakespeare scholar, William J. Rolfe, he observed:

> it's all along of Harpers and Lippincott. They ought to drop every other
> venture & throw everything into Shakespeare. Who cares for their
> twaddling Magazines? The only special comfort I can give you is that in
> your marrowbones you should be grateful that you don't live within
> earshot of your publisher. A man's tongue is more rasping than his pen –
> a pen sticks deep & ink festers, but the tongue lays bare whole
> hand-breadths of quivering nerves. 'Mr. Lippincott, you put the price of
> the book too high.' 'Too high!! the price has nothing to do with it; your
> book wouldn't sell if I put the price at seventy-five cents.' As I think I
> once said to you, how I revere the memory of Campbell who gave as a
> toast 'Napoleon Bonaparte, because he once shot a publisher.'[69]

For all the ill-feeling between editor and publisher, the volumes were, nevertheless, themselves well regarded by purchasers. Writing to F. G. Fleay, the well-connected Ohio Shakespearean Joseph Crosby observed: 'you know how beautifully the works are executed. I think them a great credit to American book-making'.[70]

In all, Furness edited fifteen plays prior to his death in 1912. Lippincott's plant was destroyed by a fire in 1899 and the plates of *Macbeth* and *Hamlet* were among the materials lost. Furness decided to take advantage of this to produce revised editions and he co-opted his son – also named Horace Howard – to work on the *Macbeth* revision. Pleased with the result, he drew his son more closely into the enterprise and Furness Jr produced his own editions of *Richard III* (1907), *Julius Caesar* (1913), *King John* (1919), and *Coriolanus* (1928). He had begun work on *Henry V* at the time of his own death in 1930. Some time before he died Furness Jr realised that the task of bringing the edition to completion was more than he could accomplish – indeed, between them, father and son managed to produce a total of just nineteen volumes (no mean achievement, given the scope of the project, but still amounting to less than half the canon). On the advice of Professor Felix Schelling, Furness approached Matthew Black and Matthias Shaaber of the University of Pennsylvania (whose work on the four folios we have previously encountered), seeking their assistance with the project. Black and Shaaber edited *Richard II* and *2 Henry IV*, but were unable to dedicate sufficient time to the project to advance it much further. In 1932, the MLA became the edition's sponsor, appointing Joseph Quincy Adams of the Folger Shakespeare Library as general editor. Under this arrangement, a further six volumes appeared. By the middle decades of the twentieth century, however, the project was foundering, though it was revived in 1973, when the MLA agreed to act directly as the edition's publisher. Texts of *As You Like It*, *Measure for Measure* and *Antony and Cleopatra* appeared in 1977, 1980 and 1990 respectively. At the close of the twentieth century, the edition was being directed by the New Variorum Shakespeare Committee, membership of which included (for varying terms): Thomas L. Berger, A. R. Braunmuller, William C. Carroll, Richard Knowles, Anne Lancashire, Leah S. Marcus, Scott McMillin, Mary Beth Rose and Paul Werstine. Overseen by this committee the edition was again energetically pursued, with scholars commissioned to work on new and revised texts.

James M. Gibson has observed of Furness that he 'brought to fledgling American scholarship a new prestige and reputation during the decade of the 1870s'.[71] During the same decade, another American, William J. Rolfe, also began producing editions of Shakespeare. Where Furness' texts were aimed at an advanced scholarly audience, Rolfe's work was produced, in the first instance, with the general reader in mind. Rolfe was himself a schoolmaster and though, as Henry W. Simon has noted, his texts 'were not at first advertised as school editions . . . the qualifications of the editor and the reasonable price made them eminently fitted for careful classroom study'.[72] His 'Shakespeare for the School and Family' edition, published by Harpers, sold for 90 cents per play or for $3 per four-play volume.[73] Rolfe was, as Richard Altick has put it, 'for better or worse . . . the principal intermediary between Shakespeare and generations of bored American schoolboys' (and, we might add, schoolgirls).[74] Whether his readers were bored or not, the fact remains that Rolfe's editions, issued in various series and by different publishers over the course of about four decades, were immensely popular. One series was published under the title the 'Friendly Edition of Shakespeare' – a name suggested to the editor by Mary Cowden Clarke who, as a consequence, was dubbed by Rolfe its 'godmother'.[75] Churchill observed that

Rolfe's 'proved far the most popular edition of Shakespeare in America', noting that it could 'be found in the homes of thousands who have never seen any other edition'.[76]

The success of Rolfe's texts indicates the extent to which Shakespeare had penetrated the US high-school curriculum by the closing decades of the nineteenth century. In this same period, third-level American education was moving through a period of considerable change. Daniel Coit Gilman founded Johns Hopkins University in 1876 and, as Gerald Graff has noted, his vision for the university 'called for specialized departments and courses of study after the German pattern'.[77] Gilman's model was enormously influential and was quickly followed by many well-established American universities (and by newer institutions, such as the University of Chicago, founded in 1892). In the very same year as Hopkins was established, Harvard appointed Francis James Child to the university's first professorship in English. James Russell Lowell had lectured on Shakespeare at Harvard as early as 1863, but this had been in his capacity as Professor of Modern Languages and his lectures did not form part of the regular undergraduate curriculum.[78] In a lecture delivered to the Edinburgh Philosophical Institute in 1883, Lowell observed: 'I never open my Shakespeare but . . . I find myself wishing that there might be professorships established for the study of his works.'[79] It would be some time before chairs specifically dedicated to Shakespeare studies would be set up in the US, but in the closing decades of the century Shakespeare was certainly being taught at American universities as part of the standard curriculum – both Child and his successor at Harvard, George Lyman Kittredge, regularly gave classes on the playwright's works. It was Kittredge, Louis Marder notes, 'who made Shakespeare popular at Harvard. He had a great influence on thousands of students from 1888 to 1936.'[80] At the very end of his career, Kittredge produced his own edition of Shakespeare, published by Ginn of Boston. Kittredge had used Rolfe's texts in the classroom and some of Rolfe's punctuation was adopted by Kittredge in his own edition.[81]

Shakespeare entered the American university curriculum at a time when the academic world was becoming increasingly professionalised. Graff notes that, in 1850, there were a total of eight graduate students in the US, in all subjects. By 1875, the year before Gilman established Johns Hopkins, that figure had risen to just 399, but, by 1908, the number was almost 8,000.[82] Where Kittredge had airily dismissed the fact that he did not have a PhD by asking 'Who could have examined me?', by the turn of the century American university English departments were increasingly being staffed by professional scholars who had undergone an extended formal course of graduate training.[83] In terms of Shakespeare editing, what this meant was that the days of the erudite amateur – a Furness or a Verplanck, for example – were largely coming to an end. At the same time as the academic world became more professionalised, so too did scholarly resources begin to improve. Morris Bishop reported that 'the first President of the University of North Carolina kept the University Library in an upstairs bedroom of his house for twenty years' and the Columbia Shakespearean Brander Matthews recalled of his own undergraduate years at the university in the 1870s:

> We were not urged to use the library; indeed it might be asserted that any utilization of its few books was almost discouraged. The library was open only for one or two hours a day, after one o'clock when most of us had gone home to our luncheons. I, for one, never climbed its stairs to avail myself of its carefully guarded treasures; and I doubt if any one of my classmates was more daring in adventuring himself within its austere walls, lined with glazed cases all cautiously locked.[84]

In the following decade, however, Justin Winsor (himself a Shakespearean bibliographer of some repute) proposed a metaphorical shift from the equivalent of North Carolina's upstairs spare bedroom to a location that Matthews and his luncheoning fellows would have found more congenial: 'The library should be to the college much what the dining room is to the house – the place to invigorate the system under cheerful conditions with a generous fare and a good digestion.'[85] Winsor concluded his article by observing that the 'college library . . . is starting on a new career' and, certainly, by the closing decades of the century, such libraries were gradually becoming both more welcoming and much more highly professionalised and intellectually ambitious.[86]

At the same time as American universities were strengthening their holdings, private American book collectors were pursuing their interests ever more energetically. In the preface to his edition of Shakespeare, Richard Grant White made a point of observing that all the quotations in his edition were taken from original sources, with the exception of 'two of the earlier quartos and two or three extremely rare books, copies of which have not yet floated over to us' (§502, I, p. xxii).[87] As the nineteenth century drew to a close, the tide of early modern books floating westward across the Atlantic rose to a considerable swell and increasingly these texts began to make their way from private hands into public institutions.[88] Furness, father and son, amassed a considerable Shakespearean library which was, eventually, presented to the University of Pennsylvania. Marsden J. Perry of Rhode Island collected an impressive array of Shakespeare materials, including all four folios, a selection of early quartos, and the Edward Gwynne Pavier volume which Pollard had found so striking when he had examined it in London.[89] Perry eventually abandoned his collecting activities when he failed to obtain the Duke of Devonshire's collection of quartos, sold at auction in 1914. He was outbid on that occasion by Henry E. Huntington and, about five years later, he sold the bulk of his Shakespeare library to the Philadelphia book dealer A. S. W. Rosenbach for a reputed $500,000.[90] Rosenbach subsequently sold the cream of the collection on to Henry Clay Folger.

The names of Huntington and Folger dominate the early modern book market in the opening decades of the twentieth century. Through the activities of these two men an extraordinary array of rare books made their way across the Atlantic. In 1917, it was estimated that in the previous six years Huntington had spent about $6,000,000 on his collection. Ten years later the library (which then amounted to some 100,000 volumes) was thought to have cost Huntington in total as much as $20,000,000. Huntington turned the library over to the public in 1920 and it has served as a major scholarly resource ever since. As Carl L. Cannon observed in 1941: 'the Huntington Library ranks with the British Museum and the Bodleian in English literature before 1641 and possesses 700 unique titles or editions in that period'.[91] Folger was Huntington's great rival in the field of book collecting, though they maintained friendly relations and sometimes arrived at a gentlemen's agreement in relation to particular auction materials which both wished to purchase. Folger first became interested in the original printings of Shakespeare's plays when he bought a copy of the 1876 Halliwell–Phillipps reduced facsimile of the First Folio, published in an American edition in 1887. He was struck by the discrepancies between the First Folio text and the text of modern editions and he also developed an interest in variations between different copies of the same early edition – the result of early modern press correction procedures. It was this later interest which prompted Folger to begin amassing multiple copies of the folios, in addition to a considerable collection of the early quartos. Antony James West notes that

> in a campaign worthy of an executive who rose to the top of the Standard Oil Company, he was not satisfied to wait for copies to come on the market. True to his practice as an oil-man, he initiated exploration for them. In May 1915, he wrote to A. H. Mayhew in Charing Cross Road giving him a list of thirty-five Folio owners from Lee's *Census*. He commissioned Mayhew to write to each of them to 'ask whether his copy is for sale, and if so what value he puts on it'.[92]

The exact number of First Folios which Folger acquired is a matter of some dispute, but it possibly amounts to something in the region of eighty – about one third of all known surviving copies.[93] Like Huntington, Folger ultimately placed his collection in the public domain. The foundation stone of the Folger Shakespeare Library was laid in 1930 and Folger himself died just two weeks later. With the opening of the Folger library in Washington DC – symbolically located little more than a block away from the Capitol buildings – east-coast US early modern scholars had a facility available to them which (in Shakespearean terms at least) matched what west-coast scholars enjoyed at the Huntington. In addition, eastern scholars could also make use of the J. Pierpont Morgan library in New York City – housing a collection strong in early modern holdings and estimated, in 1934, to be worth something in the region of $17,000,000.

The increasing accumulation of early Shakespeare texts in American libraries may be reflected in a publishing programme initiated under the auspices of the New York Shakspere Society in 1888 and running through to 1908. The general editor for this project was Appleton Morgan and the initial aim of the series was to print editions of the plays which had first appeared in quarto, in parallel with their corresponding First Folio texts. A subsequent issue presented parallel reprints of restoration adaptations with their Shakespearean counterparts. The initial volumes received high praise in an article entitled 'What edition of Shakespeare shall I buy?', published first in the *Christian Union* and then reprinted in *Shakespeariana*. The reviewer lamented the 'dead wars' of rival editors, in which 'oceans of ink, if not of blood, were shed' and praised Morgan and his fellow editors for presenting an unmediated text which freed readers to make their own textual choices. In a striking anticipation of some of the claims that would be made for electronic editions at the close of the twentieth century, the reviewer observed that Morgan had 'designed a new plan of editing the great dramatist . . . viz., not to edit him at all, but to give the facts and let the reader edit for himself'.[94] The *Christian Union* was, however, excessively generous in its assessment of the project. Harrison Ross Steevens, by contrast, observed of the volumes that the 'introductions are elaborate and, as a whole, very badly proportioned. In some large claims are made, and defended out of all relation to their importance in the history of the play itself.'[95] Some of the series' editors, including Morgan himself, were also guilty of a certain amount of pseudo-antiquarian textual sleight-of-hand. Emma Smith has noted Morgan's equivocal method of presenting a translation of a German *Hamlet* source text in a way which might lead the reader to conclude that it was a lost earlier version of the play, supposedly written by Thomas Kyd:

> In 1908 Appleton Morgan introduced a parallel text of the 1604 quarto of *Hamlet* and an imagined text of the Ur-Hamlet, complete with a suitably smudged mocked-up title page bearing the date 1597. Morgan's introduction is evasive on the origins of this originary text, although he refers to *Der Bestrafie Brudermord*, arguing that 'here at last we find a vestige of the very ur-Hamlet we are searching for; and that, if we retranslate this Brudermord back into English we will arrive at a very fair conception indeed of what that required ur-Hamlet was like'. This explanation emphasises that finding the fugitive ur-text is an imperative and its discovery is 'required'. And the result of this compulsion is the Bankside-Restoration text, produced as a companion volume to another dual *Hamlet*, a parallel text of the First Quarto and Folio editions. *Hamlet* becomes a multiple play, and in the interests of completeness the full suite of *Hamlet*s must include the elusive Ur-Hamlet.

Morgan's evasiveness about the actual origins of his Ur-text *Hamlet* is compounded by the fact that he 'silently antiquated his text by mimicking a sixteenth-century use of u/v and i/j' and by printing the text in gothic lettering.[96]

   The achievements of the Bankside editors may have been less than impressive, but other American editors were, at the same time, forging ahead with genuinely valuable work. Late in life, Furness senior commented in a public lecture in Boston that the city was 'the home of two editresses (instance unprecedented in Shakespearean annals!)'.[97] The two women in question were Charlotte Porter and Helen A. Clarke. They were not the first female editors of Shakespeare (that distinction goes to Mary Cowden Clarke or, more properly – if also more dubiously – to Henrietta Bowdler), but they can be said to have been the first women not to have worked in conjunction with a male associate and their contribution to Shakespeare scholarship was indeed significant.[98] Porter had served as editor of the periodical *Shakespeariana* and, jointly with Clarke, had founded a magazine entitled *Poet Lore*, which was devoted to Shakespeare and Browning. Under the auspices of their magazine, the editors produced study guides for Shakespeare plays, issuing, in 1901, an independent volume dedicated to the study of *Macbeth*. Rolfe observed of Porter and Clarke's work in this area that 'The programmes for Shakespeare Study . . . are the best I have ever seen – indeed, they are so much superior to the others, that I know of none . . . that deserves to be counted even second to them.'[99]

In 1903, Porter and Clarke issued the twelve volume 'Pembroke Shakespeare' and in the same year, they 'embarked on a greatly elaborated First Folio edition with introductions to the plays and poems, notes, emendations and variorum readings, literary illustrations, and selected criticism, an edition which grew to 40 volumes and was completed in 1912'.[100] The editors explained the difference between their two editions in their preface to the Pembroke text:

> For those who are interested in following out a further deeper study, they have prepared the more exhaustive information and critical apparatus supplied in their 'First Folio' edition. What is given here, however, is meant to be equally sound, but a shorter cut to a like end. The same text is furnished, with other of the same advantages also, but the design has been in general to devise a slighter equipment to suit the requirements of the general reader.
>
> (§915, I, p. iii)

The impact of Porter and Clarke's editorial work is registered in the fact that Walter Raleigh, Oxford's first professor of English literature, was quite concerned about the implications their Folio Shakespeare project might have for the the First-Folio-based edition he himself was seeking to initiate at Oxford University Press. Writing to Charles Cannan at the press on 24 January, 1905, Raleigh comments: 'This is a hard business. It's exactly the book. I could do without the introductions, and the side-notes are often unnecessary and sometimes wrong. But the rest is all right, and I think, is exactly what is needed.' He concludes the letter by observing ruefully 'I don't see a way past . . . these two advanced ladies.'[101] Raleigh's collaborator on the project was David Nichol Smith, who observed of the Porter and Clarke edition that the 'disgusting thing is that there is some reason for talking about a "new and thoroughly American lead"' in Shakespeare studies.[102]

Oxford wrestled with their folio-based Shakespeare for the best part of four decades, without ever managing to bring it to publication.[103] Press correspondence from these years provides a clear indication of the rising dominance of US academics in the realm of Shakespeare studies. In March 1932, for instance, R. B. McKerrow (who had assumed editorial responsibility for the edition) wrote to Kenneth Sisam, agreeing that some sort of announcement regarding the publication of the edition should be made: 'Only "a warning notice to others", as you say, seems to be needed at the moment. But unless something is said, we are almost sure to have an American embarking on a similar edition – especially now that the Folger Library has got started.'[104] Five years later, McKerrow is again worried about the prospects that his work will be preempted by US academics:

> There is another point against too much delay. Work on the
> Shakespearian texts is now extraordinarily active in America. Already
> several points which I had made in the introductions to Henry VI and
> Richard III have been published, since I wrote them, by others who have
> come upon them independently and there is always the chance of a big
> American edition being started by a group of scholars on the lines of the
> Milton and Spenser now in progress.[105]

McKerrow's sense of foreboding was not entirely unjustified. In the second half of the twentieth century in particular, the work of American editors and textual scholars increasingly assumed an important position in Shakespeare studies. Charlton Hinman's exhaustive two-volume study of the First Folio, accompanied by his painstakingly prepared photofacsimile of the First Folio – projects which could only have been undertaken at the Folger – represent perhaps the summit of that achievement. There was a certain neat symbolism, therefore, in the fact that when Oxford University Press did finally succeed in publishing a new Shakespeare edition in 1986, the press felt it necessary, within a few years, to sell the rights to the text to the US publisher W. W. Norton, who repackaged it, with introductions commissioned from a group of American academics. This reconfiguration might well have brought a smile to those nationalistic Americans who rioted outside the Astor Place theatre in the mid-nineteenth century. From an early Puritan rejection of Shakespeare, America has come so thoroughly to embrace the playwright that a significant segment of the global Shakespeare market is currently dominated by US-based publishers.[106]

8   Nineteenth-century popular editions

As increasing numbers of American editions of Shakespeare began to appear in the nineteenth century, the Shakespeare text was also being carried to far-flung corners of the British empire. In a nice example of unconscious imperial symbolism, a copy of the 1805 Alexander Chalmers edition of Shakespeare in the collection of the National Library of Scotland has bound in as its end papers waste pages taken from a book entitled *Sketches of the History of the Hindoos*.[1] Another Shakespeare edition, published in the very next year, includes an opening 'Advertisement' which notes that 'there is no part of the British Empire, or hardly a spot inhabited by a being who can read his language, in which Shaskpeare [sic], in some garb or other may not be found' (§418, I, p. v). As Gauri Viswanathan has argued, English literature served as one of the tools of empire throughout the nineteenth century (and beyond), as colonial administrators sought to inculcate in local populations a sense of the superiority of British culture. 'As early as the 1820s', Viswanathan writes, 'when the classical curriculum still reigned supreme in England despite the strenuous efforts of some concerned critics to loosen its hold, English as the study of culture and not simply the study of language had already found a secure place in the British Indian curriculum.'[2] By the end of the century, the 'Warwick Shakespeare' was advertising itself as the edition 'now in use in most of the leading Schools, Colleges, and Universities throughout the British Empire'.[3]

A sense of the scale of the expansion of Shakespeare publishing during the course of the nineteenth century is provided by the catalogue of the Shakespeare collection held at the Central Library in Birmingham. When the catalogue was published in 1971, it was noted that the collection included some 800 separate collected works editions from the nineteenth century, roughly equating to a new complete edition every six weeks for the entire span of one hundred years.[4] But these figures almost certainly do not indicate the full extent of Shakespeare publishing in the period, since it is highly unlikely that the Birmingham collection is wholly exhaustive.[5] The extent of the proliferation of British editions is registered even as early as 1819 by the

Scottish publisher Archibald Constable, when, on issuing (in conjunction with his London partners Hurst, Robinson and Co.) a new two-volume edition, he finds it necessary to include a prefatory advertisement which acknowledges that '*Editions of Shakspeare are indeed very numerous*' and that '*the Public is supplied even to repletion*' with existing texts (§459, I, p. v). Such repletion did not, however, stop Constable's presses from turning and, as the century progressed, the rate of publication of new editions continued to increase.

Several factors contributed to the acceleration of British Shakespeare publishing over the course of the nineteenth century. As stated in chapter 6, by the late 1700s the text of Shakespeare had effectively been confirmed as being in the public domain, and so was available to any publishing firm who felt that profit might be had from producing an edition of so centrally canonical a writer. There were other developments too, however, which contributed to the multiplication of texts for domestic consumption. Three issues in particular can be identified as being of especial significance in this regard: demographic and cultural changes occurring across the century; advances in printing technology; and, lastly, but most importantly, large-scale changes in the educational culture of nineteenth-century Britain.

Taking these issues in turn, then, we can begin by saying that one of the simplest reasons for the increase in publishing in this period was the fact that the population of Britain grew very considerably during the course of the nineteenth century. Between 1801 and 1851, for example, the population almost doubled.[6] More people, in simple terms, meant more readers, and more readers required more books.[7] At the same time, a culture of reading and writing began to expand in Britain from the early decades of the century. Again: to take a simple example, the introduction of the penny post in 1839 meant that a broader spectrum of British society was drawn into literate culture. As W. B. Stephens has observed, the penny post 'led to a substantial, though gradual, increase in working-class communication via the written word'.[8] Stephens further notes that the spread of evangelical Christianity in nineteenth-century Britain also contributed both directly and indirectly to a broadening of the culture of reading. As he observes:

> Puritanical objections to the stage, concerts, music halls, cards, billiards and so on, restricted acceptable leisure activities and enhanced the attraction of reading. Strict Sabbatarianism, involving the proscription (on the one day not dominated by work) of unnecessary travel and of physical activities and other pursuits permissible on weekdays, created a seventh day on which there was little to do other than to attend church

and to peruse moral and religious literature. Such severe precepts were most readily followed by middle-class families but affected others, too, and led to widespread restrictions on Sunday leisure pursuits, apart from reading.[9]

This interpenetration of religion, morality and a culture of home reading is most clearly seen in a Shakespearean context in the career of Thomas Bowdler and his sister Henrietta. Early in his life, Thomas Bowdler (who had trained as a doctor at the universities of St Andrews and Edinburgh) attended closely to the relationship between Sabbath worship and the ready availability of suitable reading matter. His nephew (also Thomas Bowdler) tells us that the points which most engaged the doctor's attention at this time were

> the providing of accommodation at the parish church for the lower orders, and instruction for their children. With these objects in view he contributed largely to an additional gallery in the Church; and he printed a selection of chapters from the Old Testament, for the use of the Church of England Sunday School Society in Swansea, to which he prefixed an Introduction, explaining the reasons for the particular selection which he had made, but containing likewise several useful and interesting remarks on some portions both of the historical and prophetical writings.[10]

Bowdler's sister, Henrietta Maria (or Harriet, as she was known within the family) was also religiously minded. She was the anonymous author of a volume entitled *Sermons on the Doctrines and Duties of Christianity*, a popular text which ran through fifty printings in about as many years. A contemporary story relates how the Bishop of London was so impressed by the book that he wrote to the unknown author care of the publisher offering him (as he assumed) a parish in his diocese.[11] At some point early in the century Harriet seems to have recognised that there were many people who might in time come to crave reading matter which extended beyond selected Bible chapters and pious sermons. While Shakespeare might well serve in this regard, it being 'universally acknowledged, that few authors are so instructive as SHAKESPEARE', nevertheless, there was a great deal in the playwright's work which, she felt, must give any religiously minded person pause, the plays containing 'much that is vulgar, and much that is indelicate', with Shakespeare, 'in compliance with the taste of the age in which he lived [inserting] some things which ought to be wholly omitted' (§422, I, p. vi). Harriet thus turned from sermonising to editing, producing a text of Shakespeare in which 'the various beauties of this writer' were 'unmixed with any thing that can raise a blush on the cheek of modesty' (§422, I, p. vii). Some seventeen plays seem to have fallen outside the circle of what the cheek of modesty could in any way bear without embarrassed colouring: *Antony and Cleopatra, All's Well that Ends Well, Coriolanus, The Comedy of Errors, Love's Labours Lost, Measure for Measure, Romeo and Juliet, The Taming of the Shrew, Two Gentlemen of Verona, Pericles, Timon of Athens, Titus Andronicus, Troilus and Cressida, The Merry Wives of Windsor* and the three parts of *Henry VI* were all wholly excluded from Harriet Bowdler's edition.

Harriet's Shakespearean venture was sufficiently successful to warrant a new edition just over a decade later. At this point, her brother (who had retired from medicine on inheriting their father's wealth) took over the role of editor, reworking Harriet's original twenty plays and adding a further sixteen. *Measure for Measure* defied his best efforts at an expurgatory cure and he substituted in its place the text of an acting version prepared in 1789 by John Philip Kemble.[12] The base text which Bowdler used was the 1813 Johnson–Steevens–Reed edition, but the doctor indicated a brisk lack of interest in textual matters, observing in his introduction that he did not 'presume to enter into any critical disputes as to certain readings of *Judean*, or *Indian*; *May*, or *Way of Life*; or any thing of that nature' (§453, I, p. xi). Within just two years, another new edition of the text was called for and, at this point, some of the major critical journals began to notice the publication. *Blackwood's Magazine* panned the edition, dismissing it as 'that piece of prudery in pasteboard'.[13] *Blackwood's* great rival at the time was Constable's *Edinburgh Review* and, as Noel Perrin has observed, 'What *Blackwood's* damned, the *Edinburgh* was apt to praise.'[14] The *Edinburgh's* review indicates neatly the extent to which Bowdler's edition had tapped into a growing vogue for family reading:

> Now it is quite undeniable, that there are many passages in Shakespeare, which a father could not read aloud to his children – a brother to his sister – or a gentleman to a lady: – and every one almost must have felt or witnessed the extreme awkwardness, and even distress, that arises from suddenly stumbling upon such expressions, when it is almost too late to avoid them, and when the readiest wit cannot suggest any paraphrase, which shall not betray, by its harshness, the embarrassment from which it has arisen. Those who recollect such scenes, must all rejoice, we should think, that Mr Bowdler has provided a security against their recurrence; and, as what cannot be pronounced in decent company cannot well afford much pleasure in the closet, we think it better, every way, that what cannot be spoken, and ought not to have been written, should now cease to be printed.[15]

While the *Edinburgh* was fulsome in its praise, the *British Critic* sided with *Blackwood's*, accusing Bowdler of having 'purged and castrated' Shakespeare, 'tattooed and be-plaistered him, and cauterized and phlebotomized him'.[16] Bowdler responded to the *Critic's* review in an open letter issued as a pamphlet, in which he observes, with what might seem like characteristic prudery, that in certain of Shakespeare plays 'some words are to be found, which are so indecent that if the Reviewer should dare to read them aloud in a company of virtuous women, he would be (or should deserve to be) immediately ordered to quit the apartment'. Later in his defence, however, Bowdler makes the point that he has simply 'done for the library what the manager does for the theatre'.[17] Bowdler has been much pilloried for his high-handed pietistic treatment of the text. It is worth remembering, however, that the context of his work was, as we have seen, precisely that of the family reading circle – a context recognised by the *Edinburgh Review*, whose one criticism of the edition was that the type was a touch too small: 'For we rather suspect, from some casual experiments of our own, that few *papas* will be able to read this, in a winter evening to their children, without the undramatic aid of spectacles.'[18] It is in the same context that Charles and Mary Cowden Clarke – both of them serious Shakespeare scholars – agreed to produce an expurgated edition for Cassell's. In the introduction to their edition, they fondly – if a touch paternalistically – imagine a domestic scene with 'the father, perhaps, reading to the rest while they pursued their several occupations; the mother and girls at their sewing; the boys with their slate or their sketching' (§595, I, p. ix).[19] Viewed in this light, Bowdler's work might be compared to the self-imposed watersheds and language regulations of modern network broadcasters, or their policy of re-editing cinema films for television transmission. Anyone who has watched British television late at night and has been solemnly warned that 'the following programme contains scenes of a sexual nature and strong language from the start and throughout' must know that Thomas Bowdler was not some sort of quaintly exceptional Victorian type.[20]

The Bowdler text was enormously successful and ran through at least twenty editions over the course of the nineteenth century. The venture prompted a wide array of alternative expurgated texts so that, by the closing decades of the century, as Noel Perrin has noted, 'Every major American publisher had a house Shakespeare expurgator ... just as every major English publisher had one.'[21] Many succeeding expurgators felt that the doctor and his sister had not gone far enough in their texts and so produced editions which were even more rigorously purged. Lewis Carroll, for instance, observed of Bowdler's edition that 'looking through it, I am filled with a deep sense of wonder, considering what he has left in, that he should have cut anything out!' Carroll worked intermittently at his own expurgated edition which he intended to publish under the title *The Girl's Own Shakespeare* – a text which was, however, never brought to print.[22]

If demographic and cultural changes served to expand the market for reading materials in the nineteenth century, it was advances in printing technology that made it possible for this market to be served more readily and, crucially, more cheaply. We have already seen in the previous chapter that, from the beginning of the century, stereotype printing greatly facilitated the production of multiple editions from a single setting of type. By 1814, printers were beginning to experiment with steam presses, with Thomas Bensley (who printed a number of Shakespeare editions) installing at his works a steam-driven machine which had been made for him by Frederick Koenig.[23] By the 1830s hand-operated machines were routinely being replaced by steam presses. In the same decade, the principle of machine manufacture was successfully applied to papermaking, and in 1837 an automated paper mill was established in Hertfordshire, with Isambard Kingdom Brunel characterising the machinery used there as 'one of the most splendid inventions of our age'.[24] By Brunel's account, the Hertfordshire plant could turn out 1,600 miles of paper a day. By the mid-century, attempts were being made to find ways of using machines in the manufacturing of type itself. In 1851, the French inventor, Pouchée demonstrated a typecasting machine at the Great Exhibition in London. Subsequently running into financial difficulty, Pouchée sold his machine to a Covent Garden printer for £100. What Pouchée did not know, sadly, was that this printer was merely a frontman, acting for a syndicate of type-founders, who promptly arranged to have the machine taken out to sea and dumped overboard. Despite the best efforts of machine-wrecking print workers, however, the general trend within the industry was towards greater levels of automation and concomitant reductions in cost. At the same time as these technological developments were moving rapidly forward, experiments were begun to attempt to find an alternative to rags as the basic raw material for paper manufacture. The first recourse of the industry was to woodpulp, but by 1857 Thomas Routledge was successfully experimenting with the use of esparto grass, imported from Spain and North Africa. Marjorie Plant has noted that the success of this material 'was almost phenomenal'.[25] By the second half of the century, the share of paper in the total cost of book production dropped from about 66 per cent to about 10 per cent, aided in part by a relaxing of the heavy duties traditionally imposed on paper.[26]

In *Shakespeare-Characters*, Charles Cowden Clarke observed that 'if Shakespeare could come among us again in the flesh . . . he would be among the first to appreciate the *great* qualities of our age of practical and mechanical science. He would never have thought disdainfully, even slightingly, of our machinery.' 'What superb things', Clarke writes, 'would he not have uttered upon our steam-enginery! How he would have glorified our locomotive power, surrounding all with the gorgeous hues of his imagination, adding beauty to utility.'[27] If a nineteenth-century Shakespeare would have glorified and celebrated the rise of enginery, he would, in a sense, simply have been repaying the machine for having contributed to his own greater glorification over the course of that century. For example, one secondary benefit of the rapid technological advances achieved by the printing industry was that from the early 1800s the production costs for publishing lavishly illustrated editions were greatly reduced. We have already noted that Rowe's 1709 text was the first Shakespeare edition to include a substantial number of illustrations. The most ambitious illustrated Shakespeare of the eighteenth century was, however, the text issued by John Boydell in eighteen parts between 1791 and 1802. Boydell's project was remarkable in its scope. Anxious to promote an English school of historical painting, the London alderman and print dealer commissioned a series of pictures on Shakespearean subjects from some of the leading artists of his day. Extraordinary sums of money were expended on the project; rejected twice by Joshua Reynolds (then president of the Royal Academy), for instance, Boydell is said to have visited Reynolds a third time, bringing with him £500 in cash, which he 'put . . . on the table, [telling] Reynolds that this was an advance, and that he was willing to meet any price the painter would choose to name'.[28] The paintings were put on display in a gallery on Pall Mall and the images were engraved for a lavish *Collection of Prints, from Pictures Painted for the Purpose of Illustrating the Dramatic Works of Shakespeare*. A smaller-scale set of engraved images were produced for inclusion in a new Steevens folio edition of the plays, which sold for £37 16s.[29] Not surprisingly, given the scale of the enterprise, the project brought financial ruin on Boydell. The alderman appealed to parliament for permission to hold a lottery to recoup his losses and the appropriate piece of legislation granting his request was drawn up on 23 March 1804.[30] The grand prize in the lottery consisted of the complete set of paintings, together with the unexpired lease on the gallery. The lottery was a resounding financial success, but John Boydell died before the prize draw took place and the proceeds came to his nephew and business partner, Josiah Boydell.

If Boydell's extravagant project was an expensive failure, it nevertheless set a fashion for lavishly illustrated editions, many of which took their bearings from the original Boydell prints. As printing technology developed, publishers were increasingly able to offer such editions at a fraction of Boydell's original price. Just five years after the last part of the Boydell–Steevens edition was issued, Thomas Bensley produced a text for Stockdale which broadly mimicked the earlier edition, but which reduced the format from folio to the cheaper imperial quarto.[31] In 1832–4 A. J. Valpy issued a fifteen-volume set, for which the illustrations were 'drawn from the one hundred and seventy plates in Boydell's edition' (§480, I, p. vi) and he specifically foregrounded the fact that, at 5s. per volume (a total cost of £3 15s.), this edition was far cheaper than Boydell's original.[32] At the close of the same decade, Charles Knight began issuing his 'Pictorial Edition of Shakspeare'. This text was published in fifty-six parts and it included, in total, not a 'hundred and seventy plates', but almost 1,000 illustrations.[33] In contrast to Valpy, Knight set his artistic sights against the precedent which Boydell had established, as he explains in *Passages of a Working Life*:

> In 1837 I began to look about me for artistic materials adapted to a
> Pictorial Edition of Shakspere. At first view, the existing stores of
> illustrations seemed almost boundless. There were embellishments to
> various editions from the time of Rowe, chiefly of a theatrical character,
> and, for the most part, thoroughly unnatural. The grand historical
> pictures of the Shakspere Gallery were not in a very much higher taste,
> furnishing a remarkable example of how painters of the highest rank in
> their day had contrived to make the characters of Shakspere little more
> than vehicles for the display of false costume.[34]

Knight's aim, by contrast, was that his illustrations should represent

> the REALITIES *upon which the imagination of the poet must have rested.*
> Of the Pictorial Illustrations many, of course, ought to be purely
> antiquarian; – but the larger number of subjects offer a combination of
> the beautiful with the real, which must heighten the pleasure of the
> reader far more than any fanciful representation, however skilful, of the
> incidents of the several dramas.[35]

Like Valpy, Knight was able to offer his lavishly illustrated edition for sale at a price much lower than Boydell's. The Pictorial Edition sold for 2s. 6d. per part, giving a total price of £7. Knight claimed that sales of the text had 'far exceeded that of any edition of Shakspere ever published'.[36] A commentator in the *Dublin Review* observed of the edition that it was 'unquestionably the best of its kind . . . [an edition] we could show to a foreigner without blush'.[37] In 1843, a three-volume Shakespeare edited by Barry Cornwall, with designs by Kenny Meadows, matched Knight's record of offering the public almost 1,000 illustrations. Both editors were then surpassed in their turn by Charles and Mary Cowden Clarke, in their 1864–9 illustrated text, described by Richard Altick as 'probably the most sumptuous edition of Shakespeare ever prepared for the popular market'.[38] The Clarkes recalled their own 'childhood delight in a picture-book and story-book in one', and pleasurably anticipated 'the joy that young readers of the present edition must feel in finding a picture at every other page' (§595, I, p. xv).

Charles Cowden Clarke described the 1860s Cassell's edition as 'a positive wonder of cheapness' and it was, in fact, in this decade that the economies effected in the printing process over the course of the first half of the century began to be reflected more generally in edition prices, which were, by the final decades of the century, truly a matter of wonder, as the cost of one-volume collected Shakespeares in particular rapidly declined.[39] Perhaps the first publisher to realise the potential for an inexpensive single-volume edition was Alexander Macmillan, a Scot who had come to London in 1839 and who had set up a publishing business with his brother Daniel. One of the firm's earliest publications was William Hugh Miller's *The Three Questions: What am I? Whence came I? Whither do I go?*[40] Later publications would be altogether less esoteric and Alexander Macmillan seems to have had a pretty sound sense of how, as a businessman, he might himself answer Miller's three questions. By the 1860s, Macmillans had formed an alliance with Cambridge University Press and the 'Cambridge Shakespeare' was being edited for the Scottish-led firm by Cambridge scholars and was being printed for them by the university press. This monumental scholarly edition will be discussed in some detail in chapter nine, but the present point of interest of the project is the fact that, while the Cambridge was underway, Macmillan thought of turning the editorial team's attention in a different direction. On 24 May 1864, he wrote to his close friend, the Glasgow publisher James MacLehose, seeking his advice and asking that the letter be treated in the strictest confidence:

> I enclose a page for a *Shakespeare*, which I fancy doing in one volume, on toned paper for 3s. 6d., very nicely bound in Macmillan's choicest cloth binding. The text to be gone over by our Cambridge editors, but done in this edition with an eye to more popular uses than they felt themselves at liberty to consider in their critical and scholarly edition. Now your judgment is always as you know precious to me, even when I cannot quite follow it. I want you to tell me whether you think I have a reasonable chance of selling 50,000 of such a book in three years. For if so I can do a

> nice stroke of business. You see it would be immeasurably the cheapest,
> most beautiful and handy book that has appeared of *any kind*, except the
> Bible.[41]

What Macmillan was proposing to MacLehose was the 'Globe
Shakespeare'.[42] The Cambridge editors objected to the name, arguing that
'"Hand Shakespeare" is much better than "Globe do", which we don't like. It
sounds claptrappy.'[43] But Macmillan understood very clearly the resonances
of the name and had a strong sense of the effect he was aiming at. '*Hand
Shakespeare* has rather a tame, ineffective sound to my ears', he responded,
'I want to give the idea that we aim at great popularity – that we are doing
this book for the *million*, without saying it. If our notion had been a very
elegant and compact edition for the swells, I would have printed it on more
expensive paper and sold it for 7s. 6d., or even more.'[44] Macmillan conceived
of the Globe as 'an edition of Shakespeare which every Englishman of the
tolerably educated classes, from the intelligent mechanic to the peer of the
realm, might gladly possess. It is fine enough for the latter, and cheap enough
for the former.'[45]

In due course *The Bookseller* advertised the Globe as a forthcoming publication, noting that

> with regard to the typography, and the paper and binding, nothing better
> could be wished, even if the published price were a guinea. The price
> announced is 3s. 6d., and we have little doubt that large numbers of
> buyers will be found, who will purchase their six or eight copies for the
> purpose of placing one in every room in their house. Taking into
> consideration the value of the text, the care taken in the production of the
> edition, and the handsome appearance of the book, there can be no
> question about its being the cheapest and best one volume Shakspeare
> ever produced.[46]

The Bookseller was probably being just a touch optimistic in imagining that
the public would go out and buy multiple copies of the Globe, just so that they
could have a complete Shakespeare to hand wherever they went about the
house. Nevertheless, sales did exceed Alexander Macmillan's expectations.
While he aimed, as we have seen, to sell 50,000 copies of the book in three
years, in fact, by 1867, the Globe had reached its fifth edition, with each
printrun amounting to 20,000 copies. So, in effect, the Globe outran expectation by a factor of two-to-one. And it continued to sell. The last edition of
the text would appear to have been produced in 1911, at which point the total
number of copies issued amounted to 244,000.[47] In addition to this, the text –
like the Johnson–Steevens–Reed edition – spawned an enormous number
of offspring, with the Globe forming the basis for a very great number of

reprint editions. The centrality of the Globe was also reinforced by the fact that many high-profile scholars standardised their Shakespeare references to the edition's line numbers. Thus, in 1877, Edward Dowden writes to Macmillans regarding one of his books: 'Don't you think a note on page 1 to this effect would be right:- The references to Act, scene & line, through-out, are to the Globe Shakespeare' and A. C. Bradley writes to the press in 1899, regarding his *Shakespearean Tragedy*, 'I will refer to the pages and columns of the Globe edition when I find it necessary to use passages from the plays.'[48]

Where Macmillan led, others quickly followed. On the second of November 1866, Alexander wrote to Globe co-editor William Aldis Wright, asking: 'Have you seen that beast Routledge: imitation, shameless imitation. He calls it the Blackfriars – it should be the Blackguard.'[49] In response to the Globe, George Routledge had issued a one-volume Shakespeare 'crown 8vo, green cloth, beautifully printed on toned paper' – the same general format as Macmillan's – which he priced at 3s. 6d. retail (the same as the Globe), but sold at 2s. 6d. wholesale, undercutting Macmillans by a penny per copy.[50] The Blackfriars was, however, the least of Macmillan's wor-ries. In October of the same year, the publisher had written to Wright ask-ing him with some astonishment: 'Have you seen the shilling Shakespeare? There are to be two – one is done – the old two shilling one on straw pa-per by Dicks and [that announced] through Warne.' Macmillan indicates that he has consulted with the Cambridge University Press printer, Clay, on the logistics of producing so cheap an edition, but has concluded that 'we cannot do it'.[51] What Macmillan and Clay could not do was quickly accomplished by not two, but three publishers, one of them being – pre-dictably, Macmillan might have thought – George Routledge. Routledge, John Dicks and Frederick Warne all had shilling Shakespeares on the mar-ket by 1868. The wholesale price of Routledge's edition was just $8\frac{1}{2}d.$, but *The Bookseller* was fulsome in its praise of the quality of the text, describ-ing it as 'a wonderful specimen of the art of typography and a marvel of cheapness'.[52]

The most successful of the three competing shilling Shakespeares was, undoubtedly, that produced by John Dicks, of which *The Bookseller* observed that it 'is perhaps the most wonderful edition yet published'.[53] The journal was so impressed that the editor wrote to Dicks to ask about the history of the text. Dicks replied:

> The 300th birthday of Shakspere first gave me the idea of issuing two plays for one penny, of which I sold about 150,000; on completion of the work, I published it in a complete volume, bound in cloth, price 2s., of

> which I sold 50,000 copies. Having achieved a great success, I decided
> upon issuing a 'Shilling Shakspere' . . . I immediately issued my 2*s*.
> edition for 1*s*, sewed in a wrapper, of which I have sold about 700,000
> copies in all, up to this time.[54]

Dicks' sales of some 700,000 copies of his cheap edition in the space of about
two years might be contrasted with the figures for the Globe, which, as we
have seen, sold about a third of this amount in the space of roughly half
a century. Even Dicks, however, did not manage to produce the cheapest
Shakespeare edition of the Victorian era. That honour would appear to go
to Ward and Lock, who published a 6*d*. Shakespeare in 1890.

Many of the cheapest editions of Shakespeare achieved their low cost by
selling advertising space in their endpapers. Dicks' edition, for example, includes adverts for Brown's Bronchial Troches, Blair's Gout and Rheumatic
Pills, Mr Francois's artificial teeth and Whight and Mann sewing machines.
Editions included in Cassell's National Library offer adverts for Schweitzer's
Cocoatina, Barber & Company's French Coffee and (appropriately, perhaps,
opposite the final page of *King Lear*), 'Neave's Food for Infants, Invalids,
Growing Children, and the Aged'.[55] By the closing decade of the century, this
practice was common enough to be the subject of parody in the *Gentleman's
Magazine*. A wonderfully witty piece entitled 'The Advertiser's Shakespeare'
appeared in the journal in March 1893, written by Edmund B. V. Christian.
Christian's bogus prospectus burlesques not only contemporary publishing
practice, but also the stone-faced absurdities of many serious editorial pro-
nouncements. Thus, for example, the prospectus purports to solve one of
the greatest Shakespearean mysteries of all time, informing the reader that
'it will be demonstrated that "Mr. W. H." was not, as has been supposed,
the Earl of Pembroke or the Earl of Southampton, but William Hurlbatt,
the great advertising shopkeeper of Shakespeare's time'. Hurlbatt, it seems,
employed Shakespeare 'to write to order plays and verses to advertise his
wares', but the advertisements have, 'owing to the carelessness of the printers
of the Folio' been omitted from the received text.[56] The prospectus gives numerous examples of the original text, as it will be restored in the Advertiser's
edition, including the following:

> King Stephen was a worthy peer,
> His breeches cost him but a crown;
> He said, 'I' faith, they are not dear;
> I bought them, certes, in London town,
> At M. N. O's shop, which is down
> By Houndsditch way.

* * *

Fear no more the heat of the sun,
  Nor the furious winter's rages;
Thou thy J-----r hast put on,
  Light, yet warm, it suits all ages;
When thy weekly task is done,
  That's the place to spend thy wages.[57]

By the latter half of the nineteenth century, then, a mass market for editions of Shakespeare had opened up and this market was being served by a great multiplicity of cheap texts. The fact that these editions sold in such great quantities is a clear indication that, by the later 1800s, the size of the reading public had expanded very considerably over the course of the century. We have already examined some of the factors which served to fuel this expansion, including general population growth and a nineteenth-century domestic culture of home reading. However, the greatest single contribution to the broadening of the reading public came from the extension of the educational franchise over the course of the century. A secondary consequence of this extension, in a Shakespearean context, was the assimilation of Shakespeare's works directly into the school curriculum, which generated its own particular publishing effect.

In the opening decades of the nineteenth century Britain lacked a formalised national school system. While the government did attempt some educational initiatives in the first half of the century, these schemes were largely ineffective. Richard Altick notes, for instance, that the Factory Act of 1833 was one of the first pieces of legislation in which the provisions 'were anything more than a dead letter from the outset' and which 'resulted in the setting up of school facilities in many factories, to which children of a certain age were required to repair two hours a day'. However, as Altick further notes, 'since the "schoolrooms" were often coal holes, and the "teachers" were firemen or equally unqualified persons, the children could hardly have received much more benefit than a change of occupation and an opportunity to sit down'.[58] In the first half of the century, then, educational initiatives were for the most part carried forward by non-governmental agencies. Chief among these was the Church of England, which established a widening network of schools from the beginning of the century onwards, under the auspices of the National Society for Promoting the Education of the Poor in the Principles of the Established Church.[59] The dominance of the established church in the field of education was challenged by two different groups: religious dissenters (broadly defined) and Benthamite Utilitarians. The British and Foreign School Society (originally established in 1808), though non-denominational, tended to attract dissenters, since the National

Society was Anglican. Competition between the National Society and the British and Foreign School Society helped to accelerate the rate at which schools multiplied in the early part of the century. As W. B. Stephens has observed:

> in 1814, the Bishop of London proclaimed that 'Every populous village unprovided with a National School must be regarded as a stronghold abandoned to the enemy' (that is the non-conformists), while a midlands vicar described British schools as 'dreadful machines', 'full fraught with moral and religious evil to Church and Country'. In Bristol rival Church and dissenting schools existed side by side, each hopefully 'built to empty [the schools] of other . . . denominations'.[60]

While Anglicans and dissenters vied with each other in establishing educational footholds throughout the country, Utilitarians, as Stephens has noted, 'were very active in parliament', where they campaigned for 'universal, free and secular state-provided elementary schools for the working classes'.[61] At the same time, they also launched educational schemes of their own. Principal among their initiatives was the Society for the Diffusion of Useful Knowledge (SDUK), which sponsored two publishing projects: the Library of Useful Knowledge (from 1827, in 6*d*. fortnightly parts) and the Library of Entertaining Knowledge (from 1829, in 2*s*. parts or at 4*s*. 6*d*. per volume).[62] Charles Knight served as publisher for many of the society's titles and he observed of them that they 'were to be manuals for self-education – clear, accurate, but not to be mastered without diligence and perseverance'.[63] As Knight's description makes clear, the SDUK's publications had a rather grimly Puritanical cast to them – the 'Entertaining Knowledge' series ran to such titles as *Insect Architecture*, *Secret Societies of the Middle Ages* and the three volumes of *Vegetable Substances*. Richard Altick has wryly observed that the series 'demonstrates that "entertaining" is a relative term'.[64] The SDUK did, however, serve an important function in revealing to commercial publishers the growing market which was opening up for moderately priced publications. By the time the society was disbanded, in 1846, many major publishers had initiated series dedicated to issuing cheap reprint editions of standard classics.[65] Thus, in September 1830, the *Athenæum*, in reviewing the inaugural volume of the 'Edinburgh Cabinet Library', was already indicating a certain wariness (and weariness) of the rate at which such series were proliferating:

> Well done Edinburgh! well done Messrs. Oliver & Boyd! – This is a worthy and welcome volume. Our satisfaction has been the greater, from the fear and trembling with which we first heard the series

announced. Another Library! – We have loathed the very name since
we waded through the National and the Juvenile, and feared we
should never again relish even Murray's delightful volumes as we were
wont.[66]

Charles Knight himself responded to the growing market which had been
opened up for popular publishing by issuing his own 'Stratford Shakespeare'
(1854–6), which he intended for 'The People', explaining that 'using this
term with reference to literature, I understand, chiefly, that vast aggregate
of persons who have become readers of books during the last quarter of a
century' (§497, I, p. ix). The objective of the Stratford edition was, Knight
asserts, to keep alive the spirit of Shakespeare's noble intelligence, 'to diffuse
it through every corner of the land; to make its light penetrate into the
humblest cottage; to mould even the lisping accents of the child to the
utterance of its words' (§497, I, p. ix).

We have already seen that, in the first half of the nineteenth century,
popular education was largely the province of non-governmental agencies.
These agencies received an increasing amount of financial support from
the government as the century progressed. By 1861, Palmerston's government was allocating £813,441 towards the support of education (a figure
dwarfed, however, by his military budget of £26,000,000). The extent of
education spending prompted the government to seek greater accountabil-
ity from schools and the 'Revised Code' of 1862 instituted an examination
process tied to a system of 'payment by results'. Robert Lowe, who was
responsible for the introduction of the scheme commented that, whereas
previously, 'we have been living under a system of bounties and protection;
now we propose to have a little free trade'.[67] John Roach has observed that
'Public examinations were one of the great discoveries of nineteenth-century
Englishmen. Almost unknown at the beginning of the century, they rapidly
became a major tool of social policy.'[68] The Revised Code followed, in fact,
in the tracks of several other examination schemes. British recruitment for
the Indian civil service was carried out by public examination from 1855 and
English literature formed a component of that examination programme from
the start.[69] Before the end of the decade, Oxford and Cambridge universities had been persuaded to institute a scheme of standard examinations for
secondary-level school students. Writing at the beginning of the twentieth
century, John D. Jones observed that

> The regular and systematic study of Shakespeare in English schools
> began with the establishment of these examinations. His plays were put
> among their subjects and thus found their way into schools in which their

position has been ever since growing stronger. One play has been a
subject of the Cambridge Senior and the Oxford Examination since 1858;
of the Cambridge Higher Local since 1872 and of the Junior since 1873.[70]

The incorporation of English literature in general and of Shakespeare in
particular into the educational and examination system was doubtless seen
in some quarters as little more than a pragmatic means to an end: as the
educational franchise continued to be extended, quizzing school children on
Shakespeare provided as convenient a means as any of assessing and ranking
students. For others, however, incorporating literary texts into the curriculum served a more serious cultural function. The Schools Inquiry Commis-
sion, set up under Lord Taunton in 1864 (a resonant year for Shakespeareans)
concluded its report by observing that the teaching of English literature
ought to 'kindle a living interest in the learner's mind . . . make him feel the
force and beauty of which the language is capable [and] refine and elevate
his taste'. If literature were taught in this spirit, the student would 'probably
return to it when the days of boyhood were over' and such students 'would
be very likely to continue to read Shakespeare and Milton throughout their
lives'.[71] Perhaps it was from the ranks of such cultivated former students
that John Dicks' 700,000 shilling Shakespeare customers were drawn.

If the educational system served to create a reader-base for the mass-
market commercial production of Shakespeare editions, it also prompted its
own particular publishing phenomenon. As early as 1822, the Reverend J. R.
Pitman edited a volume entitled *The School-Shakespeare; or, plays and scenes
from Shakespeare, illustrated for the use of schools, with glossarial notes, selected
from the best annotators*. Pitman's was a heavily expurgated text which included twenty-six 'complete' plays, with selected passages from nine others.
The editor observed of his volume that 'pupils may here peruse as much
of Shakspeare, as is compatible with other objects of study' (§473, p. v). As
the reading of Shakespeare became more formalised with the introduction
of standard examinations, a new genre of Shakespeare publishing emerged
in the form of editions specifically catering for the schools and examinations
market. An early example of such texts is an edition of *Henry VIII*, which
identifies its target audience as follows: 'The immediate purpose of this publication is to guide and assist young persons qualifying for the Middle-Class
Examinations, – the Henry VIII. of Shakspeare being one of the prescribed
subjects of the Oxford Examination for Midsummer 1860' (§510, 'Advertisement', p. iii). This edition could almost serve as a template for the great
wash of school Shakespeares which followed in its wake. The editor was the
Reverend John Hunter, MA, whose qualifications for the task in hand are
prominently indicated on the title page: 'Instructor of Candidates for the

Military and Civil Service Examinations, &c.; and formerly Vice-Principal of the National Society's Training Institution, Battersea'. Many later such texts would parade their editors' Oxbridge degrees and masterships at public schools on their title pages.[72] The concluding pages of Hunter's edition consist of 'Examination questions (partially answered) on passages from Henry the Eighth' (p. 169). This section of the volume includes a short quotation from the play, followed by questions such as the following:

i. Write a brief sketch of the life of Cardinal Wolsey.
ii. Give some account of the Duke of Buckingham.
iii. What figure of speech is here exemplified by the word *gold*?
iv. Explain the figurative meanings of *spanned* and *shadow*; and the force of the expressions *already*, *this instant*, and *clear*.
v. Of the forty-two words in this passage . . . how many are of Latin origin? Explain the derivation of these. What proportion of Shakspeare's English is not Saxon?
vi. Parse the passage by the ordinary or etymological method.
vii. Parse it syntactically.

The extent of the schools Shakespeare market is clearly indicated by Walter Low's catalogues of educational textbooks, published in 1871 and 1876. In the preface to the first of these catalogues, Low indicates his hope that his listing 'may prove useful to those who are battling with man's terribly aggressive foe, *Ignorance*, pointing out, as the catalogue does, the materials obtainable for carrying on the warfare'.[73] The Shakespeare entry for this first catalogue runs to:

Shakespeare's Separate Plays. 12mo. each 1 0 [i.e., 1s] Chambers
— Select Plays, Prof Brewer's Series, ed. Clark & Wright: Merchant of Venice. 12mo. 1s.; Richard II. and Macbeth. (Clarendon) each 1 6 Macmillan
— Macbeth, W. S. Dalgleish. 12mo. 1 6 Nelson
— Fifteen Select Plays, ed. J. Hunter. 12mo each 1 0 Longmans
— for Schools, edited C. Lenny. 12mo 2 6 Relfe
— The Prince's, Selections by D. Mathias. V.1 Cr. 8vo 6 0 Bentley
— Poems. 12mo. 1 0 Warne
— Classified Selections, T. Price. 12mo. 5 0 Simpkin
— Richard II. ed. H. G. Robinson. 12mo 2 0 Oliver & B.[74]

To these editions, the 1876 catalogue adds the *Household* edition (ten vols., 30s.); select plays published by Collins (including, rather arrestingly, an edition of *Richard I*); and the Rugby edition.[75]

The enduring market value of these schools Shakespeare editions can be seen by briefly looking at the extended history of two of them: Oxford

University Press's *Clarendon* series, edited primarily by William Aldis Wright and the *Pitt Press* series, edited for Cambridge University Press by A. W. Verity. In October 1863, Alexander Macmillan wrote to Wright, asking whether he could tell him of 'some one who would do me a nice popular edition of the "Tempest" for school use', providing 'a little such talk as a school boy might require'. He concluded the enquiry by asking: 'Would it not amuse yourself? Likewise be practice for higher work?'[76] Wright would not appear to have taken up the offer on this occasion, but the growing importance of the educational market seems to have remained in the forefront of Macmillan's mind. In March 1865, he wrote to Wright's Cambridge and Globe co-editor, William Clark, informing him that Charles Wordsworth, the Bishop of St Andrews, had written seeking permission to use the Globe edition 'in making a selection from Shakespeare for use in schools'. Macmillan had agreed to the request and he observed in passing that it 'is to be noted that by degrees English Literature may become a more important part of English education, and if so it would be of great consequence that really scholarly editions should be prepared for [the use of students]'.[77] By the late 1860s, the last volume of the Cambridge edition had appeared in print and Wright and Clark had committed themselves to producing the high-quality schools edition that Macmillan envisaged, for Oxford University Press. They again worked under Macmillan's direction, as he was closely involved with the Oxford press, as well as with its Cambridge counterpart. The first volume of the *Clarendon* series appeared in 1868 and Wright and Clark co-edited the first four texts, with Wright carrying on alone after Clark became incapacitated from 1871. It would appear to have taken a little time for the editors to settle on the correct pitch for the edition. In January 1869, Macmillan wrote to Wright, requesting revision in some of the materials already prepared:

> you must approach the whole thing in a different way from what you have. To secure a large sale you must adapt yourself to a large audience. You must speak the <u>wide</u> language, if you want wide sale. Set up in the marketplace & speak Arabic & see how many will hear you. I am willing to [learn?] to any extent you like. Be you the same.[78]

Wright's reply to this was rather brisk:

> What <u>do</u> you mean about speaking the wide language, talking Arabic in the marketplace, and all that? Are our notes on the Merchant of Venice & Richard the Second unintelligible, or not incoherent [sic] enough, or too brief, or have we omitted to explain anything or what? . . . We are not above learning, only do tell us what you mean by approaching the whole thing in a different way from what we have done.[79]

These early difficulties notwithstanding, the series achieved a very high level of success. The *Clarendon Macbeth*, for instance, was first issued in August 1869; by 1901 it had run through twenty-two editions and a further 10,000 copies were printed. In October 1907, total sales had reached 107,738 and another printrun (of 4,000 copies) was ordered.[80] *Julius Caesar* first appeared in April 1878 and had run to 148,310 copies by 1905.[81] In its most successful years, the series generated an income for Wright of 'as much as £1000 per annum'.[82] The books even continued to provide a modest income for Wright's heirs for several decades after his death. As late as 1931, Oxford was negotiating with Mrs Jane Evans Wright, seeking to reconfigure the royalty payments for the series. Mrs Wright agreed to a straight payment of 6*d*. per 100 books sold.[83] By the end of the 1930s, the press was beginning to think about winding down the series, as sales had dwindled very considerably.[84] By this point, the best-selling title was *1 Henry IV*, but it was averaging only 200 copies a year; *Coriolanus*, at the other end of the scale, was managing an average of just ten copies annually.[85] Despite the series' declining fortunes, it was laid to rest in a rather gentle manner. *Richard II* remained in print until 1944; *Lear* held on until 1949; *Macbeth* survived to 1950; and *Midsummer Night's Dream* finally closed out the series on 16 August 1955, when a press memo indicated: 'We are wasting our stock so will you please embulletin as out of print.' At this point, the series had been on the market for eighty-seven years.[86]

A similar extended lifespan was enjoyed by Cambridge's rival series to the *Clarendon*, the *Pitt Press Shakespeare*, edited by A. W. Verity. Verity's numbers were even more impressive than Wright's. The *Pitt Press Midsummer Night's Dream*, for example, was first issued in 1893, with an inaugural printrun of 5,000 copies. Details for subsequent printruns up to 1936 are provided in table 8.1.[87] As this table indicates, by this year, the text was already pushing towards a quarter of a million copies printed. In 1921, Verity himself wrote to the press, acknowledging receipt of the inaugural volume of John Dover Wilson and Arthur Quiller-Couch's new scholarly Cambridge edition, commenting: 'It has, to me, one merit, that it will not compete with the Pitt Press edition! That sturdy old ship seems to hold her own [course?] fairly well, despite all these new "stunts".'[88] Verity's venerable ship sailed on right up through the 1960s. In 1965, for instance, *Macbeth* was being reprinted in a run of 60,000 copies and 30,000 copies of *Hamlet* were run off in the same year.[89] By the end of the decade, however, sales of some of the volumes in the series were starting to fall away, though not quite as precipitously as in the final years of the *Clarendon* series – *Henry V*, for instance, was fluctuating between 1,000 and 3,000 copies a year 'reflecting

Table 8.1 *Printrun figures for Verity's Pitt Press edition of* Midsummer Night's Dream, *from first edition through to 1936*

Year	Printrun
1893	5,000
1894 (1)	5,000
1894 (2)	5,000
1894 (3)	2,500
1898	2,500
1900	3,000
1901	15,000
1903	5,000
1905	7,000
1908	10,000
1910 (1)	10,000
1910 (2)	10,000
1912	20,000
1917	10,000
1919	10,000
1923 (1)	10,000
1923 (2)	10,000
1924	15,000
1927	20,000
1930	15,000
1936	20,000
Total printed up to 1936	210,000

examination requirements'.[90] In 1969, the press considered terminating the series, but decided instead to grant it one last lease on life, with the price held at 7*s*. and 'production to consider economies, e.g., limp binding'.[91] The series would seem to have been allowed to run down to extinction from this point but, as in the case of the *Clarendon*, it had by that time survived in a very competitive market for the better part of an entire century.

The extended history of the *Pitt Press Shakespeare* takes us back, in some respects, to the issue with which we began this chapter: the geographical dispersal of the Shakespeare text. In 1918, Señor Juan de Goytia wrote to Cambridge, seeking permission to translate Verity's *Macbeth* into Spanish and, in 1944, Editorial Novo of La Coruña proposed reproducing Verity's texts in bilingual editions. Permission to reproduce the texts abroad was again being sought in 1960, when Jaap Bar-David, of the Bar-David Literary Agency in Tel Aviv proposed publishing (English-language) editions of

Verity's *Macbeth* and *Julius Caesar* in Israel.[92] In 1974, the Department of Education in Australia sought permission to have Verity's *Hamlet* transcribed into Braille and large print for use in public-school special classes, aimed at enabling 'blind or near blind children . . . adequately [to] adjust to the social requirements of present day society without the fear of feeling that they are in a world apart'.[93] When the future of the series was being considered at the close of the 1960s, the press canvassed the views of agents throughout a world market still shaped by the contours of the former British empire, and a variety of assessments came back to Cambridge. Brian Eccles reported that the series was 'to all intents and purposes out of the market as far as West Africa is concerned', but R. A. Griffith wrote from Trinidad and Tobago that Verity's texts were still popular at 'O' level in the Caribbean.[94] Priya Dubey insisted that the series could only continue to hold its own in India if the price could be kept to no more than 5.40 rupees, and Nancy McConnan wrote from Australia to indicate that the *Pitt Press* editions were losing ground to new bargain-price texts such as the *Signet* and *Penguin*, which were selling for about half the price of their Cambridge equivalents. Selling Shakespeare in the second half of the twentieth century had indeed become a global business and the text was fully established as a popular international commodity.

9   Nineteenth-century scholarly editions

We have seen that the rate of publication of Shakespeare editions accelerated dramatically during the nineteenth century and we have examined some of the factors which fuelled that acceleration. Most of the editions produced for the popular market over the course of the 1800s were highly derivative, with a great number of them – at least in the first half of the century – being based on the later Johnson–Steevens–Reed and Malone texts. William Miller's 1806 two-volume edition, for instance, announces that the 'text of the last edition by Mr. Reed, in twenty one volumes, octavo, has been adhered to in every respect' (§419, I, p. v) and the 'Advertisement' to Constable's 1819 edition notes that the base text chosen for reproduction is '*the well-known edition produced under the inspection of Johnson, Reed, and Steevens, which [is] universally admitted to be the most correct that has yet appeared*' (§459, I, p. vi). Malone's text also formed the basis of many editions and Gary Taylor has observed that it 'was piously reproduced by other editors for half a century'.[1] In 1856, Samuel Weller Singer noted of his own work that he 'intended that the text should be formed upon those of Steevens and Malone, compared with the early editions' (§499, I, p. vii).

We can say, then, that the eighteenth-century editorial tradition cast something of a long shadow beyond its own immediate period. But even as the base texts of these high-watermark editions were repeatedly reproduced, a strong reaction began to develop against one characteristic form of eighteenth-century editorial practice. The final Johnson–Steevens–Reed and Malone texts both ran to twenty-one volumes, swollen, in part, by a burgeoning accretion of commentary and annotation. While the *text* established by these editors was accepted as standard, a backlash set in against their sprawling apparatus. This is neatly illustrated in John Poole's *Hamlet Travestie*, published in 1810, which included annotations supposedly written 'by Dr. Johnson and Geo. Steevens, Esq. and other commentators' (title page). One sample mock annotation will provide a flavour of Poole's gentle humour at the eighteenth-century editors' expense:

(f) Rope *of onions* ——

I do not understand this. May we not, with greater propriety, read, a *robe* of onions? *i. e.* a fantastical garment ornamented with onions, in the same way as masqueraders frequently wear a domino, studded with gingerbread nuts – a dress such as Ophelia's phrenzy might naturally suggest to her.

POPE.

Rope is undoubtedly the true reading. *A rope of onions* is a certain number of onions, which, for the convenience of portability, are, by the market-women, suspended from a *rope:* not, as the Oxford editor ingeniously, but improperly, supposes, in a bunch at the end, but in a perpendicular arrangement.

For the hints afforded me in the formation of this note, and for those contained in the note upon *pickled mutton*, I am indebted to a lady celebrated at once for her literary acquirements, and for her culinary accomplishments.

JOHNSON.[2]

Poole was, of course, writing within the tradition of such late eighteenth-century parodists as T. J. Mathias, who we have already seen taking editors to task for hounding Shakespeare to death with their obsessively elaborate commentaries.[3] By the early decades of the nineteenth century, however, editors themselves were beginning to feel that the limits of commentary had been reached and that a rationalisation of the editorial apparatus was now necessary.[4] Thus Manley Wood, in his edition of 1806, observed that 'The present Editor did not set out with the design of making notes, though in a few places he could not avoid it. His purpose was to *retrench*: and to attach to his author such remarks only, from the various annotators, as are really illustrative of his dark passages' (§418, I, p. iii). Walter Scott likewise considered producing 'a sensible Shakespeare in which the useful & readable notes should be condensed and separated from the trash'.[5] He began the project (in conjunction with John Gibson Lockhart) but never brought it to fruition. Charles Knight, in the prospectus to his Pictorial Edition (1838–43), proposed to operate along similar lines:

Shakspeare demands a rational edition of his wonderful performances, that should address itself to the popular understanding, in a spirit of enthusiastic love, and not of captious and presumptuous cavilling; – with a sincere zeal for the illustration of the text, rather than a desire to parade the stores of useless learning; and offering a sober and liberal examination of conflicting opinions amongst the host of critics, in the

> hope of unravelling the perplexed, clearing up the obscure, and enforcing
> the beautiful, instead of prolonging . . . fierce and ridiculous
> controversies.[6]

The ultimate extension of this principle of retrenchment was, of course, the complete abandonment of annotation. As early as 1807, the anonymous compiler of a Johnson–Steevens–Reed Longman reprint presented the public with a clean text, observing that:

> The multiplicity of the notes with which Shakspeare has been
> overwhelmed, having been often complained of as a grievance, the editor
> determined, in the present edition, to give a simple and accurate text,
> without any commentary whatever. Most of the doubtful passages have
> been amply discussed in other editions, and may surely now be
> considered as finally decided and at rest. The correctness of the text
> secures it from obscurity.
>
> (§424, I, p. ii)

In the case of cut-price commercial reprints such as this, one might suspect a certain disingenuousness on the part of the publisher's agent in asserting that the notes have been eliminated for the best of motives. After all, a text lacking apparatus can be more cheaply and more simply reproduced and may therefore more readily return a profit. But the principle of the unannotated text was not confined exclusively to cut-price reprints. In her 1860 text, Mary Cowden Clarke – whose later edition (undertaken in conjunction with her husband), would offer 'a perfect blizzard of notes' – herself eschewed annotation.[7] She observes that

> The reader is to enjoy the comfort of reading Shakespeare's text,
> undisturbed by comment; and even uninterrupted by those marks of (a)
> (b) (c) or (1) (2) (3) which occur in annotated editions. The squabbles of
> commentators will be escaped from; the tedium of discussions will be
> avoided. Other editions may be consulted for every variety of
> information, and for reference; but this is intended for purely enjoyable
> reading – Shakespeare's book itself, and nothing else.
>
> (§507, p. vii)

The idea that a certain strand of publishing should seek to present the 'book itself, and nothing else' took firm hold in the nineteenth century, with the ultimate example of this form of edition being the unannotated *Globe Shakespeare* (discussed in the previous chapter), of which Margreta de Grazia has observed that it 'gave the impression of being no edition at all. It seemed as if nothing intervened between the reader and Shakespeare – except sheer text.' The edition appeared, de Grazia continues, 'almost transparent, as if the reader could see through the text to the mind in which it originated. One Shakespeare for one world.'[8] In the UK, the unannotated edition, supplemented by a brief glossary, became a staple of Shakespeare publishing – as evidenced, from the end of the nineteenth century by, for example, William J. Craig's Oxford University Press editions.[9]

To return to the beginning of the nineteenth century, while editors indicated a desire to avoid the petty squabbles of their eighteenth-century predecessors, they nevertheless continued to argue over exactly what should serve as the bedrock for new editions and, specifically, over the extent to which the First Folio should be privileged above other early texts. In *The Diversions of Purley*, published in 1805, Horne Tooke called for a radical return to the text of the First Folio, arguing that it was 'the only edition worth regarding'. Tooke further observed that

> it is much to be wished, that an edition of Shakspeare were given *literatim*
> according to the first Folio: which is now become so scarce and dear, that
> few persons can obtain it. For, by the presumptuous licence of the
> dwarfish commentators, who are for ever cutting him down to their own
> size, we risque the loss of Shakespeare's genuine text; which that Folio
> assuredly contains; notwithstanding some few slight errors of the press,
> which might be noted, without altering.[10]

Tooke's call resonated throughout the century and, while no one embarked on exactly the kind of edition that he proposed, several editors did afford a high priority to the First Folio text. In 1819, for instance, Thomas Caldecott issued editions of *Hamlet* and *As You Like It*, intending them as specimen texts for a complete edition (though this never materialised). Caldecott quotes Tooke's call for a folio based text with approval and observes that the First Folio 'is made the groundwork of the proposed edition and present specimen' (§456, pp. vii–viii). Additional quarto material is to be admitted, but 'Wherever the reading of the folio is departed from, the folio text is given in its place in the margin' (§456, p. viii). Charles Knight also afforded primacy to the First Folio. Knight certainly recognised the value of the quartos, but he was of the opinion that when a play appeared in an early quarto, the First Folio text likely represented a later, revised state, with the revision carried out either by the players or by Shakespeare himself. 'We are bound therefore', he suggested, 'to make the later copy the foundation of the text' (§485, I, p. xviii). Even in the case of *Lear*, where the differences between quarto and folio are particularly striking, Knight argued that 'the changes in the folio are decidedly to be preferred in nearly every instance'

(§485, I, p. xvii).[11] For giving such a high priority to the First Folio, Knight was characterised by the *Edinburgh Review* as the representative of the sect of the 'Foliantists': those 'men who stood by the first folio through sense and nonsense, believed that orthodoxy lay in literal adherence to Heminge and Condell . . . and ransacked cartloads of contemporary trash to discover any possible analogy, which might justify retaining some hopeless typographical imbroglio as sense and poetry'.[12]

The increased level of interest in the First Folio is indicated by the number of attempts that were made to reproduce it in facsimile over the course of the nineteenth century. In 1807, Francis Douce produced a page-for-page reprint of the First Folio for E. and J. Wright. Colin Franklin notes that the title page 'so faithfully imitated that of 1623 as to have been used by enterprising booksellers in completing an imperfect copy'.[13] Malone disliked the book because he felt that 'the idle gentlemen of the town' would think, 'Ay, now we shall have the true thing, and perfectly understand this great author, without being bewildered by the commentators.' Malone continued: 'I would like to see a paraphrase by some of these gentlemen on six pages of the first folio, after having been shut up for 12 hours in a room with this volume, and without any other book. It would probably be a very curious performance.'[14] Between 1862 and 1864, Lionel Booth issued another reprint of the First Folio, this time attempting a faithful reproduction in modern type of some of the peculiarities of the original – including broken letters, incorrect fonts, etc. As late as 1955, Fredson Bowers was willing to describe Booth's text as an 'amazingly accurate type facsimile'.[15] Booth's text seems not to have sold particularly well. By January 1870, the sheets had apparently come into the hands of George Routledge, who was offering the edition as part of his 'Clearance List', for a wholesale price of £1 10s. in a large paper quarto version or just 15s. in foolscap quarto. By July 1871 the price for the large paper edition had been reduced further, to a guinea.[16]

The Booth edition's failure to gain a ready market may possibly be attributed to the fact that a further facsimile followed hard on its heels, but this text – executed under the supervision of Howard Staunton – was created using the very latest technology: photolithography. An advertisement for the project printed in the *Publishers' Circular* noted that by 'the help of this invaluable agent' it is possible 'to obtain copies of any manuscript or printed book, so closely resembling the original as almost to defy distinction'.[17] The price of the edition was relatively high: it was released in sixteen monthly parts at 10s. 6d. a part, with the total cost amounting to 8 guineas. The *Bookseller*, however, contrasted the price favourably with the cost of acquiring an original folio, noting that the most recent copy of the First Folio to have been sold at Sotheby's – 'perfect [in] all but the verses by Ben Jonson' – had fetched £273.[18] Staunton's facsimile was sufficiently successful for it to be reissued in a reduced format by Chatto & Windus in 1876, under the supervision of J. O. Halliwell-Phillipps.

In his introduction to the Staunton facsimile reissue, Halliwell-Phillipps recurred to Tooke's call for an exclusively First-Folio-based edition and observed of Tooke that he 'was not so well read as were the [eighteenth-century] commentators, none of whom could have exhibited such an entire ignorance of the value of the Quartos' (p. vii). We have already seen the *Edinburgh Review* take Charles Knight to task for what it considered to be his excessive fidelity to the First Folio. Some of his fellow editors also criticised him, as they indicated a greater willingness to make use of the quartos in producing their own editions. Thus Howard Staunton, in the introduction to his edited text of 1858–60, noted that Knight 'was constrained to abandon [the First Folio] in thousands of instances' and he asserted that the 'truth is, that no edition of Shakespeare founded literally on the folio would be endured by the general reader in the present day' (§500, I, p. vii). The particular importance of the quarto texts was registered clearly by John Payne Collier, who set out his *Reasons for a New Edition of Shakespeare's Works* in 1842, issuing an eight-volume text over the course of the next three years. Dewey Ganzel has noted that his 'scrutiny of the quartos was more searching than that of any of his predecessors. No editor had been able to use as many quartos as Collier had at his disposal.'[19] Collier was granted privileged access to two formidable collections of Shakespeare materials: in the libraries of the Duke of Devonshire and of Lord Francis Egerton. Devonshire had purchased the John Philip Kemble collection (which included many early quartos) in 1821 for the 'near record price of £2,000' and had added to his Shakespeare holdings from other quarters as well.[20] In 1825, he purchased what was then a unique copy of the First Quarto *Hamlet*. Collier was offered breathtakingly easy access to the Duke's library:

> The moment it was mentioned to the Duke . . . that I had engaged to produce so important a work as a new edition of Shakespeare, and that frequent reference to his Grace's matchless dramatic library would be of essential service, the Duke at once insisted that I should take home with me every early edition of Shakespeare in his library, that I might be able to finish my collations at leisure, and under all possible advantages.[21]

Access to the Devonshire and Egerton collections led Collier to appreciate not only the significance of the quarto texts in themselves, but also the importance of examining different copies of the same edition of particular texts. By locating variants in such copies Collier was able to register more clearly than most of his predecessors the importance of the early modern practice of 'stop press' correction.[22] Collier's recognition of the importance of the quartos is registered in the fact that, by contrast with Knight, he chose the quarto texts of *Hamlet* and *Lear* as the basis for his edition of these plays in his 1842–4 edition.[23]

As in the case of the First Folio, a more focused interest in the early quarto texts led to the publication of facsimile editions. George Steevens had, of course, issued reprints of a selection of the quartos as early as 1766, but his texts were not entirely reliable and, in any case (as we have already seen), the new process of photographic reproduction opened the door to a completely new kind of reprint. Photolithographic facsimiles of the First and Second Quartos of *Hamlet* were issued in 1858 and 1859 respectively.[24] Between 1861 and 1871, J. O. Halliwell and William Ashbee embarked on an ambitious project which would see them publishing facsimiles of forty-seven early quartos, including, in some cases, variant issues of the same edition.[25] Somewhat surprisingly, the texts were produced not by using a photographic process, but by hand-tracing each individual letter to create lithographic plates. Fifty copies of each text were struck off by the lithographers, with the best thirty-one examples being bound for subscribers and the remaining stock being destroyed, '*such destruction being attested in each copy, and every copy being numbered in writing*'.[26] The subscription price for the series was quite high, at 5 guineas per volume, giving a total cost to subscribers of £246 15s.[27]

In 1880, F. J. Furnivall began issuing photolithographic facsimiles of the quartos, with the texts being created by William Griggs and Charles Praetorius, 'whose long experience at the India Office and the British Museum respectively, enable them to guarantee the entire faithfulness of their reproductions, though these are checked by the Editors too'.[28] His collaborators' long and distinguished public service notwithstanding, Furnivall's experience would not appear to have been an entirely happy one, as he once wrote that 'Any subscriber willing to undertake the hanging or burning of a photo-lithographer or two – to encourage the others – should apply to F. J. Furnivall.'[29] Furnivall promoted the series on the basis that the texts were not only very significantly cheaper than the Halliwell–Ashbee editions, but they also included scholarly introductions: 'what then cost *five guineas*, in a non-working form and without any information as to the original Quartos, is now buyable, in a new and workable form, for *six shillings*, with the addition of a critical Introduction to the text by a competent Shakspere scholar'.[30] The Furnivall texts were, however, not without their serious problems. W. W. Greg's 1910 assessment of the First Quarto *Merry Wives of Windsor* volume was damning:

> The Griggs facsimile can only be described as very bad. It was produced at a moderate price to meet the requirements of students, but it sacrificed most of the qualities that might have rendered it useful. It not only suffers from the dirty appearance of inferior lithographic work, but, what is worse, its text is quite untrustworthy, being not only illegible but sometimes doctored.
>
> (§1042, p. x)

From 1939 Greg himself, in conjunction with Charlton Hinman, began issuing a new series of quarto facsimiles, under the auspices of the Shakespeare Association. Bowers described the volumes as 'a necessity for scholars removed from great libraries', but also noted something of a falling off in quality as the series proceeded.[31]

We have noted the extent to which nineteenth-century editors debated the degree of primacy that should be afforded to the First Folio text in producing new editions. However, one of the greatest controversies of the century centred not on the general merits and standing of the First Folio, but on the status of a particular copy of the Second Folio. In January 1852, John Payne Collier set out an intriguing narrative in the pages of the *Athenæum*, detailing how he had bought a rather battered copy of the Second Folio from the famous London bookseller Thomas Rodd. Collier claimed that he had purchased the volume primarily with the expectation that 'it would add some missing leaves to a copy of the same impression which I had had for some time on my shelves'. Finding that the Rodd volume was also imperfect, Collier 'put the book away in a closet', but when he eventually returned to it he noticed that it contained manuscript alterations, that these were 'in an old hand-writing – probably not later than the Protectorate', and that the alterations 'applied . . . to every play'.[32] Collier raised the intriguing possibility that while some of the emendations 'may have been purely arbitrary or conjectural', others

> seem to have been justified either by occasional resort to better manuscripts than those employed by the old player-editors, or, as is not improbable, by the recital of the text at one of our own theatres when the corrector of my folio of 1623 was present, and of which recital he afterwards availed himself.[33]

The outer cover of the volume was inscribed 'Tho. Perkins, his booke'. Collier originally thought he remembered a 'Thomas Perkins' who had worked as an actor in the Renaissance theatre, but he realised that the actor in question was called Richard Perkins. 'Still', he concluded, 'Thomas Perkins might have been a descendent of Richard.'[34] The volume became identified as the 'Perkins Folio', with Perkins himself being sometimes referred to by Collier as 'the Old Corrector'.

If Collier presented a baited hook, the Shakespearean public soon bit. In the 27 March issue of the *Athenæum*, a correspondent signing himself 'J.F.K', asserted that 'Mr. Collier may be assured that his announcement has caused a great sensation throughout Shakspeare-dom.'[35] Collier's claims were rendered all the more credible by the fact that, as an editor, he had a reputation for extreme conservatism. Assessing his 1842–4 edition, the *Edinburgh Review* observed of him that 'he has a horror of novelty'.[36] Collier offered a sample set of the Perkins emendations in his *Athenæum* article and, in January of the following year, he published a detailed account of the annotations in *Notes and Emendations to the Text of Shakespeare's Plays*, a volume running to in excess of 500 pages. Collier estimated that the Perkins Folio included some 20,000 minor emendations ('the correction of literal and verbal errors' and adjustments of punctuation). 'With regard to changes of a different and more important character', Collier writes, 'it is difficult to form any correct estimate of their number':

> The volume in the hands of the reader includes considerably more than a thousand of such alterations; but to have inserted all would have swelled its bulk to unreasonable dimensions, and would have wearied the patience of most persons, not merely by the sameness of the information, but by the monotony of the language in which it was necessarily conveyed.[37]

The book quickly sold out its printrun of some 2,000 copies and a second edition was issued in March, which sold about the same.[38] We have seen that the publishers of Theobald's *Shakespeare Restor'd* and Edwards' *Canons of Criticism* cleverly configured their volumes as 'supplements' to the editions which they set out to critique. In a neat variation on this, Collier's publisher, Whittaker, 'piggybacked' *Notes and Emendations* on his own edition of 1842–4. The book was identified on its title page specifically as 'a supplemental volume to the works of Shakespeare by the same editor' and the annotations were cross-referenced to Collier's edition, making the book difficult to use unless one possessed a copy of the edition.

The Perkins volume caused a popular sensation and drew forth much comment, including an anonymous parody entitled *The Grimaldi Shakspere*, which purported to provide 'Notes and Emendations on the plays of Shakspere, from a recently-discovered annotated copy by the late Joseph

Grimaldi, Esq., Comedian' (title page). The author gleefully poked fun at Collier's early attempts to claim a copyright in the Perkins' annotations:

> No future edition of Shakspere can ever dare to appear without all these additions and corrections; and as they are all copyright, and may not be used by any one but me, it follows that the Bard is in future my private property, and all other editors are hereby 'warned off;' but it is not very likely such misguided labourers will appear after this warning; if they do, they will be stigmatized as all such 'trespassers,' deserve.

The parodist also pointed to a fact noted by many other commentators: that many of the emendations made by Perkins matched changes proposed by editors in the eighteenth century. Perkins, he suggests, 'must have been a Scotsman, as he evidently possessed the power of "second sight," looking into futurity so wondrously that he wrote with his own hand emendations in the text of his folio which were first invented by the scholars of the succeeding century'.[39] The charming silliness of Grimaldi's own emendations is nicely indicated in the following:

> There is a passage in *Richard III.* which has hitherto been received as the genuine reading. The 'First Gent.' says to Gloucester when he stops the funeral cortege of Henry VI,
>
> > 'My lord, stand back, and let the coffin pass.'

> A few moments consideration will show that this cannot be a correctly expressed line. Coffins are denied volition, and he must have used other words to make his meaning clear – such as 'let the *bearers* pass' – but we are fortunately saved all conjecture, by the true reading appearing in our Grimaldi folio of 1816, by which it appears the entire line of type has dropped out in moving the form (no uncommon occurrence in a printing office) and the ignorant mechanic in trying to repair his fault has made it what it is. This is what it should be:
>
> > 'My lord, stand back and let the parson cough.'

> This new reading fortunately requires no defensive arguments when we remember that the clergyman had been walking bareheaded and slowly through the streets of London: and that common politeness required the 'First Gent.' to save Gloucester, also a gentleman, from an unguarded approximation to his explosive lungs.[40]

In the field of genuine – as opposed to parodic – editing, Collier's revelations had the effect of tossing a bibliographic spanner into the works of Shakespeare publishing. His rival editors were initially at a loss to know exactly what status should be accorded to the 'Old Corrector's' emendations and Collier also, of course, rather coyly kept his cards close to his chest when it came to the question of just how many more annotations might still be contained in the volume. We can sense the anxiety prompted by the Perkins Folio in a pamphlet entitled *Old Lamps or New?* published by Charles Knight in the same year as Collier's *Notes and Emendations*. The pamphlet offers 'an introductory notice to the Stratford Shakspere' (title page) and Knight reveals in it that he had 'suspended the publication of this edition for some months – as we also thought it right to suspend the publication of a second volume of "The Companion Shakspere" – hearing, on all sides, that the received text of the greatest name in all literature was to be overthrown', as a result of Collier's revelations. Ultimately, Knight concludes that the Perkins emendations are not so ground-breaking as Collier claims and he wryly observes 'We are not disposed to rush frantically to cast aside our ancient possession, at the first cry of "*Who will change old lamps for new?*".'[41] One senses, however, that Knight's rejection of the Perkins Folio is made out of a pragmatic feeling that he needs to move forward with his own pub-lishing projects, rather than out of a well-founded sense of conviction. A similar kind of anxiety is apparent in the introduction to Alexander Dyce's edition of 1857. Though he damns the Old Corrector, Dyce seems unwill-ing to dismiss him completely: 'with all his ignorance and rashness, – the far greater proportion of his *novæ lectiones* being either grossly erroneous or merely impertinent, – he yet deserves our thanks for having success-fully removed some corruptions, and must be allowed the honour of hav-ing anticipated several happy conjectures of Theobald and others' (§501, I, pp. xiii–xiv). Dyce testily characterises the Perkins emendations as consisting of 'particles of golden ore' mixed with 'abundant dross' (§501, I, p. xvi).

With his editorial competitors on the back-foot, Collier prospered. Some months after the appearance of *Notes and Emendations*, he published a new one-volume edition of Shakespeare, which silently incorporated most of the Perkins emendations. In the introduction to this volume he observed that

> It is not to be understood that the Editor approves of all the changes in the text of the plays contained in the ensuing volume; but while he is doubtful regarding some, and opposed to others, it is his deliberate opinion, that the great majority of them assert a well-founded claim to a place in every future reprint of Shakespeare's Dramatic Works.
>
> (§494, p. v)

In 1858, Collier issued another new six-volume edition, 'this time with apparatus, which also did well, thanks to its incorporation and rationalization of the materials from the Perkins Folio'.[42] Collier experienced anxiety about his income throughout much of his life. At this point he must have been pleased by the fact that his Second Folio purchase (which had cost him just £1 10s.) had given rise to so many commercially successful publications.[43] 'It was', as Dewey Ganzel puts it, 'one of the most remarkable publishing coups of the nineteenth century.'[44]

By the time of his 1858 edition, however, the storm clouds had begun ominously to gather over the heads of Collier and his Old Corrector. Where Knight and Dyce sceptically hedged their bets about the status of the Perkins emendations, Samuel Weller Singer, in his edition of 1856, summarily dismissed 'the absurd and sweeping blunders of [Collier's] pseudo antique corrector' (§499, I, pp. x–xi).[45] Likewise, Howard Staunton, in his 1858–60 edition, characterised the whole business of the Perkins Folio as a 'disreputable topic', observing that such 'of its readings as are of value will be restored to their rightful owners, for the paternity of nearly all such is known; and the rest will speedily find the oblivion they so well deserve' (§500, I, p. xii). The tide of scholarly opinion was clearly turning against the acceptance of Perkins as a authentic early seventeenth-century annotator. But if the marginalia were *not* genuine, who, then, was responsible for them? In a little pamphlet entitled *Literary Cookery*, 'A Detective' (actually A. E. Brae), argued that the emendations would never have been accepted had they not been advanced under the imprimatur of Collier's reputation as a scholar:

> The presumption – the plagiarism – the vulgarity – the imbecility – of those wretched libels on the text of Shakespeare were as nothing to convince of their imposture; but had the prestige of their sponsor [been] less – had they really been dependent solely on their own merits – they would have been at once cried to scorn.

Pursuing his investigations further, the Detective came very close to dropping the heavy hand of the law on Collier's own shoulder: 'if the scent now opened be effectively followed up, it may, perhaps, at length extort a second confession, similar to Ireland's of Shakespearean forgeries'.[46] In the following year, the *Edinburgh Review* stopped short of actually pointing an accusatory finger at Collier, but delicately indicated that his account of affairs strained credulity:

> If we were told by some scholiast of ancient days, that Aristarchus the critic, while wandering in the market-place of Alexandria with his head full of Homer, had purchased a bargain of figs, and, on returning home, found them wrapt up in a papyrus containing the genuine text of the poet, we should smile at the simplicity of the myth; and yet the romance of Mr. Collier's discovery is almost as marvellous. That gentleman is

known to many of our readers as one who has devoted great part of his life to the study and elucidation of our great dramatist. By the merest accident, which might equally have occurred to any chance person, he became the purchaser of a copy of the second folio of Shakspeare (1632), which contained numerous MS. annotations.[47]

By the time his 1858 edition appeared, then, Collier was increasingly embattled and the tone of his introduction is anxious and defensive. He insists that his controversial copy of the Second Folio has been made widely available for public inspection:

> I carried it with me to two, if not three, evening assemblies of the Antiquaries of London, and I laid it open on their library-table for the examination of any persons who took an interest about it. I mentioned it to my relations and friends . . . The late Duke of Devonshire came up from Chatsworth purposely to inspect it: I left it for several days in the care of the late Earl of Ellesmere; and one of our great London publishers had it for nearly a week in his possession, that he might take opinions upon the subject. In short, it was freely inspected by every body who expressed the least anxiety to see it.
>
> (§504, p. xi)

What Collier may not have reckoned on at this point was that the volume – which had conveniently been out of circulation since he had presented it to the sixth Duke of Devonshire – would be scrutinised again, when the Duke's successor, in 1859, acceded to a request from Sir Frederick Madden that the book be released to the British Museum for examination by specialist staff.[48] They condemned it, unreservedly, as a modern forgery. The museum's findings were made public by N. E. S. A. Hamilton in 1860, in his *Inquiry into the Genuineness of the Manuscript Corrections in Mr. J. Payne Collier's Annotated Shakspeare, Folio, 1632; and of Certain Shaksperian Documents Likewise Published by Mr. Collier.* Hamilton's accusations ranged far beyond the immediate matter of the Second-Folio volume, as he noted himself:

> the facts I am now about to advert to are far graver than the question of the authenticity of . . . any particular volume. They have reference to a *series* of systematic forgeries which have been perpetrated, apparently within the last half century, and are in connection generally with the history of Shakspere and Shaksperian literature, although other subjects have occasionally been introduced.[49]

Dewey Ganzel observes that Collier 'was, in effect, accused of deliberately corrupting the manuscript collections of his patron Ellesmere, of Dulwich College, and of the State Record Office itself by introducing forgeries into them and of compounding this outrage by deluding the public with their subsequent "discovery"'. Ganzel observes that the 'impeachment of the Perkins Folio was by comparison almost trivial'.[50] Hamilton's evidence was damning and Collier was irretrievably disgraced.[51]

Late in life, at the age of eighty-six, Collier embarked on one last, small-scale subscription edition of Shakespeare, running to just sixty copies of each volume.[52] In his call for subscribers, published in the *Athenæum*, he proposed 'to issue a new edition of Shakespeare in the original small quarto size', with the notes 'as brief as possibly, never occupying more than a couple of lines, and avoiding all controversy' and Richard Knowles has observed that he did in fact 'withdraw the majority of the controversial emendations from his notorious Perkins Folio'.[53] The last volume of the edition was issued in January 1878, just after his eighty-ninth birthday. Collier died five years later and not long before his death he wrote in his journal: 'I am bitterly and most sincerely grieved that in every way I am such a despicable offender. I am ashamed of almost every act of my life.'[54]

Collier was not the only 'despicable offender' among nineteenth-century editors. John Velz notes that 'long before the Collier Controversy began' Samuel Weller Singer – who, as we have seen, was much given to condemning Collier – 'had initiated the editorial scandals of the nineteenth century by wholesale plagiarism from the tradition in his first Shakespeare edition (1826)'.[55] J. O. Halliwell, who had co-founded the Shakespeare Society with Collier, Knight and Dyce in 1840, also had a rather shady past. Granted ready access to the manuscript collections of Trinity College Cambridge, he stole some materials from the library, subsequently selling them on to the British Museum. Unlike Collier, Halliwell was able to weather the ensuing storm, as the college and the museum failed to agree terms regarding exactly what action should be taken against him.[56] He also became friendly with the wealthy antiquary, Sir Thomas Phillipps, to whom he dedicated a collection entitled *Scraps from Ancient MSS.* in 1840. Phillipps allowed Halliwell the use of his library, but Halliwell enraged him by proposing marriage to his eldest daughter, Henrietta. Phillipps refused to consent to the wedding, but the couple went ahead anyway, in defiance of Phillipps, who immediately cut off contact with them. The Phillipps estate was entailed to Henrietta under the terms of her grandfather's will and, on the death of Sir Thomas (in 1867), the couple inherited the family fortune, which provided Halliwell with a secure income to pursue his career as an independent scholar and collector. Between 1853 and 1865, Halliwell had produced one of the most lavish editions of the nineteenth century, in sixteen extensively illustrated folio volumes, with woodcuts by F. W. Fairholt. As in the case of his quarto facsimile series, the edition was strictly limited and very expensive. A total of 150 copies were produced for subscribers, after which the 'blocks and plates of the numerous woodcuts, facsimiles, and engravings, used' were destroyed. In twenty-five copies, the plates were reproduced on India paper.[57] The subscription cost for these copies was 150 guineas. For regular copies, the subscription was eighty guineas.[58] The subscription list indicates that Halliwell-Phillipps had quite a measure of success in attracting the great and the good to buy his edition. The list includes the King of Prussia, the Duke of Buccleuch and Queensbury and the Duke of Newcastle, the Earls of Burlington and Craven, the Lords Londesborough, Franham and Brooke and Professor Pyper of the University of St Andrews.[59] Halliwell-Phillipps also seems, however (perhaps appropriately, given his own past) to have acquired one or two disreputable subscribers. The accounts ledger for the edition is preserved in the library of Edinburgh University and from it we discover that one subscriber (a Mr Browne) 'became a bankrupt in 1866' and that another suffered an even worse fate: 'John Durdin was transported for forgery, & care must be taken not to send vols. 10 to 15 to any one but the legal owners, as he was a bankrupt as well.'[60] The *Athenæum* was unimpressed by Halliwell's achievement, seeing his commentary as something of a throwback to the antiquarian prolixity of the eighteenth-century tradition:

> If Mr. Halliwell really possesses powers adequate to such a task as he has assumed, he must arouse himself, – shake off his drowsy antiquarian fondness for heaping illustration upon illustration, emancipate himself from the commentator-like propensity to pick holes in the labours of other men, extend his mental vision beyond the letter of the text, and strive to amend obvious corruptions by entering into the author's spirit – not merely endeavour to prop them up by far-fetched allusions derived from a discursive, but incomplete and almost worthless reading.[61]

The *Edinburgh Review* was rather more succinct in its dismissal of the edition, observing that 'Mr. Halliwell's magnificent folios, which rejoice the eye . . . afford no solace whatever to the mind.'[62] Modern commentators have, however, been kinder: Christopher Spencer, assessing the edition's *Merchant of Venice* text for the *Variorum Handbook*, observed that it is 'more independent than most 19th-century editions'.[63]

If the Shakespeare world of the nineteenth century would seem at times to have been more than usually populated with brilliant rogues and charming rascals, it also had its less colourful and more sober-minded scholars. Chief among these were the editors of the *Cambridge Shakespeare*, who issued their enormously influential nine-volume text between 1863 and 1866. As we have already seen in the previous chapter, it was this text which formed the basis of the highly popular single volume Globe edition, published in 1864. As in the case of the Globe, the impetus for the multi-volume edition would seem to have come directly from the publisher Alexander Macmillan. Again, as with the Globe, Macmillan made use of fellow Scot, James MacLehose, as a sounding board for the project:

> I want you to be so kind as to tell me what you think of the chances for an edition of *Shakespeare*, edited like a critical edition of a classical author, with merely the text and such various readings as seemed to have value either for their appearances in early editions or from their intrinsic worth . . . The claims would be that anyone possessing it would have (1) a beautiful book in point of typography, (2) as pure and genuine a text, free from all taints of Collierism and other similar isms as can be obtained from careful scholarship and sound sense, (3) a complete list of all readings both from early editions and skilful suggestion as had any worth.

Macmillan goes on to note that the 'chief editor is Mr. Clark, our "public orator" and tutor of Trinity College, one of the most accomplished and popular men in the University'.[64] Clark would, of course, have at his disposal the excellent collection of materials which had been left to Trinity by Edward Capell.

Clark was assisted in getting the project underway by H. R. Luard, and together they issued, in 1860, a sample text consisting of act I of *Richard II*, with a preface setting out their general editorial principles. As Macmillan indicated to MacLehose, they proposed to edit the text 'in the manner in which it has been customary to edit an ancient Latin or Greek classic'. Their textual methodology was mapped out in the following terms:

> The plan we have adopted in our specimen is as follows: The text is generally formed on that of the first quarto, *every* variation in the second, third, and fourth quarto, and the first two folios being given. If the reading in the first quarto seemed satisfactory, and not in need of alteration, it has been always retained; when this text appeared faulty, it has been altered from the subsequent editions, the reading which has the greatest weight of authority being chosen. When none of the early editions give a reading that can stand, recourse has been had to the later ones; conjectural emendations have been rarely mentioned, and never admitted into the text except when they appeared in our judgment to carry certain conviction of their truth with them.

It is clear from this statement that what they aimed at was essentially an eclectic 'best text' edition, but the value of what they proposed is registered in their assertion that by their plan 'a reader will really have the same advantage as if he possessed all the early editions, and constantly referred to them for each individual passage'.[65]

Clark and Luard solicited 'advice which may lead either to the improvement or the abandonment of the whole scheme'.[66] The feedback they received must have been positive, as the project quickly advanced. Luard was 'compelled to relinquish his part' in the undertaking when he was elected to the office of Registrar and he was replaced by John Glover, an Irishman who had been appointed Librarian at Trinity College Cambridge in 1858.[67] The first volume of the edition appeared in 1863, under Clark and Glover's names. In December of the previous year, however, Glover had been presented by the college with the vicarage of Brading on the Isle of Wight. As a result of taking up the post, he yielded his role in the *Cambridge Shakespeare* to his successor at Trinity, William Aldis Wright.[68] Clark and Wright finished the edition together, with Wright playing an increasingly dominant role as the project progressed.[69] The contrast between the two men was marked. Clark was characterised by a contemporary as 'the most accomplished and urbane of dons and men' and he was the author of several travel books, including *Gazpacho* (1850) and *Peloponnesus, or Notes of Study and Travel* (1858). Wright, by contrast, was styled 'a much more secluded personage', possessed of a 'strict . . . reserve and brevity in manner and accost'.[70] Remarkably, Wright suffered so badly from writer's cramp that he was obliged to learn to write with his left hand. Cautious in his editorial attitudes, he was fond of quoting the rabbinical saying 'Teach thy lips to say "I do not know"'.[71] Wright seems to have devoted a very great deal of his time to the edition. In one letter to Alexander Macmillan, he notes that he has been to Oxford 'to do some collating at the Bodleian: worked ten hours a day on Tuesday & Wednesday and came back here last night'.[72] On another occasion, Macmillan writes to the editor 'I hope the stress of the Shakespeare has not quite killed you.'[73] Assistance sometimes came to the editors from unlikely sources. The *Publishers' Circular* for 1 July 1863 reported that notes were furnished to Clark and Wright by a Mr John Bullock, 'a brass-finisher, in Aberdeen – who has devoted his leisure to the study of English literature, for which, though still following his manual labour, he has obtained in his own locality a considerable reputation'.[74]

Macmillan had originally thought that a modest printrun of 750 copies would 'yield a decent profit' for the edition.[75] In the event, a total of 1,500 copies were printed, though it was decided not to stereotype the plates.[76] The inaugural volumes sold for 10*s*. 6*d*. each.[77] By October 1866, Macmillan was ordering a payment of £75 to Wright for his work on the final two volumes, observing 'I am very glad at the completion of this great work.'[78] The editors had largely followed the plan which Clark and Luard had originally set out in their sample text. In general, they eschewed conjectural emendation, admitting no changes to the text on the grounds that 'we think it better rhythm or grammar or sense' (§587, I, p. xii). They did, however, modernise spelling, arguing that there was no basis on which Shakespeare's own spelling might be securely recovered. Likewise, given the vagaries of early modern punctuation – 'in many places, we may almost say that a complete want of points would mislead us less than the punctuation of the Folios' (§587, I, p. xix) – they decided to accept the modern punctuation of the text as it had been developed by 'the best editors, from Pope to Dyce and Staunton' (§587, I, p. xx).

The edition was not universally applauded. In a cranky diatribe entitled *Shakespeare's Editors and Commentators*, published in 1865, W. R. Arrowsmith added the Cambridge editors to his general list of the textual damned:

> So it fares with all sort of them: professing to reverence the memory of Shakespeare, they violate his remains; the monument reared by his own genius they chip and deface, they plaster and daub . . . and to get themselves a mention, they bescribble it all over with their names. The Cambridge editors appear to spare no pains to propagate this vainglorious itch.[79]

Likewise, Dyce condemned the edition as 'wretched in the extreme . . . a *mumpsimus* edition with hieroglyphical notes'.[80] In general, however, the text was well received and its impact was enduring. *The Bookseller*, for instance, was fulsome in its praise: 'we recommend [the] "Cambridge" edition of the complete works of the poet, not only as the most valuable that has hitherto been issued, but because we think its appearance in the complete form will, in a great degree, render future editions unnecessary'.[81] Writing some one hundred years after its publication, Fredson Bowers – while offering certain criticisms of the editorial work of Clark and Wright – observed that it had 'remained up to the present the only complete text worth mentioning formed from a systematic re-examination of the textual situation'.[82] We have already noted in chapter 8 the extent to which the Globe spin-off edition dominated the textual world for many decades after its original publication. A clear indication of the undisputed centrality of Clark and Wright's work is provided by Gary Taylor, who notes that in 1948 'the American publisher Harcourt, Brace and Company conducted a poll of professors of English to determine whether to reprint the familiar Globe text or to print a new text based upon the latest scholarship; the octogenarian text won a landslide victory'.[83] Paul Werstine has observed that 'the Cambridge Shakespeare's power . . . was effectively resisted only after the Second World War'.[84] As late as 1974, G. Blakemore Evans noted in the introduction to his *Riverside* edition that the 'act and scene designations in the present text generally agree with those found in the Globe edition' (§1508, p. 40).

If the Johnson–Steevens–Reed and Malone texts dominated the first half of the nineteenth century, then the Cambridge edition was clearly the central text of the second half and, indeed, well beyond. There was, however, one major new Shakespeare project initiated just before the close of the century which would also have an enduring effect. In 1898, A. M. M. Methuen entered into discussions with Edward Dowden with a view to launching a new series of individual Shakespeare texts.[85] Dowden had been appointed to the newly founded chair of English Literature at Trinity College Dublin in 1867, at the age of just twenty-four. He was the author of several books, including the enormously influential *Shakspere, His Mind and Art* (1875) and an introductory *Shakspere Primer* (1877). Methuen wanted Dowden to serve as general editor for the new edition and the professor agreed. As they were casting about for a name for the series, Dowden suggested calling it the 'Arden Shakespeare' and Methuen responded that the name was 'distinctively attractive, and we cannot do better than follow your advice'.[86] Later Methuen discovered that there was already an American series proposing to run under the same title, but he concluded 'I don't think [this] need be any obstacle to us.'[87] The American series in question was probably Heath's of New York's *Arden* edition, which began to appear some time around 1895 and for which C. H. Herford served as general editor. Sample materials for the new British series were sent to A. W. Verity, who, as we have seen in chapter 8, edited a very successful series for Cambridge University Press. Predictably, perhaps, as a textbook editor, Verity suggested that what Dowden proposed in the way of commentary was 'a little concise'.[88]

Dowden himself produced the inaugural volume in the series, an edition of *Hamlet* published in 1899.[89] The book was not an immediate success and Methuen wrote to Dowden in June of 1900 to try to soften the effect of the bad news regarding sales figures:

> I am very sorry that the report of the sales of HAMLET is disconcerting. You must not base your calculations entirely on the preliminary sales of such a book. I think it is obvious that a scholarly edition of HAMLET cannot have an immediately large sale, and I see no reason why it should not go on selling for a long time, and you must remember that each volume of the series that appears will give a fillip to the preceding

volumes; the greater the merit, the greater the fillip. Everyone has spoken so well of your work and of the plan and appearance of the books, that I feel sure the edition will fill a void, as they say.[90]

Dowden, however, was not to be persuaded and, given what he took to be the exceptionally poor showing of his own *Hamlet* edition, he felt unable to ask others to give their time to editing volumes for the series. 'Therefore', he wrote to Methuen, 'I am disqualified to act as general editor & some one else should take that place, if the edition is to be carried on.' He ruefully concluded:

> I think you made Hamlet a beautiful book, & I suppose copies will be bought by a few persons from time to time. But I am convinced that the sales will not be such as to justify my asking any other person to do what I am unwilling to do myself.[91]

On the 29 June, Methuen replied to Dowden, observing: 'I regret exceedingly your decision, but I accept it as final. The series will go on, and will, I hope, finally succeed.'[92] The series did, indeed, go on, with W. J. Craig and, subsequently, R. H. Case assuming the general editorship. It took three decades for the canon to be completely issued. Though the series aimed beyond the schools' market, the general editors employed a procedure which, up to that point, had been largely confined to schools editions: the assignment of particular texts to a broad range of individual editors working under the supervision of a general editor. Over the course of the twentieth century, this policy would become the norm for most editions, whether scholarly or more broadly commercial. The series was also, of course, contrary to Dowden's expectations, enormously successful, prompting a second, newly edited issue between 1951 and 1982 and a third new issue from 1995.[93] In 1985, Michael Warren observed of the series that it was 'an extraordinary accomplishment' and that the *Arden* texts 'exercise extraordinary authority, so that each new volume is an important event. Actors and directors consult them, as do students, teachers, and scholars.'[94]

Dowden's inaugural *Arden* volume was published at the very cusp of the century's end. As the century was closing, so too was a certain editorial framework coming to an end. The work of Clark and Wright at Cambridge was groundbreaking in its own way, but in a sense what it really offered was the final culmination of an editorial strategy that had gradually evolved over the course of the eighteenth century. As the new century opened, a group of scholars were emerging whose bibliographic theories would effect a significant shift in the way in which editing was conceptualised and practised.

The collapse of Collier's reputation in the mid-nineteenth century had the collateral effect of destroying the Shakespeare Society. The organisation could not withstand the public disgrace of one of its founding members and guiding spirits. From the ashes of Collier's Shakespearian fellowship there eventually arose the New Shakspere Society (its newness signalled in part by a return to what was then imagined to be a more authentic spelling of the playwright's name). The founder of this new organisation set out his vision for the project in his inaugural address, delivered at the first meeting of the Society on 13 March 1874:

> what I . . . want to see [is] a really national study of Shakspere; which we
> have never had yet, which I am sure we ought to have, and which if we
> could but have, – all our young fellows being traind [sic] on Shakspere's
> thoughts and words, – we should have a much finer nation of Englishmen
> than we have now.[1]

The nationalistically minded speaker was Frederick J. Furnivall, a spelling reformer and literary enthusiast of extraordinary energy and intelligence, who founded a blizzard of clubs and societies during the course of his lifetime, all of which were, as Dewey Ganzel has put it 'lashed into vitality and periodically thrown into disarray by the egoism, wit, whim, jealousy and precocity of one of the greatest critical minds of his generation'.[2]

Furnivall himself was involved in a wide range of Shakespeare publishing projects. In the 1870s, Cassell's asked him to write a twenty-five page introduction to their new 'Leopold' edition of Shakespeare (named after the Belgian Prince Leopold, a patron of the New Shakspere Society). Furnivall eventually submitted a one-hundred-page extended essay which was subsequently spun-off into the highly successful independent volume *Shakspere: Life and Work*.[3] As we have seen in the previous chapter, he also initiated a series of quarto facsimile volumes, issued during the course of the 1880s. In addition to this series, he planned an old-spelling edition, to be produced directly under the auspices of the New Shakspere Society. In a prospectus dated 23 May 1880, Furnivall reported to the membership of the society that

> After many unsuccessful tries to find that rare being, a Publisher who was English-scholar enough to care about bringing out an old-spelling *Shakspere*, I have at length found one in MR GEORGE BELL, of London and Cambridge, who, as an old member of the Philological Society, naturally takes no mere trade view of the proposed edition. But I promist him money-help in it, either from the New Shakspere Society or myself.
>
> He has offerd to sell the Society 500 large-paper copies of an old-spelling *Shakspere's Works* (edited by me, with such help from fellow-workers in the Society as I can get,) in the style of his Singer's edition, in 8 vols., bound in cloth, for 35*s*. a copy, to be issued at not more than 2 volumes a year, so as to suit the Society's funds.[4]

The erudite Mr Bell's support notwithstanding, this edition would not appear ever to have advanced beyond the editorial drawing board and, indeed, the problems of getting old-spelling editions into print would trouble many more editors than just Furnivall. He did, however, finally begin issuing such an edition in 1904, working with a different publisher. Furnivall would seem always to have had a slightly vexed relationship with the business of editing Shakespeare and is reported as once having demanded: 'Why didn't the brute edit his own works? He could have done it in a month, and spared us poor devils the bother of centuries.' He continued, with characteristically pugilistic wit: 'There are times when I wish I could stand him up in the corner there and punch his head for him!'[5]

Furnivall's impatience with Shakespeare's failure to set his work properly in order may have had its roots in the editor's own intellectual formation. His undergraduate training had been in mathematics and the sciences and one of his ambitions in establishing the New Shakspere Society was that the study of Shakespeare should be reconceived on more rigorously scientific lines. In his inaugural address to the society, he announced that one of the primary aims of the new organisation should be 'by a very close study of the metrical and phraseological peculiarities of Shakspere, to get his plays as nearly as possible into the order in which he wrote them'. He anticipated that a great contribution to this project would be made by one of the society's founding members, Frederick Gard Fleay, who had devised metrical tests which served 'to detect the spurious passages in Shakspere's plays; to point out often the writers of them; to distinguish the works of Beaumont from those of Fletcher; to show in what plays Beaumont or Massinger helpt Fletcher, and so on'.[6] Like Furnivall, Fleay had received mathematical training as an undergraduate (he subsequently served as an Anglican minister, but re-signed in 1884 and became a schoolteacher) and he too firmly believed in the application of scientific principles to the study of Shakespeare's texts, observing somewhat extravagantly of his own metrical tests that

> The great need for any critic who attempts to use [them] is to have a thorough training in the Natural Sciences, especially in Mineralogy, classificatory Botany, and above all, in Chemical Analysis. The methods of all these sciences are applicable to this kind of criticism, which, indeed, can scarcely be understood without them.[7]

The conclusions reached by Fleay on the basis of his scientifically super-saturated tests were nothing short of astonishing. *Titus Andronicus*, he an-nounced, was written by Marlowe; *Romeo and Juliet* was written in the first instance by Peele, though Shakespeare re-worked part of it; *Richard III* was also an original composition of Peele's, adapted by Shakespeare; *Taming of the Shrew* was a joint production of Shakespeare and Lodge.[8] He felt his theory regarding *Julius Caesar* was so unsettling that he thought it only fair to steel his readers before revealing the details, warning that: 'My theory as to this play is so unlike anything hitherto advanced that I shall begin by stating it; so that the startled reader may have it in his power to shut the book at once, if the hypothesis seems to him too absurd to be entertained.' He went on to argue that the 'play as we have it is an abridgement of Shake-speare's play, made by Ben Jonson'.[9] As Hugh Grady has nicely observed, Fleay offered 'a strange, empiricist deconstruction *avant la lettre*'.[10]

It is not entirely clear to what extent Fleay himself fully believed in his fanciful theories. A. H. Bullen, for example, once related an anecdote of an encounter with Fleay, during the course of which Bullen 'objected to some peculiarly far-fetched theory', only to be told by Fleay that 'it was not to be taken too seriously'. Bullen reminded Fleay that 'he originally announced this theory in a school-edition of *King John*' and 'mildly expostulated with him for mystifying schoolboys'.[11] Whether schoolboys much cared about being mystified by a disintegrationist Shakespeare editor is hard to say, but the greater effect of Fleay's project, sponsored by Furnivall, was to draw a certain amount of scorn upon the New Shakspere Society itself. In particular, the organisation attracted the witheringly critical attention of Algernon Swinburne, who included a parody of the society's proceedings as an appendix to his *Study of Shakespeare* (1880). Swinburne derided the tendency of the society's members to abandon traditional aesthetic criteria of judgement, as his fictitious reporter of 'the Proceedings on the First Anniversary Session of the Newest Shakespeare Society' writes:

only the most presumptuous of readers could imagine the possibility of Shakespeare's concern or partnership in a play which had no more Shakespearean quality about it than mere poetry, mere passion, mere pathos, mere beauty and vigor of thought and language, mere command of dramatic effect, mere depth and subtlety of power to read, interpret, and reproduce the secrets of the heart and spirit.

The stone-faced supposed science of Fleay's metrical analysis is lashed by Swinburne in the account of a paper delivered by a certain 'Mr. F.', whose conclusions were borne out 'at some length by means of the weak-ending test, the light-ending test, the double-ending test, the triple-ending test, the heavy-monosyllabic-eleventh-syllable-of-the-double-ending test, the run-on-line test, and the central-pause test'. Ultimately, Swinburne concludes (with a wink toward such nineteenth-century institutions as the Society for the Diffusion of Useful Knowledge), that the work of the society will stand beside the 'inestimable commentaries' of the 'Polypseudocriticopanto-dapomorosophisticometricoglossematographicomaniacal Company for the Confusion of Shakespeare and Diffusion of Verbiage Unlimited'.[12]

If Swinburne was witheringly sarcastic in public, he was scabrously scatological in private, circulating among his friends verses dedicated to 'Fartiwell & Co.' and the 'Shitspeare Society'.[13] The personal animosity between Swinburne and Furnivall deepened, with Furnivall reacting to the poet's jibes, 'like an angry monkey' (as William Aldis Wright put it), dubbing Swinburne 'Pigsbrook' (from swin/e-b/o/urne).[14] Swinburne responded in kind by renaming Furnivall 'Brothel-dyke' (from *fornix* and *vallum*). Sparks from the conflagration set practically the whole world of British Shakespeare studies alight, as Halliwell-Phillipps and various other scholars were drawn into the dispute.[15] In time the New Shakspere Society – like the predecessor it had aimed to replace – fell victim to the fires of controversy and collapsed irretrievably. In one sense, Furnivall's organisation was never destined to achieve much more than adding a few more flaming threads to the richly colourful tapestry that is nineteenth-century Shakespeare scholarship. In another sense, however, the turn towards science which characterised the New Shakspere project was of real significance, in that it anticipated a much more serious and more coherently founded scholarly endeavour which began to take shape in the opening decades of the next century.

Furnivall was in the habit of frequenting the ABC tearoom close to the British Museum. In his late years, the elderly controversialist would sometimes be joined at his table by younger men. Among the visitors were W. W. Greg and his friend R. B. McKerrow.[16] The two men did not share

Furnivall's enthusiasm for metrical tests (though Greg would write of Fleay that, while his 'works are a constant exasperation to students', they were 'only to be neglected at their peril') but they did share his interest in science.[17] This was particularly true of McKerrow, who had studied engineering at King's College London, before joining the family business of Brunlees & McKerrow. Coming into an inheritance, he abandoned engineering and entered Trinity College Cambridge, where he studied literature. He retained an interest in science, however, purchasing a microscope later in life and subscribing to a lending-library for slides, in addition to preparing his own specimens.[18] It was during his time at Trinity that McKerrow established a close friendship with Greg, whom he 'had first known . . . on the rifle-range at Harrow' when they were both schoolboys.[19] Greg's family background was in economics rather than the physical sciences. His grandfather, James Wilson, had founded the *Economist* in 1843, and Greg himself, as a young man, was being groomed to take over the editorship of the journal.[20] His undergraduate career was, however, undistinguished. He secured only a pass degree at Cambridge and was thus 'debarred . . . from reading the Moral Sciences Tripos, which included Political Economy'.[21] He did stay on an additional year in order to study economics, but it was already clear that his real focus lay elsewhere. He retained, however, both a financial interest in the *Economist* and a general interest in mathematics and science, reading Whitehead and Russell's *Principia Mathematica* as the volumes appeared in print, and styling one of his own later publications *A Calculus of Variants*.

Greg and McKerrow shared an enthusiasm for Renaissance literature, especially plays, and, even as undergraduates, they were already discussing 'projects for editing Elizabethan drama and the textual methods to be used'.[22] Trinity College, with the Edward Capell collection in the Wren Library and with William Aldis Wright holding the office of Vice-Master, must have been a congenial place in which to imagine such projects. Greg would, in fact, serve as Librarian in the college between 1907 and 1913 and one of his achievements during the period of his tenure was the production of a catalogue for the Capell collection.[23] As it happened, his position brought him, on one occasion, into direct conflict with Aldis Wright (himself, of course, formerly Librarian at Trinity):

> Greg began to clear away 'the muddle of pictures, &c., hanging on the
> Wren cases and the conglomeration under glass'. One version portrays
> Wright retiring top-hatted and furious from the 'very sharp conversation'
> that ensued, his 'I am the Vice-Master' having been overtrumped by

Greg's 'But I am the Librarian'; but Mr. Hurry [sub-librarian under Greg] has the authentic text – 'This is a library and not a museum for coins, spearheads, and other oddments.'[24]

This encounter was, however, untypical, and, in later years, Greg acknowledged the regard in which he held Wright, noting that he 'had great veneration as well as affection for the old man, and . . . owed him a lot'.[25]

In the opening years of the new century, Greg and McKerrow were both living in London, where they made the acquaintance of A. W. Pollard. Pollard was some years older than the other two. He was closely involved with the Bibliographical Society, for which he served as honorary secretary between 1893 (the society's second year) and 1934.[26] He also served as editor of the society's journal, *The Library*. Pollard had entered the service of the British Museum in 1883, being presented on his first day with the 'Ninety-One Rules of Cataloguing [and] a barrowload of books received under the Copyright Act to which to apply them'. In order to supplement his income, Pollard took on additional paid work, including editing two of John Wyclif's Latin works for a series being published by Furnivall.[27] Between 1919 and his retirement in 1924, Pollard served as Keeper of Printed Books at the Museum. F. P. Wilson notes that the 'duumvirate' of Greg and McKerrow 'with the accession of A. W. Pollard [became] a triumvirate' and between them the three men would dominate the arena of bibliograpic studies and editing during the first several decades of the twentieth century.[28] The close personal friendship that existed between the three (and which was later extended to Pollard's disciple John Dover Wilson) is significant, in that it served to lend a coherence to their project which other bibliographic endeavours – particularly in the field of Shakespeare editing – had signally lacked. Thus, F. P. Wilson justly further observes that the fact that the triumvirate 'were friends, "a happy band of brothers", will not be a matter of indifference to the future historian of Shakespearian studies, as he passes to them after narrating the enmities of Pope and Theobald, Steevens and Malone, Collier and Dyce, Furnivall and Halliwell-Phillipps'.[29]

McKerrow made an early attempt to put into practice the principles which he and Greg had sought to work through as undergraduates when he edited the complete works of Thomas Nashe in a series of volumes issued between 1904 and 1910.[30] At the same time Greg was gleefully lambasting an older generation of scholars for their unsystematic, untheorised, and generally sloppy performance as editors. He was, as John Dover Wilson later put it, 'the *enfant terrible* of English scholarship'. In 1906, for example, he – to quote again from Wilson – 'served up Churton Collins as a Thyestean repast to readers of the *Modern Language Review*.'[31] Collins was professor of English at the University of Birmingham and was general editor of the *Arnold School Shakespeare* series. He had just published an edition of the works of Robert Greene. Greg observed of the Greene edition that 'It is impossible to pretend that it is even moderately satisfactory', going on to detail its flaws at great length. He declared that it 'is high time that it should be understood that as long as we entrust our old authors to arm-chair editors who are content with secondhand knowledge of textual sources, so long will English scholarship in England afford undesirable amusement to the learned world'. He concluded his review by observing that Collins' edition would 'serve until a better is produced, but to put forward careless and superficial work of this kind as a final edition is a gross insult to English scholarship'.[32]

Where Greg criticised Collins for contenting himself with secondhand knowledge of his textual sources, he himself and his companions – the 'New Bibliographers' as they were to become known – sought the minutest possible engagement with original printed texts. They attempted to trace, as closely as they could, the precise lineage of the printed volume and, to this end, they aimed to bring a forensic mindset to bear in examining the physical book. Greg was thus led to redefine bibliography as 'the study of books as material objects', suggesting that the discipline 'deals with books as more or less organic assemblages of sheets of paper, or vellum or whatever material they consist of, covered with certain conventional but not arbitrary signs, and with the relation of the signs in one book to those in another'.[33] The examination of the material book should, in his view, be conducted along properly scientific lines (by contrast, we might say, with the supposed science of the uncertain and mercurial verse tests that the New Shaksperians had sought to employ). Laurie E. Maguire has pointed out that, in an early address to the Bibliographical Society, Greg used 'the nominal or adjectival form of "science" twenty-eight times'. Maguire concludes by observing that 'What the New Bibliographers offered was a do-it-yourself detective kit for Elizabethan drama.'[34] A sense of the extraordinary faith that the group placed in their powers of bibliographic detection can be gathered from a characterisation of McKerrow by Greg, the witty bravado of which might be thought to border almost on the blasphemous: 'I am persuaded that, had he stood on Sinai when Moses received the graven tables, he would have there and then sat down to hunt the tell-tale flaw that would reveal the method of production – and he would have found it.'[35]

A simple, but elegant, example of the effectiveness of the forensic approach to secular (as opposed to sacred) texts is provided in an early study of Greg's, detailed here by F. P. Wilson:

Which is the earlier of two editions of *The Elder Brother*, both dated 1637? The Cambridge editors of Beaumont and Fletcher could not tell, but Greg found the proof in one reading. In Q1 an improperly adjusted space-lead had produced a mark before the word *young* which the compositor of Q2 mistook for an apostrophe, *'young*. The economy of the proof shows the workman's confidence in his tools.[36]

Likewise, in a directly Shakespearean context, we have already seen (in chapter 2) the way in which Greg was able to establish, by examining the watermarks of the paperstock, that some of the Pavier quarto title pages bore false dates.[37] A nice example of the clash of the old and new critical cultures is provided in Pollard's response to the introduction to Sidney Lee's 1902 Clarendon Press facsimile of the First Folio – a grand undertaking, the first three numbered copies of which were presented respectively to Edward VII, the German Emperor and the US President.[38] Lee asserted in his introduction that 'The main part of the First Folio was printed in Jaggard's printing-office near St Dunstan's Church, but the work was done expeditiously, and probably some presses of Jaggard's friends were requisitioned for parts of the volume' (§914, p. xv). Focusing clearly on the book as material object, Pollard responded decisively:

> It is almost inconceivable . . . that this should have been the case, as not only the same type and the same ornaments, but even the same brass rules, may be found in use in different parts of the book, whereas had separate printers been employed, each would certainly have used his own rules, and probably his own type and ornaments.[39]

Where Lee was content to speculate, Pollard took the trouble to examine the physical evidence. The crowning achievement of this line of forensic analysis is undoubtedly Charlton Hinman's monumental study of the First Folio, which traces in minute detail the book's progression through the Jaggards' printing shop.

The detective work of the New Bibliographers was not, however, intended to be an end in itself. As we have already noted, their ultimate objective was to establish the precise lineage of the texts which concerned them. F. P. Wilson has identified this project as being the most significant advance which New Bibliography effected within Shakespeare studies:

> The most important contribution that critical bibliography has made to the textual criticism of Shakespeare is its insistence upon the importance of discovering all that can be known or inferred about the manuscript from which the printer set up his copy, and all that can be known or inferred about what happened to the manuscript in the printing-house,

and upon the corollary that once it has been established that one text is more authoritative than another, that text shall be chosen as the copy-text and no alterations admitted into it without consideration of the bibliographical evidence.[40]

From an editorial perspective, the aim of the New Bibliographers was to determine exactly what text lay behind each printed edition, thereby establishing the precise relationship between any given set of early printed texts. As Greg himself indicated, the key question to be answered in this context was: 'What was the nature of the copy that the printer had before him when he was setting up the type?'[41] The editor should, as John Dover Wilson put it, attempt to 'creep into the compositor's skin and catch glimpses of the manuscript through his eyes' (§1139, p. xxx).

If the nature of the copy from which the compositor worked could be coherently identified then, as F. P. Wilson has noted, it would be possible to establish which early text had the greatest authority; the editor would then be obliged to adopt that edition as copy text, departing from it only in strictly limited circumstances.[42] The ultimate intent of this approach was to eliminate eclecticism from the editorial process – that business of ladling together 'butter from alternate tubs of unknown manufacture', as John Dover Wilson evocatively described it.[43] Such eclecticism had blighted even Clark and Wright's landmark edition. Fastidious as they had generally been as editors, the Cambridge scholars lacked the kind of precise investigative methods that would have enabled them properly to weigh the competing authority of some of the earliest editions of Shakespeare's plays.[44] As a result, they sometimes found themselves placing their editorial feet unsteadily aboard two different textual vessels. Wilson thus takes them to task for their unresolved havering between, for example, the Second Quarto and First Folio texts of *Hamlet* in both the Globe and, subsequently, the Cambridge edition:

> They have confidence in neither text; they halt between them, and are unable to make definite choice of either because they are ignorant of the character of both. And if further proof of this be needed, it is furnished by their other edition of *Hamlet*, that published two years later in *The Cambridge Shakespeare*, which differs from its predecessor in 102 readings, 89 of which go in favour of Q2 and 10 in favour of F1. This looks like tardy repentance, until the changes are examined and found to be almost without exception mere trivialities. Nor is any principle evident behind them; they seem nothing but the veerings of a weather-vane.[45]

A series of developments led the New Bibliographers to believe that they could, with increasing confidence, identify the exact nature of the copy which lay behind the individual plays in the Shakespeare canon. Editors had known, at least since the time of Malone, that some of the plays included in the First Folio were reproduced not directly from manuscript sources, but rather from the early printed quartos.[46] The practice of using quarto texts in this way had tended to cast something of a shadow over the First Folio volume, since Heminge and Condell famously claimed in their address to the reader that

> where (before) you were abus'd with diuerse stolne, and surreptitious copies, maimed, and deformed by the frauds and stealthes of iniurious impostors, that expos'd them: euen those, are now offer'd to your view cur'd, and perfect of their limbes; and all the rest, absolute in their numbers, as he conceiued thẽ.
>
>   (A3r)

Malone and his successors regarded this claim as indicating that Heminge and Condell – the supposed guardians of the Shakespeare canon – could not be trusted, since, on the one hand, they asserted that the previously published texts were now being systematically replaced by alternatives whose genuineness was guaranteed, while, on the other, they were, in fact, simply recycling some of these prior texts in their own edition. Doubts over the reliability of the volume were compounded, of course, by Fleay's disintegrationist burrowing away at its very foundations, insistently suggesting that virtually all of the plays were a compound of dispersedly produced materials.

Pollard came to the rescue of the First Folio in 1909, when, in *Shakespeare Folios and Quartos*, he offered a rereading of the word 'diuerse' in the above passage. Pollard suggested that the 'diuerse . . . copies' to which Heminge and Condell referred need not necessarily encompass *all* of the quartos printed before 1623. It may be, he argued, that 'only some of the quartos ought to be treated as "stolne and surreptitious"'. Identifying this limited set of texts and labelling them the 'bad quartos', Pollard noted that 'no use was made of these in printing the Folio, good texts being substituted for the bad ones'.[47] Margreta de Grazia has observed that 'No passage in Shakespeare's plays was ever interpreted to greater consequence' and Pollard's study was immediately hailed as a work of great significance.[48] Greg welcomed it as 'by far the most systematic and critical work that had yet appeared on the subject and one that marked the opening of a new era in Shakespearian studies'.[49]

The effect of Pollard's rereading of the First Folio 'Address' was to restore faith in the bona fides of Shakespeare's earliest 'editors', banishing 'the gloomy [doctrine] of the old criticism' that 'Heminge and Condell were either knaves in league with Jaggard to hoodwink a gullible public, or else fools who did not know how to pen a preface.'[50] More importantly, Pollard also restored the integrity of the First Folio volume itself, as he apparently established that the texts presented there were trustworthy and authentic. Peter Alexander concluded that the First Folio represented 'the honest and painstaking effort of men who, though not expert bibliographers, were well informed, and who by the very choice of the Quartos they reprinted showed their knowledge as well as their limitations'.[51] Pollard's proposition of the distinction between the 'good' and 'bad' quartos received confirmation just a year later, when Greg tentatively suggested an explanation for how one of the bad texts – the First Quarto *Merry Wives* – might have found its way into print. As we have seen in chapter 1, Greg proposed that the foreshortened version of the play might have been assembled from memory by an actor who had played the part of the Host. Greg's theory – again, as we have already noted – was quickly extended by others to encompass the entire range of 'bad' texts.[52]

The establishment of a clear distinction between the good and bad quartos laid the foundation for attempts to ascertain the precise nature of the copy which underlay the plays included in the First Folio. In the year following Greg's edition of the First Quarto *Merry Wives*, Percy Simpson published a short book entitled *Shakespearian Punctuation*, in which he attempted 'to expound and classify the earlier methods of punctuation', suggesting that a formal logic could be seen at work in the pointing of the First Folio.[53] While Simpson himself did not necessarily intend to suggest that this, in some instances at least, might offer evidence of the playwright's own hand at work, some scholars did interpret his conclusions in this way. Pollard, for example, in an analysis of the Third Quarto *Richard II* based on Simpson's work, observed that

> No printer could have invented this exquisitely varied punctuation. Is there any room for doubt that it gives the lines as Shakespeare trained his fellows to deliver them? Is there any greater room for doubt that it gives us the lines as Shakespeare punctuated them himself as he wrote them down while he heard the accents in which Richard, as he conceived him, was to speak them? These colons and commas take us straight into the room in which *Richard II* was written and we look over Shakespeare's shoulder as he penned it.[54]

Likewise, John Dover Wilson, again drawing on Simpson, declared that a 'careful study of *Hamlet*, Q2, confirmed me in the faith, since the pointing of that text, a miracle of subtlety and dramatic appositeness, could not possibly be ascribed to the compositor, whose crudity and inexpertness were evident in every line of the play'.[55]

Simpson's work on punctuation was followed five years later by what appeared to be another important breakthrough. In 1916, Edward Maunde Thompson, co-founder of the Palaeographical Society and Director of the British Museum, published a study of an obscure play entitled *Sir Thomas More*, preserved in Harleian ms. 7386 in the museum's collection. The play was the production of several playwrights working in collaboration and, as early as 1871, Richard Simpson had suggested that one of the hands might be Shakespeare's.[56] Turning a systematic eye to one particular section of the manuscript (identified as the work of 'Hand D'), Thompson discovered *'with a lively interest that I recognized in the handwriting of the addition certain features which I had already noted in Shakespeare's signatures'. 'A careful study of the MS. ensued'*, Thompson tells us.[57] It was not an easy business, as *'The task may be compared to that of attempting to identify a face in the dark by the dim light of a lucifer match'*, but, in *Shakespeare's Handwriting*, Thompson *'set out* [his] *reasons for concluding that at length we have found what so many generations have vainly desired to behold – a holograph MS. of our great English poet'*.[58] Thompson's monograph was followed, in 1923, by a collection entitled *Shakespeare's Hand in the Play of Sir Thomas More*, edited by Pollard. The importance of the discovery from an editorial point of view is indicated by Pollard in his Preface to the volume:

> It is here contended that the writing of the three pages is compatible with a development into the hand seen in Shakespeare's considerably later extant signatures and explains misprints in his text; [and] that the spelling of the three pages can all be paralleled from the text of the best editions of single plays printed in Shakespeare's life.[59]

What the *More* manuscript appeared to offer was, again, a glimpse over Shakespeare's shoulder, as he is in the act of creation. By tracing the patterns of his handwriting and the peculiarities of his spelling an editor would be able not only to detect his hand beneath the printed page in those editions produced directly from his manuscripts, but such an editor would also be able to detect errors in the printed text arising from predictable compositorial misreadings of the Shakespearean script.

To revert to Laurie E. Maguire's conceit, the New Bibliographers were beginning to assemble quite a comprehensive detective kit for the Shakespearean editor. McKerrow added the next piece of apparatus in a pair of articles published in 1931 and 1935. In 'The Elizabethan Printer and Dramatic Manuscripts' he contemplated the fact that the standard of

Renaissance play-text printing appeared, in general, to be lower than that of other kinds of printing from the same period. Seeking a reason for this, he concluded that

> the explanation is a very simple one, namely, that in the case of plays the printer very often did not get anything like so clean a copy to work from as he did in the case of other books; he did not in fact get a fair-copy at all, but as a general rule, the author's original from which the fair copy had been prepared.[60]

The fair copy, McKerrow reasoned, would have been too valuable a property to have been sent to the printshop, as it would have been the company's working text and would also likely have borne the approving signature of the Master of the Revels – the crucial licence to perform the work.

In his 1756 *Proposals for a New Edition of Shakespeare*, a deeply pessimistic Samuel Johnson had observed of Shakespeare's plays that

> no books could be left in hands so likely to injure them, as plays frequently acted, yet continued in manuscript: no other transcribers were likely to be so little qualified for their task as those who copied for the stage . . . no other editions were made from fragments so minutely broken, and so fortuitously reunited.[61]

What McKerrow now offered, however, was the altogether more optimistic possibility that, in some cases at least, what we may have inherited from the Renaissance are printed texts based not on badly reconstituted theatrically mangled fragments, but rather based directly on Shakespeare's own hand-written manuscripts. In his second article McKerrow further developed a point which he had made in passing in his original piece, where he proposed that 'no copy but a good, orderly, and legible one could possibly serve as a prompt-copy'.[62] Envisaging a clear distinction between authorial foul papers, on the one hand, and theatrical prompt copy, on the other, McKerrow attempted to sketch out those features which might characterise these two types of manuscript. Focusing particularly on the issue of naming, and arguing that the pragmatics of theatrical performance would require a manuscript that was coherent and consistent throughout, he set out his proposition as follows: 'Simply, I think, that a play in which the names are irregular was printed from the author's original MS., and that one in which they are regular and uniform is more likely to have been printed from some sort of fair copy, perhaps made by a professional scribe.'[63] By following McKerrow's suggestion, an editor would be able, relatively easily, to distinguish between a printed edition based on authorial manuscript and an edition based on a prompt-copy transcription of the author's papers.

The cumulative effect of this series of apparent discoveries – all achieved under the general auspices of the New Bibliography – was to make it seem as if the editor of Shakespeare could cultivate a kind of textual x-ray vision, making it possible to see the precise manuscript lying beneath the surface of the printed text. Or, to adopt John Dover Wilson's more earthy metaphor, 'to peel off, as it were, the dirt left upon its surface by the craftsmen who last had sight of [the manuscript] and were responsible for its perpetuation in printer's type'.[64] Armed with a knowledge of the text's precise transmission history, the editor would then be able to make finely calibrated decisions regarding how the text should be treated in producing a new edition.

The new textual dispensation which we have tracked emerging over the course of the early decades of the twentieth century had a profound impact on Shakespeare editing, shaping in one way or another virtually all editions produced during the course of the century. The force of the new thinking was felt in the first instance in major Shakespeare projects initiated at the Oxford and Cambridge university presses in the early decades of this era. Oxford set a new edition in train as early as 1904, when Walter Raleigh, having just been appointed as the first ever professor specifically of English literature at Oxford, wrote to Charles Cannan at Oxford University Press, suggesting that he undertake a major new Shakespeare project for the press. Raleigh's vision was that the edition should be 'an exact reprint of the Folio, play by play, at a moderate price' and he thought it would 'supplant, and would deserve to supplant, the best mixed texts, such as the Cambridge Shakespeare'. 'Back to the Folio', he asserted, 'will, I believe, be the motto of the next important edition.'[65] Raleigh's position was, in fact, something of a throwback to the early nineteenth century. As we have already seen in the previous chapter, Horne Tooke had, in 1805, called for 'an edition of Shakspeare . . . given *literatim* according to the first Folio'.[66] Nineteenth-century editors – including even First Folio-enthusiast Charles Knight – had, however, recognised that any worthwhile edition of Shakespeare needed to take account of at least some of the quarto texts. Raleigh's lack of textual expertise would appear to have been recognised by Cannan, who wrote to J. C. Smith, sounding him out on the project in general and seeking advice on who might serve as Raleigh's textual editor. Smith responded: 'The only man I would really recommend (from personal acquaintance) for such work is D. Nichol Smith.'[67] Smith was an apt choice for the job, since he had substantial experience with editing and had served as Raleigh's assistant at the University of Glasgow, during Raleigh's tenure of the Glasgow English professorship.[68] He contributed editions of *Henry VIII* and *King Lear* to Charles H. Herford's Warwick Shakespeare. Raleigh later commented, somewhat quixotically, of their Glasgow collaboration: 'I brought Nichol Smith here . . . I'm a gas man myself, but I don't allow any other gas men on the premises.'[69] They would seem, in some respects, to have made as unlikely a pairing as Clark and Wright, with the flamboyant Raleigh, at 6 foot 6 inches, towering over his less extravagant scholarly minded collaborator.

Smith was pleased to take up the invitation to work on the edition, writing to Raleigh:

> I dare not refuse, though I confess that there are moments when I doubt my competence. I almost shirk the responsibility. But I won't, I am too proud for that. To be asked to be the first to edit Shakespeare as he should be edited is something to justify a little elation.

But he also immediately pulled against Raleigh's intention of simply re-producing the First Folio. He shared Raleigh's goal of textual purity, but saw this as being pursued in the context of a mixed economy of copy texts: 'I hope that in the Press edition there will be no jumbling of texts and that the folio or the quarto will be followed consistently throughout each single play.'[70] At about this time, Smith was offered the Goldsmith's readership at Oxford and he moved to the university 'expecting that Shakespeare was to be [his] main work for the next dozen years or more'.[71] He proceeded with the project energetically at first and by November 1906 had completed three texts: *King Lear*, *Measure for Measure*, and *Henry V*. Henry Frowde wrote to the secretary of the press from London, asking 'Shall we begin composition at once and issue single plays as ready? or shall we wait until N. Smith sees the end and issue first in (say) nine volumes, cutting up afterwards?' Frowde was anxious 'to begin publication pretty soon, to knock Harrap and Collins'.[72] A specimen page was produced by the press in 1907, but no other printing would appear to have been carried out.[73] By August 1910, Smith had added *The Tempest* and *Two Gentlemen of Verona* to his list of completed texts and the press was envisaging a finished edition of six volumes of 500 pages each, or three volumes on India paper.[74]

As Smith was progressing with his work, he kept a close eye on the first fruits of the New Bibliography, which were just then beginning to appear in print. In later years, he wrote to Greg: 'I remember the excitement with which I read your articles in The Library on "False dates in Shakespearian Quartos" and in the following year Pollard's Folios and Quartos.' At the same time, however, all was not well in Smith's relationship with Raleigh, as he would explain to Greg:

problems arose in legions. Raleigh used to say that once I had got the plan on the page the rest would follow easily. Whenever I presented him with a problem he never seemed to me quite to see it, and if I presented him with more than one he soon grew weary.

Smith eventually came to feel that he was 'knocking [his] head against a stone wall'. The edition was, he thought, 'a mill-stone', which he did not feel he had the courage to throw off, though, in time, he said, 'it gradually dropped from my neck'.[75]

By 1920, the project appeared to be dead in the water. In that year, Kenneth Sisam wrote to R. W. Chapman, Secretary to the Delegates of the press, suggesting that Oxford consider reissuing the Lee First Folio facsimile. Chapman replied that such an undertaking would be too costly and that a reissue would be unfair to the original subscribers. He further commented: 'For twenty years we have been trying to edit Shakespeare on scientific lines, but all editors have fallen by the wayside. It is of course very difficult, though I doubt if it is as difficult as they suppose.' Chapman was himself a scholar of considerable repute, who had assisted Simpson both in his work on Shakespeare's punctuation and in teaching bibliography at Oxford; he also himself edited important editions of Samuel Johnson and Jane Austen.[76] He did not think at this point that an Oxford edition was wholly a lost cause, though he seemed wary of the rate at which the editorial landscape was changing as the New Bibliography moved quickly forward. As he commented to Sisam: 'I still hope to publish a Shakespeare; but perhaps we had better wait till this dust settles and see what it leaves standing.'[77] Early in 1927, the press made an approach to Pollard regarding the Shakespeare project, but nothing of consequence happened as a result of the contact.[78]

In November 1929, the press had moved on to soliciting aid from another of the leading lights of the New Bibliography, when it approached McKerrow. McKerrow worried a little about his age – he was, by this time, fifty-seven years old – but he accepted the invitation nonetheless, writing to Chapman:

> Perhaps I ought to decline and advise you to find some younger man, but, as I told you, to edit an Oxford Shakespeare was once an ambition of mine – though necessarily abandoned nearly 20 years ago – and as the chance has come I don't think I can refuse it. Probably whoever you found to do it would take most of the rest of his life over it, and as one gets on one is perhaps less inclined to waste time![79]

McKerrow rearranged his work duties at the publishing firm of Sidgwick and Jackson to make more time for the edition. He also declined an invitation to succeed Pollard as editor of *The Library*, again, to preserve as much time as he possibly could for the Shakespeare project.[80]

In a letter to Kenneth Sisam at the press, McKerrow set out his general plan for the edition:

> Text. Follow as closely as reasonably possible one early text. Emendations only admitted into text when this is obviously corrupt and the emendations can be, to some extent, at least justified. Nothing admitted merely because it seems to be an improvement. Collations of all early texts, including in some cases Restoration quartos (as possibly embodying stage tradition), but no editor's readings except in places of real difficulties. Eighteenth-century editors' stage-directions, scene divisions and indications of locality, to be given in footnotes only, not in text.
>
> Explanatory (mainly glossarial) notes as footnotes. Occasional parallels from other plays or elsewhere when definitely enlightening – not inserted to show that the editor is aware of them! Notes on topical references where necessary. Discussion of special difficulties at end of play or vol.[81]

As the project took shape, McKerrow planned several innovative features for the edition. The plays were to be reproduced in chronological order, rather than, as was traditionally the case in most collected editions, in the order of First Folio presentation. Old spelling was to be retained, as was 'Old punctuation when it isn't a nuisance'.[82] There was also a suggestion that, in the case of plays where early texts of competing authority had survived, both early versions might be reproduced in parallel.[83] The text of the 'bad' quartos was to be included at the end of the edition.[84]

The mood at Oxford University Press in the early years of the 1930s was highly optimistic, with Kenneth Sisam declaring that McKerrow's would be 'an epoch-making work' that it would not 'be very easy to displace . . . in the next century'.[85] In April 1932, the press formally announced in *The Times Literary Supplement* that the edition was in preparation. John Dover Wilson wrote to Chapman in response to the announcement, declaring that an 'authoritative edition of Shakespeare by R. B. McKerrow will put the crown on the new scholarship & be the greatest edition of our age'.[86] McKerrow continued to make solid progress with his texts and David Nichol Smith returned to the project, invited by the press to read McKerrow's introductions, on the grounds that 'he went a considerable way once in preparing a major edition for us, and so knows the kind of problem that arises in practice'.[87] The introductory materials, together with the notes, were, in fact, to be the cause of a certain amount of friction between McKerrow and the press officials. Oxford had always been a little concerned about exactly what market they would be aiming to sell the edition into. In their earliest correspondence, Sisam had warned McKerrow on the subject of annotation: 'Don't be too rigorous in the standard of learning assumed, because we shall hope to sell some copies to retired American business men. I am told the average young man in America who comes up to take a University course in English has seldom heard the name of Milton.'[88] What the press was aiming for, in part, was what it styled a 'Gentleman's Shakespeare'. McKerrow rejected the idea, observing to Sisam that what they envisaged 'was really a contradiction in terms, for no gentleman would read Shakespeare in old spelling!'[89] Sisam nevertheless still worried about the size of the market that the edition might hope to capture, writing to McKerrow (but shifting away a little from the previously invoked Gentleman Reader):

> I am speaking, of course, only as a publisher looking at the prospects of the book, but I think every move towards making the edition one for textual critics only must carry with it a sacrifice of the general educated reader – the non-professional reader of Shakespeare – without whom the public is rather strictly limited these days.[90]

Eventually, Greg weighed into the dispute, having been asked to look at some specimen pages. He cautioned Sisam:

> You must not aim at two things at once. If the Clarendon Press publishes a (textual) critical edition it ought to remain the standard for a long while to come. And I think you have got the right man to do it. But it is no use trying to get him to make a popular edition, & I think it would be a mistake to aim at that. It will only be of real interest to the reader interested in the criticism of text & such a reader doesn't want pap.

On a more commercially consoling note, Greg suggested that McKerrow's edition should have a greater general appeal than the Clark and Wright Cambridge edition and he concludes 'I shouldn't think that has sold so badly in the long run.'[91]

By 1936, McKerrow had made sufficient progress that he was beginning to feel inconvenienced by the accumulation of finished materials. On 10 January, he wrote to Sisam: 'I am very anxious to get something into print this year as the mass of copy is getting a nuisance!'[92] By the middle of 1936, he had acquired an assistant to help him in his work: Alice Walker. She had, McKerrow observed, 'an eagle eye for every kind of inconsistency and sloppiness'.[93] Greg, too, thought her possessed of 'a very acute brain'.[94] By December, McKerrow was sufficiently impressed with Walker to suggest that her name 'should appear on the half-titles of the plays of which she undertakes the collation'. He further noted that 'if she continues to give me as much help as she is giving me at present . . . her name should in vols. from Vol IV onwards appear with mine on the general title, either as assistant editor or joint-editor as seems appropriate'.[95]

In January of the following year, McKerrow returned to the question of publication, registering alarm at a suggestion from the press that they wished to see 'five vols. . . . in a finished state before beginning to print'. He appealed to Sisam that he 'should like to see two or three vols. out, but even if they were only printed it would be something'. He could, he observed 'at any rate use them for reference'. To encourage the press, he noted that, if some of the material were to be set in print (rather than remaining in his tangled mass of manuscripts), 'there would be no difficulty in someone else carrying on when I die or get beyond work, – at any rate with the assistance of Miss Walker who completely understands the principles on which I have been working (even if she doesn't always quite agree with them!)'.[96] Sisam responded sympathetically, indicating that the press would be willing to set the first two volumes in print provided that McKerrow could confirm that the manuscript of volume three would quickly follow.[97] The press proceeded with this plan and proofs of the initial volumes were run off.[98]

McKerrow became concerned at the extent to which his general introduction on the treatment of the text had 'grown & grown as the work progressed', achieving what he described as 'a fearful length'.[99] Ultimately, it was decided that this material should be spun off into a wholly separate volume, entitled *Prolegomena for the Oxford Shakespeare: A Study in Editorial Method*, which was finally published in 1939. McKerrow noted in his Preface that

> Editors, while often very conscious of the imperfections in the work of their predecessors, appear for the most part to have regarded their task as the solution of a series of hardly related problems, each of which could be dealt with separately as it arose, and to have troubled themselves very little about laying down any general principles for their own guidance or securing any uniformity in the treatment of their author's writings as a whole.[100]

McKerrow himself, by contrast, aimed at setting out a coherent account of the procedures and principles which he intended to adopt in producing his edition. It was, in essence, a kind of New Bibliographic handbook for the editing of Shakespeare – the first Shakespearean editorial manual of its kind.[101] Greg later systematised and modified McKerrow's principles in the opening section of his own *Editorial Problem in Shakespeare* volume, first published in 1942.

As the decade drew to a close, McKerrow's health deteriorated. Chapman wrote to Humphrey Milford in March 1939, giving a pen-picture of a scholar worn down by age and illness, but still possessed of a determination to make progress with the edition: 'We had a visit from McKerrow yesterday. He called himself "an old man", and he certainly looks flabby and walks stiffly. But he is wonderfully recovered – he was at one time given up – and he may do it after all.'[102] McKerrow himself seemed to recognise that he was unlikely to see the project through to conclusion and in May he wrote to Sisam, observing: 'I think that if I were able to look after at least 4 or 5 vols. myself, you might well consider allowing Dr Walker to finish it without appointing anyone else.'[103] On 20 January 1940, however, Chapman received the following brief telegram from McKerrow's wife, Amy: 'My husband passed away this morning.'[104] He was the first of the 'triumvirate' to die, though he would be followed by Pollard just four years later.

Following McKerrow's death, Sisam met with Alice Walker to discuss the extent of the materials that had already been prepared, and to explore the possibility that she might continue with the project herself, as McKerrow had wished. Sisam formed the opinion that Walker was 'very competent as well as accurate, clear headed, and not likely to be getting tied into knots unnecessarily'.[105] She indicated a willingness to proceed with the edition and Sisam wrote to Greg and to E. K. Chambers, asking whether they would be prepared to act as informal advisors to Walker. He assured Greg that 'she wants good counsel rather than trouble research or spade work'. His tone in writing to Greg was sombre, inflected both by the mood of the times and by a sense that the New Bibliography might by now have reached its high-water mark:

> we cannot blind our eyes to the fact that the great age is passing, now that McKerrow is gone, Pollard is not available, and both you and Chambers have many other things to do; and the new generation don't seem to be of quite the same calibre. So I hope that, with all reservations about your time and health, you will agree to give a hand, for I really believe that, with a little encouragement, we can carry the job through; and in these black days, I hate to think of any great work of learning foundering which could be kept alive.[106]

Greg readily agreed to help. He was optimistic regarding the enduring legacy of the New Bibliography: 'If scholarship survives at all, I think the work of our generation may bear fruit & that the lines of advance we have seen laid down may be carried on to greater purpose by younger men.' But he shared

Sisam's sense of foreboding concerning the war, observing 'I am not very confident that any thing worth having will survive the present débacle.'[107]

Despite the best intentions of Walker, Sisam, Chambers, Greg, and even the redoubtable Nichol Smith, who rejoined the project yet again (to complete the 'three veterans who have undertaken to act as an Advisory Committee'), the project faltered once more.[108] Trevor Howard-Hill has suggested that 'the intensification of the war apparently suspended interest in the edition' at Oxford University Press.[109] At much the same time, Walker ran into considerable difficulty at Royal Holloway College, where she was serving as Registrar and Secretary to the Principal, Janet Bacon. An acrimonious dispute led Walker and Bacon to resign from their posts at Holloway and they retired together to Welcombe in Devonshire – a turn of events which proved to be extremely disruptive to Walker's textual work. By 1950, Walker had begun to publish on bibliographic topics once again, but when Oxford thought to revive the Shakespeare edition, they placed the project in the hands of G. I. Duthie.[110] In an odd echo of her earlier experience with McKerrow, Walker was drawn back into the edition in 1955, to serve as Duthie's co-editor, and when Duthie's health failed in 1957 she once again assumed the position of de facto editor.

Not long after reassuming responsibility for the project, Walker re-entered the academic realm, becoming Reader in Textual Criticism at Oxford in 1959. She was by now nearly sixty years of age and had not been involved in teaching for almost three decades. The strain her new position placed on her was considerable, as Trevor Howard-Hill has noted:

> The burden of teaching was exacerbated by her own thoroughness and
> sense of responsibility to her students but also by the increasing number
> of graduate students admitted to Oxford University during the 1960s.
> She found little time for her own work, notably the Oxford Shakespeare,
> which she had hoped that the Oxford appointment would facilitate.[111]

In January 1965, Walker applied for sabbatical leave from Oxford, noting in her application that 'every year has made it necessary for me to provide an increasing number of classes. My own work (the preparation of an Old Spelling edition of Shakespeare for the Clarendon Press) is in consequence shockingly in arrears.'[112] At around this time, the press switched from their original plan of issuing a set of multi-text volumes to proposing to publish the texts singly – a mode of publication which, as we shall see, had served their Cambridge counterparts well. Walker's edition of *Coriolanus* was advertised as imminent in 1964, but it never appeared in print.[113] By the closing years of the 1960s, Walker began to develop serious health problems and the project would appear to have slipped away from her. Howard-Hill notes that, when he visited her in 1972 at the behest of the press, 'she simply did not want to talk about the edition'.[114] Quite apart from the many logistical difficulties which she faced, it is possible that she simply lost faith in the edition. We have seen McKerrow indicate that, while Walker completely understood the principles he was following, she did not necessarily always agree with them. In particular, she would seem not to have shared his enthusiasm for the notion of producing a modern old-spelling edition.[115] Certainly, the only Shakespeare texts that she ever did publish – for Dover Wilson's Cambridge edition – were in modernised spelling. So she may ultimately have come to feel that she was struggling against the odds to produce an edition, the fundamental principles of which were contrary to her own thinking. By the time Walker died in 1982, Oxford University Press had already made a completely new start on the project, appointing Stanley Wells to produce a wholly new edition.[116] The 1986 'Oxford Shakespeare' produced jointly by Wells, Gary Taylor, John Jowett and William Montgomery will be discussed in the next chapter.

 While Oxford was persistently struggling to get its edition off the ground, Cambridge was having greater success initiating a similar flagship project. Cambridge University Press made a later start than its Oxford counterpart and, crucially, the Cambridge press decided from the beginning that it would issue individual plays as they were ready, rather than waiting until a large chunk of the canon had been completed, in order to be able to publish a multi-volume set. The background to the two projects was remarkably similar. Raleigh proposed his edition to Oxford shortly after he had been the inaugural appointee to Oxford's first chair fully dedicated to English literature. Cambridge's new edition was placed in the hands of Arthur Quiller-Couch ('Q'). Q was the second, rather than the first, holder of Cambridge's King Edward VII Professorship of English Literature (founded in 1910), but his predecessor had been the classicist, A. W. Verall. S. C. Roberts has commented that when Verall 'was succeeded by one who was primarily known as a novelist and anthologist, classical dons raised their eyebrows'.[117] Textual scholars may also have raised an eyebrow or two at Q's appointment to the Cambridge project, as he had little experience of scholarly editing. His attitude to the Shakespeare text was that of an enthusiast – an enthusiast who had first been introduced to the playwright by being clattered on the head by a volume of one of Knight's popular editions. When he was a young boy, Q and his sister had been travelling in their family's 'four-wheeled dog-cart', with their father 'on foot some paces behind, reading a book', when, suddenly,

> without warning the near hind-wheel detached itself and we children
> were gently slid in a ditch, a small avalanche of books scattered on top of
> us. Out of these, while my father inspected the damage and our man
> trotted off on the mare with harness dangling, to fetch help from a
> wheelwright (luckily near), I picked a small volume (the first in a handy
> set of Knight's Shakespeare) and started, amid the brambles, to read *The
> Tempest*. It was my first reading in Shakespeare, 'all a wonder and a wild
> surmise', and this first love may account for a life-long preference of *The
> Tempest* above all his plays, even those esteemed his greatest.[118]

Like Raleigh, Q needed a partner who could tackle the hard graft of
textual criticism. A. R. Waller, Secretary to the Syndics of the press, had
been following a series of articles in *The Times Literary Supplement*, written
jointly by Pollard and a young John Dover Wilson, and Wilson appeared to
him to be the man for the job.[119] Pollard and Wilson had struck up a surrogate
father–son relationship under very difficult circumstances. Pollard lost both
his sons, Geoffrey and Roger, in the First World War and Wilson's father
died in the same year. 'It seemed natural', Wilson later wrote, 'that we should
adopt each other.'[120] When Waller invited Wilson to join Q in the project,
Wilson immediately wrote to Pollard for guidance, receiving the following
reply, full of sound advice:

> I don't think you will ever produce a standard text of Shakespeare. I hope
> you won't, as it would mean giving up too much of your life to it. If the
> Cambridge Press wanted you to produce a real standard text to cut out
> the Globe and any rivals to it you would have to give at least ten years to
> it. But you ought to be able to produce a provisional text which will be
> better than anything existing, though not sufficiently demonstrably so to
> cut 'em all out. Three bits of advice: (1) Don't accept or refuse any fee
> they offer till you've consulted me; (2) reserve your freedom to produce
> another text if you please later on; (3) get all the advice you can as to
> textual principles before starting, but don't try to edit Shakespeare by
> committee.[121]

The original contract for the edition stipulated that the editors would deliver
seven plays per year to the press. Q thought this figure 'rather much' and
so 'altered the seven to six in red ink'.[122] Even this figure would prove to
be comically over-optimistic. As Wilson later commented – reflecting on
the fact that he initially considered the project simply a digression from
other work – in time, 'the magnitude of this parergon, so lightly undertaken,
revealed itself and it became clear that not more than two plays could be
produced even in the best of years'.[123]

The differences of attitude between Q and Wilson were clear from the very start. Q proposed that they begin the series with *The Tempest*, not because it was the first play in the First Folio collection, or even because it was his favourite play, but rather because, as he put it, 'I know a little about ships.'[124] Wilson later revealed that 'Q's first idea was that each volume should be a pretty little book that ladies could carry to picnics.'[125] In holding this vision, Q was not wholly out of step with the objectives of the press. Waller – like his counterparts at Oxford – was anxious, from a commercial point of view, that the edition should appeal to as wide a market as possible. In a letter of July 1920, he attempted gently to convey this concern to Wilson:

> Publishers, even University Presses, are not primarily philanthropists. Unless we can make some books pay, we cannot publish contributions to learning which we know will not pay. We are not endowed like the Chicago University Press. Hence, if the commercial souled Waller presses the business aspect of things, remember him in your prayers and think kindly of him.

> Bibliographical learning will make the new Shakespeare of permanent value & sought after by scholars. Hence the desire of the syndics for your help. The proportion of people who will buy the book for its bibliographical learning is about 1 in the 100: it is by giving the 90 & 9 something they will pay us for that will enable us to satisfy the One.[126]

In 1925, Q indicated that he would be bowing out of the project, as his eyesight was failing.[127] Wilson suggested to the press that he was willing either to continue on his own or to collaborate with 'a critic of similar standing to Sir A. Quiller Couch, for example Sir Henry Newbolt, Mr. de la Mare or Mr. John Baily'.[128] These proposals came to nothing and Wilson ultimately took on the whole burden of the series himself, pleased, perhaps, to have a freer hand in setting the agenda for the work.

From the outset, Wilson was determined to produce an edition that would be informed by the latest bibliographical thinking. 'By the aid of these new tools', he wrote in his 'Textual Introduction' to the inaugural *Tempest* volume (1921), 'time-honoured textual cruxes have been attacked and fresh ones brought to light' (§1139, xliii). At the same time, however, he was aware of the fact that many of the methods he was employing were largely untried from the practical perspective of actually editing texts. Adopting a sea-faring vocabulary of which Q would doubtless have approved, Wilson noted that, in launching the series, they had put forth 'upon an uncharted ocean with a set of brand-new instruments, which had never been used for such a voyage before or, indeed, for editorial seamanship of any kind'. It had been impossible,

Wilson continued, 'to tell how these instruments would work, whether the voyage would be one of real discovery or of shipwreck'. Casting a backward glance over the first decade's worth of textual sailing in 1930, he concluded that, while the edition was not yet 'in sight of land . . . the adventure is no longer haunted by fears of immediate or ultimate disaster'.[129]

Where the other New Bibliographers tended to be cautiously conservative in their thinking, Wilson was altogether more energetically speculative, often building extravagant theories on relatively shallow evidential foundations. Finely splicing praise with critique, W. W. Greg, in the prefatory remarks to his Clark lectures of 1939, observed of Wilson that 'he has himself done much to promote the advancement of our knowledge by the alertness of his critical imagination, and at the same time perhaps something to embarrass it by the very fertility of the same quality'.[130] More evocatively, Greg compared some of Wilson's more fanciful theories to the erratic flight of a hot-air balloon that has slipped its moorings:

> Reading him I am constantly reminded of a story in the papers a few years ago. A company of French soldiers were tethering a captive balloon in a high wind, when the monster got out of hand. The men were swept off their feet. Some let go and were dashed to the ground, others held on and were carried away. Even so, under the fascination of Professor Wilson's ingenuity, I am ever in doubt whether to let go and risk a nasty fall, or to cling desperately and be borne I know not whither.[131]

The imaginative complexity of Dover Wilson's theorising is nicely indicated in his two-volume study of *The Manuscript of Shakespeare's 'Hamlet' and the Problems of its Transmission*, published in 1934. Wilson's reading of the history of the First Folio text was that it was the result of a double transcription. In his view, a theatrical scribe had produced a transcript intended to serve as prompt-copy and this text had, in its turn, been transcribed a second time to produce copy for the Jaggards' compositors. Wilson proposed that the first of these transcribers 'would inevitably have drawn attention to the inordinate length of the play', with the result that 'the prompter might well have laid the completed transcript before Shakespeare with an intimation that it must be cut down by at least 200 lines, especially Burbadge's part, if anything further was to be done with it'.[132] In cutting Burbage's part, Shakespeare, Wilson suggests, likely tinkered with other parts of the text as well, making both large-scale and smaller-scale changes. When the final prompt-book version of the play was being retranscribed for the First Folio, the second scribe further changed the text, drawing on his memory of having seen the play in production at the Globe. 'Such a supposition',

Wilson suggests, 'would explain the preposterous "O, o, o, o" after "The rest is silence".' The scribe

> had vivid memories of *Hamlet* on the stage, and was perhaps a fond admirer of the greatest actor of the age. If so, it would be easy to understand how he came to add to his text the dying groans – no doubt very effective – of his hero, that he might 'lose no drop of the immortal man'.[133]

These suppositions, and the theories founded on them, are fascinating, but Wilson advances scant evidence to support his conclusions.[134]

Wilson's imaginative turn of mind was also much in evidence in his handling of stage directions, which were at times positively Shavian in their detailed complexity.[135] At II.ii of *Hamlet*, for example, Wilson adds the stage direction: '*Hamlet, disorderly attired and reading a book, enters the lobby by the door at the back; he hears voices from the chamber and pauses a moment beside one of the curtains, unobserved*' (§1153, p. 43).[136] In the opening scene of *Titus Andronicus*, Wilson supplies the following direction: '*An open place in Rome, before the Capitol, beside the entrance to which there stands the monument of the Andronici. Through a window opening on to the balcony of an upper chamber in the Capitol may be seen the Senate in session*' (§1160, p. 3). Stanley Wells comments rather dryly in response to the conclusion of this direction: 'Not too easily, I should have thought.'[137] While admiring Wilson's 'attempts to indicate action, costume, properties, and so on', Wells nevertheless observes that he 'goes further than is necessary . . . which has caused his edition to date rather rapidly'.[138]

The mixture of extravagance and keen insight provided by Wilson in the textual introductions to his New Shakespeare editions was noted at Oxford, where a wary eye was constantly kept on developments at Cambridge.[139] When Kenneth Sisam sent McKerrow's introductions to Nichol Smith in 1933, he observed in a parenthetical comment: 'I feel that in twenty years' time, when we hope that this will still be the standard text, the references to Dover Wilson will seem disproportionate.'[140] McKerrow's own view of Wilson was more nuanced and, generally, more sympathetic. In a letter to Sisam dated 20 May 1933, he observes: 'one can't ignore D. W.'s work . . . it is too ingenious & too plausible and besides it always has some foundation'. He concludes that 'In most cases it seems to me that his superstructure is much too big for his facts, but his theories will undoubtedly be discussed and I don't see that one can ignore them.'[141] In a subsequent letter to Sisam, McKerrow observes that 'the truth is that D. W. is a clever and ingenious fellow! I don't by any means always agree with his views but he <u>had</u> noticed a lot of queer things in the plays which probably indicate something or other.'[142]

For all his theoretical waywardness, Dover Wilson was also determinedly pragmatic and he was wholly committed to bringing the series successfully to a conclusion. He revealed his pragmatic bent in a letter which he wrote to G. V. Smithers in the 1950s. Smithers had been supposed to produce an overall glossary to accompany the edition and had signally failed to deliver the goods. An exasperated Wilson demanded whether he would ever finish the work, commenting on his own experience:

> Two or three life-times are insufficient for the proper editing of Shakespeare, and I know it well enough. Had I lingered over Hamlet alone as long as I ought to have done, and should like to have done, I should still be at it. But I pushed on – with all my imperfections on my head, and with the critics always at my heels, and with their criticism too often justified, – in the belief that an edition of the complete works by one mind might be serviceable for the present generation and that anything of value it might contain would get built up into later editions of others.[143]

Wilson soldiered on with the edition year after year, drawing in a trio of assistants as the project advanced to a conclusion. These were J. C. Maxwell, G. I. Duthie and Alice Walker – who resumed her textual work to help Wilson with his edition of *Othello*, then edited *Troilus and Cressida* for the series herself in 1957. With a certain sense of triumph and relief, Wilson was able to write to Dick David at Cambridge University Press in February 1966 and declare:

> The President of the U.S.A. delivers a State of the Union message at the beginning of every year; and it is my habit, you may recollect, to follow his practice (more than 2000 miles off) by writing a state-of-the-New Shakespeare message to my President. And I do so at the beginning of 1966 with the more confidence that the edition is now complete, the copy for the Sonnets having been revised and accepted by your Mr Burbidge.

It had taken Wilson the best part of a half century, from start to finish, and he was barely able to continue working by the end, as he reported to David: 'it was [finished] only just in time, as the eyes have faded so far that they couldn't see a line of type any more'. [144]

The inordinate length of time that it had taken to get the whole edition into print meant that, by the time Wilson was done, the books themselves were already looking decidedly old-fashioned. Cambridge University Press planned a reconfiguration of the texts in an attempt to recapture ground lost

to, for example, Methuen's *Arden Shakespeare*. David (who was himself, as
it happens, an Arden editor) explained this to Wilson not long after his final
text was submitted:

> with the passage of the years the design of the original edition and
> particularly the size of type has come to be found less attractive by
> potential purchasers who compare it unfavourably with e.g., the Arden,
> and in addition they are not very well geared to economical printing. The
> Arden edition, our chief rival, has now gone into paperback; if we are to
> continue to compete with it we must meet it on its own ground.
> Mansbridge therefore in America . . . has been experimenting with the
> possibility of photographing the existing texts, magnifying the
> photograph and printing from them a larger page. Because students the
> world over are now more inclined to buy paperbacks than hardbacks we
> have thought of binding such a photographic reprint primarily in
> paper . . . ; but the problem is basically no more than the representation
> of the existing edition in a more attractive form.[145]

The process of producing the reconfigured paperback edition turned 'into a
crash programme' following the appearance of the *New Penguin Shakespeare*,
which was published in softback format.[146]

The ultimate intention at Cambridge had been to crown the series with
a single-volume edition, uniting all the texts. Long-standing questions regarding the potential market for the edition resurfaced, however, when this
last phase of the project was finally being considered. David noted the 'most
formidable' difficulty which the press faced was their 'uncertainty about just
which audience we should aim at'. He continued:

> We think that there is no possible method of producing the one-volume
> without entirely re-setting the type, and this will mean a very substantial
> capital expense. We shall not, therefore, be able to compete in price with,
> for example, the complete Oxford or three or four other editions which
> have been printing and re-printing for many years and have long ago paid
> off their capital costs . . . We shall have, therefore, to sell our edition on
> merit rather than cheapness, and in the ordinary household it is clear, I
> am sorry to say, that cheapness is more important than a good text. After
> all the book is only used for solving crossword puzzles.

One possibility canvassed at the press was that 'a very lavish volume, or
perhaps three volumes, on handmade paper' might be produced in the first
instance, to be sold 'at a high price' and that this might serve to 'pay off the
capital costs of re-setting'. David admitted, however, that the press feared

'the danger of falling between every conceivable stool' and plans for the single-volume edition would appear quietly to have been shelved.[147]

Wilson died in 1969, just three years after the appearance of his final volume. He was eighty-eight years old and it is hard not to feel that it was only his longevity and good health that had meant that his extraordinary editorial feat could have been achieved at all. His work had not been completed even two full decades when Cambridge University Press initiated a entirely new edition to replace it. In one sense, then, it might be said that his achievement was hardly enduring. But, as Harold Jenkins has noted, 'the importance of his edition lies rather in its demonstration of new possibilities and methods'.[148] To revert to Wilson's own sea-going metaphor, where the triumvirate of Greg, McKerrow and Pollard had charted a new course for editing Shakespeare in the twentieth century, Wilson can be said to have been the first to take to the water and to bring an edition founded on New Bibliographic principles securely into the final harbour of print.

In endeavouring to put into practice the techniques and theories evolved by the New Bibliography, John Dover Wilson was breaking new ground and was helping to institute a new editorial dispensation. As Wilson's own edition slowly took shape over the course of almost half a century, the general methods he was deploying gradually gained ground and became an established part of editorial practice. From about the mid-century, most new editions were heavily influenced by New Bibliographic thinking. This was certainly true of the *Arden Shakespeare*, which was relaunched in 1951, initially under the general editorship of Una Ellis-Fermor. Fermor herself, however, though a sound scholar and critic, was not a textual specialist and many of the volume editors also lacked extensive experience of editing. As a result, *Arden* 2 became something of an uneven affair, with some texts, such as A. R. Humphreys' *Much Ado About Nothing*, being 'edited with scrupulous care for the bibliographical history of the text and what can be conjectured about the nature of the underlying manuscript', but other texts being far less rigorously executed.[1]

The impact of the New Bibliography on mainstream Shakespeare publishing can clearly be seen in another edition which appeared in print in 1951: Peter Alexander's Collins text of the complete works. Alexander was a native Glaswegian, who became Regius Professor of English Language and Literature at the city's university in 1935 – a post which had in the past been filled by A. C. Bradley and by Walter Raleigh, with the latter holding the Glasgow chair just prior to initiating his ill-fated Oxford Shakespeare project.[2] In common with many other twentieth-century bibliographers, Alexander had strong family connections with the world of science. His uncle Tommy Alexander was Professor of Civil Engineering successively at Imperial College in Tokyo and at Trinity College Dublin. A second uncle, also named Peter Alexander, lectured in mathematics at Queen Margaret College in Edinburgh. J. C. Bryce has observed that the latter uncle's 'namesake-nephew never knew him except by posthumous fame, but by the time he left school he had read at least some of his uncle's works, which included papers on Fourier's theorems and on kinetics and a systematic *Treatise on Thermodynamics*'. The English professor retained a lifelong interest in mathematics and joked about 'looking forward to a retirement spent in tackling some of the famous problems that had exercized the masters'.[3]

Alexander established his reputation as a bibliographer in the 1920s, initially with a series of articles in *The Times Literary Supplement*. Building on Pollard's work in *Shakespeare's Folios and Quartos*, he suggested that *The first part of the contention betwixt the two famous houses of Yorke and Lancaster* (1594), *The true tragedie of Richard Duke of Yorke* (1595) and *The Taming of a Shrew* (1594) should be added to the list of Shakespearean bad quartos. In 1929, Alexander published a more considered study of the *Henry VI* plays and of *Richard III* as part of Pollard and Dover Wilson's Cambridge University Press 'Shakespeare Problems' series. In an introduction to the volume, Pollard characterised the book as 'a fine attempt to bring new light to bear on problems which have been discussed almost to weariness' and as 'the best contribution to his subject that has yet been made'.[4] In his own Preface, Alexander observed that: 'Like other students of Shakespeare, I owe to Professor Pollard the sense of a new style and new spirit in textual criticism.'[5]

In 1944, the publishing firm of Collins approached Alexander in connection with a Shakespeare edition. Collins had been one of the giants of Scottish publishing in the previous century, at one point giving employment to about 700 people, and they had offices in both Glasgow and London.[6] They had been reissuing the same complete works of Shakespeare for the best part of a century and they estimated that 'several million copies must have been sold'.[7] By the mid-forties, the company was uncertain as to whether it wished simply to continue reissuing this original edition or if it should instead have the text revamped by a contemporary scholar. Alexander was called in to advise on the matter. In his response to the company's queries, he noted the manner in which the textual scene had changed in recent decades, registering the extent to which a new editorial regime had become established, but also expressing some reservations about the blind enthusiasm of some editors for the new orthodoxies:

> Since your text was produced, and this applies to the Globe and Oxford texts, criticism has reassessed the value of the authorities on which every text must rest. The Quarto readings have gone up in the general estimation. Dover Wilson in his pioneer edition (the New Cambridge) showed the way and he has been followed by the Temple and Penguin editors and the Americans. In my opinion the swing over has gone too far even in Dover Wilson's text; with some others all balance has been lost.[8]

Alexander met with George F. Maine at the press on 21 September 1944 and, following the meeting, Maine wrote to the senior directors of the company outlining the alternatives of either reprinting the old text with an updated glossary and other supporting materials – work which Alexander was willing to carry out anonymously – or commissioning Alexander to 'undertake the editorship of the present volume, which would then bear his name'. Maine pointed out that 'Practically every new edition of Shakespeare published either here or in America during the last ten years bears as its hallmark of scholarship the name or names of the editors who worked on it'; he further noted that while 'this has little weight with the general public, it is a recommendation when the book is required by universities and schools'.[9] It was quickly agreed that a re-edited text bearing Alexander's name was the preferred option and Maine arranged terms with the Glasgow professor. He was to be paid 500 guineas for the work, part of which would be spent on employing two assistants. Alexander estimated that the work would take a total of 2,000 hours and he proposed 'to divide it into twelve sections to be completed in twelve monthly parts'.[10] Maine further agreed with Alexander that a second version of the text would be produced, to be spun off into the 'Collins Classics' series. This version would run to four volumes: '(1) Comedies (2) Histories (3) Tragedies and (4) the remainder of the Tragedies and the poems'.[11]

The 2,000 hours that Alexander estimated for the project amounted to the equivalent of just 250 working days – an absurdly inadequate span of time given the scale of what was involved. We will recall that Arthur Quiller-Couch thought that Cambridge's requirement that he and Dover Wilson might edit seven plays a year was 'rather much', but Alexander was proposing to produce a complete-works volume in the space of somewhat less than a year.[12] Given these circumstances, it seems unlikely that Alexander built his text absolutely from the ground up – certainly, he himself describes the edition as a 'revision of the text of Shakespeare that Messrs. Collins first published nearly ninety years ago' (§1300, p. v). Fredson Bowers has suspected that certain errors drifted into Alexander's text from the original Collins edition, as he notes that the editor's 'penetrating mind gives us, often, our best readings, but these may be mixed with faulty ones not weeded out with sufficient rigor from the old Collins text that served as basis'.[13] Even if Alexander attempted to save time by taking the old Collins edition as his base text, he still failed to deliver his work on time. On 27 January 1949 – three years after the project ought, by Alexander's reckoning, to have been completed – Maine was writing to the editor asking for 'the date when you will complete your work on the new single volume edition' and also asking for a progress report on the multi-volume text. 'Unless I can give satisfactory answers to these questions very quickly', he concludes, 'I shall be very unpopular, so please do what you can to help me.'[14] In October of the same year, Maine wrote to Alexander again, asking for the return of proofs and also 'whether work had been commenced on the Glossary'.[15] While the scale of the task might have made Alexander slow to deliver, he was certainly far from inactive and Bryce reports that, during the course of the time when he was working on the edition, Alexander's 'study lights were often seen burning between 3 and 4 a.m.'. Bryce also notes that as 'an arithmetician and with no grudge' the editor later worked out 'that the toil had brought him a farthing an hour'.[16]

The new Collins edition finally appeared in print in 1951. In the prefatory matter to the volume, Alexander explicitly aligned himself with the pioneering work of Pollard, McKerrow and Greg, noting that their 'study of Elizabethan books and theatrical documents in the light of collateral evidence hitherto neglected or misinterpreted enabled them to redraw on more probable and intelligible lines the history of the versions in which Shakespeare's work is transmitted to us' (§1300, p. v). Alexander had also been in touch directly with Dover Wilson and he was gratified to find that they seemed to be operating on the same wavelength, as he recounted to Maine: 'Dover Wilson has been at work this last six months or so on Rich iii & I'm glad to say he reports that any differences between our findings on this most troublesome text are trifling.'[17] In his acknowledgements to his own volume, Alexander noted that he had 'consulted with advantage' the volumes of Dover Wilson's edition which had thus far appeared in print, continuing that his debt to the edition 'is not the least I have to acknowledge; for whenever I have ventured to disagree with him on general principles or their particular application, I have not spared myself the expense of second thoughts' (§1300, p. vi). Dover Wilson's own contacts at Cambridge University Press did not particularly welcome the new edition – undoubtedly viewing it as a potential competitor to the New Cambridge text (which, at the time of course, they imagined would ultimately be issued in a single-volume version). In a letter to Dover Wilson, Cambridge University Press Manager Richard David dismissively observed of Alexander: 'I see that his one-volume edition of Shakespeare is now being advertised by Collins as forthcoming, with a good deal of gush about this being the first modern edition to embody all the results of the bibliographers. I suspect it will be full of misprints.'[18]

Though the one-volume text was in print by 1951, the four-volume edition remained to be completed and the press grew increasingly anxious about Alexander's failure to bring the project to a conclusion. Maine had made the disastrous decision of having the text of the plays set in type in advance of receiving the introductory materials. The consequence of this was that, since the books were not being printed in-house, the publishers were having to pay rental on the standing type. Maine pleaded with Alexander to finalise the edition, warning him that 'a storm is brewing and is about to break',[19] but Alexander temporised, explaining that just as the single-volume edition was finished 'a spate of stuff textual & otherwise came out', and observing:

> I greatly regret not having been able to take advantage of it. The new edition that Sisson is doing will; & they'll see the reviewers know all about it too. I was hoping we might just get something into the American printing to anticipate this, but as you can see all this needs thought & care & so time.

He ruefully concluded: 'I have been too ambitious to get it all right by my way of it, & such ambition is doubtless a sin.'[20]

The Comedies volume of the Classics edition was finally published in 1954 – the same year, as it happens, as C. J. Sisson's complete works volume.[21] The history plays appeared in the following year. By 1957, however, the tragedies volumes still had not been finalised and I. G. Collins himself was writing to Alexander, pointing out once again that the 'price of type metal and the rent we pay to the "outside" printer for the space occupied by this time combine to make this an astonishingly high figure over the years'. Collins offered Alexander a supplementary payment of £50 to employ someone to assist him in working on the glossary, and he attempted to set firm dates for submission of the completed materials.[22] Alexander failed to meet the new deadlines, but by the following year (1958), a new development had occurred. Heritage Press of New York contracted to produce an American edition using the Collins Classics text. Mrs H. Macy of Heritage began pressing for the work to be finished and her sense of urgency seemed to communicate itself clearly to Alexander, as he commented in a letter to the press: 'with Mr. Young's American lady friend cracking her whip or reaching down her gun, we had better get something to the printer quick before she bumps off the pianist'.[23] The concluding volumes of the Classics edition finally appeared in 1958.

The Heritage text was to include introductory matter by Tyrone Guthrie (on the comedies), George Rylands (on the tragedies) and James G. McManaway (on the histories). McManaway was then director of the Folger Library and Mrs Macy was able to report to Collins that he considered Alexander's edition to be 'the finest reading text available'.[24] At least one reviewer of the Heritage edition agreed, with M. C. Bradbrook observing that it was 'probably the most central and generally acceptable of versions recently produced'.[25] The Alexander edition itself certainly attained a very high degree of commercial and critical success and Gary Taylor has described it as the 'most esteemed and influential British edition of the twentieth century'.[26] The text was reprinted many times and served as the basis of a number of other commercial editions, published under licence from Collins, in much the same way as Macmillan's Globe text had also spawned a shoal of different versions. As late as 1978, the Alexander text was producing respectable sales figures of roughly 10,000 copies a year.[27]

At around this time, the edition received an additional boost, as it was chosen to serve as the text for the BBC TV series of the complete plays. BBC Publications decided to issue its own set of individual play texts, with Introductions by John Wilders and with the cuts made in production indicated in the margins. Collins agreed to provide the base text for these volumes at cost price (using the plates of their Classics edition), with the BBC to pay a royalty of $2\frac{1}{2}$ per cent of the selling price on the first 7,500 copies of each volume, rising to 3 per cent thereafter.[28] Collins sought to use the deal as an occasion for raising the profile of their own edition. The BBC agreed that a reference to the Alexander text would be incorporated in the credit sequence of their programmes and they also agreed to the inclusion of a short paragraph in their own volumes indicating that they were based on Alexander's edition. Collins proposed the following text for this acknowledgement:

> The Alexander Text of The Complete Works of William Shakespeare, edited by the late Professor Peter Alexander, is widely regarded as the standard reference text and was chosen by the BBC as the basis for its current major production of the complete plays. The complete Alexander Text is published in one volume by William Collins Sons & Company Ltd under the title 'The Alexander Text of the Complete Works of Shakespeare'.[29]

David Lester of BBC Publications responded to this proposal by indicating that the BBC's 'Production people were not too happy with [the] suggestion.'[30] In the end, Collins' self-promoting claim that the edition was 'widely regarded as the standard reference text' was dropped from the acknowledgement.

The BBC's own edition would not appear to have sold particularly well – certainly, by April 1979, Bill McLeod of Collins was writing to Tony Kingsford at the BBC observing that 'I take it, from the royalty statements I have seen, that you will not be too excited about the performance of the volumes.'[31] Collins themselves did, however, manage quite successfully to piggyback a revamped Alexander edition on the publicity surrounding the launch of the television series. As part of the deal they had struck with the BBC, Collins acquired exclusive rights to some production stills from the plays. They used these images to create a new cover for the Alexander text, producing what was referred to internally at Collins as the 'TV wrapped edition'. This volume performed well in the UK and elsewhere, though Collins were blocked from selling it into the US market. The BBC refused to sanction a US edition which made use of their images because the corporation's American partners, Time-Life, and their own American publishers, Mayflower Books, were not prepared to face competition from such an edition. The broadcasters were also considering the possibility of repaying their US commercial sponsors – the petrol corporation Exxon – by providing 'a very substantial quantity of the BBC books at a rock bottom price for distribution to its customers and agents'.[32]

The BBC connection helped the Alexander edition to gain a new lease on life in the late 1970s. In 1994 the edition was further revamped, when a team of academics from Alexander's old university in Glasgow provided a fresh set of introductions to the plays and Collins relaunched the text. The volume included an introductory essay on 'Shakespeare's Theatre', by Anthony Burgess – one of the very last pieces by the novelist to appear in print. The new edition also corrected an amusingly apt typographical error which had persisted in the text since its first printing. At line 61 of act v, scene iii, the Doctor in *Macbeth* had for forty years ruefully wished to be from the madhouse of 'Duninsane away and clear'.[33]

While the BBC and the Glasgow School of English contrived to revivify Alexander's text in the late 1970s and early 1990s, in the mid-1970s, the future of the edition had not looked quite so certain. At the time, Collins had cast about for a possible replacement text that might help to keep them securely in the Shakespeare market. A project which caught their eye at the time was a new text which was advertised as forthcoming in the US from Houghton Mifflin. This Boston-based company had published a Richard Grant White edition under the title *The Riverside Shakespeare* in 1883. Now they issued a prospectus for a new edition which would again use this title, with G. Blakemore Evans of Harvard serving as textual editor. In 1973, Collins approached Houghton Mifflin with a view to becoming the UK publisher of the text and initially the American company expressed some interest in the proposal. In January of the following year, however, Richard N. Clark wrote to Collins from Boston to indicate that there was no possibility of the two companies striking a deal:

> When I saw Mr. King last October, I promised him a look at this title, assuring him rights would be available. But the situation is changed. We have a new London-based sales operation about to start up, and the principals in that operation have asked us to withhold volume rights from any British house. As a result, I cannot do what I said I would – i.e., let you consider the book. Please accept my apologies.[34]

The fact that Collins were looking to an American edition as a possible alternative to the Alexander text indicates the extent to which the new editorial dispensation had by this time become firmly established in the US as well as in the UK. We have seen in chapter 9 how the editorial pendulum began to swing westward during the nineteenth century. A similar movement occurred in the twentieth century, when a British dominance in textual studies – established through the work of the New Bibliographers – was gradually supplanted by an American ascendancy. The emergence of advanced American textual scholarship was facilitated by the rise of the Modern Language Association, the professional body for American literary scholars, which supported many large-scale editorial initiatives. The person most responsible for transplanting New Bibliographic ways of thinking across the Atlantic was Fredson Bowers, son of the founder of the 'F. E. Bowers Company, Inc . . . a manufacturer of carburettors and motor parts'.[35] Bowers completed his PhD at Harvard, under the direction of George Lyman Kittredge, who served as one of the general editors of the second phase of the *Variorum Shakespeare* and whose own edition of the complete works was published by Ginn of Boston. In 1937, W. W. Greg observed in a letter to David Nichol Smith that he had

> had a long talk yesterday with a young American, Dr. F. T. Bowers by name, who has a play he wants the Malone Society to print. The editorial matter is more extensive than we have usually printed in the past, and although he is willing to reduce this to more normal limits, I am not sure that shorn of its more expansive and conjectural trappings, it would of itself retain much interest . . . He is going to be up in Oxford about the middle of August & it would be kind if you would allow him to call on you. He is a very nice fellow.[36]

The play in question was *The Fary Knight*, attributed to Thomas Randolph and preserved in a Folger manuscript. In the event, Bowers published his edition of the text with the University of Virginia Press rather than with the Malone Society.

Bowers' achievement in editing *The Fary Knight* was hardly epoch-making, but several of his other publishing projects were enormously influential. In 1949 his *Principles of Bibliographical Description* appeared and Bowers dedicated the book to Greg. The volume has been described by G. Thomas Tanselle as 'one of the great books in the history of bibliography'.[37] At the same time, Bowers was instrumental in founding the journal *Studies in Bibliography*. In the third issue of the annual (1950–1), Bowers published Greg's 'Rationale of Copy-Text', an essay which was to exert profound influence on textual editing for the next several decades. It was in this article that Greg first proposed a division between the 'accidental' and 'substantive' components of texts, arguing that an editor who faced a published text which had been partially revised by its author might opt to choose the substantive changes from the revised text while still retaining the accidentals of the earliest authoritative printed text, on the basis that the earlier text was likely to be closer to the author's practice in such features as orthography and punctuation.[38] Bowers championed Greg's view in the US and his own text of the works of Thomas Dekker – the inaugural volume of which appeared in 1953 – was the first edition to employ Greg's system. Reviewing the complete edition in *Shakespeare Survey* in 1961, Arthur Brown commented that 'Bowers's methods differ in almost every important respect from those of previous editors. He is quite deliberately putting into practice the accumulated theory of fifty years of textual scholarship.'[39] In more general terms, Bowers certainly shared Greg's conception of bibliography itself as a kind of hard-headed forensic science, commenting in one public lecture that 'strict bibliography . . . rests on the impersonal interpretation of physical facts according to rigorous laws of evidence'.[40]

The only Shakespeare text which Bowers himself produced was an edition of *The Merry Wives of Windsor*, which he published in Alfred Harbage's Pelican series.[41] He did, however, discuss the problems associated with the Shakespeare text in his volume *On Editing Shakespeare and the Elizabethan Dramatists*, based on his Rosenbach Lectures, delivered at the University of Pennsylvania in 1954. Reviewing this volume, Greg characterised Bowers as 'one who has thought on the questions at issue perhaps more profoundly than any other American scholar'.[42] His greater significance from a Shakespearean point of view may be seen, however, as lying in his promoting New Bibliographic theories and techniques in the US and in fostering the work of American textual scholars – Charlton Hinman was, for example, his first ever PhD student (graduating from the University of Virginia in 1941, having completed a study of *The Printing of the First Quarto of Othello*).[43] Tanselle has justly observed that, when Greg died in 1959, Bowers became 'unquestionably the most prominent bibliographical and textual scholar in the English-speaking world'.[44]

We have already seen that, by the early 1970s, modern American editions were sufficiently well regarded in the UK that Collins were investigating the possibility of becoming co-publishers of Houghton-Mifflin's American *Riverside* edition. Indeed, Oxford University Press also considered bidding to become the UK publishers of the text.[45] At the time of its appearance the *Riverside* was hailed by William C. McAvoy in *Shakespeare Quarterly* as 'a superb work, more than sufficient for the most advanced scholar and student and yet at the same time quite appropriate for the general reader', and he concluded that the volume was 'textually the best edition of Shakespeare yet to appear'.[46] The edition certainly enjoyed a very high degree of success in North America, achieving a dominant market position on college campuses and, crucially, serving as one of the standard reference texts for many American scholars.[47]

Like Bowers, the *Riverside* textual editor G. Blakemore Evans had contributed a volume to Harbage's Pelican series: an edition of *Richard III* published in 1959. He commenced work on the *Riverside* in the following year, though the thought of editing 'Shakespeare's complete works had occupied [his] mind and been a kind of dream long before' this.[48] As a Shakespearean textual scholar, Evans had a pleasing historical pedigree. His mother was a cousin of W. J. Craig, who had edited the complete works for Oxford University Press (and whose text remained in print for decade after decade as the press failed to get a new edition off the ground). While Evans was still an undergraduate, his father presented him with a number of books which had belonged to Craig, including a copy of Thomas Hawkins' *The Origins of the English Drama* which had been a gift to Craig from fellow Irishman Edward Dowden.[49] Dowden was, of course, the founding general editor of the *Arden Shakespeare* and Craig had succeeded him to the general editorship of the series.[50] Evans' old-school heritage notwithstanding, his edition is solidly executed within the parameters of the New Bibliographic paradigm, which he describes in his introduction to the volume as 'a fresh and comparatively "scientific" approach to the problems presented by the text' (§1508, p. 34). Evans' indebtedness to the New Bibliographic approach had been clearly signalled in a chapter on 'Shakespeare's Text: Approaches and Problems' which he contributed to the 1971 Cambridge University Press *New Companion to Shakespeare Studies*, in which he maps out the significance for editors of the concepts of foul papers, prompt copy, good and bad quartos, memorial reconstruction, and other central New Bibliographic ideas.

One innovative aspect of the *Riverside* was Evans' attempt to effect a compromise between original and modernised punctuation and spelling. Where punctuation was concerned, Evans noted that he very early decided to give as much weight as was reasonable in a modernized text to the special characteristics of the punctuation in each of the chosen copy-texts. If not Shakespeare's, it was at least the work of his contemporaries, men in whom the rhythms and special emphases of his language were alive and immediately felt. By a policy of selective modernization I believed I was able to retain something of the fluidity and cohesiveness of the original without imposing on the text as a whole either a merely antiquarian faithfulness or the Iron Maiden of modern logical punctuation.[51]

Likewise Evans observed that while his text was basically a modern-spelling edition, he had made an attempt 'to preserve a selection of Elizabethan spelling forms that reflect, or may reflect, a distinctive contemporary pronunciation, both those that are invariant in the early printed texts and those that appear beside the spellings familiar today and so suggest possible variant pronunciations of single words' (§1508, p. 39). Among the spelling forms retained in the *Riverside* edition are such words as: bankrout (for bankrupt), murther (murder), vild (vile) and strook (struck). Evans' decision to handle punctuation and spelling in this way was not universally well received. Stanley Wells observed of the *Riverside* that 'its wealth of ancillary material makes it the ideal desert-island Shakespeare', but he also felt that Evans had taken textual compromise to its *reductio ad absurdum*, noting that his editorial policy rested 'upon the fallacious assumption of a far greater degree of correlation between spelling and pronunciation in both Elizabethan and modern English than is justified by the evidence'.[52]

Wells had himself served as Associate Editor of the highly successful *New Penguin Shakespeare* series.[53] In 1977, Oxford University Press approached him with the aim of, once again, trying to get a complete works edition off the ground. As we have seen in the previous chapter, the Oxford edition which had been initiated by Walter Raleigh in 1904 had finally run irretrievably into the sand some time in the 1960s, under the stewardship of Alice Walker. Oxford now proposed to adopt a wholly new approach. Wells was to become a full-time employee of the press from January 1978, so he would not suffer from the distractions of academic employment.[54] The press were prepared, in the first instance, to invest as much as £250,000 in the project, in the hope of bringing the work to fruition within five years and in the expectation that 'the editions, particularly the one-volume Complete Works, would prove solid cash cows for the coming decades'.[55] In the event, the project required both more resources and more time than the press initially envisaged. Gary Taylor was appointed Assistant Editor from March 1978, rising to joint General Editor in 1984. John Jowett joined the project in 1981 and William Montgomery was taken on from 1984.[56] Ultimately, in addition to the four editors, the edition employed 'two full-time production assistants, and half a dozen part-time proof-readers, keyboarders, and copy editors'.[57] Complete collected-works volumes in both original and modernised spelling appeared in 1986; this was a little later than had been planned, but it was still a remarkable achievement, given the scale of the work that had been undertaken and also Oxford University Press' previous track record with Shakespeare projects.[58] It was, as one reviewer put it, 'slightly short of a miracle that [the editors] accomplished so much in so little time'.[59]

In explaining the rationale behind the new edition, Wells very usefully surveyed the state of Shakespeare publishing at the time when the Oxford project was initiated:

> The Cambridge edition, edited by John Dover Wilson and others, was acknowledged even by its publishers to be out of date . . . The Arden edition was still in progress, but its earliest volumes, and its general style of presentation, dated from the early 1950s. The New Penguin edition was serving a general readership well, but was not uniformly ambitious in its scholarship; the Pelican and Signet editions were considerably less ambitious, sparser in their annotations, and seemed more American than English in their general orientation . . . So far as complete editions were concerned, there were the Alexander text, admirable in its way, but dating from 1951 (and unattractively printed), the collected Signet and Pelican editions, the rather eccentric Sisson text of 1954, and the Riverside, of 1974, which has a textual policy with which I am not in sympathy.[60]

The Oxford team built their text from the ground up – in contrast to many other important contemporary editions. As Wells observed: 'Even *The Riverside* . . . was I understand compiled from earlier editions, pasting them up and this was also true of some of the multi-volume editions in *The Arden*.'[61] The Oxford editors were also determined from the start that the new edition would make use of the very latest bibliographic and editorial thinking, agreeing that they 'wanted actually to put into practice the consequences of current textual study, not to evade decisions on the grounds that this would be the "safe" policy'.[62] At a textual studies conference in 1985, Wells declared (with a certain uncharacteristic extravagance) that, once the Oxford edition appeared, 'the editorial tradition [would] suffer a series of blows from which, I hope, it will never recover'.[63] While this is something of an overstatement, it nevertheless is the case that, as Richard Proudfoot has observed, the Oxford project was 'probably the most radical attempt to re–edit Shakespeare since the eighteenth century'.[64]

The innovative approach of the edition was evidenced in a variety of different ways. The editors followed through on McKerrow's original plan – and broke with most previous collected works editions – by presenting the texts in their presumed chronological order of composition.[65] They also changed the titles of some of the plays back to what they considered to be their Renaissance originals. Thus *Henry VIII* became *All is True*, *2 Henry VI* became *The First Part of the Contention*, and *3 Henry VI* became *Richard Duke of York*. These changes made the volume somewhat difficult to navigate, as David Bevington noted in his review of the edition in *Shakespeare Quarterly*: 'in practical terms, this edition has no pity on the reader who wants to find a play. I've been dipping in it for months now, and I can never figure out where any play is going to be.' Bevington further observed that he did not see that the changes were 'even remotely worth the confusion that would occur if we moved to these new ways of citing the plays'.[66] In addition to changing the play titles, the editors also changed the names of some of the characters. *Cymbeline*'s Imogen became Innogen, on the grounds that the Folio compositors had misread their manuscript, 'due to the simplest of minim errors'.[67] Hamlet's Voltemand became Valtemand, the Second Quarto's spelling being 'preferred as closer to authorial incidentals' and Owen Glendower received an authentic Welsh touch up, to keep a welcome in the valleys as Owain Glyndŵr.[68] This latter alteration was accompanied by another name change in the same play which proved to be highly controversial, as Falstaff became Oldcastle. The switch had been signalled by Gary Taylor in an article published in *Shakespeare Survey* in 1985. Here, Taylor had marshalled the evidence incontrovertibly indicating that the character had originally been called 'Oldcastle', with Shakespeare's company having been forced into the change as a result of pressure brought to bear by the contemporary descendants of the historical Sir John Oldcastle (one of whom was at the time serving as the queen's Lord Chamberlain). In his 1985 essay, Taylor argued that editors who refused to restore the original name cared 'more about the integrity of the preservation and intellectual authority of a cultural tradition than about the recovery and restoration of the original authoritative *logos*'.[69] This is perhaps true, but the change also led to a confusing inconsistency in the edition as a whole, since Falstaff remained Falstaff in the second Henry IV play and in *The Merry Wives of Windsor*.

The Falstaff/Oldcastle emendation was one of a number of headline-grabbing innovations in the edition. Another was the inclusion of the text of a supposed newly discovered Shakespeare poem. This development was once again signalled in advance by Gary Taylor, who summarised the evidence for identifying the poem as Shakespeare's in a *Times Literary Supplement* article in 1985. The poem was included in the Bodleian Library's Rawlinson Poetical Manuscript 160 and the scribe who compiled the manuscript had attributed it to Shakespeare. Taylor argued that the poem's 'vocabulary, imagery, style – everything which scholarly jargon lumps together as "internal evidence" – is at least compatible with Shakespeare's authorship, and at most independently suggestive that it could hardly have been written by any other known poet'.[70] In the same issue of the journal, however, Robin Robbins challenged the ascription, predicting that when 'all the newspaper publicity dies down, we will be left with a poem that at most could be included in a section of Dubiosa'.[71] Stanley Wells has noted that the controversy over the poem 'became an international media event of astonishing proportions and a number of scholars applied themselves with great assiduity to the task of disembarrassing Shakespeare of responsibility for the poem'.[72] After the appearance of the Oxford edition, Thomas Pendleton (among others) argued strongly against the poem's Shakespearean provenance, observing that:

> No element of the language of 'Shall I die?' has been established with anything approaching likelihood as Shakespeare's. But the opposite demonstration is, I submit, quite possible: in a dozen or more particulars, the language of 'Shall I die?' can be shown with extreme probability not to be Shakespeare's.[73]

With its short lines and insistent rhyming scheme, the poem was much parodied, with David Bevington offering the following burlesque in his *Shakespeare Quarterly* review of the edition:

> As I query this theory
> And ponder this blunder
>   'Tis plain we've been taken.
>
> This is not from the quill
> Of magnificent Will
>   But of Sir Francis Bacon.[74]

If the editors offered a wholly new text in 'Shall I die?', they provided a rewritten version of an old text in *Pericles*. The surviving early edition of this play – published in quarto in 1609 – has long been recognised as problematic and, indeed, Heminge and Condell failed to include the play in the First Folio. The work may have been co-authored by Shakespeare and George Wilkins, who published a novella entitled *The Painfull Adventures of Pericles Prince of Tyre* in 1608. The Oxford editors essentially decided to treat both the 1609 quarto and the novella as imperfect 'reported' versions of the play. (In the old-spelling edition, they 'also provided . . . a truly conservative text, in the form of a diplomatic reprint of Q'.[75]) On this basis, they made far greater use of the novella than any previous editors had done. In reviewing the edition, Brian Vickers noted that the Oxford scholars took their theory 'as giving them *carte blanche* for versifying passages from the novel and then including them in the text of the play, as being by "Shakespeare and Wilkins"' and he concluded that it seemed 'particularly highhanded to include their pastiche in a volume for the general reader without any indication of who has written what'.[76] Bevington similarly observed that the 'statistical probability that the editors are reconstructing anything like what appeared on-stage seems to me something approaching zero'.[77] Rather less controversially, the Oxford edition became the first British complete-works volume to include a text of another Shakespeare collaboration: *The Two Noble Kinsmen*, co-written with John Fletcher.[78] After the edition appeared, Wells and Taylor indicated that, in retrospect, they should also have included *Edward III*, on the basis that the 'evidence that Shakespeare was the author of at least part of that play is now very strong, stronger indeed than the evidence for his authorship of the two passages from *Sir Thomas More*' (which they also included in their edition).[79]

One of the most controversial decisions made by the Oxford editors related to their handling of *King Lear*. *Lear* is one of a number of plays for which a substantive quarto version pre-dates the Folio text. In the case of some of these plays the two texts generally match each other closely, but they also differ in a number of significant respects. The First Folio text of *Lear*, for example, includes 100 lines not present in the quarto, but it lacks almost 300 lines which the quarto does include. In addition, several speeches are differently assigned in the two versions and there are somewhat less than a thousand further verbal variants.[80] To take another example, the First Folio text of *Othello* has about 160 lines more than the First Quarto, published in 1622. The First Quarto also has a handful of lines lacking in the folio and the two texts again also diverge in about a thousand individual readings.[81] When the Second Quarto of *Othello* was issued in 1630, it is clear that whoever prepared the text for publication registered the differences between the First Quarto and the First Folio texts. Responding to the variants this 'editor' produced a composite text which conflated the two earlier editions.[82] The preparer of the Second Quarto *Othello* thus anticipated the practice of the vast majority of editors of dual-text plays. The general theory governing the orthodox editorial approach was that the quarto and the First Folio versions must represent texts which were each somewhat imperfect, but in different ways. By conflating the texts, it was argued, the damage in each could be repaired by reference to the other.

While a conflationist consensus prevailed over the course of the centuries, there were a number of scholars who challenged the logic of the strategy. Charles Knight, for instance, noted in his 1838–43 edition that, as far as the quarto-only material in *Lear* was concerned, it would be easy to argue that 'in the folio edition the original play was cut down by the editors'. He felt, however, that this was an inadequate explanation, since 'this theory would require us to assume, also, that the additions to the folio were made by the editors' and these additions, he argues 'comprise several such minute touches as none but the hand of the master could have superadded' (§483, Tragedies, I, p. 393). Knight thus intimated that Shakespeare himself had revised the play, but, despite this belief, as Steven Urkowitz notes, he still printed a conflated text.[83] The idea that Shakespeare revised his work was one strand of the complex set of arguments advanced by those in the New Shakspere Society who sought to disassemble the Shakespeare canon into what they imagined were its diverse and complicated component parts. At the beginning of the twentieth century, their theories were resoundingly dismissed by E. K. Chambers in an essay entitled 'The Disintegration of Shakespeare'. Chambers characterised the group as offering 'results hardly less perturbing than those with which the Baconians and their kin would make our flesh creep'.[84] Chambers' attack on theories of Shakespearean revision in the context of his broader blast against disintegration proved to be decisive for much of the twentieth century. As Grace Ioppolo has noted, his 'reverberatingly harsh condemnation . . . effectively silenced modern discussion of revision'.[85] Interest in the idea did, however, persist on the fringes of Shakespeare scholarship. Thus, for example, Nevill Coghill, in his 1964 study, *Shakespeare's Professional Skills*, suggested that the differences between the First Quarto and First Folio *Othello* reveal themselves 'in many cases to be *serially connected*; the connections are in fact *thematic*, and this is a fact that must affect our judgment in the matter of whether or not they are revisions'.[86] Coghill believed both that the changes were revisions and that they were authorial.

Coghill's arguments (and the work of others who supported him, such as E. A. J. Honigmann) were generally passed over at the time, in large measure because Chambers' denunciation of disintegration continued to reverberate in scholarly circles.[87] In the closing quarter of the century, however, the critical climate began to change. At the World Shakespeare Congress in Washington, DC in 1976, Michael Warren, arguing in favour of authorial revision, 'urged a bifurcation of the traditional conflated text of *King Lear*'.[88] Four years later, Gary Taylor published an article in *Shakespeare Survey* in which he noted that the issue of the war was handled very differently in the two versions of *Lear*, with Cordelia's French connections, in particular, being significantly downplayed in the folio text. Reviewing the alterations made in the First Folio, Taylor concluded that it was 'hard to believe that such a succession of interrelated changes happened by accident, and it would be churlish (let alone unnecessary) to attribute them to anyone but Shakespeare'.[89] Also in 1980, Steven Urkowitz published a book-length study of the texts of *Lear* in which he argued that

> the Quarto was printed from Shakespeare's foul papers, and the Folio was printed from the Quarto version that was carefully brought into agreement with the official promptbook. The promptbook itself embodied all of Shakespeare's own revisions, including additions, cuts, substitutions, and rearrangements . . . the vast majority of the changes found in the Folio must be accepted as Shakespeare's final decisions.[90]

In April of this same year, Taylor, Urkowitz and Warren, together with Randall McLeod, forcefully made the case for Shakespeare as a revising dramatist at the textual seminar of the Shakespeare Association of America conference at Cambridge, Massachusetts.[91] During the course of the session, Stanley Wells announced his conversion to the revisionist cause.[92] Wells would subsequently write of the traditional editorial practice of conflation that its effects resemble 'that which would be achieved by an art expert faced with two versions of a portrait who had decided that the best way to represent them would be by superimposing one upon the other, even if in the process he made the sitter appear to have four eyes'.[93]

With both Taylor and Wells firmly located in the revisionist camp, it was inevitable that the Oxford edition would reflect emergent conceptions of Shakespeare as a revising playwright. The Oxford editors presented their readers with two separate versions of *Lear*: *The History of King Lear*, based on the First Quarto, and *The Tragedy of King Lear*, based on the First Folio. Wells has noted that he had himself 'resisted the suggestion that we should print the two texts in parallel' because he 'felt that it should be possible to read *King Lear* for itself alone, undistracted by scholarly alternatives'.[94] Having provided double texts of *Lear* the question arose as to what the editors should do with those other plays where there was significant variation between a substantive early quarto and the First Folio text, and where a case had been made for seeing the variations as representing authorial revision. In the instance of *Hamlet*, the editors presented an unconflated First Folio text, with the unique Second Quarto speeches being included in an appendix of 'Additional Passages'.[95] Their *Othello* was also based on the unconflated First Folio text, but 'in the Notes, and the list of rejected

Quarto readings' they placed 'an asterisk before those readings most likely to have been affected by revision'.[96] Looking back on their work in 1990, Wells and Taylor noted that, by then, it seemed obvious to them that they 'should have included two versions of *Hamlet*, as well as . . . *King Lear*' and Wells subsequently observed that 'if we'd had world enough and time and money, then we would have produced multiple texts of several other plays'.[97]

By the time the Oxford edition appeared in print the revisionists had, as Grace Ioppolo has put it, 'achieved a *coup d'état* which offers a new constitution for how scholars read, study, and teach Shakespeare's canon and also redefines the canon itself'. Having surveyed the many variations across Shakespeare's substantive texts, Ioppolo confidently declared that the 'only canonizer and constituter of Shakespeare's texts, in all their infinite revisable variety, is Shakespeare himself'.[98] Others, however, have not been so convinced. In a detailed study of the Second Quarto and First Folio *Hamlet*, Paul Werstine has argued that it would be remarkable if the variations between the substantive texts 'represented only authorial changes of mind'. And he continues: 'There are a great many other ways in which variation can be produced in printed texts – scribal transcription, unauthorized playhouse cuts or additions, printing-house errors, to name only three.' 'Can we realistically expect', Werstine asks,

> to identify the source of every variant of the hundreds between the quarto and Folio texts of such plays as *Hamlet* or *Othello*? When it is so difficult to prove or disprove authorship of an entire play or even a whole canon, there is little chance of conclusively demonstrating that Shakespeare's must have been the hand that originally wrote the eighty or so lines in the Folio text of *Hamlet* that have no counterparts in the second-quarto version. Nor are we likely ever to know whose hand(s) cut the more than two hundred lines from the second-quarto text that do not appear in the Folio; in the very nature of the case, there is simply no evidence for determining the authorship of cuts.[99]

Werstine's general conclusions have been supported by Ernst Honigmann – himself an early and energetic supporter of the revisionist position.[100] In his 1996 book *The Texts of 'Othello' and Shakespearian Revision* (intended as a companion volume to his Arden 3 edition of *Othello*) Honigmann partly repudiated his earlier strong revisionist stance. Attempting to map out the likely transmission history of *Othello* as closely as possible, he notes the extent to which variants may have entered the text through sources other than authorial revision. The scribe of the First Quarto text, he suggests, 'may . . . have chosen to save himself work by skipping longer passages . . . which cannot be regarded as accidental omissions'. Likewise, he observes that the First Quarto compositor 'seems to have tampered with the text in many ways, omitting lines for which casting off had left insufficient space, perhaps adding lines of his own devising, re-lining the verse and, unless someone else is to blame, misreading many words'. Looking beyond *Othello*, Honigmann remarks that, in the case of *Lear*, 'the relationship of revision to corruption . . . has not so far been dealt with satisfactorily: it would not be too difficult to show that at least some of the "revision" could qualify no less readily as corruption'.[101] In his 1993 parallel-text edition of the First Quarto and the First Folio *Lear*, René Weis had reached essentially the same conclusions, observing that the 'most we can safely say about Q and F *Lear* is that they differ in several important ways, and that these do not necessarily form part of a systematic revision' (§1650, p. 34). The sudden fall in the value of revisionist stock is perhaps indicated by the fact that, in 1990, Wells and Taylor indicated that they had had in mind to publish, possibly in a paperback volume, 'paired modern-spelling texts not only of *King Lear* and *Hamlet*, but also of *Othello* and *Troilus*, thus bringing together in one affordable book full versions of all four plays where authorial revision is most likely and most substantial'. With perhaps a certain air of hopefulness, they observed that they would 'still be happy to provide such a volume should the press want to publish it'.[102] Neither Oxford University Press nor any other press has appeared willing to take them up on their offer.

Many of the innovations of the Oxford edition discussed so far in this chapter have what we might identify as an essentially 'local' character to them, which is to say that, though they were controversial, they did not involve a fundamental challenge to the modern principles of editing theory and practice as evolved through the New Bibliography.[103] One innovation of the Oxford editors did, however, run counter to the orthodox position of the New Bibliographic tradition. Greg and his colleagues had always stressed the supreme and unique centrality of the author to the editorial project.[104] So Fredson Bowers, for instance, proclaimed that the 'great principle of the search for authorial integrity, which is to say for authenticity, remains forever constant'.[105] Just at the time when the Oxford text was being compiled, however, this view came under sustained scrutiny. In a pioneering volume entitled *A Critique of Modern Textual Criticism* (first published in 1983), Jerome J. McGann strongly argued for seeing the author as but one element within a greater field of productive textual relations. McGann insisted that 'Authority is a social nexus, not a personal possession' and he proposed that

> if authority for specific literary works is initiated anew for each new work by some specific artist, its initiation takes place in a necessary and integral historical environment of great complexity. Most immediately . . . it takes place within the conventions and enabling limits that are accepted by the prevailing institutions of literary production – conventions and limits which exist for the purpose of generating and supporting literary production.

Or, to put it more simply: 'literary works are not produced without arrangements of some sort'.[106] McGann was among those thanked by the Oxford editors in the prefatory acknowledgements to the *Textual Companion* to their edition and his conception of textual authority is clearly consonant with their thinking.[107] In his 1723–5 edition, Alexander Pope had accused the King's Men of 'either lopping, or stretching' Shakespeare's text, 'to make him just fit for their Stage' (§194, I, p. xviii), in the process initiating a persistent strain of anti-theatricalism among Shakespeare editors. The Oxford team, by contrast, foregrounded the fact Shakespeare's plays were, first and foremost, just that: *plays*, and plays achieve their ultimate form in theatrical performance. As Gary Taylor noted, echoing McGann: 'dramatic texts are necessarily the most socialized of all literary forms'. The Oxford editors therefore proposed to depart from the normative editorial practice of adopting as copy-text that edition which was considered closest to the author's own intentions. Instead they would 'prefer – where there is a choice – the text closer to the prompt-book of Shakespeare's company' (in practice, this tended to mean privileging the First Folio over the authoritative quarto texts where making a choice was necessary, thus reversing the New Bibliographically inspired trend noted by Alexander).[108] In addition to privileging theatrically inflected source texts, the Oxford edition also employed a format which emphasised continuity of performance, in that act and scene breaks were indicated 'in a typographically unobtrusive manner designed to make it easy to read the plays without unwarranted interruptions'.[109] The volume's designer, Paul Luna, has noted that 'there was some tension between [the] editorial principles and what OUP had been used to selling: very traditional-looking, compact single-volume editions with very clear act and scene divisions and tucked-in line-numbering, abbreviated speech prefixes, little differentiation between verse and prose'. The press were anxious, Luna reveals, that the edition risked looking 'a bit too academic, too far from the norm'.[110]

The Oxford editors noted that 'it is the texts as they were originally performed that are the sources of [Shakespeare's] power' and that their aim in the edition was to attempt to present these texts 'with as much fidelity to his intentions as the circumstances in which they have been preserved will allow'

(§1604, p. xiii). A certain logical contradiction exists between the two elements of this formulation, between, that is, performance and intention. The issue of intention has, for decades, been highly contentious within critical and textual scholarship, and it becomes an even more slippery concept within a McGannian framework.[111] McGann himself has repeatedly insisted that he never wished to 'unseat the author as source of authority and meaning', but it is necessarily the case that his conception of the social text effects a certain bifurcation of authority, between the author's own intentions, on the one hand, and the greater social frameworks which enable the text to have a public existence, on the other.[112] Authority, in this context, might be said to have twin focal points, and sometimes these focal points fail to coincide. The Oldcastle–Falstaff conflict helps to bring this issue more clearly into view. The Oxford editors reject 'Falstaff' in *1 Henry IV*, on the grounds that the change was imposed on the author by the political establishment, so they restore the original name of 'Oldcastle'. But the change *was* made in the text (the theatre being, of course, a social institution and therefore subject to social regulation) and 'Falstaff' is what some Renaissance audiences at least would be likely to have heard – so, from one perspective, this can be argued to be the socialised form of the text. The Oxford editors' withdrawal from a full conception of socialisation in this instance, and their privileging of authorial intent over the social text, is, in fact, wholly understandable. If the text is not in some primary sense anchored in what are conceived of as the author's intentions, it is hard to see quite where it can be anchored. The horizon of the social text is, we might say, infinite and, as George Walton Williams has pointed out, genuinely cleaving to the theatrical text, 'carried to its logical extreme would exalt to the position of substantive authority the most recent production of the RSC' (or, indeed, we might say, any other current theatrical production), since that would be the apotheosis of the socialized, theatrical tradition.[113] The Oxford editors thus sometimes find themselves predictably caught between contradictory impulses. McGann's theories are important and valuable, but they do not always make for easy editorial choices.

We have seen that the Oxford team produced an edition that was bold, innovative, and experimental. Thomas L. Berger has said of the text that, while it caused 'minor and major irritations to a generation of Shakespeareans', it also 'had the effect of making us review, rethink, and in many cases modify our ideas about what should constitute the text of an edition of any particular play'.[114] David Bevington likewise has commented that he 'learned more about editing from these scholars at the Oxford Shakespeare than from anyone since Fredson Bowers, even if some of that learning has come about through reacting violently'.[115] The aims of the editors were not always fully understood at the time when the edition appeared, however, since much of the scholarship which supported their editorial decisions was published in the wake of the edition itself. This included the edition's *Textual Companion*, which did not become available until more than a year after the edition had appeared in print. In reviewing the Oxford text in 1989, Brian Vickers complained vigorously about the amount of supporting materials which had yet to be published: 'I may have missed some but already the list of work on which key points depend but which are only "forthcoming", we know not when or where, is the longest I have ever encountered, and leaves a whole series of unpleasant holes in the structure of the argument.'[116] In the following year, Wells and Taylor explained that 'Completed articles and even monographs justifying some of our new ideas were set aside in order to focus on bringing the edition itself to a conclusion', and that, once work on the edition itself had largely been concluded and the team had broken up to go their separate ways, Stanley Wells had been 'left with one helper to put the *Companion* to bed'.[117] The effect of the edition's cart appearing while the discursive horse was still in the process of being groomed was that many of the editors' decisions were not immediately understood and the Oxford editors suffered something of the same fate as Edward Capell, whose volumes of notes appeared belatedly, after his edition had already been in print for some years.[118]

This was not the only publishing problem experienced by the Oxford team. As a matter of tradition, up to the closing decades of the twentieth century, British editions of the complete works had tended to be published without notes, while American editions invariably were annotated. From the start of the Oxford project, both the editors and the press had envisaged that Oxford University Press would produce an annotated edition and that this would provide them with a clear point of entry into the hugely important American market, enabling them to compete on level terms with the *Riverside* (and with other popular American editions, such as David Bevington's).[119] As a bonus, they would also sell the annotated edition into the UK market, where they would have a clear advantage over bare-bones complete works volumes, such as the Alexander. At the last moment, however, Oxford University Press America suffered a crisis of confidence. With a sales force of only around nineteen people, they felt unable to mount an effective campaign against the *Riverside* and so they decided against taking on the new edition. The flight of the troops in the field in America would seem to have spread panic among the generals back at Great Clarendon Street in Oxford. The publishers now decided to drop the annotations, together with individual play introductions of six to eight thousand words each which were already in the process of being written. These substantial introductions were replaced with short one-page alternatives and the text was launched into the UK market as a traditional British unannotated edition. The retreat from America effectively meant that the Oxford editors lost any possibility that their edition might enjoy genuine popular success on a large scale.

The press at Oxford did not, in fact, wholly abandon the American market. With their US sales force unwilling to take on the Oxford edition, they entered into negotiations with the American publisher Norton, who agreed to publish the Oxford editors' text in a repackaged form. Stephen Greenblatt was brought in to serve as general editor and a team of US-based academics provided annotations and introductions to the individual plays. Despite Wells and Taylor's various public explanations of how, in retrospect, they themselves might have improved the edition, the Norton text offered no advance on the original, from a textual point of view. In his 'General Introduction', Greenblatt wrote of the Oxford editors' glancing 'longingly at the impractical but alluring possibility of including two texts of *Hamlet*, *Othello*, and *Troilus*' (§1706, p. 73). Impracticality seems to have trumped scholarly longing in the case of Greenblatt's publishers, since no other plays received the dual-text treatment in the new edition. Norton did, however, find space for one additional text: a conflated version of *King Lear*. The deconflated *Lear*s were also retained, but they were now printed in parallel, despite Wells' repeated assertions of the value of keeping them wholly separate. The 'Additional Passages' format for the Second Quarto-only material in *Hamlet* was abandoned, with the passages being incorporated into the main text, creating, in effect, another conflated edition (albeit with the material in question being set in italics and separately numbered). 'Shall I Die?' was retained, though a 'Textual Note' prefacing the 'Various Poems' section of the volume offered the opinion that 'independent analysis of the poem's language carried out by statisticians of the poem make[s] attribution to Shakespeare possible, though not particularly likely' (§1706, p. 1994). The Norton editors added another 'new' Shakespeare poem, *A Funeral Elegy for Master William Peter*, now generally regarded as the work of John Ford.[120] Oldcastle returned to his original designation as Falstaff, though, inconsistently, Innogen failed to regain her textual maiden name.

To list the differences between the Oxford and Norton editions in this way may seem to suggest that the American text is a betrayal of the British original. This is not entirely fair and, certainly, the Norton edition has its own clear merits. Martha Tuck Rozett, for instance, has observed that the best introductions in the volume 'not only provoke the reader's curiosity but also serve as models of the critical process'.[121] At the same time, however, it *is* hard not to feel that the Norton represents a retreat from the radical attitude of the Oxford editors. The signature note of the Oxford edition was its willingness to take risks. The editorial team strongly resisted adopting a 'business as usual' attitude to the task of editing Shakespeare. They opposed what Wells has characterised as the 'timorous conservatism' which leads to 'a reluctance to emend and to an undue subservience to the editorial tradition'.[122] Taylor has also neatly anatomised the logic of inertia which tends to prevail in the editing of high-profile canonical texts:

> Critics do not object when an edition like *The Riverside Shakespeare*
> departs from its predecessors in hundreds of individual readings, because
> such scholarly labours increase one's confidence in the text, while at the
> same time making no difference to its interpretation. But when the same
> labours lead an editor to propose restoring both early versions of *King
> Lear*, or the original name of Shakespeare's most famous comic character,
> then some critics will object that the changes are impractical simply
> because they make so much difference. This attitude creates a situation in
> which the results of textual scholarship are always trivial, because if the
> results are *not* trivial they will be disregarded . . . Hence, Shakespeare's
> editors continue to produce texts which, in one way or another, they do
> not believe in; each succumbs to the weight of tradition, and thereby adds
> to the weight on any subsequent editor. At some point this vicious cycle
> must be broken.[123]

The Norton, from this perspective, is very clearly an edition which has succumbed to the weight of tradition. By contrast, the very least that can be said of the *Oxford Shakespeare* is that it represented a brave attempt to break the very cycle to which Taylor here refers.

Conclusion
Twenty-first century Shakespeares

In an interview revisiting the Oxford edition, published in 2001, Stanley Wells commented that 'If we'd started editing *The Oxford Shakespeare* in 1988 instead of publishing it then, it would have been a very different edition.'[1] Wells may be pointing here to the fact that, just at the time when the Oxford text appeared, some of the foundational principles of twentieth-century editing were being seriously interrogated. We have seen that Greg and his colleagues conceived of themselves as engaged in a form of scientific project. They believed that, together, they had established certain fundamental facts about Renaissance dramatic texts and that these facts served as the fixed points by which an editor's course could be charted. To summarise briefly the narrative set out in detail in chapter 10: the New Bibliographers believed that the early Shakespeare quartos could be neatly divided into the good and the bad, that the bad were arrived at by an illicit process of memorial reconstruction and could thus be discounted; they believed that, of the remaining quarto and First Folio texts, some were based on authorial 'foul papers' and some were based on promptbooks, and that these were clearly distinguishable manuscript categories; they believed that, in the case of any given printed text, the underlying manuscript could be relatively easily identified by searching for certain cues, characteristic of the two textual forms; they also believed that Hand D in the *Thomas More* manuscript was Shakespeare's holograph and that it provided clues to the characteristics of the author's handwriting and to the kinds of compositorial misreadings that it might prompt. All of these certainties came under scrutiny in the final years of the twentieth century.

In fact, as early as 1937, H. T. Price had questioned Greg's fundamental assertion of the scientific status of bibliography.[2] The scientific paradigm is founded on two key principles: replication and falsification. Scientific results, to be accepted, must be capable of being reproduced by a range of different investigators and the theory that the scientist seeks to establish must be open to tests which, potentially, could prove it to be false. Much of the work of the New Bibliographers involved speculating on what might have happened in a particular writing space or theatre or printshop more than three centuries ago – a very useful enterprise undoubtedly, but not, strictly speaking, a truly scientific endeavour, not least because, as R. C. Bald has put it: the 'past is an experiment that cannot be repeated'.[3] Of course, whether bibliography can *properly* be described as a science is in one sense little more than a matter of nomenclative nicety. But it does point to a broader and more fundamental issue. The New Bibliographers sought to reduce the chaos of documents and evidence surviving from the Renaissance theatre to some kind of order; they sought to classify, to separate good quartos from bad, foul papers from prompt-copy, the true text from scribal or compositorial or theatrical corruption. But, as Marion Trousdale has pointed out, the evidence under scrutiny may simply not lend itself to being reduced to order quite so readily. As she observes, while 'critical bibliography may carry as its validation a flag on which consistently applied principles of investigation are blazoned as method, method itself does not appear to have been anything about which the Elizabethans in the order of their social processes seem particularly concerned'. As she further notes: 'the early documents that remain show little trace of that order upon which the methods of critical bibliography depend'.[4]

A nice example of what Trousdale has in mind is the manuscript book commonly referred to as 'Henslowe's Diary' – a rich source of information on the structure, management and finances of the Renaissance theatre. Henslowe's book is a kind of accounts ledger for the Rose and Fortune theatres, but it is also much more than this, as it additionally contains the accounts for an iron-smelting business in Sussex, owned by Henslowe's brother John, together with notes on family matters, details of property transactions, accounts relating to Philip Henslowe's pawn brokerage, recipes for medications, accounts of where Henslowe sent his horse to grass, an odd miscellany of practical advice on such topics as how to 'make A fowle ffalle downe' and how to 'know wher a thinge is y^t Is stolen', and some highly esoteric material that hardly seems even comprehensible to a casual modern eye.[5] The very page numbering and general manner of use of the volume are neatly indicative of how the oddly Borgesian quality of early modern systematisation simply does not mesh with modern conceptions of ordering and classification. John Henslowe, R. A. Foakes tells us,

> had the curious habit of numbering from 1 to 100, then beginning again by adding one, so that he wrote '101' as '1001', and '125' as '10025'. . . .
> When Philip Henslowe began to use [the book], he reversed it, and began his entries from what had been, for John, the end of the book. However, it

is worth noting that, although Philip used the book in this way for most of his entries, running in the opposite direction to John's foliation, nevertheless for certain entries he turned the book round, and used it in the same way as John.[6]

Trying to map a grid of consistency on to documents of this kind is a very stiff proposition. Returning more directly to the theatre itself, we find Trousdale asking a series of useful and searching questions: 'Did all prompt-copies follow the same format? Were there certain regular procedures followed for entering and exiting the stage?' and, with a nod to A. E. Housman's famous editorial metaphor: 'Was there in fact an idea of constancy such as the one we necessarily follow as editors tracking down fleas?'[7] If, as Trousdale intimates here, the Renaissance theatre generally lacked standard procedures and methods of working, then the modern bibliographer's hopes of imposing classification schemes on the texts that survive from such a theatre may well, ultimately, be frustrated. Certainly, scholars such as Paul Werstine and William B. Long have noted that the manuscript playbooks that have survived from the Renaissance simply do not fall neatly into the clear categories evolved by Greg and his colleagues (nor can they so easily be distributed into these categories using the simple tests devised by McKerrow).[8] Werstine has observed that no 'good quarto' 'has ever been shown to have been set from "foul papers" because the marks that have been used to identify "foul papers" as printer's copy are also to be found in extant "promptbooks"', and he has concluded that 'in the dozens of play manuscripts from the sixteenth and seventeenth centuries, there are no complete manuscripts in single authorial hands that bear out the features of Greg's foul papers, and no theatrical manuscripts survive in the perfectly disambiguated state that, for Greg, must have marked every promptbook'.[9] Likewise, as we saw in chapter 1, Werstine (among others) has strongly challenged the division of the quartos themselves into the good and the bad, castigating 'the nearly absurd simplicity of Pollard's system of classification'. He has also declared that Greg's neat explanation of the origins of the 'bad' quartos in memorial reconstruction 'by an actor or actors identified with specific parts has never proved an adequate explanation for the genesis of any "bad" quarto; the case for such reconstruction has always broken down and has needed to be supplemented by secondary hypotheses'.[10] Taking the central instances of *Merry Wives of Windsor*, *Hamlet*, *Henry V* and *Romeo and Juliet*, Werstine has concluded that 'twentieth-century Shakespeare textual criticism has not been able to maintain the memorial-reconstruction hypothesis on the basis of qualitative evidence in any of [these] four quartos'.[11]

By the closing decade of the twentieth century, then, both the self-conception and some of the defining landmark discoveries of the New Bibliography were being seriously called into question. The classification of the quartos, memorial reconstruction, the methods for identifying the manuscript copy underlying a printed text, and the division of such copy into the exclusive categories of foul papers or prompt-copy – all of these certainties were challenged. Even the ascription to Shakespeare of the Hand D passages of *Sir Thomas More* did not seem entirely assured. In editing a volume dedicated to the problem, T. H. Howard-Hill asserted, in 1989, that a weighing of the arguments 'tips the balance in favour of Shakespeare', but he also had to concede that it is 'an index of the complexity of the *More* problem – and possibly of the insufficiency of evidence good enough to bring issues to closure – that however plausible and well supported a case may be, opposing arguments rear themselves immediately'.[12] In a 1976 article reviewing the *More* evidence, Paul Ramsey had unequivocally declared that 'We had best . . . barring some extraordinary new evidence or arguments, put those three pages on a shelf for fascinating curiosities rather than on the critic's or editor's work table.'[13] In a sense, however, part of the problem by the century's end was that so very much was now being removed from the editor's work table. To return once again to Dover Wilson's sea-faring conceit, we might say that, if the New Bibliographers sought to create a kind of theoretical chart which would enable editors to plot their textual course, then by the close of the century most of the fixed landmarks on this chart appeared to be fast receding beneath the waves.

The prevailing lack of a clear editorial consensus is mirrored in much of the Shakespeare publishing of the time. Generally speaking, most editors – especially those involved in large-scale commercial series – continued to follow the paradigms of the New Bibliography. In a sense, they had little alternative, for how else were they to be guided in undertaking their task, especially if they worked with a non-specialist audience in mind?[14] And, in any case, the prime desideratum of most publishers – even, as we have seen, university presses – is for an uncomplicated text that will appeal to a wide readership (and gain significant sales in the educational market). At the same time, the general editors of many of the more advanced Shakespeare series felt the need in some way to reflect the shifting new climate in their texts. So, for example, when the Arden edition was relaunched for the third time in 1995, the general editors took the decision to include reduced photofacsimiles of the attenuated quartos in those editions for which a 'bad' quarto existed – a significant departure from the Pollardian view that 'the epithets "stolne and surreptitious" may be applied with any desirable amount of scorn and contempt' to the short quartos.[15] In a similar manner, the *New Cambridge Shakespeare* (the successor to Dover Wilson's edition) began issuing separate edited versions of the short texts in a supplementary series titled 'The Early Quartos', diplomatically characterising them as 'abbreviated' texts and declaring them to be 'indispensable to advanced students of Shakespeare and of textual bibliography' (§1602, p. v). In 1993 Harvester-Wheatsheaf (since absorbed into Prentice Hall) launched a new series, wholly dedicated to providing largely unedited versions of the earliest texts, with a heavy emphasis (at least initially) on the short quartos. The series was much criticised, but it is noteworthy that the volume introductions drew heavily on the writings of those scholars who were interrogating the central tenets of the New Bibliography.[16]

The general editors of the Shakespearean Originals series sought to draw attention to the earliest versions of the plays in their individual specificity, arguing that they wished to see each particular version 'as a work of art in its own right rather than as an analogue to the received text' (§1636, p. 10). This emphasis on specific versions in their original forms, disjoined from the received modern version which had evolved through four centuries of editorial fashioning, was reflected in other publishing projects in the same period.[17] In 2002, for instance, Jesús Tronch-Pérez published

A Synoptic *Hamlet*: A Critical-Synoptic Edition of the $\frac{\text{Second Quarto}}{\text{and First Folio}}$ *Texts of Hamlet*.

Tronch-Pérez's text disjoins the Second Quarto and First Folio *Hamlet* – so often conflated in mainstream editions – but presents them simultaneously on the same page, so that it becomes possible either to read them individually or to read differentially between them.[18] The text has a disconcerting feel to the reader accustomed to the page layout of the standard edition (or even to those accustomed to the facing-page dual-text layout of such editions as the René Weis parallel *Lears*).

While certainly radical in many of its innovations, the Tronch-Pérez edition is also in some respects rather conventional, in that it presents a modernised text in which perceived errors are emended. Many other commentators who wished to foreground the unique integrity of the early texts sought, by contrast, to retreat from even the most minimalist form of editorial intervention. In a 1985 essay on 'Textual Problems, Editorial Assertions in Editions of Shakespeare', Michael Warren complained about the manner in which all edited texts 'sit between the student or the scholar and the peculiar originals from which they derive, and present themselves as the thing itself'. Even diplomatic reprints (in which the text is transcribed in as close as possible a form to the original) are, from Warren's point of view, unsatisfactory, since they serve to mask certain key elements of the original. As he argues:

> In such an edition of a Shakespeare text, important textual features relevant to interpretive activity would still be lost: doubtful type would need to be identified; spacings would be altered; the justification of lines would be concealed; the adjustments of line length in verse or its conversion into prose consequent upon unsatisfactory casting-off of copy would be disguised; distinctive ligatures and the peculiarities of spelling that are merely consequences of the exigencies of type would be masked.[19]

Warren's argument here has much in common with the position adopted by the bibliographer Randall McLeod, whose work has consistently exposed the extent to which the practical logistics of setting a book into type produce their own unique meaning effects – effects which can either be obscured or misinterpreted (or both) in edited reproductions. One of McLeod's neatest examples of this process in action is his demonstration that the very spelling of Shakespeare's name may well have been determined by the practicalities of typesetting. In an italic fount, the 'k' of '*Shak*' will kern forward off its typebody and the long 's' of '*ʃpeare*' will similarly kern backward off *its* typebody. Thus, if the two letters are set immediately beside each other, the kerning descenders will make contact and the type will be damaged. For this reason, the space between the two letters 'must be filled with types whose face is without descenders', such as the letter 'e'.[20] So it may possibly be the case, McLeod argues, that the medial 'e' in Shak*e*speare is a product of the exigencies of setting metal type. McLeod makes this claim in an article entitled 'Un-Editing Shak-speare' and the general thrust of his work is that editing is, essentially, an impossible task, as even the best-intentioned of editors will necessarily tend either to miss certain crucial bibliographical features of their texts or, even if they do notice them, they will be unable to replicate their meanings in their own editions. All editors are thus, in McLeod's view, inevitably prone to misreading and/or misrepresenting the texts which they edit.

Taken to its logical conclusion, the implication of the position adopted by McLeod and Warren would be that any text should only ever be read in its original edition.[21] This is, of course, a wholly impractical proposition and Warren himself has offered an alternative possibility in his 1989 *King Lear*. In this edition, Warren provides a series of photofacsimile texts, including a bound parallel text of the First Quarto and First Folio and unbound texts of the First Quarto, Second Quarto and First Folio, together with facsimiles of a selection of variant pages. Warren thus makes available a version of the original range of texts to readers who would find it difficult to access them directly in their diverse locations.[22] The *Complete* King Lear was one of several facsimile projects initiated during this period: Michael Allen and Kenneth Muir edited a collection of *Shakespeare's Plays in Quarto*, published in 1981; D. S. Brewer issued facsimiles of the Second, Third and Fourth Folios under the direction of Marvin Spevack in 1985; Archival Facsimiles issued a facsimile of Charles I's copy of the Second Folio in 1987; Peter Blayney produced a new edition of Hinman's Norton facsimile of the First Folio in 1996; Routledge/Thoemmes published a boxed set of facsimiles of all four folios in 1997; and, of course, as we have already noted, the *Arden* publishers began to include facsimiles of the short quartos in the relevant texts of their relaunched series from 1995. Most of the folio facsimiles were expensive productions, with the Routledge/Thoemmes set running to £650 and the Blayney–Hinman Norton First Folio costing £120. In 1995, however, Applause Books issued a paperback edition of the First Folio, prepared by Doug Moston and retailing in the US for just $45. This volume was subsequently taken up by Routledge, who issued it in the UK for a price of £32.50. In 2001, Octavo released what was, in relative terms, the cheapest ever version of the First Folio – a digital facsimile on CD, sold for the slightly gimmicky but astonishingly cheap price of just $16.23.

Facsimile publishing gives the appearance of offering unmediated access to something that is very close to the original text – hence the appeal for a scholar such as Warren. But facsimiles are still, in fact, *editions*, even if they purport simply to provide a faithful reproduction of the original.[23] Anyone who takes responsibility for preparing a facsimile is required to make an important set of choices, which effectively amount to editorial decisions. As Gary Taylor has observed, in preparing a facsimile, it is necessary to

> choose which copies of which editions of which works to photograph; whether to reproduce a single extant copy, or to compose an 'ideal' copy using either formes or pages from several copies; whether to photograph corrected or uncorrected states of press-variant formes; which photographic process to use; what apparatus to provide.

Taylor further notes that photography 'communicates its own message: that what you see is real, accurate, genuine'.[24] But sometimes, of course, this is, in the most literal sense, simply not true. The Routledge/Thoemmes facsimiles of the four folios, for example, are essentially a reissue of the facsimiles published by Methuen at the beginning of the twentieth century, using the original Methuen photographs.[25] But these photographs were 'cleaned', in order to remove the show-through of type from the reverse side of each page. The cleaning process eliminated some bibliographical features of the book and also, in places, affected some of the letters in the text.[26] In this sense, what the facsimile offers is precisely not 'real, accurate, genuine'. The same is true even of Warren's meticulously produced *Lear*s. In his review of the edition in *Shakespeare Quarterly*, Paul Werstine noted that, in the parallel-text segment, 'some agent has intervened by altering the photographs of F1 . . . the rules have been stripped from the F1 columns and gray space has been added so that their width seems to match that of the Q1 pages'. 'The visual effect', Werstine suggests, 'is to stabilize both texts in opposition to each other and thus to endow each with a specious integrity.'[27] Even the camera lens, then, does not provide an unmediated text.

So far we have seen that the interrogation of New Bibliographic systems of classification led both, on the one hand, to a renewed interest in texts previously dismissed as wholly peripheral and, on the other, to a privileging of specific original versions of texts and a mistrust of the process of editorial refashioning. The challenging of New Bibliographic orthodoxies in the field of textual studies also coincided with a wider set of theoretical shifts in the field of literary criticism more generally. We have already noted the manner in which the editors of the Oxford Shakespeare were influenced by Jerome J. McGann's notion of the social text. McGann did not (any more than the Oxford editors) seek utterly to displace the author from the centre of the textual universe – in a sense, he wished simply to bring the other planets in the authorial solar system into the editor's field of vision. For other theorists, however, McGann's position would have been seen – to extend the metaphor – as being regressively Ptolemaic; from their perspective, what was required was a radical break with the auctorocentric view of the textual cosmos. Thus, Roland Barthes (in)famously proclaimed the 'death of the author' and Michel Foucault pointedly asked 'what is an author?'. These theorists fully rejected the primacy of the author as the unique initiating source of meaning, which is to say, they eschewed the notion that texts originate with isolated creative agencies who precede the works which they create. For Barthes, the author is always *posterior*, and the greater field of textuality always *precedes* the author:

> a text is not a line of words releasing a single 'theological' meaning . . . but a multi-dimensional space in which a variety of writings, none of them original, blend and clash. The text is a tissue of quotations drawn from the innumerable centres of culture . . . the writer can only imitate a

> gesture that is always anterior, never original. His only power is to mix
> writings, to counter the ones with the others, in such a way as never to
> rest on any one of them.[28]

For Foucault, operating within the same paradigm, the function of the author is not to generate meaning, but to close it down to a limited and narrowly defined set of values. Thus, Foucault argues, the author 'is a certain functional principle by which, in our culture, one limits, excludes, and chooses; in short, by which one impedes the free circulation, the free manipulation, the free composition, decomposition, and recomposition of meaning'.[29]

For some Renaissance scholars, these somewhat abstruse philosophical postulates had a clear practical resonance.[30] In a seminal essay entitled 'What is a Text?' (consciously playing, of course, on the title of Foucault's own essay), Stephen Orgel observed that we assume 'that the authority of a text derives from the author', but he continues: 'self-evident as it may appear, I suggest that this proposition is not true: in the case of Renaissance dramatic texts it is almost never true, and in the case of non-dramatic texts it is true rather less often than we think'.[31] Orgel and others noted the extent to which Renaissance dramatists relied heavily on a shared pool of pre-existing texts in fashioning their own works. From this perspective, Barthes' dictum that any given text 'is a tissue of quotations drawn from the innumerable centres of culture' has a certain ring of literal truth. A number of commentators also noted the extent to which Renaissance writing culture itself differed considerably from modern-day practice. Jeffrey Masten, for example, argued that our typical contemporary image of the individual Renaissance dramatist working alone on his own unique script simply does not square with the normative culture of the period, where 'collaboration was the . . . dominant mode of textual production'.[32] Even a writer who did work alone was operating within a paradigm very different from the modern conception of authorship. As we noted in the very first chapter of this book, the Renaissance dramatist ceased to have any legal interest in his work once he delivered it to the theatre company. The notion of authors legally possessing a 'copyright' in their work was – again as we have seen in an earlier chapter – very largely a by-product of eighteenth-century legal disputes concerning the duration and extent of publishers' exclusive rights to the texts that they had purchased or inherited.

What this line of argument attempts to indicate is the extent to which the textual culture of the Renaissance period differs from that of our own time. So, we might say, just as we should resist a New Bibliographic tendency to impose the logical consistency of modern classification schemes on the fragmentary complex evidence that survives from the Renaissance theatre, so we should also resist a broader tendency to view the culture of literary production of that theatre in terms of our own textual practices. But the question that arises in the present context, of course, is just how these – to some extent rather nebulous – ideas might be brought fruitfully to bear on the practical business of editing texts. Or, to put it another way: what would an edition produced from within this kind of theoretical framework actually look like?

The answer to this question lies as much in the realm of technology as it does in that of textual theory. Postmodern theorists (to use a broad, portmanteau phrase) see Renaissance textuality as a dispersed field, in which texts weave together and interpenetrate, with the author serving as little more than an immediate point of focus (rather than a definitive source of authority). In the closing decades of the twentieth century, a number of scholars registered the filiations between this model of textuality and the developing contours of a new textual dispensation which was prompted by the emergence of the computer-based electronic text.[33] The hypertext system of connecting multiple documents, in particular, seemed to offer a useful analogue to the way in which Renaissance dramatic texts were open-ended and interconnected, lacking a unique, solitary source of authority. As George Landow, pioneering theorist of electronic textuality, has observed, once 'placed within a hypertext environment, a document no longer exists alone. It always exists in relation to other documents.' Hypertext thus, Landow argues, 'does not permit a tyrannical, univocal voice', but rather 'transforms any document that has more than one link into a transient center'.[34] The characteristic features of hypertext – identified by Landow as 'multivocality, open-endedness, multilinear organization, greater inclusion of nontextual information, and a fundamental reconfiguration of authorship, including ideas of authorial property, and of status relations within the text' – clearly resonate both with 'postmodern' theory and with late twentieth-century conceptions of the defining characteristics of Renaissance textuality.[35]

Thus far, so much (more) theory. But, again, we might ask how all of this would look in the practical realm of an actual edition. This question is partially answered by a spin-off of the *Arden Shakespeare*, issued in 1997. Under the general direction of Jonathan Bate, Arden issued a CD edition which included the Arden 2 edited texts, together with facsimiles of: the First Folio, eighteen complete first quartos, one First Quarto fragment (*Passionate Pilgrim*), two second quartos, the remnant of a lost quarto edition of *1 Henry IV*, and the deposition scene from the Fourth Quarto

Richard II. In addition, the package also included Abbott's *Shakespearian Grammar*, Partridge's *Shakespeare's Bawdy*, Onions' *Shakespeare Glossary*, and generous selections from Bullough's *Narrative and Dramatic Sources*. Crucially, all of these resources are interlinked, so that by marking out a particular passage in one of the Arden texts the user can summon up the equivalent passage in the facsimile(s) or in the source texts (likewise, individual words in the text are linked to Partridge and Onions). Bate and his colleagues did not necessarily share Landow's sense of the electronic text's critical role in vanquishing the 'tyrannical, univocal voice' of the author – this was still very much the *Arden Shakespeare* – but locating the edited text as one version among many does have the de-centring effect that Landow predicts. A kind of equivalence is effected between the Shakespearean texts and their 'sources' and between different textual versions of particular plays.

A more elaborate electronic project than the Arden has been undertaken at the Massachusetts Institute of Technology, under the direction of Peter Donaldson. For copyright reasons, access to the full version of the package has been limited to MIT and its contributing partners (such as the Folger Shakespeare Library and the Shakespeare Centre and Birthplace Trust), but a sample segment has also been made available on the Internet.[36] As in the case of the *Arden* CD, the 'Shakespeare Interactive Archive' provides edited texts of the plays (both the Mowat and Werstine Folger edition and the *Arden* edition), together with high-quality facsimiles of all the early texts. But, in addition, it also includes the text of later adaptations of the plays, material from theatrical promptbooks, pictures and illustrations based on the texts or on performances of the plays, and video of a large number of Shakespeare films, making it a true multi-media facility. In the case of the Archive, the Shakespeare text is located within a network of versions that extend over several centuries and across a broad field of different forms of reproduction (print, performance, painting, film, etc.), once again disrupting the notion of a central, stable authorially sanctioned text. As Donaldson himself has observed: 'Multimedia hypertext reconfigures the relationship between an authoritative cultural *source* (a Shakespeare play) and its belated, aesthetically- and culturally-divergent contemporary *versions*, changing the ways we think about such matters as "the original text" and its reproduction in "authoritative" versions and productions.'[37] Again: the greater textual or cultural field becomes more important than any single – original, or authoritative, or would-be definitive – text.

The archival model deployed in the MIT project has far-reaching implications and we might say that, where Barthes proclaimed the death of the author, certain theorists of electronic textuality may well be darkly whispering the last rites in the ear of the editor also. Kathryn Sutherland has mapped out some of the implications of the electronic archive as follows:

> All those judgements which dog the editor of literary works (best text, copytext, final intention, and so on), and which are endemic to the book, can be postponed indefinitely within the electronic environment. Where the satisfactions of book-bound communication are determined by closure – selecting the crucial information, the decisive examples, discarding the extraneous – those of the electronic medium are open-ended. The one offers the pleasurable illusion of completedness, the other holds out the promise of more, a never-to-be satisfied craving . . . In place of selection and the need or even art of choosing, the computer reinstates a sense of the nearly infinite range of possibilities which exists in life.

In the realm of electronic textuality, Sutherland tells us, 'the reader or user . . . takes on the role of editor, choosing to define connections between documents in a variety of temporary ways'.[38] The dull duty of the editor, as Pope characterised it, may well, it seems, have come to an end with the advent of the computer.

In a way, this would be a fitting place to conclude our long journey – to reach our terminus at the computer terminal, so to speak. We began this history with the very first printed texts of Shakespeare, produced on a version of Gutenberg's fifteenth-century printing press; there would be a certain symmetry in ending it at the dawn of a new era, with the computer text in the ascendant and the book declared obsolete. Along the way, we have traced the extended history of Shakespeare editing, from the tinkering of printing-house functionaries in the seventeenth century through to the complex theoretical models of the New Bibliographers and their descendants. If this study charts the birth of Shakespeare editing then there might well, again, be a certain nice sense of symmetry in finishing at the point where the editor, like the book, and the author, has been pronounced dead. But, in fact, things are a little more complicated than this. The computer text has its own particular set of problems and, in any case, rumours of the death of the book (not to mention the demise of the editor, and maybe even of the author too) have undoubtedly been greatly exaggerated.

We might first consider the problematics of the electronic text. The basic form of printing technology that Gutenberg invented remained in service with relatively minor changes right up to the end of the eighteenth century. Certainly, a first-generation fifteenth-century printer transported into a late eighteenth-century printshop would have had little enough difficulty adjusting to the then current methods of working. By contrast, the speed with which computing technology has changed is a positive blur. The problem with this astonishing rate of acceleration is that it is accompanied by an equally astonishing rate of obsolescence.[39] Gary Taylor has pointed out that the *Oxford Shakespeare* made use of computer files that had been compiled in the 1960s, when Trevor Howard-Hill was producing the *Oxford Shakespeare Concordances*. The files were prepared 'in a computer language which, by the late 1970s, only one computer in the world could still read'. The pace of change has, of course, intensified quite considerably in the intervening decades. And, as Taylor has further noted, as 'maintaining legibility becomes more expensive, *we will be able to afford the maintenance of legibility for fewer and fewer files*'.[40] It is already the case that some of the earliest commercial Shakespeare CD products will not open on current-specification computers. The best computer projects are also labour-intensive in a way that makes them extraordinarily expensive. The original retail price of the *Arden Shakespeare* CD was £2,500, exclusive of purchase tax. This figure was quickly reduced, but the price still remained at a level that placed the package outside the reach of individual (as opposed to institutional) purchasers. It is difficult to imagine how the problem of cost might be overcome, since, in order to be useful, electronic texts need to be very carefully tagged and checked – a much more complicated process than routine typesetting. (In an oddly ironic sense, producing computer texts sometimes seems to require the same kind of labour-intensive resources as the mediaeval scriptorium.) Taking a broad view of this issue, David Scott Kastan has observed that 'the apparent freedom of the electronic text is undermined by the not-inconsiderable costs of hardware, rights, data entry', and, in the case of material delivered over the Internet, of 'site design and maintenance (to say nothing of the obvious difficulty of persuading anyone to pay for access, leading a number of electronic publishing ventures . . . to be abandoned and others to be reconceived by their administrators as loss leaders)'.[41]

These are practical problems; they may, in time, be solved. After all, the Lumière brothers thought that *their* invention would be a nine-day's wonder with no realistic long-term commercial future. But the electronic text raises other issues too. John Lavagnino has observed of archival electronic projects that what 'proponents of these systems have imagined is that they would be transparent: they would not interpose an editor between the sources and the reader'. A 'pure' electronic Shakespeare would logically, then (in contrast to the *Arden* and MIT projects), tend to exclude edited texts from its archival dataset (or, at least, 'modern' edited texts, since all texts are in some sense edited). But, as Lavagnino goes on to argue, eliminating the editor 'implies that these sources themselves are always transparent, are never concealing something that scholarship can help us to perceive', and he continues:

> This idea, that we require no form of help with original documents, is not really very different from the idea that literary criticism is unnecessary because our untutored reactions to literary works are more authentic, and those reactions are likely to be repressed or distorted if we hear any discussion of what the texts mean.

'To refrain from editing', Lavagnino concludes, 'is an easy way to alleviate our nagging professional worries about being wrong; but it also means that we lose the opportunity to be right about anything, and to give other readers the benefit of our perceptions.'[42] We *can* do without editors, in other words, just as Dante-the-pilgrim could presumably have done without Virgil, but we might still want to ask what we forgo in refusing their services.

Another difficulty with the electronic text relates to the issue of exactly what constitutes reading. For the cyber-utopian, to read electronically – in the fullest sense – is to engage in what essentially amounts to a form of channel-surfing, pursuing a unique readerly pathway (in the Barthesian sense) across a multiplicity of resources. Thus, writing of the segmented and openly configured electronic work of interactive fiction (IF), Andrew Gibson has observed that

> whilst there may be a linear default path through IF – a clear, sequential plot – that plot cannot be thought of as in any respect the essence of the narrative in question. Rather, it exists as simply one among myriad possibilities, a kind of Platonic ideal of the narrative line which is never that of the actual narrative as it emerges or fails to emerge under the user's control.[43]

IF is, of course, designed to work in precisely this way; that is the point of its very mode of conception. But will Shakespeare be read like this? Or, more to the point, perhaps, just how many people will want to surf the archive of *Hamlet*, in preference to reading the tragedy of *Hamlet* (even if they have to read the latter in a unitary text whose very unitariness must be placed under question)?

In an odd way, this extended discussion of textual theory and electronic textuality brings us back, finally, to Arthur Quiller-Couch, the bluff Cornishman who served as John Dover Wilson's co-editor for the first eight volumes of Cambridge's *New Shakespeare*. In later years, we will recall, Dover Wilson revealed that 'Q's first idea was that each volume [in the Cambridge series] should be a pretty little book that ladies could carry to picnics'.[44]

Of course, Dover Wilson's scholarly and theoretical zeal turned the series into something quite different, something far more intellectually ambitious. But Q's instinct was not entirely wide of the mark either. Shakespeare has remained in print for centuries and his work has set in motion an accelerating train of publishing. This has happened in part, as we have seen in chapter 8, because his work has been incorporated into the educational system and so, in a sense, generations have been compelled to read his work. But Shakespeare has also been in print – and so much in print – because people have *wanted* to read his work. Richard Altick, in *The Common Reader*, retells the story of an encounter between E. E. Kellett and an unnamed pork-butcher in a crowded railway carriage:

> The butcher, looking about him, observed that there was no room except on the luggage rack. 'I fear you speak upon the rack', Kellett replied, 'where men enforcèd do speak anything.' The butcher's face lit up. 'That's Portia', he replied; 'I read Shakespeare, or something about him, every night after business.' For the next two hours the men engaged in a lively discussion, during which the butcher exhibited a wide and sound knowledge of Shakespeare's plays.[45]

There will always be a need for advanced scholarly editions of Shakespeare's works and these editions will be closely shaped both by prevalent textual theories (editorial models derived from classical and biblical studies, New Bibliography, hypertext theory . . .) and by prevalent textual forms (quarto, folio, tricesimo-secundo, floppy disk, CD, World Wide Web . . .). But there will also be a need for editions for Kellett's pork-butcher and for Q's picnicking ladies – indeed, these are, in many respects, precisely the editions (and readers) that have sustained Shakespeare's popularity since the early eighteenth century. It was to serve such readers that the folio format was abandoned, that John Dicks produced his shilling Shakespeare, that publishers in the late twentieth century recycled out-of-copyright editions to sell at 99*p*. a play. It may well be that the cyberenthusiasts are correct and that Q's ladies and Kellett's butcher will ultimately find themselves surfing a dispersed electronic Shakespearean archive rather than actually reading a pocket-sized printed book, so that the very phrase 'Shakespeare in print' may come in time to lose its meaning completely and seem a quaint anachronism. But, then again, maybe not.[46]

PART II | Appendix

Introduction to the appendix

Scope

Compiling an exhaustive listing of all of the editions of Shakespeare ever published would be an impossible task. Quite apart from the vast investment of time and resources that would be required, many of the more ephemeral editions simply have not survived, or survive only in odd volumes scattered in a wide array of libraries around the globe. The chronological appendix to this volume could not aspire to be exhaustive and in some respects it does not even aim to be in any real sense thoroughly comprehensive. The primary aim of the appendix is to provide as full a reckoning of the early editions as ever possible. Beyond the early editions, the listing seeks to present a sampling of Shakespeare publishing in more recent centuries. The sample provided is inevitably coloured both by the particular concerns of the text of *Shakespeare in Print* itself (see the general introduction to this volume) and by the concerns of the bibliographical tools which were used in compiling the listing. More will be said on this topic below.

In terms of the early publishing history of Shakespeare's texts, the appendix aims to provide a complete listing of all single-text Shakespeare volumes (which is to say, volumes containing only one play, or one poem or group of poems) up to 1709.[1] It also seeks to log all complete plays/collected-works editions published up to 1821. These cut-off points inevitably have a certain arbitrary cast to them, but there is, nevertheless, a logic motivating my choice of dates. The earliest quarto editions of Shakespeare's texts were published in advance of the folios and they initiated largely independent strands of publishing which ultimately ran in parallel with the folios. From 1709, this pattern tends to shift. Rowe's edition of that year had the effect of centralising the collected edition, not least because it initiated the Tonson cartel's policy of producing market-leading 'celebrity-edited' collected-works editions. Single-play texts certainly continued to appear, of course, but they tended in large measure to be spin-offs from the collected-works series. Thus, for example, the Foulis Glasgow edition of *Hamlet*, published in 1756, clearly indicates on its title page that it is 'according to Mr. Pope's second edition'. There were, of course, exceptions to this general rule, with Charles Jennens publishing innovative editions of *Lear, Hamlet, Macbeth, Othello* and *Julius Caesar* in the early 1770s and Thomas Caldecott producing editorially valuable texts of *Hamlet* and *As You Like It* in the early nineteenth century. The appendix aims to register texts of this kind, while omitting other single-text editions (with the exception of one particular class of texts, to be discussed below). By the late nineteenth century a new trend emerged, whereby texts from the canon were released in individual volumes which, together, constituted a collected- or selected-works edition. A good many of these series *are* included in the appendix, with details being provided of the names of the editors and the dates of publication of the individual volumes.

The eighteenth century, I have suggested, witnessed the centralising of the collected edition. It also witnessed what might be characterised as the emergence of a theoretically self-conscious tradition of Shakespeare editing – what Random Cloud has styled 'the birth of editing'.[2] Shakespeare had been edited before, of course. Someone, after all, had to assemble and organise the texts that were included in the First Folio volume, and all Shakespeare publishing in the period up to 1709 involved textual decisions of one kind or another. So, for example, whoever created the compositor's copy for the 1630 Second Quarto edition of *Othello* did so by systematically comparing the First Quarto and First Folio editions, creating a conflated text from the two of them. But it was in the eighteenth century that named editors first began to set out in their texts an explicit editorial programme – a programme that was open to debate and that, in practice, *prompted* debate, so that Shakespeare editing emerged as a distinct scholarly field, laying the foundations, in the process, of the more general field of English secular editing.[3] At the same time, a second, parallel, development occurred. If the costly leviathan folios had been accompanied by a shoal of cheaper minnow quartos, so the high-profile, expensive, celebrity-edited eighteenth-century collected-works editions served as the base text for smaller-format, cheaper editions – sometimes produced by the Tonson cartel, sometimes by other English or, more likely, Irish and Scottish, publishers, with an eye for the profits to be made from cheap editions of Shakespeare. Thus, as indicated in chapter 3, expensive leather-bound first editions sat in state in the libraries of country mansions, while cheaper spin-off versions of the same text found their way to the servants' quarters.

The appendix aims to trace as much of this history as it possibly can. All collected-works editions published up to 1821 are logged here. The choice of 1821 is intended to signal what might be characterised as a 'long eighteenth century' for Shakespeare editing. Margreta de Grazia and others have argued for seeing Edmond Malone as a pivotal figure in the editorial tradition. He represents the culmination of eighteenth-century editorial scholarship and, at the same time, his work serves as the bedrock for subsequent Shakespearean textual scholarship. The year 1821 is the one in which James Boswell's revision of Malone's edition appeared, providing a text which was reproduced again and again and again over the course of the nineteenth century. In 1877, for example, Horace Howard Furness commented that, as far as annotated editions were concerned, 'none surpasses the Variorum of 1821, which is unfortunately somewhat scarce and decidedly expensive; it is, however, the basis of all other modern editions'.[4] In this sense, intellectually, 1821 seems an appropriate date to serve as a cut-off point for attempting to log all collected editions. As indicated in the opening paragraph above, for purely practical reasons, *some* such date needs to be chosen and the date selected necessarily needs to come relatively early in the nineteenth century, since it was over the course of this century that Shakespeare publishing went into overdrive and accelerated at an unprecedented rate. As indicated in chapter 8, a rapid increase in the population of Britain, a progressive broadening of the educational franchise, and a significant shift in the economics of printing (with the advent, particularly, of the stereotype process and of cheap paper) meant both that the demand for editions rose sharply and that servicing that demand became an ever cheaper proposition. At the same time, a native tradition of Shakespeare publishing emerged in the United States, so that editions proliferated on both sides of the Atlantic. A chronological appendix of the kind included here can do little more than provide some representative snapshots of this tidal wave as it sweeps past.

Beyond 1821, then, the appendix ceases attempting to log every collected-works edition that appeared in print. The basis on which post-1821 editions are chosen is discussed in the next paragraph but, before leaving the eighteenth century, I should note one exception to the general rule that single-text editions receive minimal representation in the appendix beyond 1709. In chapter 6 of this book I have made a case for the importance of Scottish and Irish editions in widely disseminating and popularising Shakespeare's work. These editions helped Shakespeare to gain a foothold not just in Scotland and Ireland, but also in those regions of Britain which lay off the beaten track of the London trade's regular distribution routes. Irish editions in particular also served to provide the American market with cheap texts of Shakespeare in the period before a native American Shakespeare publishing tradition had been established. For these reasons, I have attempted to include in my listing as many eighteenth-century Scottish and Irish editions as I have been able to trace. The qualification offered in this last sentence is, however, important to note. There is a great likelihood that other editions were published which have not survived, or which have not yet found their way into the ESTC database, which has been the primary finding mechanism for this segment of the appendix.[5] Thus, for example, an undated Dublin text of *King John*, published by D. Chamberlaine, announces itself as being a 'second edition', but I have been unable to trace any other edition of this play produced by Chamberlaine (or, indeed, by any other eighteenth-century Irish publisher).

In the period beyond 1821 I have been guided in selecting editions, in the first instance, by the *Variorum Handbook* – a resource compiled by Richard Hosley, Richard Knowles and Ruth McGugan for editors working on the *New Variorum Shakespeare* series.[6] This *Handbook* provides a listing of the broad range of editions which variorum editors might be expected to consult when producing their own texts. The listing does not confine itself to editions which are editorially significant, but also includes texts which editors may find useful in other ways. For example, it includes quite a number of schools editions, on the grounds that they contain valuable annotations. John Velz has described the *Handbook* as 'of incalculable value to anyone who contemplates research among Shakespeare editions, past or present, or indeed to librarians contemplating building Shakespeare collections'.[7] The *Handbook* provides the skeleton for the appendix, post-1821 – and, indeed, much of the flesh as well (though in many cases more detailed information is provided here than in the *Handbook*). All of the texts included in the *Handbook* are also included here and these entries are supplemented by those texts and editions which have found a place in the chapters of *Shakespeare in Print*. The general thrust of this book has been to foreground the editions which helped to popularise Shakespeare as well as those which contributed to the advancement of the editorial tradition. For this reason, a text such as J. R. Pitman's 1822 *School-Shakespeare* volume finds a place in my listing, on the grounds that it appears to be the first Shakespeare volume produced specifically with the educational market in mind. Likewise, Ward and Lock's 1890 *Sixpenny Shakespeare* also finds a place here, as it would seem to be the cheapest complete edition published during the course of the nineteenth century. As a general rule, every edition discussed in *Shakespeare in Print* is included in the appendix. The handful of exceptions to this rule are signalled in the endnotes to the individual chapters.

One thing that should be noted here is that some of the entries in the *Variorum Handbook* refer to incomplete series – often schools editions in which only a select number of texts were produced. The *Handbook* does not always specify exactly how many volumes were included in these series, and establishing the full set of texts is not always easy. The Folger has not paid the same scrupulous degree of attention to such series as it has to editions published in the period up to the early nineteenth century and in many cases it holds only partial sets – often, confusingly, with multiple copies of the individual volumes (160 miscellaneous William J. Rolfe volumes, published by Harpers, for example). In theory, under the terms of British copyright legislation, the British Library should hold a complete set of all such editions published in the UK. And, again in theory, the National Library of Scotland – by the same logic – should also possess a full set of such texts (the National Library of Scotland has effectively enjoyed copyright deposit status since 1709). Sadly, this seldom enough proves to be the case in practice. Thus, for example, very few of John Hunter's single-play editions (aimed at the educational market), published by Longmans in the 1860s and 1870s are held by the Folger. The British Library has twenty-four of the texts, but a search of the National Library of Scotland catalogue turned up an additional four and also revealed that the Scottish library lacked nine of the volumes held in London. Even a combination of the two sets of holdings may not provide a complete record of texts. In the case of such series, then, the reader is warned that the material reproduced here should be treated with a certain degree of caution: I have tried to trace as many volumes as possible, but have often had to do so by juggling a number of incomplete sets and there is no guarantee that a conflated list of holdings from multiple institutions will have produced a complete record of any given series. In the case of texts produced by one particular editor – Rolfe – I have been forced to admit defeat and have cut the Gordian knot by simply assigning a single number to the entire set of texts.

Before passing on to a discussion of some more particular matters relating to the appendix, two classes of text specifically excluded from the listing should be registered here. I do not include here any translations of Shakespeare's works into other languages (though I do register some of the early English-language editions published in continental Europe). As indicated in the general introduction to this volume, extending the remit of this project to include translations simply proved to be too complicated, not least because many of the earliest translations are partial or are in some way unsatisfactory. It is also quite difficult in many instances to track down some of the earliest texts. In *His Exits and His Entrances* Louis Marder mentions several early translations into various languages which I have been unable to trace at any of the libraries with major Shakespeare collections. In the end, I have been forced to concede that Shakespeare in translated print is a project for others to take up, while this volume concentrates exclusively on English-language texts.

Another class of texts which I have attempted to exclude from this appendix is that of theatrical adaptations, since the primary focus of *Shakespeare in Print* is the publication history of Shakespeare's own texts. Fixing an exact boundary line between original and adaptation has proved, however, to be a somewhat tricky task. I have, for instance, included some Restoration texts which, while not wholly faithful to Shakespeare's originals, nevertheless confine adaptation to moderations or modernisations of language, combined with the marking up of text which would typically be cut in performance. Interventions of this kind are, it can be argued, not so very far removed from the kinds of changes that Pope initiated under the index of editing. Likewise, at the end of the eighteenth century, I have included 1794 Boston texts of *Hamlet* and *Twelfth Night*, since, even though they reproduce texts which were amended for performance, they are also the first ever Shakespearean texts to be published in America. As a general rule of thumb, what I have tried to exclude are texts which engage in anything that might be regarded as a significant rewriting or restructuring of the text. So: the reader will find some borderline texts here, such as Restoration players' quartos, but will not find, for example, the Dryden and Davenant *Tempest* or Nahum Tate's *King Lear*.[8]

As a final comment on inclusions and exclusions, I should note that, in addition to tracing the history of the standard, accepted Shakespearean canon, I have also attended to editions of *Two Noble Kinsmen* and *Edward III*, both of which have increasingly been accepted as having been substantially co-authored by Shakespeare. I have also traced the early history of the apocryphal plays included in the second issue of the Third Folio. Of these texts, only *Pericles* has, of course, been accepted as having a substantial Shakespearean component; however, these plays have been more closely associated with the canon than the other apocrypha (texts such as *The Merry Devil of Edmonton* or *Fair Em*, which have never been part of a collected-works edition) and they have been included in a significant number of editions. 'Bad' quartos have been tracked in the listing, in addition to their more respectable siblings (see also below), but I have not logged editions of either the early *King John* (attributed in its first edition to 'W. Sh.' and in its second to 'W. SHAKESPEARE') or of *The Taming of a Shrew*, both of which vary sufficiently from their Shakespearean counterparts to be treated as wholly separate (if complexly related) entities.

When the listing of complete plays or collected editions up to 1821 was cross-checked against Jaggard's *Shakespeare Bibliography*, a number of anomalies were identified. These are editions which appear in Jaggard without an indication of location, and which I have been unable to trace. All of these editions were checked against the following catalogues and databases: ESTC (where applicable), Folger Shakespeare Library, British Library, Bodleian Library, National Library of Scotland, Birmingham Central Library, COPAC (a consortium of British and Irish academic libraries, including Cambridge University and Trinity College Dublin), the Library of Congress and WorldCat. It seems likely that these are ghost entries in Jaggard, though perhaps some of them may yet come to light somewhere.

Regularisation and format

For individual text editions up to 1709 and for collected plays/complete editions up to 1821 the full title of the edition, as it appears on the title page, is provided. Beyond these dates, standardised titles only are used. In reproducing the titles, original spelling is retained, with the exception of the use of 'VV' and 'vv' for 'W' and 'w'. Long 's' has also been regularised. Typography for all titles – including capitalisation – is standardised, using minimal capitalisation (where there is a colon in the title, I have followed the practice of capitalising the word which follows it). In the case of names of monarchs, indications of number are given in lower case (e.g., 'King Richard the second', in §20), since most numbers in the titles themselves are given in lower case. Where words in a title have been hyphenated owing to a line break, the hyphen has been removed. With a small number of exceptions (indicated in the listing itself) title-page information is derived either directly from the volumes themselves or, in the case of some of the earliest editions, from printouts from the STC microfilm collections.

For the period up to 1709, attribution of authorship is included in the publication details line. The name has been included in the title itself in those cases where it appears medially in the title *or* where there might conceivably be some significance in the relationship of the name to the title – e.g., 'corrected and augmented By W. Shakespere'. Identifications of publishers and printers are derived from the title pages themselves. Where this material is either absent or is provided in attenuated form (e.g., 'V. S.' for Valentine Simmes) the information provided is derived, for texts published before 1800, from either Greg, *Bibliography* or from the STC (generally via ESTC records) and, for later editions, from Jaggard's *Shakespeare Bibliography*. Abbreviations for play titles follow the conventions established in the MLA *Handbook*. Sixteenth- and seventeenth-century quarto editions are numbered according to the conventional practice which makes no distinction between variant and standard texts. Where variant texts exist, both versions are here additionally numbered in their own separate sequences. As the terminology 'good quarto'/'bad quarto' has been much interrogated, the designations 'long quarto' and 'short quarto' – abbreviated to 'LQ' and 'SQ' – have been adopted here.

Collected editions are identified, for the most part, by the name of the editor. In the case of first editions, the full name is given; subsequent editions are listed under the editor's surname and include a number indicating which edition is being registered. Where an editor's name is known but does not appear on the title page, the name is enclosed in square brackets. Where no editor has been identified (or where, in an extended sequence, the editor's name has effectively become irrelevant), either the name of the publisher (or printer) or (in the case of editions published outside the island of Britain) the place of publication is used as a means of identification. For series comprised of individual-text volumes, I have simply given the date range for the complete series where the entire sequence was the work of a single editor (or editors working together on the entire sequence). Where individual texts in a series have different editors, I have given the date of first publication of each text, together with the name of the editor.

I have registered the format of editions up to my 1821 cut-off date. In general, I have relied on ESTC records (and, post-1800, on Jaggard) for this information, though, in a few instances, I have given a different size, when the examination of a volume has led me to query the ESTC record and my query has been confirmed by a library catalogue entry (for example: George Grierson's Dublin editions are sometimes identified by ESTC as octavo, sometimes as duodecimo, despite the fact that they are of uniform size). I have not tracked format beyond 1821, since standard sizes become increasingly difficult to assign as technological advances in book production accelerate from the mid-nineteenth century onward.

Multiple entries within a given year are arranged alphabetically. For those individual years where a combination of collected- and single-text editions are being logged, the single texts are listed first. Where a run of entries for a particular year spans more than one page, the first line on each subsequent page repeats the year, printed within square brackets (as an aid to navigation). Multiple collected editions in a single year are arranged alphabetically on the basis of their identifying designation, unless there is some basis for arranging them chronologically (under 1734–5, 'Walker' comes before 'Tonson *et al.*' because Walker initiated his edition in advance of Tonson). Where a series of individual volumes is being logged using MLA abbreviations, if no other ordering principle is in play (such as date of issue or series number) the texts are arranged alphabetically by MLA designation and not by the expanded title to which the designation refers (hence *Ado* is listed before *Ant.*, despite the fact that it expands to *Much Ado About Nothing*).

Where a speculative year of publication has been suggested for undated or misdated editions, the year is followed by '(?)'. Where the listing has a confirmed entry or entries for a particular year and a speculative entry for the same year, the speculative entries follow the confirmed entries. So – to make this clearer – entries for 1595 are followed by a separate entry for 1595 (?). There is one exception to this general rule: 1599 (?) *precedes* 1599 because the incomplete copy of *Passionate Pilgrim* logged under 1599 (?) is thought to have been printed before the edition of the same work which is logged under 1599. In the case of entries for editions which were published over a span of years, where the start year coincides with the year of publication of another edition, the single year comes first, the extended period second. Thus: 1750 precedes 1750–1 (note also that the determining factor is the *start* year, thus, while 1797 precedes 1797–1801, 1797–1801 itself precedes 1798). Where two series of publications have the same start year, the series with the earlier finish year is placed first. Thus: 1803–4 precedes 1803–5.

The volumes examined for this appendix were consulted at the following libraries: University of St Andrews Library, University of Edinburgh Library, National Library of Scotland, British Library, University of London Library, Cambridge University Library, Trinity College Cambridge Wren Library, Oxford University Bodleian Library, Birmingham Central Library, Shakespeare Centre Library, National Library of Ireland, Trinity College Dublin Library, Folger Shakespeare Library, Library of Congress, University of Michigan Library. In the case of a small number of entries, last minute queries could not be dealt with by returning in person to the particular library in question. In these instances, the information provided here is as supplied by the libraries themselves. These cases are noted in the listing.

References to the ESTC relate to the commercially available version of the database as it was constituted in the period when the appendix was being compiled – approximately 1998–2002. WorldCat was used in the final stages of compiling the appendix, to attempt to untangle outstanding problems.[9] All references to WorldCat therefore refer to the database as it stood in the closing months of 2002. Unless otherwise stated, references to the Folger catalogue are to the card index held in the library, not to the electronic catalogue ('Hamnet'). References to the *Variorum Handbook* are to the original 1971 edition, cross-checked against an advance printout of the 2002–3 revision (lacking confirmed final page numbers).

The indices

The appendix is provided with its own separate set of indices. Four of the five indices have been fairly straightforward to compile. The index of publishers has, however, been a more complex undertaking. Imprints often provide variant spellings for the names of printers and publishers. In some cases, it is easy enough to spot a variant – Valentine Sims and Valentine Simmes seem clearly enough to be the same person. Other cases, however, are not so simple. Could 'F. Coles' (*Venus and Adonis*, 1675) be the 'Francis Coules' whose name appears in some other *Venus and Adonis* imprints? Probably. Henry R. Plomer, in the *Dictionary of Booksellers and Printers* covering the years 1641–67, gives both Coles and Cowles as variant surnames for Francis Coules. However, Plomer also notes that it 'is likely that there was more than one publisher of this name and that the [variant] imprints may refer to father and son'.[10] It is also sometimes difficult to tell just how many names are being registered in an imprint. For example: the names 'C. Rivington' and 'J. Rivington' each appear several times in imprints, as does the name 'J. and F. Rivington', but, in 1778, the name 'J. F. and C. Rivington' appears and is subsequently repeated several times. It seems reasonable to assume that this name refers to three individuals and not two – what we would now write as 'J., F. and C. Rivington'. Again, however, the situation is not necessarily quite so straightforward as this. The 1726–75 printers' dictionary reveals that there were, in fact, three Charles Rivingtons and at least two – and possibly three – John Rivingtons, so it is not always necessarily clear quite which J. or C. Rivington a particular imprint may be referring to.[11] The hydra-headed quality of some imprints arises, of course, precisely from the fact that printing and publishing often tended to be family businesses, handed down from generation to generation. Familial connections pose other problems for an indexer too. 'T. Payne' becomes in due course 'T. Payne and Son', before shifting to 'T. Payne, jun.', then finally reverting to 'T. Payne'. This would seem to indicate a father and son sharing the same name, with the son, in a kind of bibliographical oedipal moment, finally displacing the father. But does this mean that later 'T. Payne's should be indexed under 'T. Payne, jun.'? Can we, in fact, be certain that the later T. Payne is the son and not the father? Even outside the realm of family imprints there are complexities. The 'Longman' name appears in this appendix in ten different imprints: Longman; M. Longman; T. Longman; T. N. Longman; Longman & Co.; Longmans, Green; Longmans, Green & Co.; Longman, Hurst, Rees & Orme; Longman, Hurst, Rees, Orme & Brown; Longman & Rees. Condensing this information into a set of coherent index entries is no easy matter. Other odd problems also arise: are the 'J. and J. Fairbairn' of an edition published in 1795 the same as the 'I. and I. Fairbairn' of an edition published three years previously, given that the substitution of 'I' for 'J' would have been fairly anachronous by the closing decade of the eighteenth century? Are one of these (two?) (four?) Fairbairns the Fairbairn of the 'Fairbairn and Anderson' imprint that begins to appear from 1819?

As far as I possibly can, I have checked ambiguous imprints against the dictionaries of printers and publishers produced under the auspices of the Bibliographical Society. However, readers should treat the publishers' index included here simply as a finding aid for using the appendix and should exercise caution when using the index to locate information about specific publishers. Readers interested in the Shakespearean output of a particular publisher (or, more accurately, the segment of that output logged in this listing) should check for variants on the name being investigated and look at the full set of entries indexed under the name and any possible variants. The publishers' index is intended to serve as a point of entry into the appendix, not as a fully researched document in its own right.

Chronological appendix

Explanatory note

2° – folio	8° – octavo	16° – sextodecimo
4° – quarto	12° – duodecimo	24° – vicesimoquarto

Ff – folios
Qq – quartos

Where the individual entries are annotated, the annotation is preceded by a bullet point (•)

Open bullet points (○) are used to indicate editions which appear to be ghost entries in Jaggard's *Bibliography*.

Year	Title and details	No.
No date	**Locrine (apocryphal) Q0**	1

• This text – if it existed – does not survive. It is presumed to exist on the basis of Q1's advertising itself as 'Newly set foorth, ouerseene and corrected'.

No date	**1 Henry IV Q0**	2

• Only a fragment consisting of a single sheet of four leaves survives of this edition.

1593	**Venus and Adonis 1**	3

Venvs and Adonis.

[Signed 'William Shakespeare' in dedication. London: Richard Field. 4°]

1594	**2 Henry VI (variant) Q1**	4

The first part of the contention betwixt the two famous houses of Yorke and Lancaster, with the death of the good Duke Humphrey: And the banishment and death of the Duke of Suffolke, and the tragicall end of the proud Cardinall of Winchester, with the notable rebellion of Iacke Cade: And the Duke of Yorkes first claime vnto the crowne.

[Anon. London: by Thomas Creed, for Thomas Millington]

	Lucrece 1	5

Lvcrece.

[Signed 'William Shakespeare' in dedication. London: by Richard Field, for Iohn Harrison. 4°]

[1594]   **Titus Andronicus Q1**   6

*The most lamentable Romaine tragedie of Titus Andronicus: As it was
plaide by the right honourable the Earle of Darbie, Earle of Pembrooke,
and Earle of Sussex their seruants.*

[Anon. London: by Iohn Danter, and are to be sold by Edward
White & Thomas Millington]

           Venus and Adonis 2   7

Venvs and Adonis.

[Dedication signed William Shakespeare. London: by Richard
Field. 4°]

1595   **3 Henry VI (variant) O1 [octavo]**   8

*The true tragedie of Richard Duke of Yorke, and the death of good
King Henrie the sixt, with the whole contention betweene the two houses
Lancaster and Yorke, as it was sundrie times acted by the Right
Honourable the Earle of Pembrooke his seruants.*

[Anon. London: by P. S. for Thomas Millington; P. S. is Peter
Short]

           Locrine (apocryphal) Q   9

*The lamentable tragedie of Locrine, the eldest sonne of King Brutus,
discoursing the warres of the Britaines, and Hunnes, with their
discomfiture: The Britaines victorie with their accidents, and the death
of Albanact. No lesse pleasant then profitable. Newly set foorth,
ouerseene and corrected.*

['By W. S.' London: by Thomas Creede]

1595 (?)   **Venus and Adonis 3**   10
           • Surviving copy (STC 22356, Folger – STC number is also
shelfmark number) lacks quire A.

[STC suggests R. Field for J. Harrison, 1595. 8°]

1596   **Edward III Q1**   11

*The raigne of King Edward the third: As it hath bin sundrie times
plaied about the Citie of London.*

[Anon. London: Printed for Cuthbert Burby]

           Venus and Adonis 4   12

Venvs and Adonis.

[Dedication signed William Shakespeare. London: by R. F. for
Iohn Harison; R. F. is Richard Field. 8°]

1597   **Richard II Q1**   13

*The tragedie of King Richard the second. As it hath beene publikely
acted by the right honourable the Lorde Chamberlaine his seruants.*

[Anon. London: by Valentine Simmes for Androw {sic} Wise]

[1597] **Richard III (variant) Q1** 14

The tragedy of King Richard the third. Containing, his treacherous plots against his brother Clarence: the pittiefull murther of his inuocent [sic] nephewes: his tyrannicall vsurpation: with the whole course of his detested life, and most deserued death. As it hath beene lately acted by the right honourable the Lord Chamberlaine his seruants.

• Greg suggests in *Editorial* (p. 87, n. 4) that only sheets A to G were printed by Simmes, the remainder probably being printed by Peter Short.

[Anon. London: by Valentine Sims, for Andrew Wise]

Romeo and Juliet (variant) (SQ) Q1 15

An excellent conceited tragedie of Romeo and Iuliet. As it hath been often (with great applause) plaid publiquely, by the right honourable the L. of Hunsdon his seruants.

• Danter printed quires A-D only. The remainder was printed by Edward Allde.

[Anon. London: Printed by Iohn Danter]

1597 (?) **Love's Labour's Lost Q0** 16

• This text – if it existed – does not survive. It is presumed to exist on the basis of Q1's advertising itself as 'Newly corrected and augmented'. Freeman and Grinke, in 'Four New Shakespeare Quartos?' (p. 18) have noted an entry in a manuscript catalogue of the (now largely lost) Viscount Conway library which lists an edition of *Love's Labour's Lost*, giving a date of 1597.

1598 **1 Henry IV Q1** 17

The history of Henrie the fovrth; With the battell at Shrewsburie, betweene the King and Lord Henry Percy, surnamed Henrie Hotspur of the north. With the humorous conceits of Sir Iohn Falstalffe [sic].

See §2 above for another early edition, only a fragment of which survives.

[Anon. London: by P. S. for Andrew Wise; P. S. is Peter Short]

Love's Labour's Lost Q1 18

A pleasant conceited comedie called, loues labors lost. As it was presented before her highnes this last Christmas. Newly corrected and augmented By W. Shakespere.

• Capitalisation of 'By' in attribution of authorship is retained here, but it should be noted that the attribution itself is a separate line, printed in italics.

['By W. Shakespere', as above. London: by W. W. for Cutbert Burby; W. W. is William White]

[1598]   Lucrece 2   19

Lvcrece.

[Dedication signed William Shakespeare. London: by P. S. for
Iohn Harrison; P. S is Peter Short. 8°]

Richard II Q2   20

*The tragedie of King Richard the second. As it hath beene publikely
acted by the right honourable the Lord Chamberlaine his seruants.*

['By William Shake-speare'. London: by Valentine Simmes for
Andrew Wise]

Richard II Q3   21

*The tragedie of King Richard the second. As it hath beene publikely
acted by the right honourable the Lord Chamberlaine his seruants.*

['By William Shake-speare'. London: by Valentine Simmes, for
Andrew Wise]

Richard III (variant) Q2   22

*The tragedie of King Richard the third. Conteining his treacherous
plots against his brother Clarence: the pitiful murther of his innocent
nephewes: his tyrannicall vsurpation: with the whole course of his
detested life, and most deserued death. As it hath beene lately acted by
the right honourable the Lord Chamberlaine his seruants.*

['By William Shake-speare'. London: by Thomas Creede, for
Andrew Wise]

1599 (?)   Passionate Pilgrim 1   23

• Surviving copy (STC 22341.5, held at the Folger and
shelfmarked as STC 22342) lacks title page. STC suggests 1599 as
publication date. Appears to predate 1599 edition listed below.

[No indication of authorship. STC suggests London: T. Judson for
W. Jaggard. 8°]

1599   Edward III Q2   24

*The raigne of King Edward the third. As it hath bene sundry times
played about the Citie of London.*

[Anon. London: by Simon Stafford, for Cuthbert Burby]

1 Henry IV Q2   25

*The history of Henrie the fovrth; with the battell at Shrewsburie,
betweene the king and Lord Henry Percy, surnamed Henry Hotspur of
the north. With the humorous conceits of Sir Iohn Falstalffe [sic].
Newly corrected by W. Shake-speare.*

['by W. Shakespeare', as above. London: by S. S. for Andrew Wise;
S. S. is Simon Stafford]

[1599] **Passionate Pilgrim 2** 26

['By W. Shakespeare'. London: for W. Iaggard and are to be sold by
W. Leake. 8°]

Romeo and Juliet (LQ1) Q2 27

*The most excellent and lamentable tragedie, of Romeo and Iuliet.
Newly corrected, augmented, and amended: As it hath bene sundry
times publiquely acted, by the right honourable the Lord Chamberlaine
his seruants.*

[Anon. London: by Thomas Creede, for Cuthbert Burby]

Venus and Adonis 5, 5a 28 (neuer), 29 (& neuer)

Venvs and Adonis.

• Two editions in this year, with minor variations on title page.
One has A2r catchword 'neuer', the other '& neuer'. The former
edition printed by Peter Short; the latter by R. Bradock. Farr, in
'Shakespeare's' (p. 229), suggests that Bradock printed from the
Short edition.

[Dedication signed William Shakespeare. London: for William
Leake. 8°]

1600 **2 Henry IV Q1, Q1a** 30, 31 (with new sheet)

*The second part of Henrie the fourth, continuing to his death, and
coronation of Henrie the fift. With the humours of Sir Iohn Falstaffe,
and swaggering Pistoll. As it hath been sundrie times publikely acted by
the right honourable, the Lord Chamberlaine his seruants.*

• In a second issue in the same year gatherings E3–4 are cancelled
and replaced with a complete sheet of four leaves to make good the
omission of a passage corresponding to III.i.

['Written by William Shakespeare'. London: by V. S. for Andrew
Wise and William Aspley; V. S. is Valentine Simmes]

Henry V (variant) Q1 32

*The cronicle history of Henry the fift, with his battell fought at Agin
Court in France. Togither with Auntient Pistoll. As it hath bene sundry
times playd by the right honorable the Lord Chamberlaine his seruants.*

[Anon. London: by Thomas Creede, for Tho. Millington and Iohn
Busby]

2 Henry VI (variant) Q2 33

*The first part of the contention betwixt the two famous houses of
Yorke and Lancaster, with the death of the good Duke Humphrey:
And the banishment and death of the Duke of Suffolke, and the tragical
end of the prowd Cardinall of Winchester, with the notable rebellion
of Iacke Cade: And the Duke of Yorkes first clayme to the
crowne.*

[Anon. London: by Valentine Simmes for Thomas Millington]

[1600] **3 Henry VI (variant) Q, ed 2**   34

The true tragedie of Richarde Duke of Yorke, and the death of good
King Henrie the sixt: With the whole contention betweene the two
houses, Lancaster and Yorke; as it was sundry times acted by the right
honourable the Earle of Pembrooke his seruantes.

[Anon. London: by W. W. for Thomas Millington. W. W. is
William White]

Lucrece 3, 3a   35 (London,), 36 (London.)

Lvcrece

• Two issues in the same year, one with 'London,' instead of
'London.' on title page. In the latter E3 is incorrectly signed B3.
Farr, 'Shakespeare's' (p. 248) suggests that the 'London.' edition
was printed from the 'London,'.

[Dedication signed William Shakespeare. London: by I. H. for
Iohn Harison; I. H. is John Harrison III, publisher is John
Harrison I. 8°]

Merchant of Venice Q1   37

The most excellent historie of the merchant of Venice. With the
extreame crueltie of Shylocke the Iewe towards the sayd merchant, in
cutting a iust pound of his flesh: And the obtayning of Portia by the
choyse of three chests. As it hath beene diuers times acted by the Lord
Chamberlaine his seruants.

['Written by William Shakespeare'. London: by I. R. for Thomas
Heyes; I. R. is James Roberts]

Merchant of Venice Q2   –

• 1619 quarto falsely dated for this year – see entry under 1619
below.

Midsummer Night's Dream Q1   38

A midsommer nights dreame. As it hath beene sundry times publickely
acted, by the right honourable, the Lord Chamberlaine his seruants.

['Written by William Shakespeare'. London: for Thomas Fisher;
printer was probably Richard Bradock]

Midsummer Night's Dream Q2   –

• 1619 quarto falsely dated for this year – see entry under 1619
below.

Much Ado About Nothing Q   39

Much adoe about nothing. As it hath been sundrie times publikely acted
by the right honourable, the Lord Chamberlaine his seruants.

['Written by William Shakespeare'. London: by V. S. for Andrew
Wise, and William Aspley; V. S. is Valentine Simmes]

[1600] **1 Sir John Oldcastle (apocryphal) Q1**   40

The first part of the true and honorable historie, of the life of Sir John Old-castle, the good Lord Cobham. As it hath been lately acted by the right honorable the Earle of Notingham Lord High Admirall of England his seruants.

[Anon. London: by V. S. for Thomas Pauier; V. S. is Valentine Simmes]

1 Sir John Oldcastle (apocryphal) Q2   –

• 1619 quarto falsely dated for this year – see entry under 1619 below.

Titus Andronicus Q2   41

The most lamentable Romaine tragedie of Titus Andronicus. As it hath sundry times beene playde by the right honourable the Earle of Pembrooke, the Earle of Darbie, the Earle of Sussex, and the Lorde Chamberlaine theyr seruants.

[Anon. London: by I. R. for Edward White; I. R. is James Roberts]

1601 **[The Phoenix and the Turtle 1]**   42

Loves martyr or, Rosalins complaint. Allegorically shadowing the truth of loue, in the constant fate of the phænix and turtle. A poeme enterlaced with much varietie and raritie; now first translated out of the venerable Italian Torquato Cæliano, by Robert Chester. With the true legend of famous King Arthur, the last of the nine worthies, being the first essay of a new Brytish poet: collected out of diuerse authenticall records. To these are added some new compositions, of seuerall moderne writers whose names are subscribed to their seuerall workes, vpon the first subiect: viz. the phænix and turtle.

[Poem is signed 'William Shake-speare'. London: for E. B.; E. B. is Edward Blount. 4°]

1602 **Henry V (variant) Q2**   43

The chronicle history of Henry the fift, with his battell fought at Agin Court in France. Together with Auntient Pistoll. As it hath bene sundry times playd by the right honorable the Lord Chamberlaine his seruants.

[Anon. London: by Thomas Creede, for Thomas Pauier]

Merry Wives of Windsor (variant) Q1   44

A most pleasaunt and excellent conceited comedie, of Syr Iohn Falstaffe, and the merrie wiues of Windsor. Entermixed with sundrie variable and pleasing humors, of Syr Hugh the Welch knight, Iustice Shallow, and his wise cousin M. Slender. With the swaggering vaine of Auncient Pistoll, and Corporall Nym. By William Shakespeare.

[1602]   *As it hath bene diuers times acted by the right honorable my Lord Chamberlaines seruants. Both before her maiestie, and else-where.*

['By William Shakespeare', as above. London: by T. C. for Arthur Iohnson; T. C. is Thomas Creede]

Richard III (variant) Q3   45

The tragedie of King Richard the third. Conteining his treacherous plots against his brother Clarence: The pittifull murther of his innocent nephewes: His tyrannicall vsurpation: With the whole course of his detested life, and most deserued death. As it hath bene lately acted by the right honourable the Lord Chamberlaine his seruants. Newly augmented, By William Shakespeare.

• Capitalisation of 'By' in attribution of authorship is retained here, but it should be noted that the attribution itself is a separate line, with 'William Shakespeare' in italics.

['By William Shakespeare', as above. London: by Thomas Creede, for Andrew Wise]

Thomas Lord Cromwell (apocryphal) Q1   46

The true chronicle historie of the whole life and death of Thomas Lord Cromwell. As it hath beene sundrie times publikely acted by the right honorable the Lord Chamberlaine his seruants.

['Written by W. S.' London: for William Iones; printer is Richard Read]

Venus and Adonis 7, 8, 9   –
Venvs and Adonis.

• Three texts of the poem bear the date 1602 on their title pages, but STC suggests that the dates are incorrect. The editions are distinguishable by minor variations on the title pages and, in one instance, by a catchword variation (noted in individual entries). See entries under 1607 (?), 1608 (?) and 1610 (?). For an account of these editions, see Farr, 'Shakespeare's'.

1602 (?)   **Venus and Adonis 6**   47

• Surviving copy (STC 22359, Bodleian – shelfmark Arch.Gg.4(2)) lacks title page. Handwritten title page gives 'London. Printed by I.H. for Iohn Harison', but this simply copies the imprint of an edition of *Lucrece* bound in the same volume. On the basis of the printer's ornaments, Farr, 'Shakespeare's' (p. 229) suggests that the printer was R. Bradock.

[Dedication signed William Shakespeare. STC speculates R. Bradock for W. Leake. 8°]

1603   **Hamlet (variant) (SQ) Q1**   48

The tragicall historie of Hamlet Prince of Denmarke by William Shake-speare. As it hath beene diuerse times acted by his highnesse

seruants in the Cittie of London: As also in the two vniuersities of
Cambridge and Oxford, and else-where.

['By William Shake-speare', as above. London: for N. L. and
John Trundell; N. L. is Nicholas Ling; printer is Valentine
Simmes.]

1604   1 Henry IV Q3   **49**

The history of Henrie the fourth, with the battell at Shrewsburie,
betweene the king, and Lord Henry Percy, surnamed Henry Hotspur of
the north. With the humorous conceits of Sir Iohn Falstalffe [sic].
Newly corrected by W. Shake-speare.

• 'Newly corrected by W. Shake-speare' printed together on a
separate line, with Shakespeare's name italicised.

['by W. Shake-speare', as above. London: by Valentine Simmes, for
Mathew Law]

1604/5   Hamlet (LQ1, LQ1a) Q2, Q2a   **50 (1604), 51 (1605)**

The tragicall historie of Hamlet, Prince of Denmarke. By William
Shakespeare. Newly imprinted and enlarged to almost as much againe
as it was, according to the true and perfect coppie.

• One state of the title page gives the date as 1604, this was
subsequently revised to 1605.

['By William Shakespeare', as above. London: by I. R. for N. L.;
I. R. is James Roberts; N. L. is Nicholas Ling]

1605   London Prodigal (apocryphal) Q   **52**

The London prodigall. As it was plaide by the kings maiesties seruants.

['By William Shakespeare'. London: by T. C. for Nathaniel Butter;
T. C. is Thomas Creede]

Richard III (variant) Q4   **53**

The tragedie of King Richard the third. Conteining his treacherous
plots against his brother Clarence: The pittifull murther of his innocent
nephewes: His tyrannicall vsurpation: With the whole course of his
detested life, and most deserued death. As it hath bin lately acted by the
right honourable the Lord Chamberlaine his seruants. Newly
augmented, By William Shake-speare.

• Capitalisation of 'By' in attribution of authorship is retained
here, but it should be noted that the attribution itself is a separate
line, with Shakespeare's name italicised.

['By William Shake-speare', as above. London: by Thomas Creede,
and are to be sold by Mathew Lawe]

1607   Lucrece 4   **54**

Lvcrece.

[Dedication signed William Shakespeare. London: by N. O. for
Iohn Harison; N.O. is Nicholas Okes. 8°]

[1607]   **The Puritan (apocryphal) Q**   55

*The pvritaine or the widdow of Watling-streete. Acted by the Children
of Paules.*

['Written by W. S.'. London: by G. Eld]

1607 (?)   **Venus and Adonis 7**   56

• Imprint gives 1602. See unnumbered 1602 entry above. A2r
catchword is 'and'.

[Dedication signed William Shakespeare. London: for William
Leake. STC suggests printer R. Raworth and date 1607. 8°]

1608   **1 Henry IV Q4**   57

*The history of Henry the fourth, with the battell at Shrewseburie,
betweene the king, and Lord Henry Percy, surnamed Henry Hotspur of
the north. With the humorous conceites of Sir Iohn Falstalffe [sic].
Newly corrected by W. Shake-speare.*

• 'Newly corrected by W. Shake-speare' printed together on a
separate line and italicised.

['by W. Shake-speare', as above. London: for Mathew Law]

Henry V (variant) Q3   –

• Falsely dated quarto issued in 1619 – see entry for 1619
below.

King Lear Q1   58

*M. William Shak-speare: His true chronicle historie of the life and
death of King Lear and his three daughters. With the vnfortunate life
of Edgar, sonne and heire to the Earle of Gloster, and his sullen and
assumed humor of Tom of Bedlam: As it was played before the kings
maiestie at Whitehall vpon S. Stephans night in Christmas hollidayes.
By his maiesties seruants playing vsually at the Gloabe on
Bancke-side.*

['M. William Shak-speare', as above. London: for Nathaniel
Butter; printer is Nicholas Okes]

King Lear Q2   –

• Falsely dated quarto issued in 1619 – see entry for 1619 below.

Richard II Q4, Q4a   59, 60 (additional scene)

*The tragedie of King Richard the second. As it hath been publikely
acted by the right honourable the Lord Chamberlaine his seruantes.*

Variant title:

*The tragedie of King Richard the second: With new additions of the
parliament sceane, and the deposing of King Richard. As it hath been
lately acted by the kinges maiesties seruantes, at the Globe.*

[1608] • Q4 introduced the 'abdication scene', which was not present in earlier editions. The reset title page drew explict attention to this new material.

['By William Shake-speare'. London: by W. W. for Mathew Law; W. W. is William White]

Yorkshire Tragedy (apocryphal) Q1   61

A Yorkshire tragedy. Not so new as lamentable and true. Acted by his maiesties players at the Globe.

['Written by W. Shakespeare'. London: by R. B. for Thomas Pauier; R. B. is Richard Bradock]

1608 (?) **Venus and Adonis 8**   62

• Imprint gives 1602. See unnumbered 1602 entry above. A2r catchword is 'ther'.

[Dedication signed William Shakespeare. London: for William Leake. STC suggests printer H. Lownes and date 1608. 8°]

1609 **Pericles Q1, Q2**   63 (Enter), 64 (Eneer)

The late, and much admired play, called Pericles, Prince of Tyre. With the true relation of the whole historie, aduentures, and fortunes of the said prince: As also, the no lesse strange, and worthy accidents, in the birth and life, of his daughter Mariana. As it hath been diuers and sundry times acted by his maiesties seruants, at the Globe on the Banck-side.

• A new edition was issued in the same year. The text was reset and the editions are generally distinguished by the fact that in line 3 on A2r one text reads 'Enter Gower', the other 'Eneer Gower'.

['By William Shakespeare'. London: for Henry Gosson; printer of at least part of the text appears to have been William White]

Romeo and Juliet (LQ2) Q3   65

The most excellent and lamentable tragedie, of Romeo and Juliet. As it hath beene sundrie times publiquely acted, by the kings maiesties seruants at the Globe. Newly corrected, augmented, and amended.

[Anon. London: Printed for Iohn Smethwick]

Sonnets 1, 1a   66 (Aspley), 67 (Wright)

Shake-speares sonnets. Neuer before imprinted.

• Variant title page 'By G. Eld for T. T. and are to be solde by Iohn Wright'

['Shake-speares', as above. London: By G. Eld for T. T. and are to be solde by William Aspley; T. T. is Thomas Thorpe. 4°]

Troilus and Cressida Q, Qa   68, 69 (with preface)

The historie of Troylus and Cresseida. As it was acted by the kings maiesties seruants at the Globe.

Variant title:

The famous historie of Troylus and Cresseid. Excellently expressing the beginning of their loues, with the conceited wooing of Pandarus Prince of Licia.

• Two issues in the same year. In the second issue, a single fold replaces the original title page and provides a preface – entitled 'A neuer writer, to an euer reader. Newes.' – which claims that the play was 'neuer clapper-clawd with the palmes of the vulger'. Variant title as above is for second issue.

['Written by William Shakespeare'. London: by G. Eld for R. Bonian and H. Walley]

1610 (?)   **Venus and Adonis 9**   70

• Imprint gives 1602. See unnumbered 1602 entry above. Title page only remains (STC 22360b, British Library – shelfmark Harley 5990/134).

[Dedication, if printed, does not survive. London: for William Leake. STC suggests date 1610. 8°]

1611   **Hamlet (LQ2) Q3**   71

The tragedy of Hamlet Prince of Denmarke. By William Shakespeare. Newly imprinted and enlarged to almost as much againe as it was, according to the true and perfect coppy.

['By William Shakespeare', as above. London: Printed for Iohn Smethwicke; printer appears to be Valentine Simmes]

Pericles 'Q'3 [octavo paper, arranged in quires of four]   72

The late, and much admired play, called Pericles, Prince of Tyre. With the true relation of the whole history, aduentures, and fortunes of the sayd prince: As also, the no lesse strange, and worthy accidents, in the birth and life, of his daughter Mariana. As it hath beene diuers and sundry times acted by his maiestyes seruants, at the Globe on the Banck-side.

['By William Shakespeare'. London: by S. S.; printer, for part of the text at least, appears to have been Simon Stafford]

[The Phoenix and the Turtle 2]   73

The anuals [sic] of Great Britain. Or, a most excellent monument, wherein may be seene all the antiquities of this kingdome, to the satisfaction both of the vniuersities, or any other place stirred with emulation of long continuance. Excellently figured out in a worthy poem.

[Poem signed 'William Shake-speare'. London: for Mathew Lownes. Printer Edward Allde. 4°]

[1611] **Titus Andronicus Q3** 74

The most lamentable tragedie of Titus Andronicus. As it hath svndry times beene plaide by the kings maiesties seruants.

[Anon. London: for Eedward [sic] White]

1612 **Passionate Pilgrim 3, 3a** 75 (with Shakespeare's name), 76

The passionate pilgrime. Or certaine amorous sonnets, betweene Venus and Adonis, newly corrected and augmented, By W. Shakespere. The third edition. Where-unto is newly added two loue-epistles, the first from Paris to Hellen, and Hellens answere backe againe to Paris.

• Capitalisation of 'By W. Shakespere' retained as in the original, but note that this appears as a separate line, italicised (as are other parts of the title). A second title page exists for this edition, which omits Shakespeare's name.

['By W. Shakespere', as above. {London}: by W. Iaggard. 8°]

Richard III (variant) Q5 77

The tragedie of King Richard the third. Containing his treacherous plots against his brother Clarence: The pittifull murther of his innocent nephewes: His tyrannicall vsurpation: With the whole course of his detested life, and most deserued death. As it hath beene lately acted by the kings maiesties seruants. Newly augmented, By William Shake-speare.

• Capitalisation of 'By' in attribution of authorship is retained here, but it should be noted that the attribution itself is a separate line, with Shakespeare's name printed in italics.

['By William Shake-speare', as above. London: by Thomas Creede, and are to be sold by Mathew Lawe]

1613 **1 Henry IV Q5** 78

The history of Henrie the fourth, with the battell at Shrewseburie, betweene the king, and Lord Henrie Percy, surnamed Henrie Hotspur of the north. With the humorous conceites of Sir Iohn Falstaffe. Newly corrected by W. Shake-speare.

• 'Newly corrected by W. Shake-speare' printed together on a separate line, with Shakespeare's name italicised.

['by W. Shake-speare', as above. London: by W. W. for Mathew Law; W. W. is William White]

Thomas Lord Cromwell Q2 79

The true chronicle historie of the whole life and death of Thomas Lord Cromwell. As it hath beene sundrie times publikely acted by the kings maiesties seruants.

['Written by W. S.' London: by Thomas Snodham]

1615   **Richard II Q5**   80

The tragedie of King Richard the second: With new additions of the
parliament sceane, and the deposing of King Richard. As it hath been
lately acted by the kinges maiesties seruants, at the Globe.

['By William Shake-speare'. London: for Mathew Law]

1616   **Lucrece 5**   81

The rape of Lvcrece. By Mr. William Shakespeare. Newly reuised.

• This edition adds marginal notes summarising action.

['By Mr. William Shakespeare', as above. London: by T. S. for
Roger Iackson; T. S. is Thomas Snodham. 8°]

1617   **Venus and Adonis 10**   82

Venvs and Adonis.

[Dedication signed William Shakespeare. London: for W. B.; W. B.
is William Barrett; printer is William Stansby. 8°]

1619   **Thomas Pavier's attenuated Shakespeare 'collection'**   83

• Consists of the following individual texts:

Henry V (variant) Q3   84

The chronicle history of Henry the fift, with his battell fought at Agin
Court in France. Together with ancient Pistoll. As it hath bene sundry
times playd by the right honourable the Lord Chamberlaine his seruants.

[Anon. London: for T. P.; dated 1608]

2 Henry VI (variant) Q3 and 3 Henry VI (variant) Q, edn 3   85

The whole contention betweene the two famous houses, Lancaster and
Yorke. With the tragicall ends of the good Duke Humfrey, Richard
Duke of Yorke, and King Henrie the sixt. Diuided into two parts: And
newly corrected and enlarged.

['Written by William Shake-speare, Gent'. London: for T. P.; n.d.]

King Lear Q2   86

M. William Shake-speare, his true chronicle history of the life and
death of King Lear, and his three daughters. With the vnfortunate life
of Edgar, sonne and heire to the Earle of Glocester, and his sullen and
assumed humour of Tom of Bedlam. As it was plaid before the kings
maiesty at White-Hall, vpon S. Stephens night, in Christmas hollidaies.
By his maiesties seruants, playing vsually at the Globe on Banck-side.

['M. William Shake-speare', as above. London: for Nathaniel
Butter; dated 1608]

Merchant of Venice Q2   87

The excellent history of the merchant of Venice. With the extreme
cruelty of Shylocke the Iew towards the saide merchant, in cutting a

[1619] *iust pound of his flesh. And the obtaining of Portia, by the choyse of three caskets.*
['Written by W. Shakespeare'. London: by J. Roberts; dated 1600]

Merry Wives of Windsor (variant) (SQ2) Q2   88

A most pleasant and excellent conceited comedy, of Sir Iohn Falstaffe, and the merry wives of Windsor. With the swaggering vaine of Ancient Pistoll, and Corporall Nym.

['Written by W. Shakespeare'. London: for Arthur Johnson; dated 1619]

Midsummer Night's Dream Q2   89

A midsommer nights dreame. As it hath beene sundry times publikely acted, by the right honourable, the Lord Chamberlaine his seruants.

['Written by William Shakespeare'; London: by Iames Roberts; dated 1600]

Pericles Q4   90

The late, and much admired play, called, Pericles, Prince of Tyre. With the true relation of the whole history, aduentures, and fortunes of the saide prince.

['Written by W. Shakespeare'. {London:} for T. P.; dated 1619]

1 Sir John Oldcastle (apocryphal) Q2   91

The first part of the true and honorable history, of the life of Sir Iohn Old-castle, the good Lord Cobham. As it hath bene lately acted by the right honorable the Earle of Notingham Lord High Admirall of England, his seruants.

['Written by William Shakespeare'. London: for T. P.; dated 1600]

Yorkshire Tragedy (apocryphal) Q2   92

A Yorkshire tragedy. Not so new, as lamentable and true.

['Written by W. Shakespeare'. {London:} for T. P.; dated 1619]

1620 **Venus and Adonis 11**   93

Venvs and Adonis.

[Dedication signed William Shakespeare. London: for I. P.; I. P. is John Parker. 8°]

1622 **1 Henry IV Q6**   94

The historie of Henry the fourth. With the battell at Shrewseburie, betweene the king, and Lord Henry Percy, surnamed Henry Hotspur of the north. With the humorous conceits of Sir Iohn Falstaffe. Newly corrected. By William Shake-speare.

• Note that the attribution to Shakespeare is a separate line, with Shakespeare's name printed in italics.

[1622]   ['By William Shake-speare', as above. London: by T.P. and are to
be sold by Mathew Law; T. P. is Thomas Purfoot]

Othello Q1   95

*The tragœdy of Othello, the Moore of Venice. As it hath beene diuerse
times acted at the Globe, and at the Black-Friers, by his maiesties
seruants.*

['Written by William Shakespeare'. London: by N. O. for Thomas
Walkley; N. O. is Nicholas Okes]

Richard III (variant) Q6   96

*The tragedie of King Richard the third. Contayning his treacherous
plots against his brother Clarence: The pittifull murder of his innocent
nephewes: His tyrannicall vsurpation: With the whole course of his
detested life, and most deserued death. As it hath been lately acted by the
kings maiesties seruants. Newly augmented. By William Shake-speare.*

• 'By William Shake-speare' printed as a separate line, with
Shakespeare's name italicised.

['By William Shake-speare', as above. London: by Thomas
Purfoot, and are to be sold by Mathew Law]

1622 (?) **Romeo and Juliet (LQ3, LQ3a) Q4, Q4a**   97 (anon), 98

*The most excellent and lamentable tragedie, of Romeo and Ivliet. As it
hath beene sundrie times publikely acted, by the kings maiesties seruants
at the Globe. Newly corrected, augmented, and amended.*

• No evidence as to date of publication. But it would appear to
postdate Q3. STC suggests 1622 for both issues.

[Variant title pages: Anon; 'Written by W. Shake-speare'. London:
Printed for Iohn Smethwicke]

1623   **The First Folio, F1**   99 (without *Tro.*), 100 (blank), 101 (Prologue)

*Mr. William Shakespeares comedies, histories, & tragedies. Published
according to the true originall copies.*

• Issued in three distinct states: lacking *Troilus and Cressida*;
including *Troilus and Cressida*, opening with a crossed out page
from a previous printing; including *Troilus and Cressida* and with a
'Prologue' substituted for the crossed-out page. First printing of:
Tmp.; *TGV*; *MM*; *Err.*; *AYL*; *Shr.*; *AWW*; *TN*; *WT*; *Jn.*; *1H6*; *H8*;
Cor.; *Tim.*; *JC*; *Mac.*; *Ant.*; *Cym.*

['Mr. William Shakespeares', as above. London: by Isaac Iaggard,
and Ed. Blount]

1624   **Lucrece 6**   102

The rape of Lvcrece. By Mr. William Shakespeare. Newly reuised.

['By Mr. William Shakespeare', as above. London: 'by I. B. for
Roger Iackson'; I. B. is John Beale. 8°]

1625 (?) Hamlet (LQ3) Q4 103

The tragedy of Hamlet Prince of Denmarke. Newly imprinted and inlarged, according to the true and perfect copy lastly printed.

• Printed after 1611 and before 1637. STC suggests *c*. 1625.

['By William Shakespeare'. London: by W. S. for Iohn Smethwicke; W. S. is William Stansby]

1627 Venus and Adonis 12 104

Venvs and Adonis.

[Dedication signed William Shakespeare. Edinburgh: by Iohn Wreittoun. 8°]

1629 Richard III (variant) Q7 105

The tragedie of King Richard the third. Contayning his trecherous plots, against his brother Clarence: The pittifull murther of his inocent nepthewes [sic]: *His tiranous vsurpation: With the whole course of his detested life, and most deserued death. As it hath beene lately acted by the kings maiesties sernauts* [sic]. *Newly agmented* [sic]. *By William Shake-speare.*

• Attribution is on a separate line, with Shakespeare's name italicised.

['By William Shake-speare', as above. London: by Iohn Norton, and are to be sold by Mathew Law]

1630 Merry Wives of Windsor (LQ1) Q3 106

The merry wives of Windsor. With the humours of Sir Iohn Falstaffe, as also the swaggering vaine of Ancient Pistoll, and Corporall Nym. Written by William Shake-Speare. Newly corrected.

['Written by William Shake-Speare', as above. London: by T. H. for R. Meighen; T. H. is Thomas Harper]

Othello Q2 107

The tragœdy of Othello, the Moore of Venice. As it hath beene diuerse times acted at the Globe, and at the Black-Friers, by his maiesties seruants.

['Written by William Shakespeare'. London: by A. M. for Richard Hawkins; A. M. is Augustine Mathewes]

Pericles Q5, Q5a   108, 109 (with location)

The late, and much admired play, called Pericles, Prince of Tyre. With the true relation of the whole history, aduentures, and fortunes of the sayd Prince.

• Second issue of this edition in this year. The title page is the same, except that it gives details of the location of Robert Bird's shop.

['Written by Will. Shakespeare'. London: by I. N. for R. B.; I. N. is John Norton the younger and R. B. is Robert Bird]

[1630]   **Venus and Adonis 13**   110

Venvs and Adonis.

[Dedication signed William Shakespeare. London: by J. H. and are
to be sold by Francis Coules; J. H. is John Haviland. 8°]

1630–6 (?)   **Venus and Adonis 14**   111

• Surviving copy (STC 22365, Bodleian – shelfmark Arch.Gg.3)
lacks title page.

[Dedication signed William Shakespeare. STC suggests
J. Haviland, sold by F. Coules, *c.* 1630–6. 8°]

1631   **Love's Labour's Lost Q2**   112

*Loues labours lost. A wittie and pleasant comedie, as it was acted by his
maiesties seruants at the Blacke-Friers and the Globe.*

['Written by William Shakespeare'. London: by W. S. for Iohn
Smethwicke; W. S. is William Stansby]

Taming of the Shrew Q1   113

*A wittie and pleasant comedie called the taming of the shrew. As it
was acted by his maiesties seruants at the Blacke Friers and the
Globe.*

['Written by Will. Shakespeare'. London: by W. S. for Iohn
Smethwicke; W. S. probably William Sheares]

1632   **1 Henry IV Q7**   114

*The historie of Henry the fourth: With the battell at Shrewesbury,
betweene the king, and Lord Henry Percy, surnamed Henry Hotspur of
the north. With the humorous conceits of Sir Iohn Falstaffe. Newly
corrected, By William Shake-speare.*

• Capitalisation of 'By' in attribution is retained here, but it should
be noted that the attribution is on a separate line, with
Shakespeare's name italicised.

['By William Shake-speare', as above. London: by Iohn Norton,
and are to bee sold by William Sheares]

Lucrece 7   115

The rape of Lvcrece. By Mr. William Shakespeare. Newly Revised.

['By Mr. William Shakespeare', as above. London: by R. B. for
Iohn Harrison; R. B. is Richard Badger. 8°]

The Second Folio, F2   116 (Allot), 117 (Smethwick),
                                       118 (Hawkins), 119 (Aspley), 120 (Meighan)

*Mr. William Shakespeares comedies, histories, and tragedies. Published
according to the true originall coppies. The second impression.*

• Variant title pages exist, each one indicating a different publisher, as follows: 'for Iohn Smethwick', 'for Richard Hawkins', 'for William Aspley', 'for Richard Meighen'. All copies bear the colophon 'Printed at London by Thomas Cotes, for John Smethwick, William Aspley, Richard Hawkins, Richard Meighen, and Robert Allot, 1632'.

['Mr. William Shakespeares', as above. London: by Tho. Cotes, for Robert Allot, etc., as above]

1634   Richard II Q6   **121**

The life and death of King Richard the second. With new additions of the parliament scene, and the deposing of King Richard. As it hath beene acted by the kings majesties servants, at the Globe.

['By William Shakespeare'. London: by Iohn Norton]

Richard III (variant) Q8   **122**

The tragedie of King Richard the third. Contayning his treacherous plots, against his brother Clarence: The pitifull murder of his innocent nephewes: His tyranous vsurpation: With the whole course of his detested life, and most deserued death. As it hath beene acted by the kings maiesties seruants.

['Written by William Shake-speare'. London: Printed by Iohn Norton]

Two Noble Kinsmen Q   **123**

The two noble kinsmen: Presented at the Blackfriers by the kings maiesties servants, with great applause.

• Authorship details set out as below on the title page.

Written by the memorable Worthies of their time;
Mr. *John Fletcher,* and   ⎫
Mr. *William Shakespeare.* ⎬ Gent.
                                              ⎭

[Ascription as above. London: by Tho. Cotes, for Iohn Waterson]

1635   Pericles Q6   **124**

The late, and much admired play, called Pericles, Prince of Tyre. With the true relation of the whole history, adventures, and fortunes of the said prince.

['Written by W. Shakespeare'. London: by Thomas Cotes]

1636   Venus and Adonis 15   **125**

Venvs and Adonis

[Dedication signed William Shakespeare. London: by I. H. and are to be sold by Francis Coules; I. H. is John Haviland. 16° in 8s]

1637   Hamlet (LQ4) Q5   **126**

The tragedy of Hamlet Prince of Denmark. Newly imprinted and inlarged, according to the true and perfect copy last printed.

[1637]   ['By William Shakespeare'; London: by R. Young for John Smethwicke]

Merchant of Venice Q3   127

The most excellent historie of the merchant of Venice. With the extreame crueltie of Shylocke the Iewe towards the said merchant, in cutting a just pound of his flesh: And the obtaining of Portia by the choice of three chests. As it hath beene divers times acted by the Lord Chamberlaine his servants.

• Another issue of this edition is dated 1652. A cancel is substituted for A1, providing, on the verso, a list of actors' names and an advertisement for books 'Printed and solde by William Leake'. See 1652 below.

['Written by William Shakespeare'. London: by M. P. for Laurence Hayes; M. P. is Marmaduke Parsons]

Romeo and Juliet (LQ4) Q5   128

The most excellent and lamentable tragedie of Romeo and Juliet. As it hath been sundry times publikely acted by the kings majesties servants at the Globe. Written by W. Shake-speare. Newly corrected, augmented, and amended.

['Written by W. Shake-speare', as above. London: by R. Young for John Smethwicke]

1639   ### 1 Henry IV Q8   129

The historie of Henry the fourth: With the battell at Shrewsbury, betweene the king, and Lord Henry Percy, surnamed Henry Hotspur of the north. With the humorous conceits of Sir Iohn Falstaffe. Newly corrected, By William Shake-speare.

• Capitalisation of 'By' is retained, but note that the word itself is on a separate line, with Shakespeare's name below it on another separate line.

['By William Shake-speare', as above. London: by John Norton, and are to be sold by Hvgh Perry]

1640   ### Poems   130

Poems: Written by Wil. Shake-speare. Gent.

['by Wil. Shakespeare', as above. London: by Tho. Cotes, and are to be sold by Iohn Benson. 8°]

1652   ### Merchant of Venice Q3a (reissue of Q3)   131

The most excellent historie of the merchant of Venice: With the extreame cruelty of Shylocke the Jew towards the said merchant, in cutting a just pound of his flesh: And the obtaining of Portia by the choyce of three chests.

• See above 1637

['Written by William Shakespeare'. London: for William Leake]

1655 **King Lear Q3** 132

M. William Shake-speare, his true chronicle history of the life and death of King Lear, and his three daughters. With the vnfortunat life of Edgar, sonne and heire to the Earle of Glocester, and his sullen assumed humour of Tom of Bedlam. As it was plaid before the kings maiesty at Whit-hall [sic], *vpon S. Stephens night, in Christmas hollldaies* [sic]. *By his maiesties servants, playing vsually at the Globe on the Bank-side.*

['M. William Shake-speare', as above. London: Printed by Jane Bell, and are to be sold at the East-end of Christ-Church]

Lucrece 8 133

The rape of Lucrece committed by Tarquin the sixt; and the remarkable judgments that befel him for it. By the incomparable master of our English poetry, Will: Shakespeare Gent.

• Also published in the same volume: *The banishment of Tarquin. Or, the reward of lust*, by J. Quarles.

['Will: Shakespeare', as above. London: by J. G. for John Stafford and Will Gilbertson; J. G. is John Gismond. 8°]

Othello Q3 134

The tragœdy of Othello, the Moore of Venice as it hath beene divers times acted at the Globe, and at the Black-Friers, by his majesties servants.

['Written by William Shakespears'. London: for William Leak]

1663 **The Third Folio (first issue), F3a** 135

Mr. William Shakespeares comedies, histories, and tragedies. Published according to the true original copies. The third impression.

['Mr. William Shakespeare's, as above. London: for Philip Chetwinde]

1664 **The Third Folio (second issue), F3b** 136

Mr. William Shakespear's comedies, histories, and tragedies. Published according to the true original copies. The third impression. And unto this impression is added seven playes, never before printed in folio. viz. Pericles Prince of Tyre. The London prodigall. The history of Thomas Ld. Cromwell. Sir John Oldcastle Lord Cobham. The puritan widow. A York-shire tragedy. The tragedy of Locrine.

• A second issue of F3a, but with *Pericles* and the six apocryphal plays added, as indicated in the title.

['Mr. William Shakespear's', as above. London: for P. C.; P. C. is Philip Chetwinde]

1673 **Macbeth Q** 137

Macbeth: A tragedy. Acted at the Dukes-Theatre.

• The text performed at the Duke's was Davenant's adaptation.
This text is, in fact, based on that reproduced in the folios.

[Anon. London: for William Cademan]

| 1675 | **Venus and Adonis 16, 16a** | **138, 139 (Hodgkinsonne)** |

Venus and Adonis.

• Two editions in the same year, with minor variations in title-page
epigraph and in imprint (as below).

[Dedication signed William Shakespeare. London: printed by
Elizabeth Hodgkinson, for F. Coles, T. Vere, J. Wright, and
J. Clark; variation: Hodgkinson given as 'Hodgkinsonne'. 8°]

| 1676 | **Hamlet (LQ5) Q6** | **140** |

*The tragedy of Hamlet Prince of Denmark. As it is now acted at his
highness the Duke of York's Theatre.*

• Some rewriting and amending by Sir William D'Avenant, with
passages to be cut in theatrical performance marked in the text.

['By William Shakespeare'. London: By Andr. Clark, for
J. Martyn, and H. Herringman; four line imprint]

| '1676' | **Hamlet (LQ6) Q7** | **141** |

• Title and details as previous *Hamlet* entry (§140), of which it is a
reprint, also dated 1676, though it may have been published some
years later.

['By William Shakespeare'. London: by Andr. Clark, for J. Martyn,
and H. Herringman; five line imprint]

| 1679 | **Two Noble Kinsmen** | **142** |

• Included in

*Fifty comedies and tragedies written by Francis Beaumont and John
Fletcher, all in one volume. Published by the authors original copies, the
songs to each play being added.*

[London: by J. Macock, for John Martyn, Henry Herringman, and
Richard Marriot. 2°]

| 1681 | **Othello Q4** | **143** |

*Othello, the Moor of Venice. A tragedy, as it hath been divers times
acted at the Globe, and at the Black-Friers: And now at the Theater
Royal, by his majesties servants.*

['Written by William Shakespear'. London: for W. Weak {in error
for Leake?}, and are to be sold by Richard Bentley and M. Magnes]

| 1683 | **Hamlet (LQ7, LQ7a) Q8, Q8a** | **144, 145 (Heringham)** |

*The tragedy of Hamlet Prince of Denmark. As it is now acted at his
highness the Duke of York's Theatre.*

• Some copies mistakenly give 'Heringham' instead of 'Heringman' in imprint. Some rewriting and amending by Sir William D'Avenant, with passages to be cut in theatrical performance marked in the text.

['By William Shakespeare'. London: Printed for H. Heringman and R. Bentley]

1684 **Julius Caesar Q1** 146

Julius Cæsar. A tragedy. As it is now acted at the Theatre Royal.

['Written by William Shakespeare'. London: by H. H. Jun. for Hen. Heringman and R. Bentley and sold by Joseph Knight and Francis Saunders; H. H. is Henry Hills]

1685 **The Fourth Folio, F4**

147 (Bentley), 148 (Chiswell), 149 (Herringman only)

Mr. William Shakespear's comedies, histories, and tragedies. Published according to the true original copies. Unto which is added, seven plays, never before printed in folio: viz. Pericles Prince of Tyre. The London prodigal. The history of Thomas Lord Cromwel. Sir John Oldcastle Lord Cobham. The puritan widow. A Yorkshire tragedy. The tragedy of Locrine. The fourth edition.

• Issued with three imprints, as indicated below.

['Mr. William Shakespear's', as above. London: for H. Herringman, E. Brewster, and R. Bentley; for H. Herringman, E. Brewster, and R. Chiswell; for H. Herringman]

1687 **Othello Q5** 150

Othello, the Moor of Venice. A tragedy. As it hath been divers times acted at the Globe, and at the Black-Friers: And now at the Theatre Royal, by his majesties servants.

['Written by William Shakespear'. London: for Richard Bentley and S. Magnes]

1691 **Julius Caesar Q2 (?) – see 1695 (?) below** 151

Julius Cæsar. A tragedy. As it is now acted at the Theatre Royal.

['Written by William Shakespeare'. London: for Henry Herringman, and Richard Bentley]

1695 **Hamlet (LQ8, LQ8a) Q9, Q9a** 152, 153 (Bentley)

The tragedy of Hamlet Prince of Denmark. As it is now acted at the Theatre Royal, by their majesties servants.

• Two issues in the same year, with variant imprint (as below). Some rewriting and amending by Sir William D'Avenant, with passages to be cut in theatrical performance marked in the text.

[1695]   ['By William Shakespeare'; London: Printed for H. Herringman, and R. Bentley; and sold by R. Bentley, J. Tonson, T. Bennet, and F. Sanders; variant: Printed for R. Bentley]

Othello Q6   154

Othello, the Moor of Venice. A tragedy. As it hath been divers times acted at the Globe, and at the Black-Friers: And now at the Theatre Royal, by his majesties servants.

['Written by William Shakespear'. London: for Richard Bentley]

1695 (?) Julius Caesar Qq3–5   155, 156, 157

Julius Cæsar. A tragedy. As it is now acted at the Theatre Royal.

• These three editions are undated and had been thought to fall between Q1 (1684) and the 1691 quarto. Velz ('Pirate Hills') suggests that they may have been published later than this and ESTC proposes 1695 as a possible date. A fourth text, once thought to have belonged to the sequence, has been identified by Velz as having been produced from a copy of one of these quartos, marked up from a Rowe edition, possibly Rowe 3. See 1715 (?) below.

['Written by William Shakespeare'. London: by H. H. Jun. for Hen. Herringman and R. Bentley and sold by Joseph Knight and Francis Saunders; H. H. Jun. is Henry Hills the younger]

1700   1 Henry IV Q9   158

K. Henry IV. With the humours of Sir John Falstaff. A tragic-comedy. As it is acted at the Theatre in Little-Lincolns-Inn-Fields by his majesty's servants. Revived, with alterations. Written originally by Mr. Shakespear.

• A theatrical text, cut by Thomas Betterton, but with no additions. The identification of 'R.W.' as Richard Wellington is taken from Dawson, 'Copyright', p. 28.

['with Alterations . . . Written originally by Mr. Shakespear', as above. London: Printed for R. W. and sold by John Deeve. R. W. is Richard Wellington]

c. 1700   The 'Fifth Folio', 'F5'   159

Some time around 1700 a section of the F4 text amounting to perhaps twenty-five sheets was reprinted and combined with remaining sheets from F4 to produce a hybrid edition.

1703   Hamlet (LQ9 to LQ13) Q10 Q14
          160 (N47406), 161 (N47407), 162 (N47455), 163 (N69093), 164 (T51530)

The tragedy of Hamlet Prince of Denmark. As it is now acted by her majesties servants.

• Several versions of this text were issued, with the type apparently reset each time. They can be distinguished from each other by a range of relatively minor typographical errors. Five texts are registered here, on the basis of 5 separate ESTC records (N47406, N47407, N47455, N69093, T51530). However, ESTC also records a variant in one of these (N47455) so the sequence may not be exhaustive. Some rewriting and amending by Sir William D'Avenant, with passages to be cut in theatrical performance marked in the text.

['By William Shakespeare'. London: for Rich. Wellington and E. Rumball]

1705	**Othello Q7**	**165**

Othello, the Moor of Venice. A tragedy. As it hath been divers times acted at the Globe, and at the Black-Friers: And now at the Theatre Royal, by her majesties servants.

['Written by W. Shakespear'. London: for R. Wellington]

1707	**[Lucrece; Venus and Adonis]**	**166**

Poems on affairs of state, from 1620. to this present year 1707. Many of them by the most eminent hands.

['Mr. Shakespear' included in list of authors on title page and poems identified as his in volume. London: n.p. 8°]

1709	**Nicholas Rowe 1**	**167, 168 (9 vol issue)**

The works of Mr. William Shakespear; in six volumes. Adorn'd with cuts. Revis'd and corrected, with an account of the life and writings of the author. By N. Rowe, Esq.

• The Folger has a nine-volume issue of this edition, with cancel title pages (PR2752 1709b cop. 1 sh. col.). The title page reads:

The works of Mr. William Shakespear; in nine volumes. Adorn'd with cuts. Revis'd and corrected, with an account of the life and writings of the author. By N. Rowe, Esq.

[London: Printed for Jacob Tonson. 8°, 6 vols., 9 vols.]

	Rowe 2	**169**

• Title and imprint as Rowe 1 (6 vol.) above.

[1709]	**Poems**	**170**

A collection of poems, viz. I. Venus and Adonis. II. The rape of Lucrece. III. The passionate pilgrim. IV. Sonnets to sundry notes of music.

['By Mr. William Shakespeare'. London: for Bernard Lintott. 8°]

This is the cut-off point for the complete listing of single-text editions

1710   Poems   **171**

*The works of Mr. William Shakespear. Volume the seventh.
Containing, Venus & Adonis. Tarquin & Lucrece and his miscellany
poems. With critical remarks on his plays, &c. to which is prefix'd an
essay on the art, rise and progress of the stage in Greece, Rome and
England.*

[London: Printed for E. Curll and E. Sanger. 8°]

1711   Two Noble Kinsmen   **172**

• Included in:

*The works of Mr. Francis Beaumont, and Mr. John Fletcher; in seven
volumes. Adorn'd with cutts. Revis'd and corrected: With some account
of the life and writings of the authors.*

[London: for Jacob Tonson. 8°, 7 vols.]

1711–12 Thomas Johnson *A Collection of the Best English Plays* 1   **173**

A collection of the best English plays.

• A ten-volume collection, extended by a further two volumes
(*c.* 1714–18). Plays were issued singly as well as in sets. Volumes I
and II contained plays by, or adapted from, Shakespeare, as below
(with individual title page dates noted). Some sets may vary in
their general configuration. For all texts listed here, the individual
play title page falsely gives the place of publication as London,
with no publisher's name being provided. The general imprint
from volume I is given below. As the plays were also issued
separately, individual numbers are assigned to each title. The other
Shakespearean plays included in the collection are
adaptations.

Vol. I: **174** *JC* (1711); **175** *Mac.* (1711); **176** *Ham.* (1710); **177** *Oth.*
(1710)

Vol. II: **178** *1H4* (1710); **179** *Wiv.* (1710)

[The Hague: T. Johnson. 8°]

1714   Rowe 3

• There are three versions of this edition, in the order listed below.
The second adds a 'table of the most sublime passages'; the third
incorporates Curll's edition of the poems as a ninth volume of the
set. The imprints also vary, as indicated.

                                                                                                                        180

*The works of Mr. William Shakespear; in eight volumes. Adorn'd with
cutts. Revis'd and corrected, with an account of the life and writings of
the author, by N. Rowe, Esq.*

[London: for Jacob Tonson. 12°, 8 vols.]

181

[1714]   *The works of Mr. William Shakespear; in eight volumes. Adorn'd with*
          cutts. Revis'd and corrected, with an account of the life and writings of
          the author, by N. Rowe, Esq; to this edition is added, a table of the most
          sublime passages in this author.

          [London: for J. Tonson, to be sold by J. Knapton and
          D. Midwinter, A. Betsworth, W. Taylor, T. Varnam and J. Osborn
          and J. Browne. 12°, 8 vols.]

182

          The works of Mr. William Shakespear; in nine volumes: With his life,
          by N. Rowe esq; adorned with cuts. To the last volume is prefix'd, I. An
          essay on the art, rise, and progress of the stage, in Greece, Rome, and
          England. II. Observations upon the most sublime passages in this
          author. III. A glossary, explaining the antiquated words made use of
          throughout his works.

          [London: for J. Tonson, E. Curll, J. Pemberton and K. Sanger and
          to be sold by J. Knapton and D. Midwinter, A. Betsworth,
          W. Taylor, T. Varnam and J. Osborn and J. Browne. 12°, 9 vols.]

1715 (?) **Julius Caesar**   183

          • Probably a forgery, intended to give the appearance of belonging
          to a sequence of undated quartos published sometime in the 1690s.
          See 1695 (?) above.

          [London: by H. H. Jun for Hen. Herringman and R. Bentley. 4°]

1720–22   Thomas Johnson *A Collection of the Best English Plays* 2   184

          • A reissue of Johnson's 1711–12 collection (§173). Few complete
          and unmixed sets of this issue survive. The British Library copy
          (1345.b.16–25) has the first issue general title page in volumes I
          and X and the second issue general title page in the other volumes
          of the set. Details below for volume II are taken from this set.
          Glasgow University holds a copy of volume I only of the set
          (S.M.3059). The general title page advertises that it includes *Julius*
          Caesar, *Macbeth*, *Hamlet* and *Othello* – as per the original issue.
          However, in the Glasgow copy (which may have been rebound),
          the latter two texts are not included and are replaced by an
          adaptation of *Coriolanus* and Addison's *Cato*. Dates given are those
          provided on the individual play title pages. Owing to the
          uncertainty surrounding the issue, only one number is assigned
          here. The other Shakespearean plays included in the collection are
          adaptations.

          Vol. I: *JC* (1711); *Mac.* (1711); [*Ham.*]; [*Oth.*]
          Vol. II: *1H4* (1721); *Wiv.* (nd)

1721   **Hamlet**   185
          [Dublin: George Grierson. 8°]

[1728] volumes provided (i) the text of the poems (based on Gildon's supplement to Rowe and including the additional materials incorporated in that volume, and (ii) the text of the apocryphal plays that had been included in F3b. The latter volume is sometimes included as a ninth volume to the original Tonson set. Imprints sometimes vary in the individual volumes of these various sets.

198, 199 (with apocrypha)

The works of Shakespear. In eight volumes. Collated and corrected by the former editions, by Mr. Pope. The second edition.

[London: J. Tonson. 12°, 8 vols., but see above]

200

The works of Mr. William Shakespear. In ten volumes. Publish'd by Mr. Pope and Dr. Sewell.

[London: for J. and J. Knapton, J. Darby, A. Bettesworth, J. Tonson, F. Fayram, W. Mears, J. Pemberton, J. Osborn and T. Longman, B. Motte, C. Rivington, F. Clay, J. Batley, Ri{chard} Ja{mes} and B. Wellington. 12°, 10 vols.]

1730	**Merry Wives**	201

[Dublin: for A. Bradley. 12°]

1730 (?)	**Henry V**	202

• Paged 285–382 and probably part of a larger edition, which has not been identified. Text is in the British Library – 640.h.29.(3.) – but is not included in ESTC. BL catalogue suggests it was published in Dublin in 1730.

1731	**Hamlet**	203

[Dublin: by S. Powell for Thomas Moore. 8°]

	1 Henry IV	204

[Dublin: Thomas Moore. 12°]

	Othello	205

[Dublin: Thomas Moore. 12°]

○ Jaggard, *Bibliography* (p. 499) lists a J. & P. Knapton edition of the plays (a Pope edition) for this year, in 9 vols., 8°, without giving a location. The edition is not in ESTC and I have been unable to trace it.

1733	**Lewis Theobald 1**	206

The works of Shakespeare: in seven volumes. Collated with the oldest copies, and corrected; with notes, explanatory, and critical: By Mr. Theobald.

[London: for A. Bettesworth and C. Hitch, J. Tonson, F. Clay, W. Feales, and R. Wellington. 8°, 7 vols.]

1734–5 **Walker**   207

Dramatick works of William Shakespeare.

• Plays originally published singly, in parts, then gathered into volumes. Folger Shakespeare Library catalogue notes that, in some instances, individual plays were issued in two or more editions and therefore, 'no two sets will be the same, individual plays differing as to edition'.

[London: Robert Walker. 12°, 7 vols.]

Tonson *et al.*   208

The works of Shakespeare. In eight volumes.

• Plays originally published singly. Folger Shakespeare Library catalogue notes that, in some instances, individual plays were issued in two or more editions and therefore, 'no two sets will be the same, individual plays differing as to edition'. Title page for collected set mistakenly gives date as 1625.

[London: for J. Tonson, and the rest of the proprietors. 12°, 8 vols.]

1735   **Julius Caesar**   209

[Dublin: by Theo Jones, for William Smith. 12°]

1736   **Tonson reissue of Walker stock**   210

• Some of Robert Walker's Shakespeare stock (see 1734–5 above) was reissued in this year, apparently at Tonson's initiative, but in many cases with title pages lacking imprint other than 'London'. It is not possible to establish exactly how many titles were reissued in this way, so only one number has been assigned here.

1739   **1 Henry IV**   211

[Dublin: by R. Reilly for John Smith and Abraham Bradley. 12°]

Henry VIII   212

[Dublin: by R. Reilly for Abraham Bradley. 12°]

Julius Caesar   213

[Dublin: by M. Rhames for J. Smith. 12°]

Julius Caesar   214

• Same edition as previous entry, except with a different title page? Both editions have 83 pages. No library holds both texts and ESTC provides no information on whether they are related.

[Dublin: by M. Rhames for Abraham Bradley. 12°]

[1739] **King Lear** 215
[Dublin: by R. Reilly for John Smith and Abraham Bradley. 12°]

Macbeth 216
[Dublin: J. Smith, Abraham Bradley. 12°]

Merry Wives of Windsor 217
[Dublin: Abraham Bradley. 12°]

Richard III 218
• ESTC lists a unique copy, held by Dublin City Libraries
(7A Newenham pamphlets xxxix[2]). Details taken from ESTC
record only.
[Dublin: Abraham Bradley. 12°]

Timon of Athens 219
[Dublin: by R. Reilly for Abraham Bradley. 12°]

Dublin 2 220
*The works of Shakespeare: In seven volumes. Collated with the oldest
copies, and corrected; with notes explanatory, and critical. By
Mr. Theobald.*
[Dublin: John Smith, Abraham Bradley. 12°, 7 vols.]

1740 **Theobald 2** 221
*The works of Shakespeare: In eight volumes. Collated with the oldest
copies, and corrected: With notes, explanatory, and critical: By
Mr. Theobald.*
[London: H. Lintott, C. Hitch, J. and R. Tonson, C. Corbet,
R. and B. Wellington, J. Brindley, and E. New. 12°, 8 vols.]

1741 **As You Like It** 222
[Dublin: A. Reilly for Abraham Bradley. 12°]

Hamlet 223
[Dublin: by S. Powell for Philip Crampton. 12°]

1743–44 **[Thomas Hanmer] 1** 224
*The works of Shakespear. In six volumes. Carefully revised and
corrected by the former editions, and adorned with sculptures designed
and executed by the best hands.*
[Oxford: Printed at the Theatre – for the university press. 4°,
6 vols.]

1745 **'Hanmer' 2** 225
*The works of Shakespear. In six volumes. Carefully revised and
corrected by the former editions.*

• This edition was issued in response to Hanmer's Oxford text of the previous year (§224). It reproduced Hanmer's edition, with indications of his indebtedness to Tonson editors.

[London: J. and P. Knapton, S. Birt, T. Longman, H. Lintot, C. Hitch, J. Brindley, J. and R. Tonson and S. Draper, R. and B. Wellington, E. New, and B. Dod. 8°, 6 vols.]

1746   **1 Henry IV**   226

[Dublin: for Philip Crampton. 12°]

1747   **Othello**   227

[Dublin: for Peter Wilson. 12°]

Romeo and Juliet   228

[Dublin: W. Brien and R. James. 12°]

'Hanmer' 3   229

The works of Shakespear in nine volumes with a glossary. Carefully printed from the Oxford edition in quarto, 1744.

• This edition was bought out by the Tonson cartel and was reissued with a cancel title page – see next entry.

[London: John Osborn. 12°, 9 vols.]

'Hanmer' 3/Tonson   230

The works of Shakespear in nine volumes. With a glossary. Carefully printed from the Oxford edition in quarto, 1744.

[London: J. and P. Knapton, S. Birt, T. Longman and T. Shewell, H. Lintott, C. Hitch, J. Brindley, J. and R. Tonson and S. Draper, R. Wellington, E. New, and B. Dod. 12°, 9 vols.]

William Warburton   231

The works of Shakespear in eight volumes. The genuine text (collated with all the former editions, and then corrected and emended) is here settled: Being restored from the blunders of the first editors, and the interpolations of the two last: With a comment and notes, critical and explanatory. By Mr. Pope and Mr. Warburton.

[London: J. and P. Knapton, S. Birt, T. Longman and T. Shewell, H. Lintott, C. Hitch, J. Brindley, J. and R. Tonson and S. Draper, R. Wellington, E. New, and B. Dod. 8°, 8 vols.]

Dublin 3   232

The works of Shakespear in eight volumes. The genuine text (collated with all the former editions, and then corrected and emended) is here settled: Being restored from the blunders of the first editors, and the interpolations of the two last; with a comment and notes, critical and explanatory. By Mr. Pope and Mr. Warburton.

[Dublin: R. Owen, J. Leathley, G. and A. Ewing, W. and J. Smith, G. Faulkner, P. Crampton, A. Bradley, T. Moore, E. and J. Exshaw. 12°, 8 vols.]

1748   **Merchant of Venice**   233
[Dublin: printed and sold by Richard James. 12°]

Othello   234
[Dublin: Peter Wilson. 12°]

'Hanmer' 4   235
The works of Shakespear in nine volumes. With a glossary. Carefully printed from the Oxford edition in quarto, 1744.
[London: J. and P. Knapton, S. Birt, T. Longman and T. Shewell, H. Lintott, C. Hitch, J. Brindley, J. and R. Tonson and S. Draper, R. Wellington, E. New, and B. Dod. 12°, 9 vols.]

1748 (?)   **1 Henry IV**   236
• ESTC suggests 1748. Folger catalogue suggests 1748–52.
[Dublin: Augustus Long. 12°]

1749   **Hamlet**   237
[Dublin: James Dalton. 12°]

1750   **Hamlet**   238
[Dublin: Peter Wilson. 12°]

Julius Caesar   239
[Dublin: James Dalton. 12°]

Macbeth   240
[Dublin: Augustus Long. 12°]

Romeo and Juliet   241
[Dublin: W. Brien and R. James. 12°]

Romeo and Juliet   242
[Dublin: James Dalton. 12°]

Two Noble Kinsmen   243
• Edited by Thomas Seward and included in volume ten of:
The works of Mr. Francis Beaumont, and Mr. John Fletcher. In ten volumes. Collated with all the former editions, and corrected. With notes critical and explanatory. By the late Mr. Theobald, Mr. Seward of Eyam in Derbyshire, and Mr. Sympson of Gainsborough.
[London: J. and R. Tonson and S. Draper. 8°]

Scheurleer reissue of Johnson, *Collection* 2   244
A select collection of the best modern English plays. Selected from the best authors.

• H. Scheurleer, Jr reissued remaindered sheets of Thomas
Johnson's collection of plays (see above, 1711–12 and 1720–2). The
Shakespeare texts included in volumes I and II of the Folger copy
of Scheurleer's edition (PR1241 S3 Cage) are listed below. Note
that this configuration is somewhat different from that of the
1711–12 and 1720–2 entries given above. The imprints from the
individual play title pages in the set are also included below. The
only dated title page is *Hamlet* (1720). Owing to the uncertainty
surrounding the issue, only one number is assigned here.

Vol. I: *JC* (Company of Booksellers); *Mac.* (for the Company);
Wiv. (for the Company)

Vol. II: *Ham.* (T. Johnson); *Oth.* (for the Company).

1750 (?) • The following editions are all undated. Long is known to have
been active in Dublin between 1748 and 1752. ESTC suggests
1750 for these editions.

As You Like It   245

[Dublin: Augustus Long. 12°]

2 Henry IV   246

[Dublin: Augustus Long. 12°]

Much Ado About Nothing   247

[Dublin: Augustus Long. 12°]

1750–51 **'Hanmer' 5**   248

*The works of Shakespear in nine volumes. With a glossary. Carefully
printed from the Oxford edition in quarto, 1744.*

[London: J. and P. Knapton, S. Birt, T. Longman, H. Lintott,
C. Hitch, J. Hodges, J. Brindley, J. and R. Tonson and S. Draper,
B. Dod, and C. Corbet. 12°, 9 vols.]

1751   **Othello**   249

[Dublin: Peter Wilson. 12°]

1752   **Theobald 3**   250

*The works of Shakespeare: In eight volumes. Collated with the oldest
copies, and corrected: with notes, explanatory, and critical:
By Mr. Theobald. The third edition.*

[London: J. and P. Knapton, S. Birt, T. Longman, H. Lintot,
C. Hitch, J. Hodges, J. Brindley, J. and R. Tonson and S. Draper,
B. Dod, and C. Corbet. 12°, 8 vols.]

1753   **Merry Wives of Windsor**   251

[Dublin: James Dalton. 12°]

[1753] **[Hugh Blair/John Reid] 1** 252

The works of Shakespear. In which the beauties observed by Pope,
Warburton, and Dodd, are pointed out. Together with the author's life;
a glossary; copious indexes; and, a list of the various readings.

• Editor's identity uncertain – see chapter 6. An edition of this text
was subsequently issued with the fictitious London imprint of
A. Manson, R. Dilton, J. Thomson, P. Alnwick, W. Nelson,
S. Darnton and H. Gray. The edition was undated and Jaggard,
Bibliography (pp. 500–1) suggests a date of 1753 and this
speculative date is repeated in ESTC. However, a clear relationship
exists between this edition and editions issued in 1769 under the
separate imprints of Donaldson, Ruddiman, and Balfour. See note
under 1769 for further details.

[Edinburgh: by Sands, Murray and Cochran for W. Sands,
Hamilton & Balfour, Kincaid & Donaldson, L. Hunter, J. Yair,
W. Gordon, and J. Brown. 12°, 8 vols.]

1754 **Julius Caesar** 253
[Dublin: printed by and for William Sleater. 12°]

Othello 254

• This is one of three texts listed for James Knox. In this edition
and in the 1756 *Julius Caesar* volume, a further three Shakespeare
editions 'printed and sold' by Knox – *King Lear*, *Macbeth*,
Richard III – are listed. A similar list included in the 1755 *Hamlet*
also includes *Romeo and Juliet*. These texts are not logged by
ESTC, nor do they appear in the British Library or National
Library of Scotland catalogues.

[Glasgow: James Knox. 8°]

1755 **Hamlet** 255, 256 (with adverts)
• ESTC includes two entries for a 1755 Ewing *et al. Hamlet*. The
difference would appear to be that one (ESTC N32799) includes
two final leaves containing adverts for George Grierson. The single
copy of this listed is located at the Rivera Library, University of
California Riverside (SpC PR1245.C64).

[Dublin: G. and A. Ewing, W. Smith, J. Exshaw, and R. James. 12°]

Hamlet 257
[Glasgow: James Knox. 8°]

1756 **Julius Caesar** 258
[Glasgow: James Knox. 8°]

1757 **Theobald 4** 259

The works of Shakespeare: In eight volumes. Collated with the oldest
copies, and corrected: With notes, explanatory, and critical: By
Mr. Theobald.

[London: C. Hitch and L. Hawes, H. Lintot, J. and R. Tonson,
J. Hodges, B. Dod, J. Rivington, M. and T. Longman, J. Brindley,
C. Corbet and T. Caslon. 12°, 8 vols.]

1758   **Julius Caesar**   260
         [Glasgow: n.p. 12°]

1759   **Hamlet**   261
         [Glasgow: n.p. 12°]

         1 Henry IV   262
         [Glasgow: n.p. 12°]

         Macbeth   263
         [Dublin: Hulton Bradley. 12°]

         Merry Wives   264
         [Glasgow: n.p. 12°]

         Twelfth Night   265
         [Dublin: James Hoey, Junior. 12°]

1760   **'Hanmer' 6**   266
         *The works of Shakespear: In nine volumes with a glossary. Carefully
         printed from the Oxford edition in quarto, 1744.*
         [London: C. Hitch and L. Hawes, J. and R. Tonson, B. Dod,
         J. Rivington, R. Baldwin, T. Longman, S. Crowder and Co.,
         C. Corbet, and T. Caslon. 12°, 9 vols.]

1760 (?) **Poems**   267
         Poems on several occasions by Shakespeare.
         • Imprint is false and the text is undated. ESTC suggests possibly
         published in Edinburgh in 1760.
         [London: sold by A. Murden, R. Newton, T. Davidson,
         C. Anderson, W. Nelson, and S. Paterson. 12°]

1761   **2 Henry IV**   268
         [Dublin: Hulton Bradley. 12°]

         Macbeth   269
         [Cork: Eugene Swiney. 12°]

         Measure for Measure   270, 271 (Walsh)
         • Some copies have the following stamped on title page: 'Sold by
         G. Walsh, 19 Wood-Quay'. ESTC suggests that the Walsh reissue
         may have been 1795.
         [Dublin: Hulton Bradley. 12°]

[1761]   **Measure for Measure**   272
         [Dublin: Sarah Cotter. 12°]

         Othello   273
         [Dublin: for G. and A. Ewing, W. Smith, J. Exshaw, and A. James.
         12°]

         ['Blair/Reid'] 2   274
         The works of Shakespear.
         [Edinburgh: A. Kincaid & J. Bell, J. Brown, W. Gordon,
         C. Wright, and R. Fleming. 12°, 8 vols.]

1762   **Coriolanus**   275
         [Dublin: R. Watts & W. Whitestone. 12°]

         Julius Caesar   276
         [Dublin: Cusack Greene. 12°]

         Merchant of Venice   277
         [Dublin: T. Dyton. 12°]

         Theobald 5   278
         The works of Shakespeare: In eight volumes. Collated with the oldest
         copies, and corrected: With notes, explanatory, and critical: By
         Mr. Theobald.
         [London: C. Hitch and L. Hawes, J. and R. Tonson, B. Dod,
         G. Woodfall, J. Rivington, R. Baldwin, T. Longman, S. Crowder
         and Co., W. Johnston, C. Corbet, T. Lownds, and T. Caslon. 12°,
         8 vols.]

1763   **Othello**   279
         [Cork: Phineas and George Bagnell. 12°]

1764   **Othello**   280
         [London: Halhed Garland; Dublin: John Exshaw. 12°]

         Romeo and Juliet   281
         [London: Halhed Garland; Dublin: John Exshaw. 12°]

1765   **Hamlet**   282
         [Dublin: for W. and W. Smith, J. Exshaw, and A. Ewing. 12°]

         Samuel Johnson 1   283
         The plays of William Shakespeare, in eight volumes, with the
         corrections and illustrations of various commentators; to which are
         added notes by Sam. Johnson.
         [London: J. and R. Tonson, C. Corbet, H. Woodfall, J. Rivington,
         R. Baldwin, L. Hawes, Clark and Collins, W. Johnston, T. Caslon,
         T. Lownds, and the executors of B. Dodd. 8°, 8 vols.]

[1765]   **Johnson 2**   284

The plays of William Shakespeare, in eight volumes, with the corrections and illustrations of various commentators; to which are added notes by Sam. Johnson.

[London: J. and R. Tonson, H. Woodfall, J. Rivington, R. Baldwin, L. Hawes, Clark and Collins, T. Longman, W. Johnston, T. Caslon, C. Corbet, T. Lownds, and the executors of B. Dodd. 8°, 8 vols.]

1766   **Merchant of Venice**   285

[Dublin: B. Corcoran. 12°]

Dublin 4   286

The plays of William Shakespeare, in ten volumes. With the corrections and illustrations of various commentators. To which are added, notes by Samuel Johnson, LL. D.

[Dublin: A. Leathley, C. Wynne, P. Wilson, J. Exshaw, H. Saunders, J. Potts, S. Watson, J. Mitchell, and J. Williams. 12°, 10 vols.]

Foulis   287 (8°), 288 (12°)

The works of Shakespear. In eight volumes. Collated and corrected by the former editions, by Mr. Pope. Printed from his second edition.

• Plays were issued singly from 1752, then collected into an 8° set which was reissued in the same year in 12°.

[Glasgow: Robert and Andrew Foulis. 8°, 8 vols. in 16 parts; 12°, 8 vols.]

Steevens Twenty Plays   289

Twenty of the plays of Shakespeare, being the whole number printed in quarto during his life-time, or before the restoration, collated where there were different copies, and publish'd from the originals, by George Steevens, Esq, in four volumes.

Vol I: *MND* (1600); *Wiv.* (1619, 1630, 1602); *Ado* (1600); *MV* (1600); *LLL* (1631)

Vol II: *Shr.* (1631); *Lr.* (1608); *Jn.* (1611); *R2* (1615); *1H4* (1613); *2 H4* (1600)

Vol III: *H5* (1608); *2 and 3 H6* (nd); *R3* (1612); *Tit.* (1611); *Tro.* (1609)

Vol IV: *Rom.* (1597, 1609); *Ham.* (1611); *Oth.* (1622); *Son.* (1609); *Leir* (1605)

[London: J. and R. Tonson in the Strand; T. Payne, at the Mews-gate, Castle-Street; and W. Richardson, in Fleet Street. 8°, 4 vols.]

1767   **Othello**   290

[Dublin: Bart. Corcoran. 12°]

[1767]   **Martin & Wotherspoon**   291

*The works of Shakespeare. In ten volumes. With corrections and
illustrations from various commentators.*

[Edinburgh: Martin & Wotherspoon. 12°, 10 vols.]

Theobald 6   292

*The works of Shakespeare: In eight volumes. Collated with the oldest
copies, and corrected; with notes, explanatory, and critical: By
Mr. Theobald. Printed verbatim from the octavo edition.*

[London: H. Woodfall, C. Bathurst, J. Beecroft, W. Strahan, J. and
F. Rivington, J. Hinton, Davis and Reymers, R. Baldwin, Hawes,
Clarke, and Collins, R. Horsfield, W. Johnston, W. Owen,
T. Caslon, T. Longman, E. and C. Dilly, C. Corbett, T. Cadell,
E. Johnson, B. White, G. Keith, J. Hardy, T. Lowndes, T. Davies,
J. Robson, T. Beckett, F. Newberry, and Robinson and Roberts.
12°, 8 vols.]

1768   **Hamlet**   293
[Edinburgh: Martin & Wotherspoon. 12°]

King Lear   294
[Edinburgh: Martin & Wotherspoon. 12°]

Macbeth   295 (84pp), 296 (72pp)

• Two versions of this text would appear to have been produced.
The British Library holds a copy (11765.a.25) in which the
signature line on the first page of the play text itself reads 'Vol. I B',
with the play text paged from 14 (on the second page) through to
84, with lyrics for the songs included at pages 80–3 and a general
note on the play included at pages 83–4. The National Library of
Scotland has an edition (5.1415 (23)) which simply has 'A' on the
signature line of the first page of the play text itself, with the play
text numbered from 2 (on the second page) through to 72. The
lyrics for the songs are included at pages 68–71, and a general note
on the play is included at pages 71–2. The latter edition may also
be included in the British Library collection. ESTC provides a
shelfmark of E-01124 for a British Library copy, but no text was
available from this reference number at the time when this
chronology was being compiled.

[Edinburgh: Martin & Wotherspoon. 12°]

Merchant of Venice   297, 298 (end vol. 9th)

• The National Library of Scotland holds two versions of this
edition. In one – shelfmark 5.1009(3) – the final page (80) ends
'END OF THE MERCHANT OF VENICE'; in the other –
shelfmark 00.8/2.2(8) – p. 80 ends 'END OF VOLUME

[1768]   NINTH'. In both cases, the play is followed by an unpaged leaf advertising 'PLAYS and FARCES Printed and Sold By MARTIN & WOTHERSPOON, *Edinburgh*'.

[Edinburgh: Martin & Wotherspoon. 12°]

Merry Wives of Windsor   299

[Edinburgh: Martin & Wotherspoon. 12°]

Othello   300

[Edinburgh: Martin & Wotherspoon. 12°]

Richard III   301

[Edinburgh: Martin & Wotherspoon. 12°]

Romeo and Juliet   302

[Edinburgh: Martin & Wotherspoon. 12°]

Birmingham 1   303

The works of Shakespear, from Mr. Pope's edition.

[Birmingham: Printed and sold by Robert Martin; and by R. Goadby, in Sherborne, M. Morgan in Lichfield, T. Smith in Wolverhamton {sic}, A. Donaldson in London, R. Bond in Glocester, and by all Country Booksellers. 8°, 9 vols.]

Edward Capell   304

Mr William Shakespeare his comedies, histories, and tragedies, set out by himself in quarto, or by the players his fellows in folio, and now faithfully republish'd from those editions in ten volumes octavo; with an introduction: Whereunto will be added, in some other volumes, notes, critical and explanatory, and a body of various readings entire.

• Individual volumes are dated either 1767 or 1768 but the full set was issued together in 1768.

[London: by Dryden Leach for J. and R. Tonson. 8°, 10 vols.]

Johnson 3   305

The plays of William Shakespeare, in eight volumes, with the corrections and illustrations of various commentators; to which are added notes by Sam. Johnson.

[London: H. Woodfall, C. Bathurst, J. Beecroft, W. Strahan, J. and F. Rivington, J. Hinton, Davis and Reymers, R. Baldwin, Hawes, Clarke and Collins, R. Horsfield, W. Johnston, W. Owen, T. Caslon, T. Longman, E. and C. Dilly, C. Corbett, T. Cadell, E. Johnson, B. White, G. Keith, J. Hardy, T. Lowndes, T. Davies, J. Robson, T. Becket, F. Newbery, and Robinson and Roberts. 8°, 8 vols.]

1768/70 (?) **Birmingham 2**   306

The works of Shakespeare, with illustrations.

• Undated. ESTC suggests 1770. Shakespeare Centre Library catalogue suggests 1768/70. Folger catalogue notes that 'Proposals for this edition were published on 22 May 1769. Boden disappears from the Birmingham directories in 1771. Plays were to be issued separately, one every fortnight. No more than five volumes of what would have been a nine-volume edition were ever published'.

[Birmingham: by N. Boden, and sold by Mr. Williams in Shrewsbury; Mr. Taylor in Stafford; Mr. Smith in Newcastle; Mr. Morgan in Lichfield; Mr. Shelton in Tamworth; Mr. Smart in Walsall and Wolverhampton; Mr. Sharp in Warwick; Mr. Keating in Stratford; Mr. Luckman in Coventry; Miss Boden in Bridgnorth; Mr. Hodson in Burton; Mr. Clare in Bewdley; Mr. Berrow in Worcester; Mr. Sellick in Bristol; Mr. Sibbald in Liverpool; Mr. Broster in Chester; and Mr. Houldgate in Sheffield. 12°, 5 vols. issued {of a proposed 9}]

1769   ['Blair/Reid'] 3

307 (Donaldson), 308 (Ruddiman), 309 (Manson), 310 (Balfour)

The works of Shakespear. In which the beauties observed by Pope, Warburton, and Dodd, are pointed out. Together with the author's life; a glossary; copious indexes; and, a list of the various readings. In eight volumes.

• A note in the Folger card catalogue for their copy of this edition (PR2725 1769a) – which has a Ruddiman imprint – reads as follows: 'In 1769 Alex. Donaldson and Wal. Ruddiman shared the printing of this ed., each doing 4 vols. Two states of the title exist: this one with Ruddiman in imprint, another with Donaldson. A remainder with cancel titles, names A. Manson and 6 others in the undated imprint.' A further issue in this sequence also exists, with a 1769 John Balfour imprint. An examination of these issues confirms that the same set of sheets is involved in each case. Variations in type wear may well indicate that the Donaldson and Ruddiman issues were run off in advance of the Manson *et al.* and the Balfour – though this is suggested here only tentatively. The Manson imprint is false.

[Three Edinburgh imprints: Alexander Donaldson; Wal. Ruddiman and Company; John Balfour. Bogus London imprint: A. Manson, R. Dilton, J. Thomson, P. Alnwick, W. Nelson, S. Darnton and H. Gray. 8°, 8 vols.]

1770   Hamlet   311
[Edinburgh: A. Donaldson. 12°]

[1770]	**1 Henry IV**	312

• ESTC lists a unique copy of this edition at the Essex Institute, Salem, Massachusetts (822.S52.25). Details taken from ESTC record only.

[Edinburgh: A. Donaldson. 12°]

	2 Henry IV	313

[Edinburgh: A. Donaldson. 12°]

	3 Henry VI	314

[Edinburgh: A. Donaldson. 12°]

	King Lear	315

• Charles Jennens' edition.

[London: by W. and J. Richardson and sold by B. White. 8°]

	Richard II	316

[Edinburgh: A. Donaldson. 12°]

	Richard III	317

[Edinburgh: A. Donaldson. 12°]

	Tempest	318

[Edinburgh: A. Donaldson. 12°]

	Winter's Tale	319

[Edinburgh: A. Donaldson. 12°]

1770 (?)	**King John**	320

• This date is suggested by ESTC. The Trinity College Dublin copy (196.q.48 no. 7) is kept in an envelope with 'not before 1775' written on it. The Birmingham Central Library copy (S331.175 Shakespeare library) has '[c. 1750]' pencilled on the title page. The title page says 'second edition', but I have been unable to trace another Chamberlaine *King John*.

[Dublin: D. Chamberlaine. 12°]

1770–71	**'Hanmer' 7 [second Oxford edition]**	321

The works of Shakespear. In six volumes. Adorned with sculptures. The second edition.

[Oxford: Clarendon. 4°, 6 vols.]

1771	**Poems**	322

Shakespeare's poems: Containing, I. Venus and Adonis. II. The rape of Lucrece. III. The passionate pilgrim. IV. Sonnets.

[Dublin: Printed by T. Ewing. 8°]

[1771] **['Blair/Reid'] 4**   **323 (8°), 324 (Strand), 325 (St. Paul's)**

*The works of Shakespear. In which the beauties observed by Pope,
Warburton, and Dodd, are pointed out. Together with the author's life;
a glossary; copious indexes; and, a list of the various readings.*

• The Folger catalogue identifies three versions of this edition.
Initially issued in 8°, it was reimposed in 12° in sixes. This latter
version was reissued again, with the imprint address amended
from 'corner of Arundel-Street, Strand' to '48, East corner of
St. Paul's Church-yard', Donaldson having moved premises.

[London and Edinburgh: A. Donaldson. 8° or 12°, 8 vols.]

Dublin 5   **326**

*The plays of Shakespeare from the text of Dr. S. Johnson. With the
prefaces, notes, &c of Rowe, Pope, Theobald, Hanmer, Warburton,
Johnson, and select notes from many other critics. Also, the introduction
of the last editor Mr. Capell; and a table shewing his various readings.*

[Dublin: Thomas Ewing. 8°, 6 vols.]

1772   **Theobald 7**   **327**

*The works of Shakespeare. In twelve volumes. Collated with the oldest
copies, and corrected: With notes, explanatory and critical: By Mr
Theobald.*

[London: R. Crowder, C. Ware, and T. Payne. 12°, 12 vols.]

1773   **Hamlet**   **328**

• Charles Jennens' edition.

[London: by W. Bowyer and J. Nichols and sold by W. Owen. 8°]

Macbeth   **329**

• Charles Jennens' edition.

[London: by W. Bowyer and J. Nichols and sold by W. Owen. 8°]

Othello   **330**

• Charles Jennens' edition.

[London: by W. Bowyer and J. Nichols and sold by W. Owen. 8°]

Bell (1)   **331**

*Bell's edition of Shakespeare's plays, as they are now performed at the
theatres royal in London; regulated from the prompt books of each
house by permission; with notes critical and illustrative; by the authors
of the Dramatic Censor.*

• The publication history of Bell's editions is complex. They have
been mapped here on the basis of the information provided in
Burnim and Highfill's *John Bell*. The coherence of this narrative
serves, however, to mask the convoluted nature of Bell's
undertakings, in which series overlap and supplement each other,

[1773]   with control of the editions frequently passing from Bell's own
           hands. Some individual Shakespeare texts were also recycled into
           Bell's 'British Theatre' series. Burnim and Highfill suggest (1) an
           initial 1773 five-volume release of the plays in the current
           theatrical repertoire; (2) a second release of these volumes, dated
           1774; (3) a supplement to the second release, creating a complete
           works set by adding a further four volumes (vol. IX being the
           poems), though in some cases complete sets include 1773 texts
           rather than 1774; (4) a new series, issued by numbers, dated from
           1775 to 1778; (5) an edition issued by James Barker using a mixture
           of Bell stock and new impressions, commencing in 1794 (Burnim
           and Highfill do not suggest a terminal date, but dated Barker title
           pages range from 1794 to 1796); (6) a further Barker/Bell issue,
           undated, but probably appearing between 1797 and 1801; (7) a Bell
           issue of the Johnson–Steevens text, dated 1785–8; (8) a George
           Cawthorn issue of Bell's Johnson–Steevens text, dated 1804.
           Individual Bell entries here are keyed to this list.

           The plays included in the initial five volumes are as follows (details
           from Folger copy PR2752.1774a.C1):

           Vol. I: *Mac.*; *AYL*; *Oth.*; *AWW*.

           Vol. II: *Lr.*; *Rom.*; *MV*; *Cym.*; *Ado.*

           Vol. III: *R3*; *Wiv.*; *Ham.*; *Tmp.*; *MM*.

           Vol. IV: *Jn.*; *1H4*; *2H4*; *H5*; *H8*.

           Vol. V: *JC*; *Tim.*; *WT*; *Cor.*; *TN*.

           [London: John Bell and C. Etherington. 12°, 5 vols.]

Johnson–George Steevens 1   332

*The plays of William Shakespeare. In ten volumes. With the corrections
and illustrations of various commentators; to which are added notes by
Samuel Johnson and George Steevens. With an appendix.*

[London: C. Bathurst, J. Beecroft, W. Strahan, J. and F. Rivington,
J. Hinton, L. Davis, Hawes, Clarke and Collins, R. Horsfield,
W. Johnston, W. Owen, T. Caslon, E. Johnson, S. Crowder,
B. White, T. Longman, B. Law, E. and C. Dilly, C. Corbett,
W. Griffin, T. Cadell, W. Woodfall, G. Keith, T. Lowndes,
T. Davies, J. Robson, T. Becket, F. Newbery, G. Robinson,
T. Payne, J. Williams, M. Hingeston, and J. Ridley. 8°, 10 vols.]

Theobald 8   333

*The works of Shakespeare: In eight volumes. Collated with the oldest
copies, and corrected: With notes, explanatory, and critical: By Mr.
Theobald. Printed verbatim from the octavo edition.*

[London: C. Bathurst, J. Beecroft, W. Strahan, J. and F. Rivington,
J. Hinton, L. Davis, Hawes, Clarke, and Collins, R. Horsfield,
W. Johnston, W. Owen, T. Caslon, E. Johnson, S. Crowder,

B. White, T. Longman, B. Law, E. and C. Dilly, C. Corbett,
W. Griffin, T. Cadell, W. Woodfall, G. Keith, T. Lowndes, T.
Davies, J. Robson, T. Becket, F. Newbery, G. Robinson, T. Payne,
J. Williams, M. Hingeston, and J. Ridley. 12°, 8 vols.]

1774   **Julius Caesar**   334

• Charles Jennens' edition

[London: by W. Bowyer and J. Nichols and sold by W. Owen. 8°]

Bell (2)   335

*Bell's edition of Shakespeare's plays, as they are now performed at the
theatres royal in London; regulated from the prompt books of each
house by permission; with notes critical and illustrative; by the authors
of the Dramatic Censor.*

• See 1773 above. 'The second edition' on title page.

[London: John Bell and C. Etherington. 12°, 5 vols.]

Bell (3)   336 (supplement), 337 (1774 complete), 338 (1773 complete)

• See 1773 above. Title as Bell (2) above. A supplement of four
volumes serves to make (2) a complete set; also serves as a
supplement to Bell (1).

[London: John Bell and C. Etherington. 12°, 4 vols. serving to
create complete 9 vol. sets]

1775–78   **Bell (4)**   339

• See 1773 above. This series consists of an issue of the plays,
published individually at 6*d*. each, initially on a weekly basis,
beginning on 30 September, 1775. The final text in the sequence
would appear to have been issued in 1778. I can find no record of
volume title pages having been issued for gathering the separate
texts into a complete sets. Publishing details below are taken from
Folger copy of *Antony and Cleopatra* (bound in PR1241.B47 v.11
cage).

[London: for John Bell and C. Etherington. 12°]

1776   **Hamlet**   340

[Glasgow: R. and A. Foulis. 12°]

Macbeth   341

[Glasgow: n.p. 12°]

1777 (?)   ○ Jaggard, *Bibliography* (p. 504) lists an undated Theobald edition
which he assigns to this date. I have been unable to identify this
edition and Jaggard does not provide a location for the text.

1778   **Two Noble Kinsmen**   342

• Edited by George Colman and included in vol. X of

[1778]   *The dramatick works of Beaumont and Fletcher; collated with all the former editions, and corrected; with notes, critical and explanatory, by various commentators; and adorned with fifty-four original engravings. In ten volumes.*

[London: T. Evans, P. Elmsley, J. Ridley, J. Williams and W. Fox. 8°]

Johnson–Steevens[–Isaac Reed] 2   343, 344 (with supplement)

The plays of William Shakspeare. In ten volumes. With the corrections and illustrations of various commentators; to which are added notes by Samuel Johnson and George Steevens. The second edition, revised and augmented.

• In 1780 Edmond Malone added two supplementary volumes to this edition, providing an account of the English theatre; a reprint of Arthur Brooke's translation of *Romeus and Juliet*; a new edition of the poems; and the text of the apocryphal plays included in the second issue of F3.

[London: C. Bathurst, W. Strahan, J. F. and C. Rivington, J. Hinton, L. Davis, W. Owen, T. Caslon, E. Johnson, S. Crowder, B. White, T. Longman, B. Law, E. and C. Dilly, C. Corbett, T. Cadell, H. L. Gardener, J. Nichols, J. Bew, J. Beecroft, W. Stuart, T. Lowndes, J. Robson, T. Payne, T. Becket, F. Newbery, G. Robinson, R. Baldwin, J. Williams, J. Ridley, T. Evans, W. Davies, W. Fox, and J. Murray. 8°, 10 vols.]

1779   **Macbeth**   345

• Details from ESTC record, which lists two locations: William Andrews Clark Library, University of California, Los Angeles (*PR3657.G31 1772) and University of Toronto (Fisher S52.A6M3 1779). ESTC notes that this edition is not included in Gaskell's *Bibliography*.

[Glasgow: Andrew Foulis. 8°]

1784   **Samuel Ayscough 1**   346

Stockdale's edition of Shakespeare, including in one volume the whole of his dramatic works; with explanatory notes compiled from various commentators.

[London: J. Stockdale. 8°]

1785   **Macbeth**   347

[Dublin: R. Marchbank. 12°]

Johnson–Steevens[–Reed] 3   348

The plays of William Shakspeare. In ten volumes. With the corrections and illustrations of various commentators; to which are added notes by Samuel Johnson and George Steevens. The third edition, revised and augmented by the editor of Dodsley's collection of old plays.

[London: C. Bathurst, J. Rivington and Sons, T. Payne and Son,
L. Davis, W. Owen, B. White and Son, T. Longman, B. Law,
T. Bowles, J. Johnson, C. Dilly, J. Robson, G. G. J and J. Robinson,
T. Cadell, H. L. Gardner, J. Nichols, J. Bew, W. Stuart, R. Baldwin,
J. Murray, A. Strahan, T. Vernor, J. Barker, W. Lowndes, S. Hayes,
G. and T. Wilkie, Scatcherd and Whitaker, T. and J. Egerton,
W. Fox, and E. Newbery. 8°, 10 vols.]

1785–88 **Bell (7)** 349

Dramatick writings of Will. Shakspere, with notes of all the various
commentators; printed complete from the best editions of Sam. Johnson
and Geo. Steevens.

• See 1773 above.

[London: J. Bell. 12°, 76 parts, forming 20 vols.]

1786–94 (?) **Joseph Rann 1** 350

The dramatic works of Shakspeare, in six volumes; with notes by
Joseph Rann, A. M. vicar of St. Trinity, in Coventry.

• Terminal date for edition is unclear. vols. I–IV dated,
respectively, 1786, 1787, 1789, 1791. vols. V and VI undated.
ESTC notes suggested dates of 1791 and 1794.

[Oxford: Clarendon. 8°, 6 vols.]

1787–91 **Bellamy & Robarts** 351

[Plays]

• The plays in this edition seem to have been issued serially. The
Folger has a complete set, eight volumes bound in four (232054 sh.
col.). There is no general title page and the Folger catalogue notes
that this set differs from the 1791 Bellamy & Robarts edition. The
dates given are those of the plates included in the edition.

[London: Bellamy & Robarts. 8°, 8 vols.]

1788 **Macbeth** 352

[Glasgow: Robert Duncan. 8°]

1789 **Much Ado About Nothing** 353, 354 (Walsh)

• Top of title page reads 'Bell's Edition'. Some copies have the
following stamped on title page: 'Sold by G. Walsh, 19
Wood-Quay'.

[Dublin: John Parker. 12°]

1790 **Merchant of Venice** 355

[Glasgow: Robert Duncan. 12°]

Ayscough 2 356

Shakspeare's dramatic works; with explanatory notes. A new edition.
To which is now added, a copious index to the remarkable passages and
words. By the Rev. Samuel Ayscough, F.S.A. and Assistant Librarian

[1790]   *of the British Museum. Embellished with a striking likeness of*
         Shakspeare, from the original folio edition.

         [London: John Stockdale. 8°, 3 vols., the third volume provides
         Ayscough's index to the plays.]

Malone   357

The plays and poems of William Shakspeare, in ten volumes; collated
verbatim with the most authentick copies, and revised: with the
corrections and illustrations of various commentators; to which are
added, an essay on the chronological order of his plays; an essay
relative to Shakspeare and Jonson; a dissertation on the three parts of
King Henry VI.; an historical account of the English stage; and notes;
by Edmond Malone.

[London: J. Rivington and Sons, L. Davis, B. White and Son,
T. Longman, B. Law, H. S. Woodfall, C. Dilly, J. Robson,
J. Johnson, T. Vernor, G. G. J. and J. Robinson, T. Cadell,
J. Murray, R. Baldwin, H. L. Gardner, J. Sewell, J. Nichols, J. Bew,
T. Payne, jun., S. Hayes, R. Faulder, W. Lowndes, G. and T. Wilkie,
Scatcherd and Whitaker, T. and J. Egerton, C. Stalker, J. Barker,
J. Edwards, Ogilvie and Speare, J. Cuthell, J. Lackington, and
E. Newbery. 8°, 10 volumes; volume 1 in two parts]

1790/86 **'Malone'**   358

The plays of William Shakspeare. Accurately printed from the text of
Mr. Malone's edition; with select explanatory notes. In seven volumes.

• Volume I dated 1790, remaining volumes 1786. Malone
disclaimed any connection with or responsibility for this text.

[London: J. Rivington and Sons, L. Davis, B. White and Son,
T. Longman, B. Law, H. S. Woodfall, C. Dilly, J. Robson,
J. Johnson, T. Vernor, G. G. J. and J. Robinson, T. Cadell,
J. Murray, R. Baldwin, H. L. Gardner, J. Sewell, J. Nichols, J. Bew,
T. Payne Jun., S. Hayes, R. Faulder, W. Lowndes, G. and T. Wilkie,
Scatcherd and Whitaker, T. and J. Egerton, C. Stalker, J. Barker,
J. Edwards, Ogilvie and Speare, J. Cuthell, J. Lackington, and
E. Newbery. 12°, 7 vols.]

1791   **Poems**   359

The poems of Shakspeare. To accompany Jones's edition of
Shakspeare's drama.

[Dublin: William Jones. 8°]

Bellamy & Robarts 1   360, 361 (BCL variant)

The plays of William Shakspeare, complete in eight volumes.

• Birmingham Central Library has a variant copy of this edition
(757862–67), with 'pages reset' ([Fredrick], *Bibliography*
Catalogue, III, p. 3).

[London: Bellamy and Robarts. 8°, 8 vols.]

[1791]   **Dublin 6/Ayscough 3**   362

Shakspeare's dramatic works; with explanatory notes. To which is now added, a copious index to the remarkable passages and words. By the Rev. Samuel Ayscough, F.S.A. and Assistant Librarian of the British Museum. Embellished with a striking likeness of Shakspeare, from the original folio edition, and another from the collection of his Grace the Duke of Chandos. A new edition.

[Dublin: William Jones. 8°, 3 vols., the third volume provides Ayscough's index to the plays.]

1791–1802   **Boydell/Steevens**   363

The dramatic works of Shakspeare revised by George Steevens.

[London: by W. Bulmer and Co. Shakspeare Printing Office, for John and Josiah Boydell, and George Nicol; from the types of W. Martin. 2°, 18 parts forming 9 vols.]

1792   **Cymbeline**   364

• The Ambrose Eccles text of *Cymbeline*, issued as part of a two volume set with *King Lear* in 1793 (see below), would appear to have originally been issued singly in 1792. WorldCat indicates that the Harry Ransom Library at the University of Texas, Austin, has a copy of this edition.

Gordon *et al.*   365

The dramatic works of William Shakespear printed complete from the best editions of Samuel Johnson George Stevens [sic] and E. Malone to which is prefixed the life of the author.

[Edinburgh: for W. Gordon. N. R. Cheyne. I. & I. Fairbairn. & Silvester Doig; London: I. Lackington; Leith: W. Coke; Stirling: W. Anderson. 12°, 8 vols.]

○ Jaggard, *Bibliography* (p. 506) lists an edition in two volumes published in London this year, with Ayscough's index, without giving a location. I have been unable to trace this edition.

1793   **Cymbeline**   366, 367 (set with Lear), 368 (1794 reissue)

• Edited by Ambrose Eccles. Published as one of a two–volume set with London *Lear* text listed below. The set was reissued by G. G. and J. Robinson, C. Dilly, and T. Payne in 1794. See also 1792.

[London: Lackington, Allen & Co. 8°]

Cymbeline   369, 370 (set with Lear)

• Edited by Ambrose Eccles. Published as one of a two–volume set with the Dublin *Lear* text listed below.

[Dublin: by Zachariah Jackson for A. Grueber. 8°]

Hamlet   371

[Paisley: John Neilson. 12°]

[1793]   **King Lear**   372
• Edited by Ambrose Eccles. See also §366–8 above.
[London: Lackington, Allen & Co. 8°]

King Lear   373
• Edited by Ambrose Eccles. See also §369, 370 above.
[London {probably Dublin}: for C. Dilly. 8°]

Romeo and Juliet   374
[Dublin: P. Wogan. 12°]

Johnson–Steevens[–Reed] 4   375
The plays of William Shakspeare. In fifteen volumes. With the corrections and illustrations of various commentators. To which are added, notes by Samuel Johnson and George Steevens. The fourth edition. Revised and augmented (with a glossarial index) by the editor of Dodsley's collection of old plays.
[London: T. Longman, B. Law and Son, C. Dilly, J. Robson, J. Johnson, T. Vernor, G. G. J. and J. Robinson, T. Cadell, J. Murray, R. Baldwin, H. L. Gardner, J. Sewell, J. Nicholls, F. and C. Rivington, W. Goldsmith, T. Payne Jun., S. Hayes, R. Faulder, W. Lowndes, B. and J. White, G. and T. Wilkie, J. and J. Taylor, Scatcherd and Whitaker, T. and J. Egerton, E. Newbery, J. Barker, J. Edwards, Ogilvy and Speare, J. Cuthell, J. Lackington, J. Deighton, and W. Miller. 8°, 15 vols.]

1794   **Hamlet**   376
• This entry and the next (*Twelfth Night*) were the first Shakespeare texts to be published in America. Both are abridged acting texts, 'as performed at the theatre in Boston', based on Bell's theatrical texts (see 1773 above).
[Boston: for David West and John West. 12°]

Twelfth Night   377
• See previous entry (*Hamlet*).
[Boston: for David West and John West. 12°]

Dublin 7   378
The plays and poems of William Shakspeare, in sixteen volumes. Collated verbatim with the most authentick copies, and revised: With the corrections and illustrations of various commentators; to which are added, an essay on the chronological order of his plays; an essay relative to Shakspeare and Jonson; a dissertation on the three parts of King Henry VI. An historical account of the English stage, and notes; by Edmond Malone.
[Dublin: John Exshaw. 12°, 16 vols.]

1794–6 (?) Bell (5)/Barker   **379**

• See 1773 and 1775–8 above. James Barker reissued Bell (4),
drawing partly on Bell stock which had been sold at auction in
1793, following Bell's bankruptcy. I can find no record of volume
title pages having been issued for gathering the separate texts into a
complete set. Publishing details below are taken from Folger copy
of 1794 *King Lear* (PR2819.1794b sh. col.).

[London: Printed (by assignment) for J. Barker. 12°]

1795 'Blair[/Reid]' 5   **380 (Edinburgh), 381 (Glasgow)**

*The works of William Shakespeare, in eight volumes. In which the
beauties observed by Pope, Warburton, and Dodd, are pointed out.
Together with the author's life, a glossary, copious indexes, and, a list of
the various readings.*

• Issued with a variant imprint in the same year. The Folger
catalogue notes that 'Even the title-page was printed from the same
setting of type, with imprint changed.'

[Edinburgh: Bell & Bradfute, J. Dickson, W. Creech,
J. & J. Fairbairn, and T. Duncan; variant imprint: Glasgow:
J. & A. Duncan, J. & M. Robertson, and J. & W. Shaw. 12°,
8 vols.]

Philadelphia/[Joseph Hopkinson?]   **382**

*The plays and poems of William Shakspeare. Corrected from the latest
and best London editions, with notes, by Samuel Johnson, L.L. D. to
which are added, a glossary and the life of the author. Embellished with
a striking likeness from the collection of his Grace the Duke of Chandos.*

[Philadelphia: Printed and sold by Bioren & Madan. 12°, 8 vols.]

1795 (?) • Hulton Bradley's edition of *Measure for Measure* may have been
reissued in this year with the name 'G. Walsh' stamped on the title
page. See 1761 above.

1796 Bellamy & Robarts 2   **383**

The plays of William Shakspeare, complete, in eight volumes.

• ESTC notes that some texts included in this edition are reissued
from the 1791 Bellamy & Robarts edition.

[London: Bellamy and Robarts. 8°, 8 vols.]

1797 Longman *et al.*   **384**

The plays of William Shakspeare. In six volumes.

[London: T. Longman, B. Law, C. Dilly, J. Robson, J. Johnson,
G. G. & J. Robinson, R. Baldwin, H. L. Gardner, J. Sewell,
W. Richardson, J. Nichols, F. & C. Rivington, J. Edwards,
T. Payne, Jun., S. Hayes, R. Faulder, W. Lowndes, B. & J. White,

[1797]   G. & T. Wilkie, J. & J. Taylor, J. Scatcherd, T. Egerton, E.
Newbery, W. Bent, J. Walker, W. Clarke & Son, J. Cuthell, J. Nunn,
J. Lackington & Co., T. Kay, J. Deighton, W. Miller, Vernor &
Hood, Cadell & Davies, Murray & Highley, and Lee & Hurst. 8°,
6 vols.]

Longman *et al.*   385

The plays of William Shakespeare, accurately printed from the text of
Mr. Steevens's last edition, with a selection of the most important notes.
In eight volumes.

[London: T. Longman, B. Law, C. Dilly, J. Johnson, G. G. and
J. Robinson, R. Baldwin, H. L. Gardner, J. Sewell, W. Richardson,
J. Nichols, F. and C. Rivington, T. Payne Jun., R. Faulder,
W. Lowndes, B. and J. White, G. and T. Wilkie, J. and J. Taylor,
J. Scatcherd, T. Egerton, E. Newbery, W. Bent, J. Walker,
W. Clarke and Son, J. Barker, J. Edwards, D. Ogilvy and Son,
J. Cuthell, J. Nunn, J. Anderson, J. Lackington and Co., T. Kay,
J. Deighton, W. Miller, Vernor and Hood, Cadell and Davies,
Murray and Highley, and Lee and Hurst. 12°, 8 vols.]

Robinson *et al.*   **386, 387 (reset), 388 (quarto edition?)**

The works of William Shakespeare, containing his plays and poems; to
which is added a glossary. In seven volumes.

• In one Folger copy (PR2752 1797b2 Sh. Col.) 'To the Public' is
'reset, signed Vol. 1. b, and on different paper'. ESTC (record no.
ESTC N66869) lists an edition of this text in 4° format, giving as
the only example a copy held at the McMaster University Mills
Memorial Library (RB C629–35). The Research Collections
Librarian at Mills confirms that an examination of the volumes
inclines him to think that the format is 'probably quarto', but
concedes that the volumes may be 'octavo in 4s'. As a matter of
caution, I have assigned an additional number to account for the
possibility that a quarto edition was issued.

[London: G. G. & J. Robinson, R. Faulder, B. & J. White, J.
Edwards, T. Payne, Jun., J. Walker, & J. Anderson. 8°, 7 vols.]

○ Jaggard, *Bibliography* (p. 507) lists an Edinburgh edition for this
year, which he speculatively attributes to Martin and Wotherspoon.
He also lists a twelve-volume London edition for this year. He
gives no location for either edition and I have been unable to trace
them.

1797–1801   Charles Wagner   **389, 390 (reissue)**

The dramatic works of William Shakspeare. In eight volumes. With an
account of the life of the author written by Mr. Rowe. Published by
Charles Wagner. A. M. Professor of the Carolinum at Brunswick.

• The first English edition published in continental Europe. The date range here corresponds with that indicated by the individual volumes in the British Library copy (11766.c.16). Jaggard (p. 508) suggests that it was reprinted in 1799–1801, identifying a copy at Birmingham Central Library. The Birmingham library has a copy (26224), for which it gives a date of 1801 only and library staff confirm that all volumes in this set are dated 1801.

[Brunswick, Germany: Charles Wagner. 8°, 8 vols.]

1797-1801 (?)   **Bell (6)**   391

• See 1773 and 1794(–96?) above. Burnim and Highfill suggest that James Barker issued a further set of Bell-based texts in this period.

1798   **Baldwin** *et al.*   392

The plays of William Shakespeare, accurately printed from the text of Mr. Steevens's last edition.

[London: Printed by H. Baldwin and Son for C. Dilly, J. Johnson, G. G. and J. Robinson, R. Baldwin, H. L. Gardner, J. Sewell, W. J. and J. Richardson, J. Nichols, F. and C. Rivington, T. Payne, R. Faulder, W. Lowndes, G. Wilkie, J. and J. Taylor, J. Scatcherd, T. Egerton, E. Newbery, W. Bent, J. Walker, W. Clarke and Son, J. Barker, J. Edwards, D. Ogilvy and Son, J. Cuthell, R. Lea, J. Nunn, J. Lackington and Co., T. Kay, J. Deighton, J. White, W. Miller, Vernor and Hood, Cadell and Davies, T. N. Longman, C. Law, Murray and Highley, and Lea and Hurst. 12°, 9 vols.]

Morrison   393

The dramatic writings of Will. Shakespeare. With introductory prefaces to each play. Printed complete from the best editions.

[Perth: R. Morrison and Son. 12°, 9 vols.]

Ogilvie   **394, 395 (BCL variant), 396 (10 vols.)**

The dramatic writings of Will. Shakespeare. With introductory prefaces to each play. Printed complete from the best editions.

• Same edition as previous entry (§393), but with different title page. The Birmingham Central Library [Fredrick], *Bibliography . . . Catalogue* lists a second Ogilvie edition (16110) for this year, also in nine volumes, but 'differ[ing] . . . in some details'. A further version, in ten volumes, would also appear to have been issued (ESTC notes a complete edition of this issue only at the Bodleian – Vet.A5f.885–894).

[London: D. Ogilvie and Son. 12°, 9 vols. or 10 vols., as above]

[1798–1800]   Vernor & Hood/Harding

397, 398 (2nd issue, ill), 399 (2nd issue, non-ill)

The plays of William Shakspeare.

• Plays issued individually 1798–99, with separate title pages, headed 'Harding's edition'. Collected into set, with volume title pages dated 1800. Folger catalogue identifies two further issues of these sheets, one with illustrations, the other without.

[London: by T. Bensley for Vernor and Hood, E. Harding, and J. Wright. 12°, 12 vols., probably originally issued in 38 parts.]

1799–1802   Tourneisen   400

The plays of William Shakspeare. With the corrections and illustrations of various commentators. To which are added, notes by Samuel Johnson and George Steevens. A new edition. Revised and augmented (with a glossarial index) by the editor of Dodsley's collection of old plays.

[Basil {sic}, Germany: J. J. Tourneisen. 8°, 23 vols.]

1800   Taylor   401

The works of Shakespeare.

[Berwick: John Taylor. 12°, 9 vols.]

○ Jaggard, *Bibliography* (p. 508) lists an edition in nine volumes published by Sharpe in this year, without giving a location. I have been unable to trace this edition.

1801   ○ Jaggard, *Bibliography* (p. 506) lists an eight-volume edition published in Zurich in this year, without giving a location. I have been unable to trace this edition.

1802–04   Boston 1   402, 403 (Folger variant)

The dramatick works of William Shakespeare. Printed complete with Dr. Samuel Johnson's preface and notes. To which is prefixed the life of the author.

• Originally issued to subscribers in sixteen parts. Folger has a variant copy (PR2752 1802–1804b Sh. Col.) in which *Tmp.* and *TGV* (vol. I) 'are of a different printing'.

[Boston: Munroe and Francis {first eight volumes}; Oliver and Munroe, and Belcher and Armstrong {vol. IX}. 12°, 9 vols.]

1803   Johnson–Steevens–Reed 5   404

The plays of William Shakspeare. In twenty-one volumes. With the corrections and illustrations of various commentators. To which are added, notes, by Samuel Johnson and George Steevens. The fifth edition. Revised and augmented by Isaac Reed, with a glossarial index.

• This edition was much reprinted. The two editions which immediately follow here were reprinted from it and the titles of

[1803]   several subsequent entries will indicate the extent of its
         reproduction. As this was, effectively, the last new text in the
         Johnson–Steevens–Reed sequence, I am discontinuing the
         numbering with this edition. The 1813 edition of the text was
         advertised as the 'sixth edition', but it was completed after Isaac
         Reed's death (in 1807) by William Harris. Harris does little more
         than correct errors in the 1803 text.

         [London: J. Johnson, R. Baldwin, H. L. Gardner, W. J. and
         J. Richardson, J. Nichols and Son, F. and C. Rivington, T. Payne,
         R. Faulder, G. and J. Robinson, W. Lowndes, G. Wilkie,
         J. Scatcherd, T. Egerton, J. Walker, W. Clarke and Son, J. Barker
         and Son, D. Ogilvy and Son, Cuthell and Martin, R. Lea,
         P. Macqueen, J. Nunn, Lackington, Allen and Co., T. Kay,
         J. Deighton, J. White, W. Miller, Vernor and Hood, D. Walker,
         B. Crosby and Co., Longman and Rees, Cadell and Davies,
         T. Hurst, J. Harding, R. H. Evans, S. Bagster, J. Mawman, Blacks
         and Parry, R. Bent, J. Badcock, J. Asperne, and T. Ostell. 8°,
         21 vols.]

J. Johnson *et al.*   405

*The plays of William Shakspeare, accurately printed from the text of
the corrected copy left by the late George Steevens, Esq. With glossarial
notes. In ten volumes.*

[London: J. Johnson, R. Baldwin, H. L. Gardner, W. J. and
J. Richardson, J. Nichols and Son, F. C. and J. Rivington, T. Payne,
R. Faulder, G. and J. Robinson, W. Lowndes, G. Wilkie,
J. Scatcherd, T. Egerton, J. Walker, W. Clarke and Son, J. Barker
and Son, D. Ogilvy and Son, Cuthell and Martin, R. Lea,
P. M'Queen, J. Nunn, Lackington, Allen and Co., T. Kay,
J. Deighton, J. White, W. Miller, Vernor and Hood, D. Walker,
B. Crosby and Co., Longman and Rees, Cadell and Davies,
T. Hurst, J. Harding, R. H. Evans, S. Bagster, J. Mawman, Blacks
and Parry, R. Bent, J. Badcock, J. Asperne, and T. Ostell. 8°,
10 vols.]

J. Johnson *et al.*   406

*The plays of William Shakspeare, accurately printed from the text of
the corrected copy left by the late George Steevens, Esq. With glossarial
notes. In nine volumes.*

• Johnson's Preface omitted.

[London: J. Johnson, R. Baldwin, H. L. Gardner, W. J. and
J. Richardson, J. Nichols and Son, F. C. and J. Rivington, T. Payne,
R. Faulder, G. and J. Robinson, W. Lowndes, G. Wilkie,
J. Scatcherd, T. Egerton, J. Walker, W. Clarke and Son, J. Barker
and Son, D. Ogilvy and Son, Cuthell and Martin, R. Lea,
P. M'Queen, J. Nunn, Lackington, Allen and Co., T. Kay,

J. Deighton, J. White, W. Miller, Vernor and Hood, D. Walker,
B. Crosby and Co., Longman and Rees, Cadell and Davies,
T. Hurst, J. Harding, R. H. Evans, S. Bagster, J. Mawman, Blacks
and Parry, R. Bent, J. Badcock, J. Asperne, and T. Ostell. 12°,
9 vols.]

○ Jaggard, *Bibliography* (p. 509) lists another Boydell edition for
this year, in two folio volumes. He gives the Birmingham
Shakespeare collection as his only location, but no such text is
included in the Birmingham catalogue. The dedication of the
Steevens' Boydell edition is dated 1803 and a two-volume set of the
prints was issued with a title-page date of 1803 and a dedication
dated 1805.

1803–4   **Sharpe**   407

The plays of William Shakspeare, in miniature.

• Title page reads 'Sharpe's edition'.

[London: John Sharpe and H. D. Symonds. 24°, 9 vols.]

1803–5   **Wynne** *et al.*   408

The plays of Willliam Shakspeare.

[London: Wynne and Scholey, and J. Wallis. 8°, 10 vols.]

1804   **Bell (8)/Cawthorn**   409

• See 1773 above. George Cawthorn would appear to have acquired
some of the stock of Bell's 1785–8 edition in 1796. In 1804 he
reissued these texts under his own imprint.

[London: for and under the direction of George Cawthorn. 12°,
20 vols.]

Turnbull   410

The plays of William Shakespeare. In nine volumes.

[Edinburgh: Thomas Turnbull. 12°, 9 vols.]

1804–13   **Leipsick**   411

The plays of William Shakspeare, accurately printed from the text of
Mr. Steeven's [sic] *last edition, with a collection of the most important*
notes.

[Leipsick: Gerhard Fleischer the Younger. 16°, 20 vols.]

1805   **Merchant of Venice**   412

• Edited by Ambrose Eccles

[London: Lackington, Allen & Co. 8°]

Chalmers   413, 414 (without plates), 415 (1812 reissue)

The plays of William Shakspeare, accurately printed from the text of
the corrected copy left by the late George Steevens, Esq. with a series of
engravings, from original designs of Henry Fuseli, Esq. R. A. Professor

[1805]   *of Painting: And a selection of explanatory and historical notes, from
the most eminent commentators; a history of the stage, a life of
Shakspeare, &c. By Alexander Chalmers, A. M.*

• Also issued without the Fuseli plates, in nine volumes (and with
minor changes to signatures and pagination). Reissued in 1812,
with volumes 1–6 reprinted, but volumes 7–9 identical and
including plates.

[London: F. C. and J. Rivington, J. Johnson, R. Baldwin,
H. L. Gardner, W. J. and J. Richardson, J. Nichols and Son,
T. Payne, R. Faulder, G. and J. Robinson, W. Lowndes, G. Wilkie,
Scatcherd and Letterman, T. Egerton, J. Walker, W. Clarke and
Son, J. Barker and Son, D. Ogilvy and Son, Cuthell and Martin,
R. Lea, P. Macqueen, Lackington, Allen and Co., T. Kay, J.
Deighton, J. White, W. Miller, Vernor and Hood, D. Walker,
C. Law, B. Crosby and Co., R. Pheney, Longman, Hurst, Rees, and
Orme, Cadell and Davies, J. Harding, R. H. Evans, S. Bagster,
J. Mawman, Blacks and Parry, J. Badcock, J. Asperne, and T.
Ostell. 8°, 10 vols.]

Scott   416

The plays of William Shakespeare. In nine volumes.
[London: John Scott. 24°, 9 vols.]

1805–9   **[Joseph Dennie] 1**   417

*The plays of William Shakspeare. In seventeen volumes. With the
illustrations of various commentators. To which are added, notes, by
Samuel Johnson and George Steevens. Revised and augmented by
Isaac Reed, Esq. With a glossarial index.*

• First American variorum edition. Imprints vary across the
individual volume title pages. Imprint below taken from vol. 1.

[Philadelphia: C. and A. Conrad & Co. Philadelphia; Conrad,
Lucas, & Co. Baltimore; Somervell and Conrad, Petersburg; and
Bonsal, Conrad, & Co. Norfolk. 12°, 17 vols.]

1806   **Manley Wood**   418

The plays of William Shakspeare, with notes of various commentators.
[London: George Kearsley. 8°, 14 vols.]

Miller   419

The dramatic works of William Shakspeare. Complete in two volumes.
[London: William Miller. 8°, 2 vols.]

1807   **Ayscough**   420

*The dramatic works of William Shakspeare: With explanatory notes.
To which is added, a copious index to the remarkable passages and
words, by Samuel Ayscough.*

[1807]   [London: John Stockdale, W. J. and J. Richardson, J. Walker,
R. Faulder and Son, Scatcherd and Letterman, Longman and Co.,
Crosby and Co., Lackington and Co., Cadell and Davies, J.
Harding, J. Mawman, J. Booker, G. Robinson, E. Lloyd, W. Earle,
and J. Booth. 8°, 3 vols., the third volume provides Ayscough's
index to the plays.]

Boston 2   421

*The dramatick works of William Shakespeare. Printed complete with
Dr. Samuel Johnson's preface and notes. To which is prefixed the life of
the author.*

[Boston: Munroe & Francis. 12°, 9 vols.]

[Henrietta/Thomas Bowdler]   422

The family Shakespeare. In four volumes.

• First systematically expurgated edition. Contains twenty plays
only, as follows:

Vol. I: *Tmp.*; *MND*; *Ado*; *AYL*; *MV*

Vol. II: *TN*; *WT*; *Jn.*; *R2*; *1H4*

Vol. III: *2H4*; *H5*; *R3*; *H8*; *JC*

Vol. IV: *Mac.*; *Cym.*; *Lr.*; *Ham.*; *Oth.*

[Bath: by R. Cruttwell, Bath, for J. Hatchard, London. 12°, 4 vols.]

Francis Douce   423

*Mr. William Shakespeares comedies, histories, & tragedies. Published
according to the true originall copies.*

• First type facsimile.

[London: E. & J. Wright. 2°]

Longman *et al.*   424

*The plays of Shakspeare. Printed from the text of Samuel Johnson,
George Steevens, and Isaac Reed.*

[London: Longman, Hurst, Rees, and Orme, and William Miller;
Edinburgh: A. Constable and Co. 8°, 12 vols.]

Stockdale   425

*The plays of William Shakspeare from the corrected text of Johnson
and Steevens. Embellished with plates.*

[London: John Stockdale. 4°, 6 vols.]

Wynne *et al.*   426 (Folger d), 427 (Folger e, 10 vol), 428 (Folger f)

The plays of William Shakspeare.

• Appears to have been produced using standing type from the
1803–5 Wynne edition. The Folger has three different issues of
this edition – PR2752 1807d, e and f. In d, the frontispiece portrait

of Shakespeare is identified as 'S. Harding delin. LeGoun sculpt'.
e is in ten volumes, rather than eight, with the portrait identified as
'Jn. Thurston delin. Cha. Warren sculpt'. In f the identification of
the portrait is 'engraved by J. Thomson from the original picture
in the possession of Mr. Richardson'. These details supplied by the
Folger. Jaggard, *Bibliography* (p. 511) also lists a four-volume
version of this edition, but I have been unable to trace it.

[London: Peter Wynne and Son and Robert Scholey. 8°, 8 vols./
10 vols.]

1808 **John Britton**   **429**

*Mr. William Shakespeares comedies, histories, & tragedies. Published
according to the true originall copies.*

• Second type facsimile.

[London: by E. & J. Wright for Vernor & Hood. 2°, 4 vols.]

1809 **Avignon**   **430**

*William Shakspeare's selected plays, from the last edition of Johnson
and Steevens; with brief explanatory notes, extracted from various
commentators.*

• In the Folger copy (PR2752 1809d copy 1), vols. 5 and 6 are
bound together. Contains nine plays, as follows:

Vol. I: *Tmp.*; *MV*

Vol. II: *1H4*; *2H4*

Vol. III: *Cor.*; *Rom.*

Vol. IV: *Lr.*; *Mac.*

Vol. V: *Ham.*

Vol. VI: *Oth.*

[Avignon. Seguin Frères. 12°, 6 vols.]

Vernor *et al.*   **431 (Folger c1), 432 (Folger c2), 433 (12°)**

*The plays of William Shakespeare, from the correct edition of Isaac
Reed, Esq.*

• Title page indicates 'stereotype edition'. Probably the first
Shakespeare edition produced by this method. The Folger has
three distinct issues of this edition, all apparently using the same
plates, but with variations in signatures, and presence or absence of
half titles and plates. One issue (PR2752 1809c3 cop. 1 sh. col.) is
reimposed in 12s. The other two issues (c1 and c2) are
distinguished by the fact that in c2 the first gathering of
preliminaries is unsigned, the signing picking up with 'c'; in c1, the
preliminaries are signed 'b'. These details supplied by the Folger.
Jaggard, *Bibliography* (p. 511) also lists a four-volume Vernor *et al.*
edition which he assigns to this year, but I have been unable to
trace it.

[London: Vernor, Hood and Sharpe, Poultry; and Taylor and Hessey, Fleet Street. 8° or 12°, 12 vols.]

○ Jaggard, *Bibliography* (p. 511) lists a twelve-plays edition published by Mitchell in Newcastle in this year, which he describes as the 'first Newcastle-on-Tyne edition'. I have been unable to trace it.

1810   **[Joseph Dennie] 2**   434

The plays of William Shakspeare, from the text of Johnson and Steevens.

• Reading version of the first American variorum

[Philadelphia: C. and A. Conrad & Co.; Baltimore: Conrad, Lucas, & Co.; Petersburg: Somervell and Conrad; Norfolk: Bonsal, Conrad, & Co. 8°, 8 vols.]

○ Jaggard, *Bibliography* (p. 511) lists a nine-volume London edition published by Sharpe in this year, which I have been unable to trace.

1810–12 **Boston 3**   435

The works of William Shakspeare. In nine volumes. With the corrections and illustrations of Dr. Johnson, G. Steevens, and others, revised by Isaac Reed.

[Boston: Munroe, Francis, & Parker; New York: Ezra Sargeant; Philadelphia: Hopkins & Earle. 12°, 9 vols.]

1811   **Ayscough**   436

The dramatic works of William Shakspeare; with explanatory notes; in four volumes. Embellished with one hundred and twenty-three copper plates.

[London: John Stockdale. 8°, 4 vols.]

Forsyth   437

The plays of Shakspeare. Printed from the text of Samuel Johnson, George Steevens, and Isaac Reed.

[London: James Forsyth; Edinburgh: John Grieg. 12°, 9 vols.]

Nichols et al.   438

The plays of William Shakspeare, accurately printed from the text of the corrected copy left by the late George Steevens, Esq. With glossarial notes, and a sketch of the life of Shakspeare. In eight volumes.

• An additional title page is included with the preliminary matter, as follows:

The plays of William Shakspeare. In eight volumes.

London: Printed for F. C. & J. Rivington and Partners

[1811] [London: J. Nichols and Son, F. C. and J. Rivington, J. Stockdale, W. Lowndes, G. Wilkie and J. Robinson, T. Egerton, J. Walker, J. Nunn, W. Clarke and Son, J. Barker and Son, J. Cuthell, R. Lea, Lackington and Co., J. Deighton, J. White and Co., C. Law, B. Crosby and Co., W. Earle, J. Gray and Son, G. Robinson, Longman and Co., Cadell and Davies, J. Harding, R. H. Evans, J. Booker, S. Bagster, J. Mawman, Black and Co., J. Richardson, J. Booth, Newman and Co., R. Pheney, R. Scholey, J. Asperne, J. Faulder, R. Baldwin, Cradock and Joy, J. Mackinlay, J. Johnson and Co., Gale and Curtis, and Wilson and Son, York. 12°, 8 vols.]

Nichols *et al.*   439

The plays of William Shakspeare, accurately printed from the text of the corrected copy left by the late George Steevens, Esq. with a series of engravings, from original designs of Henry Fuseli, Esq. R.A. Professor of Painting: And a selection of explanatory and historical notes, from the most eminent commentators; a history of the stage, a life of Shakspeare, &c. By Alexander Chalmers, A. M. A new edition.

[London: J. Nichols and Son, F. C. and J. Rivington, J. Stockdale, W. Lowndes, G. Wilkie and J. Robinson, T. Egerton, J. Walker, W. Clarke and Son, J. Barker, J. Cuthell, R. Lea, Lackington and Co., J. Deighton, J. White and Co., B. Crosby and Co., W. Earle, J. Gray and Son, Longman and Co., Cadell and Davies, J. Harding, R. H. Evans, J. Booker, S. Bagster, J. Mawman, Black and Co., J. Richardson, J. Booth, Newman and Co., R. Pheney, R. Scholey, J. Asperne, J. Faulder, R. Baldwin, Cradock and Joy, J. Mackinlay, J. Johnson and Co., Gale and Curtis, G. Robinson, and Wilson and Son, York. 8°, 9 vols.]

Nichols *et al.*   440

The plays of William Shakspeare, accurately printed from the text of the corrected copy left by the late George Steevens, Esq. with glossarial notes. A new edition, in ten volumes.

[J. Nichols and Son, F. C. and J. Rivington, T. Payne, R. Faulder, J. Stockdale, W. Lowndes, G. Wilkie and J. Robinson, Scatcherd and Letterman, T. Egerton, J. Walker, W. Clarke and Son, J. Barker and Son, J. Cuthell, R. Lea, Lackington, Allen, and Co., J. Deighton, J. White and Co., C. Law, B. Crosby and Co., Longman and Co., Cadell and Davies, J. Harding, R. H. Evans, J. Booker, S. Bagster, J. Mawman, Black, Parry, and Kingsbury, J. Richardson, J. Booth, Newman and Co., R. Pheney, R. Scholey, J. Asperne, R. Baldwin, Cradock and Joy, and J. Johnson and Co. 12°, 10 vols.]

○ Jaggard, *Bibliography* (p. 512) lists three editions for 1811 which I have been unable to trace: two in eight volumes, by J. Walker (24°) and William Miller (12°) and one in twelve volumes, 12°, by Cowie & Co.

1812   **Chalmers reissue**   —

• Chalmers text of 1805 reissued in this year. See §413 above.

1812–15 **Tegg**   441

The dramatic works of William Shakespeare.

[London: for Thomas Tegg. 8°, 12 vols.]

1813   **Nichols** *et al.*   442

The plays of William Shakspeare. In twenty-one volumes. With the corrections and illustrations of various commentators. To which are added notes by Samuel Johnson and George Steevens. Revised and augmented by Isaac Reed, with a glossarial index. The sixth edition.

[London: J. Nichols and Son, F. C. and J. Rivington, J. Stockdale, W. Lowndes, G. Wilkie and J. Robinson, T. Egerton, J. Walker, Scatcherd and Letterman, W. Clarke and Sons, J. Barker, J. Cuthell, R. Lea, Lackington and Co., J. Deighton, J. White and Co., B. Crosby and Co., W. Earle, J. Gray and Son, Longman and Co., Cadell and Davies, J. Harding, R. H. Evans, J. Booker, S. Bagster, J. Mawman, Black and Co., J. Black, J. Richardson, J. Booth, Newman and Co., R. Pheney, R. Scholey, J. Murray, J. Asperne, J. Faulder, R. Baldwin, Cradock and Joy, Sharpe and Hailes, Johnson and Co., Gale and Co., G. Robinson, C. Brown, and Wilson and Son, York. 8°, 21 vols.]

Williams/Delaplaine   443, 444 (Eastburn), 445 (miniature)

The plays of William Shakspeare. Complete in one volume. Accurately printed from the text of Isaac Reed, Esq.

• First US single volume edition. Some copies include the name 'Eastburn, Kirk & Co. New York' on title page.

[Boston: Charles Williams; Philadelphia: Joseph Delaplaine. 8°]

• A second edition in six miniature volumes was published in the same year, details as follows:

The plays of William Shakspeare. In six volumes. Printed from the text of Isaac Reed, Esq.

[Boston: Charles Williams; Philadelphia: Joseph Delaplaine. Miniature, 6 vols.]

1813–14 **Whittingham**   446

The dramatic works of William Shakspeare.

[Chiswick: C. Whittingham. 16°, 7 vols.]

1814   **Vienna**   447

The plays of William Shakspeare, accurately printed from the text of Mr. Steevens's last edition, with a selection of the most important notes.

[Vienna: Anton Doll. 16°, 20 vols.]

○ Jaggard, *Bibliography* (p. 512) lists both a Williams Boston edition and a Cowie & Co. London edition for this year, without giving locations. The Williams edition is not included in Westfall's listing in *American*. I have been unable to trace either of these two editions.

1815 **Whittingham & Arliss** 448

The dramatic works of William Shakspeare. With a life of the poet; the preface by Dr. Johnson; and a glossarial index. In seven volumes.

[London: Whittingham and Arliss. 12°, 7 vols.]

1816 **Proprietors** 449

The works of William Shakspeare, in sixteen volumes. Collated verbatim with the most authentic copies, and revised, with the corrections and illustrations of various commentators; to which are added, an essay on the chronological order of his plays; an essay relative to Shakspeare and Jonson; a dissertation on the three parts of King Henry VI., an historical account of the English stage, and notes, by Edmond Malone.

[London: Printed for the Proprietors. 8°, 16 vols.]

1817 **Oliver & Boyd** 450

The plays of Shakspeare. Printed from the text of Samuel Johnson, George Steevens, and Isaac Reed.

[Edinburgh: Published by Oliver and Boyd; Sold by Law and Whittaker, London; and William Turnbull, Glasgow. 12°, 9 vols.]

1817 (?) **Maurice** 451

The dramatic works of Shakspeare. In eight volumes.

• Plays are provided with individual title pages, with a variety of imprints.

[London: printed by D. S. Maurice and sold by all booksellers in town and country. 12°, 8 vols.]

1817–18 **Durell** 452

The dramatic works of William Shakespeare, in ten volumes. With the corrections and illustrations of Dr. Johnson, G. Steevens, and others, revised by Isaac Reed, Esq.

[New York: Henry Durell. 8°, 10 vols.]

1818 **Bowdler 2** 453

The family Shakespeare, in ten volumes; in which nothing is added to the original text; but those words and expressions are omitted which cannot with propriety be read aloud in a family.

[London: Longman, Hurst, Rees, Orme, and Brown. 12°, 10 vols.]

[1818]   **Whittingham**   454

The dramatic works of William Shakspeare. Whittingham's edition.

[Chiswick: by C. Whittingham, for Sherwood, Neely, and Jones.
16°, 7 vols.]

Whittingham   455

The dramatic works of William Shakspeare. Whittingham's edition.

• Birmingham Central Library [Fredrick], *Bibliography* . . .
Catalogue suggests that this edition is an 'impostor', having 'the
title page of Whittingham's Edition, but [being] printed by
Maurice for J. Bumpus' (I, p. 9).

[Chiswick: by C. Whittingham, for Sherwood, Neely, and Jones –
but see note above. 16°, 9 vols.]

1819   **Hamlet and As You Like It**   456, 457 (reissue)

• Edited by Thomas Caldecott. Reissued in 1820. Caldecott's
original intention was to publish a complete edition, of which these
texts were to serve as a sample. Second edition published in 1832
(included below).

[London: John Murray, 1819. 8°]

Allason *et al.*   458

The plays of Shakespeare, carefully revised from the best editions.

[London: W. Allason, J. Maynard; Edinburgh: W. Blair. 12°,
9 vols.]

Hurst *et al.*   459

*The plays of Shakspeare. Printed from the text of Samuel Johnson,
George Steevens, and Isaac Reed. In two volumes.*

• The original Scottish publisher would appear to have been
Ballantyne.

[London: Hurst, Robinson, and Co.; Edinburgh: Archibald
Constable and Co. 8°, 2 vols.]

Robertson *et al.*   460

*The plays of Shakespeare, printed from the texts of Samuel Johnson,
George Steevens, and Isaac Reed.*

[Edinburgh: James Robertson, Fairbairn and Anderson, Stirling
and Slade; London: G. and W. B. Whittaker and Thomas and
Joseph Allman. 12°, 9 vols.]

1820   **Black & Son**   461

The dramatic works of Shakspeare. Complete in three volumes.

[London: J. Black and Son. 12°, 3 vols.]

[1820] **Bowdler 3** 462

The family Shakspeare, in ten volumes; in which nothing is added to the original text; but those words and expressions are omitted which cannot with propriety be read aloud in a family.

• Folger catalogue notes that this edition was either stereotyped from the same setting of type as Bowdler 2 above (§453), or was made up from remainder sheets of that edition 'except *Measure*, which is reedited and much altered and contains cancels. All preliminaries newly printed, with Preface dated 1820'.

[London: Longman, Hurst, Rees, Orme, and Brown. 12°, 10 vols.]

Walker *et al.* **463, 464 (Folger variation)**

The dramatic works of William Shakespeare, from the correct edition of Isaac Reed, Esq., with copious annotations.

• Would appear to have been produced using the same plates as 1809 Vernor & Hood above (§431). The Folger has a second issue of this with minor variations in signatures (PR2752 1820d2 sh. col.).

[London: J. Walker, G. Offor, Sharpe and Sons; Edinburgh: J. Sutherland; Dublin: J. Cumming. 8°, 12 vols.]

1820 (?) **Leipsic** 465

The dramatic works of William Shakspere. With a life, and glossary.

[Leipsic: Brothers Schumann. 24°, 8 vols.]

Limbird 466

The complete dramatic works, and miscellaneous poems of William Shakspeare. With glossarial notes & life by N. Rowe.

[London: J. Limbird. 8°]

1821 **Black and Whittaker** 467

The dramatic works of Shakspeare. Complete in three volumes.

[London: Alexander Black and G. and W. B. Whittaker. 12°, 3 vols.]

Bumpus *et al.* 468

The dramatic works of Wm. Shakspeare. Correctly given from the text of Johnson & Steevens. With a preface, by Samuel Johnson, LL.D and a complete glossarial index.

[London: J. Bumpus, Andrews, Butler, Sharpe, Reid, Clarke. 16°, 9 vols.]

Collins & Hannay 469

The dramatic works of William Shakespeare, in ten volumes. With the corrections and illustrations of Dr. Johnson, G. Steevens, and others, revised by Isaac Reed, Esq.

• Appears to have been stereotyped from the same plates as 1817–18 Durell edition (§452).

[New York: Collins & Hannay. 8°, 10 vols.]

[1821]   **Malone–James Boswell**   470

*The plays and poems of William Shakspeare, with the corrections and
illustrations of various commentators: Comprehending a life of the poet,
and an enlarged history of the stage, by the late Edmond Malone. With
a new glossarial index.*

[London: F. C. and J. Rivington, T. Egerton, J. Cuthell, Scatcherd
and Letterman, Longman, Hurst, Rees, Orme, and Brown, Cadell
and Davies, Lackington and Co., J. Booker, Black and Co.,
J. Booth, J. Richardson, J. M. Richardson, J. Murray, J. Harding,
R. H. Evans, J. Mawman, R. Scholey, T. Earle, J. Bohn, C. Brown,
Gray and Son, R. Pheney, Baldwin, Cradock, and Joy, Newman
and Co., Ogles, Duncan, and Co., T. Hamilton, W. Wood,
J. Sheldon, E. Edwards, Whitmore and Fenn, W. Mason, G. and
W. B. Whittaker, Simpkin and Marshall; R. Saunders, J. Deighton
and Sons, Cambridge; Wilson and Son, York, and Stirling; and
Slade, Fairbairn and Anderson, and D. Brown, Edinburgh. 8°,
21 vols.]

Sherwin   471

*The dramatic works of William Shakspeare; to which are added his
miscellaneous poems.*

[London: Sherwin & Co. 8°]

Walker *et al.*   472

*The dramatic works of William Shakspeare, to which are added his
miscellaneous poems. In six volumes.*

• Appears to have been stereotyped from same plates as Walker
et al. 1820 above (§463), but with a different frontispiece.

[London: J. Walker; J. Richardson and Co.; J. Sharpe and Son;
J. Johnston; Also R. Griffin and Co. Glasgow. 12°, 6 vols.]

This is the cut-off point for the complete listing of collected editions.

1822   **J. R. Pitman**   473

• Probably the first extensive Shakespeare text produced
specifically for schools. Included heavily expurgated texts of
AWW; *Ant.*; *AYL*; *Cor.*; *Cym.*; *Ham.*; *1H4*; *2H4*; *Lr.*; *Mac.*; *MV*;
MND; *Ado*; *Oth.*; *R3*; *Rom.*; *Shr.*; *Tmp.*; *TN*; *WT*; *Jn.*; *MM*; *TGV*;
H8; *JC*; *Tim.* and selected passages from *Err.*; *H5*; *1H6*; *2H6*; *3H6*;
LLL; *Wiv.*; *R2*; *Tro.*, together with twelve of the sonnets.

[London: C. Rice]

1822–23 **Pickering**   474

Plays.

• Printed in 'Diamond' type, the smallest edition which had yet
appeared. Pages measure approximately 83mm x 46mm.

[London: by Corrall for William Pickering. Issued in thirty-six parts, gathered into nine vols.]

1825   **Hamlet**   475

• Reprint of Q1. The first of two extant copies of Q1 had been discovered two years previously.

[London: Payne and Foss]

Harness   476, 477 (reprint)

• This edition was reprinted in 1830. The original edition would seem to be relatively rare. WorldCat lists just eight locations: the university libraries at Montevallo, Yale, Duke, Oregon, Brown, Carson Newman, Wisconsin (Milwaukee) and the Free Library of Philadelphia. Details here taken from WorldCat.

[London: Saunders and Otley. 8 vols.]

1826   **Samuel Weller Singer 1**   478

Plays.

[Chiswick: by Charles Whittingham. 10 vols.]

1832   **Hamlet and As You Like It**   479

• Edited by Thomas Caldecott. See 1819 above.

[London: printed for the editor by William Nicol.]

1832–4   **A. J. Valpy**   480

Works.

[London: A. J. Valpy. 15 vols.]

1836   **[O. W. B. Peabody]**   481

Plays.

[Boston. Hilliard, Gray & Co. 8°, 7 vols.]

1838   **Thomas Campbell**   482

Plays.

[London: Edward Moxon.]

1838–43   **Charles Knight 1**   483

Works.

[London: C. Knight & Co. 56 parts forming 8 vols.]

1842–44   **John Payne Collier 1**   484

Works.

[London: Whittaker. 8 vols.]

Knight 2   485

Works.

[London: Charles Knight and Co. 12 vols.]

1843   **Barry Cornwall [pseud. for Bryan Waller Procter]**   486
Works.
[London: Robert Tyas. 3 vols.]

1844   **Sir Thomas More**   487
• Edited by Alexander Dyce. First publication of the play. Dyce's
edition includes some readings now lost owing to the deterioration
of the ms.
[London: Shakespeare Society]

1844–47 **Gulian C. Verplanck**   488
Plays.
[New York: Harper & Brothers. 138 (?) parts, forming 3 vols.]

1846   **Two Noble Kinsmen**   489
• Edited by Alexander Dyce and included in his *Works of Beaumont
& Fletcher*, vol. 11. Dyce also included a text of the play in his 1866
Shakespeare edition.
[London: Edward Moxon]

1848   **William Gilmore Simms/Apocryphal**   490
• First American edition of the apocryphal plays.
[New York: G. F. Cooledge & Brother]

1849   **Bowdler US**   491
• First American edition of Bowdler's text, in one volume.
[Philadelphia: Jesper Harding]

1851–52 **William Hazlitt**   492
Plays.
[London: Routledge. 4 vols.]

1851–56 **Henry N. Hudson 1**   493
Works.
[Boston: James Munroe & Co. 11 vols.]

1853   **Collier 2**   494
Plays.
[London: William White]

1853–65 **James Orchard Halliwell[-Phillipps]**   495
Works.
[London: C. & J. Adlard. 16 vols.]

1854   **'Nicolaus Delius 1'**   496
Works

• Text and all commentary, notes, etc. in English. The revised edition of the *Variorum Handbook* notes that this 'identification now seems to be erroneous. The title page reads "Edited by Dr. D.____" Jaggard mis-identifies as "The first edition edited by Delius." The title page also reads "The text regulated by . . . the recently discovered folio of 1632" – i.e., Collier's Perkins Folio; Delius on the contrary was severely skeptical of [Collier's Perkins-influenced text], refused to treat the Sonnets biographically, and spelled Sh.'s name "Shakspere".' I have followed the revised *Handbook* in not adjusting the Delius edition numbers in the light of this discovery.

[Leipzig: Baumgärtner]

1854–56	**Charles Knight, Stratford**	497

Works.

[London: Thomas Hodgson. 10 vols.]

1854–61	**Delius 2**	498

Works.

• Text in English, with commentary in German.

[Elberfeld: Friderichs. 7 vols.]

1856	**Singer 2**	499

Plays.

[London: Bell and Daldy. 10 vols.]

185[6]–60	**Howard Staunton**	500

Plays.

[London: Routledge. Issued serially in fifty parts, beginning in December 1856, then collected into three volumes, with title pages dated 1858, 1859, 1860]

1857	**Alexander Dyce 1**	501

Works.

[London: Moxon. 6 vols.]

1857–66	**Richard Grant White**	502

Works.

[Boston: Little, Brown. 12 vols.]

1858	**Hamlet**	503

• Photolithographic facsimile of Q1

[Privately printed in a limited edition at the direction of the Duke of Devonshire]

[1858]   **Collier 3**   504
Works.
[London: Whittaker. 6 vols.]

1859   **Hamlet**   505
• Photolithographic facsimile of Q2
[Privately printed in a limited edition at the direction of the Duke
of Devonshire]

Romeo and Juliet   506
• Parallel text of first and second quartos, edited by Tycho
Mommsen. Text in English, with German commentary.
[Oldenberg: Gerhard Stalling; London: Williams & Norgate]

1859–60 **Mary Cowden Clarke**   507 (1 vol.), 508 (2 vols.)
Works.
[New York: Appleton. Issued serially in fortnightly parts,
beginning in 1859, then issued in one volume and in two volumes]

1860–73 (?)   **John Hunter**   509
• The *Variorum Handbook* provides a speculative date range of
1860–93 and notes that Hunter's 'editions of the separate plays in
various schools series were apparently reissued and revised
irregularly' (p. 78, repeated in revised edition). I have attempted
here to establish a base-line set of first-edition texts edited by
Hunter for Longman, Green & Co. The listing here is based on the
complete holdings of the British Library (11763.b.9) and on
additional volumes found at the National Library of Scotland. One
of the additional volumes included below – *Othello* – is, in fact,
missing from the National Library of Scotland collection and so
details are taken from the library's computer catalogue. This may
not be a complete record – note, for instance, that parts 2 and 3 of
Henry VI are listed here, but not part 1.
510 *H8* (1860); 511 *JC* (1861); 512 *MV* (1861); 513 *Ham.* (1865);
514 *Lr.* (1865); 515 *Tmp.* (1865); 516 *AYL* (1869); 517 *Mac.* (1869);
518 *Oth.* (1869); 519 *R2* (1869); 520 *R3* (1869); 521 *Ant.* (1865); 522
Cor. (1870); 523 *MND* (1870); 524 *TN* (1870); 525 *1H4* (1871); 526
2H4 (1871); 527 *H5* (1871); 528 *Jn.* (1871); 529 *Cym.* (1872); 530
WT (1872); 531 *Rom.* (1872); 532 *Err.* (1873); 533 *2H6* (1873); 534
3H6 (1873); 535 *LLL* (1873); 536 *TGV* (1873); 537 *Tim.* (1873).
[London: Longmans, Green & Co. 28 vols.?]

1861–71 **Edmund William Ashbee/J. O. Halliwell[-Phillipps]**   538
facsimiles
• Collection of lithographic facsimiles of the early quarto editions.
Titus Andronicus (1594) was not included as it had not been
discovered at the time of issuing of the series.

539 *1H4* (1599; 1861); **540** *Per.* (1609 – edn with first SD 'enter Gower'; 1862); **541** *R2* (1597; 1862); **542** *R3* (1597; 1863); **543** *R3* (1605; 1863); **544** *Tro.* (1609; 1863); **545** *MND* (1600; 1864); **546** *Oth.* (1622; 1864); **547** *MND* ('1600' – Pavier quarto; 1865); **548** *Ado* (1600; 1865); **549** *Rom.* (1599; 1865); **550** *R3* (1602; 1865); **551** *MV* ('1600' – Pavier quarto; 1865); **552** *Ven.* (1593; 1866); **553** *Luc.* (1594; 1866); **554** *Rom.* (1597; 1866); **555** *1H4* (1598; 1866); **556** *Tit.* (1600; 1866); **557** *2H4* (1600; 1866); **558** *2H4* (1600 – with gatherings E3-4 cancelled and replaced; 1866); **559** *Wiv.* (1602; 1866); **560** *Wiv.* (1619; 1866); **561** *Ham.* (1603; 1866); **562** *1H4* (1613; 1867); **563** *Ven.* (1594; 1867); **564** *R3* (1598; 1867); **565** *H5* (1602; 1867); **566** *1H4* (1608; 1867); **567** *Ham.* (1604; 1867); **568** *Lr.* ('1608' – Pavier quarto; 1867); **569** *Tit.* (1611; 1867); **570** *H5* (1600; 1868); **571** *Ham.* (1605; 1868); **572** *Lr.* (1608; 1868); **573** *Per.* (1611; 1868); **574** *Rom.* (nd; 1868); **575** *R2* (1598; 1869); **576** *LLL* (1598; 1869); **577** *Rom.* (1609; 1869); **578** *Ham.* (1611; 1870); **579** *MV* (1600; 1870); **580** *R2* (1608; 1870); **581** *H5* (1608; 1870*); **582** *R2* (1615; 1870); **583** *1H4* (1604; 1871); **584** *Per.* (1609 – edn with first SD 'eneer Gower'; 1871); **585** *R3* (1612; 1871). Introductory volume published in 1871, containing preface, list of contents, and three title pages.

* The Folger also has a copy (PR2752 1861–1871 Sh. Col. no. 35a) of an Ashbee facsimile of the 1608 quarto of *H5* without the usual Ashbee title page, printed on both sides of the paper (instead of, as is usual, one side).

[London: privately printed. 48 vols., including introductory volume]

1862–4 **Lionel Booth F1** 586
• Type facsimile.
[London: for Lionel Booth. 3 vols.]

1863–6 **William George Clark, John Glover and William Aldis Wright** 587

Cambridge 1
Works.
[Cambridge and London: Macmillan & Co.. 9 vols.]

1864 **Coriolanus** 588
• Photolithographic facsimile of F1 text, together with an edition of the play and extracts from North's Plutarch.
[London: John Russell Smith.]

Delius 3 589
Works.
• Text in English, with commentary in German.
[Elberfeld: Friderichs. 7 vols.]

[1864]   **Globe**   **590**
Works.
[Cambridge and London: Macmillan & Co.]

Thomas Keightley   **591**
Plays.
[London: Bell and Daldy. 6 vols.]

John B. Marsh, Reference Shakspere   **592**
Plays.
[London: Simpkin, Marshall & Co.; Manchester: John Heywood.]

1864–6   **Staunton facsimile**   **593**
• Facsimile of F1, using either photo–lithography or
photo–zincography.
[London: Day & Son. Issued serially from 1864, gathered into a
single volume, dated 1866]

1864–7   **Dyce 2**   **594**
Works.
[London: Chapman and Hall. 9 vols.]

1864–9 (?)   **Charles and Mary Cowden Clarke**   **595**
Plays.
[London: Cassell, Petter, and Galpin. Issued serially in 270 weekly
parts, gathered into 3 vols., undated]

1867   **Dicks**   **596, 597 (paper)**
• Bound in cloth, priced 2s. Subsequently reissued with a paper
cover as 'Dick's Shilling Shakespeare'.
[London: Dicks]

Knight, Pictorial   **598**
Works.
[London: Routledge. 8 vols.]

1868–97 **Clark and Wright/Clarendon**   **599**
• Series of individual editions (Clark worked on the first four
only), published as the Clarendon Shakespeare. Expurgated and
intended for use in schools.
600 *MV* (1868); **601** *R2* (1869); **602** *Mac.* (1869); **603** *Ham.* (1872);
604 *Tmp.* (1874); **605** *Lr.* (1875); **606** *AYL* (1877); **607** *MND*
(1877); **608** *JC* (1878); **609** *Cor.* (1879); **610** *R3* (1880); **611** *H5*
(1881); **612** *TN* (1885); **613** *Jn.* (1886); **614** *H8* (1891); **615** *Ado*
(1894); **616** *1H4* (1897).
[Oxford: Clarendon. 17 vols.]

1870–3 **Hudson** 617

• The revised edition of the *Variorum Handbook* adds an entry for this edition, noting that 'Later reissues bear the name "Hudson's School Shakespeare" on the spine. In fact these three volumes are an early run anticipating Hudson's single-vol. school editions of individual plays. Much if not most of the commentary that appears in those school eds . . . originates in these vols., and should be dated accordingly.' Details given here are taken from the Library of Congress online catalogue.

Plays.

[Boston: Ginn brothers. 3 vols.]

1870 (?) – 1911 (?) **William J. Rolfe** 618

• Considerable confusion seems to surround Rolfe's publishing ventures. Jaggard indicates forty octavo volumes published by Harpers between 1871 and 1896, but a more complex picture of overlapping projects (including revisions) is registered in the *Variorum Handbook*, which, *inter alia*, notes that the Folger 'owns 160 copies published by Harper and Bros. from 1872–1907' (p. 82, repeated in revised edition). As I have been unable to unravel these editions I have simply assigned a single number here.

1871–1928 **Horace H. Furness and Horace H. Furness Jnr., variorum project** 619

• See also 1936–55 and 1977– below.

620 *Rom.* (1871); **621, 622** *Mac.* (1873; revised edn, HHF jun., 1903); **623** *Ham.* (1877; 2 vols.); **624** *Lr.* (1880); **625** *Oth.* (1886); **626** *MV* (1888); **627** *AYL* (1890); **628** *Tmp.* (1892); **629** *MND* (1895); **630** *WT* (1898); **631** *Ado* (1899); **632** *TN* (1901); **633** *LLL* (1904); **634** *Ant.* (1907); **635** *R3* (1908; HHF jun.); **636** *JC* (1913; HHF jun.); **637** *Jn.* (1919; HHF jun.); **638** *Cor.* (1928; HHF jun.).

[Philadelphia: J. B. Lippincott & Co.]

1872 **Delius 4** 639

Works.

• Text in English, with commentary in German.

[Elberfeld: Friderichs. 2 vols.]

1872 (?)–83 **Charles E. Moberly *et al.*, Rugby** 640

• The volumes listed here are those included in the Folger collection. The total number corresponds with that suggested by the *Variorum Handbook*. The *Handbook* notes that the texts are heavily expurgated, but also notes that 'Furness quoted their commentaries extensively' (p. 83, repeated in revised edition).

641 *H5* (nd; Charles E. Moberly; title page says 'new edition'); **642** *AYL* (1872; Moberly; title page says 'new edition'); **643** *Cor.* (1872; R. Whitelaw); **644** *Mac.* (1872; Moberly); **645** *Ham.* (1873; Moberly); **646** *Lr.* (1876; Moberly); **647** *Tmp.* (1876; J. Surtees Phillpotts); **648** *Rom.* (1880; Moberly); **649** *MND* (1881; Moberly); **650** *Oth.* (1883; E. K. Purnell).

[London: Rivingtons. 10 vols.?]

1873–5 **Samuel Neil *et al.*, English Classics**   651

• All volumes undated. Date range here taken from the *Variorum Handbook* (p. 83 and revision). Texts in this series would appear to be simply a reissue of those in the Collins School and College Classics series (next entry), with different title pages and covers. The *Handbook* seems a touch confused about these two editions. It attributes the English Classics series to Morris *et al.*, but this is likely because Morris edited the first of the School and College Classics volumes. Assuming that the English Classics edition is a repackaged version of the School and College Classics edition, I have simply assigned one number to it here and I also assume that the full list of volumes is as given under School and College Classics below.

[London and Glasgow: William Collins, Sons, & Co. 15 vols.]

1873–9 **Samuel Neil *et al.*, Collins School and College Classics**   652

• See also previous entry.

653 *R2* (1873; D. Morris); **654** *MV* (1874; Morris); **655** *R3* (1874; William Lawson); **656** *H8* (1875; Lawson); **657** *Lr.* (1875; W. B. Kemshead); **658** *Tmp.* (1875; Morris); **659** *AYL* (1876; Samuel Neil); **660** *Mac.* (1876; Neil); **661** *Ham.* (1877; Neil); **662** *JC* (1877; Neil); **663** *Cor.* (1878; James Colville); **664** *H5* (1878; Neil); **665** *Jn.* (1878; F. G. Fleay); **666** *MND* (1878*; Neil); **667** *Rom.* (1879; Neil).

* The Folger also has a copy of this edition with an undated title page.

[London and Glasgow: William Collins, Sons, & Co. 15 vols.]

1875–6 **Dyce 3**   668

Works.

[London: Chapman & Hall. 9 vols.]

1875–8 **Collier 4**   669

• Includes *Edward III* – the first (?) collected Shakespeare edition to do so.

Works.

[Maidenhead: privately printed. Issued serially in forty-three parts to subscribers, gathered into 8 vols.]

1876 **Halliwell-Phillipps reduced facsimile** 670
• Produced using either photo–lithography or photo–zincography. Partially a reproduction of §593.
[London: Chatto & Windus.]

1877 **Leopold** 671
• Introduction by Frederick J. Furnivall. Includes *Edward III* and *Two Noble Kinsmen*.
[London, Paris and New York: Cassell, Petter & Galpin.]

1879 **Hamnet** 672
Plays.
• Edited by Allan Park Paton, who believed that capitals in the text of F1 provided an indication of where emphasis should be placed in lines – a theory sporadically revived during the course of the twentieth century. The edition was discontinued after ten volumes.
[Edinburgh: Edmonston. 10 vols.]

1879–91 **W. Wagner and L. Proescholdt** 673
Works.
• English text and notes.
[Hamburg: Karl Grädener. 12 vols.]

1880–1 **Hudson/Harvard** 674
Works.
[Boston: Ginn & Heath. 20 vols.]

1880 (?)–1891 (?) **W. Griggs and C. Prætorius quarto facsimiles** 675
• Photolithographic facsimiles. Most volumes were undated; where dates are provided they are included below. The series was numbered and texts are listed here in their number order. As in the case of the Ashbee–Halliwell sequence, *Titus Andronicus* (1594) was not included as it had not been discovered at the time of issuing of the series.

676 *Ham.* (1603; F. J. Furnivall); **677** *Ham.* (1604; Furnivall); **678** *MND* (1600; J. W. Ebsworth); **679** *MND* ('1600' – Pavier quarto; Furnivall); **680** *LLL* (1598; Furnivall); **681** *Wiv.* (1602; no. 6 – first edition, undated, but identified as 1881; P. A. Daniel); **682** *Wiv.* (no. 6 – second edition, dated 1888 on title page. Issued following the destruction of the greater part of the stock of the original edition in a fire at Griggs's warehouse. A different copy of the quarto was photographed for the second edition; Daniel); **683** *MV* ('1600' – Pavier quarto; Furnivall); **684** *1H4* (1598; Herbert Evans); **685** *2H4* (1600; Evans); **686** *PP* (1599; Edward Dowden); **687** *R3* (1597; Daniel); **688** *Ven.* (1593; Arthur Symons); **689** *Tro.* (1609; H. P. Stokes); **690** *Ado* (1600; Daniel); **691** *A Shrew* (1594; Furnivall); **692** *MV* (1600; Furnivall); **693** *R2* (1597 – Devonshire

copy; Daniel); **694** *R2* (1597 – Huth copy; W. A. Harrison); **695** *R2*
(1608; 1888; Harrison); **696** *R2* (1634; 1887; Daniel); **697** *Per.* (1609
– Q1; 1886; P. Z. Round); **698** *Per.* (1609 – Q2; 1886; Round); **699**
2H6 (*Whole Contention* 1; 1619; 1886; Furnivall); **700** *3H6* (*Whole
Contention* 2; 1619; 1886; Furnivall); **701** *Rom.* (1597; 1886; Evans);
702 *Rom.* (1599; 1886; Evans); **703** *H5* (1600; 1886; Symons); **704**
H5 (1608; 1886; Symons); **705** *Tit.* (1600; nd; Symons); **706** *Son.*
(1609; nd; Thomas Tyler); **707** *Oth.* (1622; 1885; Evans); **708** *Oth.*
(1630; 1885; Evans); **709** *Lr.* (1608; 1885; Daniel); **710** *Lr.* ('1608' –
Pavier quarto; 1885; Daniel); **711** *Luc.* (1594; nd; Furnivall); **712**
Rom. (nd; 1887; Evans); **713** *2H6* (*Contention*; 1594; 1889;
Furnivall); **714** *3H6* (*True Tragedy*; 1595; 1891; Tyler); **715** *Famous
Victories of Henry the Fifth* (1598; 1887; Daniel); **716** *Troublesome
Raigne of John, King of England* (1591; 1888; Furnivall); **717** *The
Second Part of the Troublesome Raigne of King John* (1591; 1888;
Furnivall); **718** *R3* (1602; 1888; Daniel); **719** *R3* (1622; 1889;
Daniel).

[London: W. Griggs/C. Prætorious. 43 vols., plus one volume
reissued]

1883   **White 2/Riverside**   **720, 721 (6 vols.)**
        Works.

        [Boston: Houghton, Mifflin & Co. . 3 vols.; also published in a
        six-volume set in the same year]

        Charles Wordsworth, History Plays 1   **722**
        [Edinburgh & London: Blackwood. 3 vols.]

1885   **Hamlet**   **723**
        • Edition by George MacDonald, based on F1 text, with Q2-only
        passages printed in smaller type at the foot of the page.

        [London: Longmans, Green]

1886–91 **E. K. Chambers *et al.*, Falcon**   **724**
        • A difficult edition to track. The Folger has seven of the volumes
        listed below: *JC*, *MV*, *1H4*, *R3*, *H5*, *Tmp.*, *Shr.* The British
        Library set is missing. The remaining records below are taken from
        the WorldCat database. WorldCat notes that the *Taming of the
        Shrew* lists a total of fourteen volumes for the series, including an
        edition of *As You Like It*, which it suggests may never have been
        issued.

        725 *JC* (1886; H. C. Beeching); **726** *MV* (1887; Beeching); **727**
        1H4 (1889; O. Elton;); **728** *2H4* (1889; A. D. Innes); **729** *R3* (1889;
        W. H. Payne Smith); **730** *TN* (1889; H. Howard Crawley); **731** *Ado*
        (1890; A. W. Verity); **732** *Cor.* (1890; Beeching); **733** *H5* (1890;
        Innes); **734** *Jn.* (1890; Elton); **735** *R2* (1891; E. K. Chambers); **736**
        Tmp. (1891; A. C. Liddell); **737** *Shr.* (1891; Crawley).

        [London: Rivingtons or Longmans, Green & Co. 13? vols.]

1887   **Halliwell-Phillipps reduced facsimile – US edition**   738
• American edition of §670.

[New York: Funk & Wagnalls]

1888–9 (?)   **National**   739
• Type facsimile. West, *First Folio*, volume I gives these dates.
British Library catalogue suggests 1904. All three volumes in the
British Library set (C.108.m.5) are date-stamped '11 Ja 1904'.

[London: William McKenzie. 3 vols.]

1888–90 **Henry Irving and Frank A. Marshall**   740
Works.

[London: Blackie & Son. 8 vols.]

1888–1905 (?)   **K. Deighton (and C. H. Tawney)**   **741 (Grey), 742 (Red)**
• It appears that the original issues were with grey covers, with
later reissues in red.

743 *Ado* (1888); **744** *H5* (1888); **745** *R3* (1888; Tawney); **746** *Cym.*
(1889); **747** *Oth.* (1889); **748** *Tmp.* (1889); **749** *TN* (1889); **750** *WT*
(1889); **751** *JC* (1890); **752** *Jn.* (1890); **753** *Mac.* (1890); **754** *MV*
(1890); **755** *R2* (1890); **756** *Ant.* (1891); **757** *AYL* (1891); **758** *Cor.*
(1891); **759** *Ham.* (1891); **760** *Lr.* (1891); **761** *MND* (1891); **762**
1H4 (1893); **763** *2H4* (1893); **764** *Rom.* (1893); **765** *H8* (1895); **766**
TGV (1905*).

* May possibly be a reissue, but no other date is recorded in the
copy examined.

[London: Macmillan. 24 vols.]

1888 – 1906   **Appleton Morgan, gen. ed., Bankside**   767
• Reprints of texts originally printed in quarto, with parallel F1
texts. The *Comedy of Errors* volume offers the F1 text in parallel
with the Globe text – it was intended as part of a projected issue of
sixteen volumes, which was not proceeded with. The listing here
indicates which quarto text was reproduced. See also Bankside
Restoration at 1907–8 below.

768 *Wiv.* (1602; 1888; Morgan); **769** *A Shrew* (1594; 1888; Albert
R. Frey); **770** *MV* (1600; 1888; William Reynolds); **771** *Tro.* (1609;
1889; Morgan); **772** *Rom.* (1597; 1889; B. Rush Field); **773** *Ado*
(1600; 1889; Wm. H. Fleming); **774** *Tit.* (1600; 1890; Morgan); **775**
MND (1600; 1890; Reynolds); **776** *Oth.* (1622; 1890; Thomas R.
Price); **777** *Lr.* (1608; 1890; Alvey Agustus Adee); **778** *Ham.* (1603;
1890; Edward P. Vining); **779** *1H4* (1598; 1890; Fleming); **780** *2H4*
(1600; 1891; Fleming); **781** *Per.* (1609; 1891; Morgan); **782** *R3*
(1597; 1891; Elias A. Calkins); **783** *H5* (1600; 1892; Henry Paine
Stokes); **784** *R2* (1597; 1892; Alfred Waites); **785** *The Life and
Death of King John* (1591; 1892; Morgan); **786** *2H6* (1594; 1892;

Charles W. Thomas); **787** *3H6* (1595; 1892; Morgan); **788** *LLL*
(1598; 1906; Isaac Hull Platt); **789** *Err.* (F1; 1894; Morgan).

[New York: Shakespeare Society of New York; London: Trübner &
Co. 22 vols.]

1890	**Ward & Lock's 'Sixpenny Shakespeare'**	**790**

[London and New York: Ward, Lock & Co.]

1890 – 1936 (?)   **A. W. Verity** *et al.*, **Pitt Press**   **791**
   • Between the Folger, National Library of Scotland and British
   Library, I have traced a total of seventeen vols., as below. Details
   for the Newbolt and Sampson *Romeo and Juliet* are taken from the
   National Library of Scotland online catalogue, as the volume itself
   could not be traced. As far as I can tell, the post 1905 volumes are
   first editions.

   792 *Ado* (1890); **793** *MND* (1893); **794** *TN* (1894); **795** *JC* (1895);
   796 *Son.* (1895); **797** *Tmp.* (1896); **798** *Lr.* (1897); **799** *MV* (1898);
   800 *AYL* (1899); **801** *R2* (1899); **802** *H5* (1900); **803** *Mac.* (1901);
   804 *Ham.* (1904); **805** *Cor.* (1905); **806** *Ado* (1923; George
   Sampson); **807** *Cym.* (1923); **808** *Rom.* (1936; arranged by Francis
   Newbolt, edited by Sampson).

   [Cambridge: Cambridge University Press. 17 vols?]

1891   **Hamlet**   **809**
   • Parallel text of Q1 and Q2, with the F1 text running across the
   bottom third of both pages. Edited by Wilhelm Vietor.

   [Marburg: N. G. Elwert'sche]

1891 (?)   **William James Craig, Oxford**   **810**
   Works.

   [Oxford: Clarendon Press.]

1891–3   **William Aldis Wright, Cambridge 2**   **811**
   Works.

   [London: Macmillan. 9 vols.]

1893   **Dallastype**   **812**
   • A facsimile of F1, using the 'Dallastype' photographic process.
   Fifty-seven parts were envisaged, but it seems unlikely that the
   project progressed very far. The British Library has just three
   parts: Preliminaries; part one of the *Tempest*; part two of the
   Tempest and part one of *Two Gentlemen of Verona*. Dallas clearly
   intended to spin off the photographic plates into a variety of
   different F1 publishing projects. In addition to the twin-text
   Tempest listed at 1895 below, the British Library also has a
   Dallastype facsimile of the complete F1 *Tempest* text (11764.m.12).

[1893] An advert on the final page of this latter volume indicates, under the title 'Scheme of Publication', that no fewer than fourteen versions of the project were envisioned.

[London: D. C. Dallas. Envisaged as 57 parts]

Charles Wordsworth, History Plays 2   813

[London: Remington. 3 vols.]

1893 (?) – 1938 (?) **Charles H. Herford, gen. ed., Warwick**   814

• Later texts here do not appear to be either reissues or second editions. Perhaps the series lapsed and was revived? The Folger has eighteen titles and a search at the British Library yielded a further six, a total of twenty-four. *Variorum Handbook* (revised edition) suggests a speculative total of twenty-five volumes. A search on WorldCat provided details of a further volume: *Othello*. Details for this volume are taken from WorldCat. See also the note on Herford's Heath's [American] Arden below.

815 *Ado* (nd; J. C. Smith); **816** *Ham.* (nd; E. K. Chambers); **817** *H5* (nd; G. C. Moore Smith); **818** *H8* (nd; D. Nichol Smith); **819** *Mac.* (nd; Chambers); **820** *MND* (nd; Chambers); **821** *R3* (nd; George Macdonald); **822** *TN* (nd; Arthur D. Innes); **823** *JC* (1893; Innes); **824** *R2* (1893; C. H. Herford); **825** *AYL* (1894; J. C. Smith); **826** *Cym.* (1897; Alfred J. Wyatt); **827** *MV* (1897; H. L. Withers); **828** *Tmp.* (1897; F. S. Boas); **829** *Cor.* (1898; Chambers); **830** *Jn.* (1900; G. C. Moore Smith); **831** *Lr.* (1902; D. Nichol Smith); **832** *1H4* (1904; Frederick W. Moorman); **833** *Oth.* (1920; Herford); **834** *WT* (1926; Herford); **835** *2H4* (1928; Herford); **836** *Ant.* (1934; A. E. Morgan and W. Sherard Vines); **837** *LLL* (1936; Morgan and Vines); **838** *Rom.* (1936; J. E. Crofts); **839** *Tro.* (1938; Bonamy Dobrée).

[London: Blackie & Son. 25? vols.]

1894–6 **Israel Gollancz, Temple**   840

[London: J. M. Dent & Co. 40 vols.]

1895   **Tempest – Dallastype**   841

• 'Edited with a glossarial index by Frederick A. Hyndman and D. C. Dallas', with an introduction by F. J. Furnivall. Modern text drawn from a Charles Knight edition faces a facsimile of F1. Probably intended as the first number of a series – the end pages include an advert for a *Merry Wives* volume 'To be published December 1895 uniform with the Present Work.' However, the British Library catalogue indicates 'no more published'. See also 1893 above.

[London: George Redway]

1895 (?) – 1932 (?)   **Charles H. Herford, Heath's [American] Arden**   842

　　• This is a difficult series to track. The Folger set is incomplete and
　　I have been unable to locate a set of the texts at the British Library,
　　Library of Congress or National Library of Scotland. The details
　　provided here are taken from WorldCat, which lists a total of 155
　　records for Heath's Arden series. Dates given are, as far as can be
　　established, for the first edition of each volume, though this may
　　not be wholly accurate in each instance. In the latter stages of the
　　project, Heath's began re-issuing the original texts with revisions
　　by other scholars; these revised volumes are not listed here. A clear
　　relationship would appear to exist between this series and
　　Herford's 'Warwick Shakespeare' (see above). Both series would
　　seem to have been interrupted in 1904; the Arden resumed in 1913,
　　but the Warwick seems not to have recommenced until 1920.
　　Before 1904, the series mirror each other very closely – almost
　　all matching volumes have the same editor and the dates of issue
　　are very close. After the hiatus, the series diverge. Some
　　Americanisation of the language occurs in the Arden texts.

　　843 *Ado* (date unknown; J. C. Smith); **844** *AYL* (1895; Arthur D.
　　Innes); **845** *Ham.* (1895; E. K. Chambers); **846** *JC* (1896; Innes);
　　847 *R3* (1896; George MacDonald); **848** *TN* (1896; Innes); **849**
　　Cym. (1897; Alfred John Wyatt); **850** *MND* (1898; Chambers); **851**
　　MV (1898; H. L. Withers); **852** *H5* (1899; G. C. Moore Smith);
　　853 *Mac.* (1899; Chambers); **854** *Tmp.* (1899; Frederic S. Boas);
　　855 *Cor.* (1900; Chambers); **856** *H8* (1900?; David Nichol Smith);
　　857 *Jn.* (1900?; G. C. M. Smith); **858** *R2* (1900?; Herford); **859**
　　Tim. (1900?; Ernest Hunter Wright); **860** *Lr.* (1902; D. N. Smith);
　　861 *1H4* (1904; Frederic William Moorman); **862** *Rom.* (1913;
　　Robert Adger Law); **863** *WT* (1915; H. B. Charlton); **864** *LLL*
　　(1917; Charlton); **865** *2H4* (1918; L. Winstanley); **866** *Oth.* (1924;
　　Herford and Raymond MacDonald); **867** *Ant.* (1926; Harold
　　Newcomb Hillebrand); **868** *Err.* (1928; Thomas Whitfield
　　Baldwin); **869** *TGV* (1931; Charles Washburn Nichols); **870** *Tro.*
　　(1932; Robert Metcalf Smith).

　　[New York: D. C. Heath. 28? vols.]

1896　　**Thomas Donovan, English History Plays**   871

　　• 'Taking Shakespeare's ten chronicles as a basis, nearly all the
　　gaps that he left in the continuity of his English history are here
　　filled in with plays written by his contemporaries' (Preface, v).
　　Plays are condensed for performance. Includes, in vol. I: *Jn*;
　　Edward III; *R2*; *1* and *2H4*, condensed as a single play; *H5*; in vol.
　　II: *1H6*; *2H6*; *3H6*; *R3*; *H8*.

　　[London: Macmillan. 2 vols.]

1899   **Charles H. Herford, Eversley**   872
        Works.
        [London: Macmillan. 10 vols.]

1899 – 1931 **(Edward Dowden) W. J. Craig and R. H. Case, gen eds.,**
             Arden 1   873

   874 *Ham.* (1899; Dowden); **875** *Rom.* (1900; Dowden); **876** *Lr.*
   (1901; Craig); **877** *Tmp.* (1901; Morton Luce); **878** *JC* (1902;
   Michael Macmillan); **879** *Cym.* (1903; Dowden); **880** *H5* (1903;
   Herbert Arthur Evans); **881** *MM* (1903; H. C. Hart); **882** *Oth.*
   (1903; Hart); **883** *AWW* (1904; W. Osborne Brigstocke); **884** *Shr.*
   (1904; R. Warwick Bond); **885** *Tit.* (1904; H. Bellyse Baildon); **886**
   Wiv. (1904; Hart); **887** *MND* (1905; Henry Cunningman); **888** *MV*
   (1905; Charles Knox Pooler); **889** *Tim.* (1905; K. Deighton); **890**
   Ant. (1906; Case); **891** *LLL* (1906; Hart); **892** *TGV* (1906;
   Warwick Bond); **893** *TN* (1906; Morton Luce); **894** *Tro.* (1906;
   Deighton); **895** *Err.* (1907; Cunningham); **896** *Jn.* (1907; Ivor B.
   John); **897** *Per.* (1907; Deighton); **898** *R3* (1907; A. Hamilton
   Thompson); **899** *1H6* (1909; Hart); **900** *2H6* (1909; Hart); **901** *3H6*
   (1909; Hart); **902** *Ven., Luc., PP, PhT* (1911; Pooler); **903** *Mac.*
   (1912; Cunningham); **904** *R2* (1912; John); **905** *WT* (1912; F. W.
   Moorman); **906** *AYL* (1914; J. W. Holme); **907** *1H4* (1914; R. P.
   Crowl and A. E. Morgan); **908** *H8* (1915; Pooler); **909** *Son.* and *LC*
   (1918; Pooler); **910** *Cor.* (1922; Craig and Case); **911** *2H4* (1923;
   R. P. Crowl); **912** *Ado* (1924; Grace R. Trenery).
   [London: Methuen. 39 vols.]

1901–4 **W. E. Henley [and Walter Raleigh], Edinburgh Folio**   913
        • Issued in a limited edition of 1,000 numbered copies.
        Works
        [London: Grant Richards. Forty parts for 10 vols.]

1902   **Lee F1 facsimile**   914
        • Collotype facsimile, introduction by Sidney Lee. Lee's *Census*
        was issued as a matching volume.
        [Oxford: Clarendon Press]

1903   **Charlotte Porter and Helen A. Clarke, Pembroke**   915
        Works
        [New York: Thomas Y. Crowell. 13 vols.]

1903–12 **Charlotte Porter and Helen A. Clarke, American First Folio**   916
         [New York: Thomas Y. Crowell & Co. 40 vols.]

1904   **Methuen F4 facsimile**   917
        • Produced using photo-zincography.
        [London: Methuen]

[1904]   **Personal Shakespeare**   918
• Introduction by Esther Wood, biographical study by Goldwin Smith. Added to the revised edition of the *Variorum Handbook*, which characterises it as an 'early critical old-spelling ed., presenting an edited F1 text with additions from the "earliest complete" Qq in the places where the Globe ed. makes such additions, and with Globe stage directions'. Details here taken from WorldCat.

[New York: Doubleday, Page & Co. 15 vols.]

1904–7   **[A. H. Bullen,] Stratford**   919
Works.

[Stratford: Shakespeare Head Press; New York: Duffield & Company. 10 vols.]

[1904–8] **E. K. Chambers, Red Letter**   920, 921 (Gresham reissue)
• According to the *Variorum Handbook* (p. 88, repeated in revised edition), this series was originally issued by Blackie, then reissued, possibly using the same plates, by Gresham.

[London: Blackie/Gresham. 39 vols.]

1904 and 1908–12   **F. J. Furnivall, W. G. Boswell-Stone**
                    (and F. W. Clarke), Old Spelling   922
• *Variorum Handbook* notes that the series 'was discontinued, then picked up by another publisher' (p. 88, repeated in revised edition). *Love's Labour's Lost* was reissued by the new publisher in 1907 and so is included here twice. The revised edition of the *Variorum Handbook* suggests '13 (17?) vols.'. I have seen twelve at the British Library. WorldCat adds a further two – *Comedy of Errors* and *Midsummer Night's Dream* – in addition to the 1907 *Love's Labour's Lost*. Details of these three volumes are taken from WorldCat.

923 *LLL* (1904); **924** *LLL* (1907); **925** *Ado* (1908); **926** *AWW* (1908); **927** *AYL* (1908); **928** *Err.* (1908); **929** *MND* (1908); **930** *MV* (1908); **931** *Tmp.* (1908); **932** *Wiv.* (1908); **933** *WT* (1908); **934** *1H4* (1909); **935** *2H4* (1909); **936** *Jn.*(1909); **937** *H5* (1912).

[*LLL* (1904): London: Alexander Moring; other volumes: London: Chatto; New York: Duffield & Co.]

1904 (?)–1924 (?)   **William Briggs, gen ed. (University) Tutorial**   938
• *Variorum Handbook* (both editions) does not specify number of volumes. The listing here is a combination of Folger and British Library holdings. Two different editions of both *R3* and *Rom.* would appear to have been issued.

939 *Ado* (nd; S. E. Goggin); **940** *Ant.* (nd; F. Allen); **941** *AWW* (nd; A. J. F. Collins); **942** *Cor.* (nd; Collins); **943** *Cym.* (nd; A. R. Weekes); **944** *Err.* (nd; D. J. Donovan); **945** *Ham.* (nd; Goggin);

946 *1H4* (nd; Collins); **947** *2H4* (nd; Collins); **948** *H5* (nd; Collins); **949** *H8* (nd; G. E. Hollingworth); **950** *Jn.* (nd; Collins); **951** *Lr.* (nd; Goggin); **952** *Mac.* (nd; Goggin); **953** *MND* (nd; A. F. Watt); **954** *MV* (nd; Goggin); **955** *Oth.* (nd; Donovan); **956** *R2* (nd; Watt); **957** *R3** (nd; B. I. Evans); **958** *R3** (nd; William J. Rolfe); **959** *Rom.** (nd; Evans) **960** *Rom.** (nd; Rolfe); **961** *Shr.* (nd; Donovan); **962** *TGV* (nd; R. W. Faint); **963** *Tmp.* (nd; Weekes); **964** *TN* (nd; H. C. Duffin); **965** *WT* (nd; Collins); **966** *AYL* (1909; Weekes); **967** *JC* (1909; Watt); **968** *LLL* (1924; M. M. Wheale).

[London: W. B. Clive, University Tutorial Press. 28 plays, 30 vols.?]

1905	**George Brandes, Garrick**	969

Works.

[London: Heinemann. 12 vols.]

Lucrece facsimile	970

• Produced by Sidney Lee

[Oxford: Clarendon Press]

Methuen F3b facsimile	971

[London: Methuen]

Venus and Adonis facsimile	972

• Produced by Sidney Lee

[Oxford: Clarendon Press]

1906	**William Allan Neilson**	973

Works.

[Boston and New York: Houghton Mifflin]

1906–9	**Sidney Lee, gen. ed., Renaissance**	974

• Annotations and general introduction by Sidney Lee; introductions by various others, as indicated below. Individual volumes are numbered; the order of listing here is that of the volume numbers.

975 *Err.* (1907; Edmund Gosse); **976** *TGV* (1907; Richard Garnett); **977** *LLL* (1907; Lee); **978** *MV* (1907; Theodore Watts-Dunton); **979** *AWW* (1907; Andrew Lang); **980** *MND* (1907; George E. Woodberry); **981** *Shr.* (1907; Alice Meynell); **982** *Wiv.* (1907; Austin Dobson); **983** *Ado* (1907; Hamilton W. Mabie); **984** *AYL* (1907; George P. Baker); **985** *TN* (1907; Maurice Hewlett); **986** *MM* (1907; Andrew J. George); **987** *Per.* (1907; Algernon Charles Swinburne); **988** *Cym.* (1907; Arthur Symons); **989** *WT* (1907; Jean Jules Jusserand); **990** *Tmp.* (1907; Henry James); **991** *1H6* (1907; Adolphus William Ward); **992** *2H6* (1907; Ward); **993** *3H6* (1907; Ward); **994** *R3* (1907; William P. Trent);

995 *R2* (1907; George Saintsbury); **996** *Jn.* (1907; Garnett); **997** *1H4* (1908; Augustine Birrell); **998** *2H4* (1908; Birrell); **999** *H5* (1908; Lee); **1000** *H8* (1908; Edward Dowden); **1001** *Rom.* (1908; J. Churton Collins); **1002** *Tit.* (1908; Brander Matthews); **1003** *JC* (1908; Lee); **1004** *Ham.* (1908; George Santayana); **1005** *Tro.* (1908; Walter Raleigh); **1006** *Oth.* (1908; William E. Henley); **1007** *Mac.* (1908; Henry Charles Beeching); **1008** *Lr.* (1908; William Archer); **1009** *Tim.*(1908; Herbert Paul); **1010** *Ant.* (1908; Lee); **1011** *Cor.* (1909; Lee); **1012** *Son.* (1909; John Davidson); **1013** *Poems I* (*Ven.*, *Luc.*, *PP*; 1909; Alfred Austin, for all poems); **1014** *Poems II* (*LC*, *PhT*; 1909).

[New York: George D. Sproul. 40 vols.]

1906 (?) – 1926 (?)   **Hudson, Ebenezer C. Black** *et al.*, **New Hudson**   1015

• Introduction and notes taken from Henry Norman Hudson. This is the full extent of the British Library holdings. The Folger has fewer volumes.

1016 *AYL* (1906; Black and Andrew Jackson George); **1017** *MV* (1906; Black and George); **1018** *H5* (1908; Black and George); **1019** *JC* (1908; Black and George); **1020** *Mac.* (1908; Black and George); **1021** *Err.* (1909; Black and George); **1022** *Ham.* (1909; Black and George); **1023** *MND* (1910; Black and Moses Grant Daniell); **1024** *Lr.* (1911; Black); **1025** *TN* (1911; Black); **1026** *Ado* (1914; Black); **1027** *R2* (1916; Black); **1028** *R3* (1916; Black); **1029** *Cor.* (1916; Black); **1030** *Rom.* (1916; Black); **1031** *Jn.* (1916; Black); **1032** *1H4* (1922; Black); **1033** *2H4* (1924; Black); **1034** *Oth.* (1926; Black and Agnes Knox Black).

[Boston: Ginn & Co. 19 vols.?]

1907–8   **Morgan, gen. ed., Bankside Restoration**   1035

• Restoration adaptations printed on facing pages with the equivalent Shakespeare text (generally F1). See also Bankside at 1888–1906 above.

1036 Shadwell *Timon* (1678; 1907; Willis Vickery); **1037** Dryden *All for Love* (1678; 1908; Francis A. Smith); **1038** D'Avenant, *Law against Lovers* (1662; 1908; Frank Carpenter); **1039** conjectural Kyd *Hamlet* facing Q2 *Hamlet* (1908; Morgan); **1040** Dryden *Tempest* (1676; 1908; Frederick W. Kilbourne).

[New York: Shakespeare Society of New York. 5 vols.]

1909   **Methuen F2 facsimile**   1041

[London: Methuen]

1910   **W. W. Greg, Shakespeare's Merry Wives of Windsor 1602**   1042

[Oxford: Clarendon]

1910 (?) – 1918 (?)   **J. H. Lobban, Granta**   **1043**

> • This has been a difficult edition to track. The Folger does not appear to possess a complete set and the British Library set is missing. *Variorum Handbook* does not specify number of volumes (either edition). Details provided here are taken from the WorldCat database.
>
> **1044** *WT* (1910); **1045** *Mac.* (1911); **1046** *TN* (1911); **1047** *MND* (1913); **1048** *MV* (1913); **1049** *JC* (1915); **1050** *Ado* (1916); **1051** *Cym.* (1916); **1052** *Tmp.* (1916); **1053** *Ant.* (1917); **1054** *Cor.* (1917); **1055** *H5* (1917); **1056** *R2* (1918).
>
> [Cambridge: Cambridge University Press. 13 vols.?]

1911–12 **W. J. Craig, Oxford**   **1057**

> Works.
>
> [London: Oxford University Press. 3 vols.]

1911–13 **William A. Neilson and Ashley H. Thorndike, gen. eds., Tudor**   **1058**

> **1059** *AYL* (1911; Martha Hale Shackford); **1060** *1H4* (1911; Frank Wadleigh Chandler); **1061** *H5* (1911; Lewis F. Mott); **1062** *1H6* (1911; Louise Pound); **1063** *Mac.* (1911; Arthur C. L. Brown); **1064** *MV* (1911; Harry Morgan Ayres); **1065** *Rom.* (1911; Neilson and Thorndike); **1066** *Ado* (1912; William W. Lawrence); **1067** *AWW* (1912; John J. Lowes); **1068** *Cor.* (1912; Stuart P. Sherman); **1069** *Err.* (1912; Frederick Morgan Padelford); **1070** *2H4* (1912; Elizabeth Deering Hanscom); **1071** *H8* (1912; Charles G. Dunlap); **1072** *Jn.* (1912; Henry M. Belden); **1073** *LLL* (1912; James F. Royster); **1074** *Lr.* (1912; Virginia C. Gildersleeve); **1075** *MM* (1912; Edgar C. Morris); **1076** *MND* (1912; John W. Cunliffe); **1077** *Oth.* (1912; Thomas M. Parrott); **1078** *R2* (1912; Hardin Craig); **1079** *R3* (1912; George B. Churchill); **1080** *Shr.* (1912; Frederick Tupper Jr.); **1081** *TGV* (1912; Martin W. Sampson); **1082** *TN* (1912; Walter Morris Hart); **1083** *Tro.* (1912; John S. P. Tatlock); **1084** *WT* (1912; Laura J. Wylie); **1085** *Ant.* (1913; George Wyllys Benedict); **1086** *Cym.* (1913; Will D. Howe); **1087** *Ham.* (1913; George Pierce Baker); **1088** *2H6* (1913; Charles H. Barnwell); **1089** *3H6* (1913; Robert Adger Law); **1090** *JC* (1913; Robert M. Lovett); **1091** *Per.* (1913; C. Alphonso Smith); **1092** *Son.* and *LC* (1913; Raymond M. Alden); **1093** *Tim.* (1913; Robert Huntington Fletcher); **1094** *Tit.* (1913; Elmer Edgar Stoll); **1095** *Tmp.* (1913; Herbert E. Greene); **1096** *Ven., Luc. and other poems* [*PP, PhT*] (1913; Carleton Brown); **1097** *Wiv.* (1913; Fred P. Emery).
>
> [New York: Macmillan. 39 vols.]

1917–28 **Wilbur L. Cross and C. F. Tucker Brooke (and Willard**   **1098**
Higley Durham), gen. eds., Yale

1099 *Ado* (1917; Brooke); **1100** *Ham.* (1917; Jack R. Crawford);
1101 *1H4* (1917; Samuel B. Hemingway); **1102** *Lr.* (1917; William
Lyon Phelps); **1103** *Rom.* (1917; Durham); **1104** *H5* (1918; Robert
D. French); **1105** *1H6* (1918; Brooke); **1106** *Mac.* (1918; Charlton
M. Lewis); **1107** *MND* (1918; Durham); **1108** *Oth.* (1918;
Lawrence Mason); **1109** *Tmp.* (1918; Chauncey B. Tinker); **1110**
WT (1918; Frederick E. Pierce); **1111** *AYL* (1919; Crawford); **1112**
JC (1919; Mason); **1113** *Tim.* (1919; Stanley T. Williams); **1114**
Ant. (1921; Henry Seidel Canby); **1115** *2H4* (1921; Hemingway);
1116 *R2* (1921; Llewellyn M. Buell); **1117** *Shr.* (1921; Henry Ten
Eyck Perry); **1118** *Wiv.* (1922; George van Santvoord); **1119** *TN*
(1922; George Henry Nettleton); **1120** *2H6* (1923; Brooke); **1121**
3H6 (1923; Brooke); **1122** *MV* (1923; Phelps); **1123** *Son.* (1923;
Edward Bliss Reed); **1124** *Cor.* (1924; Brooke); **1125** *Cym.* (1924;
Hemingway); **1126** *TGV* (1924; Karl Young); **1127** *H8* (1925; John
M. Berdan and Brooke); **1128** *LLL* (1925; Cross and Brooke); **1129**
Per. (1925; Alfred R. Bellinger); **1130** *AWW* (1926; Arthur E.
Case); **1131** *Err.* (1926; French); **1132** *MM* (1926; Durham);
1133 *Tit.* (1926; A. M. Witherspoon); **1134** *Jn.* (1927; Williams);
1135 *R3* (1927; Crawford); **1136** *Tro.* (1927; N. Burton Paradise);
1137 *Ven., Luc. and the minor poems* (1928; Albert Feuillerat).

[New Haven: Yale University Press. 39 vols.]

1921–66 **(Arthur Quiller-Couch and) John Dover Wilson, gen. ed.,**   **1138**
New Shakespeare

• Quiller-Couch withdrew from the project in 1925.

1139 *Tmp.* (1921); **1140** *TGV* (1921); **1141** *Wiv.* (1921); **1142** *Err.*
(1922); **1143** *MM* (1922); **1144** *Ado* (1923); **1145** *LLL* (1923); **1146**
MND (1924); **1147** *AYL* (1926); **1148** *MV* (1926); **1149** *Shr.*
(1928); **1150** *AWW* (1929); **1151** *TN* (1930); **1152** *WT* (1931); **1153**
Ham. (1934); **1154** *Jn.* (1936); **1155** *R2* (1939); **1156** *1H4* (1946);
1157 *2H4* (1946); **1158** *H5* (1947); **1159** *Mac.* (1947); **1160** *Tit.*
(1948); **1161** *JC* (1949); **1162** *Ant.* (1950); **1163** *1H6* (1952); **1164**
2H6 (1952); **1165** *3H6* (1952); **1166** *R3* (1954); **1167** *Rom.* (1955;
George Ian Duthie and Wilson); **1168** *Per.* (1956; J. C. Maxwell);
1169 *Oth.* (1957; Alice Walker and Wilson); **1170** *Tim.* (1957;
Maxwell); **1171** *Tro.* (1957; Walker); **1172** *Cor.* (1960); **1173**
Cym. (1960; Maxwell); **1174** *Lr.* (1960; Duthie and Wilson);
1175 *H8* (1962; Maxwell); **1176** *Son.* (1966); **1177** *Poems*
(1966).

[Cambridge: Cambridge University Press. 39 vols.]

1925–29 (?) **George B. Harrison and Francis H. Pritchard,** 1178
            'New Readers'

• *Variorum Handbook* (either edition) does not indicate number of volumes. The listing here is a combination of the Folger and British Library holdings.

1179 *AYL* (1925); **1180** *H5* (1925); **1181** *JC* (1925); **1182** *Lr.* (1925); **1183** *Mac.* (1925); **1184** *MND* (1925); **1185** *MV* (1925); **1186** *R2* (1925); **1187** *Tmp.* (1925); **1188** *TN* (1925); **1189** *Ado* (1926); **1190** *Cor.* (1926); **1191** *Ham.* (1926); **1192** *1H4* (1926); **1193** *2H4* (1926); **1194** *WT* (1926); **1195** *Jn.* (1927); **1196** *Oth.* (1927); **1197** *Wiv.* (1928); **1198** *Shr.* (1929).

[London: George G. Harrap & Co. 20 vols.?]

1925–47 (?) **Henry Newbolt, gen. ed., Teaching of English Series** 1199

• The Folger has thirteen volumes; the British Library has the same thirteen, together with an additional eight, giving a total of twenty-one, as below. The edition of *Romeo and Juliet* listed below has a different style cover from the other texts in the series and does not include the series title. It does, however, include the usual 'General Editor's Preface'. The copyright page indicates that the edition was 'First published, June 1937'. From an advert on the back cover of this text it would appear that the series was repackaged as 'Nelson's Sixpenny Shakespeare', with the general editorship attributed to Richard Wilson. The 6*d.* texts had paper covers rather than the original cloth.

1200 *R3* (1923; Evelyn Smith); **1201** *1H4* (1925; Smith); **1202** *Mac.* (1925; Smith); **1203** *MND* (1925; Smith); **1204** *R2* (1925; Newbolt); **1205** *Ado* (1926; Smith); **1206** *AYL* (1926; Smith); **1207** *Cor.* (1926; Smith); **1208** *JC* (1926; John Hampden); **1209** *Lr.* (1926; Smith); **1210** *MV* (1926; Smith); **1211** *Tmp.* (1926; Hampden); **1212** *TN* (1926; Smith); **1213** *H5* (1927; Smith); **1214** *2H4* (1928; Hampden); **1215** *H8* (1928; Smith); **1216** *Jn.* (1928; Hampden); **1217** *Ham.* (1930; Hampden); **1218** *Rom.* (1937; A. J. J. Ratcliff); **1219** *Oth.* (1941; Nora Ratcliff); **1220** *Ant.* (1947; Nora Ratcliff).

[London and Edinburgh: Thomas Nelson & Sons]

1930 **John Dover Wilson, Hamlet** 1221

• Produced as a limited edition, with illustrations by Edward Gordon Craig. Details here taken from British Library online catalogue.

[Weimar: Cranach]

1934–6 **Maurice R. Ridley, New Temple** 1222

• Forty volumes of texts were issued, together with an additional volume: *William Shakespeare: A Commentary*, by Ridley and John Norman Bryson (1936).

[London: J. M. Dent; New York: E. P. Dutton. 40 vols.]

1935–7   **Guy Boas, gen. ed., New Eversley**   1223
1224 *Ant.* (1935; Boas); **1225** *Cor.* (1935; V. de Sola Pinto); **1226**
Ham. (1935; Adrian Alington); **1227** *1H4* (1935; M. Alderton
Pink); **1228** *2H4* (1935; Pink); **1229** *H5* (1935; Dorothy Margaret
Stuart and E. V. Davenport); **1230** *JC* (1935; F. Allen); **1231** *Lr.*
(1935; F. E. Budd); **1232** *Mac.* (1935; Pink); **1233** *MND* (1935; ed.
C. Aldred, intro. Walter de la Mare); **1234** *MV* (1935; P. H. B.
Lyon); **1235** *Oth.* (1935; Boas); **1236** *R2* (1935; ed. Lionel Aldred,
intro. St. John Irvine); **1237** *Rom.*(1935; Boas); **1238** *Tmp.* (1935;
Edward Thompson); **1239** *TN* (1935; N. V. Meeres); **1240** *WT*
(1935; Boas); **1241** *Ado* (1936; Budd); **1242** *AYL* (1936; Cicely
Boas); **1243** *Cym.* (1936; Boas); **1244** *R3* (1936; Lionel Aldred);
1245 *H8* (1937; ed. M. St. Clare Byrne, intro. Boas); **1246** *Jn.*
(1937; Meeres).
[London: Macmillan. 23 vols.]

1936   **Titus Andronicus**   1247
• The first quarto of *Titus* was discovered in 1904. This facsimile,
produced for the Folger Shakespeare Library, was the first such
edition of the text to be published.
[New York and London: Charles Scribner's Sons]

George Lyman Kittredge   1248
Works.
[Boston: Ginn]

1936–41   **Karl J. Holzknecht and Norman E. McClure, Selected**   1249
Plays
Vol. I: *R2*; *1H4*; *Ado*; *JC*; *Ham.*; *WT.*
Vol. II: *Err.*; *Rom.*; *MND*; *H5*; *Lr.*; *Ant.*; *Tmp.*
Vol. III: *R3*; *AYL*; *TN*; *Oth.*; *Mac.*; *Cym..*
Vol. IV: *Jn.*; *MV*; *MM*; *Cor.*; *H8*; *Son.*
[New York: American Book Co.; London: Appleton-Century.
4 vols.]

1936–55   **C. F. Tucker Brooke, Joseph Q. Adams, Mathias A. Shaaber,**
Felix E. Schelling, George Lyman Kittredge, gen. eds.,
New Variorum Shakespeare   1250
• See also 1871–1928 above and 1977– below.

1251 *1H4* (1936; Samuel Burdett Hemingway); **1252** *Poems* (1938;
Hyder Edward Rollins); **1253** *2H4* (1940; Matthias A. Shaaber);
1254 *Tro.* (1953; Harold N. Hillebrand); **1255** *R2* (1955; Matthew
W. Black).
[Philadelphia: Lippincott]

1937–59 **G. B. Harrison, Penguin 1**   **1256**
Works.
[Harmondsworth: Penguin. 37 vols. – *1*, *2*, and *3H6* in one volume]

1938–70 **Ralph E. C. Houghton, gen. ed., New Clarendon**   **1257**
• Details of *Othello* volume taken from WorldCat.
1258 *JC* (1938; Houghton); **1259** *MV* (1938; Ronald F. W.
Fletcher); **1260** *R2* (1938; John M. Lothian); **1261** *TN* (1938; J. C.
Dent); **1262** *Mac.* (1939; Bernard Groom); **1263** *MND* (1939; F. C.
Horwood); **1264** *Tmp.* (1939; J. R. Sutherland); **1265** *AYL* (1941;
Isabel J. Bisson); **1266** *H5* (1941; Fletcher); **1267** *2H4* (1946;
William R. Rutland); **1268** *Ham.* (1947; George Rylands); **1269**
Rom. (1947; Houghton); **1270** *1H4* (1952; Bertram Newman); **1271**
Ado (1954; Philip Wayne); **1272** *Cor.* (1954; B. H. Kemball-Cook);
1273 *WT* (1956; S. L. Bethell); **1274** *Lr.* (1957; Houghton); **1275**
Ant. (1962; Houghton); **1276** *R3* (1965; Houghton); **1277** *Oth.*
(1968; Horwood and Ralph Edward Cunliffe); **1278** *MM* (1970;
Houghton).
[Oxford: Clarendon. 21 vols.?]

1939–40 **Herbert Farjeon, Limited Editions Club**   **1279**
• Individual volumes provide either 'The text of the First Folio,
with Quarto insertions, edited and amended where obscure by
Herbert Farjeon' or 'The text of the First Folio edited and
amended where obscure by Herbert Farjeon'. Commentary is
provided on a folded sheet inserted in each volume. Only 1950
copies were issued.
[New York: Limited Editions Club. 37 vols.]

1939–75 **W. W. Greg and Charlton Hinman quarto facsimiles**   **1280**
• Volumes were numbered. Order followed here is that of the
numbering system.
1281 *Lr.* (1608, Pied Bull; 1939); **1282** *MV* (1600, Hayes; 1939);
1283 *Wiv.* (1602; 1939); **1284** *Ham.* (1604/5; 1940, reissued
Clarendon, 1964); **1285** *Per.* (1609; 1940); **1286** *Rom.* (1599; 1949);
1287 *Ham.* (1603; 1951); **1288** *Tro.* (1609; 1952); **1289** *H5* (1600;
1957); **1290** *LLL* (1598; 1957); **1291** *3H6* (1595; 1958); **1292** *R3*
(1597; 1959); **1293** *R2* (1597; 1966); **1294** *1H4* (1598; 1966); **1295**
Ado (1600; 1971); **1296** *Oth.* (1622; 1975).
[London: Shakespeare Association and Sidgwick & Jackson. From
1957, Oxford: Clarendon Press. 16 vols.]

1942 **William Allan Neilson and Charles Jarvis Hill**   **1297**
Works.
[Cambridge, MA: Houghton Mifflin]

1944   **Viking Portable Shakespeare**   1298
• The text used is that of Kittredge's 1936 edition (§1248).
Originally issued by Viking in 1944 and subsequently reissued a
number of times. The text was issued by Penguin in 1977. I have
been unable to track down a copy of the Viking original. Details
here taken from the Penguin edition.

Complete text of: *Ham., Mac., Rom., JC, MND, AYL, Tmp.*
Selections from: *MV, Oth., TN, Shr., Lr., TGV, MM, Ado, LLL,
AWW, WT, Jn., R2, Wiv., 1H4, 2H4, H5, 1H6, 2H6, 3H6, R3,
H8, Tro., Cor., Ant.* Songs from the plays. Sonnets.

[New York: Viking; subsequently Harmondsworth: Penguin]

1946   **Kittredge, Sixteen Plays of Shakespeare**   1299
• Plays issued individually, 1939–45, then collected into a single
volume. Plays included are (in order of appearance in the collected
volume): *Tmp., Ado, MND, MV, AYL, TN, R2, 1H4, H5, Rom.,
JC, Mac., Ham., Lr., Oth., Ant.*

[Boston: Ginn & Co.]

1951   **Peter Alexander**   1300
Works.

[London and Glasgow: Collins]

Hardin Craig   1301
Works.

[Chicago, Atlanta, Dallas, New York: Scott, Foresman & Co.]

1951–82 **Una Ellis-Fermor, Harold F. Brooks, Harold Jenkins,   1302
Brian Morris, gen. eds., Arden 2**
1303 *LLL* (1951; Richard David); **1304** *Mac.* (1951; Kenneth
Muir); **1305** *Lr.* (1952; Muir); **1306** *Tit.* (1953; J. C. Maxwell);
1307 *Ant.* (1954; M. R. Ridley); **1308** *H5* (1954; J. H. Walter);
1309 *Jn.* (1954; E. A. J. Honigmann); **1310** *Tmp.* (1954; Frank
Kermode); **1311** *Cym.* (1955; J. M. Nosworthy); **1312** *JC* (1955;
T. S. Dorsch); **1313** *MV* (1955; John Russell Brown); **1314** *R2*
(1956; Peter Ure); **1315** *2H6* (1957; Andrew S. Cairncross); **1316**
H8 (1957; R. A. Foakes); **1317** *Oth.* (1958; Ridley); **1318** *AWW*
(1959; G. K. Hunter); **1319** *Tim.* (1959; H. J. Oliver); **1320** *1H4*
(1960; A. R. Humphreys); **1321** *Poems* (1960; F. T. Prince); **1322**
Err. (1962; Foakes); **1323** *1H6* (1962; Cairncross); **1324** *Per.* (1963;
F. D. Hoeniger); **1325** *WT* (1963; J. H. P. Pafford); **1326** *3H6* (1964;
Cairncross); **1327** *MM* (1965; J. W. Lever); **1328** *2H4* (1966;
Humphreys); **1329** *TGV* (1969; Clifford Leech); **1330** *Wiv.* (1971;
Oliver); **1331** *AYL* (1975; Agnes Latham); **1332** *TN* (1975; J. M.
Lothian and T. W. Craik); **1333** *Cor.* (1976; Philip Brockbank);
1334 *MND* (1979; Brooks); **1335** *Rom.*(1980; Brian Gibbons); **1336**

Ado (1981; Humphreys); **1337** *R3* (1981; Anthony Hammond); **1338** *Shr.* (1981; Morris); **1339** *Ham.* (1982; Jenkins); **1340** *Tro.* (1982; Kenneth Palmer).

[London: Methuen. 38 vols.]

1953	**Herbert Farjeon and Ivor Brown, New Nonesuch**	**1341**
	Works	
	[London: Nonesuch, 1953. 4 vols.]	
1954	**C. J. Sisson**	**1342**
	Works.	
	[London: Odhams]	

1954–60 (?)   **Helge Kökeritz and C. T. Prouty, gen. eds., New Yale**   **1343**
• Listed below are the total number of volumes that I have been able to find. *Variorum Handbook* (either edition) does not specify number of volumes.

1344 *AYL* (1954; S. C. Burchell); **1345** *Mac.* (1954; Eugene M. Waith); **1346** *MM* (1954; Davis Harding); **1347** *Rom.* (1954; Richard Hosley); **1348** *Shr.* (1954; Thomas G. Bergin); **1349** *TN* (1954; William P. Holden); **1350** *Ant.* (1955; Peter G. Phialas); **1351** *H5* (1955; R. J. Dorius); **1352** *Tmp.* (1955; David Horne); **1353** *Tro.* (1956; Jackson J. Campbell); **1354** *R2* (1957; Robert T. Petersson); **1355** *JC* (1959; Alvin Kernan); **1356** *MV* (1960; A. D. Richardson III).

[New Haven: Yale University Press. 13 vols.]

1955	**Helge Kökeritz and C. T. Prouty Yale F1 facsimile**	**1357**

• Produced using photo–lithography.

[New Haven: Yale University Press]

1956–67 **Alfred Harbage, gen. ed., Pelican**   **1358**
1359 *Cor.* (1956; Harry Levin); **1360** *Mac.* (1956; Harbage); **1361** *MM* (1956; R. C. Bald); **1362** *WT* (1956; Baldwin Maxwell); **1363** *Ham.* (1957; Willard Farnham); **1364** *1H4* (1957; M. A. Shaaber); **1365** *2H4* (1957; Allan Chester); **1366** *H5* (1957; Louis B. Wright and Virginia Freund); **1367** *R2* (1957; Matthew W. Black); **1368** *Ado* (1958; Josephine Waters Bennett); **1369** *Lr.* (1958; Harbage); **1370** *Oth.* (1958; Gerald Eades Bentley); **1371** *TN* (1958; Charles T. Prouty); **1372** *Tro.* (1958; Virgil K. Whitaker); **1373** *AYL* (1959; Ralph M. Sargent); **1374** *MND* (1959; Madeleine Doran); **1375** *MV* (1959; Brents Stirling); **1376** *R3* (1959; G. Blakemore Evans); **1377** *Tmp.* (1959; Northrup Frye); **1378** *Ant.* (1960; Maynard Mack); **1379** *JC* (1960; S. F. Johnson); **1380** *Per.* (1961; James G. McManaway); **1381** *Rom.* (1960; John E. Hankins); **1382** *Son.* (1961; Douglas Bush and Harbage); **1383** *Jn.* (1962; Irving

Ribner); **1384** *LLL* (1963; Harbage); **1385** *Wiv.* (1963; Fredson
Bowers); **1386** *AWW* (1964; Jonas A. Barish); **1387** *Cym.* (1964;
Robert B. Heilman); **1388** *Err.* (1964; Paul A. Jorgensen); **1389**
TGV (1964; Berners A. W. Jackson); **1390** *Shr.* (1964; Richard
Hosley); **1391** *Tim.* (1964; Charlton Hinman); **1392** *1H6* (1966;
David Bevington); **1393** *H8* (1966; F. David Hoeniger); **1394** *Poems*
(1966; Richard Wilbur and Harbage); **1395** *2H6* and *3H6* (1967;
Robert K. Turner and George Walton Williams); **1396** *Tit.* (1967;
Gustav Cross).

[Baltimore: Penguin. 38 vols.]

1957–8 **John Munro, London**   1397

[London: Eyre & Spottiswoode. 6 vols.]

1959–69 **Louis B. Wright and Virginia A. LaMar, Folger 1**   1398

• Thirty-seven play volumes were issued, together with a *Sonnets*
volume, a *Poems* volume, and a *Sonnets and Poems* volume. In
addition, Wright and LaMar also published a volume entitled *The
Folger Guide to Shakespeare* (1969).

[New York: Washington Square. 40 vols.]

1963–8 **Sylvan Barnet, gen. ed., Signet**   1399

1400 *AWW* (1963; Barnet); **1401** *AYL* (1963; Albert Gilman); **1402**
Ham. (1963; Edward Hubler); **1403** *JC* (1963; William and Barbara
Rosen); **1404** *Lr.* (1963; Russell Fraser); **1405** *Mac.* (1963; Barnet);
1406 *MND* (1963; Wolfgang Clemen); **1407** *Oth.* (1963; Alvin
Kernan); **1408** *R2* (1963; Kenneth Muir); **1409** *Tro.* (1963; Daniel
Seltzer); **1410** *WT* (1963; Frank Kermode); **1411** *Ado* (1964; David
L. Stevenson); **1412** *Ant.* (1964; Barbara Everett); **1413** *MM* (1964;
S. Nagarajan); **1414** *R3* (1964; Mark Eccles); **1415** *Rom.* (1964; J.
A. Bryant, Jr.); **1416** *Son.* (1964; edited by William Burto,
introduction by W. H. Auden); **1417** *TGV* (1964; Bertrand Evans);
1418 *Tit.* (1964; Barnet); **1419** *Tmp.* (1964; Robert Langbaum);
1420 *Err.* (1965; Harry Levin); **1421** *1H4* (1965; Maynard Mack);
1422 *2H4* (1965; Norman N. Holland); **1423** *H5* (1965; John
Russell Brown); **1424** *LLL* (1965; John Arthos); **1425** *MV* (1965;
Kenneth Myrick); **1426** *Per.* (1965; Ernest Schanzer); **1427** *Tim.*
(1965; Maurice Charney); **1428** *TN* (1965; Herschel Baker); **1429**
Wiv. (1965; William Green); **1430** *Cor.* (1966; Reuben Brower);
1431 *Jn.* (1966; William H. Matchett); **1432** *Shr.* (1966; Robert B.
Heilman); **1433** *TNK* (1966; Clifford Leech); **1434** *1H6* (1967;
Lawrence V. Ryan); **1435** *2H6* (1967; Arthur Freeman); **1436** *Cym.*
(1968; Richard Hosley); **1437** *3H6* (1968; Milton Crane); **1438** *H8*
(1968; S. Schoenbaum); **1439** *Narrative Poems* (1968; edited by
Burto, introduction by William Empson).

[New York: New American Library. 40 vols.]

1967– **T. J. B. Spencer, gen. ed., Stanley Wells, assoc. ed., New Penguin**   **1440**

• The *Cymbeline* edition remained unpublished at the time when this volume went to press.

1441 *Cor.* (1967; G. R. Hibbard); **1442** *JC* (1967; Norman Sanders); **1443** *Mac.* (1967; G. K. Hunter); **1444** *MND* (1967; Wells); **1445** *MV* (1967; W. Moelwyn Merchant); **1446** *Rom.*(1967; Spencer); **1447** *Ado* (1968; R. A. Foakes); **1448** *AYL* (1968; H. J. Oliver); **1449** *1H4* (1968; P. H. Davison); **1450** *H5* (1968; A. R. Humphreys); **1451** *Oth.* (1968; Kenneth Muir); **1452** *R3* (1968; E. A. J. Honigmann); **1453** *Shr.* (1968; Hibbard); **1454** *TGV* (1968; Sanders); **1455** *Tmp.* (1968; Anne Righter [Anne Barton]); **1456** *TN* (1968; M. M. Mahood); **1457** *MM* (1969; J. M. Nosworthy); **1458** *R2* (1969; Wells); **1459** *WT* (1969; Ernest Schanzer); **1460** *AWW* (1970; Barbara Everett); **1461** *Tim.* (1970; Hibbard); **1462** *H8* (1971; Humphreys); **1463** *Jn.* (1971; R. L. Smallwood); **1464** *Luc.* (1971; J. W. Lever); **1465** *Err.* (1972; Wells); **1466** *Lr.* (1972; Hunter); **1467** *Wiv.* (1973; Hibbard); **1468** *Per.* (1976; Philip Edwards); **1469** *Ant.* (1977; Emrys Jones); **1470** *2H4* (1977; Davison); **1471** *TNK* (1977; N. W. Bawcutt); **1472** *Ham.* (1980; Spencer, with an introduction by Anne Barton); **1473** *1H6* (1981; Sanders); **1474** *2H6* (1981; Sanders); **1475** *3H6* (1981; Sanders); **1476** *LLL* (1982; John Kerrigan); **1477** *Son. and LC* (1986; Kerrigan); **1478** *Tro.* (1986; Foakes); **1479** *Narrative Poems* (1989; Maurice Evans); **1480** *Tit.* (2001; edited by Sonia Massai, with introduction and commentary by Jacques Berthoud).

[Harmondsworth: Penguin. 40 vols.]

1968 **Hinman facsimile of F1**   **1481**

• Produced using photo–lithography.

[New York: Norton]

1969 **Alfred Harbage, gen. ed., Pelican 2**   **1482**

Works.

[Baltimore, MD: Penguin]

1971–85 (?) **Macmillan**   **1483**

• This is a difficult series to make sense of. WorldCat lists twenty-one titles published under the 'Macmillan Shakespeare' series between 1971 and 1985 (as below). Some of these volumes were reissued in 1992. In addition, Macmillan also issued some of the same titles, edited by either Roderick Wilson or Jeffrey Evans, between 1985 and 1995. I have not logged the Wilson and Evans volumes. Details below are taken from WorldCat.

1484 *Mac.* (1971; D. R. Elloway); **1485** *MND* (1971; Norman Sanders); **1486** *Tmp.* (1971; A. C. Spearing and J. E. Spearing);

1487 *TN* (1971; E. A. J. Honigmann); **1488** *Ham.* (1973; Nigel
Alexander); **1489** *AYL* (1974; Peter Hollindale); **1490** *JC* (1974;
Elloway); **1491** *R3* (1974; Richard Adams); **1492** *Rom.* (1974; James
Gibson); **1493** *1H4* (1975; Hollindale); **1494** *Lr.* (1975; Philip
Edwards); **1495** *R2* (1975; Adams); **1496** *Shr.* (1975; Robin
Christopher Hood); **1497** *H5* (1976; B. A. Phythian); **1498** *MV*
(1976; Christopher Parry); **1499** *2H4* (1981; Tony Parr); **1500** *Ado*
(1982; no editor identified); **1501** *WT* (1982; Parry); **1502** *Ant.*
(1984; Jan McKeith and Richard Adams); **1503** *Oth.* (1984; Celia
Hilton and R. T. Jones); **1504** *Cor.* (1985; Parr).

[Basingstoke: Macmillan. 21 vols.?]

1971   **George Lyman Kittredge and Irving Ribner**   1505, 1506 (Ginn)

• Plays were issued singly between 1966 and 1969, with the
imprint: Waltham, MA: Blaisdell, then collected into a complete
works volume, with Wiley and Ginn imprints, as below. These
details taken from WorldCat.

Works.

[New York: John Wiley & Sons; some copies have imprint
Waltham, MA: Ginn]

1973   **Hardin Craig (David Bevington revision)**   1507

• This text was a revision of Hardin Craig's 1951 edition.

Works.

[Glenview, IL: Scott, Foresman & Co.]

1974   **G. Blakemore Evans, gen. ed., Riverside 1**   1508

[Boston: Houghton Mifflin]

1977   **Stephen Booth, Facsimile edition of the Sonnets**   1509

[New Haven: Yale University Press]

1977–   **New Variorum**   1510

• See also 1871–1928 and 1936–55 above. *Winter's Tale*, edited by
Robert Turner and Virginia Haas was close to being ready for
publication at the time when this present volume went to press. In
the period 1997–2003, the following scholars served for varying
terms on the New Variorum Shakespeare Committee: Thomas L.
Berger, A. R. Braunmuller, William C. Carroll, Richard Knowles,
Anne Lancashire, Leah S. Marcus, Scott McMillin, Mary Beth
Rose, Paul Werstine.

1511 *AYL* (1977; Richard Knowles); **1512** *MM* (1980; Mark
Eccles); **1513** *Ant.* (1990; Marvin Spevack).

[New York: Modern Language Association]

1978–84 **John Wilders (literary consultant), BBC TV** 1514
• Text based on Alexander's 1951 edition, with notes on the scene
breaks and cuts made in the BBC TV production.
[London: BBC. 37 vols.]

1980– **Bevington 2** 1515
Works.
[Glenview, IL: Scott, Foresman & Co.]

G. A. Wilkes, gen. ed., Challis 1516
• Added in the revised edition of the *Variorum Handbook*, which
includes a quote indicating that the series is 'Designed specifically
for the Australian reader'. Details provided here are taken from
WorldCat.

1517 *Mac.* (1980; A. P. Riemer); **1518** *Tmp.* (1980; Wilkes); **1519**
Lr. (1982; E. A. M. Colman); **1520** *Oth.* (1982; Christopher
Bentley); **1521** *Ham.* (1984; Wilkes); **1522** *Ant.* (1985; Riemer);
1523 *1H4* (1987; Colman); **1524** *Tro.* (1987; Riemer); **1525** *WT*
(1989; Riemer).
[Sydney: Sydney University Press]

1981 **Michael Allen and Kenneth Muir, Shakespeare's Plays in** 1526
Quarto: A Facsimile Edition of Copies Primarily from the
Henry E. Huntington Library
[Berkeley: University of California Press]

1982– **Stanley Wells, gen. ed., Oxford** 1527
• Details of the 2001 and 2002 texts provided by Stanley Wells,
who noted that *1H6* was about to go to press at the time when this
volume was being completed.
1528 *H5* (1982; Gary Taylor); **1529** *Shr.* (1982; H. J. Oliver); **1530**
Tro. (1982; Kenneth Muir); **1531** *JC* (1984; Arthur Humphreys);
1532 *Tit.* (1984; Eugene M. Waith); **1533** *Ham.* (1987; G. R.
Hibbard); **1534** *1H4* (1987; David Bevington); **1535** *Tmp.* (1987;
Stephen Orgel); **1536** *Jn.*(1989; A. R. Braunmuller); **1537** *TNK*
(1989; Waith); **1538** *Wiv.* (1989; T. W. Craik); **1539** *LLL* (1990;
Hibbard); **1540** *Mac.* (1990; Nicholas Brooke); **1541** *MM* (1991;
N. W. Bawcutt); **1542** *Ado* (1993; Sheldon P. Zitner); **1543** *AWW*
(1993; Susan Snyder); **1544** *AYL* (1993; Alan Brissenden); **1545**
MV (1993; Jay L. Halio); **1546** *Ant.* (1994; Michael Neill); **1547**
Cor. (1994; R. B. Parker); **1548** *MND* (1994; Peter Holland); **1549**
TN (1994; Roger Warren and Wells); **1550** *WT* (1996; Orgel); **1551**
Cym. (1998; Warren); **1552** *2H4* (1998; René Weis); **1553** *H8* (1999;
Halio); **1554** *Lr.* (2000; Wells [based in part on a text prepared with
Gary Taylor]); **1555** *R3* (2000; John Jowett); **1556** *Rom.*(2000;

Jill L. Levenson); **1557** *3H6* (2001; Randall Martin); **1558** *Err.*
(2002; Charles Whitworth); **1559** *2H6* (2002; Warren); **1560** *Poems*
(2002; Colin Burrow).

[Oxford: Clarendon]

1984–   **Philip Brockbank, Brian Gibbons, A. R. Braunmuller,**   **1561**
         Robin Hood, gen. eds., New Cambridge

• Details for 2002 text provided by the press. *Tro.* was in
production when this present volume was being completed.

1562 *MND* (1984; R. A. Foakes); **1563** *Oth.* (1984; Norman
Sanders); **1564** *R2* (1984; Andrew Gurr); **1565** *Rom.* (1984;
G. Blakemore Evans); **1566** *Shr.* (1984; Ann Thompson); **1567**
AWW (1985; Russell Fraser); **1568** *Ham.* (1985; Philip Edwards);
1569 *TN* (1985; Elizabeth Story Donno); **1570** *MV* (1987; M. M.
Mahood); **1571** *Ado* (1988; F. H. Mares); **1572** *Err.* (1988; T. S.
Dorsch); **1573** *JC* (1988; Marvin Spevack); **1574** *2H4* (1989;
Giorgio Melchiori); **1575** *Ant.* (1990; David Bevington); **1576** *1H6*
(1990; Michael Hattaway); **1577** *H8* (1990; John Margeson); **1578**
Jn. (1990; L. A. Beaurline); **1579** *TGV* (1990; Kurt Schlueter);
1580 *2H6* (1991; Hattaway); **1581** *MM* (1991; Gibbons); **1582** *H5*
(1992; Gurr); **1583** *Lr.* (1992; Jay L. Halio); **1584** *Poems* (1992;
John Roe); **1585** *3H6* (1993; Hattaway); **1586** *Tit.* (1994; Alan
Hughes); **1587** *Son.* (1996; ed. by Evans, intro. by Anthony Hecht);
1588 *1H4* (1997; Herbert Weil and Judith Weil); **1589** *Mac.* (1997;
Braunmuller); **1590** *Wiv.* (1997; David Crane); **1591** *Edward III*
(1998; Melchiori); **1592** *Per.* (1998; Doreen Delvecchio and Antony
Hammond); **1593** *R3* (1999; Janis Lull); **1594** *AYL* (2000;
Hattaway); **1595** *Cor.* (2000; Lee Bliss); **1596** *Tim.* (2001; Karl
Klein); **1597** *Tmp.* (2002; David Lindley).

• The 'Early Quartos' series:

1598 *Q1 Lr.* (1994; Halio); **1599** *Q1 R3* (1996; Peter Davison); **1600**
A Shrew 1594 (1998; Stephen Roy Miller); **1601** *Q1 Ham.* (1998;
Kathleen O. Irace); **1602** *Q1 H5* (2000; Gurr).

[Cambridge: Cambridge University Press]

1985   **Marvin Spevack, Brewer facsimiles of Ff2–4**   **1603**
        [Cambridge: D. S. Brewer, 3 vols.]

1986   **Stanley Wells and Gary Taylor, with John Jowett and**   **1604**
        William Montgomery, Oxford
        [Oxford: Clarendon]

        Wells and Taylor, with Jowett and Montgomery, Oxford   **1605**
        Original-Spelling
        [Oxford: Clarendon]

1987 **Archival Facsimiles facsimile of F2** 1606

• A photographic reproduction of Charles I's copy. West, in *First Folio*, v. 1, p. 169 says that this edition 'is not easy to find'. The British Library has a copy – LB.31.c.11071.

[Alburgh: Archival Facsimiles]

1988 **David Bevington ed., Bantam** 1607

• Issued in a variety of different formats: single volume complete works; six volume complete works set; multiple-text volumes, by genre (*Four Tragedies, Four Comedies, Three Early Comedies, Late Romances, Three Classical Tragedies*); individual plays (sometimes with more than one text included in the same volume – e.g., *1, 2 and 3 Henry VI, King John* and *Henry VIII*). For simplicity's sake – and because Bevington edited all volumes – one number is issued here.

[New York: Bantam. Various combinations of volumes, as indicated above]

1989 **Michael Warren, ed., The Complete King Lear** 1608

• Includes unbound facsimiles of Q1, Q2 and F1 *Lear* texts, together with a bound parallel text of Q1 and F1 *Lear*.

[Berkeley: University of California Press]

Two Noble Kinsmen 1609

• Edited by Fredson Bowers and included in Bowers (gen. ed.), *The Dramatic Works in the Beaumont and Fletcher Canon*, VII.

[Cambridge: Cambridge University Press]

1989–91 **John F. Andrews, Guild** 1610

• Volumes (mostly) contained paired texts. *Hamlet* and *Romeo and Juliet* were issued individually, to take advantage of the success of current film versions of the plays and of the film *Shakespeare in Love*. Details given here are taken from WorldCat. The editor himself provided details of the *All's Well* and *Cymbeline* volumes. At the time when this volume was being completed there were no immediate plans to extend the series.

1611 *Ham.* (1989); **1612** *Rom.* (1989); **1613** *AYL* and *TN* (1989); **1614** *2H4* and *H5* (1989); **1615** *Ham.* and *Tro.* (1989); **1616** *JC* and *Ant.* (1989); **1617** *MND* and *TGV* (1989); **1618** *R2* and *1H4* (1989); **1619** *Rom.* and *Tit.* (1989); **1620** *Shr.* and *Wiv.* (1989); **1621** *Son.* and *Poems* (1989); **1622** *AWW* and *MM* (1990); **1623** *Err.* and *Ado* (1990); **1624** *1H6* and *2H6* (1990); **1625** *3H6* and *R3* (1990); **1626** *Oth.* and *Mac.* (1990); **1627** *Tim.* and *Per.* (1990); **1628** *Lr.* and *Cor.* (1991); **1629** *MV* and *LLL* (1991); **1630** *Jn.* and *H8* (1992); **1631** *Cym.* and *WT* and *Tmp.* (1992).

[New York: Doubleday. 21 vols.]

1991	Paul Bertram and Bernice W. Kliman, The Three Text Hamlet: Parallel Texts of the First and Second Quartos and First Folio	1632

[New York: AMS]

1992	Bevington 3	1633

Works.

[New York: HarperCollins]

1992–6	Graham Holderness and Bryan Loughrey, gen. eds., Shakespearean Originals	1634

• Lightly edited transcriptions of early editions.

1635 *Ham.* (1603; 1992; Holderness and Loughrey); **1636** *H5* (1600; 1992; Holderness and Loughrey); **1637** *A Shrew* (1594; 1992; Holderness and Loughrey); **1638** *Ant.* (F1; 1995; John Turner); **1639** *Lr.* (1608; 1995; Holderness); **1640** *MV* (1600; 1995; Annabel Patterson); **1641** *Oth.* (1622; 1995; Andrew Murphy); **1642** *Rom.* (1597; 1995; Cedric Watts); **1643** *TN* (F1; 1995; Laurie E. Osborne); **1644** *JC* (F1; 1996; James Rigney); **1645** *Mac.* (F1; 1996; Rigney); **1646** *MM* (F1; 1996; Grace Ioppolo); **1647** *MND* (1600; 1996; T. O. Treadwell); **1648** *R3* (1597; 1996; John Drakakis).

[Hemel Hempstead: Harvester Wheatsheaf/Prentice Hall. 14 vols.]

1992–	Barbara A. Mowat and Paul Werstine, New Folger	1649

• Twenty-seven volumes issued to date. Expected year of completion is 2009.

[New York: Washington Square]

1993	René Weis, ed., King Lear: A Parallel Text Edition	1650

[London: Longman]

1993–	John F. Andrews, ed., Everyman	1651

• Texts edited by Andrews, with forewords by various commentators (mainly actors). Authors of forewords listed below. There were no immediate plans to extend the series when this volume was being completed.

1652 *Ant.* (1993; Tony Randall); **1653** *Ham.* (1993; Derek Jacobi); **1654** *JC* (1993; John Gielgud); **1655** *Lr.* (1993; Hal Holbrook); **1656** *Mac.* (1993; Zoe Caldwell); **1657** *MND* (1993; F. Murray Abraham); **1658** *MV* (1993; Kelly McGillis); **1659** *Rom.* (1993; Julie Harris); **1660** *MM* (1994; Tim Pigott-Smith); **1661** *Tmp.* (1994; Gielgud); **1662** *TN* (1994; Alec McCowen); **1663** *Oth.* (1995; James Earl Jones); **1664** *WT* (1995; Adrian Noble); **1665** *Ado* (1996; Kevin Kline); **1666** *AYL* (1997; Michael Kahn); **1667** *Cor.* (1998; Charles Dance).

[London: J. M. Dent. 16 vols.]

| 1995 | Anne Barton and John Kerrigan, executive eds., Editions and Adaptations of Shakespeare | 1668 |

• Available on CD and via the Internet.

[Cambridge: Chadwyck-Healey]

| | Doug Moston, Applause facsimile of F1 | 1669 |

[New York: Applause]

| 1995– | David Scott Kastan, Richard Proudfoot and Ann Thompson, gen. eds., Arden 3 | 1670 |

1671 *Ant.* (1995; John Wilders); **1672** *H5* (1995; T. W. Craik); **1673** *Tit.* (1995; Jonathan Bate); **1674** *Lr.* (1997; R. A. Foakes); **1675** *Oth.* (1997; E. A. J. Honigmann); **1676** *Son.* (1997; Katherine Duncan-Jones); **1677** *TNK* (1997; Lois Potter); **1678** *JC* (1998; David Daniell); **1679** *LLL* (1998; H. R. Woudhuysen); **1680** *Tro.* (1998; David Bevington); **1681** *2H6* (1999; Ronald Knowles); **1682** *Tmp.* (1999; Virginia Mason Vaughan and Alden T. Vaughan); **1683** *1H6* (2000; Edward Burns); **1684** *H8* (2000; Gordon McMullan); **1685** *Wiv.* (2000; Giorgio Melchiori); **1686** *3H6* (2001; John D. Cox and Eric Rasmussen); **1687** *1H4* (2002; Kastan); **1688** *R2* (2002; Charles R. Forker).

[Walton-on-Thames: Thomas Nelson & Sons]

| 1996 | Peter Blayney, Norton facsimile of F1, second edition | 1689 |

• The 1968 text, including Hinman's introduction and apparatus, with an additional introduction by Peter Blayney.

[New York: Norton]

| | Bernice Kliman, The Enfolded Hamlet | 1690 |

• Reproduces Q2 and F1 on the same page. Published as an 'extra issue' of *The Shakespeare Newsletter*.

| 1996– | John Russell Brown (*et al.*), Applause | 1691 |

• Details taken from WorldCat.

1692 *JC* (1996; Maurice Charney and Stuart Vaughan); **1693** *Lr.* (1996; Brown); **1694** *Mac.* (R. A. Foakes and Brown); **1695** *MND* (1996; Brown, John Hirsch and others); **1696** *Tmp.* (1996; Brown); **1697** *Ant.* (2001; Barry Gaines and Janet Suzman); **1698** *MM* (2001; Grace Ioppolo and Leon Rubin); **1699** *MV* (2001; Randall Martin and Peter Lichtenfels); **1700** *Oth.* (2001; Brown); **1701** *Rom.* (2001; Brown); **1702** *TN* (2001; Brown).

[New York: Applause]

| 1997 | Jonathan Bate, consulting ed., Arden Shakespeare – CD version | 1703 |

• Arden 2 texts, with electronic facsimiles of F1 and some quartos, together with other materials.

[Walton-on-Thames: Thomas Nelson]

	Bevington 4	1704
	Works.	
	[New York/London: Longman.]	

	G. Blakemore Evans, with J. J. M. Tobin, gen. eds., **Riverside 2**	1705
	Works.	
	[Boston: Houghton Mifflin]	

	Stephen Greenblatt, gen. ed., Norton	1706
	• Based on the 1986 Oxford edition (but see chapter 11 for an account of revisions made in the Norton text).	
	[New York: Norton]	

| | **Routledge/Thoemmes reprint of Methuen Ff1–4 facsimiles** | 1707 |
| | [London: Routledge/Thoemmes. Boxed set of 4 vols.] | |

1998	**Kastan, Proudfoot and Thompson, gen. eds., Arden Complete**	1708
	• Reproduces a mixture of Arden 2 and Arden 3 texts.	
	Works.	
	[Walton-on-Thames: Thomas Nelson & Sons]	

| | **Moston, Routledge facsimile of F1** | 1709 |
| | [London: Routledge] | |

1999	**Rowe 1709 Facsimile**	1710
	• Introduction by Peter Holland	
	[London: Pickering & Chatto. 7 vols.]	

2001	**Octavo Electronic facsimile of F1**	1711
	• Produced in CD and Internet versions.	
	[Oakland, CA: Octavo]	

| 2002 | **Jesús Tronch-Pérez, ed., A synoptic Hamlet: A critical-synoptic edition of the second quarto/and first folio texts of Hamlet** | 1712 |
| | [SEDERI/University of Valencia Press] | |

Index 1
By play/poem title

Index 2
By series title

This index only lists series which have a particular identifying title. Other series can be accessed by checking the editor's name in the index of editors. 'Series' here refers to editions issuing in single-text volumes. The index lists partial as well as complete editions.

Index 3
By editor

Includes names of those who have written introductions to texts edited by others.

Where the names of other editors and commentators are included in titles, these names are also indexed here. Where an editor is wholly responsible for a selection of texts issued under a series title, only the number of the series itself is given here.

Index 4
By publisher

Includes printer and/or sales agent, where shown in imprint.

Index 5
By place of publication (excluding London)

Where editions clearly identify a principal publisher, followed by a list of selling agents, only the location for the principal publisher is included here. For series where all volumes are published in the same location only the main series number is given, rather than the numbers for each individual volume. 'Chiswick' is treated as a London imprint.

Notes

Introduction

1. 'Shall Shakespeare', p. 169.
2. 'Shakspeare', p. 92.
3. Bowers, *On Editing*, p. 101.
4. Velz, 'Research', p. 51.
5. See de Grazia, *Verbatim*, Martin, *Edmond Malone*, Seary, *Lewis Theobald*; Jarvis, *Scholars* and Walsh, *Shakespeare, Milton*.
6. See Sherbo, *Achievement, Birth, Samuel Johnson, Isaac Reed.*
7. In terms of book-length studies, the single noteworthy exception that comes to mind is James M. Gibson's 1990 volume on Horace Howard Furness and the New Variorum Shakespeare. One might, I suppose, also include Dewey Ganzel's 1982 account of the career of John Payne Collier (*Fortune and Men's Eyes*), but this is a significantly flawed work – see chapter 9. Important shorter studies have been published by such scholars as Richard Knowles and John Velz.
8. See, as representative publications, McGann, *Critique* and *Textual Condition* and McKenzie, *Bibliography* and 'Typography'.
9. Leah Marcus has offered an alternative model for editorial history – see her *Unediting*.
10. Parrish, 'Whig'.
11. McKerrow, *Treatment*, p. 113.
12. See Maw, 'Hornet's Nest', p. 25.
13. See Jarvis, *Catalogue*. The Rowe edition in question did, however, lack most of its plates.
14. For full details of the Dicks and Macmillan editions mentioned in this paragraph, see chapters 8 (Dicks) and 9 (Macmillan).
15. 'Shall Shakespeare', p. 169.
16. The Cambridge Shakespeare was, in fact, spun off into the enormously successful Globe edition. But – as I indicate in chapter 8 – even the Globe figures fail significantly to match those of the Dicks.
17. I learned of Dicks, in the first instance, from a passing reference in an article by Richard Altick, entitled 'From Aldine to Everyman: Cheap Reprint Series of the English Classics 1830–1906' (see pp. 9–10). I cannot recall ever having come across a reference to Dicks in scholarly materials relating directly to Shakespeare publishing.
18. See Rodgers, 'Pope'.
19. John Sutherland made these comments during the course of a plenary address at the 'Remarking the Text' conference, held at the University of St Andrews in July 2002.
20. Routledge Archives, University of London, item no. 8.
21. For these details, see Collison-Morley, *Shakespeare in Italy*.

22. The Cambridge University Press Shakespeare files include some very interesting material on the reprinting and repackaging of Cambridge editions in India for the local market.
23. It is worth noting in this regard that the Boydell edition of Shakespeare, which was part of a larger project involving paintings and etchings, has itself prompted several book-length studies – see Bruntjen, Friedman, Hutton and Nelke and Pape and Burwick.
24. On the Scott and Carroll editions, see chapters 8 (Carroll) and 9 (Scott).
25. J. W. C., article, p. 365.
26. The Simplified Speling Society was founded in 1908 by W. W. Skeat and F. J. Furnivall. The list of vice presidents included Percy Simpson and H. G. Wells. Among the society's other publications was the pamphlet *I Hav Lurnt to Spel*, by William Archer. This *Hamlet* text, in common with the Mills and Boon *Henry V* also mentioned in this paragraph, is not included in the chronological appendix to this volume.
27. Wilson, *Milestones*, pp. 178, 179.
28. Mills and Boon merged with its North American equivalent Harlequin in 1971. The British company advertised in 1968 that its readers 'come from that large group of people who are bored with tales of sex, violence and sadism and just want a pleasant book' (quoted in Bedell, 'Mills', p. 47) – something which seems curiously at odds with their having issued an edition of *Henry V*.
29. Full-text comic-book editions of *Othello*, *Macbeth* and *King Lear* were issued by Oval Projects in the UK in the 1980s. Comic-book versions of some plays had already been issued in the US in the 1960s, in the 'Classics Illustrated' series, published by Gilbertson. Neil Gaiman's *Dream Country* (1991) and *The Wake* (1997), published by DC Comics, draw heavily on Shakespearean materials (including Shakespeare's own life, in the case of *The Wake*). On the BBC and Exxon, see chapter 11.
30. The volume was compiled by Ann Thompson, Thomas L. Berger, A. R. Braunmuller, Philip Edwards and Lois Potter.

1 The early quartos

1. In 1592, Shakespeare's father was asked to assist in valuing the goods and chattles of Richard Field's father, Henry, the Stratford tanner. The assessors valued his possessions at 'the modest sum of £14 14s' (Kirkwood, 'Richard Field', p. 1).
2. Jaggard, *Shakespeare: Once a Printer*. The general outlines of his theory are set out at pp. 2–4. In fairness to Jaggard, it should be pointed out that he was also the author of the monumental *Shakespeare Bibliography*, which he intended as an exhaustive listing of Shakespeare editions and of materials relating to Shakespeare; the book was a considerable achievement and proved invaluable when the present volume was being prepared. Jaggard's account of Shakespeare's lost years had been anticipated by William Blades in *Shakspere and Typography*. Blades offered a novel explanation for Shakespeare's supposed reluctance to see his plays into print: 'sickened with reading other people's proofs for a livelihood, he shrunk from the same task on his own behalf' (p. 35).
3. On Jonson, see Douglas A. Brooks, *From Playhouse to Printing House*, pp. 51–2 and chapter 3.
4. Ibid., p. 55 and Dutton, 'Birth', p. 161. Note, however, that Lukas Erne challenges the standard narrative of Shakespeare's indifference to print publication in his *Lines to Time: Shakespeare and Literary Drama* (forthcoming from Cambridge University Press).

5. Robertson, *Genuine*, p. 34.
6. Johnson, 'Book-prices', p. 92. For the price of the *Sonnets* collection, see p. 110.
7. Rowe's edition (§167), I, p. x. Rowe notes that the supposed payment was 'A Bounty very great, and very rare at any time, and almost equal to that profuse Generosity the present Age has shewn to *French* Dancers and *Italian* Eunuchs.'
8. These figures are drawn from Kirkwood, 'Richard Field', p. 13. W. W. Greg notes that, over the course of the sixteenth century, the lines of demarcation became clearer: 'before the end of the sixteenth century, printers, though they continued to produce books on their own account, had become very largely trade-printers, the bulk of whose output was commissioned by other stationers who possessed no presses of their own' (*First Folio*, p. 47).
9. Somewhat unusually, Field was granted the sole right to print this text in the following year, with no limitation of time. See Feather, 'Rights in Copies', p. 193.
10. Greg, 'Elizabethan Printer', pp. 106, 107–8, 108.
11. Osborn, 'Edmond Malone and Oxford', p. 325. The volume is part of the Malone collection, held at the Bodleian Library.
12. F. S. Ferguson notes, in 'Relations', that 'most of [Wreittoun's] books are now among the rarest productions of the Scottish press' (p. 194). Lee, in the introduction to his *Venus and Adonis* facsimile, speculates that Wreittoun may have used an early edition of the poem owned by Drummond of Hawthornden as his copy text (§972, pp. 69–70).
13. See John Roe's 1992 Cambridge edition of the *Poems* (§1584), p. 294.
14. Heywood, *Apology*, G4r–G4v.
15. Katherine Duncan-Jones argues very persuasively for Shakespeare's direct involvement in the publication, in 'Was the 1609 *Shake-speares Sonnets* Really Unauthorized?' She maps out the publisher, Thomas Thorpe's, close connections with other writers such as Jonson, Marston, and Chapman in close detail and notes that, as in the case of the earlier narrative poems, the *Sonnets* volume was published at a time when the theatres were closed owing to an outbreak of the plague.
16. These poems were the sonnets identified as 138 and 144 in the 1609 edition and three poems taken from the 1598 edition of *Love's Labour's Lost*.
17. Heywood, *Apology*, G4v. Note, however, that the reading of Heywood's comments in this paragraph (which matches Duncan-Jones' reading in her edition of the sonnets) is heavily disputed by MacD. P. Jackson. Jackson argues that, when Heywood writes that Shakespeare 'since, to do himself right, hath published [his poems] in his own name', he is actually referring to the appearance of Shakespeare's name on the title page of the third edition of *Passionate Pilgrim* and not to the 1609 *Sonnets* volume – see p. 370 of his review of the Duncan-Jones' *Sonnets* volume.
18. For the principal contending theories regarding the extent of Shakespeare's involvement with the publication of the 1609 volume, see Berger and Lander, 'Shakespeare in Print', pp. 397–8.
19. For a more complex reading of the evidence concerning the publishing of Shakespeare's sonnets, see Duncan-Jones (ed.), *Shakespeare's Sonnets*, esp. pp. 3–6, where she posits the relevance to the debate of a 1600 Stationers' Register entry covering '*sonnetes* by W.S.' (p. 3). Duncan-Jones speculates that this entry may either point to a lost edition of the poems or may have been intended as a 'blocking entry' in response to the second edition of *Passionate Pilgrime*.
20. Hallett Smith, in 'No Cloudy Stuffe', argues against taking Benson's preface seriously, noting that he 'was merely writing a blurb. And, like many other blurb-writers, he was

more concerned with getting some fine-sounding words to attract customers than he was with accurately describing the offered book' (p. 20). Smith traces Benson's indebtedness to Thomas May's prefatory poem to Joseph Rutter's *The Shepheards Holy-Day*, which Benson had published in 1635.

21. The exact extent of the regendering is mapped out by de Grazia in 'Scandal', pp. 35–6. In the context of the alterations Benson did carry out, de Grazia asks: 'If Benson had wished to censure homoerotic love, why did he not omit the notoriously titillating master-mistress sonnet (20)? Or emend the glamorizing sonnet 106 that praises the beloved – in blazon style, part by part – as the "master" of beauty? Or the sexually loaded sonnet 110 that apologizes to a specifically male "god of love" for promiscuity of a decidedly "preposterous" cast?' (p. 36).

22. For a useful account of the publications history of the poems in the eighteenth century, see Alexander, 'Province'.

23. The clearest account of this process is provided by Peter Blayney, in 'Publication', esp. pp. 403–4.

24. Brooks, *From Playhouse to Printing House*, p. 10. But see also Barbara A. Mowat's 'Constructing the Author', which delineates paradigms of authorship that clearly did exist in the early modern period.

25. On collaboration as a normative practice in the writing of Renaissance plays, see Masten, *Textual Intercourse*. For the contractual obligations incurred by one late Renaissance playwright – Richard Brome – see Wickham, Berry and Ingram (eds.), *English Professional Theatre*, pp. 650–1 and 657–64.

26. Wells and Taylor, *Textual Companion*, p. 33. Scott McMillin notes that 'The leading acting companies were paying £5 or £6 for a new play in 1598, with the price going up sharply to £10, even to £20 by 1613' ('Playwrighting', p. 227).

27. Blayney gives this as 'a typical price, though by no means invariable', in 'Publication' (p. 411), where he provides a speculative reconstruction of the economics of quarto play publishing. See also Johnson, 'Book-prices', p. 91; Johnson notes that in 1594/5, the *True Tragedy of Richard Duke of York* was commanding a price of 8*d*.

28. Alfred Hart, in *Stolne and Surreptitious Copies*, notes that 'Up to the year 1600, two-thirds of all the printed plays written for the public theatres or acted between the years 1587 and 1600 did not have the authors' names on their title-pages, though the names of the authors of many of these plays were certainly known to the play-going, and perhaps to many of the play-reading public. Lyly, Peele, Greene, Kyd, Marlowe, Shakespeare, Heywood, Drayton and others contributed to the long list of nameless plays. It is correct to state that anonymity was the rule rather than the exception' (p. 6). David Scott Kastan does, however, make clear that the name of the author gradually comes to assume a greater significance, eventually displacing the name of the theatre company, which figures prominently on most early playbook title pages. Writing specifically of Shakespeare and the King's Men, he observes: 'year by year on the bookstalls the commercial cachet of an old acting company weakened, while the commercial cachet of an old playwright grew' (*Shakespeare and the Book*, p. 40).

29. Hoppe, *The Bad Quartos of Romeo and Juliet*, p. 27. Details of Danter's career are drawn from this source and from Plomer, 'The Printers of Shakespeare's Plays and Poems', and Danter's entry in McKerrow, *Dictionary*, pp. 83–4.

30. Leishman (ed.), *Three Parnassus Plays*, p. 184. On the identification of Ingenioso as Nashe, see pp. 70–1.

31. Ibid., pp. 247 (first quote), 248.

32. See Greg, *Bibliography*, entry no. 117 (I, p. 197).

33. In fact Danter printed only the first four sheets (A-D) of this edition. Sheets E-K were probably printed by Edward Allde. See Hoppe, *Bad Quartos*, p. 3 and Henning, 'The Printer of *Romeo and Juliet*, Q1', pp. 363–4.

34. It should be noted, however, that the kind of information provided on Renaissance play-text title pages is altogether less clear-cut and stable than is implied here. See Berger's excellent 'Shakespeare in Caroline England'.

35. References here are to the New Cambridge Shakespeare edition of the play, edited by G. Blakemore Evans (§1565).

36. There are also less marked differences between the F1 and quarto versions of *2 Henry IV*, *Troilus and Cressida* and *Othello*, and between the First Folio and Second Quarto *Hamlet*.

37. Pollard, *Folios and Quartos*, p. 80. Challenges to Pollard's choice of terminology are numerous – see, e.g., Cloud, 'Marriage'. The texts classified by Pollard as 'bad' are *Romeo and Juliet* (1597), *Henry V* (1600), *Merry Wives of Windsor* (1602), *Hamlet* (1603) and *Pericles* (1609). In 1919, W. W. Greg, in '*Titus Andronicus*' added the fly scene in the F1 version of that play. Peter Alexander brought *A Shrew* (1594), *The First Part of the Contention / 2 Henry VI* (1594) and *Richard Duke of York / 3 Henry VI* (1595) within the classification in a series of *TLS* articles in 1924 and 1926 and in *Shakespeare's 'Henry VI' and 'Richard III'* (1929). E. K. Chambers added *King Lear* in *William Shakespeare* (1930) and D. L. Patrick included *Richard III* (1597) in *The Textual History of 'Richard III'* (1936). There is some speculation that there may also have been a 'bad' quarto of *Love's Labour's Lost* which has not survived; the quarto of 1598 advertises itself as 'Newly corrected and augmented' on its title page.

38. Hoppe, *Bad Quartos*, p. 59.

39. Hoppe, *Bad Quartos*, p. 60. It is noteworthy that the 1825 edition of Q1 *Hamlet* unequivocally states that it is 'an accurate reprint from the only known copy of this Tragedy as originally written by Shakespeare, which he afterwards altered and enlarged' (§475, unpaged). An alternative line of argument suggested that Shakespeare began by producing revisions of the work of other dramatists, which he then subsequently further revised. For a still useful account of the roots of this theory see Alexander, *Shakespeare's 'Henry VI' and 'Richard III'*, chapter 3.

40. Theobald also believed that the actors contributed significantly to the corruption of the text.

41. See Ganzel, *Fortune and Men's Eyes*, pp. 14–16.

42. Quoted in Gibson, *Philadelphia Shakespeare Story*, p. 190.

43. For sermons, see William Matthews, 'Shorthand', pp. 248–9 and 'Reporters', pp. 491–8.

44. Heywood, *Pleasant Dialogves*, p. 249

45. See, in addition to the articles noted in the previous note, Matthews' 'Peter Bales'. A useful summary of his arguments against stenography is provided in 'Correspondence', pp. 227–8. For a nice example of the 'afterlife' of the stenography debate, see Gary Blackwood's children's book *The Shakespeare Stealer*. The issue of stenography has been raised again in more recent times by Adele Davidson – see in particular her 'Some by Stenography' and '*King Lear* in an Age of Stenographical Reproduction'.

46. Giordano-Orsini, 'Thomas Heywood's Play', p. 338. Matthews makes the point that Heywood's comments might have been prompted by the popularity of stenography in the 1630s: 'in [the] twenty-nine years [between 1608 and 1637] shorthand had progressed enormously in scope and popularity. Individual reporters had achieved considerable fame, and the art gave employment to numerous writing masters, some of whom taught

in the neighbourhood of the theatres. In 1608 Heywood might have been unaware of stenography but could hardly have been so in 1637' ('Shorthand', p. 245).

47. Greg was not, in fact, the first commentator to argue that 'memorial reconstruction' might account for the existence of one of the short quartos. As early as 1857 Tycho Mommsen had advanced a broadly similar theory in relation to *Hamlet*. Mommsen speculated that he 'discern[ed] two hands employed, one after the other . . . the one being probably that of an actor, who put down, from memory, a sketch of the original play, as it was acted, and who wrote very illegibly; the other that of a bad poet . . . who, without any personal intercourse with the writer of the notes, availed himself of them to make up this early copy of "Hamlet"' ('"Hamlet", 1603', p. 182).

48. Maguire, *Suspect Texts*, pp. 75–6.

49. Werstine, 'Narratives', p. 79.

50. Wilson, 'Copy', p. 178.

51. Ibid., p. 177.

52. Bowers, 'Today's Shakespeare Texts', p. 45.

53. Blayney, 'Publication', p. 385.

54. Ibid., p. 389. Of Shakespeare's plays, Blayney comments that most 'had a relatively undistinguished publishing history before 1623. It is true that three of them (*Richard II*, *Richard III* and *1 Henry IV*) were reprinted with a frequency which almost (but not quite) brought them into the class of runaway best-sellers such as *Mucedorus* and Heywood's *If You Know Not Me*. But to balance against these successes there were *The Merry Wives of Windsor* (1602, reprinted 1619), *The Merchant of Venice* and *A Midsummer Night's Dream* (both 1600, reprinted 1619), *2 Henry IV* and *Much Ado about Nothing* (both 1600, reprinted 1623), and *Love's Labour's Lost* (1598, reprinted 1623). These books were not total failures – they were, after all, ultimately reprinted – but the facts indicate that the contemporary demand was not particularly great' (p. 82). We might contrast these reprint figures with the publishing record of Henry Smith's sermons, which are estimated to have run through 127 editions between 1591 and 1637 – see Henderson and Siemon, 'Reading', p. 214.

55. Maguire, *Suspect*, p. 281. With regard to the short Shakespeare quartos, Maguire concludes that *Hamlet* is 'Possibly MR [memorial reconstruction], but if so, a very good one' (p. 256); that *Merry Wives of Windsor* is 'probably MR' (p. 286); that if *Pericles* is 'a reported text, it is a very good one' (p. 295) (she means, I take it, in the context of memorial reporting – as a text, *Pericles* is generally regarded as very poor); and that the other texts are not memorially reconstructed. See also Werstine, 'Narratives' and 'Century'. For an alternative view, see Irace, *Reforming the 'Bad' Quartos*.

56. Urkowitz, 'All things', p. 116.

57. Urkowitz has been central in reviving a more narrowly conceived version of the authorial revision hypothesis originally advanced by Pope. Many scholars have agreed that the variants in the 1608 and 1623 versions of *King Lear* can be attributed to authorial revision. See Urkowitz, *Shakespeare's Revision of 'King Lear'* and Taylor and Warren (eds.), *The Division of the Kingdom*. For the most ambitious exposition of the revision hypothesis see Grace Ioppolo, *Revising Shakespeare*. See also chapter 11, pp. 251–5.

58. Elizabeth Eisenstein, in her account of the history of the rise of print, notes that 'one must wait until a full century after Gutenberg before the outlines of new world pictures begin to emerge into view' (*Printing Press*, I, p. 34).

59. For a general account of reading practices in the Renaissance, see Hackel, 'Great Variety'.

60. Altick, *Common Reader*, p. 22. Julie Stone Peters also notes that there 'were books that people felt they needed before they could allow themselves to buy playbooks: books for

the carrying out of business (agriculture, domestic economy); books for the care of the soul. In the countryside, readers were more likely to buy books of entertainment better suited to reading aloud: books of dialogue, for instance, not in need of scenic trappings' (*Theatre*, p. 33).

61. Blayney, 'Publication', pp. 414, 415.
62. Letters from Sir Thomas Bodley to Thomas James, dated 1 January 1612 and 15 January 1612, in Wheeler (ed.), *Letters*, pp. 219, 222.
63. Chambers, *William Shakespeare*, p. 197.
64. Ibid., p. 194.
65. Bennett, *English Books*, III, p. 201.
66. Blayney, 'Publication', p. 415.
67. Quoted in Hackel, 'Rowme', p. 118. Sasha Roberts notes, in 'Reading the Shakespearean Text', that 'Several women owners . . . recorded their names in Folger Folios: Rachell Paule (1650), Olivea Cotton (*c*. 1675) and Elizabeth Hutchinson (*c*. 1700), Mary [?]Watkin and Mary Child (1675), and Elizabeth Brockett (1702)' (p. 303).
68. See Thompson and Roberts (eds.), *Women Reading Shakespeare*, pp. 11–12. The letter itself is included in their collection at pp. 12–14.
69. All quotations taken from Sisson, 'Shakespeare Quartos as Prompt-Copies', p. 138. See also Mowat, 'Culture', p. 213.
70. Sisson speculates that the printed text of *Saint Christopher* may never have existed and may simply have been a convenient fiction for Cholmeley's Men (p. 142). It should be noted here, of course, that, as Stanley Wells notes in his Oxford edition of *King Lear*, the non-Shakespearean *True Chronicle History of King Leir* was also available in print at the time, having been published in 1605 – see §1554, p. 56.
71. Middleton, *Mayor*, V.i, p. 69. See also Sisson, 'Shakespeare Quartos as Prompt-Copies', p. 135.
72. Greg, *First Folio*, p. 160. For a discussion of quartos known to have been used as prompt-books, see Baskervill, 'Prompt Copy' and Thomson, 'Quarto'. Later in the century, in the 1670s and 1680s, a copy of the third folio was used at Smock Alley in Dublin as a promptbook. A copy of the First Folio had similarly been used at Padua in the 1630s or 1640s. See Shattuck, *Shakespeare Promptbooks . . . Catalogue*, pp. 7–8.
73. Quoted from Taylor, *Reinventing*, p. 7.
74. Moseley, 'The Stationer' in Beaumont and Fletcher, *Comedies and Tragedies*, g2r.
75. Taylor, *Reinventing*, p. 21.
76. Dobson, *Making of the National Playwright*, p. 28. Berger, in 'Shakespeare in Caroline England', makes the interesting argument that, in the early Stuart period by contrast, editions of Shakespeare retained an 'Elizabethan' cast to their title pages in order to 'recapture the rapture of an earlier, simpler world' (p. 337).
77. In 1673, an edition of *Macbeth* appeared, with the title page indicating that it was 'A Tragedy. Acted at the Dukes-Theatre' (§137, title page). In fact, the text performed at the Dukes was an adaptation by Davenant, while the text reproduced in the 1673 quarto was actually based on the Folio text, which had most recently been published in the third folio of 1663/4.
78. Spencer, 'Restoration', p. 785; see also Spencer, *Shakespeare Improved*, pp. 174–85.
79. Spencer, 'Restoration', p. 777.
80. Barbara Mowat has noted the influence of the players' quartos on Nicholas Rowe's edition of 1709 and the extent to which this influence has persisted in the editorial tradition and she has observed that 'our tendency to ignore the players' quartos in our study of the history of Shakespeare texts may need to be rethought' ('Form', p. 106).

81. Paul, 'Mr. Hughs' Edition', p. 441.
82. Shattuck, *Shakespeare Promptbooks . . . Catalogue*, p. 8. Richard Knowles has added a new section on 'Theater Editions', the revised edition of the *Variorum Handbook*. Such editions continue to appear. In 2001, Edward Hall and Roger Warren's adaptation of the *Henry VI* plays in two parts, entitled *Rose Rage*, was published by Oberon books. (Neither this text, nor the film editions mentioned in the next paragraph, have been included in the chronological appendix to this volume.)
83. I am grateful to John Kerrigan, the editor of the Penguin *Sonnets* volume, for passing this information on to me.
84. Quoted in Wells and Taylor, *Textual Companion*, p. 37. On the Jonson folio more generally, see Brady and Herenden (eds.), *Ben Jonson's 1616 Folio* and Douglas A. Brooks, *From Playhouse to Printing House*, chapter 3. On the trope of work versus play, see Peters, *Theatre*, p. 207.

2 Early collected editions

1. Pollard, 'A Literary Causerie', p. 528. Marsden J. Perry paid £7,000 for the volume, subsequently selling it to A. S. W. Rosenbach, who in turn sold it to Henry Clay Folger, for a price of $100,000 – see Cannon, *American Book Collectors*, p. 327.
2. See Pollard, *Folios and Quartos*, pp. 83–4. A further set of the quartos turned up in the early 1940s in the Girsby Manor home of Sir John St Vigor Fox. For a rather overheated account of this discovery, see J. E. Hodgson's pamphlet *The Remarkable Story of the Shakespearian Quartos of 1619*.
3. Pollard, 'A Literary Causerie', p. 529.
4. Quoted in Curwen, *History of Booksellers*, p. 391.
5. Greg, 'False Dates', esp. pp. 122–5.
6. Neidig, 'Shakespeare Quartos', p. 6.
7. Ibid., pp. 9–10.
8. Stevenson, 'Shakespearian Dated Watermarks', pp. 159, 160.
9. Details of the careers of William and Isaac Jaggard are largely taken from Willoughby, *A Printer of Shakespeare*.
10. My thanks to Lukas Erne for bringing this set of collaborations to my attention.
11. See Chambers, *William Shakespeare*, I, p. 135.
12. See chapter 1, pp. 19–20.
13. Pavier also had at least a slender claim to the rights to *Titus Andronicus*, which had been assigned to him by Thomas Millington in 1602. However, Edward White seems also to have claimed the play (his name, together with Millington's, had been included on the title page of Danter's original 1594 edition of the text, as a seller of the book). In any event, Pavier did not include *Titus* in his quarto collection.
14. Greg, *First Folio*, p. 67.
15. Johnson, 'Thomas Pavier', p. 38.
16. On 4 August 1626, Pavier's widow transferred his publishing rights to Edward Brewster and Robert Bird and the transfer included 'Mr. Paviers right in Shakesperes plaies or any of them'. Subsequently, on 8 November 1630, Robert Bird transferred rights in a selection of plays to Richard Cotes. This transfer specifically names *Pericles* as one of the copies included in the transaction. See Dawson, 'Copyright', p. 17.
17. In fact, Thomas Hayes' son, Lawrence, re-entered the copy for *Merchant* on 8 July 1619, publishing an edition of the play himself in 1637. See Greg, *First Folio*, p. 65.
18. Johnson, 'Thomas Pavier', p. 35.

19. Ibid., p. 25.
20. See Jackson, 'Counterfeit Printing'. Berger, in 'Looking', p. 327, includes parallel illustrations of the title pages of the 1600 *Henry V* and *Midsummer Night's Dream* and their Pavier counterparts.
21. Quoted from Wells and Taylor, *Textual Companion*, p. 36.
22. It is just conceivable that they may have heard of the collection from Jaggard himself, since one of the benefits which he gained in taking over James Roberts' business was the exclusive right to publish playbills. See note 34 below.
23. Johnson, 'Thomas Pavier', p. 40.
24. Berger and Lander speculate, in 'Shakespeare in Print', that this may have been one of the reasons why no definite action would appear to have been taken against Pavier: 'whoever felt their interests damaged by the quartos may have been willing to countenance the appearance of apparently old playbooks on the grounds that they might actually help create a market for a new, authoritative edition' (p. 405).
25. Quoted from Chambers, *William Shakespeare*, II, p. 172.
26. Greg, *First Folio*, p. 1. Charles Connell's little volume *They Gave Us Shakespeare*, while rather lightweight and hagiographical, nevertheless provides some useful background information on Heminge and Condell.
27. My thanks to Gabriel Egan for bringing this to my attention and for providing me with the reference indicated in the next note. Dr Egan has written about this topic in 'Tap-house'.
28. Chambers, *Elizabethan Stage*, II, p. 421.
29. These plays were: *The Tempest, Two Gentlemen of Verona, Measure for Measure, Comedy of Errors, As You Like It, All's Well that Ends Well, Twelfth Night, King John, 1 Henry VI, Henry VIII, Coriolanus, Timon of Athens, Julius Caesar, Macbeth, Antony and Cleopatra, Cymbeline* and *Taming of the Shrew* (if we accept that this is clearly a different play from the 1594 *Taming of a Shrew*).
30. Orgel, 'Kinds', p. 109.
31. Prynne, *Histrio-Mastix*, 'To the Christian Reader'. Prynne may have had the Second rather than the First Folio in mind in making this comment, since it had appeared in 1632, just a year before *Histrio-Mastix*.
32. It is noteworthy that, following the appearance of the Fourth Folio in 1685, it would be a full century before another single-volume collected edition appeared – Stockdale's large octavo edition of 1784, which had very small print. For the second Stockdale edition, published in 1790, an additional title page was provided so that the text could be bound in two volumes 'in order to remove the objection made by some to the bulk of the volume' (§356, Preface, a4r).
33. Hinman, *Printing and Proof-reading*, I, p. 48.
34. Jaggard petitioned for this right in 1593, following the death of John Charlwood. The Court of Assistants decided that they would 'have consideracon to prefer him in this suite before another' if he could obtain the consent of Charlwood's widow, or if she died or married out of the Company. In the event, Alice Charlwood married James Roberts. See Willoughby, *Printer*, pp. 42–3. But see also Willoughby, *Printing*, pp. 2–3.
35. Blayney, *First Folio*, p. 4. Kastan has added a further practical reason for Jaggard's involvement: 'Heminge and Condell contracted with the Jaggards to print the folio because the Jaggards were willing to do it. Few stationers would have been eager or even able to undertake a project the size of the Shakespeare folio. The commitment of resources and the impossibility of any quick profits would make it an unattractive venture for any but the most ambitious publishers' (*Shakespeare and the Book*, pp. 57–8).

36. The texts of these plays reproduced in the Folio were not, however, those which had been published by Johnson and Butter. Johnson's *Merry Wives* was a variant text and the Folio syndicate replaced it with a text of their own. The Folio text of *Lear* also differs from the Butter Quarto; some have argued that it represents an authorial revision of the earlier version – see Taylor and Warren (eds.), *Division* and Ioppolo, *Revising*.
37. See Willoughby, *Printer*, p. 4.
38. Blayney, §1689, p. xxviii. Kastan argues in *Shakespeare and the Book*, however, that Blount was probably a latecomer to the venture – see p. 61.
39. Greg, *First Folio*, p. 18.
40. Kastan, *Shakespeare and the Book*, p. 62.
41. The entry in fact reads 'The thirde parte of Henry yᵉ sixt', but this almost certainly refers to the play conventionally styled *1 Henry VI* – possibly it is being identified here as the third play of the sequence to be registered.
42. Blayney, *First Folio*, p. 21.
43. The *Oxford Shakespeare* editors note that 'no textual theory can make it credible that Shakespeare wrote the bulk of the first nine scenes [of the play] and . . . a variety of evidence points to George Wilkins as his probable collaborator' (Wells and Taylor, *Textual Companion*, p. 557).
44. Kastan discusses the question of the inclusion of *Henry VIII* at p. 67 of *Shakespeare and the Book*.
45. See Blayney, *First Folio*, p. 1.
46. General details here are taken from the *Cardenio* entry in Dobson and Wells, *Oxford Companion*, p. 66–7. Theobald claimed to have had access to as many as four manuscripts, but his claims have aroused suspicion, not least because he failed to include the play in his own edition of Shakespeare and no manuscripts of the play appeared in *The Catalogue of the Library of Lewis Theobald, Deceas'd* (October 1744), when his library was disposed of at auction. Brean S. Hammond has offered some very tentative evidence that one of the manuscripts may have been held by the Covent Garden Theatre, which was destroyed by fire in 1808.
47. From Blayney, *First Folio*, p. 8, where the relevant pages of the catalogue are included in facsimile.
48. For a summary timetable of the volume's progress through the Jaggard printshop, see Hinman, *Printing and Proof-reading*, I, p. 363.
49. Satchell, 'Spelling', p. 352.
50. Hinman, *Printing and Proof-reading*, II, p. 513. Hinman also noted, as other commentators had done, that a certain John Shakespeare of Warwickshire was apprenticed to Jaggard in 1610, taking up his freedom in 1617. 'It is pleasant to wonder', Hinman writes, 'if the man who set more than half of the Folio into type [Compositor B] was by any chance this same John Shakespeare' (p. 513). Blayney is, however, dismissive of the idea, noting that John Shakespeare was not mentioned in William Jaggard's will 'and probably worked elsewhere after serving out his term' (*First Folio*, p. 11).
51. See Blayney, §1689, pp. xxxiii–xxxiv, which includes details of the most important recent studies, and also pp. xxxv–xxxvii, which provide details of the work carried out by each compositor.
52. These general details are taken from Smith, 'Eternal', who provides a full account of the development of the collator. Smith notes that 'It should be emphasized that Hinman's unit specialized in cryptanalytic work and not photographic analysis . . . Thus, the aerial photography experiment was something that Hinman "heard," perhaps from a neighboring

unit or a colleague elsewhere in the intelligence community, and not something that he observed directly' (p. 137).

53. Tanselle, 'Bowers', p. 34, quoting William H. Bond.
54. These details taken from a Mico Engineering Company leaflet on the collator. My thanks to Betsy Walsh at the Folger Shakespeare Library for tracking down this material for me.
55. West, in *Shakespeare*, observes that 'No other book is even in the same league in generating such broad interest and detailed study' as the First Folio (p. 41).
56. The ground had, to some extent, been broken by Willoughby in *The Printing of the First Folio of Shakespeare*.
57. A Folio sheet consists of two pages set side-by-side and these two pages together make up a single forme. Like most books of its size, the First Folio was made up of quires consisting of three sheets folded together. Sheet one of the first quire therefore has pages 1 and 12 on the 'outside' of the sheet (the 'outer forme') and pages 2 and 11 on the 'inside' of the sheet (the 'inner forme'). The outer forme of sheet two has pages 3 and 10 and the inner pages 4 and 9; the outer forme of sheet three has pages 5 and 8 and the inner pages 6 and 7.
58. If the book had been set page by page and in page order, then the following would have had to be set before any printing could begin: (i) the right hand page of the outer forme of sheet one (p. 1); (ii) left hand page of inner forme sheet one (p. 2); (iii) right hand outer sheet two (p. 3); (iv) left hand inner sheet two (p. 4); (v) right hand outer sheet three (p. 5); (vi) left hand inner sheet three (p. 6); (vii) right hand inner sheet three (p. 7). Only by stage (vii) would an entire forme have been set and ready for imposition. Blayney notes that 'as the person who can be said to have "discovered" setting by formes, Hinman had not yet had the opportunity to realize what subsequent studies have shown, namely that it was the *usual* way of setting the text of books in folio (and fairly common in quarto printing too)' (§1689, p. xxxii).
59. 'Casting off' was the process whereby a printer divided up his copy into the segments that he estimated would fill the individual pages of the printed book.
60. Hinman, *Printing and Proof-reading*, I, pp. 507–509.
61. Taylor, 'General Introduction', in Wells and Taylor, *Textual Companion*, p. 51.
62. For a classic early exposition of the problem, see R. B. McKerrow's 'Suggestion'. McKerrow's work in this area is discussed in chapter 10, pp. 219–21.
63. See, in particular, Werstine, 'Narratives'. William B. Long is scathing about the lack of direct attention that has been paid to surviving Renaissance manuscript playbooks and the misguided theorising to which this lack of attention has given rise: 'in seeking to establish the nature of the manuscripts which lay behind printed editions, editors expend great quantities of ink discussing "promptbooks" and what they should reveal as they babble on, constructing a screen of flimflam, weaving explanations out of their imaginations while ignorantly (or arrogantly or both) ignoring even the mention of the existence of these surviving playbooks. . . . It is obviously much easier (and probably more fun) to conjure up explanations of the provenance of a text without being fettered by surviving historical evidence' ('Precious Few', p. 415). See also Long's 'A bed / for woodstock'. As long ago as 1932, Charles Read Baskervill, in discussing a quarto marked up for performance, noted that the theatrical annotator failed to make certain changes which would seem intuitively necessary in the creation of a prompt book ('Prompt Copy', pp. 50–1).
64. Hinman, *Printing and Proof-reading*, II, p. 521.
65. Why the printers should have skipped over the second part of *Henry IV* as well as the first is hard to say, especially given that this play was owned by a member of the Folio

syndicate – William Aspley. It had been published in quarto in 1600, so copy would, presumably, have readily been available. John W. Schroeder speculates that Jaggard may have been 'reluctant to print the last half of a two-part play whose first half was in Law's keeping' (*Great Folio*, p. 99).

66. Hinman, *Printing and Proof-reading*, II, p. 523.
67. Greg, *First Folio*, p. 449.
68. The Droeshout engraving of Shakespeare's portrait included in the preliminaries of the volume is also found in three distinctive states. See Hinman, *Printing and Proof-reading*, I, pp. 248–9.
69. Blayney, in *First Folio*, offers the most comprehensive account of the likely cost of the book. He observes that: 'The real answer to the question of how much the Folio cost . . . is a range rather than a price. In London, unbound copies would usually have cost 15s., while bound copies would have cost about 16s.–17s. in limp forel, 17s.–18s. 6d. in forel-covered boards, and about £1 in plain calf' (p. 32). The most comprehensive account of sale prices for all four folios is provided in West, 'Sales and Prices'. Details of clerical income are taken from Altick, *Common Reader*, p. 22.
70. See West, *Shakespeare*, p. 58. Extending this price analysis, West notes that by the first decade of the twentieth century the price of the First Folio had risen to the equivalent of 96,000 loaves of bread.
71. Hinman, §1689, p. xix.
72. Blayney, §1689, p. xxxiii.
73. Willoughby, *Printer*, p. 180.
74. Dawson, 'Copyright', p. 19. The most extensive analysis of the variant states of the title page is provided by William B. Todd, in 'Issues and States'. Todd notes that, of 163 extant title pages, 125 give Allot's name; 16 Smethwick's; 7 Aspley's; 9 Hawkins'; 6 Meighen's (p. 95).
75. For example, Stanley Wells notes in his Oxford edition of *King Lear* that the printers of the Second Quarto *Lear* 'attempted, with some success, to correct typographical mistakes, to make punctuation more intelligible, and to supply needed stage directions' (§1554, p. 81). Likewise, Jonathan Bate observes in his Arden *Titus Andronicus* that Q2 *Titus* 'has greatly improved punctuation and makes some corrections which suggest a real attentiveness to the text' (§1673, p. 113). Someone involved in preparing the Second Quarto *Titus* felt compelled to write some extra lines for the play, since the bottom of the final two leaves of the copy of the First Quarto that was used by the compositors as copy had been torn away – see, in addition to Bate's edition pp. 113–14, Bolton, 'Authentic Text'.
76. Nicoll, 'Editors', p. 165 and pp. 165–6.
77. Black and Shaaber, *Editors*, pp. 20, 97, 33.
78. Ibid., p. 48; on metre, see pp. 41–2 and p. 46.
79. Werstine, 'William Shakespeare', p. 256.
80. Williams, 'Publishing', p. 594.
81. Farr, 'Philip Chetwind', p. 134.
82. Ibid., p. 160.
83. Lounsbury, *Text*, p. 114.
84. Black and Shaaber, *Editors*, pp. 20–1.
85. Ibid., p. 50.
86. Farr, 'Philip Chetwind', p. 160.
87. De Beer (ed.), *Diary*, III, p. 459 and note 3.
88. Dawson, 'Copyright', pp. 21–2.
89. Dawson, 'Bibliographical', p. 99 and pp. 99–100.

90. Black and Shaaber, *Editors*, p. 59.
91. Dawson, 'Bibliographical', pp. 94–102.
92. Rasmussen, 'Anonymity', p. 318. Rasmussen further notes that 'a significant number of emendations previously attributed to Rowe, Pope, and Theobald turn out to have been anticipated by F5' (p. 320).

3 The Tonson era 1: Rowe to Warburton

1. Lynch, *Jacob Tonson*, p. 1. Except where otherwise stated, details of Tonson's career as a publisher are taken from Lynch.
2. Ibid., p. 126.
3. See chapter 2, pp. 54–5. As noted there, the logic of the surviving records indicate only a half share of these rights were acquired by Martin and Herringman. But their claim to a full share in these rights seems to have been accepted.
4. See Dawson, 'Copyright', pp. 25–6.
5. Lynch, *Jacob Tonson*, p. 67.
6. See Franklin, *Domesticated*, p. 9. The convenience of the new size is registered in the dedication to Tonson's edition of Beaumont and Fletcher, published in 1711. This edition was also in octavo and the writer of the dedication hopes that the dedicatee (the Duke of Devonshire) will 'approve of Publishing these Authors in the same Portable Volume, as *Shakespear* has so successfully appeared in' (§172, I, A2r–v).
7. Boase, 'Illustrations', p. 87.
8. Holland, §1710, I, p. xxii.
9. Black and Shaaber, *Editors*, p. 59.
10. Announcement regarding Rowe's edition (unpaged). Tonson was publisher of the *Gazette*.
11. Smith, *Eighteenth Century*, p. 31.
12. There is some dispute regarding exactly which quarto edition Rowe used – Jackson, 'Rowe's Edition' suggests 1676 (p. 466), as does Mowat, 'Form' (p. 106), but Dawson, *Four Centuries* suggests 1703 (p. 6).
13. Smith, *Eighteenth Century*, pp. 32–3. It is perhaps more likely that he used the Second Folio since, as West notes in 'Sales', a Second Folio but not a First was included in the sale of Rowe's books (p. 493).
14. See Mowat, 'Rowe', pp. 318–19.
15. See McKenzie, 'Typography and Meaning', esp. p. 81. Holland notes that Rowe 'made the plays conform to contemporary theatrical practice and that necessitated the careful definition of each play's act form. Given that most of Shakespeare's plays were written for a theatre where act divisions were not marked in performance but the performance ran continuously, Rowe is imposing a shape often against the grain of the text's own articulation of its shape' (§1710, I, p. xiv).
16. Mowat, 'Rowe', p. 317.
17. For alternative ordering practices in the Renaissance period, see Sisson, 'Prompt-Copies', who notes that 'the speakers' names in early printed plays are generally set out in the order of their appearance, as in modern programmes. So it is, for example, in *The Disobedient Child* and *Damon and Pythias*, both 1571, *Apius and Virginia*, 1575, *All for Money*, 1578, and *The Conflict of Conscience*, 1581' (p. 132).
18. Hume, 'Before the Bard', p. 51.
19. He was also taken to court by Pope for publishing an unauthorised edition of Pope's correspondence – see Rose, *Authors*, pp. 58–66.

20. Straus, *Unspeakable Curll*, p. 4.
21. Sherbo, *Birth*, p. 1.
22. Quoted in Lynch, *Jacob Tonson*, p. 131.
23. Straus, *Unspeakable Curll*, p. 44.
24. Dawson, *Four Centuries*, p. 9.
25. Ford, *Shakespeare*, p. 11.
26. On the new artwork, see Boase, 'Illustrations', pp. 87–8.
27. Johnson, 'Catalogue', unpaged.
28. Ford, *Shakespeare*, pp. 3–4.
29. Dawson, *Four Centuries*, p. 9.
30. Lynch, *Jacob Tonson*, p. 115.
31. Geduld, *Prince*, pp. 20, 140.
32. Announcement regarding Pope's edition (*Weekly Journal*), p. 927.
33. Announcement regarding Pope's edition (*The Evening Post*), third page.
34. See Peck, *New Memoirs*.
35. Sherburn (ed.), *Correspondence*, II, p. 142.
36. Smith, *Eighteenth Century*, p. 36.
37. Seary, *Theobald*, p. 143.
38. McKerrow, 'Treatment', p. 102.
39. Lounsbury, *Text*, pp. 108–9.
40. McKerrow, 'Treatment', pp. 104–5.
41. Smith, *Eighteenth Century*, p. 36; Lounsbury, *Text*, p. 110.
42. On Pope's selection criteria for his 'shining passages' and the influence of Gildon's supplementary volume to Rowe's edition on his choices, see Dixon, 'Pope's Shakespeare'.
43. Walsh, *Shakespeare, Milton*, p. 131. See also Brown, 'Little fellow'.
44. Rogers, 'Subscribers', p. 7. Rogers provides a very interesting analysis of the subscribers which the edition did attract.
45. Ibid., p. 17.
46. Schoenbaum, *Lives*, p. 119.
47. Theobald, *Tragedy*, Bb3r, italics as in original.
48. Walsh, *Shakespeare, Milton*, p. 133.
49. Theobald, *Shakespeare Restor'd*, p. 134.
50. Quoted in Seary, *Theobald*, p. 87. A parody, whose implied author was Swift, figured Pope and Theobald as biblical siblings; Pope grew 'exceeding fair, and comely . . . and in Favour with God and Man; and he became a Rhymer of Rhymes in those Days. But *Theobald* his Brother was a meek Man, and skilled in all the Learning of the Heathens' (*Dean Jonathan's Parody*, p. 3).
51. *Dunciad*, p. 9. The poem was issued in a variety of editions including, in 1729, *The Dunciad Variorvm. With the Prolegomena of Scriblerus*, which provided the poem with an extended spoof apparatus, thus broadening the attack to embrace the whole business of textual criticism and annotation. The opening note in the 'variorum' suggests that the title of the poem should be 'Dunc*e*iad' 'as the Etymology evidently demands' (p. 1); the note is mischievously attributed to 'THEOBALD'.
52. Seary, *Theobald*, p. 97.
53. See Theobald, *Shakespeare Restor'd*, p. 193: 'The Alteration of a *Letter*, when it restores Sense to a corrupted Passage, in a *learned Language*, is an Atchievement that brings Honour to the *Critick* who advances it: And Dr. BENTLEY will be remember'd to Posterity for his Performances of this Sort, as long as the World shall have any Esteem for the Remains of *Menander* and *Philemon*.'

54. Bentley also disastrously ventured into the field of English literature, when he produced an edition of *Paradise Lost* in 1732. D. C. Greetham notes that 'By postulating an amanuensis who had – perhaps deliberately – misrepresented what Milton dictated, Bentley was able to indulge in a level of conjecture that he would never have allowed in his classical work' (*Textual Scholarship*, pp. 318–19). Thomas Newton, who published an edition of Milton's poem in 1749, characterised the performance as 'the dotages of Dr Bentley' and observed that Bentley 'was more sagacious in finding faults, than happy in mending them; and if he had confined himself only to the former, he might have had better success; but when he attempted the latter . . . he commonly made most miserable bungling work' (Newton (ed.), *Paradise Lost*, I, a3r). Theobald's comments on Bentley following the appearance of the Milton edition are rather more circumspect than his earlier praise for the editor – see the Preface to Theobald's edition, §206, I, pp. xxxix–xl.
55. West, in 'Sales', neatly indicates how this change can be mapped in eighteenth-century-book auction catalogues, in which a shift occurs 'from an organizing principle of "Latin and theological works first" to one of "English works first and no distinction between theological and secular works"; at the same time the dominating proportion of books shifted from theological to secular, with the latter ultimately dwarfing the former' (p. 488).
56. Walsh, *Shakespeare, Milton*, p. 34.
57. Theobald does on one occasion make what may be a sly oblique reference to Pope's religion, when he observes in the Preface to his edition of Shakespeare that 'His Libels have been thrown out with so much Inveteracy, that, not to dispute whether they *should* come from a Christian, they leave it a Question whether they *could* come from a *Man*' (§206, I, p. xxxvi).
58. On the *Double Falsehood*, see chapter 2, note 46.
59. Theobald, *Double Falsehood*, Preface (unpaged).
60. Seary, *Theobald*, pp. 123–4. See Sherburn (ed.), *Correspondence*, III, pp. 241–5.
61. Seary, *Theobald*, pp. 123–4, fn. 74, drawing on Bodleian ms. Rawl. D. 729 and Folger ms. S. a. 163.
62. Ibid, drawing on Folger ms. S. a. 161.
63. Sherburn (ed.), *Correspondence*, II, pp. 82, 118.
64. From the Warburton and Theobald correspondence included in Nichols, *Illustrations*, II, p. 257.
65. Quoted in Smith, 'Shakespearean Commentaries', p. 221. The writer was George Montague and the quote is taken from W. S. Lewis (ed.), *Horace Walpole's Correspondence* (New Haven: Yale University Press, 1941), IX, p. 20.
66. Smith, 'Shakespearean Commentaries', p. 231.
67. Ibid., p. 234.
68. Jarvis, *Scholars*, p. 69.
69. McKerrow, *Treatment*, p. 111.
70. See Corballis, 'Copy-text'.
71. Lounsbury, *Text*, p. 524.
72. Seary, *Theobald*, p. 135.
73. Jarvis, *Scholars*, p. 95.
74. Ibid., p. 101.
75. *Weekly Oracle*, p. 144.
76. A set of trial pages for the Rowe edition survives in the collection of the British Library – shelfmark C.175.m.1. See Holland's introduction to §1710, I, p. xiii.
77. Quoted in Gondris, 'Farrago', p. 128.

78. Similar debates were played out in the late twentieth century also. In 1968, Edmund Wilson bitterly railed against MLA-sponsored editions which he found to be pedantic, arcane and unreadable, freighted with materials which would only be of interest to a 'very small group of monomaniac bibliographers' ('Fruits', p. 10).

79. Collins, 'Porson', p. 104. The editors of the 1863–66 Cambridge edition also recognised the value of Theobald's work, characterising him as 'incomparably superior to his predecessors, and to his immediate successor, Warburton, although the latter had the advantage of working on his materials. He was the first to recal [sic] a multitude of readings of the first Folio unquestionably right, but unnoticed by previous editors' (§587, I, p. xxxi). Likewise, in his 1908 Harvard lecture on Shakespeare, Horace Howard Furness observed of Theobald that he was 'an admirable and widely read classical scholar' whose 'power of unraveling a tangled sophistication of the printers amounted almost to inspiration' (*On Shakespeare*, pp. 22, 23).

80. McKerrow, *Treatment*, p. 109.

81. Jones, *Theobald*, pp. 181–2.

82. Quoted in Geduld, *Prince*, p. 23.

83. There was one other significant new edition published in the interval between Theobald and Warburton, Sir Thomas Hanmer's text of 1745. This edition will be considered in chapter 5.

84. Nichols (ed.), *Illustrations*, II, p. 96.

85. See Warburton, 'Shakespeare'.

86. Nichols (ed.), *Illustrations*, II, p. 129.

87. Far from sequestering materials of Warburton's for a second edition, Theobald, in fact, greatly reduced the amount of Warburton's notes included in his edition of 1740.

88. Quoted in Smith, 'Shakespearean Commentaries', p. 220.

89. *Hamlet* examples taken from Walsh, *Shakespeare, Milton*, pp. 153 and 164. Other examples from Marder, *His Exits*, p. 101.

90. Nichol, 'Editors', p. 174.

91. Walsh, *Shakespeare, Milton*, p. 163.

92. Grey, *A Word*, p. 2.

93. Edwards, *Supplement*, p. 9.

94. Marder, *His Exits*, pp. 102–3.

4 The Tonson era 2: Johnson to Malone

1. In these years, Theobald's edition was reissued three times by the cartel and Thomas Hanmer's edition four times. On Hanmer, see chapter 5, pp. 110–14.

2. 'Proposals', included in Johnson, *Observations*, unpaged.

3. Curwen, *History*, p. 59.

4. Quoted in Dawson, 'Copyright', p. 32.

5. Quoted in Marder, *His Exits*, p. 104.

6. Quoted in Rivington, *Publishing Family*, p. 69. Johnson had, however, a shrewd enough head for business in other respects, as he took Tonson to task for selling the edition at a price below the subscription rate, thus undercutting the editor himself, whose payment took the form of subscription copies – see *Publishing Family*, p. 70.

7. Johnson, *Proposals*, pp. 3–4.

8. McKerrow, *Treatment*, pp. 113–14.

9. Eastman, 'Texts', p. 191.

10. Walsh, *Shakespeare, Milton*, p. 175.

11. Eastman, 'Laity', pp. 1114, 1115.
12. Ibid., pp. 1116, 1121.
13. Franklin, *Domesticated*, p. 26.
14. See Schoenbaum, *Documentary*, p. 242.
15. Belanger, 'Publishers and Writers', p. 18.
16. See Richard Tonson's *DNB* entry.
17. Quoted from Samuel Pegge's memoir of Capell, included in Nichols (ed.), *Illustrations*, I, p. 474.
18. Ibid., pp. 476, 474.
19. See Greg, *Catalogue*, p. 164.
20. Seary, *Theobald*, p. 124, note 74, drawing on Folger ms. S. a. 163. On Johnson's payment, see Sherbo, *Samuel Johnson*, p. 10; on Theobald, see above, chapter 3, p. 71.
21. Franklin, *Domesticated*, p. 28.
22. See Pegge, in Nichols (ed.), *Illustrations*, I, p. 472.
23. Taylor, *Reinventing*, p. 143.
24. See Martin, *Malone*, p. 39; Boswell, 'Advertisement' to the 1821 Boswell-Malone edition (§470, I, p. xxii).
25. Halliwell[-Phillips], *Few Words*, p. 10. See also Joseph Crosby's comments to Joseph Parker Norris, in Velz and Teague (eds.), *One Touch*, pp. 75, 226. In a letter dated 30 May 1875, Crosby observes 'when you once see the old Scholar's meaning, it sticks to you, & you can bet on it. What little I have of Capell has done me great good' (p. 75). Alice Walker came to his defence in the twentieth century, in 'Edward Capell and his Edition of *Shakespeare*'.
26. Thomas Newton had abandoned the received text of *Paradise Lost* in his edition of 1749 – perhaps as a result of the controversy regarding Richard Bentley's edition of 1732. He was explicitly conscious of the different demands of Shakespearean and Miltonic editing. By contrast with Shakespeareans, he observes, 'we who undertake to publish Milton's Paradise Lost are not reduced to [such] uncertainty; we are not left floting [sic] in the wide ocean of conjecture, but have a chart and compass to steer by; we have an authentic copy to follow in the two editions printed in his own life-time, and have only to correct what may be supposed to be the errors of the press, or mistakes occasioned by the author's blindness' (I, a2r–a2v).
27. Review of Capell, *Monthly Review*, p. 483.
28. McKerrow, *Treatment*, p. 116.
29. See Crosse, 'Charles Jennens', p. 239.
30. Urkowitz, 'Base', pp. 36, 37.
31. Velz, in Hosley, Knowles and McGugan, *Variorum Handbook*, p. 66.
32. Velz, 'Research', p. 55.
33. Crosse, 'Charles Jennens', p. 240.
34. Steevens, review in *Critical Review*, pp. 436, 439, 438.
35. Cross, 'Charles Jennens', p. 238.
36. Quoted in Marder, *His Exits*, p. 109.
37. Schoenbaum, *Lives*, p. 211.
38. Sherbo, *Achievement*, p. xi.
39. Nichols (ed.), *Illustrations*, V, p. 428.
40. Sherbo, *Achievement*, p. 1.
41. See above, chapter 3, pp. 62–3.
42. 'Advertisement' to the 1793 Johnson–Steevens–Reed edition, (§375, I, p. vii).
43. For the publishing date of the Johnson edition, see Wheatley, 'Johnson's', p. 298.

44. All quotations from Steevens, 'Proposals', unpaged.
45. Franklin, *Domesticated*, p. 34.
46. Blagden discusses the commercial logic of drawing a large number of publishers into individual publishing projects in 'Trade Sales'. Plant, in *Book Trade* notes that such partnerships became less common in the nineteenth century, in part because of changes in company law: 'The time was coming when publishers would not be so anxious to pass on part of their risks. From the [1860s] onwards the risks borne by publishing and other companies were greatly reduced by the provisions for limited liability. Although Latham's edition of Johnson's *Dictionary* was published in 1866 by a partnership it was the very rarity of such a form of publication by that time which called attention to it' (p. 430).
47. Collins, dedication to Capell, *Notes*, I, a2r, a2v. See also Collins, *A Letter to George Hardinge*.
48. Evans, 'Rough Notes', p. 44.
49. *Etymologist*, p. 33.
50. Quoted in Sherbo, *Factotum*, p. 9.
51. 'Fairly early in his career as bookseller, editor, and writer in a number of genres, Robert Dodsley did contemporary historians of the early English drama a great service by editing and publishing a twelve-volume *Select Collection of Old Plays* in 1744 . . . A second edition was published, well after Dodsley's death, by his younger brother James, in 1780. The work, bearing the words "Corrected and Collated with the Old Copies" on the title page, was printed by John Nichols, but the editor, Isaac Reed, as was his wont, preferred anonymity. In his Preface Reed acknowledged "that aid – offered him, in the politest manner, by a gentleman to whom he is under many great obligations, besides his communications to this work. When it is known, that to him the publick are indebted for all the notes signed with the letter S, the reader will regret that there are not a greater proportion of the whole number under that signature." S was George Steevens, the number and extent of those notes virtually make him co-editor' (Sherbo, *Achievement*, p. 97).
52. Ibid., p. 25.
53. Sherbo, 'Steevens' 1785', p. 241.
54. Woodson, 'Printer's Copy', p. 209.
55. Sherbo, *Factotum*, p. 89.
56. Review, *Monthly Review*, pp. 168, 169.
57. Ritson, proposals, in *Remarks*, unpaged.
58. Ritson, *Remarks*, p. ii.
59. Ritson, *Cursory Criticisms*, pp. vii, 35.
60. Martin, *Malone*, pp. 168–9.
61. Quoted in Sherbo, *Birth*, pp. 140–1. Details of the number of Ritson's notes used by Steevens taken from the same source, p. 140.
62. The names included here are all, as Steevens himself explains, taken from the list of actors included in the First Folio.
63. Martin, *Malone*, pp. 13, 15–16.
64. Quoted in Wheatley, 'Shakespeare's Editors', p. 165.
65. On Malone's borrowing of *Romeus and Juliet* in exchange for allowing Capell to see his copy of *A Shrew*, see Walker, 'Edward Capell', p. 137.
66. See Grebanier, *Great Shakespeare Forgery*, pp. 203–10.
67. Nichols (ed.), *Illustrations*, V, p. 463.

68. Jones (ed.), *Isaac Reed Diaries*, p. 181, entry for 13 September 1790.
69. Martin, *Malone*, p. 133.
70. De Grazia, *Verbatim*, p. 2.
71. On Malone's choice of base text, see Jarvis, *Scholars*, p. 185.
72. Ibid., p. 187.
73. De Grazia, *Verbatim*, p. 6.
74. Jarvis, *Scholars*, p. 187.
75. De Grazia, *Verbatim*, p. 54.
76. Review of Capell's three volumes of notes, *Monthly Review*, p. 484. This review was published in 1783 and therefore refers to Malone's earlier Shakespearean work, rather than to his edition. But the same arguments apply to the edition – Evans, in 'Rough Notes', observes of the 1790 text that 'Malone completes [Steevens'] steal from Capell, particularly in the matter of stage directions' (p. 45). See also chapter IX of Hart, *Edward Capell*.
77. Malone, proposals, unpaged.
78. Martin, *Malone*, p. 177.
79. See Boswell's 'Advertisement' to the edition (§470, I, p. vi).
80. Sherbo, *Birth*, p. 168
81. Sen, 'Malone's', p. 390.
82. Quoted in Marder, *His Exits*, p. 131. John Payne Collier also took the edition severely to task in *Reasons*, especially pp. 21–8. Collier asserts that 'Boswell (to say nothing of Malone) performed his duty of collation with almost criminal inattention' (p. 26).
83. Smith, *Eighteenth Century*, p. 57. Smith's neglect of the Cambridge and Globe editions may possibly have been a consequence of his involvement in a rival Oxford edition (which was eventually aborted) – see chapter 10, pp. 221–3.
84. Holt, *An Attempt*, pp. iv–v.
85. Heath, *Revisal*, p. vi.
86. Bell's 1786–8 edition, 'Reasons *for Printing this* WORK, *and* Observations *on it's* [sic] *Propriety*' (§349, I, unpaged). Mathias, *Pursuits*, pp. 93, 96. Where Mathias characterised the critics as dogs, George Steevens imagined them as sheep. Having borrowed Malone's edition of the 1600 edition of *Lucrece*, he returned it with a drawing pasted on the flyleaf: 'a bust of Shakespeare is shown with the words written on a label proceeding from his lips: "Would that I had all my commentators in Lipsbury pinfold!"' (Lee, 'Introduction' to *Lucrece*, §970, pp. 44–5, n. 1).
87. Mathias, *Pursuits*, p. 101. Interestingly, only Capell is fully exempted from Mathias' satire. Other editors 'From Capell steal, yet never own the theft, / And then desert him of his store bereft' (pp. 89–90) and Capell himself is characterised as '*the Patron* of SHAKSPEARE' (p. 91).
88. Ibid., p. 91. Mathias was prescient. An advert for Valpy's 1832 edition notes that 'The Work will be handsomely printed, hot-pressed, and bound in cloth.'

5 Copyright disputes: English publishers

1. Belanger, 'Tonson, Wellington', p. 195; Blagden, 'Trade Sales', p. 250.
2. See Feather, 'Publishers', p. 24.
3. Blagden, 'Trade Sales', p. 255.
4. The term 'copyright' is used throughout this chapter as a matter of convenience. In fact the word 'copyright' came into use only very gradually over the course of the eighteenth

century. The first recorded use would appear to be in Pope's transactions with the book trade in 1727 – see McLaverty, *Pope*, p. 237.

5. Rose, 'Author', p. 53.
6. Steinberg, *Five Hundred Years*, p. 109.
7. On the rigorous exercise of these powers by the second Surveyor, Sir Roger L'Estrange, see Patterson, *Copyright*, p. 135.
8. Astbury, 'Renewal', p. 296.
9. Quoted in Rose, *Authors*, p. 32.
10. Kernan, *Printing Technology*, p. 59.
11. See Feather, *History*, p. 73.
12. Feather, 'Publishers', p. 5.
13. Feather, 'Book Trade in Politics', p. 36.
14. McLaverty, *Pope*, p. 238.
15. Kernan, *Printing Technology*, p. 100.
16. Ford, *Shakespeare*, p. 47.
17. Letter from Johnson to Professor Charles Mackie, dated 10 October 1728, Edinburgh University archives ms. La.II.91. All quotations from the Johnson–Mackie correspondence are taken from this file.
18. McDougall, 'Litigation', p. 3.
19. Feather, 'English Book Trade', p. 57.
20. See note 17.
21. See Johnson, 'Catalogue', unpaged.
22. Ford, *Shakespeare*, pp. 51–2.
23. See chapter 3, p. 63.
24. Review of Pope's edition, p. 2075. All subsequent quotations taken from the same page.
25. Ibid., 27 March 1725, p. 2081.
26. *Cotes Weekly Journal*, no. 1, front page.
27. Ibid., no. 7, final page.
28. Ibid., no. 1, front page.
29. Quoted in Patterson, *Copyright*, p. 153.
30. See Atto, 'Society'.
31. Dawson, 'Copyright', p. 30.
32. Wiles, *Serial*, p. 226. This was, in fact, not an exceptional practice – see Alden, 'Pills', p. 21.
33. Dawson, *Four Centuries*, p. 13.
34. Quotations are from an extended advertisement included at the end of Walker's edition of *2 Henry IV*.
35. Bald, 'Early Copyright', p. 89.
36. From Walker's advertisement included at the end of *Othello* (both quotations).
37. Dawson, *Four Centuries*, p. 13.
38. Advertisement included with Tonson's edition of *All's Well*.
39. Dawson, *Four Centuries*, p. 13; from an advert included at the end of Walker's edition of *Locrine*.
40. Dawson, 'Walker's', pp. 63–7.
41. Nicoll, *Garrick*, p. 16.
42. Dawson, 'Walker's', p. 81.
43. Hume, 'Before the Bard', p. 54.
44. Bunbury (ed.), *Correspondence*, p. 81.
45. Dawson, 'Warburton, Hanmer', p. 41, n. 6.

46. Irene G. Dash notes that Hanmer 'found lines objectionable that apparently had been inoffensive to his predecessor. Differences in the men as well as in the times played a part: Pope's responses to the text were those of a poet – an artist not easily shocked by bawdy or innuendo – Hanmer's were those of a man of taste and sensibilities who belonged to a specific culture group and who mirrored their standards in his edition' ('Culture', p. 271).
47. Sherburn (ed.), *Correspondence*, IV, p. 475. Warburton fell out as bitterly with Hanmer as he had done with Theobald. See Bunbury (ed.), *Correspondence*, pp. 86–90 for the full, rather tedious, details.
48. Carter, *History*, I, p. 301.
49. Allentuck, 'Editor's Notes', p. 288.
50. Bunbury (ed.), *Correspondence*, p. 84.
51. Ibid., pp. 87–8.
52. Carter, *History*, I, p. 304.
53. Maw, 'Hornet's Nest', p. 25.
54. Nichols, *Castrated Letter*, p. 22.
55. Hervey, *Letter*, p. 24.
56. Ibid., p. 23.
57. Dawson, 'Copyright', p. 32.
58. See Sherbo, 'Warburton'. Kliman, in 'Samuel Johnson', suggests that the job of producing the annotations may have been undertaken by Johnson, partly as a compensation for Tonson's blocking the proposed Johnson–Cave edition. Her proposal is certainly very interesting, but it rests, as she herself acknowledges, very largely on circumstantial evidence.
59. See chapter 4, p. 80.
60. Cave himself was clearly conscious of the pricing issue. In his 'Proposals' (in Johnson, *Remarks*), he priced his own set at £1 5s. for subscribers, and included a note which read: 'It is hoped that the Undertakers of this Edition will be thought entitled to some Regard, when it is considered that the Price of Mr *Pope*'s was six Guineas, Mr *Theobald*'s two, and Sir *T. H.*'s three Guineas' (unpaged).
61. Quoted in Dawson, 'Copyright', p. 32.
62. Donaldson, *Some Thoughts*, p. 20. I say 'if this account is to be believed' because Donaldson, as will become clear in the next chapter, was not a disinterested party.
63. Donaldson, *Considerations*, p. 14.
64. Ibid., p. 14.
65. It is noteworthy that 'J. Osborn' is one of the names included in the imprint of the Tonson cartel's third edition of Nicholas Rowe's text, published in 1714, and also in one version of the imprint of their 1728 second edition of Pope's text. If this J. Osborn is John Osborn, then it may be that he felt he had some claim to the text by virtue of having been in some way connected with the cartel.
66. See Carter, *History*, I, p. 408.
67. Franklin, *Domesticated*, p. 31.
68. Ibid., p. 30.
69. Thompson, 'Boydell', pp. 20–1. On Boydell, see chapter 8, pp. 173–4.
70. Burnim and Highfill, *Bell*, p. 9.
71. Alexander, 'Province', p. 358. On the illustrations to the Bell editions, see Byrne, 'Bell's', p. 65.
72. Burnim and Highfill, *Bell*, p. 3.
73. Perrin, *Legacy*, pp. 94–5.
74. Marder, *His Exits*, p. 109.

75. Altick, *Common Reader*, p. 54. Left-over stock from the Shakespeare edition would seem to have been used to replace some of the texts originally included in the 'British Theatre' series – see Cameron, *Bibliography*, pp. 2–5.
76. The move was connected with the establishment of 'Bell's British Letter Foundry' – see Burnim and Highfill, *Bell*, p. 5.
77. Review of Bell, p. 156.
78. Knight, *Shadows*, p. 277.
79. Altick, *Common Reader*, p. 54.

6 Copyright disputes: Scottish and Irish publishers

1. See Rose, *Authors*, p. 83.
2. Quoted in Lynch, *Scotland*, p. 321.
3. Stockwell, 'Dublin Pirates', p. 31.
4. Quoted in ibid., p. 32.
5. Quoted in Phillips, *Printing*, p. 15.
6. Cole, *Irish Booksellers*, p. 16.
7. One might contrast Hamilton's view with that of a French visitor to Dublin in 1734, who observed: 'The better to form a Judgment of the Taste of the People, in Matters of Learning, I have past some Hours in a Booksellers Shop, whereof there is a great many in the Capital. I have found there is no City in *Europe*, (ceteris paribus) where there be so many good Pieces printed, and so few bad' (quoted in Pollard, *Dublin's Trade*, pp. 110–11).
8. Cole, *Irish Booksellers*, p. 1.
9. Feather, 'English Book Trade', p. 57, and see also p. 64.
10. See Pollard, *Dublin's Trade*, p. 134.
11. Quoted in Ward, *Prince*, p. 18. Cole notes that Edmond Malone 'was a frequent subscriber to Dublin reprints like the 1775 Johnson's *Dictionary* and the Dublin *Dante* . . . and he had 148 Irish editions in his library, many of them multi-volumed and most of them reprints' (*Irish Booksellers*, p. 19).
12. McDougall, 'Litigation', p. 5.
13. M. Pollard, however, questions whether the export trade was ever as significant as some contemporary British commentators suggested: 'While certain members of the Dublin trade made illegal attempts to supply [Britain and the colonies] by the complicated and hazardous method of book-smuggling, I consider the financial suffering caused to the London trade by this intrusion on their home market to have been relatively small. Much greater was the loss of a large part of the Irish market through the Dubliners' ability to reprint cheaply' (*Dublin's Trade*, p. vi).
14. Quoted in Dix, 'Irish', p. 75. On disputes regarding Dublin reprints of Richardson's work, see also Ward, *Prince*, pp. 18–20.
15. English editions of Shakespeare certainly seem to have made their way to Ireland during the course of the seventeenth century. Pollard notes that the library of Edward Conway, second Viscount of Killultagh contained close to 10,000 works 'including some 2,000 titles under the heading of literature and romances with a number of Shakespeare quartos' (*Dublin's Trade*, p. 63). In 1698, John Dunton came to Ireland with '*A General Collection of the most Valuable Books, Printed in* England, *since the Fire in* London *in 66. to this very time*', including a '*Great Variety of Scarce Books. – A Collection of Pamphlets, in all Volumes: – And a Parcel of Manuscripts, never yet in Print*'. These books and manuscripts

were sold at a series of auctions in Dublin. Included in a list of some of the books auctioned is 'Shakespears *Works*' (Dunton, *Dublin Scuffle*, pp. 108–9).

16. Plomer, *Dictionary*, p. 134.

17. Plomer, Bushell, and Dix, *Dictionary*, p. 387.

18. Hammond, 'King's Printers', pp. 88–89.

19. See Phillips, *Printing*, p. 16.

20. That no Shakespeare texts were published in Ireland until the 1720s can probably be attributed to the fact that, from the mid-sixteenth century through to the end of the seventeenth century, Irish printing was (at least broadly speaking) the monopolistic preserve of Dublin's single 'king's printer', whose primary concern was with official publishing. By the time Grierson was appointed, the remit of the king's printer had been largely confined to official government printing and the trade had begun significantly to expand. For a detailed account of this history, see Pollard, *Dublin's Trade*, chapter 1.

21. If M. Pollard's figures (derived from an analysis of subscription lists for the later period 1740–9) can be taken as a guide, this seems like a relatively low number of subscribers. Pollard found that, while subscriptions in the 1740–9 sample ranged from fewer than 100 to greater than 1,200, the average was 380 – see *Dublin's Trade*, pp. 118–20.

22. §195: first three titles from a joint Grierson–Ewing list included at the end of volume I; final title from a separate Grierson list included at the end of volume VIII.

23. It should be noted that the numbers given in the opening sentences of this paragraph relate only to those Irish editions which have been logged in the ESTC database. As I indicate in the introduction to the chronological appendix to this volume, it seems likely that other editions were published in Ireland in this period which have not survived (or which have not yet been identified). For this reason, the figures quoted here should be taken as offering very rough guides only.

24. Writing of popular printing in Ireland between 1750 and 1850, Niall Ó Ciosáin notes the dominance of Dublin in terms of production and trade: 'Pedlars would have bought their goods, including books, in Dublin, and travelled along a national road system which radiated from Dublin' (*Print*, p. 55).

25. See Fenning, 'Catholic Press', pp. 21–2. Fenning notes that Swiney seems to have had some sort of connection with the Dublin printer, Bartholomew Corcoran, whose religious illustrations Swiney incorporated into his 1766 edition of Sadler's *Daily Exercise*. Corcoran was also a Shakespeare publisher, producing editions of *Merchant of Venice* (1766) and *Othello* (1767).

26. Information drawn from an advertisement included in Swiney's 1761 edition of *Macbeth* (§269). All of these texts had appeared in Irish editions in advance of Swiney's advertisement, with the exception of *Coriolanus*, which would seem to have appeared for the first time in an Irish edition in the following year. Thomas Sheridan's adaptation, *Coriolanus: or, the Roman Matron*, was, however, published by M. Williamson in Dublin in 1757.

27. Pollard, in *Dublin's Trade*, notes that in 1722 Smith was expelled from the university 'ostensibly for celebrating Lord Molesworth's election to Parliament by kindling a bonfire and refusing to obey authority's command to put it out' (p. 198).

28. Grierson may have followed the same practice – the verso of the final leaf of his 1726 *Hamlet* has the catchword 'OTHEL-' and the Trinity College Cambridge copy of the text (Munby d.37[5]) has an *Othello* title page bound with it, with a date of 1726. No copy of a 1726 Grierson *Othello* has been logged by ESTC. The page numbers in the *Hamlet* do not correspond with those of the 1725–6 collected edition, but the Folger

Shakespeare Library catalogue notes that the *Hamlet* text is composed of overrun sheets from the larger edition 'with some reimposition and new page numbers'.

29. Shelfmark: I6551Dubl. – only volumes I and VI of the set have survived. I am, of course making the assumption (perhaps unwarranted) that the excisions were made in the eighteenth century. The Library has no provenance records for the volumes (unlike its Scottish counterpart, the National Library of Ireland's collection does not have its roots in the deposit requirements specified in the 1710 copyright act).

30. It was from this Dublin edition that Christoph Martin Wieland made his translation of Shakespeare into German in the 1760s. See Meisnest, 'Wieland's', pp. 16–18.

31. All quotations from Exshaw, *Proposals*, unpaged.

32. Somewhat anomalously, one Shakespeare text had been published in Scotland before this: a 1627 edition of *Venus and Adonis*, issued in Edinburgh by John Wreittoun.

33. If this is true, it holds good only for collected editions. Individual play editions rose to a peak of fourteen in the decade of the 1750s. The equivalent figures for the 1720s, 1730s, and 1740s are eleven, thirteen, and nine respectively. The figure for the 1760s is twelve, after which individual-play publishing dropped away almost completely. But, again, these figures need to be treated with caution (see note 23 above).

34. A useful compendium of information on Shakespeare and Scotland is provided in the National Library of Scotland exhibition catalogue *Shakespeare: An Exhibition of Printed Books*.

35. Except where otherwise stated, general details of Foulis' career are taken from Murray, *Foulis*.

36. *Robert and Andrew Foulis: An Exhibition*, p. 1.

37. See Campbell, 'Francis Hutcheson'; Duncan, *Notices*, p. 10.

38. Murray (ed.), *Letters*, p. 2.

39. Wilson, in fact, subsequently established an English branch of the foundry at Two-Waters in Hertfordshire and this facility was ultimately taken over by the Caslons in 1850. See Glasgow Bibliographical Society, *Catalogue*, p. 20.

40. Curwen, *History*, p. 453

41. Ibid.

42. Quoted in Duncan, *Notices*, p. 21.

43. Murray, *Foulis*, suggests (p. 49) that the larger set was issued in 1757, as does the *Shakespeare: An Exhibition* catalogue (p. 24), possibly following Murray. I have found no evidence that this is correct. Full details of the two issues are provided in Gaskell, *Bibliography*, pp. 270–3.

44. See ibid., p. 273.

45. Quoted in Duncan, *Notices*, pp. 19–20.

46. Hosley, Knowles and McGugan, *Variorum Handbook*, p. 63. Richard Knowles and Christopher Spencer found far fewer emendations in their analysis of *As You Like It* and *Merchant*, concluding 'For our plays the edition was apparently not worth collating.'

47. See Crawford (ed.), *Scottish Invention*.

48. See McDougall, 'Litigation', p. 14.

49. *Unto the Right Honourable the Lords of Council and Session*, p. 30.

50. 'Answers for John Reid', printed with *Unto the Right Honourable*, p. 30.

51. Appendix listing 'books claimed by the petitioner [Donaldson], which he alledges were sent from his shop to the printing-house, and taken from thence by Mr. Reid', included in *Unto the Right Honourable*, p. 40.

52. See Skinner, *Notable Family*, p. 14 and Plomer, *Dictionary*, p. 299. General details of Donaldson's career are taken from these sources.

53. Donaldson, *Catalogue*, p. 46, items 1113 and 1114.
54. *Unto the Right Honourable*, p. 1.
55. Quoted in Walters, 'Booksellers', p. 291.
56. The full text of the letter is included in ibid., pp. 290–1.
57. Ibid., p. 301.
58. [Donaldson], *Some Thoughts*, p. 24.
59. Ibid., p. 18.
60. Ibid., p. 20.
61. See chapter 5, pp. 114–15.
62. [Donaldson], *Considerations*, pp. 13–14.
63. ESTC records indicate that these editions are extremely rare; possibly Donaldson may have issued other texts in the series, which either have not survived or have not yet been identified.
64. Quoted in Walters, 'Booksellers', p. 302.
65. See McDougall, 'Litigation', p. 4.
66. See Curwen, *History*, p. 63.
67. McDougall, 'Litigation', p. 5.
68. On Home, Shakespeare, and the evolution of English as a university subject in Scotland, see Rhodes, 'Rhetoric'.
69. Quoted in McDougall, 'Litigation', pp. 7, 6.
70. Quoted in Rose, *Authors*, p. 83.
71. McDougall, 'Litigation', p. 9.
72. Feather, 'Publishers', p. 20.
73. Walters, 'Booksellers', p. 303.
74. Feather, 'Publishers', p. 20.
75. Sales figures taken from Patterson, *Copyright*, p. 172.
76. Feather, 'Publishers', p. 20.
77. See Rose, *Authors*, p. 96.
78. Quoted in Rose, 'Author', p. 68.
79. For a clear mapping out of the exact decisions reached in the Lords' ruling, see Patterson, *Copyright*, p. 175.
80. Altick, 'Aldine', p. 6.
81. See 'Reminiscences of James Donaldson by James Campbell, Printer 1853', in Skinner, *Notable Family*, p. 16.
82. Quoted in Patterson, *Copyright*, p. 179.
83. Gray, 'Alexander Donaldson', pp. 197, 202.
84. Review of Bell's edition, p. 155.
85. See Cole, *Irish Booksellers*, p. 149.
86. Ibid., p. 152.
87. Ó Ciosáin notes that the dissolution of the Irish parliament also hit the printing trade more directly, in that it led to 'the decline of printing for the administration' (*Print*, p. 56).
88. Cole, *Irish Booksellers*, p. 153.
89. See Martin, *Malone*, pp. 142–3.
90. See Cole, *Irish Booksellers*, p. 59.
91. Willoughby, 'Reading', p. 52.
92. See Lorenz, *Hugh Gaine*, pp. 27–8.
93. Cole, *Irish Booksellers*, pp. 55–6.
94. See Cole, *Irish Booksellers*, pp. 45, 156.

7 American editions

1. Churchill, 'America', p. xiv.
2. See Hughes, *History*, pp. 14, 19.
3. Simon, *Reading*, p. 7.
4. Dunn, *America*, pp. 29–30.
5. List of books, unpaged.
6. See Willoughby, 'Colonial', p. 51, Bolton, *Harvard*, pp. 435–6.
7. See Wright, *Literary Culture*, p. 188.
8. See Willoughby, 'Colonial', p. 52.
9. See Westfall, *American*, p. 30.
10. See Willoughby, 'Colonial', p. 48.
11. Cannon, *American*, p. 16.
12. Quoted in Willoughby, 'Colonial', p. 56.
13. Dunn, *America*, p. 125.
14. Printing came to Catholic Spanish America earlier than this. As David D. Hall notes in Amory and Hall, *History*, 'the Bishop of Mexico established in 1539 the first printing office in the New World, using it to issue books of religious instruction' (I, p. 14). Except where otherwise stated, general information on early American printing is taken from Amory and Hall.
15. Wroth, 'North America', pp. 324–5, 325.
16. See Amory and Hall, *History*, pp. 18–19. Hall notes that 'the number of Indian imprints had reached approximately twenty-eight by 1730' (p. 19).
17. Wroth, 'North America', p. 20, pp. 319–20.
18. For all general details included in the paragraph, see ibid., pp. 326–9, 338–9.
19. Quoted in Westfall, *American*, pp. 79–80.
20. See Westfall, *American*, pp. 81–3. The fact that some of the notes are copied unthinkingly from Bell is indicated by, for instance, the following note on Sir Andrew, on p. 7 of the *Twelfth Night* text: 'The requisites we have mentioned for *Slender*, in *The Merry Wives*, will suit this child of whim, save that he should possess sprightlier, more disengaged simplicity' (§377).
21. See chapter 6, pp. 139–40.
22. Dunn, in *America* (pp. 224–5), has observed that:

> the entrance of Shakespeare into the conservative American stronghold of traditional education, under the respectable aegis of Hugh Blair, is one of the pleasant little jokes of our history. Hugh Blair was a famous Edinburgh preacher and professor; these facts spelled safety for anything he might write and publish. He had occupied successively the famous pulpit of the Presbyterian High Church in Edinburgh and the newly created Chair of Rhetoric and Belles Lettres in Edinburgh University. He had retired in 1783 from his lectureship and put his lectures into book form. This Scotch preacher and teacher, friend of Hume and Adam Smith, made frequent use of Shakespeare both in his lectures and in the book for which they furnished the basis.
>
> To be sure Shakespeare is handled with the usual eighteenth century prejudices. He is scolded for not knowing the rules of poetry. But he is lauded, too, and generously quoted. 'Touching the heart', Blair declares, 'is Shakespeare's great excellency.' Shakespeare is a bulwark of virtue and morality instead of a seduction of the devil. His characters make speeches which 'are at once *instructive* and affecting'. He is 'great' and 'altogether unrivalled' in

tragedy and comedy. Thus by way of the Scotch Presbyterian, Blair, Shakespeare as 'great', as 'instructive' and 'touching the heart' enters, unchallenged, into the educational scheme of America.

23. Westfall, *American*, p. 90.
24. John Velz notes, in 'Research', that the lack of an international copyright agreement between the US and the UK greatly facilitated the recycling of British editions in America in the nineteenth century (the US did not accept international copyright law until 1891). Velz observes: 'Dozens of these piracies appeared in the course of the century' (p. 53).
25. See Westfall, *American*, p. 98.
26. A subscribers list is included in volume VIII of the Shakespeare Centre Library copy of this edition – 39/1802-4 (accession no. 1506).
27. Advertisement for Dennie's edition, pp. 46, 47.
28. Notices regarding Dennie's edition (10 March), p. 79.
29. See, for example, Notices (14 April), p. 119.
30. Westfall, *American*, p. 107.
31. These details taken from Westfall, *American*, p. 103. I was unable to locate a subscribers list in the copy of the edition which I consulted – Folger PR2752 1807–08 C.2 sh. col.
32. See Sherzer, 'American', p. 644.
33. Westfall, *American*, p. 114.
34. See Plant, *Book Trade*, p. 299.
35. Kubler, *Stereotyping*, pp. 42–5.
36. On Foulis, Tilloch and Stanhope, see Kubler, *Stereotyping*, pp. 58–63.
37. On Wilson, see Turner, 'Andrew Wilson'.
38. See Westfall, *American*, pp. 117–18; Sherzer, 'American', p. 650.
39. See Hosley, Knowles and McGugan, *Variorum Handbook*, p. 72. See also Scheide, 'Earliest', p. 333. Scheide suggests that it may be possible that Peabody used the Parker copy of the First Folio.
40. Westfall, *American*, p. 127.
41. Sherzer, 'American', pp. 658, 659.
42. Knowles, 'Dates', p. 190. Harvey, *Verplanck*, notes that 'Even as early as 1859, it was hard to obtain' and she doubts whether more than a dozen complete sets have survived (p. 221).
43. Sherzer, 'American', pp. 662, 663.
44. Hudson, *Essays*, p. 3.
45. Rankin, *Shakespearean Interpreter*, pp. 35–6. General details of Hudson's career are taken from Rankin.
46. Hudson, *Lectures*, I, p. vi.
47. Gould, Review, p. 203.
48. Ibid., p. 201.
49. Prospectus, unpaged.
50. Unpaged advertisement included as the final page of Hudson, *Essays*.
51. See Levine, *Highbrow/Lowbrow*, p. 23.
52. See Churchill, 'America', p. xxx.
53. Levine, *Highbrow/Lowbrow*, p. 63.
54. A list of those killed and wounded is included in *Account of the Terrific and Fatal Riot*, pp. 28–30.
55. Cannon, *American*, p. 319; see also Winsor, *Bibliography*, pp. 5–9. For Lenox, see Cannon, *American*, pp. 72–3.
56. Quoted in Winsor, *Bibliography*, pp. 7–8.

57. [Lowell], 'White's Shakspeare', pp. 246, 259.
58. British Library add ms. 55029, letter dated 24 July 1875.
59. Westfall, *American*, p. 153.
60. Churchill, 'America', p. xxxv.
61. Quoted in Gibson, *Philadelphia*, p. 15.
62. Savage, 'Shakspere', p. 348.
63. Gibson, *Philadelphia*, p. 59. Except where otherwise stated, all general details of Furness' career are taken from Gibson.
64. H. H. F. J. (ed.), *Letters*, II, pp. 54–5.
65. Quoted in Gibson, *Philadelphia*, p. 61.
66. On the Cambridge edition, see chapter 9, pp. 202–6.
67. Furness, 'New Variorum', p. 109.
68. Gibson, *Philadelphia*, pp. 69–70.
69. H. H. F. J. (ed.), *Letters*, I, p. 177.
70. Quoted in Velz, 'New Information', p. 290.
71. Gibson, *Philadelphia*, p. 111.
72. Simon, *Reading*, p. 114.
73. See prospectus, verso of cover (unpaged).
74. Altick, *Cowden Clarkes*, p. 202.
75. Cowden Clarke, *Long Life*, p. 228.
76. Churchill, 'America', p. xxxvii.
77. Graff, *Professing*, p. 58. Except where otherwise stated, general details regarding American higher education are taken from Graff.
78. Brander Matthews noted of Charles Murray Nairne, who taught him English literature at Columbia in the late 1860s and whose title was 'Professor of Moral and Intellectual Philosophy and English Literature', that it 'was not only a chair that he filled, or even a settee; it was a series of settees, rising row on row' (*These Many Years*, p. 109).
79. Quoted in Dunn, *America*, pp. 245–6.
80. Marder, *His Exits*, p. 184.
81. See Hosley, Knowles and McGugan, *Variorum Handbook*, p. 82.
82. See Graff, *Professing*, p. 26.
83. Kittredge quoted in ibid., p. 66.
84. Bishop quoted in Graff, *Professing*, p. 26; Matthews, *These Many Years*, p. 107.
85. Winsor, 'College Library', p. 8.
86. Ibid., p. 14.
87. At least one copy of the First Folio was lost during the course of this sea voyage. See West, *Shakespeare*, p. 33.
88. An indication of the extent of early Shakespeare holdings in the US in the second half of the nineteenth century is provided by Winsor, *Bibliography*, esp. pp. 17–19.
89. See chapter 2, p. 36.
90. See Cannon, *American*, p. 328. Except where otherwise stated, material on American book collectors included in this paragraph and the next is taken from Cannon. The extent of Rosenbach's importance as a trader in early Shakespeare is indicated by an illustration included in his *Books and Bidders*. The photograph shows a window at Rosenbach's Philadelphia premises, with a display of copies of all four folios, together with a selection of quartos. In front of the display is a sign reading 'SHAKESPEARE Exhibition of Original Editions of the works of William Shakespeare Price of the Collection $985,000^{00}' (facing p. 86).
91. Cannon, *American*, p. 313.

92. West, *Shakespeare*, p. 48.
93. See Blayney, *First Folio*, pp. 45–6, 42.
94. 'What Edition', p. 487.
95. Steevens, 'American', p. 365.
96. Smith, 'Ghost', pp. 186–7. For another instance of a bogus title page reproduced in a Bankside text, see Gellert, 'Davenant's'. One interesting feature of the Bankside edition was that the lines in the plays were numbered individually from the beginning through to the end of the text. The series thus anticipated the 'through line numbering' (TLN) system adopted by Charlton Hinman in his 1968 facsimile edition of the First Folio. My thanks to Marvin Spevack for drawing my attention to this feature of the Bankside texts.
97. Furness, *On Shakespeare*, p. 25.
98. A photograph pasted on to the inside cover of a copy of Porter and Clarke's edition of *Midsummer Night's Dream* held in the Folger (PR2755.P6.A3.v8. sh. col.) is perhaps – wittingly or unwittingly – emblematic of the traditional position of women editors of Shakespeare. In the picture, Porter and Clarke are kneeling behind a set of iron railings, reaching through the bars to hold the top corners of a copy of the First Folio. One of their own volumes rests against the book. I am indebted to Jeanne Addison Roberts for drawing this image to my attention, for discussing Porter and Clarke with me, and for providing me with a copy of her unpublished article 'Women Editors'. General details of the women's careers are derived from Roberts' essay.
99. Quoted in Roberts, 'Women Editors', p. 4.
100. Quoted from Roberts, 'Women Editors', p. 1.
101. OUP ms. CP/ED/000019. Porter and Clarke's opening sentence in the inaugural volume of their series might have struck a jarring note for the nationalistically minded English reader: '"The Tempest" may be said to be Shakespeare's one American play' (§915, *Tempest*, p. vii).
102. OUP ms. CP/ED/000019, letter from D. Nichol Smith to Walter Raleigh, dated 1 March 1905. In 1922, following A. S. W. Rosenbach's purchase of the Burdett-Coutts copy of the First Folio, *Punch* ran a cartoon in which 'Uncle Sam' is shown carrying off the volume, while regretting that he was unable to acquire Shakespeare's skeleton as well. A reproduction of the *Punch* cartoon is included in West, *Shakespeare*, p. 45. In the following year, at a London auction, Bernard Quaritch outbid Rosenbach for another copy of the First Folio and 'the audience applauded with as much national fervor as if an invasion had been stemmed', though the book nevertheless still ended up in the US, as Quaritch sold it on to Eddie Newton of Philadelphia (Wolf and Fleming, *Rosenbach*, p. 185).
103. See chapter 10, pp. 221–9.
104. OUP ms. CP/ED/000018, letter dated 27 March 1932. McKerrow's anxiety might be contrasted with the *Cambridge Review*'s comment in its obituary for William Aldis Wright, who co-edited the famous Cambridge Shakespeare in the 1860s, that 'Professors of English in American Universities have been known to say that the pointing out to them of his venerable and characteristic figure at work in the Trinity Library was as exciting an experience as their first view of Westminster Abbey' (Obituary, p. 466).
105. OUP ms. CP/ED/000018, letter dated 3 January 1937.
106. One neat indication of the transatlantic shift in Shakespeare studies is provided by Antony James West. Logging the redistribution of copies of the First Folio across the twentieth century, West provides figures which demonstrate almost an exact inversion between UK and US First Folio holdings between 1902 and 2000. In 1902, 66 per cent

of surviving copies of the First Folio were located in the UK, with 23 per cent in the US. By 2000, the equivalent figures were 20 per cent and 64 per cent. See West, *Shakespeare*, p. 140, table 2C.

8 Nineteenth-century popular editions

1. Call number NG.1577.d.1. The pages are probably taken from Quintin Craufurd's *Sketches of the history, religion, learning, and manners of the Hindoos. With a concise account of the present state of the native powers of Hindostan*, first published in 1788, reissued in 1790 and published in an enlarged second edition by Thomas Cadell in 1792.
2. Viswanathan, *Masks*, p. 3. The situation with regard to Shakespeare is, however, complex and does not always involve one-way cultural trafficking – see Loomba 'Cultural Difference' and 'Shakespearian Transformations'.
3. Advertising leaflet, unpaged.
4. [Waveney], *Shakespeare Bibliography*, I, p. xi.
5. The collection was instituted in the first instance in 1864, but most of the original stock was lost in a fire in January 1879. The library reopened in June 1882 and a total of some 40,000 items had been amassed in the Shakespeare collection by 1971. See [Waveney], *Shakespeare Bibliography*, I, p. ix.
6. See Plant, *Book Trade*, p. 446.
7. I say 'in simple terms' because, of course, the number of readers is not contingent on absolute population figures, but rather is determined by the degree of literacy in the population and the extent to which those who are literate can afford access to books. However, demographic shifts were to a large extent accompanied by an expansion in the educational franchise, as I will indicate in the final section of this chapter.
8. Stephens, *Education*, p. 150.
9. Ibid., p. 148.
10. [Bowdler], *Memoir*, pp. 328–9.
11. See Perrin, *Legacy*, p. 69.
12. See Daiches, 'Presenting', p. 94. By the third edition (1820), Bowdler had managed to create his own text from Shakespeare's original.
13. Quoted in Perrin, *Legacy*, p. 83.
14. Perrin, *Legacy*, pp. 83–4.
15. Review, pp. 52–3.
16. The review, which primarily concerned itself with Thomas Caldecott's editions of *Hamlet* and *As You Like It*, was published in April 1822. It was reproduced in Bowdler's *Letter*, from where it is quoted here (p. 7).
17. Bowdler, *Letter*, pp. 15, 31.
18. Review, p. 54. Perrin notes that 'Four months after the review, Owen Rees of Longmans & Co. reported to Dr. Bowdler that a new edition "in octavo with large type for *papas*" was in the works' (*Legacy*, pp. 84–5).
19. For a contemporary critique of the Cowden Clarkes expurgations, see Jaques, *Modern Corruptions*.
20. As Colin Franklin observes in 'Bowdlers': 'Passions are restrained, most days of most lives, impulses disciplined. We are all Bowdlers, in no position to mock' (p. 243).
21. Perrin, *Legacy*, p. 109.
22. Ibid., p. 105.
23. See Plant, *Book Trade*, p. 274. All general details of technological advances in printing in this paragraph are taken from Plant.

24. Plant, *Book Trade*, p. 329.
25. Ibid., p. 336.
26. In *Passages of a Working Life*, Charles Knight observes that 'The 13th of August, 1836, was a remarkable day in the annals of the press of this country, for on that day two Acts of Parliament received the Royal Assent, which materially influenced all the commercial arrangements for rendering knowledge, political or literary, more accessible to the bulk of the people. The first of these (c. 52), was to reduce the duties on first-class paper from three-pence per pound to three-halfpence, so that the former tax of three-halfpence upon second-class paper should apply to paper of all descriptions. The second of these (c. 76), was to reduce the stamp on newspapers from fourpence to a penny' (II, pp. 248–9). The paper duty was fully repealed in 1861.
27. Charles Cowden Clarke, *Shakespeare-Characters*, pp. 518–19.
28. Hammerschmidt-Hummel, 'Promoting', p. 34.
29. See Thompson, 'Boydell', pp. 21–2. On Steevens' role in the project, see Wenner, *George Steevens*.
30. Friedman, *Boydell's*, p. 88.
31. See Franklin, *Domesticated*, p. 54.
32. The contrast with the price of the Boydell edition is made in the first of four pages of adverts included in the front matter of volume I of the set. The prices given for Boydell in the advert are £95 and £190. I presume these must have been the contemporary second-hand prices for copies of the Steevens edition and the *Collection of Prints* respectively. If this is correct, then the price of each had increased approximately threefold.
33. According to one advertisement, the comedies included 335 illustrations, the histories 304 and the tragedies and poems, 271, with a supplementary volume offering a further eighty-four woodcuts (Advertisement for 'Mr. Knight's Editions of Shakspere', *Quarterly Literary Advertiser*, p. 79).
34. Knight, *Passages*, II, pp. 283–4.
35. Knight, Prospectus, p. 2.
36. See advertisement for 'Mr. Knight's Editions', *Quarterly Literary Advertiser* (for both pricing and quotation).
37. Review, p. 330.
38. Altick, *Cowden Clarkes*, p. 199.
39. Ibid.
40. See Bell, *George Bell*, p. 20. The book was co-published by Bell.
41. Quoted from Macmillan (ed.), *Letters*, pp. 171–2.
42. It is often assumed that the Globe was simply a reconfigured version of the larger Cambridge edition. This is not strictly true. As the Cambridge text was only partially completed when the Globe was being prepared, the editors used, for part of their base text, a copy of Knight's Stratford edition. See McKitterick, *History*, II, p. 394.
43. Letter to Alexander Macmillan from William Aldis Wright, dated 8 July 1864, BL add. ms. 55015.
44. Macmillan (ed.), *Letters*, p. 175. *The Bookseller* agreed with Macmillan, observing that the title 'does not appear to us to be inappropriate or too ambitious', Notices, p. 836.
45. Alexander Macmillan, letter to booksellers, unpaged.
46. 'Globe Edition', p. 587.
47. This figure was arrived at by tracking the Globe through the Cambridge University Press prizing books, which span the period from 1862 through to the late 1930s. Printrun figures for the text appear in volumes 17/3 through 17/9, 17/14 and 17/16.

48. Letter from Edward Dowden to George Macmillan, dated 4 August 1877, BL add. ms. 55029; letter from A. C. Bradley to George Macmillan, dated 30 August 1899, BL add. ms. 55017. In 1931, R. B. McKerrow noted of 'traditional numbering for Shakespeare' that 'the standard is the Globe' (OUP ms. CP/ED/000019, letter from McKerrow to Kenneth Sisam, dated 17 Sept 1931). As late as 1998, Globe line numbers were added to the Routledge reprint of the Halliwell-Phillipps/Staunton First Folio facsimile, prepared by Doug Moston.

49. Letter from Alexander Macmillan to William Aldis Wright, dated 2 November 1866, BL add. ms. 55386. The extent of Routledge's publishing interest in Shakespeare is indicated by the firm's publication book covering the years 1858–81, which provides an account of some (but not all) of the Shakespeare editions published by the firm in those years. The index provides entries for Hazlitt's Shakespeare; an edition of Knight's pictorial; two versions of Campbell's Shakespeare; a Staunton edition; and a Routledge edition in fifty parts (see University College London Library, Routledge archives, item 8, volume 3).

50. For the wholesale price of the Globe, see Morgan, *Macmillan* p. 76. The Routledge figures are taken from a trade catalogue issued by the publisher in January 1870 (pp. 68, 81), held at the University of London Library. This is the earliest catalogue held by the library. I am presuming that the wholesale price would not have been higher than this at the end of 1866.

51. Letter from Alexander Macmillan to William Aldis Wright, dated 17 October 1866, BL add. ms. 55386.

52. See Routledge trade catalogue, January 1870, p. 37; 'Shilling Shakespeares', p. 451.

53. 'Shilling Shakespeares', p. 451.

54. Ibid.

55. Henry Morley (ed.), *King Lear* (London: Cassell & Co., 1888), advert facing p. 192. These Cassell's editions have not been included in the chronological appendix to this volume.

56. Christian, 'Advertiser's', pp. 310, 308.

57. Ibid., p. 310.

58. Altick, *Common Reader*, p. 148.

59. See Stephens, *Education*, pp. 5–6. Except where otherwise stated, general information on education in the nineteenth century is taken from Stephens. It should be pointed out here that much of the material in this paragraph pertains only to England and Wales. Just as Scotland retained an independent legal system after the union of 1707, so too did it retain an independent educational system.

60. Ibid., pp. 13–14.

61. Ibid., p. 14.

62. See Altick, *Common Reader*, pp. 269–70.

63. Knight, *Passages*, II, p. 56.

64. Altick, *Common Reader*, p. 270.

65. See Altick, 'Aldine' and Bennett, 'John Murray's'.

66. Review of Leslie *et al.*, *Narratives*, p. 593.

67. Quoted in Altick, *Common Reader*, p. 157. Budget figures also derived from this source.

68. Roach, *Public Examinations*, p. 3.

69. See Daiches, 'Presenting', p. 96.

70. Jones, 'Shakespeare in English Schools', p. 115.

71. Quoted in Daiches, 'Presenting', p. 96.

72. To take just a few illustrative examples: *Coriolanus* 'edited by R. Whitelaw late fellow of Trinity College, Cambridge, and Assistant Master in Rugby School' (1873); *Julius*

Caesar 'edited by Arthur D. Innes, M.A., sometime scholar of Oriel Coll. Oxford' (1895); *Julius Caesar*, 'edited by E. M. Butler, M.A., Assistant Master at Harrow School' (1896).

73. Low, *Catalogue* (1871), preface (unpaged).
74. Ibid. p. 20.
75. Low, *Catalogue* (1876), pp. 63–4.
76. Letter from Alexander Macmillan to William Aldis Wright, dated 30 October 1863, BL add. ms. 55381.
77. Letter from Alexander Macmillan to William George Clark, dated 29 March 1865, BL add. ms. 55384.
78. Letter from Alexander Macmillan to William Aldis Wright, dated 28 January 1869, BL add. ms. 55386.
79. Letter from William Aldis Wright to Alexander Macmillan, dated 29 January 1869, BL add. ms. 55015.
80. Oxford University Press, Long Book 50.
81. Long Book 270.
82. Letter from Charles Cannan to Rix & Son, solicitors, dated 13 June 1914, Long Book 48. Wright's agreement, as this same letter makes clear, was for 60 per cent of profits.
83. Letter from R. W. Chapman to Mrs Jane Evans Wright, dated 23 January 1930, Long Book 48.
84. As early as 1905, the press was beginning to think about an alternative text for schools. Part of the rationale for the projected Oxford First-Folio-based text was that it could be reconfigured into a schools edition. Walter Raleigh thus wrote to the press observing that 'this edition, as it comes to birth, can easily be adapted for the schools, and reissued in an educational edition with separate introductions short notes and glossaries for the several plays' (undated letter, stamped as received on 12 September 1905, OUP ms. CP/ED/000019). On the projected First-Folio-based Oxford edition, see chapter 10, pp. 221–9.
85. Schedule attached to a memo from A. Norrington to the Secretary of the press (R. W. Chapman) and Kenneth Sissam, dated 6 February 1939, Long Book 48.
86. Dates for the embulletining as out of print of plays taken from the following sources: *Richard II* Long Book 49; *Lear* Long Book 221; *Macbeth* Long Book 50; *Midsummer Night's Dream* Long Book 261.
87. Figures included in this table are derived from tracking the text through Cambridge University Press prizing books 10, 11, 14, 21 and 27.
88. Letter from Verity to Clay, dated 20 February 1921, Cambridge University Press 'Pitt Press Shakespeare' files (three files referenced under the number 5195). All subsequent CUP references are to these files.
89. Figures from reprint order forms.
90. Memo from CFE to TFW, DWS, RJB, PJT, dated 9 December 1968.
91. Memo from CFE to DWS, RJB, TFW, WPS, dated 10 November 1969. One solution canvassed for saving money on the series, but apparently not pursued further, was 'reprinting in India and shipping sheets from there for non-Indian markets including UK' (memo from SC to DWS/RJB, dated 13 March 1969). This proposal interestingly anticipates much current publishing practice, both in print and electronic media.
92. Letter from C. J. Clay to Señor Juan de Goytia, dated 16 April 1918; letter from Editorial Novo to the press, dated 30 October 1944; letter from Jaap Bar-David to the press, dated 3 July 1960.

93. Letter from N. McG. Johnston to George Gill & Sons, redirected to the press, dated 12 January 1967 and a similar letter from the Australian Department of Education, dated 26 November 1974.
94. Letters appended to CFE's memo of 10 November 1969 (see note 91 above).

9 Nineteenth-century scholarly editions

1. Taylor, *Reinventing*, p. 56.
2. Poole, *Hamlet Travestie*, pp. 86–7.
3. See chapter 4, pp. 99–100.
4. A similar backlash occurs in the twentieth century, but its point of focus is the textual apparatus included in scholarly editions, rather than excessive commentary. Braunmuller, in 'Shakespeares Various' quotes E. M. W. Tillyard's response to a colleague who recommended that he use the Arden edition in his teaching, because of its extensive textual notes: 'I have not forgotten the unchallengeable earnestness of his expression as he pointed to the thick little nest of variant readings and conjectures below the text . . . I no more dared question his reverence in front of the textual variants than if he had taken me for a silent walk through a cemetery, suddenly stopped, and then, pointing to a monument, remarked, "There, that's my mother's grave"' (p. 3).
5. Letter from Walter Scott to Archibald Constable, dated 25 February 1822, National Library of Scotland, ms 743, II, item 5.
6. Knight, Prospectus, p. 1.
7. Altick, *Cowden Clarkes*, p. 199.
8. De Grazia, 'Question', p. 247.
9. Interestingly, one of the reasons why the later Wells and Taylor Oxford text was reconfigured by W. W. Norton for the US market was that, as an unannotated edition, it was considered unsuitable for American students, as they were thought to need more than just the 'book itself'. On the Wells and Taylor edition, see chapter 7, p. 166 and chapter 11, pp. 247–60.
10. Tooke, *Diversions*, II, p. 52.
11. Knight did, however, acknowledge that while the quarto lines omitted in the folio are cut for 'sufficient dramatic reason', it is, nevertheless, 'truly fortunate that passages of such exquisite beauty as they for the most part are should have been preserved to us in the original publication' (§485, I, p. vii).
12. Review of various Shakespeare editions (1845), p. 366. Knight himself conceded, in *Passages of a Working Life*, that he had 'preferred perhaps a little too exclusively the authority of the folio' (II, p. 291).
13. Franklin, *Domesticated*, p. 55.
14. Quoted in Martin, *Malone*, pp. 258, 258–9.
15. Bowers, Review of Yale, p. 55.
16. These figures are taken from Routledge trade catalogues held at the University College London Library. The figures are given on p. 83 of both catalogues and both are included in item number 215 in the library's Routledge archive.
17. Advertisement for Staunton's edition, p. 752.
18. 'Shall Shakespeare Have a Monument?', p. 169. West, *First Folio*, logs this sale on p. 94.
19. Ganzel, *Fortune*, p. 87.
20. Ibid., p. 40.
21. Collier, *Reasons*, pp. 10–11.
22. Ibid., pp. 12–13.

23. Eric Rasmussen registers this difference between the two editions in his entry on 'editing' in the Dobson and Wells, *Companion*, p. 122.

24. These facsimiles were privately printed at the instigation of the Duke of Devonshire. A note inside the National Library of Scotland copy of the 1604 text (shelfmark RB.s.1993), signed by John Payne Collier and dated August 1859, reads: '40 Copies. This facsimile was executed by the direction of the Duke of Devonshire and is presented by his Grace to the Library of the Writers of [sic] the Signet, Edinburgh.' The 'Writers to the Signet' is a society of Scottish lawyers with a history stretching back over 500 years. The society's library at one time ran to 150,000 volumes, but it was reduced over the course of the twentieth century to a core of some 63,000 volumes, mostly of a legal nature – see the Introduction to *Register*. The National Library's copy of the facsimile of the First Quarto *Hamlet* (shelfmark H.28.e.17) was presented to the library itself by Collier.

25. James Orchard Halliwell assumed the additional surname Phillipps by royal letters patent in 1872, Phillipps being the surname of his estranged father-in-law (see later in this chapter). Previous references to him in this chapter have post-dated 1872. Since references in the remainder of the chapter predate his name change, I will refer to him by his original name.

26. Halliwell, *Prospectuses*, p. 13.

27. See ibid., p. 11.

28. Furnivall, Prospectus, pp. 1–2.

29. Quoted in Marder, *His Exits*, p. 120.

30. Furnivall, Prospectus, p. 1.

31. Bowers, Review of Shakespeare Quarto Facsimiles, p. 235. Bowers speculated that, while the original publishers, Sidgwick and Jackson, had used a collotype facsimile process, Oxford University Press appeared to have switched to the cheaper offset process, with a consequent loss of quality in the reproduction.

32. Collier, Letter to *Athenæum*, p. 142.

33. Ibid., pp. 142–3.

34. Collier, *Notes*, p. viii.

35. J.F.K., Letter to *Athenæum*, p. 363.

36. Review of various editions (1845), p. 332.

37. Collier, *Notes*, p. iv. As the Bibliography indicates, my own copy of *Notes and Emendations* has a cancel title page, with 'The Shakespeare Society' substituted for the 'Whittaker & Co.' as publisher. The substitute title page gives the year of publication as 1852, whereas, in fact, the volume was issued in 1853.

38. See Ganzel, *Fortune*, p. 155. Ganzel notes, however, that the publishers – against Collier's own advice – grossly overestimated the market for the second edition, printing up some 30,000 copies.

39. *Grimaldi Shakspere*, p. 3, pp. 3–4.

40. Ibid., p. 13.

41. Knight, *Old Lamps*, p. lxiii.

42. Velz, 'Collier Controversy', p. 110.

43. For the purchase price of the Second-Folio volume, see Collier, Letter, p. 142.

44. Ganzel, *Fortune*, p. 5. Other editors used Collier's work to justify their own new editions, even as they sought to debunk the Perkins Folio. In an advertisement for his own second edition, for instance, Samuel Weller Singer observed: 'Mr. Collier has put forth a volume of Notes and Emendations founded on the manuscript-corrections of an anonymous writer, in a copy of the folio edition of 1632, in which such extreme license in altering the text is taken, as would make any edition in which such changes were admitted no longer

Skakespeare [sic]. Still, a few corrections of apparent typographical errors in the old copies which had escaped observation, are suggested by the anonymous annotator, these shall have the attention due to them in the thoroughly revised text now printing; and I trust it will be found that much has been done towards its purification and amendment' (advertisement included at the end of Singer's *Shakespeare Vindicated*, pp. 1–2).

45. In *The Text of Shakespeare Vindicated*, Singer ascribed the annotations to 'some "Puck of a commentator"' and observed that 'It would not be the first time that such knavish ingenuity has misled a well-trained Shakespearian antiquary and commentator' (pp. v, vi). Singer also claimed to have had copies of the Second and Third Folios with annotations of a similar kind to those in Collier's volume (pp. vii–x).

46. [Brae], *Literary Cookery*, p. 7. Velz, in 'Collier Controversy', notes that 'Collier sought an action of libel against Brae's publisher and forced the withdrawal of the pamphlet' (p. 112).

47. Review of various editions (1856), p. 360.

48. The volume was subsequently acquired by the Huntington Library.

49. Hamilton, *Inquiry*, p. 71. The National Library of Scotland copy of the *Inquiry* (N.E.1030.c.9) includes a pasted-in letter from Hamilton to F. C. Parry, in which he observes 'I cannot any longer be a believer in Mr. Collier's good faith.'

50. Ganzel, *Fortune*, p. 276.

51. Ganzel attempts to salvage something of Collier's reputation, suggesting that, far from being the perpetrator of a fabrication, he may rather have purchased the Perkins Folio in good faith, with the annotations already in place, and may naively have chosen to believe that the marginalia were of seventeenth-century origin, when, in fact, they were much more recent. He also argues that the British Museum staff were biased against Collier and accuses them of machinations deliberately aimed at discrediting him. While Ganzel's arguments are interesting, they have been rejected by all well-informed reviewers. See, in particular, Freeman's 'A New Victim for the Old Corrector', which concludes that the book 'is so seriously flawed by its central misconception that little of it survives to be credited' (p. 393). Ganzel and Freeman subsequently engaged in a heated exchange of views in *The Times Literary Supplement*, leading Freeman to exclaim in one letter 'Shame on him' ('John Payne Collier', p. 573). The substantial body of evidence indicating that Collier perpetrated a wide range of forgeries surely counts against Ganzel's argument – see, for example, Freeman and Freeman's 'Scholarship', Dawson's 'John Payne Collier's', and Velz's 'Collier Controversy'. A study of Collier's career by the Freemans is forthcoming.

52. A note inside case I of the National Library of Scotland copy of Collier's edition (shelfmark X.173.d) reads: 'This whole Edition in sm 4to was 60 Copies Each play is complete in itself but only 59 complete Copies of all the plays were sent out to as many subscribers in G. Britain & America This is my Own Copy, N° 60; and no more complete Copies exist than 60. All the rest are Odd Numbers, but every Play is complete in itself. J. P. C.'

53. Collier, 'New Shakspeare'; Knowles, 'Dates', p. 200.

54. Quoted in Ganzel, *Fortune*, p. 1. Ganzel does not regard this confession as relating to Collier's forgeries.

55. Velz, 'Collier Controversy', p. 112.

56. For a full account of the affair, see Winstanley, 'Halliwell Phillipps'.

57. Halliwell, *Prospectuses*, p. 5.

58. There seems to be some confusion regarding these prices. Jaggard, *Bibliography*, p. 530, gives £150 and £105. Schoenbaum, *Lives*, gives £84 and £63, probably deriving his information from the *Dictionary of National Biography*. I have taken my figures directly from Halliwell, *Prospectuses*, p. 3.

59. The university library at St Andrews holds copy number five of the edition, call number sfPR2753.H2.
60. Edinburgh University Library, H.-P. Coll. 314, entries 53 and 36.
61. Review of Halliwell, p. 799. Halliwell responded to the review in *Curiosities*.
62. Review of various editions (1856), p. 359.
63. Hosley, Knowles and McGugan, *Handbook*, p. 75.
64. Quoted from Macmillan, *Letters*, pp. 52–3, 53.
65. Clark and Luard, *First Act*, pp. 3, 4, 6.
66. Ibid., p. 7.
67. §587, I, p. x; Sinker, *Biographical Notes*, p. 77. Subsequent details of Glover's career are also taken from this latter source.
68. A letter from Alexander Macmillan to Clark, dated 2 July 1863, asks: 'Did you not express a wish that the agreement should be drawn afresh adding Wright's name? If you return it to me I will have this done' – BL add. ms. 55381.
69. Wright may not have been entirely happy with the collaborative arrangement. In a letter written to W. W. Greg in 1940, David Nichol Smith gave details of an encounter he had with Wright, while visiting the Capell collection at Cambridge. Smith writes: 'He said to me – "If you edit Shakespeare, do not have a colleague", – from which, & from his interest in the old spelling, I gathered that the plan of the Cambridge Shakespeare was not wholly to his liking.' Letter of 23 November 1940, National Library of Scotland ms Acc. 3511.
70. Colvin, obituary, p. 299 (for characterisations of both editors).
71. These details from Wright's *DNB* entry, p. 597.
72. Letter from William Aldis Wright to Alexander Macmillan, dated 22 July 1864, BL add. ms. 55015.
73. Letter from Alexander Macmillan to William Aldis Wright, dated 30 June 1863, BL add. ms. 55381.
74. Notice of Cambridge edition, p. 322.
75. Macmillan, *Letters*, p. 53.
76. See McKitterick, *History*, II, p. 393.
77. Entry included in the 'English Catalogue', unpaged.
78. Letter from Alexander Macmillan to William Aldis Wright, dated 17 October 1866, BL add. ms. 55386.
79. Arrowsmith, *Shakespeare's*, p. 19.
80. Quoted in McKitterick, *History*, II, p. 393. The feeling seems to have been mutual. In a letter to Alexander Macmillan, dated 29 July 1869, Wright observes of Dyce's own text that 'of all modern editions it is the worst' – BL add. ms. 55015.
81. Notices, p. 835.
82. Bowers, 'Today's', p. 39.
83. Wells and Taylor, *Textual Companion*, p. 56.
84. Werstine, 'William Shakespeare', p. 263.
85. Algernon Methuen Marshall Stedman changed his surname from Stedman to Methuen in 1899 – just at the time when he was corresponding with Dowden (hence the slight confusion in the endnotes which follow). For the sake of simplicity, I have used the surname Methuen throughout the main text of the chapter.
86. Letter from A. M. M. Stedman to Edward Dowden, dated 15 June 1898, TCD mss. 3147–54a (1089).
87. Letter from A. M. M. Stedman to Edward Dowden, dated 8 October 1898, TCD mss. 3147–54a (1093a).

88. Letter from A. M. M. Stedman to Edward Dowden, dated 15 June 1898, TCD mss. 3147–54a (1089).
89. John Dover Wilson felt that Dowden's edition was ahead of its time, anticipating much that would be characteristic of the New Bibliography. In *What Happens in* Hamlet, he comments:

> it is a significant fact that, apart from Dr Johnson and Edward Dowden, none of the great Shakespearian critics have been editors. This has not greatly mattered in plays the purport of which is clear and undisputed, as it is with most. But in *Hamlet*, where all is in doubt, editor, commentator and dramatic critic must go to work as a committee of one. Dowden, indeed, came near to bringing it off; he might have done, had he been young enough to be fathered by Pollard and brothered by [Greg]. (p. 13)

90. Letter from A. M. M. Methuen to Edward Dowden, dated 13 June 1900, TCD mss. 3147–54a (1110).
91. Letter from Edward Dowden to A. M. M. Methuen, dated 14 June 1900 and drafted on the back of Methuen's letter to Dowden of 13 June (see previous endnote). Dowden did, however, produce two further volumes for the series: *Romeo and Juliet* (1900) and *Cymbeline* (1903).
92. Letter from A. M. M. Methuen to Edward Dowden, dated 29 June 1900, TCD mss. 3147–54a (1112).
93. Arthur Brown notes that, for the second edition of the series, the publishers initially intended simply to reproduce the original base texts with new preliminaries: 'although wiser counsels prevailed, the publishers of the Arden Shakespeare were prepared to retain in the new volumes the stereotype plates of the text as it appeared in the original Arden series, making only minor alterations where absolutely necessary' ('Editorial Problems', p. 18).
94. Warren, 'Textual Problems', p. 26.

10 The New Bibliography

1. Furnivall, Inaugural, p. ix.
2. Ganzel, *Fortune*, p. 373.
3. See Benzie, *Furnivall*, pp. 217–18.
4. Furnivall, Prospectus (old spelling), pp. 3–4.
5. Quoted in Corbin, 'Shakespeare Against his Editors', p. 396.
6. Furnivall, Inaugural, pp. vi, vii.
7. Fleay, *Shakespeare Manual*, p. 108.
8. Ibid., p. 44 (*Titus*); p. 32 (*Romeo and Juliet*); p. 30 (*Richard III*); p. 42 (*Taming*).
9. Ibid., p. 262.
10. Grady, *Modernist*, p. 63.
11. Quoted in Benzie, *Furnivall*, p. 187.
12. Swinburne, *Study*, pp. 281–2, 286, 307.
13. See Benzie, *Furnivall*, p. 202.
14. Quoted in ibid., p. 201.
15. The full details of how the tedious dispute played itself out are provided by Benzie, *Furnivall*, at pp. 199–209. The petty pointlessness of the quarrel brings to mind Jorge Luis Borges' jibe about the Falklands War: that it amounted to the equivalent of 'two bald men fighting over a comb'.

16. See Greg, 'McKerrow', p. 493.
17. Greg, ' "Hamlet" Texts', p. 384.
18. Except where otherwise stated, all general details of McKerrow's life are taken from Greg, 'McKerrow'.
19. Greg, 'McKerrow', p. 491.
20. Except where otherwise stated, all general details of Greg's life are taken from Wilson, 'Greg' and J.C.T.O. *et al.*, 'Greg'.
21. Wilson, 'Greg', p. 310.
22. Greg, 'McKerrow', p. 491.
23. See Greg, *Catalogue*.
24. J.C.T.O. *et al.*, 'Greg', p. 152.
25. Letter from Greg to David Nichol Smith, dated 26 November 1940, National Library of Scotland, ms. 19603. See also Greg, *Editorial Problem*, p. 1.
26. John Dover Wilson observes in 'Pollard' that the Bibliographical Society was Pollard's 'child in everything but its begetting' (p. 280). Except where otherwise stated, general details of Pollard's life are taken from this source and from Pollard's *DNB* entry.
27. Pollard, 'First', pp. 6, 7.
28. Wilson, 'Greg', p. 310.
29. Ibid., pp. 310–11.
30. As late as 1984, Stanley Wells would comment of this edition that it remained 'one of the most impressive of all editions of an English author' (*Re-Editing*, p. 7).
31. Wilson, 'Pollard', p. 289.
32. Greg, Review (Collins), pp. 246, 251 (final quote).
33. Greg, 'Bibliography – an Apologia', in *Collected Papers*, pp. 241, 247.
34. Maguire, *Suspect*, pp. 41, 42. The address to which she refers is 'What is Bibliography?', read before the Society in February 1912. It is included in *Collected Works*.
35. Greg, 'The Present Position of Bibliography', in *Collected Works*, p. 218.
36. Wilson, 'Greg', p. 324.
37. See pp. 37–8.
38. See Note on Lee Facsimile, p. 3.
39. Pollard, *Folios and Quartos*, p. 131.
40. Wilson, *New Bibliography*, p. 102.
41. Greg, 'The Function of Bibliography', in *Collected Works*, p. 274.
42. Both McKerrow, in *Prolegomena* (esp. pp. 10–18) and Greg, in 'The Rationale of Copy-Text' (included in *Collected Papers*) attempted to define the precise circumstances in which an editor could or should depart from the readings of the copy text.
43. Wilson, *Manuscript*, I, p. 9.
44. Pollard noted that 'It was only at the end of their labours on *Hamlet* and *King Lear* that they discovered that the *Hamlet* quartos dated 1604 and 1605 which they called Q2 and Q3 differed only in the last figure of the date on their title-pages, and that the quarto of *Lear* which they had called Q1 was in fact the second. More especially in the case of *Lear* this means that they were making their editorial decisions under a wrong theory throughout the play and encouraged themselves in an eclecticism which was contrary to their excellent principles' (Review of Wilson's *Hamlet*, p. 119).
45. Wilson, *Manuscript*, I, p. 9.
46. See §357, I, xii–xiii.
47. Pollard, *Folios*, p. 4. Charles Knight, in fact, anticipated Pollard's argument, in his 1842–4 edition, where he observes: 'The editors of the first folio, as we have seen, use in their preface the following words; – "Before, you were abused with *divers* stolen and surreptitious

copies, maimed and deformed by the frauds and stealths of injurious impostors that exposed them." It is necessary that we should examine to which of the plays published before the folio this strong charge applies. It has been thought to involve a sweeping condemnation of *all* the previous editions; – but this is not so: it applies only to "*divers* stolen and surreptitious copies" (§485, I, p. xi). His insight would not, however, appear to have registered with other editors.

48. De Grazia, 'Essential', p. 74.
49. Greg, '"Hamlet" Texts', p. 382.
50. Wilson, 'Task', p. 77.
51. Alexander, *Shakespeare's* 'Henry VI' *and* 'Richard III', p. 136.
52. See pp. 23–30, above.
53. Simpson, *Punctuation*, p. 14.
54. Pollard, *Pirates*, p. xxi.
55. Wilson, 'Thirteen', p. 407. Greg would appear never to have been convinced by such arguments. While he thought Simpson's book extremely valuable as a study in Renaissance punctuation, he suggested that it was 'unfortunately named' ('The Present Position of Bibliography' in *Collected Papers*, p. 209).
56. See Simpson, 'Extant MSS'.
57. Thompson, *Handwriting*, p. viii. Italics as in original.
58. Ibid., p. 53, viii.
59. Pollard, 'Preface' to *Shakespeare's Hand*, p. v.
60. McKerrow, 'Elizabethan', p. 264.
61. Johnson, *Proposals*, pp. 3–4.
62. McKerrow, 'Elizabethan', p. 264.
63. McKerrow, 'Suggestion', p. 464.
64. Wilson, *Manuscript*, I, p. 151.
65. Letter from Walter Raleigh to Charles Cannan, dated 4 December 1904, OUP CP/ED/000019. Raleigh had, at this time, recently assisted in preparing W. E. Henley's 'Edinburgh Folio' edition of Shakespeare, published by Grant Richards. In the 'Advertisement' to volume I, Henley observed that 'Far and away the most notable book ever issued from the press, the First Folio is not for that the most correctly printed – the freeëst from mistakes. Hence, in the beginning it was all-too lightly regarded. In a later stage of civilisation, having regained its repute, and something more, it has come to be something of a fetish, and is vested with an authority, which, as SHAKESPEARE did not correct the proofs, seems a little fantastical. Thus, though it be the basis of the present Text, the Editor of that Text has not hesitated to accept amendments when occasion demanded, nor, when occasion demanded, to make amendments on his own account' (§913, I, unpaged).
66. Tooke, *Diversions*, II, p. 52.
67. Letter from J. C. Smith to Charles Cannan, dated 19 February 1905, OUP CP/ED/000019.
68. General information on Raleigh and Smith is taken from their respective *DNB* entries.
69. This quotation is taken from a typed transcript of an article by W. L. Renwick from *The Scotsman*, included in the David Nichol Smith papers at the National Library of Scotland – ms. acc. 6802. No date is given for the article.
70. Letter from D. Nichol Smith to Walter Raleigh, dated 1 March 1905, OUP CP/ED/000019.
71. Letter from D. Nichol Smith to W. W. Greg, dated 23 November 1940, National Library of Scotland – ms. acc. 3511. All further references to this correspondence are to this file.

72. Memo from Henry Frowde to the Secretary of the Clarendon Press, dated 12 November 1906, OUP CP/ED/000019.
73. See letter from D. Nichol Smith to W. W. Greg, dated 17 November 1940.
74. Unsigned document headed 'Interview' and dated 22 August 1910, included in OUP CP/ED/000019.
75. All quotations in this paragraph taken from the letter from D. Nichol Smith to W. W. Greg, dated 23 November 1940.
76. See Simpson, *Punctuation*, p. 3 and Greg, 'Present Position of Bibliography', in *Collected Works*, p. 209. Greg characterises Chapman as 'a scholar whose enthusiasm embraces alike cancel leaves and silver spoons – both worthy objects'. For a general outline of his career, see Naiman, 'Chapman'.
77. Letter from R. W. Chapman to K. Sisam, dated 5 March 1920, OUP CP/ED/000019.
78. Pollard was, later, mildly offended that the project proceeded without him. See letter from him to R. W. Chapman, dated 13 February 1930 (?), OUP CP/ED/000018.
79. Letter from R. B. McKerrow to R. W. Chapman, dated 24 November 1929, OUP CP/ED/000018. All further OUP correspondence references are to this file, unless otherwise stated.
80. See Francis, 'Bibliographical Society', p. 20.
81. Letter from R. B. McKerrow to Kenneth Sisam, dated 15 December 1929.
82. Report of a meeting with McKerrow by Kenneth Sisam, dated 22 January 1932.
83. See letter from R. W. Chapman to Humphrey Milford, dated 17 December 1928, where Chapman observes: 'we had it in mind that where two texts must be printed, e.g. Hamlet, they would be printed en face'.
84. See McKerrow, *Prolegomena*, pp. 4–5.
85. Report of a meeting with McKerrow by Kenneth Sisam, dated 22 January 1932.
86. Letter from John Dover Wilson to R. W. Chapman, dated 14 April 1932.
87. Letter from Kenneth Sisam to R. B. McKerrow, dated 16 June 1933.
88. Typed sheets marked 'Extract from letter dated 17th December, 1929' from Kenneth Sisam to R. B. McKerrow.
89. Letter from R. B. McKerrow to Kenneth Sisam, dated 9 May 1933.
90. Letter from Kenneth Sisam to R. B. McKerrow, dated 5 December 1934.
91. Letter from W. W. Greg to Kenneth Sisam, dated 3 January 1935.
92. Letter from R. B. McKerrow to Kenneth Sisam, dated 8 January 1936.
93. Letter from R. B. McKerrow to Kenneth Sisam, dated 2 May 1936. In his *Prolegomena* volume, McKerrow observed of Walker that her 'acute and logical mind has in particular enabled me to straighten out very numerous details of method in connexion with the giving of collations, and who besides this has aided me enormously in what is perhaps the most difficult of an editor's tasks, namely, the securing of consistency in dealing with parallel problems in different plays. This requires constant reference back and forth in a large bulk of material – as well as an excellent memory – and without her help, I fear that it would have been impossible for me even to approach the uniformity of treatment which, between us, we have, I hope, achieved' (p. x).
94. Letter from W. W. Greg to D. Nichol Smith, dated 26 November 1940, National Library of Scotland, ms. 19603.
95. Letter from R. B. McKerrow to Kenneth Sisam, dated 2 May 1936.
96. Letter from R. B. McKerrow to Kenneth Sisam, dated 3 January 1937.
97. See letter from Kenneth Sisam to R. B. McKerrow, dated 4 January 1937.
98. Stanley Wells notes, in his 'Preface' to *Re-editing*, that 'Nine plays were in fact set up in type, probably from marked-up facsimiles of early editions for McKerrow to use as

working texts. They include some emendations; though we cannot be sure that McKerrow would finally have endorsed them, they are of exceptional interest as evidence of his thinking' (p. v).

99. Letter from R. B. McKerrow to Kenneth Sisam, dated 6 December 1937.
100. McKerrow, *Prolegomena*, p. v.
101. Unless, perhaps, one counts Greg's *Principles of Emendation in Shakespeare*, but this was a much slighter work, being based on the text of a British Academy lecture.
102. Letter from R. W. Chapman to Humphrey Milford, dated 28 March 1939.
103. Letter from R. B. McKerrow to Kenneth Sisam, dated 10 May 1939.
104. Telegram from Amy McKerrow to R. W. Chapman, dated 20 January 1940.
105. Letter from Kenneth Sisam to E. K. Chambers, dated 7 February 1940.
106. Letter from Kenneth Sisam to W. W. Greg, dated 22 February 1940.
107. Letter from W. W. Greg to Kenneth Sisam, dated 24 February 1940.
108. Letter from Kenneth Sisam to Miss M. Dowling, dated 16 May 1940. The letter concerns the text of an appreciation of R. B. McKerrow to be published in the *Review of English Studies* and Sisam is anxious to stress that all concerned with the Oxford Shakespeare project 'are solid in the intention that the plan should be carried out if it is humanly possible'.
109. Howard-Hill, 'Walker', p. 300. All general details concerning Walker's life are taken from this source. I am very grateful to Professor Howard-Hill for his generosity in answering queries regarding Walker's role in the Oxford project. Stephen Tabor also notes, in 'McKerrow', that the 'first priority of the Oxford University Press after the war was to replenish its back stock, and by the time resources were again made available to new projects, the Shakespeare project had lain dormant too long to be revived' (p. 208).
110. Howard-Hill, 'Walker', pp. 300–1, drawing on OUP Delegates' Minutes of 7 March 1952. Walker's work in the 1950s was widely influential. In a letter to Peter Alexander, dated 6 October 1953, G. F. Maine of Collins publishers writes: 'I am in the course of reading, with great interest, Alice Walker's excellent volume on the Textual Problems of the First Folio' (Collins file 'Shakespeare Oct 1944 – Aug 77').
111. Howard-Hill, 'Walker', p. 304.
112. Ibid., p. 304, drawing on Oxford University Registry FA 9/2/910.
113. Stanley Wells and Gary Taylor have noted that 'her text of the play was set up in proof' and that they made some use of it in working on their own Oxford edition ('Re-Viewed', p. 6).
114. Trevor Howard-Hill, personal communication.
115. Howard-Hill, 'Towards the Twenty-First Century', p. 3.
116. Wells and Taylor note in 'Re-Viewed' that Walker 'was still nominal General Editor when the press's commissioning editor for English literature, John Bell, approached Stanley Wells in 1977 with the request that he assist the press in taking a fresh look at the problem' (pp. 6–7).
117. Roberts, 'Introduction' to Quiller-Couch's *Memories and Opinions*, p. ix.
118. Quiller-Couch, *Memories and Opinions*, p. 23.
119. See Wilson, *What Happens*, pp. 10–11.
120. Wilson, 'Pollard', p. 268.
121. Ibid., pp. 293–4.
122. Wilson, *Milestones*, p. 171.
123. Wilson, *What Happens*, p. 11.
124. Letter from Arthur Quiller-Couch to John Dover Wilson, dated 7 July 1919, National Library of Scotland ms. 14317.

125. Interview with John Dover Wilson in the *Guardian*, 6 June 1968.
126. Letter from A. R. Waller to John Dover Wilson, dated 17 July 1920, National Library of Scotland ms. 14323.
127. See letter from S. C. Roberts to John Dover Wilson, dated 6 November 1925, National Library of Scotland ms. 14323.
128. Letter from John Dover Wilson to S. C. Roberts, dated 10 November 1925, National Library of Scotland ms. 14323.
129. Wilson, 'Thirteen', p. 398.
130. Greg, *Editorial Problem*, p. 1.
131. Greg, 'Present Position of Bibliography', in *Collected Papers*, pp. 218–19. Wilson responded to the jibe in *What Happens* by telling Greg (to whom he dedicated the volume) that 'if the *balloons d'essai* and the gas they contain were of my manufacture, you were yourself largely responsible for the wind' (p. 11).
132. Wilson, *Manuscript*, I, p. 171.
133. Ibid., p. 78.
134. While criticising the flawed nature of Wilson's work, Fredson Bowers nevertheless felt it important to recognise the value of his basic principle of attempting 'thoroughly to analyze the documents in which variant forms of the text are preserved . . . to arrive at a coherent theory about their origins and relations, before undertaking to edit the text according to principles consistent with an overall hypothesis dependent upon this analysis' (Bowers, *Editing Shakespeare*, pp. 4–5).
135. Q had, in fact, warned Wilson against just such a tendency at the project's inception: 'If we make a page of The Tempest feel like a page of Androcles & the Lion, we are lost men' (letter from Q to John Dover Wilson, dated 31 August 1919, National Library of Scotland ms. 14317).
136. This stage direction paves the way, of course, for Wilson's interpretation of the nunnery scene, which he mapped out in detail in *What Happens in 'Hamlet'*. Wilson's argument that Hamlet is aware that Polonius and Claudius are spying on him has heavily influenced theatre and film directors over the past several decades.
137. Wells, *Re-Editing*, p. 84.
138. Ibid., p. 68.
139. A nice indication of this interest is the fact that Oxford University Press file CP/ED/000019 includes a flyer for Cambridge's 'Shakespeare Problems' series, which also announces the new Shakespeare edition, together with a dummy dust jacket for the New Cambridge *Tempest*, with the price 'Cloth 7s. 6d. net' circled twice in pencil.
140. Letter from Kenneth Sisam to David Nichol Smith, dated 19 May 1933, OUP CP/ED/000018. Subsequent Oxford University Press correspondence quoted in this paragraph is also from this file.
141. Letter from R. B. McKerrow to Kenneth Sisam, dated 20 May 1933.
142. Letter from R. B. McKerrow to Kenneth Sisam, dated 28 June 1933.
143. Letter from John Dover Wilson to G. V. Smithers, 26 June 1956, National Library of Scotland ms. 14324.
144. Letter from John Dover Wilson to Richard (Dick) David, dated 2 February 1966, National Library of Scotland ms. 14325. All further correspondence quoted is from this file.
145. Letter from Dick David to John Dover Wilson, dated 21 February 1966.
146. Letter from Peter Burbidge, Cambridge University Press, to John Dover Wilson, dated 26 January 1968.

147. Letter from Dick David to John Dover Wilson, dated 9 February 1966.
148. Jenkins' entry on Wilson in *DNB*, p. 1094.

11 The later twentieth century

1. Bowers, 'Today's', p. 48.
2. Except where otherwise stated, all general details of Alexander's life are taken from J. C. Bryce, 'Alexander'.
3. Bryce, 'Alexander', pp. 381, 383.
4. Pollard, 'Introduction', in Alexander, *Shakespeare's*, p. 28.
5. Alexander, *Shakespeare's*, p. v.
6. See Curwen, *History*, p. 454. The company has in recent times been absorbed into the News International conglomerate.
7. Letter from G. F. Maine of Collins to Peter Alexander, dated 12 October 1944, Collins archive file 'Shakespeare Oct 1944 – Aug 77'. Further references are to this file until otherwise indicated.
8. Typed sheet, headed 'Shakespeare (Notes by Professor P. Alexander, Professor of English Literature in the University of Glasgow)', dated 5 October 1944.
9. Memo from 'D Department' to W. A. Collins, W. A. R. Collins, Lieut.-Col. I. G. Collins and Mr. F. T. Smith, dated 21 September 1944.
10. Ibid.
11. Letter from G. F. Maine to Peter Alexander, dated 27 January 1949.
12. See chapter 10, p. 230.
13. Bowers, 'Today's', p. 44. It should be noted, however, that Bowers' characterisation of the edition does not seem to be wholly accurate. He observes, for instance, that 'Alexander was brought in to rescue another editor and therefore did not have control of the operation from the beginning.' If this is true, I have found no evidence to support it in the Collins archives.
14. Letter from G. F. Maine to Peter Alexander, dated 27 January 1949.
15. Letter from G. F. Maine to Peter Alexander, dated 13 October 1949.
16. Bryce, 'Alexander', p. 401.
17. Letter from Peter Alexander to G. F. Maine, dated 20 October 1951.
18. Letter from Richard David to John Dover Wilson, dated 11 January 1951, National Library of Scotland, ms. 14324. Those involved in the Oxford edition had also been a touch sniffy in their attitude to Alexander. In a letter to E. K. Chambers dated 7 February 1940 Kenneth Sissam observes: 'I asked Miss Walker what McKerrow thought of Alexander, and she said he distrusted him on the bibliographical side, i.e. didn't think he gave enough weight to clear bibliographical evidence' (OUP archives, file. CP/ED/000018).
19. Letter from G. F. Maine to Peter Alexander, dated 27 May 1952.
20. Letter from Peter Alexander to G. F. Maine dated 29 May 1952.
21. Sisson did not, in fact, particularly foreground complex textual issues. In his preface, he noted that no 'modern editor can fail to acknowledge debts to the work during the present century of a notable band of scholars, often referred to as the London School, including A. W. Pollard, W. W. Greg, and R. B. McKerrow, who laid the foundations of bibliographical scholarship in relation to the text of Shakespeare'. But he also emphasised that his was 'above all a reader's text, with the minimum of interference with the reading' (§1342, Preface, unpaged). Sisson did, however, publish two volumes of *New Readings in Shakespeare* in 1956. The volumes were intended 'to furnish material

for the consideration of the new generation of scholars at work upon the text, in a number of enterprises now in progress or about to begin, on the long way leading to a new Authorized Version of Shakespeare' (I, p. v).

22. Letter from I. G. Collins to Peter Alexander, dated 29 February 1957.
23. Letter from Peter Alexander to Alan S. Hockley, dated 7 June 1958. 'Mr. Young' was G. B. Young of Collins.
24. Letter from G. B. Young to Mrs H. Macy, dated 11 April 1958.
25. Bradbrook, Review, p. 229.
26. Wells and Taylor, *Textual Companion*, p. 56.
27. Figure derived from a memo from David K. Boath to George Pratt, dated 12 February 1979, included in Collins file 'Shakespeare Sept 73 (to May 79)'. The actual figures are: home sales: 6,393; export sales: 2,946.
28. Letter from A. L. Kingsford of BBC Publications to W. T. McLeod of Collins, dated 28 June 1978, included in Collins file 'BBC Shakespeare, Dec. 77–Mar. 82'. The full set of terms were, of course, more complicated than this – especially as regards books sold outside the UK market. The contract for the series is included in this Collins file. Further references are to this file until otherwise indicated.
29. Memo from W. T. McLeod to M. Hyde, dated 6 September 1978.
30. Letter from David Lester to W. T. McLeod, dated 12 September 1978.
31. Letter from W. T. McLeod to Tony Kingsford, dated 18 April 1979.
32. Memo from W. T. McLeod to J. A. D. Macfarlane, dated 11 August 1978.
33. My thanks to Edwin Moore of HarperCollins for drawing this correction to my attention and for assisting me in accessing the Collins archive material.
34. Letter from Richard N. Clark to W. T. McLeod, dated 25 January 1974, Collins file 'Shakespeare Sept. 73 (to May 79)'.
35. Tanselle, 'Bowers', p. 3. Except where otherwise stated, all general details of Bowers' life are taken from this source.
36. Letter from W. W. Greg to David Nichol Smith, dated 2 August 1937, National Library of Scotland, ms. 19603.
37. Tanselle, 'Bowers', p. 40.
38. This was, of course, a conscious departure from the position established by McKerrow in his *Prolegomena*.
39. Brown, 'Studies', p. 9.
40. Bowers, *Bibliographical*, p. 20.
41. Unless one also counts his edition of Fletcher and Shakespeare's *Two Noble Kinsmen*, included in his Beaumont and Fletcher *Dramatic Works*, VII (1989) (§1609).
42. Greg, Review of *On Editing Shakespeare*, p. 101. While generally praising the volume, Greg denounced Bowers' writing style, accusing him of unhelpfully wrapping difficult subject matter 'in a fog of verbiage' (p. 104).
43. See Smith, 'Eternal', p. 130. Smith notes that one commentator referred to Hinman's collating machine as an 'electronic Bowers' (p. 132).
44. Tanselle, 'Bowers', p. 66.
45. See Wells and Taylor, 'Re-Viewed', p. 7.
46. McAvoy, 'Best', pp. 125, 114.
47. Thus, for example, in a prefatory 'Note on Texts' in his *Shakespearean Negotiations*, Stephen Greenblatt – whose New Historicist mode of analysis dominated Renaissance criticism in the closing decades of the twentieth century – declares: 'Throughout this book, except where noted, I have used *The Riverside Shakespeare*' (p. xi).

48. Evans, '*Restored*', p. 40. General information about Evans' family in this paragraph is derived from this source.
49. Craig's *DNB* entry indicates that 'Several hundred volumes from his library were presented by his sister, Mrs. Merrick Head, to the public library at Stratford-upon-Avon, where they are kept together in a suitably inscribed bookcase' (1901–11 volume, pp. 434–5). Sadly, enquires at the library indicate that no such bookcase now exists and that whatever books of Craig's remain in the library have long since been dispersed into the general collection.
50. See chapter 9, pp. 206–7.
51. Evans, '*Restored*', pp. 49–50.
52. Wells, *Writer*, p. 82; *Re-editing*, p. 19.
53. In an interview with Edward Ragg published in 2001, Wells observed of the New Penguin that '*Hamlet* and *Macbeth* sell hundreds of thousands of copies' and that his own half per cent royalty on the series 'gives [him] several thousand a year' (Ragg, 'Oxford', p. 97).
54. Wells comments in his Ragg interview that 'Oxford had had a whole history of uncompleted editions of major authors and so they lost a lot of confidence in the capacity of literary scholars to produce major editions while working as University teachers' (Ragg, 'Oxford', p. 77).
55. Ragg, *Controversies*, p. 43 (investment figure also taken from this source and derived from John Bell, who commissioned the project). I am grateful to Edward Ragg for providing me with a copy of this text and also an advance copy of his interview with Paul Luna.
56. For these general details, see Wells and Taylor, 'Re-Viewed', pp. 6–8.
57. Taylor, *Reinventing*, p. 315.
58. In addition to the collected-works volumes, the press also initiated a multi-volume series under the general editorship of Stanley Wells. Wells himself has observed that this series was launched in part because the *Arden* was perceived to be 'in the doldrums', though he notes that 'before long, stimulated no doubt by the competition, the Arden editors pulled up their socks, almost completing what is now known as Arden2 before embarking on Arden3 in 1995' (*Shakespeare: For All Time*, pp. 384–5).
59. Williams, Review, p. 115.
60. Wells, *Re-Editing*, p. 3.
61. Ragg, 'Oxford', p. 83.
62. Wells and Taylor, 'Re-Viewed', p. 8.
63. Wells, 'Revision', p. 69.
64. Proudfoot, 'Chairman's Introduction', in Wells, *Shakespeare and Revision*, p. 2.
65. See chapter 10, p. 224.
66. Bevington, 'Determining', p. 517.
67. Wells and Taylor, *Textual Companion*, p. 604. The editors provide a convincing catalogue of evidence that the form of the name consistently used in the period – including in Shakespeare's source (Holinshed) – was 'Innogen'.
68. Ibid., pp. 403, 332.
69. Taylor, 'Fortunes', p. 100.
70. Taylor, 'Poem?', p. 1447.
71. Robbins, 'Counter-arguments', p. 1450.
72. Wells, *Shakespeare: For All Time*, p. 386.
73. Pendleton, 'Non-Shakespearian', p. 328.
74. Bevington, 'Determining', pp. 518–19.
75. Wells and Taylor, *Textual Companion*, p. 559.
76. Vickers, Review, p. 408.

77. Bevington, 'Determining', p. 504.
78. The play had already been included in the American *Riverside* edition.
79. Wells and Taylor, 'Re-Viewed', p. 17.
80. See Wells, 'Once', p. 6.
81. See Honigmann, *Texts*, p. 3.
82. See Berger, 'Second Quarto'.
83. See Urkowitz, 'Base', p. 40.
84. Chambers, 'Disintegration', p. 89.
85. Ioppolo, *Revising*, p. 2.
86. Coghill, *Professional*, p. 183.
87. See Honigmann, *Stability*.
88. Taylor, *Reinventing*, p. 358. See Warren, 'Quarto and Folio'.
89. Taylor, 'War', p. 34.
90. Urkowitz, *Revision*, p. 129.
91. The seminar provided the impetus for Taylor and Warren's co-edited collection, *The Division of the Kingdoms* (1983).
92. For these general details, see Taylor, *Reinventing*, p. 358. The brief history of revisionism presented here is necessarily highly condensed and is weighted towards the context of the Oxford edition. For a more thorough account of the arguments as they developed through the scholarly literature, see the 'Annotated Bibliography 1885–1986' in Michael Warren's *Complete* King Lear (§1608) and, more generally, Ioppolo, *Revising*.
93. Wells, 'Revision', p. 93.
94. Wells, *Shakespeare and Revision*, p. 21.
95. Reflecting on the edition in 'Re-Viewed', Wells and Taylor conceded that this form of presentation was unsatisfactory, noting that it was not apparent 'until we actually saw the text in proof – that the Additional Passages format would be so unclear in this instance' (p. 17).
96. Wells and Taylor, *Textual Companion*, p. 478.
97. Wells and Taylor, 'Re-Viewed', p. 17; Ragg, 'Oxford', p. 85.
98. Ioppolo, *Revising*, pp. 3, 132.
99. Werstine, 'Mystery', p. 2.
100. In addition to *Stability*, see also Honigmann's 'Revised'.
101. Honigmann, *Texts*, pp. 48, 144–5.
102. Wells and Taylor, 'Re-Viewed', p. 17.
103. This might be said to be true even of the Oxford editors' revisionist turn, since their acceptance of revision ultimately served simply to expand the canon of conventionally conceived texts. As Jonathan Goldberg has observed: 'There are two *King Lears*, we are told, but we are also assured that the Quarto derives from Shakespeare's manuscript and that the Folio represents an authoritative revision. The kingdom has been divided, but Shakespeare reigns supreme, author now of two sovereign texts' ('Textual', p. 215).
104. This, in a sense, is the point of Greg's 'Rationale' – faced with a late revised printed text, the editor should revert to the earliest substantive printed text for accidentals, since this will produce a composite text imagined to be closest to the author's own creation.
105. Bowers, 'Unfinished', p. 11.
106. McGann, *Critique*, p. 48.
107. Wells and Taylor, *Textual Companion*, p. v.
108. Ibid., p. 15 (both quotations).
109. Wells, *Re-Editing*, p. 64.
110. Ragg, 'Much Ado'.

111. From a literary critical point of view, the classic interrogation of intentionalism is, of course, Wimsatt and Beardsley's 'Intentional Fallacy', where they observe that: 'The poem is not the critic's own and not the author's (it is detached from the author at birth and goes about the world beyond his power to intend about it or control it)' (p. 5). For discussions of intention from a New Bibliographic perspective, see Tanselle, 'Editorial Problem' and Bowers, 'Authorial'.
112. Quotation from D. C. Greetham's 'Foreword' to McGann, *Critique*, p. xiii.
113. Williams, Review, p. 108.
114. Berger, 'Second Quarto', p. 155.
115. Bevington, 'Determining', p. 502.
116. Vickers, Review, p. 406.
117. Wells and Taylor, 'Re-Viewed', p. 14.
118. See chapter 4, pp. 85–6. Ragg has also made this point in *Controversies*.
119. All details in this paragraph are taken from Ragg, 'Oxford', pp. 80–81.
120. The most insistent advocate of Shakespeare's authorship of the *Elegy* has been Donald W. Foster – see his *Elegy by W.S.* Foster withdrew the attribution in a message posted to the SHAKSPER email discussion list on 12 June 2002 (SHK 13.1514), following the publication of Gilles Monsarrat's '*A Funeral Elegy*: Ford, W.S., and Shakespeare', which argues in favour of Ford's authorship of the piece. The *Funeral Elegy* was also included in the 1997 second edition of the *Riverside* and in David Bevington's 1997 complete works edition (Professor Bevington has noted, in a personal communication, that the poem will be removed from the fifth edition of his text).
121. Rozett, Review, p. 469.
122. Wells, *Re-Editing*, pp. 3, 4.
123. Taylor, 'Fortunes', pp. 92–3. A similar point is made by Stanley Wells, in *Shakespeare: For All Time*: 'Before the [Oxford] edition appeared, information that I was working on it was apt to be received in Oxford with a curl of the upper lip and a rising of the left eyebrow along with the words, "Will it be any different from all the others?" Condescension turned in some quarters to consternation when it turned out to be very different indeed' (p. 385).

Conclusion

1. Ragg, 'Oxford', p. 93.
2. See Price, 'Towards'.
3. Bald, 'Evidence', p. 167. It should be noted here that McKerrow was, in fact, himself highly sceptical of Greg's claims that bibliography should be regarded as a science. In the *Prolegomena*, he observed that: 'Nothing can be gained, and much may be lost, by a pretence of deriving results of scientific accuracy from data which are admittedly uncertain and incomplete' (p. vii).
4. Trousdale, 'Second Look', pp. 91, 89.
5. Foakes and Rickert (eds.), *Henslowe's Diary*, p. 39. See also the odd conflation of numerology and naming schemes mapped out on p. 38.
6. Foakes (ed.), *Henslowe Papers*, I, Introduction (unpaged).
7. Trousdale, 'Diachronic', p. 313. See Housman's comment that 'A textual critic engaged upon his business is . . . like a dog hunting for fleas' ('Application', p. 132).
8. In addition to the Werstine articles quoted in this paragraph, see also Long's 'Precious Few' and 'A bed / for woodstock'. In fact, Greg himself, by the end of his career, had begun to lose faith in the editor's ability to identify easily the nature of the manuscript

which underlay a given printed text. Reviewing the third volume of Bowers' edition of Dekker in 1959, he gloomily asked: 'Is it that our hopes of being able to infer from the features of a printed text the nature of the manuscript that served as copy are fated to vanish like a dream?' (p. 415).

9. Werstine, 'Narratives', p. 81; 'William Shakespeare', p. 267. In his own Folger edition, co-edited with Barbara Mowat, Werstine adopts a similar line: 'Many of this century's Shakespeare enthusiasts have persuaded themselves that most of the quartos were set into type directly from Shakespeare's own papers, although there is nothing on which to base this conclusion except the desire for it to be true. Thus speculation continues about how the Shakespeare plays got to be printed. All that we have are the printed texts' (§1649, *2 Henry VI*, p. lv).

10. Werstine, 'Narratives', pp. 65, 81.

11. Werstine, 'Century', p. 327. For an extended discussion of the issue of bad quartos and memorial reconstruction, see chapter 1, pp. 23–30.

12. Howard-Hill (ed.), 'Introduction' to *Shakespeare and 'Sir Thomas More'*, pp. 8, 6. In 'William Shakespeare', Paul Werstine observes: 'Over the years advocates of Shakespeare as Hand D have been forced to admit that none of the evidence is conclusive' (p. 266).

13. Ramsey, 'Shakespeare', p. 346.

14. Paul Werstine has astutely observed, in 'William Shakespeare', that the 'enormous popular appeal that Shakespeare commands is associated not with the most recent theoretical construct of Shakespeare's intention but with the received text, and no editor has been able to ignore the reader's investment in and right to the received text' (p. 253). Werstine co-edits the Folger Shakespeare with Barbara Mowat, who has observed of the force of the editorial tradition (using an emblematic instance): 'What does one do, for example, about the name of Hamlet's mother? . . . Most editors . . . use Q2 as the text on which to base their editions. Yet each edition names Hamlet's mother not as she was named in Q2, but as she was named in the Folio'. Editors choose the name Gertrude rather than Gertrard, Mowat suggests, 'because it is as Gertrude that she exists and has existed for nearly three hundred years. That's who she *is* in the appreciations, criticisms, productions, and interpretations that comprise her social/cultural life' ('Problem', p. 142).

15. Pollard, *Folios*, p. 80. Arden's uncertain attitude to the new textual climate – and specifically the project of 'unediting' advocated by Macleod (throughout his work) and Marcus (most notably in *Unediting the Renaissance*) – is nicely caught in the Introduction to a collection of essays written by Arden 3 editors, in which Ann Thompson and Gordon McMullan observe: 'While, by definition, none of the contributors to this collection subscribes to the "unediting" argument, it is clear that the debates it has provoked have been of considerable value, as well as of unease, to editorial practitioners' (p. xvi).

16. Brian Vickers dismissed the series in *'Hamlet'*. Stanley Wells offers a more moderate assessment in 'Multiple Texts and the Oxford Shakespeare'. Graham Holderness and Bryan Loughrey, the general editors of the series, have defended the project in 'Misconstrued'. The present writer was responsible for the series' edition of the First Quarto *Othello*.

17. For a perceptive discussion of the problematics of valorising 'versions' over 'works', see Small, 'Why edit'.

18. The Tronch-Pérez edition was not without precedent. As early as 1883, Teena Rochfort Smith published a three-scene sample of a proposed *Four-Text 'Hamlet' in Parallel Columns*. In more recent times, Bernice Kliman published an 'Enfolded *Hamlet*', separating the Second Quarto and First Folio texts on the same page, as a special issue of *The Shakespeare Newsletter* (§1690).

19. Warren, 'Textual', pp. 27, 34–5.
20. McLeod, 'Un-Editing', p. 45. This essay is, as it happens, dedicated to Michael Warren.
21. Or, to push the logic of the position even further: in the *entire set* of the text's original edition, given the Renaissance printing practice of mixing corrected and uncorrected sheets, so that, potentially, all individual copies of any given book may vary from each other in some degree.
22. The package also facilitates certain kinds of work which cannot be carried out using the originals themselves. As Warren himself points out: 'since such books rarely (in most cases never) leave their libraries, there is no way to compare certain features of the copies without using some mode of reproduction; for instance, no library has sufficient copies of the First Quarto *King Lear* to display every forme in its variant states, and relatively few instance of formes of First Folio *King Lear* in the uncorrected state have been reproduced' (§1608, part 1, p. xxi).
23. Paul Werstine has also argued that Warren and his colleagues bring a certain anachronous mindset to the interpretation of facsimiles, observing that 'these critics read such facsimiles as if they were modern editions in which such things as the placement of stage directions and the use of punctuation had been accorded careful and thorough consideration' ('William Shakespeare', p. 269).
24. Wells and Taylor, *Textual Companion*, p. 4.
25. I am grateful to Routledge for providing me with this information, which was supplied when I was writing a review of the volumes (see next endnote).
26. See Pafford, 'Methuen' and Velz, 'Text'. For this reason, I concluded my own review of the volumes by observing that: 'Republishing these particular facsimiles was an error, and it was error compounded by failing to provide the set with a detailed introduction which could have registered the texts' provenance and history' ('Folios', p. 157). Anthony West, in *Shakespeare*, has disagreed: 'In my judgement, making readily available, in facsimile, the Second, Third, and Fourth Folios abates any error' (p. 163).
27. Werstine, Review, pp. 236–7.
28. Barthes, 'Death', p. 146.
29. Foucault, 'Author', p. 119.
30. I have written at greater length on some of the issues raised in this paragraph in 'Texts'.
31. Orgel, 'Text', p. 83.
32. Masten, *Textual*, p. 4.
33. For a particularly useful collection of essays on this issue, see Rhodes and Sawday, *Renaissance Computer*.
34. Landow, *Hypertext*, pp. 143, 11, 12.
35. Landow, 'What's a Critic to Do?', p. 36. There is a certain danger, of course, that late twentieth-century conceptions of Renaissance textuality may actually be a *product* of our own experience with electronic textuality.
36. At the time of writing, the website address is: http://shea.mit.edu/ramparts/. (Doubtless, if you are reading this in the medium to distant future, the location is no longer valid.)
37. Donaldson, 'Shakespeare', p. 125.
38. Sutherland, 'Looking', pp. 13–14, 15.
39. I recently showed a ten-year-old 5 $\frac{1}{4}$-inch floppy disk to a group of students at St Andrews. They told me they had never seen one before.
40. Taylor, 'c:\wp\file.txt', pp. 45, 48 (italics in original).
41. Kastan, *Shakespeare and the Book*, p. 130.
42. Lavagnino, 'Reading', p. 114 (all quotations).

43. Gibson, 'Interactive', p. 83.
44. Interview with John Dover Wilson in *The Guardian*, 6 June 1968.
45. Altick, *Common Reader*, pp. 243–4.
46. David Scott Kastan observes, in *Shakespeare After Theory*: 'In truth, most of us will for the foreseeable future continue to read Shakespeare's plays and teach them in edited versions, in book form rather than off a computer screen, with spelling and punctuation modernized. . . If we must admit that in actuality there is no fully acceptable way to edit Shakespeare . . . we must also admit that reading an edited text is a remarkably convenient way to engage the play, especially for students who, however naively, merely want to read it (to say nothing about actors who require a single and stable text to perform)' (p. 69).

Introduction to the appendix

1. I have omitted from my listing the possible 'new Shakespeare quartos' identified by Freeman and Grinke, on the basis of their work on the manuscript catalogue of the Viscount Conway library (the largest portion of which would appear to have been destroyed in a raid on Conway's Irish residence during the course of the 1641 uprising). The catalogue includes entries for 'Henry 4 the first and second parte[s], 1619', 'The history of Henry 5, 1617' and 'The Taminge of the Shrew by W: Sh: 1621'. Freeman and Grinke themselves note that the date of 1621 attached to *The Taming of the Shrew* may simply be 'a slip of the pen' for 1631 – the date of the first known quarto edition (p. 18). They speculate that the *Henry IV* and *Henry V* plays listed may possibly be additional texts from Pavier's 1619 selected edition (see chapter 2, pp. 36–41). On balance, this seems a touch unlikely since, as Freeman and Grinke themselves indicate, a 1619 Pavier *Henry V* text *has* survived – with a false date of 1608. It is possible, of course, that Pavier might also have produced a now-lost *Henry V* in 1617, since he did own the rights to the (variant) text, but as no quarto edition had appeared since 1602, it would surely seem odd that Pavier should produce two editions in the space of just two years and should have falsely dated one of the two. It would also seem odd that, if Pavier did produce texts of the *Henry IV* plays, these texts are not included in any of the surviving sets of the Pavier selected edition. Freeman and Grinke note that the catalogue also lists an edition of *Love's Labour's Lost* with a date of 1597. Since the earliest known quarto of this play, dated 1598, indicates on its title page that it is 'Newly corrected and augmented', it has long been thought that a previous edition must have existed, which is now lost. It may be that the Conway evidence points to a likely date for this edition, though it is not, of course, possible to have complete faith in this evidence. I have listed the supposed lost edition of the play under '1597?' in the listing, having originally listed it under 'No date'.
2. Cloud, 'Very names', p. 94.
3. Hans Zeller has observed, in 'New Approach', that 'the decisive phases in the development of English editing have been determined largely by Shakespeare scholarship' (p. 232).
4. H.H.F.J., *Letters*, p. 188.
5. The ESTC has its own particular shortcomings too, of course. See Blayney, Letter, and the replies of Snyder and Crump and McKitterick.
6. In compiling the appendix in the first instance, I used the original 1971 edition of the *Handbook*. At the time when work on this book was being concluded, Richard Knowles was revising the *Handbook* for republication. Professor Knowles very kindly provided me with an advance printout of the revised section on editions and I have cross-checked my listing against this printout. The revised edition of the *Handbook* includes a small number of new entries. Some of these I have managed to examine at libraries within Scotland, so

that the details provided in the appendix are taken from the texts themselves. In other instances, I have had to rely on electronic sources for publishing information. These latter cases are identified in the listing. I am extremely grateful to Professor Knowles for his very kind assistance with my project.

7. Velz, 'Research', p. 52.

8. Richard Knowles has commented on the proliferation of cheap 'acting' editions of the plays in the nineteenth century, characterising these texts as 'a bibliographical nightmare'. His comments provide a further indication of why these texts are excluded from this appendix: 'More often than not they are undated, evidently so that they could be kept in stock and reissued, or reprinted without change. Library catalogues often attempt to date them from cast lists frequently given in the preliminaries, but these may in some cases be several decades out of date – that is, they may have been for a recent performance when the edition first appeared in separate numbers but not when it was reprinted years or decades later. The plays were usually issued in separate numbers but often in bound volumes as well; the separate numbers were often issued by separate publishers concurrently, sometimes bearing the imprint of a series but often not. To complicate matters more, these series were occasionally merged or bought up by another publisher, so that a play issued in mid-century might very well have appeared in practically identical form much earlier in the century in another series' (revised edition of the *Variorum Handbook*). Knowles provides a listing of some of the major theatrical series. In my appendix, I include only those editions which form part of the main *Handbook* listing.

9. It should be noted, however, that WorldCat is not always fully up to date. A search for the Guild Shakespeare on WorldCat produced a record of nineteen titles. However, when I contacted the series editor, John F. Andrews, he noted that a further two volumes had been released. I am very grateful to John F. Andrews for answering queries regarding the Guild and Everyman series.

10. Plomer, *Dictionary*, pp. 49, 50.

11. See Plomer, Bushnell and Dix, *Dictionary*, pp. 214–15. Some of this complex history can be unravelled by referring to Rivington, *Publishing Family*.

Bibliography

Manuscript and archive materials

Cambridge University Press archives, Cambridge University Press. 'Pitt Press Shakespeare' files, reference no. 5195.

Cambridge University Press archives, University of Cambridge Library. Prizing books 17/3 through 17/38 (UA CUP 17/3–17/38).

Collins archives, HarperCollins, Glasgow. Files marked 'Shakespeare Oct. 1944–Aug. 77', 'Shakespeare Sept. 73 (to May 79)', 'BBC Shakespeare, Dec. 77–Mar. 82'.

Edward Dowden papers, Trinity College Dublin. Letters from A. M. M. Stedman (later A. M. M. Methuen) to Dowden and a draft of a reply from Dowden, TCD mss. 3147-54a.

Edinburgh University archives, Edinburgh University Library. Letters of Thomas Johnson to Professor Charles Mackie, ms. La.II.91.

James Orchard Halliwell-Phillipps collection, Edinburgh University Library. Accounts ledger for Halliwell edition of 1853–65, H.-P.Coll.314.

Macmillan archives, British Library. Various letters, BL add. ms. 55015, 55017, 55029, 55381, 55384, 55386.

Oxford University Press archives, Oxford University Press. Letters in connection with *The Oxford Shakespeare*, ms. CP/ED/000018, CP/ED/000019; Long Book files relating to *The Clarendon Shakespeare*, LB48, LB49, LB50, LB221, LB261, LB270.

Routledge archives, University College London Library. Routledge trade catalogues, item no. 215; Routledge Publication Books, item no. 8.

Sir Walter Scott papers, National Library of Scotland. Letter from Scott to Archibald Constable, ms. 743, II, item 5.

David Nichol Smith papers, National Library of Scotland. Letters from Smith to W. W. Greg, ms. acc. 3511; letters from Greg to Smith, ms. 19603; transcript of newspaper article, ms. acc. 6802.

John Dover Wilson papers, National Library of Scotland. Letters in connection with the Cambridge *New Shakespeare*, ms. 14317, 14323, 14324, 14325.

Printed materials

Advertisement for Joseph Dennie's edition of Shakespeare, *Port Folio*, IV: 6 (11 Feb. 1804): 46–7.

Advertisement for 'Mr. Knight's Editions of Shakspere', *Quarterly Literary Advertiser* (Dec. 1842): 79.

Advertisement for Howard Staunton's facsimile edition of F1, *Publishers' Weekly*, 8 Dec. 1863: 752.

Advertising leaflet for the Warwick Shakespeare ([London: Blackie & Sons], n.d.).

Account of the Terrific and Fatal Riot at the New-York Astor Place Opera House . . . (New York: H. M. Ranney, 1849).

Alden, John, 'Pills and Publishing: Some Notes on the English Book Trade, 1660–1715', *Lib.*, 5th series, 7 (1952): 21–37.

Alexander, Catherine M. S., 'Province of Pirates: The Editing and Publication of Shakespeare's Poems in the Eighteenth Century', in Joanna Gondris (ed.), *Reading Readings: Essays on Shakespeare Editing in the Eighteenth Century* (Madison: Fairleigh Dickinson University Press, 1998): 345–65.

Alexander, Peter, '*II. Henry VI.* and the Copy for *The Contention* (1594)' *TLS*, 9 Oct. 1924: 629–30.

'*3 Henry VI* and *Richard, Duke of York*', *TLS*, 12 Nov. 1924: 730.

'*The Taming of a Shrew*', *TLS*, 16 Sept. 1926: 614.

Shakespeare's 'Henry VI' and 'Richard III' (Cambridge: Cambridge University Press, 1929).

Allentuck, Marcia, 'Sir Thomas Hanmer Instructs Francis Hayman: An Editor's Notes to his Illustrator', *SQ*, 27 (1976): 288–315.

Altick, Richard, *The Cowden Clarkes* (Oxford: Oxford University Press, 1948).

The English Common Reader: A Social History of the Mass Reading Public 1800–1900 (Chicago: University of Chicago Press, 1957).

'From Aldine to Everyman: Cheap Reprint Series of the English Classics 1830–1906', *SB*, 11 (1958): 3–24.

Amory, Hugh and David D. Hall, *A History of the Book in America*. I: *The Colonial Book in the Atlantic World* (Cambridge: American Antiquarian Society/Cambridge University Press, 2000).

Announcement regarding Pope's edition, *The Weekly Journal, or Saturday Evening Post*, no. 155, Saturday, 18 Nov. 1721: 927.

Announcement regarding Pope's edition, *The Evening Post*, 3–5 May 1722 (no. 1992), third page.

Announcement regarding Rowe's edition, *The London Gazette*, 4523, Monday, 14 Mar. to Thursday, 17 Mar. 1708, verso.

Arrowsmith, W. R., *Shakespeare's Editors and Commentators* (London: J. Russell Smith, 1865).

Astbury, Raymond, 'The Renewal of the Licensing Act in 1693 and Its Lapse in 1695', *Lib.*, 5th series, 33 (1978): 296–322.

Atto, Clayton, 'The Society for the Encouragement of Learning', *Lib.*, 4th series, 19 (1938): 263–88.

Bald, R. C., 'Early Copyright Litigation and its Bibliographical Interest', *PBSA*, 36 (1942): 81–96.

'Evidence and Inference in Bibliography', in *English Institute Annual, 1941* (New York: Columbia University Press, 1942): 159–84.

Barthes, Roland, 'The Death of the Author', in Stephen Heath (ed. and trans.), *Image Music Text* (London: Fontana, 1977): 142–8.

Baskervill, Charles Read, 'A Prompt Copy of *A Looking Glass for London and England*', *MP*, 30 (1932–3): 29–51.

Beaumont, Francis and John Fletcher, *Comedies and Tragedies* (London, 1647).

Bedell, Geraldine, 'Mills and Boom Boom', *Observer Magazine* (15 Dec. 2002): 47–8.

Belanger, Terry, 'Tonson, Wellington and the Shakespeare Copyrights', *Studies in the Book Trade in Honour of Graham Pollard* (Oxford: Bibliographical Society, 1975): 195–209.

'Publishers and Writers in Eighteenth-century England', in Isabel Rivers (ed.), *Books and Their Readers in Eighteenth-Century England* (Leicester: Leicester University Press, 1982): 5–25.

Bell, Edward, *George Bell, Publisher: A Brief Memoir* (London: Chiswick Press, 1924).

Bennett, H. S., *English Books and Readers 1603 to 1640: Being a Study in the History of the Book Trade in the Reigns of James I and Charles I* (Cambridge: Cambridge University Press, 1970).

Bennett, Scott, 'John Murray's Family Library and the Cheapening of Books in Early Nineteenth Century Britain', *SB*, 29 (1976): 138–66.

Benzie, William, *Dr. F. J. Furnivall: Victorian Scholar Adventurer* (Norman, OK: Pilgrim, 1983).

Berger, Thomas L., 'The Second Quarto of *Othello* and the Question of Textual "Authority"', *AEB*, n.s., 2: 4 (1988): 141–59.

'Looking for Shakespeare in Caroline England', *Viator*, 27 (1996): 323–59.

Berger, Thomas L. and Jesse M. Lander, 'Shakespeare in Print, 1593–1640', in David Scott Kastan (ed.), *A Companion to Shakespeare* (Oxford: Blackwell, 1999): 395–413.

Bevington, David, 'Determining the Indeterminate: *The Oxford Shakespeare*', *SQ*, 38: 4 (1987): 501–19.

Black, N. W. and Matthias Shaaber, *Shakespeare's Seventeenth-Century Editors, 1632–1685* (New York: MLA, 1937).

Blackwood, Gary, *The Shakespeare Stealer* (Dublin: O'Brien Press, 1999).

Blades, William, *Shakspere and Typography* (London: Trübner & Co., 1872).

Blagden, Cyprian, 'Booksellers' Trade Sales 1718–1768', *Lib.*, 5th series, 5 (1950–1): 243–57.

Blayney, Peter, *The First Folio of Shakespeare* (Washington, DC: Folger Shakespeare Library, 1991).

'The Publication of Playbooks', in John D. Cox and David Scott Kastan (eds.), *A New History of Early English Drama* (New York: Columbia University Press, 1997): 383–422.

Letter to the Editor of *The Library*, *Lib.* 7th series, 1: 1 (2000): 72–4. See also responses from Henry L. Snyder and M. J. Crump and from David McKitterick at pp. 75–7 and 78 of the same issue.

Boase, T. S. R., 'Illustrations of Shakespeare's Plays in the Seventeenth and Eighteenth Centuries', *Journal of the Warburg and Courtauld Institutes*, 10 (1947): 83–103.

Bolton, C. K., *The Harvard University Library* (Cambridge, MA: 1894).

Bolton, Joseph S. G., 'The Authentic Text of *Titus Andronicus*', *PMLA*, 44 (1929): 765–88.

Bowdler, Thomas, *A Letter to the Editor of the 'British Critic'; occasioned by the censure pronounced in that work . . .* (London: Longman, Hurst, Rees, Orme and Brown, 1823).

[Bowdler, Thomas, nephew of Thomas Bowdler the editor], *Memoir of the late John Bowdler, Esq., to which is added some account of the late Thomas Bowdler, Esq. editor of the Family Shakspeare* (London: Longman, Hurst, Rees, Orme, Brown and Green, 1825).

Bowers, Fredson, *On Editing Shakespeare and the Elizabethan Dramatists* (Philadelphia: Rosenbach Foundation/University of Pennsylvania Library, 1955).

Review of the Yale facsimile of F1, *MP*, 53 (1955): 50–7.

Review of Shakespeare Quarto Facsimiles 9 and 10, *MLR*, 53 (1958): 235–6.

The Bibliographical Way (Lawrence: University of Kansas Libraries, 1959).

'Today's Shakespeare Texts, and Tomorrow's', *SB*, 19 (1966): 39–65.

'Unfinished Business', *TEXT*, 4 (1988): 1–11.

'Authorial Intention and Editorial Problems', *TEXT*, 5 (1991): 49–61.

Bradbrook, Muriel, Review of the Heritage Press edition of Peter Alexander's text, *SQ*, 10: 2 (1959): 229–30.

Brady, Jennifer and W. H. Herenden (eds.), *Ben Jonson's 1616 Folio* (Newark: University of Delaware Press, 1991).

[Brae, A. E.], writing as 'A Detective', *Literary Cookery* (London: John Russell Smith, 1855).

Braunmuller, A. R., 'Shakespeares Various' in Ann Thompson and Gordon McMullan (eds.), *In Arden: Editing Shakespeare* (London: Thomson, 2003): 3–16.

Brooks, Douglas A., *From Playhouse to Printing House: Drama and Authorship in Early Modern England* (Cambridge: Cambridge University Press, 2000).

Brown, A. D. J., 'The little fellow has done wonders', *Cambridge Quarterly*, 21 (1992): 120–49.

Brown, Arthur, 'Editorial Problems in Shakespeare: Semi-Popular Editions', *SB*, 8 (1956): 16–27.

'Studies in Elizabethan Drama since 1900', *SS*, 14 (1961): 1–14.

Bruntjen, Sven H. A., *John Boydell, 1719–1804: A Study of Art Patronage and Publishing in Georgian London* (New York: Garland, 1985).

Bryce, J. C., 'Peter Alexander, 1893–1969'. *PBA*, 66 (1980): 378–405.

Bunbury, Sir Henry (ed.), *Correspondence of Sir Thomas Hanmer, Bart* (London: Moxon, 1838).

Burnim, Kalman A. and Philip H. Highfill Jr., *John Bell, Patron of British Theatrical Portraiture: A Catalog of the Theatrical Portraits in His Editions of Bell's Shakespeare and Bell's British Theatre* (Carbondale and Edwardsville, IL: Southern Illinois University Press, 1998).

Byrne, M. St Clare, 'Bell's Shakespeare', *TLS*, 31 Jan. 1948: 65.

Cameron, William J., *A Bibliography in Short-Title Catalog Form of Bell's British Theatre 1780–1793 and Bell's English Theatre 1792* (London, Ontario: University of Western Ontario, 1982).

Campbell, T. D., 'Francis Hutcheson: "Father" of the Scottish Enlightenment', in R. H. Campbell and Andrew S. Skinner (eds.), *The Origins and Nature of the Scottish Enlightenment* (Edinburgh: John Donald, 1982): 167–85.

Cannon, Carl L., *American Book Collectors and Collecting, from Colonial Times to the Present* (New York: H. W. Wilson, 1941).

Capell, Edmund, *Notes and Various Readings to Shakespeare*, edited by John Collins (London: for the author, 1779–80), 3 vols.

Carter, Harry, *A History of Oxford University Press* (Oxford: Oxford University Press, 1975) I (no further volumes issued).

Chambers, E. K., *Elizabethan Stage* (Oxford: Clarendon Press, 1923), 4 vols.
'The Disintegration of Shakespeare', *PBA*, 1924–5: 89–108.
William Shakespeare: A Study of Facts and Problems (Oxford: Clarendon Press, 1930), 2 vols.
Christian, Edmund B. V., 'The Advertiser's Shakespeare', *Gentleman's Magazine*, Mar. 1893: 305–11.
Churchill, George B., 'Shakespeare in America', *Jahrbuch der Deutschen Shakespeare-Gesellschaft*, 42 (1906): xiii–xlv.
Clark, W. G. and H. R. Luard, *The First Act of Shakespeare's 'King Richard II'. Intended as a Specimen of a New Edition of Shakespeare* (Cambridge: Cambridge University Press, 1860).
Cloud, Random, 'The Marriage of Good and Bad Quartos', *SQ*, 4, 33 (1982): 421–31.
'"The very names of the Persons": Editing and the Invention of Dramatick Character', in David Scott Kastan and Peter Stallybrass (eds.), *Staging the Renaissance: Reinterpretations of Elizabethan and Jacobean Drama* (London: Routledge, 1991): 88–96.
See also McLeod, Randall.
Coghill, Nevill, *Shakespeare's Professional Skills* (Cambridge: Cambridge University Press, 1964).
Cole, Richard Cargill, *Irish Booksellers and English Writers* (London, Mansell, 1986).
Collier, John Payne, *Reasons for a New Edition of Shakespeare's Works, Containing Notices of the Defects of Former Impressions, and Pointing out the Lately Acquired Means of Illustrating the Plays, Poems, and Biography of the Poet* (London: Whittaker & Co., 1842).
Letter regarding the 'Perkins Folio', *Ath.*, 1266 (Jan. 1852): 142–4.
Notes and Emendations to the Text of Shakespeare's Plays, from Early Manuscript Corrections in a Copy of the Folio, 1632, in the Possession of J. Payne Collier, Esq. F.S.A. . . (London: Shakespeare Society, 1852 [for 1853]; originally published London: Whittaker & Co., 1853).
'A New Shakspeare', *Ath.*, 2463 (Jan. 1875): 52.
[Collins, John], *A Letter to George Hardinge, Esq. on the Subject of a Passage in Mr. Steevens's Preface to his Impression of Shakespeare* (London: G. Kearsly, 1777).
Collins, John Churton, 'The Porson of Shakspearian criticism', *Quarterly Review*, 175 (1892): 102–31.
Collison-Morley, Lacy, *Shakespeare in Italy* (Stratford-upon-Avon: Shakespeare Head Press, 1916).
Colvin, Sidney, obituary for William Aldis Wright, *Journal of Philology* (1914): 299–301.
Connell, Charles, *They Gave Us Shakespeare: John Heminge and Henry Condell* (Stocksfield: Oriel Press, 1982).
Corballis, Richard, 'Copy-Text for Theobald's "Shakespeare"', *Lib.*, 6th series, 7 (1986): 156–9.
Corbin, John, 'Shakespeare Against his Editors', *North American Review*, 28 Feb. 1907: 398–406.
Cotes, Cornelius, publisher's statement in *Cotes Weekly Journal: or, the English Stage-Player*, 1 (11 May 1734): 1.
Cowden Clarke, Charles, *Shakespeare-Characters; Chiefly those Subordinate* (London: Smith, Elder & Co.; Edinburgh: James Nichol, 1863).

Cowden Clarke, Mary, *My Long Life* (London: T. Fisher Unwin, 1896).

Crawford, Robert (ed.), *The Scottish Invention of English Literature* (Oxford: Clarendon Press, 1998).

Crosse, Gordon, 'Charles Jennens as editor of Shakespeare', *Lib.*, 4th series, 16 (1935): 236–40.

Curwen, Henry, *A History of Booksellers, the Old and the New* (London: Chatto & Windus, 1873).

Daiches, David, 'Presenting Shakespeare', in Asa Briggs (ed.), *Essays in the History of Publishing in Celebration of the 250th anniversary of the House of Longman 1724–1974* (London: Longman, 1974): 63–112.

Dash, Irene G., 'When the Culture Obtrudes: Hanmer's *Winter's Tale*', in Joanna Gondris (ed.), *Reading Readings: Essays on Shakespeare Editing in the Eighteenth Century* (Madison: Fairleigh Dickinson University Press, 1998): 268–80.

Davidson, Adele, 'Some by Stenography: Stationers, Shorthand, and the Early Shakespearean Quartos', *PBSA*, 90 (1996): 417–50.

   '*King Lear* in an Age of Stenographical Reproduction or "Sitting Down to Copy *King Lear* Again"', *PBSA*, 92: 3 (1998): 297–324.

Dawson, Giles E., 'The Copyright of Shakespeare's Dramatic Works', in C. T. Prouty (ed.), *Studies in Honor of A. H. R. Fairchild* (University of Missouri Studies, xxi/1) (Columbia: University of Missouri Press, 1946): 11–35.

   'Warburton, Hanmer, and the 1745 Edition of Shakespeare', *SB*, 2 (1949–50): 35–48.

   'Some Bibliographical Irregularities in the Shakespeare Fourth Folio', *SB*, 4 (1951–2): 93–103.

   'Robert Walker's Editions of Shakespeare', in Josephine W. Bennett, Oscar Cargill, and Vernon Hall Jr (eds.), *Studies in the English Renaissance Drama in Memory of Karl Julius Holzknecht* (New York, 1959): 58–81.

   Four Centuries of Shakespeare Publishing (Lawrence: University of Kansas Libraries, 1964).

   'John Payne Collier's Great Forgery', *SB*, 24 (1971): 1–26.

De Beer, E. S. (ed.), *The Diary of John Evelyn* (Oxford: Clarendon Press, 1955), 6 vols.

De Grazia, Margreta, 'The Essential Shakespeare and the Material Book', *Textual Practice*, 2: 1 (1988): 69–86.

   Shakespeare Verbatim: The Reproduction of Authenticity and the 1790 Apparatus (Oxford: Clarendon Press, 1991).

   'The Scandal of Shakespeare's Sonnets', *SS*, 46 (1994): 35–49.

   'The Question of the One and the Many: *The Globe Shakespeare*, the *Complete "King Lear"*, and the *New Folger Library Shakespeare*, *SQ*, 46: 2 (1995): 245–51.

De Grazia, Margreta and Peter Stallybrass, 'The Materiality of the Shakespearean Text', *SQ*, 44 (1993): 255–83.

Dean Jonathan's Parody on the 4th Chap. of Genesis (London: Timothy Atkins, 1729).

Dix, E. R. McClintock, 'Irish Pirated Editions', *An Leabarlann*, 2 (1906): 67–77.

Dixon, Peter, 'Pope's Shakespeare', *JEGP*, 63 (1964): 191–203.

Dobson, Michael, *The Making of the National Poet: Shakespeare, Adaptation and Authorship, 1660–1769* (Oxford: Clarendon Press, 1992).

Dobson, Michael and Stanley Wells (eds.), *The Oxford Companion to Shakespeare* (Oxford: Oxford University Press, 2001).

Donaldson, Alexander, *A catalogue of curious and valuable books, to be disposed of by way of sale (the lowest price being marked at each book), at the shop of Alexander Donaldson, the first fore-stair above the entry to the Royal Bank, Edinburgh* (Edinburgh: Donaldson, 1753).

[Donaldson, Alexander?] *Some Thoughts on the state of literary property, humbly submitted to the consideration of the public* (Edinburgh: Donaldson, 1764).

Considerations on the nature and origin of literary property wherein that species of property is clearly proved to subsist no longer than for the terms fixed by the statute 8vo Annæ (Edinburgh: Donaldson, 1767).

Donaldson, Peter, 'The Shakespeare Interactive Archive: New Directions in Electronic Scholarship on Text and Performance', in Edward Barrett and Marie Redmond (eds.), *Contextual Media* (Cambridge, MA: Massachusetts Institute of Technology Press, 1995): 103–27.

Duncan, Robert, *Notices and Documents Illustrative of the Literary History of Glasgow, during the greater part of last century* (Glasgow: Maitland Club, 1831).

Duncan-Jones, Katherine, 'Was the 1609 *Shake-speares Sonnets* Really Unauthorised?', *RES*, 34 (1983): 151–71.

Dunn, Esther Cloudman, *Shakespeare in America* (New York: Macmillan, 1939).

Dunton, John, *The Dublin Scuffle: Being a challenge sent by John Dunton, citizen of London, to Patrick Campbell, bookseller in Dublin . . .* (London: printed for the author, 1699).

Dutton, Richard, 'The Birth of the Author', in Cedric C. Brown and Arthur Marotti (eds.), *Texts and Cultural Change in Early Modern England* (Basingstoke: Macmillan, 1997): 153–78.

Eastman, Arthur M., 'The Texts from which Johnson Printed his *Shakespeare*', *JEGP*, 49 (1950): 182–91.

'Johnson's Shakespeare and the Laity: A Textual Study', *PMLA*, 65 (1950): 1112–21.

[Edwards, Thomas], *A Supplement to Mr. Warburton's Edition of Shakespear. Being the Canons of Criticism, and Glossary, Collected from the Notes in that Celebrated Work, and Proper to be Bound up with it* (London: M. Cooper, 1748).

Egan, Gabriel, 'John Heminges's Tap-House at the Globe', *Theatre Notebook*, 55 (2001): 72–7.

Eisenstein, Elizabeth, *The Printing Press as an Agent of Change* (Cambridge: Cambridge University Press, 1979), 2 vols.

'English Catalogue', *Publishers' Circular*, 1 July 1863.

The Etymologist, a comedy in three acts (London: J. Jarvis, 1785).

Evans, G. Blakemore, 'Rough Notes on Editions Collated for *1 Henry VI*', *Shakespearean Research Opportunities*, 2 (1966): 41–9.

'Shakespeare's Text: Approaches and Problems', in Kenneth Muir and S. Schoenbaum (eds.), *A New Companion to Shakespeare Studies* (Cambridge: Cambridge University Press, 1971): 222–38.

'*Shakespeare Restored* – Once Again!' in Anne Lancashire (ed.), *Editing Renaissance Dramatic Texts* (New York and London, Garland, 1976): 39–56.

Exshaw, Edward and John, *Proposals for Printing by Subscription, the Works of Shakespear in Eight Volumes* (Dublin: Exshaw, 1747).

Farr, Henry, 'Notes on Shakespeare's Printers and Publishers with Special Reference to the Poems and *Hamlet*', *Lib.*, 4th series, 3: 4 (1923): 225–60.

'Philip Chetwind and the Allott Copyrights', *Lib.*, 4th series, 15 (1934–5): 129–60.

Feather, John, 'The Book Trade in Politics: The Making of the Copyright Act of 1710', *PH*, 8 (1980): 19–44.

'The English Book Trade and the Law 1695–1799', *PH*, 12 (1982): 51–75.

'The Publishers and the Pirates: British Copyright Law in Theory and Practice, 1710–1755', *PH*, 22 (1987): 5–32.

A History of British Publishing (London: Routledge, 1988).

'From Rights in Copies to Copyright: The Recognition of Authors' Rights in English Law and Practice in the Sixteenth and Seventeenth Centuries', in Martha Wood-mansee and Peter Jaszi (eds.), *The Construction of Authorship: Textual Appropriation in Law and Literature* (Durham, NC: Duke University Press, 1994): 191–209.

Fenning, Hugh, 'The Catholic Press in Munster in the Eighteenth Century', in Gerard Long (ed.), *Books Beyond the Pale: Aspects of the Provincial Book Trade in Ireland Before 1850* (Dublin: Rare Books Group of the Library Association of Ireland, 1996): 19–31.

Ferguson, F. S., 'Relations between London and Edinburgh Printers and Stationers to 1640', *Lib.*, 4th series, 7 (1927): 145–98.

Fleay, F. G., *Shakespeare Manual* (London: Macmillan, 1876).

Foakes, R. A. (ed.), *The Henslowe Papers* (London: Scolar, 1977).

Foakes, R. A. and R. T. Rickert (eds.), *Henslowe's Diary: Edited with Supplementary Material, Introduction and Notes* (Cambridge: Cambridge University Press, 1961).

Ford, H. L., *Shakespeare 1700–1740: A Collation of the Editions and Separate Plays with some account of T. Johnson and R. Walker* (Oxford: Clarendon Press, 1935).

Foster, Donald W., *Elegy by W.S.: A Study in Attribution* (Newark: University of Delaware Press, 1988).

Foucault, Michel, 'What is an Author?', in Paul Rabinow (ed.), *The Foucault Reader* (New York: Pantheon, 1984): 101–20.

Francis, F. C., 'The Bibliographical Society: A Sketch of the First Fifty Years', in F. C. Francis (ed.), *The Bibliographical Society 1892–1942: Studies in Retrospect* (London: Bibliographical Society, 1945): 1–22.

Franklin, Colin, *Shakespeare Domesticated: The Eighteenth-Century Editions* (Aldershot: Scolar, 1991).

'The Bowdlers and their Family Shakespeare', *The Book Collector* (Summer 2002): 227–43.

[Fredrick, Waveney R. N.], *A Shakespeare Bibliography. The Catalogue of the Birmingham Shakespeare Library, Birmingham Public Libraries* (London: Mansell, 1971), 7 vols.

Freeman, Arthur, 'A New Victim for the Old Corrector', *TLS*, 22 April 1983: 391–3.

'John Payne Collier' (letter to the editor), *TLS*, 3 June 1983: 573.

Freeman, Arthur and Janet Ing Freeman, 'Scholarship, Forgery, and Fictive Invention: John Payne Collier before 1831', *Lib.*, 6th series, 15: 1 (1993): 1–23.

Freeman, Arthur and Paul Grinke, 'Four New Shakespeare Quartos? Viscount Conway's Lost English Plays', *TLS*, 5 April 2002: 17–18.

Friedman, Winifred H., *Boydell's Shakespeare Gallery* (New York: Garland, 1976).

Furness, Horace Howard, 'A New Variorum Shakspere', *N&Q*, 4th series, 5 (22 January 1870): 109.

On Shakspere, 'or, what you will' (Boston: n.p., 1908).

Furnivall, F. J., Prospectus for Shakspere Quarto Facsimiles (no place of publication, publisher, or date).

Prospectus for Proposed Edition of Shakspere in Old Spelling (dated 23 May 1880; no place of publication or publisher).

Inaugural address to the New Shakspere Society, *The New Shakspere Society's Transactions*, series 1, 1–2 (1874): v–xi.

Ganzel, Dewey, *Fortune and Men's Eyes: The Career of John Payne Collier* (Oxford: Oxford University Press, 1982).

Gaskell, Philip, *A Bibliography of the Foulis Press* (London: Rupert Hart-Davis, 1964).

Geduld, Harry M., *Prince of Publishers, A Study of the Work and Career of Jacob Tonson* (Bloomington, IN: Indiana University Press, 1969).

Gellert, James, 'Davenant's *The Law Against Lovers*: A "Lost" Herringman Quarto', *Lib.*, 6th series, 5 (1983): 57–60.

Gibson, Andrew, 'Interactive Fiction and Narrative Space', in Warren Chernaik, Marilyn Deegan, and Andrew Gibson (eds.), *Beyond the Book: Theory, Culture, and the Politics of Cyberspace* (London: Office for Humanities Computing, 1996): 79–91.

Gibson, James M., *The Philadelphia Shakespeare Story: Horace Howard Furness and the New Variorum Shakespeare* (New York: AMS, 1990).

Giordano-Orsini, G. N., 'Thomas Heywood's Play on "The Troubles of Queen Elizabeth"', *Lib.*, 4th series, 14 (1933–4): 313–38.

Glasgow Bibliographical Society, *Catalogue of the Foulis Exhibition held in the University of Glasgow, April 1913* (Glasgow: MacLehose, 1913).

'The Globe Edition of Shakspeare', *The Bookseller*, 30 Sept. 1864: 587.

Goldberg, Jonathan, 'Textual Properties', *SQ*, 37: 2 (1986): 213–17.

Gondris, Joanna, '"All This Farrago": The Eighteenth-Century Shakespeare Variorum Page as a Critical Structure', in Joanna Gondris (ed.), *Reading Readings: Essays on Shakespeare Editing in the Eighteenth Century* (Madison: Fairleigh Dickinson University Press, 1998): 123–39.

[Gould, Edward S.], Review of Henry N. Hudson's 1851–6 edition of Shakespeare, *North American Review*, 84 (1857): 183–203.

Grady, Hugh, *The Modernist Shakespeare: Critical Texts in a Material World* (Oxford: Clarendon Press, 1991).

Graff, Gerald, *Professing Literature* (Chicago: University of Chicago Press, 1987).

Gray, W. Forbes, 'Alexander Donaldson and His Fight for Cheap Books', *Juridical Review*, 38 (1926): 180–202.

Grebanier, Bernard, *The Great Shakespeare Forgery: A New Look at the Career of William Henry Ireland* (London: Heinemann, 1966).

Greenblatt, Stephen, *Shakespearean Negotiations: The Circulation of Social Energy in Renaissance England* (Los Angeles: University of California Press, 1988).

Greetham, D. C., *Textual Scholarship: An Introduction* (New York: Garland, 1994).

Greg, W. W., *Catalogue of the Books Presented by Edward Capell to the Library of Trinity College in Cambridge* (Cambridge: Cambridge University Press, 1903).

Review of John Churton Collins (ed.), *The Plays and Poems of Robert Greene*, *MLR*, 1 (1905–6): 337–41.

'On Certain False Dates in Shakespearian Quartos', *Lib.*, 2nd series, 9 (1908): 113–31 and 381–409.

'*Titus Andronicus*', *MLR*, 14 (1919): 322–3.

'The "Hamlet" Texts and Recent Work in Shakespearian Bibliography', *MLR*, 14 (1919): 380–5.

'An Elizabethan Printer and His Copy', *Lib.*, 4th series, 4 (1923–4): 102–18.

Principles of Emendation in Shakespeare (London: Humphrey Milford, 1928); a separate volume, the text originally having been included in *PBA*, 14 (London: Humphrey Milford, 1928).

A Bibliography of the English Printed Drama to the Restoration, I: *Stationers' Records; Plays to 1616: Nos. 1–349* (London: Bibliographical Society, 1939).

'Ronald Brunlees McKerrow 1872–1940', *PBA* (1940): 489–515.

The Editorial Problem in Shakespeare: A Survey of the Foundations of the Text (3rd edn, Oxford: Clarendon Press, 1954).

The Shakespeare First Folio: Its Bibliographical and Textual History (Oxford: Clarendon Press, 1955).

Review of Fredson Bowers, *On Editing Shakespeare and the Elizabethan Dramatists*, *SQ*, 7: 1 (1956): 101–4.

Review of Fredson Bowers (ed.), *The Dramatic Works of Thomas Dekker*, III, *RES*, 10 (1959): 413–15.

Collected Papers, edited by J. C. Maxwell (Oxford: Clarendon Press, 1966).

[Grey, Zachary], *A Word or Two of Advice to William Warburton; A Dealer in Many Words* (London: printed for J. L., 1746).

The Grimaldi Shakspere. Notes and Emendations on the Plays of Shakspere, from a Recently-discovered Annotated Copy by the late Joseph Grimaldi, Esq., Comedian (London: J. Russell Smith, 1853).

Hackel, Heidi Brayman, '"Rowme" of Its Own: Printed Drama in Early Libraries', in John D. Cox and David Scott Kastan (eds.), *A New History of Early English Drama* (New York: Columbia University Press, 1997): 113–30.

'"The Great Variety of Readers" and Early Modern Reading Practices', in David Scott Kastan (ed.), *A Companion to Shakespeare* (Oxford: Blackwell, 1999): 139–57.

Halliwell[-Phillips], J. O., *Curiosities of Modern Shaksperian Criticism* (London: privately published, 1853).

A Few Words in Defence of the Memory of Edward Capell, Occasioned by a Criticism in the Times Newspaper, December the 26th, 1860 (London: printed only for presentation, 1861).

Prospectuses of 1. The folio edition of Shakespeare, completed in sixteen volumes. Illustrated. 2. Facsimiles of all the quarto editions of the works of Shakespeare which were issued in the life-time of the poet. Forty-seven volumes ([London]: no publisher, *c.* 1870).

Hamilton, N. E. S. A., *An Inquiry into the Genuineness of the Manuscript Corrections in Mr. J. Payne Collier's Annotated Shakspere, Folio, 1623...* (London: Bentley, 1860).

Hammerschmidt-Hummel, H. 'Promoting', in Walter Pape and Frederick Burwick (eds.), *The Boydell Shakespeare Gallery* (Bottrop: Peter Pomp, 1996): 33–44.

Hammond, Brean S., 'Theobald's *Double Falshood*: An "Agreeable Cheat"?', *N&Q*, 229 (March 1984): 2–3.

Hammond, Joseph W., 'The King's Printers in Ireland, 1551–1919' (part 3), *Dublin Historical Record*, 11 (1949–50): 88–96.

Hart, Alfred, *Stolne and Surreptitious Copies: A Comparative Study of Shakespeare's Bad Quartos* (Melbourne: Melbourne University Press, 1942).

Hart, Hymen Harold, 'Edward Capell: The First Modern Editor of Shakespeare' (PhD dissertation, University of Illinois, 1967).

Harvey, Sara King, 'Gulian Crommelin Verplanck: A Forgotten Knickerbocker' (PhD dissertation, University of Chicago, 1934).

Heath, Benjamin, *A Revisal of Shakespear's Text, wherein the Alterations Introduced into it by the More Modern Editors and Critics are Particularly Considered* (London: W. Johnston, 1765).

Henderson, Diana E. and James Siemon, 'Reading Vernacular Literature', in David Scott Kastan (ed.), *A Companion to Shakespeare* (Oxford: Blackwell, 1999): 206–22.

Henning, Standish, 'The Printer of *Romeo and Juliet*, Q1', *PBSA*, 60 (1966): 363–4.

Hervey, Thomas, *A Letter from the Hon. Thomas Hervey, to Sir Thomas Hanmer, Bart.* (Glasgow: J. Donaldson, n.d.).

Heywood, Thomas, *An Apology for Actors. Containing Three Briefe Treatises* (London, 1612).

Pleasant Dialogves and Dramma's . . . (London: by R. O. for R. H., 1637).

H. H. F. J. [Horace Howard Furness Jr.] (ed.), *The Letters of Horace Howard Furness* (Boston and New York: Houghton Mifflin, 1922).

Hinman, Charlton, *The Printing and Proof-Reading of the First Folio of Shakespeare* (Oxford: Clarendon Press, 1963), 2 vols.

Hodgson, J. E., *The Remarkable Story of the Shakespearian Quartos of 1619* (London: Hodgson & Co., 1946).

Holderness, Graham and Bryan Loughrey, 'Shakespeare Misconstrued: The True Chronicle Historie of Shakespearean Originals', *Textus*, 9 (1996): 393–418.

[Holt, John], *An Attempt to Rescue that Aunciente, English Poet, and Play-Wrighte, Maister Williaume Shakespere . . .* (London: printed for the author, 1749).

Honigmann, Ernst, *The Stability of Shakespeare's Text* (London: Edward Arnold, 1965).

'Shakespeare's Revised Plays: *King Lear* and *Othello*', *Lib.*, 6th series, 4 (1982): 142–73.

The Texts of 'Othello' and Shakespearian Revision (London: Routledge, 1996).

Hoppe, Harry R., *The Bad Quartos of Romeo and Juliet: A Bibliographical and Textual Study* (Ithaca: Cornell University Press, 1948).

Hosley, Richard, Richard Knowles and Ruth McGugan, *Shakespeare Variorum Handbook: A Manual of Editorial Practice* (New York: MLA, 1971).

Housman, A. E., 'The Application of Thought to Textual Criticism' in John Carter (ed.), *Selected Prose* (Cambridge: Cambridge University Press, 1961): 131–50.

Howard-Hill, Trevor, '"Towards the Twenty-First Century: The Oxford Shakespeares'', *AEB* n.s. 4 (1990): 3–5.

'Alice Walker (8 December 1900–14 October 1982)', in William Baker and Kenneth Womack (eds.), *Twentieth-Century British Book Collectors and Bibliographers* (Detroit: Gale, 1999): 297–304.

Howard-Hill, Trevor (ed.), *Shakespeare and 'Sir Thomas More': Essays on the Play and its Shakespearian Interest* (Cambridge: Cambridge University Press, 1989).

Hudson, Henry N., *Lectures on Shakespeare* (New York: Baker and Scribner, 1948).

Essays on Education, English Studies, and Shakespeare (Boston: Ginn, Heath, & Co., 1882).

Hughes, Glenn, *A History of the American Theatre, 1700–1950* (New York: Samuel French, 1951).

Hume, Peter D., 'Before the Bard: "Shakespeare" in Early Eighteenth-Century London', *English Literary History*, 64 (1997): 41–75.

Hutton, Richard W. and Laura Nelke, *Alderman Boydell's Shakespeare Gallery . . .* (Chicago: David & Alfred Smart Gallery, 1978).

Ioppolo, Grace, *Revising Shakespeare* (Cambridge, MA: Harvard University Press, 1991).

Irace, Kathleen O., *Reforming the 'Bad' Quartos: Performance and Provenance of Six Shakespearean First Editions* (Newark: University of Delaware Press, 1994).

Jackson, A., 'Rowe's Edition of Shakespeare', *Lib.*, 4th series, 10 (1930): 455–73.

Jackson, MacD. P., Review of Katherine Duncan-Jones (ed.), *Shakespeare's Sonnets*, *SQ*, 50: 3 (1999): 368–72.

Jackson, William A., 'Counterfeit Printing in Jacobean Times', *Lib.*, 4th series, 15 (1935): 364–76.

Jaggard, William, *Shakespeare Bibliography: A Dictionary of Every Known Issue of the Writings of Our National Poet: And of Recorded Opinion Thereon in the English Language* (Stratford-on-Avon: Shakespeare Press, 1911).

Shakespeare: Once a Printer and Bookman (Stratford-on-Avon: Shakespeare Press, 1933).

Jaques, pseud., *Modern Corruptions of Shakespeare's Text. A Letter to a Friend on the Subject of 'Cassell's Illustrated Shakespeare'* (London: Printed for private circulation, 1869).

J. W. Jarvis & Son, *Catalogue of Books, Pamphlets, Etc. Wholly Relating to Shakespeare* (London: Jarvis, 1892).

Jarvis, Simon, *Scholars and Gentlemen: Shakespearian Textual Criticism and Representations of Scholarly Labour, 1725–1765* (Oxford: Clarendon Press, 1995).

J.C.T.O., John Dover Wilson, Alice Walker, Muriel St Clare Byrne, Fredson Bowers and F. C. Francis, 'Walter Wilson Greg: 9 July 1875 – 4 March 1959', *Lib.*, 5th series, 14: 3 (Sept. 1959): 150–74.

'J.F.K.', Letter concerning the 'Perkins Folio', *Ath.*, 1274 (27 March 1852): 363.

Johnson, Francis R., 'Notes on English Retail Book-prices, 1550–1640', *Lib.*, 5th series, 5 (1950): 83–112.

Johnson, Gerald D., 'Thomas Pavier, Publisher, 1600–25', *Lib.*, 6th series, 14 (1992): 12–50.

Johnson, Samuel, *Miscellaneous Observations on the Tragedy of Macbeth: with remarks on Sir T. H.'s edition of Shakespear. To which is affix'd, proposals for a new edition of Shakeshear* [sic], *with a specimen* (London: E. Cave, 1745).

Proposals for a New Edition of Shakespeare (London, 1756; facsimile reprint, London: Humphrey Milford, 1923).

Johnson, Thomas, 'Catalogue of English Plays', included in the end pages of Johnson's edition of Dryden and Davenant's *The Tempest* (The Hague: Johnson, 1721), unpaged.

Jones, Claude E. (ed.), *Isaac Reed Diaries, 1762–1804* (Berkeley: University of California Press, 1946).

Jones, John D., 'Shakespeare in English Schools', *Jahrbuch der Deutschen Shakespeare-Gesellschaft*, Jahrgang, 32 (1906): 113–23.

Jones, R. F., *Lewis Theobald: His Contributions to English Scholarship, with Some Unpublished Letters* (New York: Columbia University Press, 1919).

J. W. C., Article on Shakespeare editions, *Dublin University Magazine*, March 1853: 356–73.

Kastan, David Scott, *Shakespeare After Theory* (London: Routledge, 1999).

Shakespeare and the Book (Cambridge: Cambridge University Press, 2001).

Kernan, Alvin, *Printing Technology, Letters and Samuel Johnson* (Princeton: Princeton University Press, 1987).

Kirkwood, A. E. M., 'Richard Field, Printer, 1589–1624', *Lib.*, 4th series, 12 (1931): 1–35.

Kliman, Bernice W., 'Samuel Johnson and Tonson's 1745 Shakespeare: Warburton, Anonymity, and the Shakespeare Wars', in Joanna Gondris (ed.), *Reading Readings: Essays on Shakespeare Editing in the Eighteenth Century* (Madison: Fairleigh Dickinson University Press, 1998): 299–317.

Knight, Charles, Prospectus for the 'Pictorial Edition of Shakspeare' (London: Charles Knight and Co., July 1838).

Old Lamps, or New? A Plea for the Original Editions of the Text of Shakspere: Forming an Introductory Notice to the Stratford Shakspere, Edited by Charles Knight (London: n.p., 1853).

Passages of a Working Life (London: Bradbury and Evans, 1864–5), 3 vols.

Shadows of the Old Booksellers (London: Bell and Daldy, 1865).

Knowles, Richard, 'Dates for Some Serially Published Shakespeares', *SB*, 40 (1987): 187–202.

Kubler, George A., *A New History of Stereotyping* (New York: n.p., 1941).

Landow, George, *Hypertext: The Convergence of Contemporary Critical Theory and Technology* (Baltimore: Johns Hopkins University Press, 1992).

'What's a Critic to Do?' in George Landow (ed.), *Hyper/Text/Theory* (Baltimore: Johns Hopkins University Press, 1994): 1–48.

Lavagnino, John, 'Reading, Scholarship, and Hypertext Editions', *TEXT*, 8 (1995): 109–24.

Leishman, J. B. (ed.), *The Three Parnassus Plays (1598–1601)* (London: Nicholson & Watson, 1949).

Levine, Lawrence W., *Highbrow/Lowbrow: The Emergence of Cultural Hierarchy in America* (Cambridge, MA: Harvard University Press, 1988).

List of books held in the *New England Courant* offices, *New England Courant*, 48 (25 June to 2 July 1722), verso.

Long, William B., '"A bed / for woodstock": A Warning for the Unwary', *MARDIE*, 2 (1985): 91–118.

'"Precious Few": English Manuscript Playbooks', in David Scott Kastan (ed.), *A Companion to Shakespeare* (Oxford: Blackwell, 1999): 414–33.

Loomba, Ania, 'Shakespeare and Cultural Difference', in Terence Hawkes (ed.), *Alternative Shakespeares*, II (London: Routledge, 1996): 164–91.

'Shakespearian Transformations', in John J. Joughin (ed.), *Shakespeare and National Culture* (Manchester: Manchester University Press, 1997): 109–41.

Lorenz, Alfred L., *Hugh Gaine, A Colonial Printer-Editor's Odyssey to Loyalism* (Carbondale, IL: Southern Illinois University Press, 1972).

Lounsbury, T. R., *The Text of Shakespeare* (New York: Scribner, 1906).

[Lowell, James Russell], 'White's Shakspeare (second notice)', *Atlantic Monthly*, 3 (February 1859): 241–60.

Low, Walter, *A Classified Catalogue of School, College, Classical, Technical, and General Educational Works in Use in Great Britain in the Early Part of 1871 . . .* (London: Sampson Low, Son, and Marston, 1871).

A Classified Catalogue of School, College, Classical, Technical, and General Educational Works in use in the United Kingdom and its Dependencies in 1876 . . . (London: Sampson Low, Marston, Searle, & Rivington, 1876).

Lynch, Kathleen M., *Jacob Tonson, Kit-Kat Publisher* (Knoxville: University of Tennessee Press, 1971).

Lynch, Michael, *Scotland: A New History* (London: Pimlico, 1991).

McAvoy, William C., 'Best Single-Volume Shakespeare Yet', *SQ*, 27: 1 (1976): 114, 117–22 and 125.

McDougall, Warren, 'Copyright Litigation in the Court of Sessions, 1738–1749, and the Rise of the Scottish Book Trade', *Edinburgh Bibliographical Society Transactions*, part 5, 5 (1988): 2–31.

McGann, Jerome J., *A Critique of Modern Textual Criticism* (Charlottesville: University of Virginia Press, 1992; originally published Chicago: University of Chicago Press, 1983).

The Textual Condition (Princeton: Princeton University Press, 1991).

McKenzie, D. F., 'Typography and Meaning: The Case of William Congreve', in *Buch und Buchhandel in Europa im achtzehnten Jahrhundert: The Book and the Book Trade in Eighteenth-Century Europe*, Proceedings of the fifth Wolfenbüttler Symposium, 1–3 Nov. 1977, ed. Giles Barber and Bernhard Fabian (Dr. Ernst Hauswedell, Hamburg, 1981): 81–126.

Bibliography and the Sociology of Texts (London: British Library, 1986).

McKerrow, R. B., 'The Elizabethan Printer and Dramatic Manuscripts', *Lib*, 4th series, 12: 3 (1931): 253–75.

The Treatment of Shakespeare's Text by his Earlier Editors, 1709–1786 (British Academy Annual Lecture, 1933).

'A Suggestion Regarding Shakespeare's Manuscripts', *RES*, 11 (1935): 459–65.

Prolegomena for the Oxford Shakespeare: A Study in Editorial Method (Oxford: Clarendon Press, 1939).

McKerrow, R. B. (gen. ed.), *A Dictionary of Printers and Booksellers in England, Scotland and Ireland, and of foreign printers of English books, 1557–1640* (London: Bibliographical Society, 1910).

McKitterick, David, *A History of Cambridge University Press*, II: *Scholarship and Commerce, 1698–1872* (Cambridge: Cambridge University Press, 1998).

McLaverty, James (ed.), *Pope and the Early Eighteenth-Century Book-Trade* (Oxford: Clarendon Press, 1991).

McLeod, Randall, 'Un-Editing Shak-speare', *Sub-Stance*, 33/4 (1982): 26–55. See also Cloud, Random.

McMillan, Scott, 'Professional Playwrighting', in David Scott Kastan (ed.), *A Companion to Shakespeare* (Oxford: Blackwell, 1999): 225–38.

Macmillan, Alexander, printed letter to booksellers, dated 15 Oct. 1864.

Macmillan, George (ed.), *Letters of Alexander Macmillan* (London: Macmillan, 1908).

Maguire, Laurie E., *Shakespearean Suspect Texts: The 'Bad' Quartos and their Contexts* (Cambridge: Cambridge University Press, 1996).

Malone, Edmond, Proposals for a new edition of Shakespeare, dated 6 Feb. 1792 (no publisher or place of publication).

Marcus, Leah, *Unediting the Renaissance: Shakespeare, Marlowe, Milton* (London: Routledge, 1996).

Marder, Louis, *His Exits and His Entrances: The Story of Shakespeare's Reputation* (London: John Murray, 1964).

Martin, Peter, *Edmond Malone, Shakespearean Scholar: A Literary Biography* (Cambridge: Cambridge University Press, 1995).

Masten, Jeffrey, *Textual Intercourse: Collaboration, Authorship, and Sexualities in Renaissance Drama* (Cambridge: Cambridge University Press, 1997).

Mathias, T. J., *The Pursuits of Literature. A Satirical Poem in Four Dialogues* (London, 1798, 8th edn).

Matthews, Brander, *These Many Years: Recollections of a New Yorker* (New York: Charles Scribner's Sons, 1917).

Matthews, William, 'Shorthand and the Bad Shakespeare Quartos', *MLR*, 27 (1932): 243–62.

'Peter Bales, Timothy Bright and William Shakespeare', *JEGP*, 34 (1935): 483–510.

'Shakespeare and the Reporters', *Lib.*, 4th series, 15 (1935): 481–98.

'Correspondence: Shakespeare and the Reporters', *Lib.*, 4th series, 17 (1936–7): 225–30.

Maw, Martin, 'A Hornet's Nest', *Around the Globe* (1998): 25.

Meisnest, F. W., 'Wieland's Translation of Shakespeare', *MLR*, 9 (1914): 12–40.

Middleton, Thomas, *The Mayor of Quinborough: A Tragedy* (London: Henry Herringman, 1661).

Mommsen, Tycho, '"Hamlet", 1603; and "Romeo and Juliet", 1597', *Ath.*, 1528 (1857): 182.

Monsarrat, G. D., '*A Funeral Elegy*: Ford, W.S., and Shakespeare', *RES*, 53: 210 (2002): 186–203.

Morgan, Charles, *The House of Macmillan (1843–1943)* (London: Macmillan, 1943).

Mowat, Barbara A., 'The Form of *Hamlet*'s Fortunes', *Renaissance Drama*, 19 (1988): 97–126.

'Nicholas Rowe and the Twentieth-Century Shakespeare Text', in Tetsuo Kishi, Roger Pringle and Stanley Wells (eds.), *Shakespeare and Cultural Traditions* (Newark: University of Delaware Press, 1994): 314–22.

'Constructing the Author', in R. B. Parker and S. P. Zitner (eds.), *Elizabethan Theater: Essays in Honor of S. Schoenbaum* (Newark: University of Delaware Press, 1996): 93–110.

'The Theatre and Literary Culture', in John D. Cox and David Scott Kastan (eds.), *A New History of Early English Drama* (New York: Columbia University Press, 1997): 213–30.

'The Problem of Shakespeare's Text(s)', in Laurie E. Maguire and Thomas L. Berger (eds.), *Textual Formations and Reformations* (Newark: University of Delaware Press, 1998): 131–48.

'The Reproduction of Shakespeare's Texts', in Margreta de Grazia and Stanley Wells (eds.), *The Cambridge Companion to Shakespeare* (Cambridge: Cambridge University Press, 2001): 13–29.

Murphy, Andrew, 'Shakespeare's Folios', *Critical Survey*, 9: 3 (1997): 156–8.

'Texts and Textualities: A Shakespearean History', in Andrew Murphy (ed.), *The Renaissance Text: Theory, Editing, Textuality* (Manchester: Manchester University Press, 2000): 191–210.

Murray, David, *Robert and Andrew Foulis and the Glasgow Press with some account of the Glasgow Academy of the Fine Arts* (Glasgow: MacLehose, 1913).

Murray, David (ed.), *Some Letters of Robert Foulis* (Glasgow: MacLehose, 1917).

Naiman, Sandra, 'R. W. Chapman (5 Oct. 1881 – 20 April 1960)', in William Baker and Kenneth Womack (eds.), *Twentieth-Century British Book Collectors and Bibliographers* (Detroit: Gale, 1999): 40–8.

Neidig, William, 'The Shakespeare Quartos of 1619', *MP*, 8 (Oct. 1910): 145–63.

Newton, Thomas (ed.), *Paradise Lost. A Poem, in twelve books* (London: J. and R. Tonson and S. Draper, 1749), 2 vols.

Nichols, John (ed.), *Illustrations of the Literary History of the Eighteenth Century, consisting of authentic memoir and original letters of eminent persons, and intended as a sequel to the, 'Literary Anecdotes'* (London: Nichols, Son and Bentley, 1817–58), 8 vols.

[Nichols, Philip], *The Castrated Letter of Sir Thomas Hanmer* (London: for the author, 1763).

Nicoll, Allardyce, 'The Editors of Shakespeare from First Folio to Malone', in *Studies in the First Folio* (London: Humphrey Milford for Oxford University Press, 1924): 157–78.

    The Garrick Stage: Theatres and Audience in the Eighteenth Century (Manchester: Manchester University Press, 1980).

Note on the 1902 Sidney Lee facsimile of the First Folio, *The Periodical*, March 1903: 3.

Notice of the Cambridge edition, *Publishers' Circular*, 1 July 1863: 322.

Notices regarding the Cambridge and Globe editions, *The Bookseller*, 10 Dec. 1864: 835–6.

Notices regarding Joseph Dennie's edition, *Port Folio*, IV:10 (10 March 1804): 79; IV:15 (14 April 1804): 119.

Obituary for William Aldis Wright, *The Cambridge Review: A Journal of University Life and Thought*, 35: 882 (20 May 1914): 466–70.

Ó Ciosáin, Niall, *Print and Popular Culture in Ireland, 1750–1850* (Basingstoke: Macmillan, 1997).

Orgel, Stephen, 'Shakespeare and the Kinds of Drama', *Critical Inquiry*, 6 (1979): 107–23.

    'What is a Text?', in David Scott Kastan and Peter Stallybrass (eds.), *Staging the Renaissance: Reinterpretations of Elizabethan and Jacobean Drama* (London: Routledge, 1991): 83–7. Originally published in *Research Opportunities in Renaissance Drama* 26 (1981): 3–6.

Osborn, James M., 'Edmond Malone and Oxford', in W. H. Bond (ed.), *Eighteenth-Century Studies in Honor of Donald F. Hyde* (New York: Grolier, 1970): 323–38.

Pafford, J. H. P. 'The Methuen Facsimile, 1910, of the First Folio, 1623', *N&Q*, 13 (1966): 126–7.

Pape, Walter and Frederick Burwick (eds.), *The Boydell Shakespeare Gallery* (Bottrop: Peter Pomp, 1996).

Parrish, S.M., 'The Whig Interpretation of Literature', *TEXT*, 4 (1988): 343–50.

Patrick, D. L., *The Textual History of Richard III* (London: Humphrey Milford for Oxford University Press, 1936).

Patterson, Lyman Ray, *Copyright in Historical Perspective* (Nashville: Vanderbilt University Press, 1968).

Paul, Henry N., 'Mr. Hughs' Edition of *Hamlet*', *Modern Language Notes*, 49 (1934): 438–43.

Peck, Francis, *New Memoirs of the Life and Poetical Works of Mr. John Milton* (London: 1740).

Pendleton, Thomas A., 'The Non-Shakespearian Language of "Shall I Die?"', *RES*, n.s., 40: 159 (1989): 323–51.

Perrin, Noel, *Dr. Bowdler's Legacy* (London: Macmillan, 1970).

Peters, Julie Stone, *Theatre of the Book 1480–1880: Print, Text, and Performance in Europe* (Oxford: Oxford University Press, 2000).

Phillips, James W., *Printing and Bookselling in Dublin, 1670–1800* (Dublin: Irish Academic Press, 1998).

Plant, Marjorie, *The English Book Trade: An Economic History of the Making and Sale of Books* (London: George Allen & Unwin, 1939).

Plomer, Henry R., 'The Printers of Shakespeare's Plays and Poems', *Lib.*, new series, 7 (1906): 149–66.

A Dictionary of the Booksellers and Printers who were at work in England, Scotland and Ireland from 1641 to 1667 (London: Bibliographical Society, 1907).

Plomer, Henry R., G. H. Bushell and E. R. McClintock Dix, *A Dictionary of the Printers and Booksellers who were at work in England, Scotland and Ireland from 1726 to 1775* (London: Bibliographical Society, 1932).

Pollard, A. W., 'A Literary Causerie: Shakespeare in the Remainder Market', *The Academy* (2 June 1906): 528–9.

Shakespeare's Folios and Quartos: A Study in the Bibliography of Shakespeare's Plays, 1594–1685 (London: Methuen, 1909).

Shakespeare's Fight with the Pirates (London: Alexander Moring, 1917).

Review of John Dover Wilson (ed.) *Hamlet*, *Lib.* 4th series, 12 (1932): 116–120.

'My First Fifty Years', in Gwendolen Murphy (ed.), *A Select Bibliography of the Writings of Alfred W. Pollard* (Oxford: Oxford University Press, 1938): 1–15.

Pollard, A. W. (ed.), *Shakespeare's Hand in the Play of Sir Thomas More* (Cambridge: Cambridge University Press, 1923).

Pollard, M., *Dublin's Trade in Books, 1550–1800: Lyell Lectures, 1986–1987* (Oxford: Clarendon Press, 1989).

Poole, John, *Hamlet Travestie: in three acts. With annotations by Dr. Johnson and Geo. Steevens, Esq. and other commentators* (London, 1810).

Pope, Alexander, *The Dunciad, an Heroic Poem. In Three Books* (London: A. Dodd, 1728).

The Dunciad Variorum. With the Prolegomena of Scriblerus (London: A. Dod, 1729).

Price, H. T., 'Towards a Scientific Method of Textual Criticism for the Elizabethan Drama', *JEGP*, 36 (1937): 151–67.

Prospectus for *The Harvard Shakespeare* (Boston, New York, Chicago: Ginn and Heath, n.d.).

Prospectus for *Shakespeare for the School and Family* (New York: Harper & Brothers, n.d.).

Pyrnne, William, *Histrio-Mastix. The Players Scovrge, or, Actors Tragædie, divided into two parts* (London, 1633).

Quiller-Couch, Arthur, *Memories and Opinions* (Cambridge: Cambridge University Press, 1945).

Ragg, Edward, 'Controversies of the Iconic: Why do Publishers Produce Rival Editions of Classic Authors? *The Oxford Shakespeare* 1978–1987' (MA dissertation, Oxford Brookes University, 1999).

'*The Oxford Shakespeare* Re-Visited: An Interview with Professor Stanley Wells', *AEB*, n.s., 12: 2 (2001): 73–101.

'Much Ado About Everything: Designing *The Oxford Shakespeare*: An Interview with Professor Paul Luna', forthcoming in *Typography Papers*.

Ramsey, Paul, 'Shakespeare and *Sir Thomas More* Revisited: or, A Mounty on the Trail', *PBSA*, 70 (1976): 333–46.

Rankin, J. E., *The Shakespearean Interpreter, with memorial words respecting Henry Norman Hudson* (Middlebury, VT: n.p., 1886).

Rasmussen, Eric, 'Anonymity and the Erasure of Shakespeare's First Eighteenth-Century Editor', in Joanna Gondris (ed.), *Reading Readings: Essays on Shakespeare Editing in the Eighteenth Century* (Madison: Fairleigh Dickinson University Press, 1998): 318–22.

Register of the Society of Writers to Her Majesty's Signet (Edinburgh: Clark Constable, 1983).

Review of John Bell's edition (1786–8), *MR* (Aug. 1788): 155–7.

Review of Bowdler's edition (1820), *ER* (1821): 52–4.

Review of Capell's *Notes and Various Readings*, *MR* (Dec. 1783): 483–8.

Review of J. O. Halliwell's edition, *Ath.*, 1340 (2 July 1853): 796–9.

Review of the Johnson–Steevens–Reed edition (1785), *MR* (Aug. 1786): 81–94; (Sept. 1786): 161–9.

Review of Charles Knight's Pictorial Edition, *Dublin Review* (Nov. 1840): 316–31.

Review of Leslie, Jameson and Murray, *Narrative of Discovery and Adventure in the Polar Seas and Regions*, *Ath.*, 152 (25 Sept. 1830): 593.

Review of Pope's edition, *The Weekly Journal or Saturday's Post* (also known as *Mist's Journal*) (20 March 1725): 2075–6. Further comments in the issue of 27 March: 2081.

Review of various Shakespeare editions, *ER* (1845): 329–84.

Review of various Shakespeare editions, *ER* (1856): 358–86.

Rhodes, Neil, 'From Rhetoric to Belles Lettres', in Robert Crawford (ed.), *The Scottish Invention of English Literature* (Oxford: Clarendon Press, 1998): 22–36.

Rhodes, Neil and Jonathan Sawday, *The Renaissance Computer: Knowledge Technology in the First Age of Print* (London: Routledge, 2000).

Ritson, Joseph, *Remarks, Critical and Illustrative on the Text and Notes of the Last Edition of Shakspeare* (London: J. Johnson, 1783).

'The Genuine Text of Shakespeare. Preparing for the Press, an Edition of the Plays of William Shakspeare, with Notes', included in *Remarks* (1783).

Cursory Criticisms on the Edition of Shakspeare Published by Edmond Malone (London: Hookham & Carpenter, 1792).

Rivington, Septimus, *The Publishing Family of Rivington* (London: Rivingtons, 1919).

Roach, John, *Public Examinations in England, 1850–1900* (Cambridge: Cambridge University Press, 1971).

Robert and Andrew Foulis: An Exhibition in the Hunterian Museum to Commemorate the Silver Jubilee of the British Records Association (Glasgow: University of Glasgow, 1958).

Roberts, Jeanne Addison, 'Women Editors of Shakespeare (Faceless and Behind Bars)', unpublished seminar paper.

Roberts, Sasha, 'Reading the Shakespearean Text in Early Modern England', *Critical Survey*, 7: 3 (1995): 299–306.

Robertson, J. M., *The Genuine in Shakespeare: A Conspectus* (London: Routledge, 1930).

Robbins, Robin, '. . . and the Counter-arguments', *TLS*, 20 Dec. 1985: 1450.

Rodgers, Pat, 'Pope and his Subscribers', *PH*, 3 (1978): 7–36.

Rose, Mark, 'The Author as Proprietor: *Donaldson v. Beckett* and the Genealogy of Modern Authorship', *Representations*, 23 (1988): 51–85.

  Authors and Owners: The Invention of Copyright (Cambridge, MA: Harvard University Press, 1993).

Rosenbach, A. S. W., *Books and Bidders: The Adventures of a Bibliophile* (Boston: Little, Brown, 1927).

Rozett, Martha Tuck, Review of the *Norton, Riverside* and *Bevington* editions of Shakespeare, *SQ*, 48: 4 (1997): 465–72.

Satchell, Thomas, 'The Spelling of F1', *TLS*, 3 June 1920: 352.

Savage, Henry L., 'The Shakspere Society of Philadelphia', *SQ*, 3 (1952): 341–51.

Scheide, William H., 'The Earliest First Folio in America?', *SQ*, 27 (1976): 332–3.

Schoenbaum, Samuel, *William Shakespeare: A Documentary Life* (New York: Oxford University Press/Scolar Press, 1975).

  Shakespeare's Lives (2nd edn, Oxford: Clarendon Press, 1991).

Schroeder, John W., *The Great Folio of 1623: Shakespeare's Plays in the Printing House* (Hamden, CT: Shoe String Press, 1956).

Seary, Peter *Lewis Theobald and the Editing of Shakespeare* (Oxford: Clarendon Press, 1990).

Sen, Sailendra Kumar, 'Malone's Two Shakespeare Editions', *Lib.*, 5th series, 31 (1976): 390–1.

Shakespeare: An Exhibition of Printed Books (Edinburgh: National Library of Scotland, 1964).

'Shakspeare', *The Bookseller*, 29 Feb. 1864: 92–3.

'Shall Shakspeare Have a Monument?', *The Bookseller*, 31 March 1864: 169.

Shattuck, Charles H., *The Shakespeare Promptbooks: A Descriptive Catalogue* (Urbana: University of Illinois Press, 1965).

Sherbo, Arthur, 'Warburton and the 1745 "Shakespeare"', *JEGP*, 51 (1952): 71–82.

  Samuel Johnson, Editor of Shakespeare (Illinois Studies in Language and Literature 42. Urbana: University of Illinois Press, 1956).

  'George Steevens' 1785 Variorum *Shakespeare*', *SB*, 32 (1979): 241–6.

  The Birth of Shakespeare Studies: Commentators from Rowe (1709) to Boswell–Malone (1821) (East Lansing: Colleagues, 1986).

  Isaac Reed, Editorial Factotum (Victoria, BC: University of Victoria Press, 1989).

  The Achievement of George Steevens (New York: Peter Lang, 1990).

Sherburn, George (ed.), *The Correspondence of Alexander Pope* (Oxford: Clarendon Press, 1956), 5 vols.

Sherzer, Jane, 'American Editions of Shakespeare: 1753–1866', *PMLA*, 15 (1907): 633–96.

'The Shilling Shakspeares', *The Bookseller*, 1 July 1868: 451.

Simon, Henry W., *The Reading of Shakespeare in American Schools and Colleges: A Historical Survey* (New York: Simon & Schuster, 1932).

Simpson, Percy, *Shakespearian Punctuation* (Oxford: Clarendon Press, 1911).

Simpson, Richard, 'Are there any Extant MSS. in Shakespeare's Handwriting?', *N&Q*, 183 (July 1871): 1–3.

Singer, Samuel Weller, *The Text of Shakespeare Vindicated from the Interpolations and Corruptions Advocated by John Payne Collier Esq. in his Notes and Emendations* (London: William Pickering, 1853).

Sinker, Robert, *Biographical Notes on the Librarians of Trinity College* (Cambridge Antiquarian Society, 1897).

Sisson, Charles J., 'Shakespeare Quartos as Prompt-Copies with Some Account of Cholmeley's Players and a New Shakespeare Allusion', *RES*, 18: 70 (1942): 129–43.

   New Readings in Shakespeare (Cambridge: Cambridge University Press, 1956), 2 vols.

Skinner, R. T., *A Notable Family of Scots Printers* (Edinburgh: Constable Press, 1928).

Small, Ian, '"Why Edit Anything at All?" Textual Editing and Postmodernism: A Review Essay', *English Literature in Transition*, 38 (1995): 195–203.

Smith, D. Nichol, *Shakespeare in the Eighteenth Century* (Oxford: Clarendon Press, 1928).

Smith, Emma, 'Ghost Writing: *Hamlet* and the Ur-Hamlet', in Andrew Murphy (ed.), *The Renaissance Text: Theory, Editing, Textuality* (Manchester: Manchester University Press, 2000): 177–90.

Smith, Hallett, '"No Cloudy Stuffe to Puzzell Intellect": A Testimonial Misapplied to Shakespeare', *SQ*, 1: 1 (Jan. 1950): 18–21.

Smith, John Hazel, 'Styan Thirlby's Shakespearean Commentaries: A Corrective Analysis', *Shakespeare Studies*, 11 (1978): 219–41.

Smith, Steven Escar, '"The Eternal Verities Verified": Charlton Hinman and the Roots of Mechanical Collation', *SB*, 53 (2000): 129–61.

Smith, Teena Rochfort, *A Four-Text Edition of . . . Hamlet* (London: New Shakespeare Society, 1883).

Spencer, Hazelton, '*Hamlet* under the Restoration', *PMLA*, 38 (1923): 770–91.

   Shakespeare Improved: The Restoration Versions in Quarto and on the Stage (Cambridge, MA: Harvard University Press, 1927).

Spevack, Marvin, *James Orchard Halliwell-Phillipps: The Life and Works of the Shakespearean Scholar and Bookman* (Delaware and London: Oak Knoll Press and Shepheard-Walwyn, 2001).

Steevens, George, 'Proposals for a new edition of Shakespeare, dated February 1, 1766' (no publisher or place of publication).

   Review of Charles Jennens' edition of *King Lear* in *Critical Review*, 30 (Dec. 1770): 436–9.

Steevens, Harrison Ross, 'American Editors of Shakspere', in Brander Matthews and Ashley Horace Thorndike (eds.), *Shaksperian Studies by Members of the Department of English and Comparative Literature in Columbia University* (New York: Columbia University Press, 1916): 345–68.

Steinberg, S. H., *Five Hundred Years of Printing* (3rd edn, London: Pelican, 1974).

Stephens, W. B., *Education in Britain, 1750–1914* (Basingstoke: Macmillan, 1998).

Stevenson, Allan H., 'Shakespearian Dated Watermarks', *SB*, 4 (1951–2): 159–64.

Stockwell, La Tourette, 'The Dublin Pirates and the English Laws of Copyright, 1710–1801', *Dublin Magazine*, 12 (1937): 30–40.

Straus, Ralph, *The Unspeakable Curll* (London: Chapman and Hall, 1927).

Sutherland, Kathryn, 'Looking and Knowing: Textual Encounters of a Postponed Kind', in Warren Chernaik, Marilyn Deegan, and Andrew Gibson (eds.), *Beyond the Book: Theory, Culture, and the Politics of Cyberspace* (London: Office for Humanities Computing, 1996): 11–22.

Swinburne, Algernon Charles, *A Study of Shakespeare* (London: Chatto & Windus, 1880).

Tabor, Stephen, 'R. B. McKerrow (12 Dec. 1872 – 20 January 1940)', in William Baker and Kenneth Womack (eds.), *Twentieth-Century British Book Collectors and Bibliographers* (Detroit: Gale, 1999): 198–209.

Tanselle, G. Thomas, 'The Editorial Problem of Final Authorial Intention', in *Selected Studies in Bibliography* (Charlottesville: University Press of Virginia, 1979): 309–53.

'The Life and Work of Fredson Bowers', *SB*, 46 (1993): 1–154.

Taylor, Gary, 'The War in *King Lear*', *SS*, 33 (1980): 27–34.

'The Fortunes of Oldcastle', *SS*, 38 (1985): 85–100.

'A New Shakespeare Poem? The Evidence . . .', *TLS*, 20 Dec. 1985: 1447–8.

Reinventing Shakespeare: A Cultural History from the Restoration to the Present (1989; reprinted Oxford: Oxford University Press, 1991).

'c:\wp\file.txt 05:41 10-07-98', in Andrew Murphy (ed.), *The Renaissance Text: Theory, Editing, Textuality* (Manchester: Manchester University Press, 2000): 44–54.

Taylor, Gary and Michael Warren (eds.), *The Division of the Kingdom: Shakespeare's Two Versions of 'King Lear'* (Oxford: Clarendon Press, 1983).

Theobald, Lewis, *The Tragedy of King Richard the II . . . Alter'd from Shakesper, by Mr. Theobald* (London: G. Strahan, 1720).

Shakespeare Restor'd: or, A Specimen of the Many Errors as well Committed, or Unamended, by Mr. Pope in his Late Edition of this Poet . . . (London: R. Francklin, J. Woodman and D. Lyon, and C. Davis, 1726).

Double Falsehood; or, The Distrest Lovers (London: J. Watts, 1728).

Thomson, Leslie, 'A Quarto "Marked for Performance": Evidence of What?', *MARDIE*, 8 (1996): 176–210.

Ann Thompson and Gordan McMullan, 'Introduction' to Ann Thompson and Gordon McMullan (eds.), *In Arden: Editing Shakespeare* (London: Thomson, 2003): xi–xxiv.

Thompson, Ann, Thomas L. Berger, A. R. Braunmuller, Philip Edwards and Lois Potter (eds.), *Which Shakespeare? A User's Guide to Editions* (Milton Keynes: Open University Press, 1992).

Thompson, Ann and Sasha Roberts (eds.), *Women Reading Shakespeare, 1660–1900: An Anthology of Criticism* (Manchester: Manchester University Press, 1997).

Thompson, Edward Maunde, *Shakespeare's Hand* (Oxford: Clarendon Press, 1916).

Thompson, Lawrence, 'The Boydell Shakespeare: An English Monument to Graphic Arts', *Princeton University Library Chronicle*, 1: 2 (1940): 17–24.

Todd, William B., 'The Issues and States of the Second Folio and Milton's Epitaph on Shakespeare', *SB*, 5 (1952–3): 81–109.

Tooke, J. Horne, *EΠea Πterpoenta. Or, the Diversions of Purley* (London: printed for the author, 1805), 2 vols.

Trousdale, Marion, 'Diachronic and Synchronic: Critical Bibliography and the Acting of Plays' in Bernhard Fabian and Kurt Tetzeli von Rosador (eds.), *Shakespeare: Text, Language, Criticism* (Hildesheim, Zurich and New York: Olms-Weidmann, 1987): 304–14.

'A Second Look at Critical Bibliography and the Acting of Plays', *SQ*, 41 (1990): 87–96.

Turner, Michael L., 'Andrew Wilson: Lord Stanhope's Stereotype Printer', *Journal of the Printing Historical Society*, 9 (1975): 22–65.

Unto the Right Honourable the Lords of Council and Session, the Petition of Alexander Donaldson Bookseller in Edinburgh (Edinburgh: n.p. 1769).

Urkowitz, Steven, *Shakespeare's Revision of 'King Lear'* (Princeton: Princeton University Press, 1980).

'"The Base Shall to th' Legitimate": The Growth of an Editorial Tradition', in Gary Taylor and Michael Warren (eds.), *The Division of the Kingdom: Shakespeare's Two Versions of 'King Lear'* (Oxford: Clarendon Press, 1983): 23–43.

'"All things is hansome now": Murderers Nominated by Numbers in *2 Henry VI* and *Richard III*', in George Walton Williams (ed.), *Shakespeare's Speech-Headings: Speaking the Speech in Shakespeare's Plays* (Newark: University of Delaware Press, 1997): 101–19.

Velz, John W., '"Pirate Hills" and the Quartos of *Julius Caesar*', *PBSA*, 63 (1969): 177–93.

'The Text of *Julius Caesar* in the Second Folio: Two Notes', *SQ*, 20 (1969): 95–8.

'New Information About Some Nineteenth-Century Shakespeare Editions from the Letters of Joseph Crosby', *PBSA*, 71 (1977): 279–94.

'Research in Eighteenth and Nineteenth Century Editions of Shakespeare', *Literary Research Newsletter*, 2 (1977): 47–58.

'The Collier Controversy Redivivus', *SQ*, 36:1 (1985): 106–15.

Velz, John W. and Frances N. Teague (eds.), *One Touch of Shakespeare: Letters of Joseph Crosby to Joseph Parker Norris 1875–1878* (Washington, DC: Folger, *c.* 1986).

Vickers, Brian, Review of *The Oxford Shakespeare*, *RES*, 40 (1989): 402–11.

'*Hamlet* by Dogberry: A Perverse Reading of the Bad Quarto', *TLS*, 24 Dec. 1993: 24–5.

Viswanathan, Gauri, *Masks of Conquest: Literary Study and British Rule in India* (Delhi: Oxford University Press, 1998).

Walker, Alice, 'Edward Capell and his Edition of *Shakespeare*', *PBA*, 46 (1960): 131–45.

Walsh, Marcus, *Shakespeare, Milton and Eighteenth-Century Literary Editing: The Beginnings of Interpretive Scholarship* (Cambridge: Cambridge University Press, 1997).

Walters, Gwyn, 'The Booksellers in 1759 and 1774: The Battle for Literary Property', *Lib.*, 5th series, 29 (1974): 287–311.

Warburton, William, 'Shakespeare' entry in John Peter Bernard, Thomas Birch, John Lockman, and other hands, *A General Dictionary, Historical and Critical* . . . (London: G. Strahan, etc., 1739), IX: 190–1.

Ward, Robert E., *Prince of Dublin Printers: The Letters of George Faulkner* (Lexington: University of Kentucky Press, 1972).

Warren, Michael J., 'Quarto and Folio *King Lear* and the Interpretation of Albany and Edgar', in David Bevington and Jay L. Halio (eds.), *Shakespeare: Pattern Excelling Nature* (Newark: University of Delaware Press, 1978): 95–117.

'Textual Problems, Editorial Assertions in Editions of Shakespeare', in Jerome J. McGann (ed.), *Textual Criticism and Literary Interpretation* (Chicago: University of Chicago Press, 1985): 23–37.

The Weekly Oracle: or, Universal Library (London: T. Read, 1737).

Wells, Stanley, *Shakespeare: The Writer and his Work* (London: British Council/Longman, 1978).

'Introduction: The Once and Future *King Lear*', in Gary Taylor and Michael Warren (eds.), *The Division of the Kingdom: Shakespeare's Two Versions of 'King Lear'* (Oxford: Clarendon Press, 1983): 1–20.

Re-Editing Shakespeare for the Modern Reader (Oxford: Clarendon Press, 1984).

'Revision in Shakespeare's Plays', in Richard Landon (ed.), *Editing and Editors: A Retrospect* (New York: AMS, 1988): 67–97.

Shakespeare and Revision: The Hilda Hulme Memorial Lecture (London: University of London, 1988).

'Multiple Texts and the Oxford Shakespeare', *Textus*, 9 (1996): 357–74.

Shakespeare: For All Time (Basingstoke: Macmillan, 2002).

Wells, Stanley and Gary Taylor, *William Shakespeare: A Textual Companion* (Oxford: Clarendon, 1987).

'*The Oxford Shakespeare* Re-Viewed by the General Editors', *AEB*, n.s., 4: 1 (1990): 6–20.

Wenner, Evelyn Wingate, 'George Steevens and the Boydell Shakspeare' (PhD dissertation, George Washington University, Washington DC, 1952).

Werstine, Paul, 'The Textual Mystery of *Hamlet*', *SQ*, 39 (1988): 1–26.

'Narratives About Printed Shakespeare Texts: "Foul Papers" and "Bad" Quartos', *SQ*, 41 (1990): 65–86.

Review of Michael Warren (ed.), *The Complete 'King Lear'*, *SQ*, 44 (1993): 236–7.

'William Shakespeare', in D. C. Greetham (ed.), *Scholarly Editing: A Guide to Research* (New York: MLA, 1995): 253–82.

'A Century of "Bad" Shakespearean Quartos', *SQ*, 50:3 (Fall 1999): 310–33.

West, Anthony James, 'Sales and Prices of Shakespeare First Folios: A History, 1623 to the Present (Part One)', *PBSA*, 92:4 (1998): 465–528.

The Shakespeare First Folio: The History of the Book, I: *An Account of the First Folio Based on its Sales and Prices, 1623–2000* (Oxford: Oxford University Press, 2001).

Westfall, Alfred Van Rensselaer, *American Shakespearean Criticism 1607–1865* (New York: H. W. Wilson, 1939).

'What Edition of Shakespeare Shall I Buy?', *Shakespeariana* (1889): 483–91 (originally published in *The Christian Union*, 3 Oct. 1889).

Wheatley, Henry B., 'Johnson's Edition of Shakespeare', *Ath.*, 4272 (1909): 298.

'Shakespeare's Editors: 1623 to 20th Century', *Transactions of the Bibliographical Society*, XIV (1916): 145–73.

Wheeler, G. W. (ed.), *Letters of Sir Thomas Bodley to Thomas James, First Keeper of the Bodleian Library* (Oxford: Clarendon Press, 1926).

Wickham, Glynne, Herbert Berry and William Ingram (eds.), *English Professional Theatre, 1530–1660* (Cambridge: Cambridge University Press, 2000).

Wiles, R. M., *Serial Publication in England Before 1750* (Cambridge: Cambridge University Press, 1957).

Williams, George Walton, 'The Publishing and Editing of Shakespeare's Plays' in John. F. Andrews (ed.), *William Shakespeare: His World, His Work, His Influence*, 3 vols. (New York: 1985): 589–601.

Review of *The Oxford Shakespeare, Cahiers Elisabethains*, 35 (1989): 103–17.

Willoughby, E. E., *The Printing of the First Folio of Shakespeare* (Oxford: Bibliographical Society, 1932).

A Printer of Shakespeare: The Books and Times of William Jaggard (London: Allan & Co., 1934).

'The Reading of Shakespeare in Colonial America', *PBSA*, 30, part 2 (1936): 45–56.

Wilson, Edmund, 'The Fruits of the MLA', *New York Review of Books*, 26 Sept. 1968 (7–10) and 10 Oct. 1968 (6–14).

Wilson, F. P., 'Sir Walter Wilson Greg 1875–1959', *PBA*, 45 (1959): 307–34.

Shakespeare and the New Bibliography, revised and edited by Helen Gardner (Oxford: Clarendon Press, 1970).

Wilson, John Dover, 'The Copy for *Hamlet*, 1603' and 'The *Hamlet* Transcript, 1593', *Lib.*, 3rd series, 9 (1918): 153–85 and 217–47.

'The Task of Heminge and Condell', in *Studies in the First Folio* (London: Humphrey Milford/Oxford University Press, 1924): 53–77.

'Thirteen Volumes of Shakespeare: A Retrospect', *MLR*, 25: 4 (1930): 397–414.

The Manuscript of Shakespeare's 'Hamlet' and the Problems of its Transmission: An Essay in Critical Bibliography (Cambridge: Cambridge University Press, 1934), 2 vols.

What Happens in 'Hamlet' (Cambridge: Cambridge University Press, 1935).

'Alfred William Pollard 1859–1944', *PBA*, 31 (1945): 257–306.

Milestones on the Dover Road (London: Faber & Faber, 1969).

Wimsatt, W. K. and Monroe C. Beardsley, 'The Intentional Fallacy', in W. K. Wimsatt (ed.), *The Verbal Icon: Studies in the Meaning of Poetry* (Lexington: University of Kentucky Press, 1954): 3–18.

Winsor, Justin, *A Bibliography of the Original Quartos and Folios of Shakespeare with Particular Reference to Copies in America* (Boston: James R. Osgood, 1876).

'The College Library', in *Circulars of Information of the Bureau of Education*, no. 1 (Washington: Government Printing Office, 1880).

Winstanley, D. A., 'Halliwell Phillipps and Trinity College Library', *Lib.*, 5th series, 3: 2 (1947–8): 250–82.

Woodson, W. C., 'The Printer's Copy for the 1785 Variorum Shakespeare', *SB*, 31 (1978): 208–10.

Wolf, Edwin II and John F. Fleming, *Rosenbach: A Biography* (Cleveland and New York: World Publishing Company, 1960).

Wright, T. G., *Literary Culture in Early New England, 1620–1730* (New Haven: Yale University Press, 1920).

Wroth, Lawrence C., 'North America (English-speaking)', in R. A. Peddie (ed.), *Printing: A Short History of the Art* (London: Grafton, 1927): 319–69.

Zeller, Hans, 'A New Approach to the Critical Constitution of Literary Texts', *SB*, 28 (1975): 231–64.

Main index

(*Note*: the Chronological appendix has its own separate set of indices)

pilloried by Thomas Edwards 78–79
serves as base text for Johnson's
edition 83
Ward and Lock 178
Warne, Frederick 177
Warren, Alice 53, 54
Warren, Michael 207, 252, 265, 266–267, 268
Warwick Shakespeare 167
Weis, René 255, 265
Wells, George 58
Wells, H. G. 412
Wells, Mary 58
Wells, Stanley 4, 233, 247–260, 261, 422, 451
Wells, William 58
Werstine, Paul 4, 27, 53, 159–161, 206, 254, 263, 268, 459, 460
Folger Shakespeare 271
West, Antony James 162, 439, 460
West, Charlotte, Lady de la Warr 71
West, David and John 145
Westfall, Alfred Van Rensselaer 146, 148, 149, 150, 155
Which Shakespeare? A User's Guide to Editions 14
Whiston, John 131
White, Edward 22, 23
White, Richard Grant 154–155, 161
editorial methodology 154
Wilders, John 242
Wilkie, John 131
Wilkins, George, *The Painfull Adventures of Pericles Prince of Tyre* 250
Wilks, Robert 34

Williams, George Walton 257
Willis, John, *Stenography* 26
Willoughby, E. E. 51, 143
Wilson, Alexander 128
Wilson, Andrew 149
Wilson, F. P. 213, 214, 215, 216
Wilson, John Dover 10, 185, 213, 216, 218, 221, 238, 240, 274
Kessler edition of *Hamlet*
The Manuscript of Shakespeare's Hamlet 232–233
response to McKerrow's proposed edition 224
role in *New Shakespeare* 230–236
speculative mindset 28
What Happens in 'Hamlet' 448
see also *New Shakespeare*
Winsor, Justin 161
Wise, Andrew 25
Wood, Manley 189
Woodson, William C. 92
Wordsworth, Charles 184
Wortley, Edward 102
Wreittoun, John 19
Wright, William Aldis 7, 157, 184–185, 204, 211, 212
see also *Cambridge Shakespeare, Clarendon Shakespeare, Globe Shakespeare*
Wriothesley, Henry, Earl of Southampton 16–17
Wroth, Lawrence C. 145
Wycherley, William 58

Yale University 143
Yates, Justice Sir Joseph 135

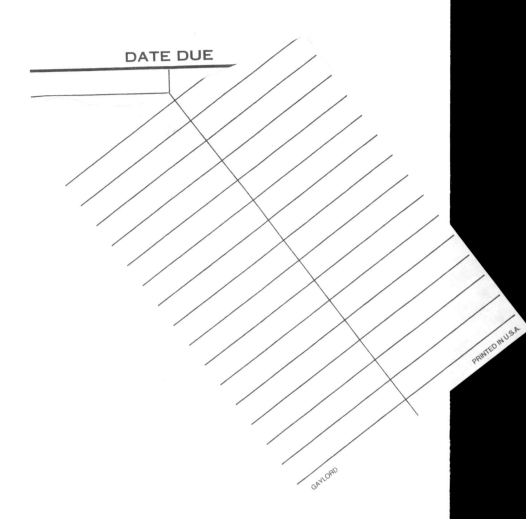

DATE DUE

GAYLORD

PRINTED IN U.S.A.